PHILOSOPHICAL FOUNDATIONS
OF TORT LAW

Philosophical Foundations
of
Tort Law

DAVID G. OWEN
Editor

CLARENDON PRESS · OXFORD

*This book has been printed digitally and produced in a standard specification
in order to ensure its continuing availability*

OXFORD
UNIVERSITY PRESS

Great Clarendon Street, Oxford OX2 6DP

Oxford University Press is a department of the University of Oxford.
It furthers the University's objective of excellence in research, scholarship,
and education by publishing worldwide in

Oxford New York

Auckland Bangkok Buenos Aires Cape Town Chennai
Dar es Salaam Delhi Hong Kong Istanbul Karachi Kolkata
Kuala Lumpur Madrid Melbourne Mexico City Mumbai Nairobi
São Paulo Shanghai Taipei Tokyo Toronto

Oxford is a registered trade mark of Oxford University Press
in the UK and in certain other countries

Published in the United States
by Oxford University Press Inc., New York

ISBN 0-19-825847-X

Printed in Great Britain by
Antony Rowe Ltd., Eastbourne

For Joan

Contents

Acknowledgments   xi

Notes on Contributors   xiii

FOREWORD: Why Philosophy Matters to Tort Law   1

    by DAVID G. OWEN

I. THE NATURE AND REALM OF TORT LAW AND PHILOSOPHY

1. The Concept of a Civil Wrong   29

    by PETER BIRKS

2. The Practice of Corrective Justice   53

    by JULES L. COLEMAN

3. The Morality of Tort Law—Questions and Answers   73

    by TONY HONORÉ

II. PRINCIPLES AND VALUES UNDERLYING TORT LAW

4. Wealth Maximization and Tort Law: A Philosophical Inquiry   99

    by RICHARD A. POSNER

5. The Uneasy Place of Principle in Tort Law   113

    by GEORGE C. CHRISTIE

6. Tort Law in the Aristotelian Tradition   131

    by JAMES GORDLEY

7. Right, Justice and Tort Law   159

    by RICHARD W. WRIGHT

8. The Idea of Complementarity as a Philosophical Basis for Pluralism in Tort Law   183

    by IZHAK ENGLARD

III. PHILOSOPHICAL PERSPECTIVES ON TORT LAW PROBLEMS

A. Responsibility and the Basis of Liability

9. Philosophical Foundations of Fault in Tort Law   201
   by DAVID G. OWEN

10. Intention in Tort Law   229
    by JOHN FINNIS

11. The Standards of Care in Negligence Law   249
    by RICHARD W. WRIGHT

12. The Seriousness of Harm Thesis for Abnormally Dangerous Activities   277
    by KEN KRESS

13. Aggregate Autonomy, the Difference Principle, and the Calabresian Approach to Products Liability   299
    by JOHN B. ATTANASIO

B. Connecting Agency and Harm: Risk, Causation, and Damage

14. Risk, Harm, and Responsibility   321
    by STEPHEN R. PERRY

15. Causation, Compensation and Moral Responsibility   347
    by CHRISTOPHER H. SCHROEDER

16. Necessary and Sufficient Conditions in Tort Law   363
    by TONY HONORÉ

17. Moments of Carelessness and Massive Loss   387
    by JEREMY WALDRON

18. Wrongdoing, Welfare, and Damages: Recovery for Non-Pecuniary Loss in Corrective Justice   409
    by BRUCE CHAPMAN

19. The Basis for Excluding Liability for Economic Loss in Tort Law   427
    by PETER BENSON

C. Victim Responsibility for Harm

20. Contributory Negligence: Conceptual and Normative Issues   461
     by KENNETH W. SIMONS

AFTERWORD: What Has Philosophy to Learn From Tort Law?   487
     by BERNARD WILLIAMS

Index   499

Acknowledgments

The idea for this book grew out of various seminars, discussions and debates at Oxford University during a lecture visit in 1991 and visiting fellowships at Corpus Christi and University Colleges, Oxford, in 1992. I am grateful to the fellows of both colleges—especially Peter Cane, Martin Matthews, and Jane Stapleton of Balliol, for their instrumental roles in arranging these visits. As I was first formulating the nature and scope of the collection, Stephen Shute and Peter Cane provided important preliminary advice that helped to shape the contours of the volume. John Finnis, Joseph Raz, and Stephen Smith were gracious in letting me participate in their seminar on the Philosophical Foundations of the Common Law, which generated ideas that contributed to the project, as did discussions with John Davies, Ronald Dworkin, John Gardner, Tony Honoré, Bernard Rudden, Simon Whittaker, and with Raymond Pfeiffer and Albert Calsamiglia, also visitors at Oxford.

The project could not have moved forward without the early support and advice of John Finnis and Peter Birks. Nor would the volume ever have amounted to more than an academic pipedream if Richard Hart had not been so enthusiastic in his support for the enterprise at its inception, and without his creative problem-solving as it moved along. Although precluded from participating more directly because of his own book project, Ernest Weinrib contributed encouragement and advice from start to finish. Richard Epstein and George Fletcher also provided input along the way, and I am grateful to them for their work. Richard Wright offered counsel on various aspects of the project in its early stages, and I am grateful for his time. I thought about inviting Pat Hubbard to participate in some manner in the creation of this collection but chose instead to invite him to use the volume in his seminar.

John Montgomery, mixing roles as law-school dean and friend, provided indispensable support in many ways. I am in debt to him, and to the University of South Carolina School of Law, for furnishing the necessary resources, including time, to complete this venture. The law library staffs at Oxford and the University of South Carolina lent valuable assistance, especially Barbara Tearle, at the former, and Mary McCormick, at the latter.

The bulk of the technical editorial work has fallen to my student assistants, Frances Barnes, Stephanie Johnston, Victoria Miller, Stephen Samuels, and Shahin Vafai, all of whom devoted long hours to assure the technical quality of the essays. Victoria Miller helped organize the editorial work at the inception of the project, and Stephanie Johnston, as technical editor, thereafter managed other aspects of the project with skill and dedication. Most of the secretarial work on the manuscript was provided by Frances Donnelly, who labored skillfully and with good humor, and whose untiring assistance was a major ingredient in the final product. I am also grateful for the secretarial assistance of Doris Cooper and DeAnna Sugrue.

The success of such a venture invariably depends, not insubstantially, upon the sacrifices, support, and encouragement of the author's family; this was no exception. Thanks to Joan, Wendy, Ethan, Megan, and my parents.

My greatest debt is to the authors, whose book this is.

Notes on Contributors

JOHN B. ATTANASIO   Dean and Professor of Law at Saint Louis University School of Law, Dean Attanasio holds a baccalaureate degree from the University of Virginia, law degrees from N.Y.U. and Yale, and a Diploma in Law from Oxford. Prior to taking the deanship at St. Louis, Dean Attanasio was Professor of Law at Notre Dame Law School. Dean Attanasio's writings include studies of the relationship between liberty and equality in law, and a casebook and treatise on American Constitutional Law (both with Redlich & Schwartz).

PETER BENSON   Associate Professor of Law at McGill University, Professor Benson studied social and political theory at Harvard, the London School of Economics and Political Science, the Institut d'Etudes Politiques de Paris, and the University of Toronto, and holds law degrees from Harvard and Toronto. His writings, examining the philosophy of tort and contract law, explore aspects of Rawls, Hegel, Kant, Grotius, and François Gény, and he is in the process of preparing a book on the philosophical aspects of contract law.

PETER BIRKS   Regius Professor of Civil Law and Fellow of All Souls College, University of Oxford, and holding doctorates from Oxford and Edinburgh, Professor Birks is the Honorary Secretary of the Society of Public Teachers of Law. Professor Birks' books include RESTITUTION: THE FUTURE; INTRODUCTION TO THE LAW OF RESTITUTION; THE LEGAL MIND (with MacCormick); THE INSTITUTES OF JUSTINIAN (ed., with McLeod); and NEW PERSPECTIVES ON THE ROMAN LAW OF PROPERTY (ed.). He is Queen's Counsel and a Fellow of the British Academy.

BRUCE CHAPMAN   Associate Professor of Law at the University of Toronto, Professor Chapman holds a Ph.D. from Cambridge and a law degree from Toronto. Professor Chapman formerly was a post-doctoral fellow at the Center for the Study of Public Choice at Virginia Polytechnic, a research associate in law and philosophy at the Westminster Institute for Ethics and Human Values, and an assistant professor in the Faculty of Law and Department of Philosophy at the University of Western Ontario. He is the editor of THE UNIVERSITY OF TORONTO LAW JOURNAL and the co-editor of JUSTICE, RIGHTS AND TORT LAW.

GEORGE C. CHRISTIE   James B. Duke Professor of Law at Duke University, Professor Christie holds law degrees from Columbia and Harvard.

Professor Christie's works include LAW, NORMS & AUTHORITY; CASES AND MATERIALS ON THE LAW OF TORTS (2d ed., with Meeks); JURISPRUDENCE: TEXT AND READINGS ON THE PHILOSOPHY OF LAW (2d ed. with Martin); and numerous articles in the areas of tort law and legal philosophy.

JULES L. COLEMAN   John A. Garver Professor of Jurisprudence and Philosophy at Yale University, Professor Coleman holds a Ph.D. in philosophy from Rockefeller University and an M.S.L. from Yale. Prior to his present position, Professor Coleman taught philosophy, and law and philosophy, at several universities. His books include RISKS AND WRONGS; PHILOSOPHY OF LAW: AN INTRODUCTION TO JURISPRUDENCE (with Murphy); MARKETS, MORALS AND THE LAW; and LAW AND PHILOSOPHY. He is editor of LEGAL THEORY and *Cambridge Studies in Philosophy and Law.*

IZHAK ENGLARD   Bora Laskin Professor of Law and former Dean of the Faculty of Law, Hebrew University, Jerusalem, Professor Englard holds law degrees from Hebrew University and the University of Paris. A member of the Israel Academy of Sciences and Humanities, Professor Englard's books include THE PHILOSOPHY OF TORT LAW; AN INTRODUCTION TO LAW; THE LAW OF TORTS—GENERAL PRINCIPLES; and THE RULE OF RES IPSA LOQUITUR IN THE LAW OF TORTS.

JOHN FINNIS   Professor of Law and Legal Philosophy at the University of Oxford, Fellow of University College, Oxford, and Professor of Law at the University of Notre Dame, Professor Finnis' books include NATURAL LAW AND NATURAL RIGHTS; MORAL ABSOLUTES; NUCLEAR DETERRENCE, MORALITY AND REALISM (with Boyle & Grisez); FUNDAMENTALS OF ETHICS; and *Commonwealth and Dependencies* in HALSBURY'S LAWS OF ENGLAND (4th ed.). He is a Fellow of the British Academy.

JAMES GORDLEY   Professor of Law at the University of California, Berkeley, Professor Gordley holds a baccalaureate degree and an M.B.A. from the University of Chicago and a law degree from Harvard. Professor Gordley's books include THE PHILOSOPHICAL ORIGINS OF MODERN CONTRACT DOCTRINE; THE CIVIL LAW SYSTEM: AN INTRODUCTION TO THE COMPARATIVE STUDY OF LAW (with von Mehren); and TOWARD EQUAL JUSTICE: A COMPARATIVE STUDY OF LEGAL AID (with Cappelletti & Johnson).

TONY HONORÉ   Having studied and taught law and legal philosophy at the University of Oxford for a half century, and formerly having held positions as Regius Professor of Civil Law, Fellow and Acting Warden of All Souls College, Fellow of Queen's College, and Fellow of New College, Oxford, Professor Honoré has authored CAUSATION IN THE LAW (2d ed., with Hart); MAKING LAW BIND—ESSAYS LEGAL AND PHILOSOPHICAL; THE QUEST FOR SECURITY; ULPIAN; TRIBONIAN; CONCORDANCE TO THE DIGEST JURISTS (with Menner); EMPERORS AND

examining differing philosophical approaches to risk creation, responsibility, and rights.

KENNETH W. SIMONS   Professor and formerly Associate Dean for Academic Affairs at Boston University School of Law, Professor Simons holds a baccalaureate degree in philosophy from Yale University and took his law degree at the University of Michigan. Professor Simons' numerous publications examine a variety of law and philosophy topics, including theoretical explorations into the nature of responsibility and defenses in both tort and criminal law.

JEREMY WALDRON   Professor of Law and Philosophy in the Jurisprudence and Social Policy Program at the University of California, Berkeley, Professor Waldron studied law and philosophy at Otago University, New Zealand and the University of Oxford, and formerly taught philosophy at Otago and political theory at Edinburgh and Oxford. Professor Waldron's books include THEORIES OF RIGHTS; NONSENSE UPON STILTS: BENTHAM, BURKE AND MARX ON THE RIGHTS OF MAN; THE RIGHT TO PRIVATE PROPERTY; and LIBERAL RIGHTS: COLLECTED PAPERS.

BERNARD WILLIAMS   White's Professor of Moral Philosophy and Fellow of Corpus Christi College, University of Oxford, and Monroe Deutsch Professor of Philosophy at the University of California, Berkeley, Professor Williams formerly was Knightbridge Professor of Philosophy at Cambridge University, and Fellow and later Provost of King's College, Cambridge. Professor Williams' books include MORAL LUCK; UTILITARIANISM—FOR AND AGAINST (with Smart); MORALITY; PROBLEMS OF THE SELF; DESCARTES: THE PROJECT OF PURE ENQUIRY; ETHICS AND THE LIMITS OF PHILOSOPHY; SHAME AND NECESSITY; and MAKING SENSE OF HUMANITY. He is a Fellow of the British Academy.

RICHARD W. WRIGHT   Professor and Norman & Edna Freehling Scholar at Chicago-Kent College of Law of the Illinois Institute of Technology, holding a baccalaureate degree from the California Institute of Technology and law degrees from Loyola Law School and Harvard University, Professor Wright formerly taught law at the Benjamin N. Cardozo School of Law, Yeshiva University. He presently is writing a book on the philosophical foundations of tort law and has published numerous articles critically examining efficiency theories of legal responsibility and exploring philosophical aspects of causation, corrective justice, and individual and joint responsibility. He is a member of the American Law Institute.

LAWYERS; and SEX LAW. He is Queen's Counsel and a Fellow of the British Academy.

KEN KRESS University Faculty Scholar and Professor of Law at the University of Iowa, Professor Kress took his baccalaureate degree at U.C.L.A, holds a law degree as well as M.A. and Ph.D. degrees in Jurisprudence and Social Policy from the University of California, Berkeley and pursued graduate studies in philosophy at Princeton. He has published numerous articles on coherence and other topics of jurisprudence, including its application to the law of torts, and is currently writing a book on the normative value of coherence.

DAVID G. OWEN Byrnes Scholar and Professor of Tort Law at the University of South Carolina, Professor Owen holds degrees in economics (Wharton) and law from the University of Pennsylvania. His books include PROSSER AND KEETON ON THE LAW OF TORTS (5th ed., with Prosser, Keeton, Dobbs & Keeton) and PRODUCTS LIABILITY AND SAFETY (3d ed., with Keeton, Montgomery & Keeton). He has explored the philosophical foundations of tort and products liability law in various articles, and he is a member of the American Law Institute.

STEPHEN R. PERRY Associate Professor of Law at McGill University, Professor Perry holds baccalaureate and law degrees from the University of Toronto, and B.Phil and D.Phil degrees in philosophy from the University of Oxford. Professor Perry has published articles on jurisprudence, political philosophy, and theoretical aspects of the law of torts. He is currently writing a book on the theoretical foundations of tort law.

RICHARD A. POSNER Chief Judge of the U.S. Court of Appeals for the Seventh Circuit and Senior Lecturer at the University of Chicago Law School, Judge Posner has authored hundreds of articles and over twenty books on law and economics, legal philosophy, and related subjects, including ECONOMIC ANALYSIS OF LAW (4th ed.); THE ECONOMIC STRUCTURE OF TORT LAW (with Landes); THE ECONOMICS OF JUSTICE; THE PROBLEMS OF JURISPRUDENCE; SEX AND REASON; LAW AND LITERATURE: A MISUNDERSTOOD RELATION; and OVERCOMING LAW.

CHRISTOPHER H. SCHROEDER Professor of Law at Duke University, with undergraduate work in religion at Princeton, a divinity degree from Yale, and a law degree from Berkeley, Professor Schroeder has served in various governmental positions, including Acting Chief Counsel, United States Senate Judiciary Committee. He is currently Deputy Assistant Attorney General in the Office of Legal Counsel of the Department of Justice. He is the author of ENVIRONMENTAL REGULATION: LAW, SCIENCE AND POLICY (2d ed., with Percival, Miller & Leape) and various articles

Foreword
Why Philosophy Matters to Tort Law

DAVID G. OWEN[*]

I. A BRIEF INTELLECTUAL HISTORY OF TORT LAW AND PHILOSOPHY

The philosophy of tort law in some ways is very old. As revealed in several of the essays here philosophical examination of tort law problems is conventionally traced to Aristotle's discussion of corrective justice in *Nicomachean Ethics* written some 2,500 years ago. Aristotle, however, provided little more than a skeletal description of the law's 'corrective' function of rectifying torts—wrongful interferences with the holdings of another—and a similarly skeletal description of how this corrective function fits together with the law's broader function of allocating a society's scarce resources among its members according to prevailing principles of distributive justice. Moving forward in time, one begins to see some fleshing in of Aristotle's corrective justice skeleton, first, by Thomas Aquinas and his medieval followers, and then by various natural law theorists of the Enlightenment, such as Hugo Grotius and Samuel Pufendorf. Late in the eighteenth century, Immanuel Kant expounded the powerful ethic of equal freedom, which he conceived to be the moral foundation of rights, justice, and law. Explicitly or implicitly, Kant's moral and legal philosophy has become a pillar for much of modern tort-law theory. Although Kant's equal freedom ethic added significant substantive content to Aristotle's corrective-justice structure, his elaboration of that content remained general and abstract. In searching for more specific content, one may travel forward in time into Anglo-American jurisprudence, where one might next note the publication in 1881 of Oliver Wendell Holmes, Jr.'s *The Common Law*, arguably the first 'modern' effort to unravel fundamental problems of the common law, including tort law, in basic philosophic terms. But the bridge between tort law and philosophy remained thereafter but lightly travelled for many decades.[1]

---

[*] Byrnes Scholar and Professor of Tort Law, University of South Carolina. Comments by Stephen Perry, Ernest Weinrib, and Richard Wright helped me frame the historical discussion in section I. Pat Hubbard did not comment on any section.

[1] One such traveller was Harvard Law School dean, James Barr Ames:

'[T]he spirit of reform which during the last six hundred years has been bringing our system of law more and more into harmony with moral principles has not yet achieved its perfect work. It

Modern Anglo-American scholarship on tort law and philosophy was preceded by, and to a large extent emerged in reaction to, important economic efficiency theories of tort liability first expounded in the 1960s and early 1970s by Ronald Coase,[2] Guido Calabresi,[3] Robert Morris,[4] and Richard Posner.[5] These important forays in tort theory, which attempted to explain the developing law of torts in economic terms, laid the foundation for a proliferation of writing on the economics of tort law that dominated the theoretical tort law scholarship in the 1970s and much of the following decade.[6] Tort law scholarship of this type, which viewed the law of torts through the consequentialist lens of economic analysis, spurred a sharp response in the 1970s from those in the academy who thought that the foundations of tort law rested more firmly on moral ground.[7] Thus, in 1970, Charles Fried published his book, *An Anatomy of Values*, in 1972 George Fletcher published his article, *Fairness and Utility in Tort Theory*,[8] in 1973 Richard Epstein published his first article on the topic, *A Theory of Strict Liability*,[9] and Jules Coleman in 1974 began his long journey into

is worth while to realize the great ethical advance of the English law in the past, if only as an encouragement to effort for further improvement': James Barr Ames, *Law and Morals*, 22 HARV. L REV. 97, 113 (1908). Consider also the observation of Professor Isaacs: 'Our progress has been marked in two ways—by the higher moral notions to which we seek to adapt our law, and by a greater ability to adapt the law to any given moral notion' : Nathan Isaacs, *Fault and Liability*, 31 HARV. L REV. 954, 978 (1918). Other scholars also explored the depths of tort law justifications along the way. *See, e.g.*, Clarence Morris, *Rough Justice and Some Utopian Ideas*, 24 HARV. L REV. 730 (1929); Glanville Williams, *The Aims of the Law of Tort*, 4 CURRENT LEGAL PROB. 137 (1951); Rev. Francis E. Lucey, *Liability Without Fault and the Natural Law*, 24 TENN. L REV. 952 (1957); Robert E. Keeton, *Conditional Fault in the Law of Torts*, 72 HARV. L REV. 401 (1959).

[2] R. H. Coase, *The Problem of Social Cost*, 3 J.L. & ECON. 1 (1960).

[3] GUIDO CALABRESI, THE COSTS OF ACCIDENTS (1970); Guido Calabresi, *Some Thoughts on Risk Distribution and the Law of Torts*, 70 YALE L. J. 499 (1961). *See also* Guido Calabresi & Douglas Melamed, *Property Rules, Liability Rules, and Inalienability: One View of the Cathedral*, 85 HARV. L REV. 1089 (1972).

[4] C. Robert Morris, Jr., *Enterprise Liability and the Actuarial Process—The Insignificance of Foresight*, 70 YALE L.J. 554 (1961).

[5] Richard A. Posner, *A Theory of Negligence*, 1 J. LEGAL STUD. 29 (1972). Scholarship on the moral and legal dimensions of economic theory deepened in the 1970s. *See, e.g.*, KENNETH J. ARROW, THE LIMITS OF ORGANIZATION (1974); RICHARD A. POSNER, ECONOMIC ANALYSIS OF LAW (1972).

[6] *See, e.g.*, William M. Landes & Richard A. Posner, *The Positive Economic Theory of Tort Law*, 15 GA. L. REV. 851 (1981). Culminating perhaps in WILLIAM M. LANDES & RICHARD A. POSNER, THE ECONOMIC STRUCTURE OF TORT LAW (1987); STEPHEN SHAVELL, ECONOMIC ANALYSIS OF ACCIDENT LAW (1987).

[7] Note the complaints of a couple of scholars at the time that 'the law has "gone a-whoring after false gods" and that all of the raving about loss absorption has blinded lawyers to the obvious concern of tort law with right and wrong' : Edward Veitch & David Miers, *Assault on the Law of Tort*, *38* M.L.R. 139, 142–3 (1975). (quoting Weir). *See* Edward Veitch, Book Review, 22 N IR. L Q 560, 563 (1971) (complaining that tort theorists as a group 'have been led by the nose by economists' too long).

[8] 5 HARV. L. REV. 537 (1972).

[9] 2 J. LEGAL STUD. 151 (1973), followed by his *Defenses and Subsequent Pleas in a System of Strict Liability*, 3 J. LEGAL STUD. 165 (1974).

tort theory scholarship with *On the Moral Argument for the Fault System.*[10] For a number of years thereafter, while the law and economics scholars churned out an increasingly elaborate body of literature, the study of tort law and philosophy percolated unobtrusively.[11]

Investigation into the philosophical roots of tort law matured in sophistication and began to take on the appearance of a discipline, albeit a nascent one, in the 1980s. Starting the decade, Izhak England in 1980 critiqued the tort theory literature of the preceding decade in *The System Builders: A Critical Appraisal of Modern American Tort Theory,*[12] and Ernest Weinrib entered the fray with his first tort law and philosophy article, *The Case for a Duty to Rescue.*[13] Then, in 1982 and 1983, a critical mass developed when a number of scholars, including Coleman,[14] Weinrib,[15] and Fletcher,[16] offered a variety of diverse views on tort law and philosophy in *Law and Philosophy.*[17] This was an important event in the evolution of tort theory for at least two reasons. For one, it was the first united opposition by leading scholars to the theretofore largely unchallenged supremacy of the economic theorists' utility and efficiency-based approaches that had become entrenched as the dominant theoretical scholarship of the time. For another, it presented side by side the radically different conceptions of corrective justice of Jules Coleman and Ernest Weinrib, whose writings on the subject came to frame and significantly shape the evolving conception of tort law and philosophy as it is broadly understood today. As the 1980s

[10] 71 J. PHIL. 473 (1974). Coleman published several more essays on tort theory in the 1970s, including Jules L. Coleman, *The Morality of Strict Tort Liability*, 18 WM. & MARY L. REV. 259 (1976).

[11] During which time Glanville Williams and B. A. Hepple published FOUNDATIONS OF THE LAW OF TORT (1976), Marshall Shapo published THE DUTY TO ACT—TORT LAW, POWER, & PUBLIC POLICY (1977), and Guido Calabresi and Philip Bobbitt published TRAGIC CHOICES (1978). *See also* John Borgo, *Causal Paradigms in Tort Law*, 8 J. LEGAL STUD. 419 (1979); Richard A. Epstein, *Nuisance Law: Corrective Justice and its Utilitarian Constraints*, 8 J LEGAL STUD. 49 (1979).

[12] 9 J. LEGAL STUD. 27 (1980). *See also* Izhak England, *Can Strict Liability Be Generalized?*, 2 OXFORD J. LEGAL STUD. 245 (1982).

[13] 90 YALE L.J. 247 (1980). Also in 1980 was David G. Owen, *Rethinking the Policies of Strict Products Liability*, 33 VAND. L. REV. 681 (1980), and William H. Rodgers, Jr., *Negligence Reconsidered: The Role of Rationality in Tort Theory*, 54 SO. CAL. L. REV. 1 (1980). The next year witnessed Gary T. Schwartz, *The Vitality of Negligence and the Ethics of Strict Liability*, 15 GA. L. REV. 963 (1981), and 1982 saw Peter Cane, *Justice and Justifications for Tort Liability*, 2 OXFORD J. LEGAL STUD. 30 (1982).

[14] Jules L. Coleman, *Moral Theories of Torts: Their Scope and Limits, Parts I & II*, 1 LAW & PHIL. 371 (1982); 2 LAW & PHIL. 5 (1983). *See also* Jules Coleman, *Corrective Justice and Wrongful Gain*, 11 J. LEGAL STUD. 421 (1982).

[15] Ernest J. Weinrib, *Toward a Moral Theory of Negligence Law*, 2 LAW & PHIL. 37 (1983).

[16] George P. Fletcher, *The Search for Synthesis in Tort Theory*, 2 LAW & PHIL. 63 (1983).

[17] *Values in the Law of Tort: A Symposium, Part I*, 1 LAW & PHIL. 369 (1982) (with an Introduction by Michael Bayles and Bruce Chapman, and essays by Jules Coleman, Theodore Benditt, Joseph Steiner, and S. C. Coval and J. C. Smith); *Part II*, 2 LAW & PHIL. 3 (1983) (with an Introduction by Michael Bayles and Bruce Chapman, and essays by Jules Coleman, Ernest Weinrib, George Fletcher, and Robert Prichard and Alan Brudner).

progressed, Weinrib and Coleman continued to refine their respective models, and more and more legal scholars joined the search for philosophical illumination of the law of torts.[18] And as the decade moved along, the philosophy of tort law scholarship increasingly evolved into explicit, systematic applications of formal philosophic principles to legal problems of responsibility for harm.[19]

Also during the 1970s and 1980s, in the halls of the philosophers, a number of scholars laid important philosophic groundwork that was indispensable to the lawyers in developing moral conceptions of tort law. Two especially important books published in the early 1970s, John Rawls' monumental *A Theory of Justice*[20] and Robert Nozick's powerful *Anarchy, State, and Utopia,*[21] offered a dramatic challenge to consequentialist and utilitarian concepts. Despite their significant differences, these two works together provided a vital infusion of neo-classical rights-based moral theory into the debate on political theory. And some philosophers in this period, notably Joel Feinberg[22] and Judith Jarvis Thomson,[23] began quite explicitly to address the issues of greatest interest to tort lawyers, those concerning moral responsibility for harming others.[24]

The 1990s decade has been shaping up as the decade of the books. There were none devoted to a deep and systematic inquiry into the philosophy of

---

[18] *See, e.g.,* Steven D. Smith, *Rhetoric and Rationality in the Law of Negligence,* 69 MINN. L. REV. 277 (1984).

[19] *See, e.g.,* RONALD DWORKIN, LAW'S EMPIRE (1986) ch. 8 ; *Symposium on Causation in the Law of Torts,* 63 CHI.-KENT L. REV. 397 (1987) (with a Foreword by Mario Rizzo, articles by Ernest Weinrib, Jules Coleman, Judith Jarvis Thomson, Michael Moore, Robert Cooter, Richard Wright, Mark Kelman, Alan Schwartz, and an Afterword by Richard Epstein). There were as well a number of important books and articles on tort theory that applied philosophical principles to tort law problems, but less formally. For example, see Marshall S. Shapo's TOWARDS A JURISPRUDENCE OF INJURY: THE CONTINUING CREATION OF A SYSTEM OF SUBSTANTIVE JUSTICE IN AMERICAN TORT LAW (1984) (report to the ABA), and Guido Calabresi's IDEALS, BELIEFS, ATTITUDES, AND THE LAW (1985).

[20] JOHN RAWLS, A THEORY OF JUSTICE (1971).

[21] ROBERT NOZICK, ANARCHY, STATE, AND UTOPIA (1974).

[22] *See, e.g.,* JOEL FEINBERG, DOING AND DESERVING (1970); J. Feinberg, *Harm and Self-Interest, in* LAW, MORALITY, AND SOCIETY—ESSAYS IN HONOUR OF H. L. A. HART (P.M.S. Hacker & J. Raz (eds.), 1977), 285.

[23] See, e.g., JUDITH JARVIS THOMSON, ACTS AND OTHER EVENTS (1977); JUDITH JARVIS THOMSON, RIGHTS, RESTITUTION, AND RISK (1986); JUDITH JARVIS THOMSON, THE REALM OF RIGHTS (1990).

[24] Also during the 1980s, tort law was critiqued from a variety of perspectives including Marxism, the Critical Legal Studies movement, pragmatism, and feminism. *See, e.g.,* THE POLITICS OF LAW (David Kairys (ed.), 1982); Richard L. Abel, *A Socialist Approach to Risk,* 41 MD. L. REV. 695 (1982); Leslie Bender, *A Lawyer's Primer on Feminist Theory and Tort,* 38 J. LEGAL EDUC. 3 (1988); David M. Engel, *The Oven Bird's Song: Insiders, Outsiders, and Personal Injuries in an American Community,* 18 LAW & SOC'Y REV. 551 (1984); Duncan Kennedy, *Distributive and Paternalist Motives in Contract and Tort Law, with Special Reference to Compulsory Terms and Unequal Bargaining Power,* 41 MD. L. REV. 563 (1982); Stephen D. Sugarman, *Doing Away with Tort Law,* 73 CAL. L. REV. 555 (1985), elegantly critiqued in David G. Owen, *Deterrence and Desert in Tort,* 73 CAL. L. REV. 665 (1985).

tort law when the present volume was first conceived in 1991. Jules Coleman promptly remedied that with his publication in 1992 of *Risks and Wrongs*.[25] There, rejecting conventional 'rational choice' liberalism, he places tort law within the broader legal system and explains its role as a means of rectifying wrongful losses, not inefficient exchanges. Tort liability, he argues, merely rectifies the wrong; it does not right it. Compensation for a tort does not serve to legitimate an unconsented-to taking; rather, it is the victim's due. Thus, he argues that tort practice is best conceived as rectification-of-wrong-done, not as a substitute for efficient contract. Also in 1992, two important symposia on tort law philosophy appeared— *Symposium on Risks and Wrongs*,[26] centering around Coleman's book, and *Symposium: Corrective Justice and Formalism—The Care One Owes One's Neighbors*.[27] The next year, 1993, witnessed the publication of a number of important collections, including *Symposium on Legal Formalism*,[28] which centered around Ernest Weinrib's work, a collection of essays on tort theory edited by Ken Cooper-Stephenson and Elaine Gibson, *Tort Theory*,[29] and Izhak England's book, *The Philosophy of Tort Law*,[30] in which he critiques once again (but more broadly and deeply) recent Anglo-American tort law theories and examines as well the European historical roots of tort philosophy.[31]

Within a few weeks of the present volume going to press, Ernest Weinrib has published his book, *The Idea of Private Law*,[32] in which he places tort law in the broader context of private law. Viewing private law from within itself, in terms of its 'internal intelligibility', Weinrib argues that the conceptual perspective of private law embodies a correlativity of rights and

[25] JULES L. COLEMAN, RISKS AND WRONGS (1992).

[26] 15 HARV. J.L. & PUB. POL'Y 621 (1992) (with a Foreword by Larry Alexander and articles by Jules Coleman, Margaret Jane Radin, Randy Barnett, Jean Hampton, David Gauthier, Steven Walt, Emily Sherwin, Kenneth Simons, Christopher Wonnell, Richard Craswell, Alan Schwartz, Richard Arneson, Stephen Perry, and Claire Finkelstein).

[27] 77 IOWA L. REV. 403 (1992) (with an Introduction by Ken Kress, an article and comment by Ernest Weinrib, and articles by Jules Coleman, Stephen Perry, Peter Benson, Richard Wright, Anita Allen and Maria Morales, Dennis Patterson, John Stick, Richard Hyland, Marlena Corcoran, and Steven Heyman).

[28] 16 HARV. J.L. & PUB. POL'Y 579 (1993) (with a Foreword by Dennis Patterson, an article and response by Ernest Weinrib, and comments by Stephen Perry, Jean Love, and Ken Kress).

[29] TORT THEORY (Ken Cooper-Stephenson & Elaine Gibson (eds.), 1993) (with essays by the following Canadian legal scholars: Ernest Weinrib, Stephen Perry, Ken Cooper-Stephenson, Bruce Chapman, J. C. Smith, Lucie Léger, Elaine Gibson, Kate Sutherland, Ted Decoste, Allan Hutchinson and Robert Maisey, Daniel Jutras, Lakshman Marasinghe, David Cohen, and Bruce Feldthusen).

[30] IZHAK ENGLARD, THE PHILOSOPHY OF TORT LAW (1993).

[31] Englard also examines specific areas of tort law practice, addressing philosophic issues in such areas as defamation, informed consent, punitive damages, economic loss, and mass torts. Importantly in terms of the present volume, Englard outlines in his book the pluralistic 'complementarity' theory of tort law which he further develops here.

[32] ERNEST J. WEINRIB, THE IDEA OF PRIVATE LAW (1995).

duties highlighting the centrality of the notion of causation of harm and the distinction between nonfeasance and misfeasance. Grounding his perspective of tort law in Aristotelian corrective justice and Kant's philosophy of right, he argues that private law should be viewed as a coherent, self-understanding enterprise. From this perspective, Weinrib further expounds his theory of tort law as a normative unit integrating the doing and suffering of harm that is resolved in bipolar litigation between the plaintiff and defendant.

This brings us to the present volume. The collection of essays here, each written especially for this volume, is designed to provide an expansive philosophic view of tort law issues by many of the scholars who have helped develop the discipline in its recent emergence from the mists of academic obscurity to its present position as a neo-quasi-discipline of its own. Part I, THE NATURE AND REALM OF TORT LAW AND PHILOSOPHY, containing essays by Peter Birks, Jules Coleman, and Tony Honoré, attempts to provide a structural framework for understanding the nature of tort law and the general types of problems involved in a philosophic inquiry into this particular domain of law. Part II, PRINCIPLES AND VALUES UNDERLYING TORT LAW, which includes essays by Richard Posner, George Christie, James Gordley, Richard Wright, and Izhak Englard, explores the variety of abstract principles and values thought by different scholars to furnish tort law with a substantive, philosophic foundation—ethics believed to provide it with normative content. In Part III, PHILOSOPHICAL PERSPECTIVES ON TORT LAW PROBLEMS, the inquiry shifts to the major tort law perplexities in need of normative help from the domain of philosophy. In the first section here, *Responsibility and the Basis of Liability*, John Finnis, Richard Wright, Ken Kress, John Attanasio, and I inquire into how philosophic concepts of responsibility for harm should be fit together with one or more of the conventional grounds of tortious liability based upon intent, negligence, or strict liability. The next section, *Connecting Agency and Harm: Risk, Causation and Damage*, contains essays by Stephen Perry, Christopher Schroeder, Tony Honoré, Jeremy Waldron, Bruce Chapman, and Peter Benson, each exploring the nature of the connections in tort law between agency, risk, and harm. In the final section of Part III, *Victim Responsibility for Harm*, Kenneth Simons switches the inquiry to the plaintiff's conduct, focusing upon the nature and significance of a victim's responsibility for causing accidental harm. Closing out the volume in an AFTERWORD, Bernard Williams reverses the inquiry of the other essays and asks what philosophers may learn from studying the law of torts.

II. THE NATURE AND REALM OF TORT LAW AND PHILOSOPHY

How law and philosophy broadly fit together is a large and controversial topic that ranges far beyond the scope of this volume. Of interest here is the much narrower question of how *tort* law may be informed by the teachings and principles of philosophy. The law of torts concerns the obligations of persons living in a crowded society to respect the safety, property, and personality of their neighbors, both as an *a priori* matter and as a duty to compensate for wrongfully caused harm, *ex post*. Tort law, in other words, involves questions of how people should treat one another and the rules of proper behavior that society imposes on each citizen for avoiding improper harm to others, and for determining when compensation for harm is due. Moral philosophy (ethics), and to some extent political philosophy, are themselves concerned with principles of proper conduct.[33] And so both fields, tort-law and philosophy, involve a search for norms of proper behavior, norms that may be used for evaluating the propriety or wrongfulness of particular instances of harmful conduct.

The essays in Part I frame the inquiry for the remainder of the volume. The issues considered in this part may be viewed as structural, in that they involve at once a micro-tort examination of the internal structure of a tort—what it is that makes a tort a tort, and a macro-tort examination of the proper placement of the law of torts within the external structure of other law—the law of property, contracts, restitution, and crimes. The nature of a tort, its necessary elements, the relation of its internal norms to broader social norms, and the objectives of a system of tort law within the broader legal system are the kinds of issues investigated in this opening part of the collection.

In *The Concept of a Civil Wrong*, Peter Birks begins the inquiry by providing a structural analysis of the nature of a tort, or 'civil wrong,' exploring where it fits within the broader structure of the common law. From this perspective, he examines how the concept of a civil wrong relates to and is distinguishable from the other common law concepts—contract, unjust enrichment, and other events. Locating tort within a scheme containing these other common law categories, a classification approach which he finds coherent, Birks proposes that tort law be viewed broadly to include all appropriate responses to tortious behavior, including the restitution of wrongful gains. By so focusing on how tort and the other common law categories differ and overlap, Birks provides insights into the nature of a civil wrong—a tort—which he defines as 'the breach of a legal duty which affects

---

[33] Epistemology, the philosophy of knowledge, helps in a more limited fashion to inform the connection between risk and responsibility, as Stephen Perry explains in his essay in Part III.

the interests of an individual to a degree which the law regards as sufficient to allow that individual to complain on his or her own account rather than as the representative of society as a whole'. Birks explains the universal requirement that the core of tort involves a breach of legal duty (a primary obligation) which generates a further duty to compensate the victim (a secondary obligation). He postulates and explores the notion that the core tort case includes three primary elements: harm, conduct, and blameworthiness. He concludes that neither harm nor blameworthiness is essential, leaving only conduct amounting to a breach of duty as the sole imperative in the core tort concept. Arguing that the remedial obligations for breach of duty in tort are policy-based, rather than logically necessary, he distinguishes tort from the other three common law categories, the remedies for which are dictated by the causative event itself. Finding that the broad formal concept of a civil wrong is weak and abstract, Birks concludes that, for a complete explanation of the concept of a civil wrong, one must turn to the policies and values lying beneath the primary duty, where principles of economic efficiency compete for recognition with ethics of liberal autonomy and moral paternalism.

In 1992, Jules Coleman published his book, *Risks and Wrongs*, where he presents corrective justice as the principle that those who are responsible for the wrongful losses of others have a duty to repair them, and where he argues that the core of tort law embodies this concept of corrective justice. In his essay here, *The Practice of Corrective Justice*, Coleman probes further into the nature of corrective justice and its role in the law of torts. Broadly viewed, corrective justice is one of the norms that apply when persons are somehow connected with the misfortunes of others, providing an important link between agents and victims. Rooting his particular conception of corrective justice in liberal political morality, Coleman maintains that the concept is properly viewed as the duty to make repair, to make good the victim's loss, but only if the loss is *wrongful*, and only if the agent is *responsible* for having brought about the loss. He claims as well that those, including himself, who maintain that the concept of corrective justice figures in tort law are committed to the claim that corrective justice has objective semantic content. This leads him to a discussion of the meta-ethics of the concept of corrective justice. Arguing for an anti-realist approach to the concept, he claims that its core content is drawn from the practices (including tort law) in which it figures. And so he speaks of the 'practice' of corrective justice. Thus Coleman contends that tort law itself helps provide content to corrective justice, while corrective justice in turn serves as a criterion for assessing existing tort practice. As for the substantive essence of corrective justice, he maintains that it contains a coherent core that includes *human agency, rectification,* and *correlativity.* Finally, Coleman explores other features of the practice of corrective justice, arguing that its content is pre-political (independent of legal and other political institutions), non-instrumental (independent of social goals, like cost avoidance), while remaining ultimately dependent on the moral, legal, and political practices already existing within the community.

Borrowing from H. L. A. Hart's approach to the criminal law, Tony Honoré poses and answers six questions that together frame much of the moral aspect of tort law. In his first essay here, *The Morality of Tort Law— Questions and Answers*, Honoré argues that the threshold aim of tort law, like the criminal law, is to minimize undesirable conduct. But he notes that other principles also constrain tort law in the pursuit of this aim. Thus *corrective* justice, based on equality, requires a harm-doer to 'put the matter right', which in tort law usually requires the payment of compensation to the victim. While fault is an important basis of responsibility for harm, Honoré's notion of 'outcome-responsibility' provides a broader form of responsibility that may generate a duty to compensate on grounds other than fault. *Distributive* justice, in Honoré's view, includes the notion that losses from risk-creating conduct should fall upon the actor commensurate with the possibility of gains he sought from the conduct. Under principles of *retributive* justice, he maintains, the penalty imposed on the defendant should not be disproportionate to the wrong. By spreading losses, insurance advances the goals of distributive justice as well as retributive justice, Honoré explains, and it helps assure that strict liability does not impose a burden on the defendant greater than his benefit or fault. In addition to the constraints of proportionality, he argues that tort responsibility should be limited to harm within the scope of the pertinent liability rules. Honoré also reasons that principles of both corrective and retributive justice suggest that responsibility should be proportioned according to the manner and extent to which the victim contributed to the harmful outcome. Finally, he contends that certain forms of state compensation schemes, such as the distribution of motoring risks to all motorists or the entire community, appear compatible with principles of risk-distributive justice. In reviewing the answers to the six questions posed at the start, Honoré explains that the tort system is justified as a means by which the state, subject to the constraints of justice, seeks to reduce undesirable conduct by treating certain individual interests as rights that the right-holder is empowered to protect when infringed by conduct marked as a civil wrong.

III. PRINCIPLES AND VALUES UNDERLYING TORT LAW

Are there principles, values, or truths of moral theory that help the law of torts establish norms of proper conduct for avoiding harm to others? If so, what might such notions be, and from whence did they derive? Is there use in organizing tort theory around the principles internal to tort law itself, such as the doctrine of foreseeability? What lessons may be learned from a study of the ethical inquiries of the great philosophers, from Aristotle to Aquinas and his followers, to Kant and Hegel? And how (if at all) might such principles help explain, justify, and guide the law of torts today? More particularly, should tort law be viewed in economic terms, as a manifestation of wealth maximization principles, or should it be viewed instead as a reflection of a moral ethic such as equal freedom? Or is it really comprehensible only in terms of the pluralistic world of conflicting values abroad in social life? These are the kinds of questions examined by the essays in Part II.

Some time ago, Richard Posner began an inquiry into the philosophical justifications for the economic explanation of law that he has developed over the years.[34] The purpose of his present essay, *Wealth Maximization and Tort Law: A Philosophical Inquiry*, is to 'restate, refine, and amplify the philosophical version' of his argument that wealth maximization is the 'best normative guide to the law of torts'. Rather than being derived from a single moral theory, such as utilitarianism, Posner argues that wealth maximization is consistent with a variety of moral theories and repugnant to none. For illustration, Posner first explains how Pareto optimality, based on the liberal notion of consent, may be roughly accomplished through the negligence system, since actors (who are also potential victims) would probably prefer a system in which the sum of liability and accident (victim) insurance costs are minimized. Next, he explains how common-sense-rule utilitarianism favors liability rules that minimize the sum of these same costs, and so maximize wealth. Nor, in Posner's view, is Aristotelian corrective justice, which seeks to rectify wrongful transactions, incompatible with wealth maximization, for the latter theory provides guidance in ascertaining the types of transactions that should be considered wrongful. Even Kantian deontology, he argues, which proscribes the use of others merely as ends, is consistent with a system of tort law which accommodates conflicting activities by maximizing their combined value, an approach which enjoins potential injurers and victims alike to accord due consideration to each other's interests. Finally, he argues that, although the wealth-maximizing damages principles of tort law do tend to ratify rather than redistribute pre-existing holdings of wealth, broad-based egalitarianism is simply unachievable as a practical matter through changes in the tort system. Thus, Posner concludes that the theory of wealth maximization

---

[34] Richard A. Posner, *Utilitarianism, Economics, and Legal Theory*, 8 J. LEGAL STUD. 103 (1979); Richard A. Posner, *The Ethical and Political Basis of the Efficiency Norm in Common Law Adjudication*, 8 HOFSTRA L. REV. 487 (1980). He continued the inquiry in RICHARD A. POSNER, THE ECONOMICS OF JUSTICE (1981), chs. 3 & 4 and RICHARD A. POSNER, THE PROBLEMS OF JURISPRUDENCE (1990), chs. 12 & 13, and investigated the particular domain of tort law in WILLIAM M. LANDES & RICHARD A. POSNER, THE ECONOMIC STRUCTURE OF TORT LAW (1987).

supports the existing system of tort law because it is rooted in, and not inconsistent with, the various moral traditions of society.

In *The Uneasy Place of Principle in Tort Law*, George Christie explores the role of principle in tort law, and he does so skeptically. Citing Coke's assertion that 'Reason is the life of the law', Christie reminds us of Holmes' rejection of this view in his famous aphorism, 'The life of law has not been logic: it has been experience'. Yet the urge of lawyers 'to find some coherent logical structure in the law', observes Christie, persists. Christie notes preliminarily the importance and difficulty of obtaining agreement on the very meaning of a particular principle and on proper methods of applying it to concrete fact situations. Examining the search for principle in the British tort-law cases concerning responsibility for economic loss, pure and otherwise, Christie traces the rise and fall of the principle of foreseeability as the controlling principle in this context. He then turns to the use and abuse of the foreseeability limitation principle in American cases, first in the economic-loss context and then in regard to parent-child recovery for lost consortium, showing how the principle has caused perhaps more confusion than helpful guidance in both contexts. But Christie rejects the nihilist (or extreme realist) view of principle as nonsense, arguing instead for a more moderate position. Because the very purpose of a legal system is to require decision-makers to justify their decisions according to some relevant criteria, Christie reasons that principle can play some role in providing criteria for decision-making. In reflecting the richly diverse goals and values of life, Christie argues that principles are more properly viewed as devices by which humans seek to achieve the good life than as ultimates or ends in themselves. Principles guide decision-making; they do not control it. He further contends that decisions in complex cases are too complicated to be made to depend upon some single normative principle, whether foreseeability or something else. Christie concludes that we must have more modest expectations of how principle may help the law of torts.

James Gordley investigates the ancient roots of tort law in his essay, *Tort Law in the Aristotelian Tradition*. Aristotle's brief account of corrective justice in *Nicomachean Ethics*, explains Gordley, was the starting point for philosophical analysis of tort law by Thomas Aquinas and Thomist scholars in medieval and early modern Europe. Gordley argues that the broader Aristotelian conception of tort theory developed by Thomas and his followers better justifies the law of torts than do the theories of modern tort-law scholars. Beginning with an explanation of corrective and distributive justice, Gordley describes how an Aristotelian–Thomistic account of the defense of necessity provides a better explanation of modern American and European tort law doctrine than do interpretations of modern scholars. Corrective justice in the Aristotelian tradition, which aims at the restoration of a pre-existing equality, links the plaintiff's right and the defendant's duty: the defendant must pay because he has used up the plaintiff's resources for his own ends. Gordley explains how Aristotle, Thomas, and Cajetan rested responsibility for accidental harm on the notion of *prudence*, which entails a weighing of risks and precautions, as in the modern approach to negligence explained by Judge Learned Hand in formulaic terms in the *Carroll Towing* case. Gordley argues, however, that the Aristotelian–Thomistic account, in which the weighing of costs and benefits is ascribed to the moral virtue of prudence, is more satisfactory than the account of modern economists whose theories rest on incentives and efficiency. Although the Aristotelian tradition never adequately addressed strict liability, Gordley contends that strict liability can be explained by the principles of that tradition: an actor should be liable if he chooses to use up another's resources for his own ends, for example by exposing others to especially high risks in order to obtain some benefit for himself.

In *Right, Justice and Tort Law*, Richard Wright explores the normative foundation of tort law. Agreeing with Ernest Weinrib that pluralist theories are by nature incoherent and indeterminate, and arguing that the utilitarian efficiency norm of maximizing aggregate social welfare is normatively deficient, Wright offers a theory of tort law based on the single foundational norm of equal freedom. He elaborates Kant's concepts of freedom and right, noting that the primary purpose of the state under Kantian theory of morality and law is to enforce each person's basic right of equal freedom. Wright then turns to a consideration of Aristotle's conceptions of corrective and distributive justice, arguing that they constitute the negative and positive aspects, respectively, of the right of equal freedom. He asserts that, as such, they are independent but compatible and comprehensive types of justice, with distinct domains, grounds, and structures. Corrective justice, he explains, applies to individual interactions and requires that the effects of such interactions on the interacting parties' resources be consistent with each party's equal negative freedom, while distributive justice focuses on a person's status as a member of the political community and requires that the community's resources be distributed to promote the equal positive freedom of each person in the community. Wright argues that tort law, being concerned with individual interactions, is grounded in corrective justice. He seeks to demonstrate that corrective justice, with its criterion of equal negative freedom, explains, justifies, and illuminates the general structure, content, and institutions of tort law, including the availability of punitive damages in appropriate cases. Finally, stressing the logical and normative correlativity of rights and duties and the bilateral structure of the rights and duties of corrective justice, Wright argues that proposed alternatives to tort law, such as compulsory no-fault insurance schemes or at-fault risk pools, which ignore this bilateral correlativity, are unjust and hence unjustifiable.

In this part of the volume, each of the essays to this point focuses upon abstract principles and values thought to underlie the law of torts. In the essay that concludes this section, *The Idea of Complementarity as a Philosophical Basis for Pluralism in Tort Law*, Izhak Englard engages a question on which the prior authors have disagreed: whether tort law is best explained in terms of a single principle or value, or whether instead it rests on a multiplicity of norms. Arguing that the reality of tort law is pluralistic, as he sought to show in an extensive analysis of tort practices in his recent book,[35] Englard explains and normatively defends this thesis in his essay here. Unimpressed by arguments of monists (such as Ernest Weinrib) and critical legal studies theorists (such as Jack Balkin) that pluralistic approaches are incoherent and unintelligible, Englard claims that positive tort law is based upon polyvalent justifications that in fact are often logically incompatible. Englard finds justificatory support for his pluralistic conception of tort law in a notion coined 'complementarity' by the Danish physicist (and quasi-philosopher) Niels Bohr to address the wave-particle duality problem of quantum mechanics. The complementarity term, explains Englard, was 'meant to convey the idea that the full understanding of physical reality may require the use of contrasting, mutually exclusive models'. Bohr believed that the significance of complementarity extended beyond atomic physics to other fields where its epistemological importance for empirical knowledge could be fruitfully employed. Exploring the ancient lineage of the principle of polar duality in such forms as *Yin* and *Yang*, Englard notes the difficulties in moving the complementarity notion from its descriptive role in explaining physical reality to the prescriptive realm of establishing norms for social life. Finally, Englard explains in a variety of contexts how the ideal vision of harmony between contrasting principles, as captured in the complementarity notion, is a helpful philosophical conception that provides a deepened understanding of tort law problems.

IV. Philosophical Perspectives on Tort Law Problems

The focus of this final part of the volume, Part III, is on philosophic notions at play within the context of particular tort law problems. The subject of tort law might fairly be said to involve the nature and extent of an actor's legal responsibility to a victim for causing harm. If so, then one important preliminary question for tort law must be how responsibility for causing harm should be defined and limited. Should it rest only upon the actor's moral desert, limited by notions of blameworthiness for acting upon

---

[35] Izhak Englard, The Philosophy of Tort Law (1993).

choices that are by some measure bad, as viewed *ex ante?* Or should the concept of tort responsibility be widened to embrace the harmful consequences of the actor's conduct, including victim needs, *ex post?* In doctrinal terms, should liability be based on fault or should it instead be strict? And how should such concepts be defined? Questions such as these are the subject of the first section of Part III. The next section in this part explores the three linking aspects of tort law that serve to connect an agent's responsibility and a victim's harm—risk, causation, and damage. The final section in Part III concerns the problem of contributory victim fault—the nature of a victim's own faulty conduct, and how it should bear on the responsibility in tort of another person also responsible for the causing the victim's harm.

A. Responsibility and the Basis of Liability

For at least a century, the basis of liability in tort law has been ordered formally according to a tripartite responsibility scale based on the culpability of the actor. On this basis, tort actions conventionally have been classified into one of the following categories: (1) intentionally inflicted harm, (2) negligently caused harm, and (3) no-fault or strict liability for causing harm. The essays in this section explore philosophical foundations of legal responsibility for causing harm to others from this vantage point, examining tort law obligations from the perspective of one or more of these three separate bases of liability grounded in fault.

The first three essays in this section examine fundamental aspects of the fault-based theories of recovery in tort—intent and negligence—each author searching in a different way for an understanding of the meaning of fault for causing harm, in both moral and legal terms. The last two essays in this section focus on responsibility for dangerous activities and things. Putting to use and trying to cope with the hazards in dangerous things has inhered in the human condition since the dawn of man. Whether the goal has been to harness and control the dangers of fire or wild animals or, more recently, of gun powder, reservoirs, or the powers inherent in the products of modern engineering, physics, and chemistry, the destructive power of such things sometimes escapes and causes harm. In cases such as these, tort law has tended to turn away from the explicitly fault-based approach of negligence doctrine toward other theories of liability called 'strict'. On what basis the person making or using the dangerous thing should be liable for resulting accidental harm, whether strictly for all such harm or merely for misadventures that result from fault, is a problem that has long confounded courts adjudicating tort claims for such losses.

Beginning the investigation here, my essay, *Philosophical Foundations of Fault in Tort Law*, inquires into the essentials of fault for causing harm that support responsibility for both intentional torts and negligence and that explain and justify the great bulk of tort-law doctrine. The inquiry centers on a consideration of the nature of human choice, action, and harm, which together illuminate the fundamentals of moral responsibility for causing harm. First considered from this perspective are the ideals of freedom, equality, and common good. Under the umbrella of equal freedom, three principles of choice—which I call the choice-end principle, the choice-harm principle, and the choice-blame principle—help explain the moral quality of harmful human behavior in various tort law contexts. In ordering the pertinent values, I argue that the equal freedom ethic is lexically prior to utility, but that utility serves a vital default function that plays a major role in ascertaining responsibility for accidental harm. When the ordering inquiry shifts from behavioral ideals to the interests subject to harm, I argue that human life and limb are properly valued more highly than property, wealth, and convenience in the context of intentional harms, but that, when the focus shifts to accident cases, the equal-freedom ethic generally requires that all interests be thrown without preference into the decisional calculus. Finally, applying these various perspectives to the philosophic essentials of fault for both intentional and accidental harm, I conclude that there is little place in moral theory for rules of strict liability in tort law, and that the great bulk of the law of torts instead is properly based on fault.

The next essay, *Intention in Tort Law*, by John Finnis, explores the particular realm of liability for intentionally inflicted harm. Investigating the nature and significance of the concept of intention at work in tort law, Finnis argues for a common sense view of the concept and against various constructive extensions of the notion employed over the years by courts and the *Restatement of Torts* that deprive the concept of its normative power. Illustrating with the spring gun cases how misuse of the intention concept may confuse analysis of tort law problems, he explains that intention plays a central role in moral assessment because of its focus on the deliberation, proposals for action, and choice that lie behind action. Simply stated, '[w]hat one intends is what one chooses'. Accordingly, he criticizes the rejection of intention by economic theorists for failing to comprehend its moral significance in tort law. Finnis critiques the concepts of intention (and related motivations) in early House of Lords opinions holding that a bad motive (intent to harm) does not render otherwise lawful conduct unlawful (tortious), and he contrasts the notion of real intention to the constructive, 'objective' formulation of the concept embodied in the *Restatement*'s 'substantially certain to result' (alternative) definition. Common morality finds normative significance in real (as opposed to constructive) intent, Finnis argues, in large part because the process of actually choosing a result endures, persists, and remains in one's will, thereby forming a permanent part of the person's character. For a person to choose to harm another person is 'the paradigmatic wrong, the exemplary instance of denial of right'. The common perception of intent conflicts with the utilitarian model, which allows intentional harm if it maximizes wealth. Yet a primary function of government, Finnis maintains, is to apply commutative justice to rectify such intentional harms by requiring the actor to repair the victim's loss. Distinguishing the fairness principles of negligence law from the concept of intent, he notes the analogical relationship between the two. Finnis concludes by reiterating that real intention should not be confused with artificial conceptual extensions, that intention as properly understood is morally significant, and that intent to harm is a *per se* wrong-making factor in any conduct.

Turning the inquiry from intentionally caused harm to accidental harm, Richard Wright in his essay here explores the Kantian–Aristotelian foundations of negligence, the most common basis of liability for accidental loss. In *The Standards of Care in Negligence Law*, Wright argues that the equal freedom norm is normatively more attractive than its chief competitor, utilitarian efficiency, contending that it also better explains the outcomes of the negligence cases. In a frontal assault on Judge Learned Hand's famous risk-utility formula, which generally is thought to reflect the utilitarian efficiency approach, Wright argues that the formula is both analytically and descriptively flawed. He examines various non-utilitarian efforts to justify or criticize the Hand formula—including those of Ronald Dworkin, Ernest Weinrib, Charles Fried, George Fletcher, and Leslie Bender—and concludes that all fall into the aggregation-of-interests trap of utilitarianism. Identifying three different aspects of the standards of care in negligence law—the risks taken into account, the (objective versus subjective) perspectives applied, and the substantive criteria of reasonableness— he argues that each of these aspects is formulated differently depending on whether the defendant's or the plaintiff's negligence is at issue, and that only the equal freedom theory can explain and justify this differing treatment. Wright concludes by surveying the standards of care in a number of recurring contexts—those involving defendants treating others as means, socially essential activities, premises liability, participatory plaintiffs, paternalistic defendants, plaintiffs' self-interested conduct, plaintiffs' self-sacrificing conduct, and failures to aid or rescue. He maintains that, consistent with the equal-freedom theory but not with the utilitarian efficiency theory, different standards of care are applied in these different situations, depending primarily on who put whom at risk for whose benefit, and on whether the person put at risk consented to the risk.

In *The Seriousness of Harm Thesis for Abnormally Dangerous Activities*, Ken Kress explores the basis of liability for activities that are in some way specially dangerous, activities that generally are classified in American tort law today as 'abnormally dangerous'. Kress challenges the conventional approach to liability in this context, which he views as based upon a notion of 'super-risk' of expected harm. By setting liability on the traditional analytic pillars of expected disvalue (probability of injury times anticipated harm) and uncommonness, the conventional analysis manifests a concern for consequentialist, utilitarian, and efficiency rationales which Kress finds inadequate if not unacceptable. Instead, he offers a solution which he calls the 'seriousness of harm thesis'. His view of the proper basis of liability in this area, majestic in its simplicity, is that the dominant factor of importance is the size of the loss if it does occur—the seriousness of harm—and only secondarily the (conditional) probability that loss will occur if the instrumentality escapes the actor's control. Kress criticizes utilitarian cost-benefit analyses on a number of grounds, and he argues that the maximin decision rule is rationally preferable under certain circumstances which he elaborates. But he ultimately rejects maximin decision-making, concluding that it provides insufficient justificatory support for a special rule of strict liability for abnormally dangerous activities. Because the abnormally dangerous activities cases are best explained in terms of seriousness of harm, Kress concludes that this thesis is superior to conventional analyses of liability in this branch of tort law.

In an article several years ago, John Attanasio offered an 'aggregate-autonomy' justification for Guido Calabresi's strict liability approach to products liability.[36] Attanasio there argued that the aggregate autonomy principle obligates product manufacturers (through liability) and other consumers (through higher prices) to surrender small amounts of wealth to provide compensation to persons severely injured in product accidents. Manufacturers should be liable for such injuries on a strict liability basis when they are the 'best deciders' under Calabresian economic theory, according to Attanasio, in order to maximize the internalization of accident costs to manufacturers and thereby promote the greatest *aggregate* autonomy in society. In his present essay, *Aggregate Autonomy, the Difference Principle, and the Calabresian Approach to Products Liability*, Attanasio further explains and develops this thesis. While the writings of John Rawls provide only general, amorphous support for a Calabresian strict-liability approach to products liability, Rawls' work (particularly the difference principle) did inspire the development of the principle of aggregate autonomy—in both, the better off are required to assist the less advantaged. Thus, although the aggregate-autonomy theory is rooted partially in Nozickian notions of freedom, the theory borrows egalitarian aspects from Rawls. 'Ultimately', Attanasio says, 'the principle of aggregate autonomy seeks to maximize the number of individuals in society who have at least some minimal level of autonomy.' More than Rawls' difference principle,

[36] John B. Attanasio, *The Principle of Aggregate Autonomy and the Calabresian Approach to Products Liability*, 74 VA. L. REV. 677 (1988).

the aggregate autonomy ethic seeks to provide for the basic needs of accident victims, and it accomplishes this by exacting small amounts of wealth from other members of society. In this manner, Attanasio concludes, the principle of aggregate autonomy helps reconcile the fundamental tension between liberty and equality.

B. Connecting Agency and Harm: Risk, Causation, and Damage

This section investigates the complex link between responsibility and harm, a link comprised of many strands. At its center is the fundamental connecting instrument of causation—the vital nexus that brings together into a tort an agent's misconduct and *resulting* harm. Viewed from the center, the question posed is 'What *caused* what?' Causation issues are colored, however, by issues of responsibility and harm that connect to it on either side. So, matters bearing on responsibility and risk need first to be understood in order to decide or even define the issue of '*What* caused what?' So, too, on the other side, tort law must decide what counts as *harm*, if the 'What caused *what?*' question is to make much sense. All three aspects of the tort law linking problem are explored within this section.

In his essay, *Risk, Harm, and Responsibility*, Stephen Perry explores the nature of risk, how it relates to harm, and ultimately how the two interconnect with responsibility in tort law. Perry begins with an inquiry into the two main conceptions of probability that are plausible candidates for understanding the moral significance of risk, which he terms the 'objective' and 'epistemic' conceptions. Emerging from the relative frequency theory of probability, the most basic understanding of the objective conception regards probabilities as just a certain kind of empirical fact in the world. Perry explains how the epistemic conception, according to the preferred reasonableness account, views probability judgments as *estimates* of objective probabilities in the relative frequency sense. Such judgments are based on inductive reasoning, and they are always relative to a given body of evidence. Perry next examines the proposition advanced recently by some theorists that subjecting another to a risk of harm, or reducing his chance of avoiding harm, should itself be viewed as a form of harm redressable in tort. He argues that lost *chance*, understood simply as a probability in the relative frequency sense, does not constitute harm in its own right, but that lost *opportunity*, understood in terms of detrimental reliance, might well do so. Finally, Perry considers when an agent whose risky conduct causes harm to another bears moral responsibility for the harm. Arguing that such responsibility should be grounded in an epistemic notion of risk, he rejects the libertarian argument that actors should be held morally accountable for the materialization of any objective risks they create, a theory that leads unacceptably to a standard of absolute liability. Instead, Perry favors a notion of 'outcome-responsibility' that is rooted in the *avoidability* of harm. Avoidability, he argues, presupposes an epistemic view of risk that would limit responsibility in tort to harm that is foreseeable. Perry concludes that this provides a moral basis for both negligence and risk-based strict liability.

'How is the fact that some actor has caused another person to suffer a loss related to a responsibility to repair the loss?' So asks Christopher Schroeder in *Causation, Compensation and Moral Responsibility,* in which he explores how causation relates to responsibility for harm and how the element of causation more generally fits in the law of torts. Arguing that a *duty to compensate* inheres in the basic structure of tort law, reflected by the maxim, 'If you break it, you pay for it', Schroeder's essay investigates the elusiveness of the search for a convincing moral rationale for the compensation duty. Pursuing the search for such a rationale, he divides the tort paradigm into its three essential elements—(1) a victim who suffers an undeserved loss, (2) a deficient actor, and (3) an action that causes the loss, and he subjects each to certain standard modes of moral evaluation. Finding each of these elements deficient in providing a justification for imposing a compensation obligation on the actor, Schroeder then explores the adequacy of the more complex human agency 'outcome-responsibility' theories of Tony Honoré and Stephen Perry. Although he recognizes that a harmful outcome may well impose responsibilities beyond simply acknowledging one's agency in producing that harm, Schroeder finds such theories inadequate to support the duty to compensate; all that outcome-responsibility can supply is a reason for a response, not for a *particular* response, and certainly not for a duty *fully* to rectify the victim's loss. Schroeder turns finally to the principle of equality that entitles each person to be treated with equal dignity and respect. Noting the usefulness of this concept in ascertaining the faultiness of conduct, as when the actor fails to respect equally the interests of the victim, Schroeder argues that even this powerful basis for ascertaining the moral quality of an act is simply incapable of supplying in addition a rationale for the duty to compensate, for requiring the actor in particular to rectify the victim's loss. He questions whether the concept of equal dignity and respect can be consistent with drawing the kind of sharp distinction contemplated by the duty to compensate on the basis of the single fact of causation. Causation by itself, he reasons, provides too slender a reed for such a sharp distinction. And so Schroeder concludes that one must look somewhere other than causation to find a justification for the duty to compensate in tort law.

In 1959, Tony Honoré and H. L. A. Hart published the first edition of their seminal work, *Causation in the Law.*[37] There, they argued that to be a cause of some event, a prior event must have been a 'causally relevant

---

[37] The work is now in its second edition. H. L. A. HART & TONY HONORÉ, CAUSATION IN THE LAW (2d edn., 1985).

condition' of the resulting event, in that the prior event was a necessary element in a set of prior and concurrent conditions that together was sufficient
to produce the result. In 1965, John Mackie applied the Hart and Honoré
approach to causal regularities—causal generalizations of *types* of events,
rather than specific events—in a theory that was sometimes applicable to
specific events as well. Critiquing Mackie's theory, and elaborating upon
the Hart and Honoré causal-relevancy approach, Richard Wright in 1985
propounded what he termed the 'NESS' (Necessary Element of a Sufficient
Set) test,[38] an approach to causation that has received wide acceptance in
recent years.

In his essay on causation here, *Necessary and Sufficient Conditions in
Tort Law*, Tony Honoré continues to unravel the elusive mysteries of causation. Taking the NESS test as the standard, he examines various ways in
which the NESS and but for tests agree and differ. In terms of their agreement, Honoré explains the importance of tying the plaintiff's harm to the
defendant's breach of duty rather than simply to the defendant's conduct,
and the necessity under both theories of formulating and answering counterfactual hypothetical questions. He then examines contexts where the two
causation theories interpret problems differently, sometimes producing the
same and sometimes different causal conclusions. From this perspective,
Honoré explores three types of 'overdetermination' cases, those involving
(1) similar causal processes culminating at the same time, (2) different
causal processes, and (3) subsequent causation of harm that already has
occurred. Finally, he inquires into problems of indeterminacy, showing that
neither causation theory adequately explains the causal perplexities of
human decision-making and behavior; neither can fully unravel the mysteries of what caused, persuaded, or provoked someone to act as he did,
but something analogous to the idea of sufficiency can aid our understanding. Honoré concludes that causation is important to tort law in that
it helps to explain puzzling events, fix the outer limits of social responsibility, and assure that liability is imposed only for (unlawful) conduct that has
changed the course of events for the worse.

The apparent unfairness of a tort regime that imposes full tort liability
upon persons whose momentary inadvertence happens to result in massive
losses is the topic of Jeremy Waldron's essay. In *Moments of Carelessness
and Massive Loss*, Waldron's investigation into the logic and fairness of the
tort system thus explores the connection and sometimes gross disparity
between the degree of a victim's loss and the degree of the actor's fault.
Pointing to the intuitive unfairness of such a system in terms of individual
desert, he considers and rejects the argument that issues of desert should be
left to the domain of retributive justice and the criminal law, where they are

---

[38] Richard Wright, *Causation in Tort Law*, 73 CAL. L. REV. 1735 (1985).

more widely accepted as being central to responsibility. A gaping disproportion between the moral character of a person's actions and the consequences attendant thereto, Waldron argues, seems to violate notions of
fairness and desert as much in tort as elsewhere in the law. He next examines the so-called annulment theory of tort law, where the goal is said to be
the simultaneous annulment of the actor's gains and the victim's losses, and
he explains its inability to resolve the fairness problem under consideration.
Nor does a distributive justice focus on the unfairness to the victim of suffering the loss help much, in Waldron's view: the mere fact that an accident
caused a disruption in the prior just distribution of goods provides no more
reason for forcing the disruption upon the actor than leaving it upon the
victim. Questioning whether the causal requirement in tort law may not be
too strong in limiting the class of persons asked to shoulder an enormous
loss to the actor and the victim, Waldron suggests that a broader insurance
approach to accident losses may be preferable to the law of torts.
Borrowing the 'penal lottery' theory of criminal punishment proposed by
David Lewis, Waldron explores the possibility of viewing a person's risky
action as imposing a chance or lottery upon potential victims. If the actor's
inadvertence in a particular case unluckily happens to cause injury—if the
victim's number is unluckily called up—then neither fairness nor desert
would seem to be much offended by placing the consequences of the lottery chosen by the actor upon his head. From this perspective, the purchase
cost of inflicting a lottery upon others is to accept the consequences oneself. By so imposing risks (of liability) on negligent actors corresponding
precisely to the risks that negligent actors impose on others, even for massive losses when they do occur, Waldron argues that the all-or-nothing
damages lottery approach of tort law may explain away the appearance of
unfairness in such liability. Even as so viewed, however, he concludes that
the tort system remains unattractive to social insurance schemes for
addressing accidental loss.

The role of tort-law damages in corrective justice generally, and for non-
pecuniary loss in particular, is the topic of Bruce Chapman's essay,
*Wrongdoing, Welfare, and Damages: Recovery for Non-Pecuniary Loss in
Corrective Justice*. Noting that the general principle of tort-law damages
traditionally has held that such damages should restore the plaintiff to the
position he would have occupied had the tort not occurred, *restitutio in
integrum*, Chapman investigates how and why this classic principle, at least
in the particular case of non-pecuniary loss, might be inconsistent with
modern tort law theories. Compensation theorists from the left would most
like to preserve scarce economic resources for the pressing financial needs
of victims, while economic theorists on the right would compensate
non-pecuniary losses only to the limited extent that persons would insure
themselves against such losses *ex ante*. Although corrective justice theory

would seem to require full compensation for unjust inflictions of non-pecuniary loss as much as for other types of losses, Chapman argues that corrective justice, although in fact requiring full compensation for the pecuniary costs of future care and future earnings loss, does *not* require compensation for non-pecuniary loss. Adopting Ernest Weinrib's conception of corrective justice, which focuses upon the inherent correlativity of the defendant's doing and the plaintiff's suffering of harm, Chapman reasons that corrective justice should only correct for wrongful losses within the space of rights, and that it should not otherwise be concerned with a victim's welfare. Explaining that money damages simply cannot repair the kind of rights damage suffered when losses are of the non-pecuniary kind, he claims that money damages in this context can only serve to increase the victim's welfare in some respect which is irrelevant to the wrongful act. Thus, because corrective justice does not support compensation for such losses, he maintains that nominal damages alone are appropriate for this type of loss. Chapman further explains that the argument for very limited damages for this type of loss is based upon money's lack of utility—its inability to restore the plaintiff's specific welfare loss within the ambit of the defendant's wrongdoing—a very different matter from how the plaintiff might actually choose to use a monetary award. He distinguishes the idea that money may have no utility in restoring the plaintiff's loss from Margaret Jane Radin's notion, based on her theory of corrective justice as redress rather than rectification, that money may be incommensurable with the victim's loss. Chapman concludes that the concept of the limited utility of money, on which all contemporary tort theories seem to be agreed, precludes awarding anything but nominal damages for non-pecuniary loss.

One of the more difficult and controversial areas of tort doctrine concerns the judicial exclusion of liability for economic losses of certain types. In particular, courts and scholars have long struggled to define the proper contexts in which the law of torts should allow recovery in negligence for pure economic loss. Notwithstanding many years of rigorous scrutiny, there is still little agreement on the nature or even the possibility of an underlying rationale for excluding such losses from tort recovery consistent with the conception of negligence as developed in this century. In *The Basis for Excluding Liability for Economic Loss in Tort Law*, Peter Benson boldly enters this quagmire of doctrine and theory, examining and ordering the different categories of economic loss through an analysis that seeks to remain internal to the law by drawing on the very principles and considerations that are present in it. In contrast to prevailing policy-based approaches, Benson (following Rawls) proposes what he calls a 'public basis of justification' that roots the analysis of doctrine in purely juridical normative considerations. He argues that there is a single rationale that explains why economic loss claims are allowed in some situations but not in others. Recovery is allowed, he contends, only where the plaintiff's claim against the defendant sounds in misfeasance: it must rest only on such interests which the plaintiff can validly assert in some legally recognized manner as 'his own', exclusive of the defendant. Only then, argues Benson, will an interest qualify as a *protected* interest for the purposes of tort law. Through this analytical prism, the economic loss cases may be seen as reconcilable on the basis of a fundamental and pervasive feature of the general conception of liability for negligence without recourse to considerations of policy or of distributive justice.

C. Victim Responsibility for Harm

It takes two to do the Tango, and it takes an actor *and a victim* to make a tort. A victim's presence at a place and time when he is collided into by an actor is always a matter of the victim's prior choices, at least in part. Perhaps the victim willingly chose to place himself in a dangerous spot to achieve a particular objective. Or perhaps that objective, or the victim's choice for some other reason, or the victim's method of acting to achieve the objective was a bad one by some measure. The question explored here, in this final section of Part III, is how the law of torts should make this measure—how tort law should determine if a *victim*'s harm-producing conduct was improper and, if so, whether that fact should relieve a tortious actor of responsibility (in whole or part) for the victim's harm.

Turning the inquiry away from the injurer and toward the victim of an accidental injury, Kenneth Simons probes the fundamentals of contributory victim fault forms of defense in *Contributory Negligence: Conceptual and Normative Issues*. While it may seem obvious that a person who carelessly steps into danger should have his recovery for damages against a negligent actor reduced or eliminated on the basis of his own fault, Simons finds that the grounds for that conclusion are far from obvious. Understanding the very notion of victim fault or negligence, in his view, raises a variety of difficult questions. First, in saying that the victim is 'at fault' or 'negligent' in failing to take a particular precaution, do we mean that the victim should have acted otherwise, that his conduct was *deficient*, and that a reduction in his damages is one way to rectify this moral failure? Or do we instead believe that the victim had a *right* not to take the precaution, but that his acceptance of a damage reduction is the legitimate price of exercising the right? On the latter view, Simons reasons, the victim's conduct would seem to be devoid of fault and so more fairly might be viewed as a form of 'plaintiff's strict responsibility'. Under either view, Simons explains, the victim's duty to use reasonable care is only conditional, in that it applies only if the victim chooses to sue the injurer. Turning to the substantive rationales for limiting a victim's recovery, Simons considers whether those rationales justify applying identical or distinct criteria to victim and injurer negligence. From this perspective, he first examines the Kantian view of negligence as based upon the injurer's unjustifiable egoism and concludes that it cannot explain limiting the victim's recovery. Next, he probes beneath the surface symmetry of the utilitarian Hand formula and finds lurking there a number of problems of aggregation that undermine its coherence when applied to victim conduct. Simons then examines a moral parity approach which he finds more promising, under which the plaintiff is bound to apply the same standard to himself as to the defendant. He also considers a forfeiture rationale, which would justify the application of very different criteria to victim and injurer negligence, then explores the effect of relaxing the assumption that the victim poses risks only to himself, and finally inspects the rationales for and implications of limiting a victim's recovery under the plaintiff's strict responsibility approach. Simons concludes that the reasons that justify providing the victim with a remedy for the injurer's negligence do not suffice to justify limiting the remedy for the victim's negligence.

V. From Tort Law to Philosophy—Passing the Baton

The essays in this volume (with one notable exception) are written by lawyers searching for meaning in the law of torts, looking for an explanation and justification for the principles and rules of tort law in another discipline, philosophy. While some interbreeding between law and philosophy has occurred over the centuries, both disciplines have remained remarkably insular even to this day. One of the great strengths of the human intellect is its ability through reason to organize facts and concepts into castle-like structures of the mind, structures that themselves contain numerous interconnected chambers of elegantly refined and ever-expanding interrelationships of thought. But the chambers and especially the castles of different intellectual disciplines have thick walls, thickened and reinforced over the centuries against outside attack, permitting separate communities of scholars to continue to live and think within and ornament their respective chambers and castles in isolated comfort. But while this type of Balkan buttressing of thought has in many ways strengthened the internal integrity of thought within the separate bastions of discipline, the resulting inbreeding spawns defects that weaken the structures, sometimes superficially but other times penetrating insidiously to the very foundations and integrity of the entire castle.

Both law and philosophy over the years in different ways have been guilty of this type of insular perspective, and at least the law has suffered from it. As perhaps is true with all disciplines, law and philosophy both in many ways have long been over-specialized and over-technical, in both their language and their concepts. And as close as tort law ought to be to moral and political philosophy, neither the lawyers nor the philosophers know very much about each other's discipline. One function of this volume, then, may be to help the two disciplines come a little bit together, in the specific realm of the law of torts. The important premise here is that both disciplines may be enriched and strengthened by learning from one another. Yet this collection cannot make claim to interdisciplinary status in any full sense, for each essay but one is written by a lawyer.[39] Although each essay purports to be a philosophical study, each is written from a tort law point of view, from the perspective of what philosophy can do for *law*, of how the *law* can benefit from borrowing the type of reflective thought that 'belongs' to philosophy. Even the title of this Foreword, *Why Philosophy Matters to Tort Law*, unabashedly makes this point.

While the effort to bring together the learning of these two separate disciplines is not at all an easy task, surely it is worth the effort. This volume continues the recent march of tort lawyers into the foreign land of philosophy, a journey begun in earnest less than a quarter century ago and only very recently acquiring any numbers or sense of real direction. With a fertile (perhaps militaristic) imagination, one might close one's eyes and envision a platoon of academic lawyers marching out of the Castle of Law across the meadows and into the Castle of Philosophy. Now that the lawyer-invaders have surveyed the philosophic booty on the inside, and picked and chosen according to each one's taste, they have marched back to their own lands to proclaim how the philosophic curiosities they have pilfered may be used to fortify the Castle of Law.

The essays to this point in the volume offer such thoughts from tort law theorists on how philosophy may help determine what tort law is, what it should be doing, and how it may better accomplish its objectives. In the volume's Afterword, *What Has Philosophy to Learn from Tort Law?*, Bernard Williams turns a philosopher's eye back in the other direction, with a look at how philosophy may benefit from examining the law of torts. Williams postulates that law generally, and tort law in particular, might be of interest to philosophers in providing a laboratory for studying instances of problem-solving under pressure, where the community must decide in a practical and conclusive way what to do about the consequences of intentional or accidental harm. In this manner, the strength of concepts and distinctions are tested by the law in a crucible of reality in a way that philosophical reflection cannot do alone. He characterizes this perspective as 'the Picture', that the law might remind philosophy of reality by revealing distinctions recognizable to common sense under pressure where much turns on the outcome. Williams anticipates that the Picture may be subject

---

[39] Although a number of the authors have received formal training in philosophy, all but Bernard Williams are teachers of the law.

to two principal objections. First is that this view *over*estimates the effects of legal concepts applied by argument within the legal process—that cases are decided on the basis of values external to the law, such as utility or wealth maximization, and that the legal concepts explicitly applied (such as negligence and proximate causation) are merely decorative rationalizations. The second objection is that the Picture *under*estimates the separateness of the concepts and processes of the law from *common sense*, such that the law's specialist ways of thinking are too removed from the kinds of extra-legal thought of interest to philosophy to provide insights in this latter realm.

Williams finds that neither objection is fatal to the Picture, for tort law necessarily forces the resolution of issues of fault and responsibility, particularly in terms of the agent's state of mind and the directness of the connection between that state of mind and the resulting harmful consequences. While he objects to attempts to ground everyday morality in ethical theory (especially in a unified monistic theory), he acknowledges the importance to a liberal society of explaining the application of power, which includes a court's application of tort law rules to resolve disputes. For this purpose, the theory generated by philosophical reflection may help both explain and improve the law. Although this way of looking at the matter largely turns it back around, into one of how philosophy can help the law, Williams reasons that this back side of his question inheres in philosophy's exploration of what the law is trying to do. Finding notions of responsibility and the voluntary (including Tony Honoré's notion of outcome responsibility) interesting to philosophy, he cautions against pushing too hard for deep and adequate theories of the voluntary and moral responsibility. Williams concludes that there is truth in the Picture, that the law provides insights into the concepts of philosophy under extreme conditions, and he observes the importance of arriving at an adequate theory (provided by law and philosophy together) of how philosophical concepts work in law.

Bernard Williams' essay serves more than as a decorative bookend from a member of a different discipline for a volume of essays about theories of the law of private wrongs. Surely it does provide important closing insights of interest to legal scholars on the reciprocal interests of the discipline of philosophy invoked by each of the lawyers writing about tort law theory. But even more importantly, it serves as an opening offer to the philosophers to enter the fray, to join battle with the lawyers, and engage the law of torts. As Williams makes clear, focusing on the relationship between philosophy and tort law reveals numerous ways in which philosophy can 'come to the rescue' of this area of the law. And while tort law might not *require* rescue[40] by philosophers, it certainly could make good use of it. Many of the philosophical concepts invoked by the lawyers in this volume, such as

[40] Yania *v.* Bigan, 155 A.2d 343 (Pa. 1959); Note, *A Comparative Study*, 52 COLUM. L. REV. 631 (1952) (examining general no-duty-to-rescue rule of Anglo-American tort law).

notions of free will, utility, and truth, have been rejected by many modern philosophers as theoretically suspect and outmoded. If, indeed, such concepts have no philosophic value for tort law problems, if they cannot meaningfully help lawyers understand how the content of tort-law doctrine should be framed, then surely it is the philosophers' job to prove this point and to teach the lawyers how instead to address the kinds of issues they confront in the law of torts.

One may sense a certain skepticism in Bernard Williams' essay about the strength of the underlying relationship between law and philosophy, a certain acceptance of the separateness of the two disciplines; there is no persuasive evidence in the essay that he perceives an important foundational link between the two. This contrasts quite sharply with the perspectives of most of the lawyers writing in the volume who either argue explicitly or postulate implicitly that the law of torts is constructed upon philosophical foundations. Perhaps this is merely wishful thinking of the doers of a shallow discipline—law—hoping to give historical and intellectual legitimacy to a craft that has served for most of its existence as little more than a kind of window dressing to 'gussy up' the raw exercise of power. Or maybe the tort lawyers sooner than the philosophers have sensed a fundamental interrelationship that really does exist between the theoretical and practical disciplines of how people ought to and must treat one another in the world. Almost all the essays in this volume are committed to the latter view, and one may sense an implicit (perhaps begrudging) discovery of at least a little of its truth in the progression of analysis in Williams' essay.

Whether the suspicions of many modern philosophers about the validity and usefulness of moral theorizing derive merely from the trends of skepticism and nihilism pervading many disciplines in the twentieth century, or whether they derive instead from true vacuousness in such concepts, is difficult to know. But know we must, if law—or philosophy in action—is to understand itself. The importance of the current study is that such philosophical suspicions, just as the tort lawyers' grand theories, can be tested with special reliability, as Williams argues, in the real-world laboratory of the law of torts. More than any other area of the law, tort law offers examples of how people should and should not treat each other—examples from nearly every context of harmful human interaction. From such myriad situations, tort law also raises important issues of how the community should use its power to respond, through the private law of civil wrongs, to complaints of persons hurt by other human beings. How the law of torts deals with such issues, and how it *ought* to deal with them, certainly *should* be matters of interest to philosophers.

Surely stumbling, the tort lawyers have run the opening lap, and the baton has now been passed.

PART I

THE NATURE AND REALM OF TORT LAW AND PHILOSOPHY

The Concept of a Civil Wrong

PETER BIRKS[*]

This essay is concerned with the common law, but it has a Roman beginning. By starting from the Roman analysis in which it had its origin, we can most easily set out the common law classification in which civil wrongs, or torts, form one important category. The concept of a civil wrong cannot be investigated other than in the context of that classification. Differentiation is not the least important aspect of the exercise.

I. THE FOURFOLD CLASSIFICATION

The second century jurist Gaius was, so far as we know, the first to advance the proposition that every obligation arises from a contract or from a wrong or from some other causal event.[1] He was attracted by a simpler proposition, without the miscellaneous third category: every obligation arises from a contract or a wrong.[2] However, he saw that that would not do, for there were indisputable instances of legal obligation handed down from the unsystematic past which arose from neither. The obligation to return a mistaken payment was a prominent example.[3]

The threefold classification—contracts, wrongs, and other events—was not the end of the Roman story. The miscellaneous third category posed a challenge. By the end of the first life of Roman law the three terms had given way to four, and the miscellany appeared to have been resolved: every obligation arises from a contract, or *as though from* a contract, or from a wrong, or *as though from* a wrong.[4] The 'as though' categories gave us the terms 'quasi-contract' and 'quasi-delict', but they cast no light on the lines drawn. The categories are not only categories of causative event but categories of explanation. We seem to see the force of the proposition that an obligation arises from contract or from a wrong, but there is no explanatory force in the parallel propositions for quasi-contract and quasi-delict. The 'as though' categories are described negatively, so that the reader only knows what these events are not. The doubts infect the two seemingly safe

* Regius Professor of Civil Law, University of Oxford, and Fellow of All Souls College, Oxford.

[1] JUSTINIAN, DIGEST 44.7.1 pr. (GAIUS, AUREA, bk. 2).   [2] GAIUS, INSTITUTES, 3.88.
[3] GAIUS, INSTITUTES, 3.91.   [4] JUSTINIAN, INSTITUTES, 3.13.

categories. Where exactly are the lines drawn? Where precisely does the explanatory force of contract and wrongs run out?

We need not pursue the Roman story here. We have only to notice that the game which Gaius started is still being played out in the common law today. The challenge is the same, and the problems closely similar. Some would prefer to go behind Gaius's starting point. That is, they would not even accept contract and wrongs. However, ever since serious and sustained thought about the common law began somewhat over a century ago,[5] most jurists have accepted the two main Roman categories of contract and wrongs or, using the French for wrongs which the common law still prefers, 'torts'. There are very few law schools which do not teach, as basic required courses—the law of contracts and the law of torts. Both topics of the law have survived well enough into modern times to earn their second Restatements.[6]

What about the miscellany beyond contract and tort? For many lawyers it is still *terra incognita*, territory unknown. But most of those who have done some exploration think that at least one more major category can be mapped, namely unjust enrichment. That produces four categories and narrows the residual miscellany: (1) contract, (2) tort, (3) unjust enrichment, and (4) other causative events. Except against those radicals who want to abolish the categories of contract and tort, that fourfold classification ought now to be secure. It seemed to become secure in 1937. In that year the American Law Institute published the Restatement of Restitution.[7] It could have been called the Restatement of Unjust Enrichment, but the American Law Institute chose to call the law of unjust enrichment 'restitution'. That is, the Restatement was named by the response to the event, not the event itself.

Taken alone, restitution is a good name, but it is not perfectly coextensive with the autonomous cause of action called unjust enrichment and it does not align properly with contract and tort. It tends to push the subject towards remedies. In fact, restitution is now often taught in courses on remedies, even though it is mostly concerned with defining causative events or, synonymously, causes of action—that is, with identifying the precise facts which render an enrichment unjust and from which the obligation to make restitution arises. Perhaps it is the bad influence of its wrongly aligned name which has cost restitution the security of a Second Restatement. The project appeared to be under way, but after two Tentative Drafts, it was

---

[5] The beginning, or perhaps the end of the beginning, of such scholarship can be conveniently marked by the foundation of two great law reviews, the *Law Quarterly Review* in 1885 and the *Harvard Law Review* in 1887.

[6] And now the beginnings of a Third Restatement for the law of torts. *See, e.g.,* RESTATEMENT (THIRD) OF TORTS: PRODUCTS LIABILITY (Tentative Draft No. 1, 1994).

[7] RESTATEMENT OF THE LAW OF RESTITUTION (1937).

abandoned.[8] Despite that hesitation, the fourfold classification of causative events—(1) contracts (consent), (2) torts (wrongs), (3) unjust enrichments, and (4) other events—is unlikely to be easily displaced, though it may be that the miscellaneous fourth category can be made to yield up further nominate events.

The question in this essay concerns the second category in this scheme, which the common law habitually calls 'torts' but which the title of the essay calls 'civil wrongs'. This classification of causative events is all-important, not only to the work of the essay, but to the structure of the common law. For, even though most common lawyers pay no conscious heed to it, this fourfold classification underlies their thinking, and the coherence of the classification is one of the foundations of the law's rationality. Every time a lawyer selects a theory of liability he draws on it, if not directly and consciously, then at least on ideas which rest upon it. It is an error, albeit one which is institutionalized in many law schools simply because different professors teach different courses, to define or reflect upon one category in isolation from the others. The reason why that error must be avoided is that a legal concept cannot be fully understood unless it is clearly differentiated from others in its field, and the exercise of differentiation remains impossible so long as a concept is studied in isolation.

II. The Thesis in a Nutshell

This essay aims both to establish a stable and properly differentiated concept of a civil wrong and to defend the coherence of the fourfold classification set out above. The latter aim is part and parcel of the exercise of differentiation. The reader may find it helpful at the outset to have some forewarning of the positions which will be taken. Subject, therefore, to the routine caveat that an outline cannot stand alone, the thesis of this paper may be enucleated as follows.

(1) A civil wrong is no more nor less than a breach of legal duty owed to a plaintiff. Core characteristics such as harm and fault are analytically inessential. However, (2) a failure to perform a contract or to fulfil an obligation to make restitution of unjust enrichment or to pay a tax or satisfy a judgment is no less capable of being described as a breach of duty than negligent injury or defamation or any other familiar tort. Hence, (3) there is a

---

[8] The A.L.I. published Tentative Drafts No. 1 and No. 2 in 1983 and 1984. The project did not proceed as the Institute hoped, and so it was temporarily suspended sometime in 1984 or 1985. *Minutes of the A.L.I. Council*, Dec. 11–14, 1985, 1(g), at 6. The project was never resumed, and the Second Restatement series is now complete. Accordingly, the best current hope for the subject of restitution is to be included in a possible Third Restatement of Remedies: telephone conversation between A.L.I. Librarian and the editor of this volume, June 24, 1994.

prima facie case for asserting that the fourfold classification—contract, wrongs, unjust enrichment, and other events—is incoherent: all four categories appear to entail breaches of duty, with the consequence that, if a wrong is a breach of duty and every breach of duty is a wrong, it must be dangerous nonsense to tolerate three categories which entail breaches of duty yet on their face purport to be something different from a wrong. However, (4) the broad concept of a civil wrong as nothing more nor less than a breach of duty does not, on closer analysis, render the fourfold classification incoherent, although it does provoke a warning that the complexity of that classification is not to be underestimated. (5) The key to the coherence of the fourfold classification lies in the difference between the possibility of describing a given event as a breach of duty and the necessity of so describing it. The three categories other than wrongs are categories of event in which it is unnecessary, though not impossible, to explain the liabilities which they cause as triggered by a breach of duty. So, for example, your liability to return a mistaken payment (a category 3 event) can be, but need not be, explained as triggered by your breach of the duty to return mistaken payments. Each of the first, third, and fourth categories exists as an independent category—or, one might say, as an independent theory of liability—because and to the extent that the law prefers to give them direct effect and does not opt to reduce them to the analysis in terms of breach of duty. (6) The practical matter which turns on the choice of whether or not to give priority to an explanation in terms of breach of duty has to do with remedies. The remedial potential of a wrong (breach of duty) is more diverse than that of any of the events in the first, third, and fourth categories.

The sixth proposition above is linked to an important sub-theme. Just as the response to crimes is a matter for policy and open to debate, within extrinsic constraints such as the renunciation of recourse to cruelty, so civil wrongs similarly dictate no particular response. Although rational debate as to the best policy will often favor compensation in money, there is no reason why, subject to the external constraints, other forms and measures of response should not also be used.

III. COMMON DISTRACTIONS

Two distractions impede analysis. One is the tendency of 'tort' to exclude equitable wrongs. The other is the misinterpretation of the association of civil wrongs with one measure of response, namely compensation for loss. This must not be elevated to the level of a logical necessity, as if any other remedy would be unnatural.

The common law is everywhere heavily marked by the ancient jurisdictional division between law and equity, although different members of the common law family have bridged the gap at different speeds. Tort developed as a common law category. Wrongs redressed in equity—such as breach of trust, knowing assistance in a fraud, and abuse of confidence—have not traditionally been regarded as torts. They have been the subject of different books and different courses. Salmond excluded breaches of equitable obligations simply on the basis of historical classification; tort was common law, and that was that.[9] In contrast, Winfield was more agonized. He defined tortious liability thus: 'Tortious liability arises from the breach of a duty primarily fixed by the law: such duty is towards persons generally and its breach is redressible by an action for liquidated damages.'[10] He clearly had some difficulty with the exclusion of breach of trust, but he excluded it nevertheless in the end on two grounds—that equity did not deal in 'liquidated damages', and that the law of trusts should be regarded as a separate department of the law.[11]

Civil wrongs are thus as a matter of history a wider category than tort. But it is difficult to find or to create any theoretical interest in or justification for the continued separation between legal and equitable wrongs.[12] If one observes the restriction of tort to common law, one confines one's discussion to a sub-set of wrongs identified by history rather than by any rational principle. That is why this essay prefers to speak of civil wrongs generally and, except where the context otherwise makes clear, uses 'tort' to denote all civil wrongs, whatever their jurisdictional root.

Not wholly unrelated to the jurisdictional division between law and equity are theories which define the notion of a civil wrong in terms of a particular kind of harm remediable by a particular measure of damages. Thus, some believe that torts necessarily entail a loss to a plaintiff compensable in money and that the remedy must be compensation for that loss.[13] However, although policy choices on those lines can be made, it should be evident that there is nothing absolute or definitive about the notion of loss reflected in awards of compensatory damages. Awards of

---

[9] From the first edition in 1907, this has survived to the present day. *See* R. F. V. HEUSTON & R. A. BUCKLEY, SALMOND AND HEUSTON ON THE LAW OF TORTS (20th edn., 1992) 14.

[10] PERCY H. WINFIELD, THE PROVINCE OF THE LAW OF TORT (1931) 32.

[11] *Id.* at 113–15.

[12] The pioneering article of P. M. North, *Breach of Confidence: Is There a New Tort?*, 12 LEGAL STUD.: J. SOC. PUB. TEACH. L. 149 (1972), opened the way for a more robust approach insisting on a full cross-over between law and equity. *Cf.* Aquaculture Corp. v. New Zealand Green Mussell Co. [1990], 3 N.Z.L.R. 299, 301, *per* Sir Robin Cooke, P.

[13] In Cassell & Co. v. Broome, [1972] A.C. 1027, Lord Reid clearly regarded the law of civil wrongs as naturally confined to compensating losses, anything else being 'highly anomalous': *id.* at 1086D. Note, however, the more cautious attitude of Lord Wilberforce: *id.* at 1114C–D. In German law the commitment to compensation is absolute. Para. 823–6 of the Bürgerliches Gesetzbuch (Civil Code) [BGB] are expressly focused on an *Ersatzpflicht* (a compensation-obligation). Zimmermann apparently regards this as the natural position of a mature system. REINHARD ZIMMERMANN, THE LAW OF OBLIGATIONS (1990), 902, 909.

exemplary and restitutionary damages—the latter sometimes disguised in other language, for example as accounts of profits or money had and received upon a waiver of tort—prove that there is no absolute objection to awards for more than a victim has suffered in loss.[14] And awards of nominal damages similarly show that the notion of a wrong is detachable in principle from the compensable harm suffered. There would be nothing incoherent in a system making the policy choice to increase the penal and deterrent functions of the law of civil wrongs by using multiple measures of damages or even by visiting beatings and other humiliations upon the defendant at the instance of the plaintiff.[15]

Jules Coleman's recent book,[16] so far as it concerns tort rather than contract, appears to give comfort to those who believe that the law of civil wrongs is and must be definitively linked to the notion of compensation for loss, since compensation for wrongful loss might be said to be its insistent theme. The true message of the book is or ought to be different, though this is rather easily overlooked. Coleman says from the beginning that he is only talking about the core of tort law, not its entirety.[17] Thus, when he touches on non-compensatory awards for wrongs, he is able to dismiss them, not as alien to the law of tort but as outside the core and the conception of corrective justice operative in that core. Thus, of restitutionary awards for wrongs he says: 'Corrective justice imposes the duty on the wrongdoer to compensate his victims . . . Restitutionary justice gives the victim the right to the wrongdoer's gains secured at her expense.'[18]

It is essential to the understanding of the nature of civil wrongs to dispel the illusion that compensation and such wrongs are intrinsically connected. Coleman is of course entitled to choose his own subject matter, though there are dangers in theorizing about a not very clearly defined part of a larger whole. In the paragraph following the assertions quoted above, he slips from distinguishing the spheres of operation of two principles of justice (compensatory and restitutionary) to dividing two categories of law: 'Tort law is the central institution for discharging the duty to repair wrongful losses; restitution is the legal remedy for repairing wrongful gains.' The latter assertion seems to say that restitutionary damages belong outside the law of tort, not merely outside his chosen core. But that cannot be right, since the categories do not match up. 'Tort' is a category of *causative event*

---

[14] *See generally* David G. Owen, *The Moral Foundations of Punitive Damages*, 40 ALA. L. REV. 705 (1989); P. B. H. BIRKS, *Civil Wrongs: A New World, in* BUTTERWORTH LECTURES 55, (1990-91), 77–98. In two recent decisions, the U.S. Supreme Court has quite rightly refused to outlaw punitive damages. Browning-Ferris Indust., Inc. v. Kelco Disposal, Inc., 492 U.S. 257 (1989); Pacific Mut. Life Ins. Co. v. Haslip, 499 U.S. 1 (1991). However, it is clear that it is not the availability of punitive damages, but only their abuse, which attracts the *Honda* Court's hostility.

[15] *See infra,* text accompanying note 46.

[16] JULES L. COLEMAN, RISKS AND WRONGS (1992).   [17] *Id* at 198.   [18] *Id* at 371.

whereas 'restitution' is a category of *response* to an event, just as is 'compensation'. The law of tort must concern itself with all responses which might be appropriate to the tortious event, and the restitution of wrongful gains is one of those responses. An account of the profits of a tort is no more outside the law of tort than are awards of compensatory or punitive damages.[19]

IV. A UNIVERSAL REQUIREMENT AND THE CORE CASE

A wrong is always a breach of duty according to the normative system which is in question. If there is no duty broken, there can be no wrong. The normative system with which we are concerned is the law. A legal wrong cannot be understood except as a breach of legal duty. A complainant may believe his life to be ruined by another's seduction of his daughter or his wife. It may be that, according to his view of morality, he has suffered a wrong. If so, his view of morality is that it includes a duty to the father or husband not to seduce or not to commit adultery. In a plural society, many might agree with him. Yet the law generally is not plural, and it is less open than morality to debate. In a court, if there is no legal duty not to seduce or not to commit adultery, he cannot complain of a legal wrong. Similarly with infringements of privacy. The public revelation of private facts or secret photographs may inflict terrible emotional pain on the victim and to many may be a moral wrong. But if the particular jurisdiction recognizes no legal duty to respect these privacy interests of other persons, their invasion cannot be a legal wrong. Again, one supermarket may set out to capture the business of another and ruin the latter's owners, but if there is no legal duty not to compete—or not to compete in the chosen mode or with the chosen purpose—there can be no legal wrong.

This universal requirement serves to introduce a two-tier structural truth about legal wrongs, namely, that the facts which constitute the breach of a legal duty will almost always, though not of absolute necessity, generate a new and different obligation.[20] If you negligently break my leg in breach of your duty to take care not to cause me foreseeable injury, your breach of that duty will generate a further obligation to pay me money. John

---

[19] It is crucial to distinguish between the cause of action which consists in the wrong, which may have different measures of response, and the entirely different cause of action in subtractive unjust enrichment, which may sometimes be available to the victim of a wrong but which will involve a re-analysis of his facts. *See* PETER BIRKS, AN INTRODUCTION TO THE LAW OF RESTITUTION (1989), 39–43, 106–7, 313–18.

[20] I take obligation in the sense of duty to make a performance to another. In a rare case the consequence of a wrong can be a personal liability of a different kind or even the creation of a proprietary interest, as appears to be the case when in breach of duty a bribe is received. Attorney-General for Hong Kong v. Reid [1933] 3 W.L.R. 1143.

Austin,[21] following Pothier,[22] called the initial legal duty a 'primary obligation' and the obligation consequential upon breach a 'secondary obligation' or a 'remedial obligation'. Austin criticized the fourfold classification examined above precisely on the ground that it failed to take this two-tier structure into account and therefore failed to notice that it doubled back on itself.[23] We will return to this criticism, which suggests a *prima facie* incoherence in the fourfold classification, later in the essay.

In the core case, of which everyone will agree that it constitutes a civil wrong, the breach of legal duty consists of the following: harm to a victim caused by conduct (either acts or omissions) of a defendant in respect of which the defendant was blameworthy. In short, the core tort case includes three principal[24] elements: (1) harm, (2) conduct, and (3) blameworthiness. For example, V's car is dishonestly taken by D; or V's legs are injured by D's negligent control of his vehicle; or V, a child for whom D is responsible, suffers brain damage because D cruelly fails to feed him; or V's reputation is damaged by untruths knowingly published by D.

It is trite philosophy that core characteristics often turn out on closer analysis to be inessential to the concept under examination. The crucial question is therefore whether each of the three core features—harm, conduct, and blameworthiness—is essential to the notion of a civil wrong.

A. Harm to the Victim

In examining the first element of a civil wrong, we first must separate the two words, 'civil' and 'wrong'. If the word 'wrong' is taken alone, it certainly does not require that there should be harm to a victim. Whether or not we hold the views which support the condemnation, we cannot deny the sense, for one who does, of holding that a wrong is committed by a person who privately smokes cannabis or reads pornographic material. Further, it is wrong, as well as stupid, for a driver to overtake as he approaches the brow of a hill, whether or not there is a car invisibly approaching. If he is lucky and gets away without a collision, his reckless driving is none the less a wrong, a moral wrong in the view of most people, and a legal wrong in most jurisdictions, albeit on the criminal side.

Although etymology is not decisive, it is interesting that the rich vocab-

---

[21] JOHN AUSTIN, LECTURES ON JURISPRUDENCE (1970), 44–7, 795–6.

[22] ROBERT J. POTHIER, A TREATISE ON THE LAW OF OBLIGATIONS (William D. Evans trans., 1826) (originally TRAITÉ DES OBLIGATIONS), ¶ 183–6. The discovery of the source of this structure in Pothier is due to Professor Bernard A. Rudden: *see* letter from Bernard A. Rudden (1990) 10 OXFORD J. LEGAL STUD. 288, commenting on Brice Dickson, *The Contribution of Lord Diplock to the General Law of Contract (1989)* 9 OXFORD J. LEGAL STUD. 441.

[23] AUSTIN, *supra*, note 21, at 796–800.

[24] The element of causation implied by the words 'caused by' in the previous sentence has no independent bearing on the present discussion.

ulary in this field omits all reference to a victim harmed. 'Wrong' and 'tort', like 'crook' and 'bent', play on the same metaphor which contrasts to 'right' and 'straight'. Wrong conduct, or, using the French word, 'tort', is twisted, a metaphor for condemned or disapproved.[25] But what is condemned need not entail harm to a victim. 'Trespass', long used outside the law to refer to the geographical line between mine and yours, steps in fact across the more elusive boundary between right and wrong.[26] Sometimes one goes too far. 'Forgive us our trespasses' implies regret for those transgressions and a will to try to stay on the right side of the line. A 'malefactor' simply does bad.[27] A 'delinquent' fails to do, without saying what; but we know that when a 'delict' is committed it is the calls of right and good conscience that are neglected.[28]

All these words merely disapprove conduct, without regard to harm done to any victim. They suppose duties not to act in certain ways. But they do not limit those outlawed acts to those which harm victims. It is neither here nor there that some people argue that there ought to be no disapproval in such cases, at least where there is no danger of harm to anyone. That is an argument about what ought and ought not be disapproved, reflecting premises as to the value of freedom. It is an argument therefore about policy, not about the natural limits of the concept of a wrong.

The lesson of this etymology is underscored by what has happened to the word 'injury'. It has become oriented to the victim, so much so that it no longer reveals whether the harm which the victim has suffered is attributable to another's wrong. But in Latin it was originally oriented the other way, *iniuria* being formed from a negative particle *in-* combined with *ius*, *iuris*, the word for 'right' or 'law', and hence something done *non iure* (non-rightly). [29]

The etymology corroborates what we would anyway infer from the modern usage of the word 'wrong', namely that, standing alone, it does not require harm to a victim. However, the addition of the word 'civil' changes that picture. A civil wrong is one in respect of which a citizen may make his own complaint, on his own account and not on behalf of the citizenship

---

[25] THE OXFORD DICTIONARY OF ENGLISH ETYMOLOGY (Charles T. Onions (ed.), 1966) [hereinafter DICTIONARY OF ETYMOLOGY], s.v. 'wrong' and 'tort'. The latter is from the Latin *torquere*, to twist. Onions draws the parallel with 'wring' and 'wrong'.

[26] DICTIONARY OF ETYMOLOGY, *supra*, note 25, s.v. 'trespass' and 'transgress'. The medieval Latin *transpassare* is the equivalent of the classical *transgredi* from which *transgressio. See* OXFORD LATIN DICTIONARY (1968), s.v. In classical Latin these words were not yet used for 'wrong'. *See id.*

[27] *Malum* = bad plus *facere* = do. *Maleficium* was used by Roman jurists as a synonym for *delictum: id.*

[28] *Delinquo*, supine *delictum* means 'to be lacking' or 'fail'. It was already used in classical Latin to mean 'fail in one's duty, offend': *id.*

[29] DICTIONARY OF ETYMOLOGY, *supra*, note 25, s.v. *Cf.* JUSTINIAN, DIGEST, 9.2.5.1 (Ulpian, Edict, bk. 18).

to which he belongs. In its opposition to 'criminal', 'civil' means that the initiative in bringing the matter to the court is taken, not by society as a whole through its customary organs or representatives, but by the victim of the wrong as the victim of the wrong. A private prosecution of a crime brought by the victim is different, for there the victim takes the initiative as the representative of society as a whole.

The word 'civil' thus supposes a plaintiff who can claim to have been the victim of the wrong. Where, for example, a defendant has created a public nuisance, no individual can sue who has not suffered special damage. Harm suffered is that which most obviously gives the individual the *locus standi* to complain of conduct disapproved by the law. However, there are cases which show that harm is not essential. For example, wrongs which are actionable in themselves (*per se*), chiefly trespass of all types, do not require proof of any harm in the sense of damage or injury.[30] It is enough that the protected interest of the plaintiff is infringed. The landowner whose land is entered is sufficiently a victim by that infringement. Again, where a fiduciary makes a gain in breach of the duty to avoid pursuing interests which might conflict with those of the beneficiary, the beneficiary's right to sue for that breach of duty and recover that gain is not dependent on proof of harm.[31] For good and sufficient reasons the law protects the beneficiary's interest in disinterested management. The infringement of that protected interest suffices to create the standing to sue. The two examples can be run together. The trespasser who makes a gain from his trespass without inflicting a loss on the landowner will have to surrender his gain to the landowner. The infringement of the protected interest supports more than a nominal remedy.[32]

It cannot be said that the law's practice in this respect is incoherent— that is, that it makes the concept of a civil wrong impossible to understand. The notion of a wrong does not intrinsically require a victim. However, it is in the nature of a civil wrong to raise a practical question: when shall an individual be allowed to complain on his or her own account and to take the benefit of the secondary or remedial obligation born of the wrong? The obvious answer is in terms of harm suffered. But it may be convenient or prudent to allow other kinds of answer. The plaintiff must be affected

---

[30] The traditional cases in English law, besides trespass, are libel and certain particular slanders (imputations of crime, professional incapacity, unchastity of a woman, and certain antisocial diseases), but there are other instances, for example, malicious exclusion of a vote, *see* Ashby v. White, 92 E.R. 126 (1909), and such exclusion from an inn, *see* Constantine v. Imperial Hotels, Ltd., [1944] K.B. 693.

[31] *See* Regal (Hastings), Ltd. v. Gulliver [1967] 2 A.C. 134 (1942); Boardman v. Phipps [1967] 2 A.C. 46.

[32] *See, e.g.,* Edwards v. Lee's Adm'r, 96 S.W.2d 1028 (Ky. 1936); Raven Red Ash Coal Co. v. Ball, 39 S.E.2d 231 (Va. 1946). *See generally* 1 GEORGE E. PALMER, THE LAW OF RESTITUTION (1978) 177–9; Hon. Mr. Justice W. M. C. Gummow, *Unjust Enrichment, Restitution and Proprietary Remedies, in* ESSAYS ON RESTITUTION (P.D. Finn (ed.), 1990), 60–67.

adversely in a manner which the law deems sufficient to identify him as a victim of the breach of duty and to give him standing to sue on his own account. Arguably, the effect on the plaintiff need not even be 'adverse'. 'Adversely' here is certainly to be understood in a weak or technical sense, so as not to exclude encroachments on protected interests which do not cause loss or harm or suffering of the conventional kind.

There is a fine line between exploiting the full potential of civil claims and smuggling criminal law into the civil courts. The line is guarded by the proposition that in civil wrongs the plaintiff must be the victim of the breach of duty, suing as victim. Suppose that a given jurisdiction provided that any resident within a town who witnessed a person vandalizing municipal property might claim £100 from that person by the same procedure as was used to recover ordinary debts. It would not be possible in that case to describe the vandalism as a civil wrong, because no plausible argument could be constructed to present the witness-claimant as its victim, any more than other members of the community.

B. Conduct

One commits a wrong or does wrong. The requirement of conduct, meaning either acts or omissions, could possibly have turned out to be attributable to the accompanying verb, not to the intrinsic notion of a wrong. But that is not so. A wrong necessarily involves acts or omissions by the alleged wrongdoer. It is not possible for a person to be in breach of duty, and *a fortiori* not possible for him to have committed a wrong, except by his own acts or omissions.

If, for example, we were to explain the vicarious liability of an employer for the wrongs of his employees as arising from a breach of duty by the employer, we would have to give that statement content by specifying the acts which he ought not to have committed or the omissions which he ought to have made good. It would come down to asserting that he was under a duty to employ safe people or to supervise effectively their every action. Vicarious liability shows that the law can make one person liable for the wrong of another, but it also shows, in the word 'vicarious' itself, that one cannot commit a wrong or be in breach of duty except by one's own acts or omissions. A 'vicarious' liability is a liability which one person takes over from another, and as such not his but that other's, just as a 'vicar' was originally a person in holy orders who occupied a place which was not his but the rector's whose substitute he was.[33]

Again, if you build a dam to make a reservoir and the dam bursts and floods the people below, it is not the event which constitutes your breach

[33] THE NEW OXFORD SHORTER ENGLISH DICTIONARY (Lesley Brown (ed.), 1993), s.v. 'vicarious', 'vicar'.

of duty but your own failure to ensure that the water did not escape and do damage. You were under a duty, if you made and kept the potentially dangerous reservoir, to ensure that the water did not escape.[34]

There are some fierce teachings in the Sermon on the Mount which might be cited to show that a wrong can be committed by thought alone, and some might argue that that would be a case of a wrong without acts or omissions. Thus the passage at Matthew 5:27-28 famously declares, 'You have learned that they were told, "Do not commit adultery". But what I tell you is this: If a man looks on a woman with a lustful eye, he has already committed adultery with her in his heart.' This is more of a problem for morality than law, since there are practical reasons why the law has to insist on the external manifestation of intent. But the suggestion that a wrong already committed in thought proves that conduct is inessential can be met by including thought within the conception of conduct. There is nothing artificial in that. Thinking is something that a person does. It lacks only the externalities of 'conduct'.

The correct conclusions are that conduct is essential, whether in the form of an act or an omission, that in principle thought suffices as a form of conduct, but that, in law as opposed to morality, there are practical reasons why it would be rash, though not absolutely impossible, to allow civil liability to attach to disapproved thought which has not yet issued in externally perceptible behavior.

C. Blameworthiness

The law can design a duty so that it may be broken only by a party who acts or omits intentionally, or so that it is broken by a party who acts or omits negligently, or so that it is broken by a party who simply acts or omits without any fault at all. These three bases of liability—fault consisting in bad intention, fault consisting in failure to take reasonable care, and no fault at all—are on closer inspection only stopping points on a sliding scale. Strict liability can be made subject to exceptional excuses. The reasonableness standard can be set at a level, say, 'best professional practice', which many people cannot attain. Even the standard set by the ubiquitous reasonable man is unattainable by many people who would not wish to claim the privileges of the insane. The liability based on intention may be distorted by discounting certain factors subjectively relevant to the formation of a wicked intent, such as a mistake of law concealing the wrongfulness of what was done or ignorance of the exceptional fragility of the victim.

There is a further complication, which arises from the occasional inter-

---

[34] The classic example, of course, is Rylands v. Fletcher (1868) L.R. 3 H.L. 330.

action of strict liability and the difficulty of proving fault. Facts which trigger strict liability can sometimes be understood as doing so via a conclusive presumption of fault. The liability is then conceived as based on fault, even though often it is in reality strict. When Joseph's brothers left Egypt they were hauled back because a silver cup was found in Benjamin's luggage, proof of dishonest taking, though the cup had been planted.[35]

There is no need to investigate here the subtleties of gradation between wicked intent and strict liability or the interaction between standards of liability and evidence. All that matters is to decide whether the word 'wrong' can be withheld from the case in which the duty is broken without proof of fault. The more difficult questions as to the nature and proof of fault will only arise if it can be so withheld.

The question is deliberately phrased as whether the word can be 'withheld', for there is a certain *prima facie* attractiveness in trying to withhold it.[36] Categories of causative event find much of their utility in their power to explain the legal responses which they cause. It is plausible therefore to suppose that the isolation of criteria of blameworthiness will provide the explanation of the remedial obligations which a wrong triggers. And there is the comfort of some etymological support. The metaphor which contrasts straight and right with twisted, bent and crooked invites us to characterize the wrongdoer and his conduct as worthy of reproach, even revulsion. And in the core case that is certainly what happens, for, in a world where happiness and well-being are precarious, the core wrongdoer is the devil's agent, one who intentionally realizes the dangers which people fear or takes no pains to avert those which might have been avoided.

However, the attempt is bound to fail. It is impossible to support the argument that 'wrong' cannot or should not extend to the case in which a breach of duty is established without proof of fault or, in other words, where the liability is strict. There are two essential reasons, though it can be said that the one merely reflects the other. One is linguistic usage. To withdraw the word 'wrong' in cases of strict liability would defy current usage. The other, more important and perhaps the explanation of the usage, is that, in countless cases in which the language of fault is used, closer analysis shows that we do in practice pay little attention to it.

A person who sells a car belonging to another commits the wrong of conversion, however careful he was in trying to verify the title of the person who sold it to him.[37] A fiduciary who successfully pursues a profit which might have tempted him to sacrifice the interests of his beneficiary commits

[35] *Genesis* 44, discussed by David Daube, Studies in Biblical Law (1947), 235 ff., 248–9.

[36] *Cf.* Jeremiah Smith, *Tort and Absolute Liability*, 30 Harv. L. Rev. 241, 254 (1917), and Nathan Isaacs, *Quasi-Delict in Anglo-American Law*, 31 Yale L.J. 571 (1922). These are discussed by Winfield, *supra*, note 10, at 207 ff. and 241 ff.

[37] 'Persons deal with the property in chattels or exercise acts of ownership over them at their peril': Fowler v. Hollins (1872) L.R. 7 Q.B. 616, 639, *per* Cleasby, B.

the wrong of breach of fiduciary duty even though he believed he was acting in the best interests of his beneficiary and thought that he had made a
full disclosure.[38] A trustee who makes an investment or disbursement which
is not authorized commits the wrong of breach of trust, even though he
may be excused in the case in which he acted both honestly and reasonably.[39] A person who publishes a story which defames another is guilty of
the wrong of defamation even if he had no means of knowing that the story
would be understood as referring to that person.[40] Someone who stores a
dangerous substance is guilty of a wrong if he allows that substance to
escape and do foreseeable damage, whether or not he took all reasonable
precautions to prevent the escape.[41] A builder who undertakes to complete
a house by a certain day is guilty of the wrong of breach of contract if the
house is not completed by that day, even if he used his best efforts to overcome the difficulties of an adverse market in labor and materials.[42]

These examples use the word 'wrong' in six different contexts, each of
which is constructed to exclude blameworthiness. Let us add one more dramatic case. A sleepwalker kills. A jurisdiction might make the rule absolute,
Thou shalt not kill. Let us say that it makes him guilty of a homicide in a
low degree, called manslaughter. The sleepwalker who kills commits that
wrong.[43] If the rule is clear, the debate will not be whether he has committed the wrong but whether the rule should be changed. So long as this
rule remains unchanged the sleepwalker has indubitably committed the
wrong. English criminal law comes close to this position in the case in
which the mind is disabled by drug abuse, although in fact it evades the
conclusion that there is no culpability at all.[44] In effect, the wrong is committed though the mind is absent. The underlying difficulties need not concern us.

What these examples show is that when the primary duty is clearly stated
and clearly broken, so that that which is proscribed is indubitably done, a

---

[38] *See* Boardman v. Phipps [1967] 2 A.C. 46.

[39] *See Re* Allsop [1914] 1 Ch. 1 (Eng. C.A.,1913); Perrins v. Bellamy [1899] 1 Ch. 797;
Trustee Act 1925, § 61 (U.K.).

[40] *See* E. Hulton & Co. v. Jones [1910] A.C. 20. After Gertz v.Robert Welch, Inc., 418 U.S.
323 (1974), negligence may now be constitutionally required in America with respect to unintended identification of the plaintiff. *See* RESTATEMENT (SECOND) OF TORTS, § 580B cmts. b and
d (1976).

[41] *See* Rylands v. Fletcher (1868) L.R. 3 H.L. 330, as modified by Cambridge Water Co.
v. Eastern Countries Leather Plc [1994] 1 All E.R. 53.

[42] *See* Davis Contractors Ltd. v. Fareham Urban Dist. Council [1956] A.C. 696.

[43] In fact, in English law he is not guilty of any crime, not because he did not perform the
act but because he lacked all intent. *See* Bratty v. Attorney-General for N. Ir. [1963] A.C. 386,
409.

[44] *See* Regina v. Lipman [1970] 1 Q.B. 152 (Eng. C.A., 1969); Director of Public
Prosecutions v. Majewski [1977] A.C. 443. The picture has been changed by the species of
recklessness recognized in Commissioner of the Police of the Metropolis v. Caldwell [1982]
A.C. 341, which makes it very easy to conclude that a deeply intoxicated person was reckless.

legal 'wrong' is committed even if the duty is so designed as to be broken without culpability. One might challenge this conclusion in one of two ways, either (1) by insisting that blameworthiness is imperfectly excluded in each of the various examples, or (2) by asserting that the word 'wrong' is incorrectly used. But neither of these two challenges is particularly convincing.

We are habitually inattentive to blameworthiness. This shows partly in the fact that we tolerate without anxiety the sliding scale between liability based on intent and absolute liability. But it shows more dramatically in the way in which we handle the commonest of all civil wrongs, namely negligence. Negligence consists in the breach of a duty of care to avoid damage. The duty is given content by the standard set by the notional reasonable man. It is broken by a defendant who fails to take the precautions that a reasonable man would take to avoid damage which a reasonable man would foresee. In practice the application of that standard is a very imperfect guide to the question whether a defendant was worthy of blame, reproach, or revulsion. The objective standard ignores the actual capacities of the defendant and, very importantly, takes no account of the fact that in the real world the reasonable man makes mistakes quite often without forfeiting his title to respect as a reasonable and careful being. Further, the near-universal practice of liability insurance has inclined the courts towards victims and discouraged attention to the issue of personal culpability.

In end result, therefore, the reality of the common law of negligence is that it imposes what is in effect strict liability for bad practice as, for example, in the control of a motor vehicle on the roads. It sets an objective standard of competence to define bad practice but does not ask whether the particular defendant was in fact worthy of reproach for the particular incident in which he fell below that standard.[45]

[45] For a brilliant account and justification, see Tony Honoré *Responsibility and Luck*, 104 LAW Q. REV. 530 (1988). For an exposition of the contrary view, that blameworthiness properly defines the core of tort responsibility, see David G. Owen, *The Fault Pit*, 26 GA. L. REV. 703 (1992). In his recent book, Professor Coleman appears to accept the substance of this analysis, but he expresses it quite differently. *See* COLEMAN, *supra*, note 16, at 216–33, 330–35. His argument that we should distinguish between 'fault in the doer' and 'fault in the doing' is problematic. And while his use of the concept of a 'wrong' as merely involving conduct that is 'invasive of a right' is not dissimilar to the position taken here, he distinguishes it from 'wrongdoing' in a curious manner. A full and fair critique of Coleman's views, however, is necessarily beyond the scope of this essay.

V. THE FOURFOLD CLASSIFICATION AGAIN:
COHERENCE AND INCOHERENCE

A. Prima Facie Incoherence

The fourfold classification will be recalled as containing (1) contracts (consent), (2) torts (wrongs), (3) unjust enrichments, and (4) other events. If a
civil wrong be no more than a breach of legal duty actionable by an individual victim on his own account, it is clear that not only category (2),
explicitly named 'wrongs', but also all three other categories in the
classification can include or give rise to wrongs. The fourfold classification
can therefore be represented as guilty of failing to observe the two-tier
structure of obligation. This is because the category of wrongs on this view
overlaps the other three categories: wrongs are all breaches of primary
obligation, and they—contract, unjust enrichment, and other obligation-
creating events—are categories of primary obligation breach of which is a
wrong, like tort, generating a secondary obligation. In short, the fourfold
classification is not treating like with like but slipping from the primary
level (contract, unjust enrichment, and other events) to the secondary level
(wrongs). A hostile critic might suggest that the fourfold classification
should try to make up its mind whether it wants to count chickens or eggs:
three chickens and a basket of eggs cannot add up to four chickens.

Meeting this challenge, the best decision at first seems to be to count only
chickens and then, separately, only eggs. In other words, we should accept
the need to distinguish very clearly between the events creating primary
obligations and the events creating secondary obligations and attempt a
thorough classification of primary obligations. Then, moving to the secondary level, we should recognize that on that level, since all secondary
obligations arise from breaches of primary obligations (wrongs), wrongs
must form the one and only generic category, subject to internal subdivi-
sion. This is what Austin recommended.[46] However, this attractive project
immediately runs into enormous difficulties.

Suppose, first, that one retains as much as possible of the original
classification. One then wants to say that primary obligations arise from (1)
contract, from (2) [a problem to be solved], from (3) unjust enrichment, and
from (4) other events. But the problem to be solved turns out to be insol-
uble. That is, it is impossible to name generically the event which creates
the primary obligations the breach of which was previously identified by
the word 'wrongs' or, more accurately, those wrongs which are not
breaches of the primary obligations in categories (1), (3), and (4).

Another more radical strategy can be attempted, jettisoning all but the

---

[46] AUSTIN, *supra*, note 21, at 796–7 & 944–8.

first category of the original classification. All primary obligations then arise from contract (with consent) or without contract because they are imposed (without consent); those imposed lie on all citizens either generally, by virtue of their citizenship, or contingently, by virtue of some event superadded to their citizenship. This runs into deeper and deeper difficulties as contingencies (employment, marriage, occupation of land, receipt of mistaken payments, taxable events) begin to be listed and sub-classified. Nor is that extraordinarily difficult game attractive, because it drives us further and further from the categories of the law as we know them. All the same we would have to play it if it was the only way to make our law make sense. But it is not.

B. The Coherence of the Fourfold Classification

In fact the fourfold classification is coherent, though the observation that it moves up and down the tiers of the two-tier structure of primary and secondary obligations is not only correct but also an important warning of the complexity of the classification and the ever-present danger of abuse.

1. Torts (Wrongs)—Category (2)

The category of civil wrongs is a category of events in which the explanation of the defendant's obligation to the plaintiff is his having committed a breach of duty. It is in their character as breaches of duty that the facts which we call wrongs account for the defendant's liability to the plaintiff. However, breach of duty (wrong) is not the only possible explanation of liability. The other categories in the classification are categories of event which can and do explain liability in other ways.

As we turn to justify the separate existence of the other three categories, we will encounter once more and have cause to emphasize an important characteristic of a civil wrong, namely that the measure of the law's response, or in other words the content of the remedial obligation triggered by the breach of duty, is in principle a mere matter of policy. The law has a free choice of what it shall be, subject only to extrinsic considerations such as the values of proportionality, determinacy, humanity, and so on. The widespread preference for compensation for loss reflects a policy choice, not a logical necessity. There is no measure of response logically dictated by the nature of a civil wrong.[47]

This contrasts with the other categories. In them the measure of the plaintiff's recovery is dictated by the causative event itself. It is not impossible, however, for the law to escape that in-built measure by, so to say, moving the entire matter into category (2) which, as we shall see, can be

[47] *See supra,* notes 13–19 and accompanying text.

done by turning from direct enforcement of the primary obligation created by the event to a policy-determined response to the wrong of failing to comply with that obligation. This important point may be illustrated by the simple case of mistaken payment. Here, the defendant's unjust enrichment itself dictates restitution and nothing else. For the wrong of failing to make restitution the defendant might, subject to constraining extrinsic considerations of the kind mentioned above, lose double the sum, or his house, or his thumbs. We will spell this out more clearly in the paragraphs which follow.

2. Unjust Enrichment—Category (3)

Every subtractive unjust enrichment (every enrichment which is obtained from the defendant in circumstances in which the law concludes that the enrichment is unjust) explains the defendant's obligation to make restitution without any necessity to characterize the defendant's conduct as a breach of duty.[48] I pay you £100 by mistake. You are enriched by subtraction from me and, subject to some fine-tuning which we may assume to be satisfied, the mistake is a factor which the law regards as sufficient to characterize your enrichment as unjust. The reason behind that conclusion is, in this case, that the plaintiff's intention to transfer was impaired. These facts provide a wholly satisfactory explanation of the obligation to make restitution. That is, the primary obligation is sufficient in itself.

It should be noted, however, that a plaintiff who relies on this explanation of the defendant's liability to make restitution puts in issue nothing which bears on anything other than the sum which has passed between the parties. The unjust enrichment cannot justify more than restitution. It provides, without the least mention of any wrong, a perfectly satisfactory explanation of the primary obligation to make restitution, but it cannot explain any other measure of response.

The law could treat unjust enrichment differently. Let us continue to use mistaken payments to exemplify all instances of subtractive unjust enrichment. The law could say, whether additionally or alternatively, that what explains the liability of the recipient of a mistaken payment is, not the primary obligation arising from the receipt, but the wrong which consists in the breach of that primary obligation—in other words, the wrong of not making the restitution which the law requires. However, in general there is no point in saying that the reason why a defendant has to make restitution is that he is in breach of his duty to make restitution. It merely restates the primary duty. The 'wrong' explanation of the duty to make restitution is thus wholly unnecessary, except under one condition. That condition is

---

[48] On 'subtractive' unjust enrichment and the difference between it and restitution for wrongs, *see supra,* note 19, and PETER BIRKS, RESTITUTION—THE FUTURE (1992), 1-25; ANDREW BURROWS, THE LAW OF RESTITUTION (1993), 21-2, 376-80.

important to understand. It is this. If the law wished to go beyond the explanatory power of the unjust enrichment itself, by, say, doubling the amount to be repaid, it would have to attach that hostile response to the *wrong* of failing to make restitution. In other words it would have to consider the event as a wrong in category (2) rather than as an unjust enrichment in category (3). It could be done. The potential for alternative analysis, focusing on breach of the primary duty to make restitution, is present in every case of subtractive unjust enrichment, but, so long as the court does for the plaintiff only that which the unjust enrichment itself can explain, the category (2) analysis is superfluous. That is, if the plaintiff is awarded only restitution there is no need to explain his claim as arising from the wrong of not making restitution.

The importance of this point can be illustrated from recent litigation in England. It is well established that in certain contracts, called *uberrimae fidei*, a party is entitled to know all material facts.[49] What are the consequences of non-disclosure? Are they limited to rescission of the contract and restitution?[50] Or can the non-disclosing party be made to make good consequential losses too? The answer given, ultimately,[51] was that the non-disclosing party was *not* liable to pay damages; liability was confined to rescission and restitution. This could mean two things. Either non-disclosure is a category (2) event—a wrong consisting in the breach of the duty to disclose—but one for which, untypically, the remedial response is confined to restitution; or, which is more likely, the receipt of a benefit after non-disclosure is a category (3) event and as such incapable of explaining anything but restitution.[52]

3. Other Events—Category (4)

The same pattern is repeated in category (4) (miscellaneous other events). We may take as examples a taxable event, such as earning income, and a

---

[49] Examples of such contracts are insurance, family arrangements, guarantee. *Cf.* G. H. TREITEL, THE LAW OF CONTRACT (8th edn., 1991) 354-9.

[50] It is unnecessary to investigate the question here whether rescission should be regarded as a species of restitution. If it is, one should not say 'rescission of the contract and restitution'.

[51] Banque Keyser Ullmann S.A. v. Skandia (U.K.) Ins. Co. [1990] 1 Q.B. 665 (Eng. C.A. 1988) (Steyn J), *aff'd sub nom.* Banque Financière de la Cité (formerly Banque Keyser Ullmann) v. Westgate Fin. [1991] 2 A.C. 249. Steyn J at first instance had held that damages were available, but he was reversed on appeal. On further appeal to the House of Lords, the decision went off on another point but Lord Templeman indicated that he agreed with the Court of Appeal: [1991] 2 A.C. at 280.

[52] The correct analysis is that it is an example of a benefit conferred by mistake, so that exploitation of the mistake is the unjust factor. However, as between contracting parties, a mistake which is attributable to silent non-disclosure by the other party normally does not trigger restitution. It is the requirement of utmost good faith (*uberrima fides*) which produces the exceptional contrary result. *Cf.* Sybron Corp. v. Rochem Ltd. [1985] A.C. 761.

judgment.[53] These events create primary obligations. Those primary obligations can be and are directly enforced. The defendant's liability to pay the tax or the sum due under the judgment does not have to be explained by invoking the wrong of failing to pay. If that wrong were invoked, the reason would once again have to be the desire to reach beyond the explanatory power of the causative event itself. The wrong of failure to make punctual payment might be visited with divers penalties extrinsic to the primary obligation explicable by the event itself.

4. Contracts (Consent)—Category (1)

Category (1) is much the most difficult, partly because the history is deceptive. The fact that the primary tier of contractual obligation always has to be studied in order to establish the circumstances in which there can be a secondary obligation from the wrong of breach would not, on the present account, justify creating a category distinct from wrongs. The question is whether the law enforces contractual obligation as opposed to obligations from the wrong of breach. Only an affirmative answer can justify the separate category.

It is easy to see that a contract is capable of being sufficient explanation of liability in itself, rather than as the primary superstructure above the wrong of breach of contract. Indeed some systems do not think in terms of the wrong of breach of contract but only in terms of the primary obligation flowing from the contract itself. However, it is less easy to say with confidence whether and when our law relies on that analysis and when, by contrast, it insists, usually without thinking about it, on a category (2) analysis in terms of the wrong of breach of contract. Formally, the victory of the action of *assumpsit* over the action of debt in Slade's Case (1602)[54] was a victory of the category (2) analysis, since the wording of *assumpsit* emphasized the wrong of breach of contract: the defendant was to show why, whereas he promised (*assumpsit*), he wickedly broke his promise.[55] But the wording of the forms of action is notoriously deceptive. It would not be safe to place much analytical weight on it. Arguably modern common law still deals in category (1) obligations (primary obligations from contract) where fixed sums of money are promised—that is, in respect of

---

[53] Providing an exhaustive list would be a challenge. Salvage rewards provide one other example, and there is an ill-defined group of cases which the late Professor Stoljar christened 'unjust sacrifice': S. J. Stoljar, *Unjust Enrichment and Unjust Sacrifice*, 50 M.L.R. 603 (1987).

[54] 4 Co. Rep. 91 (1602), but now much more fully reported in JOHN H. BAKER AND S. F. C. MILSOM, SOURCES OF ENGLISH LEGAL HISTORY (1986) 420.

[55] The conservative Walmsely J, even after *Slade*, complains that one consequence of this was to throw open the measure of recovery: '[I]n an action on the case the plaintiff shall recover everything in damages; and that is uncertain, because the jury may give him a greater or lesser sum in damages, while in an action of debt he shall recover the debt certain.' *See* Wright v. Swanton (1604) in SOURCES OF ENGLISH LEGAL HISTORY, *supra*, note 54, at 441, 442. This exactly expresses the difference, discussed above, between categories (1) and (2).

contractual debts—and where the contract is regarded as specifically performable. For the rest, it appears to deal only in category (2) obligations (secondary obligations arising out of the primary wrong of breach of contract). In other words the correct conclusion must be that for most purposes the common law approaches contract through the wrong of breach of contract. In effect it adds breach of contractual duty to the list of torts. But for some purposes it still orders the defendant to keep his covenant, directly enforcing the primary obligation generated by the contract itself.

VI. CONCLUSION: THE DISTINCT CATEGORY OF CIVIL WRONGS

According to the view taken in this essay, civil wrongs remain a distinct category of obligation-creating event within the fourfold classification of such events. The concept of a civil wrong is abstract and broad. A wrong is the breach of a duty. A legal wrong is the breach of a duty recognized by law (a legal duty). A civil wrong is the breach of a legal duty which affects the interests of an individual to a degree which the law regards as sufficient to allow that individual to complain on his or her own account rather than as the representative of society as a whole. Obligations arising from wrongs are explained and justified as responses to breach of duty. The reason why we have other categories of causative event is that there are three classes of event which create primary obligations which are directly enforced and to which the notion of breach of duty (wrong) is irrelevant.

The content of the remedial or secondary obligation triggered by a wrong is for the law to decide as a matter of policy constrained only by extrinsic considerations. Wrongs themselves dictate no fixed measure of response. It follows that it is unnecessary to insist on a compensable harm and incorrect to orient the idea of a wrong towards the victim on the model of 'injury'. Harm enters the picture on the back of the word 'civil' because of the need to explain why the plaintiff has standing to sue on his or her own account. But that standing can be recognized on grounds other than harm suffered.

Because the concept of a civil wrong is broad and abstract, its explanatory power is weak. To say that a consequence follows certain conduct because that conduct is a breach of a primary duty is to offer a formal explanation but not a satisfying one. The real explanation has to be completed in every case from the policies and values underlying the recognition of the primary duty which is in question. It is there that economic efficiency has to contest the field with liberal autonomy and moral paternalism, for the primary duties lie on the frontiers of law, politics and philosophy.

The Practice of Corrective Justice

JULES L. COLEMAN*

In a recent book,[1] I set out the contours of a conception of corrective justice, and tentatively explored aspects of its relationship to Anglo-American tort law. I argued that corrective justice is the principle that those who are responsible for the wrongful losses of others have a duty to repair them, and that the core of tort law embodies this conception of corrective justice. One could object to my argument on at least two grounds. One might accept my characterization of corrective justice, but deny that, so conceived, it is reflected in our tort practices,[2] or one might reject my conception of corrective justice.

In obvious ways, this second concern is more fundamental. Perhaps I see so much (or so little) corrective justice in tort law simply because I have such a confused idea about what corrective justice is. In any case, the extent to which I see corrective justice in tort law surely depends on my understanding of it; the same is true of any would-be corrective justice account of tort law—Weinrib's, Fletcher's, and Epstein's, as well as mine. So it is only natural to ask whether any of us is right about the content of corrective justice. And that requires an account of what it means to say that a particular conception of a concept like corrective justice is correct, as well as an account of the adequacy conditions of such a judgment.

In this brief essay, I want to tackle some of these meta-ethical concerns. Before doing so, however, I want to outline the way in which corrective justice figures in my general approach to political philosophy.

I. CORRECTIVE JUSTICE AND POLITICAL MORALITY

As I see it, the fundamental question of practical reason is: what ought I do? What I ought to do depends on what there are good reasons for me to

---

* John A. Garver Professor of Jurisprudence, Yale Law School. I am grateful to Stephen Perry and Brian Leiter for several discussions of previous drafts of this chapter. I am especially indebted to Perry, who, I believe, is the best young scholar working on the moral foundations of tort law. His criticisms of my work have been the fundamental stimulus in its continued development. I am also grateful to Joseph Raz whose sympathetic prodding has brought out more in my thinking on these topics than was probably there to begin with.

[1] JULES L. COLEMAN, RISKS AND WRONGS (1992).

[2] Or that it is reflected in tort law to the extent I take it to be.

do.[3] In the kind of liberal political morality I defend, the fact that events affect individual welfare or well-being is normatively important because effects on individual welfare are the kinds of things that provide agents with reasons for acting. That others have experienced a loss in welfare or well-being, or are in a situation in which they are likely to do so, is the kind of fact about them that can provide me with reasons for acting: reasons for coming to their aid, for example.

This particular project of liberal political philosophy is to connect reasons for acting with the effects of events on welfare or well-being. There are at least four variables that figure in this project. If we focus on events that negatively or adversely affect welfare ('losses' or misfortunes), the four factors involved in the inquiry are: (1) the moral character of the loss; (2) the relationship between the loss and those thought to have a reason to act in virtue of it; (3) the nature of the principles that create reasons for acting, that connect losses with agents; and (4) the nature and content of the reasons the principles supply.

Here are some (hopefully, intuitive) examples of how the inquiry works. If individuals suffer loss as a result of a hurricane or a natural disaster of some other sort, this fact about them creates a reason for acting in each of us who stands in a certain relationship to them. Typically, it is enough that each of us be a member of the same political or geographic community in order that a hurricane or natural disaster affecting any one of us provide a reason for the rest of us to do something about it. The duty we have is to come to the aid of those who are victims of the hurricane, and it is a duty each of us has. So, to put the case of a hurricane or other natural disaster in terms of the four factors mentioned above:

(1) With respect to the moral character of the loss, it is not necessary that we characterize or think of the loss as an injustice or a wrong. The fact that it is a simple but substantial misfortune appears to suffice. (2) With respect to the relationship of those said to have a reason for acting, for doing something about the plight of hurricane victims, there is no requirement that those who have reason to act must have caused or otherwise been responsible for bringing about the damage. Instead, the relationship is one of proximity—between those members of the community spared the disaster and those suffering it, and between the spared members and the disaster which could have (and nearly did) hit them. (4) With respect to the nature and content of the duty (or reason) for acting, it is, first, a duty that falls on individuals quite generally, and, second, it is a duty to come to the aid of those in need,

---

[3] To say that what I ought to do depends on the reasons that apply to me is not to say that the justification of everything I do is settled by reason and reason alone. There are many choices I am justified in making for which I cannot offer conclusory reasons. Still, reasons figure prominently in determining what I ought to do.

especially one's neighbors, to help repair their loss or to alleviate its consequences. The exact nature of the duty depends on (3) the particular principle, norm, or moral practice that grounds it.

Some might defend the duty to aid hurricane victims as being a matter of charity; others might see it as a matter of beneficence, and others as a matter of fairness or even distributive justice. If the duty to come to the aid of hurricane victims is a matter of distributive justice, for instance, it is plausible to suppose that it falls on all and only those members of the political community governed by the relevant conception of distributive justice. If, in contrast, the duty to aid is a matter of charity, it may extend beyond political boundaries and be otherwise independent of membership in a particular political community. Whether grounded in principles of charity or distributive justice (or something else altogether), the duty to come to the aid of hurricane victims is *agent-general* in that it applies to each person within the relevant political or moral community.

Sometimes our actions affect the welfare of others in ways that create *agent-specific* reasons for acting, reasons that apply to us and not to everyone. If I promise to meet you for lunch tomorrow, then I have a reason for acting in a particular way that others do not have. I have a reason to show up. If others have a reason to show up, it might be because they, too, have promised you to do so: it cannot be that they have a reason to show up for lunch because I promised you that I would. The norms that give rise to the reason I have for showing up are constitutive of the practice of promising. If I fail to show up, then I have a reason to apologize that no one else has. If you have lost something by relying on my showing up, then I may have a reason to make good your losses as well.

Ordinary norms of decency and civility can also give rise to agent-specific reasons for acting. Suppose that I unintentionally knock you down on a crowded city street and accidentally bloody your nose. Though my conduct is not intentional, perhaps not even negligent or otherwise careless, I may have a host of responsibilities with respect to your care, comfort, and welfare. I may have a duty to lift you to your feet (if you cannot get up on your own), call for help if you cannot get up at all, wait with and attend to you until help arrives, and so on. Coming to your aid in such circumstances is a matter of common decency. My having a reason to come to your aid does not depend on your loss being wrongful or unjust; it is simply undeserved and unfortunate, and connected in some way to what I have done. Nor does my reason for coming to your aid depend on my having done something wrong or blameworthy, though it appears to depend on my being very weakly (causally) responsible for what happened to you. Causal *responsibility*, however, is not a necessary condition of my having a reason to come to your aid. Had I been hurled into you by a gust of wind, I might have similar responsibilities towards you. In that case, my responsibilities to you would have nothing to do with my being an agent with respect to your injury.

Sometimes duties to come to the aid of another that derive from conventions of common decency are based on agency (as in the case in which I unintentionally knock you down); sometimes they derive from fault (as when I carelessly knock you down); other times they derive from causation without responsibility (as in the case when the wind hurls me into you); but on other occasions, duties to come to another's aid will require neither agency, fault nor causation. Thus, individuals in the vicinity of the accident may have a duty to help you up or to seek aid for you, and so on. It may be enough that those in the vicinity be capable of helping and of doing so at no great personal inconvenience. Neither fault, nor agency, nor even the weakest form of causal connection, is *necessary* to ground a duty to aid. On the other hand, if I have a special, stronger, or more stringent reason for helping—such that the inconvenience of waiting around with you for help to arrive would not excuse me from my responsibilities—that may be because I am causally connected to you or your injury in ways in which onlookers are not.

None of this is intended to be earth shaking or terribly novel. What we ought to do depends in part on what we owe others (and ourselves). What we owe others depends in part on what happens to them, how fortune shines on them, how our agency affects their welfare, what relationships we bear to one another, and so on. The specific duties we have towards others depends on the principles that apply to us and the moral and other practices in which we are engaged. The principle of corrective justice is simply one of the norms that applies when we are somehow connected with the misfortunes of others.

II. The Meta-Ethics of Corrective Justice

A. *Understanding Corrective Justice*

The principle of corrective justice imposes agent-specific reasons for acting. To put this in terms of the four factors outlined above: according to (3) corrective justice, (4) the duty is to make repair, to make good the victim's loss, (1) but only if the loss is *wrongful*, and (2) only if he is *responsible* for having brought about the loss.

Whereas common decency may require that I lift you to your feet if I knock you down unintentionally through no fault of my own, the requirement that I make good your losses (should any arise) invokes the principle of corrective justice. And because it does, while I may have a responsibility to lift you to your feet even if I have done nothing wrong or violated no right of yours, my having a duty to rectify your loss depends on my having acted wrongfully in some way. Moreover, whereas civility and decency may impose a duty to come to the aid of those whose mishaps you have witnessed and can do something about reasonably easily, corrective justice imposes an agent-specific reason for acting that falls only to those whose agency is responsible for the harm done, and whose responsibility the harm is.

Put this way, the analysis is incomplete in three ways. First, corrective justice requires an analysis of what is to count as a loss. There is an important difference between being harmed and not being benefitted by the actions of others. Secondly, it requires an account of what makes a loss wrongful, for the duty to repair under corrective justice is restricted to wrongful losses.[4] Thirdly, it requires a theory of responsibility, for the duty to make repair under corrective justice falls only to those who are responsible for the losses for which repair is sought.[5]

Most legal theorists who have been interested in corrective justice have been interested in it in so far as it might figure in an account, explanation, or interpretation of various legal practices, especially tort law, and, to a lesser extent, contract law. For such theorists, corrective justice provides an alternative to the prevailing economic analysis of the common law. As it happens, corrective justice accounts of tort law have not been as successful in capturing the imagination of the legal audience as those based on economic efficiency.

One reason for this is that there are very few systematic accounts of tort law based on corrective justice, and it is fair to say that the field is in its relative infancy. Another reason, frankly, is that the legal community has found various economic approaches more persuasive or compelling than those based on corrective justice. Finally, whereas proponents of economic analysis appear to agree upon one conception of economic efficiency—so there is only one 'economic theory' of tort law[6]—there appears to be substantial disagreement among moral theorists of torts about the content and demands of corrective justice.

---

[4] Whereas I have only provided a conceptual account of wrongfulness in my previous work, I have begun the task of providing a normative account of how we are to understand 'fault' or wrongfulness. *Cf.* Jules L. Coleman & Arthur Ripstein, *Mischief and Misfortune* (1995) (unpublished manuscript on file with authors).

[5] Of course, wrongfulness, responsibility, and loss are elements in *my* conception of corrective justice. Whether they figure in the correct conception of corrective justice, and do so in the way I allege they do, is the issue before us. In fact, I do not here defend my conception of corrective justice. Rather, I take up the more basic question of how we ought to think about defending or exploring a particular conception of corrective justice.

[6] I have argued that there are in fact several different conceptions of economic efficiency. *Cf.* JULES L. COLEMAN, *Efficiency, auction and exchange, in* MARKETS, MORALS AND THE LAW 67 (1988). Even economic analysts who agree on a single conception of efficiency differ with respect to its implications for tort law.

Those who have offered corrective justice accounts of tort law differ with respect to: (1) the conditions of responsibility; (2) whether in order to invoke corrective justice, losses must be wrongful; (3) what makes conduct wrongful within the ambit of corrective justice—and more. It is hard for an approach to tort law to gain widespread acceptance when disagreement about what that approach is committed to is apparently so widespread.

Widespread disagreement about its content raises an even more fundamental worry about the principle of corrective justice, and that worry is that corrective justice lacks semantic content; or, if it has semantic content, that its content is subjective, not objective. In either case—no semantic content, or subjective content—there is a problem for the legal theorist who invokes the concept of corrective justice as a substantive moral ideal and not just as a vehicle for expressing approval of certain arrangements and disapproval of others.

To understand the issues at stake, we first have to indicate ways in which tort theorists who invoke the concept of corrective justice are committed to its having objective semantic content; then we need to explain why substantial disagreement about what that content is invites either a skeptical or subjectivist interpretation of corrective justice.

B. Understanding Meta-ethics

In order to meet these demands, it may be helpful if we draw some preliminary distinctions—first, between cognitive and non-cognitive interpretations of a concept or predicate (or an entire discourse); and secondly, between subjective and objective interpretations of semantic content. A discourse is cognitive if the majority of its syntactically specified declarative judgments are fact-stating or truth value worthy. Sentences in a cognitive discourse are typically either true or false. Cognitivists about moral discourse—ethical cognitivists—believe that moral judgements are typically either true or false. Non-cognitivists deny that the sentences of a discourse are truth value worthy; non-cognitive discourses are not fact-stating. Ethical non-cognitivists believe that moral judgements are normally neither true nor false; rather than describing moral facts, moral judgements express attitudes of approval or disapproval. An ethical non-cognitivist, then, might believe that moral predicates like corrective justice are used to express approval of certain institutional arrangements and to disparage others.

The next distinction is between objectivist and subjectivist interpretations of a concept or predicate (or an entire discourse). Suppose that ethical non-cognitivists are mistaken about moral discourse, in which case most moral judgements will turn out to be either true or false. What makes them true or false? On an objectivist interpretation, the truth of moral judgements is independent of how particular speakers or theorists regard it. On a subjectivist view, moral judgements are true provided they accurately report the speaker's (or theorist's) beliefs or views. A subjectivist view about corrective justice, then, would amount to the claim that the content of the concept is fixed by the speaker's or theorist's beliefs about what that content is. For an objectivist, what individuals take to be the case has no bearing on what is the case; for a subjectivist, what is the case is fixed by the beliefs of particular persons. Whatever the differences between objectivists and subjectivists are, it is important to keep in mind that both are cognitivists about moral predicates.

With these roughly characterized distinctions in hand, we can return to the principle of corrective justice. Judging by the role it plays in their scholarship, tort theorists who invoke the concept of corrective justice treat it as objective. Tort theorists are cognitivists and objectivists about corrective justice. This is because legal theorists who invoke the concept of corrective justice mean to treat it as a substantive moral ideal, and not just as a vehicle for expressing approval of certain arrangements and disapproval of others. This means that they believe the concept of corrective justice has cognitive content.[7] They believe, moreover, that some conceptions of corrective justice are more plausible than others; some might even believe that there is one (and only one) correct conception of it, and so on. This means they believe that the content of corrective justice is, in a suitable sense, objective. Not every conception of corrective justice is equally good.

It is a commonplace that in order for a predicate or a discourse to admit of an objectivist interpretation, there must be some considerable agreement or convergence regarding the core use of the concept(s). The lack of convergence or coherence is normally seen as inviting some or other form of skeptical interpretation: either non-cognitivist or subjectivist. To understand the importance of convergence to objectivity, we need to introduce one further set of distinctions: those between realist and various forms of anti-realist accounts of the metaphysics of (moral) properties.

Roughly, a realist believes that the existence and character of properties or predicates, including moral ones, are logically and constitutively independent of human minds (beliefs) and evidence. The moral 'world' is logically and constitutively independent of how we humans regard it, the beliefs we have about it, and the evidence we can adduce in favor of those beliefs.

The anti-realist denies what the realist asserts. He claims that the (moral) world is fixed by human practices and beliefs. For the anti-realist, the way

---

[7] No doubt, in defending or rejecting tort practice as satisfying or failing to measure up to the demands of corrective justice, tort theorists typically mean to be expressing their pleasure or disfavor with current legal arrangements. But they mean to be doing so because current practice either satisfies or fails to satisfy certain substantive constraints that specify the cognitive content of corrective justice. The expressive function of corrective justice is conceptually connected to its cognitive content—or at least it is for those tort theorists who invoke it as a standard for evaluating existing tort practice.

the world is is not logically or constitutively independent of our beliefs about it or the evidence one can adduce in favor of those beliefs.

All moral realists are cognitivists and objectivists about moral discourse. The situation is more complex for the anti-realist. Realists are committed to two claims: that there are moral facts, and that they are mind- or evidence-transcendent. Some anti-realists are non-cognitivists. They deny that there are moral facts at all. If there are no moral facts, then moral discourse cannot refer to such facts. Therefore, moral discourse is not fact-stating. Anti-realists need not deny the existence of moral facts, however. In order to qualify as anti-realist, a theory need deny only that such facts are objective in the way realism takes them to be. That is, an anti-realist need deny only that (moral) facts are mind- or evidence-transcendent. So anti-realists can be either non-cognitivists or cognitivists.

Must a cognitivist anti-realist be a subjectivist? The answer is no. Even though this kind of anti-realist denies that (moral) facts are objective in the realist sense, he need not deny that facts can be objective in some other sense. Of course, the burden then falls to the anti-realist to specify the relevant sense of objectivity. We may distinguish among three senses of objectivity. At one extreme is the strong objectivity of the realist. Facts or properties that are objective in this sense are mind- (belief) or evidence-transcendent. They do not depend on human practices or the ways in which humans regard them. At the other extreme is minimal objectivity. Facts or properties that are objective in this sense do depend on human practices, beliefs, and evidence. Something is the case in this sense provided that it is how most competent language users and observers regard it. Facts are objective in this sense because they take the judgment of what is the case out of the 'hands' of particular speakers or observers and place it in the hands of the community as a whole. Minimal objectivity is therefore normally associated with forms of conventionalism. From both minimal and strong objectivity we can distinguish modest objectivity. Facts or properties are modestly objective provided their content is fixed by how they would be regarded by individuals under idealized or appropriate epistemic conditions.

These various notions of objectivity play useful explanatory roles; in particular, they provide (different) accounts of the possibility of mistake, growth, disagreement and the like. Someone can be wrong in his judgement according to minimal objectivity if his judgement departs from what most people take to be the case. On the other hand, one consequence of minimal objectivity is that most people cannot (logically) be wrong. (What is the case just is what most people take it to be.) Someone can be wrong in his judgement according to modest objectivity provided his judgement departs from what it would have been under ideal conditions of judgement. Moreover, modest objectivity allows that everyone could be wrong in their judgement provided the judgements they reach diverge from those they would have reached under ideal conditions of observation and judgement. It is straightforward how a realist would explain both local and general mistake.

There are at least three (and probably more) conceptions of objectivity: strong, minimal, and modest. Different concepts of objectivity may be suitable to different domains. Someone may hold the view that mid-sized physical objects, e.g. tables and chairs, are strongly objective, whereas moral properties are either minimally or modestly objective. The kind of objectivity involved in some discourses, e.g. science, may be the strong objectivity of realism, whereas that involved in legal discourse may be something considerably weaker.

Whichever concept of objectivity is at work in a domain of discourse, the important point for our present purposes is that convergence is a precondition of objectivity of any sort. First, for the anti-realist-non-cognitivist, moral predicates lack cognitive content, so the question whether that content is objective simply does not arise. Secondly, for the anti-realist-subjectivist, moral predicates are not objective simply because they are reports of the beliefs or judgements of minimally competent language users and observers. Thirdly, for the anti-realist-conventionalist (or minimal objectivist), the objectivity of moral predicates depends on actual convergence of usage among the majority of competent language users and judgers. Fourth, for the anti-realist ideal-observer theorist (or modest objectivist), the objectivity of moral predicates depends on individual judgement converging under ideal epistemic or observation conditions.

Though realism holds that the existence and character of moral predicates are logically and constitutively independent of human beliefs and practices, the realist is also committed to convergence over time, as a pragmatic if not as a conceptual matter. Moral predicates are to figure in the explanations of our beliefs and judgements. If those beliefs and judgements do not converge over time, then it is implausible to suppose that strongly objective properties can explain our beliefs. For if such properties did exist, then the (long-term) divergence of our beliefs and judgements would appear inexplicable. This is not to say that convergence would be enough to establish that strongly objective properties lie behind our judgements, but it does suggest that the absence of convergence gives us cause to worry that such properties do exist.

Of course, divergence in judgement and belief can have a variety of different sources: disagreement about relevant facts, cognitive shortcomings, prejudice, and the like. So disagreement as such does not undermine realism. But this simply implies that realism is committed to a form of conditional convergence: for moral properties to be strongly objective, it is likely necessary that judgements and beliefs about their instantiation made under certain conditions, e.g. full information, rationality, etc., would converge over time.

C. Meta-ethical Approach to Corrective Justice

Convergence or coherence regarding the core of a concept (and its instantiations) is a precondition of objectivity; and thus it is a precondition of the objectivity of corrective justice. That is why the apparent widespread disagreement among tort theorists about the content of corrective justice invites the worry that corrective justice lacks objective semantic content. Either corrective justice is just a name we give to certain institutional arrangements we wish to praise, or else it is a gloss we put on our own theories about it: a gloss we mean for others to treat as objective, but which we in the end cannot fully defend by appeal to general reason, principle, or practice. This is the fear that disagreement invites, and the one I mean to allay.

Like others, I am committed to the objectivity of corrective justice. Unlike others, however, I take this meta-ethical worry about the objectivity of corrective justice very seriously. I do not believe that it can go unanswered, and I mean to answer it. Moreover, because I am an anti-realist about moral properties and moral discourse generally, the kind of answer I want to pursue must reflect my view that the content of corrective justice depends on human practices, beliefs, and evidence. So, I am both an anti-realist and an objectivist about corrective justice. For me, then, the content of corrective justice depends on the practices in which it figures, but it is not fully fixed by how I or anyone else happen to regard it.

Some of my critics have wanted me to defend my conception of corrective justice by deriving it in some way from a set of first principles, from more basic principles of justice; while others have objected to my emphasis on what I have called 'middle level theory': that is, my emphasis on extracting principles and norms from existing practices, including legal ones. In fact, I have not tried to defend my conception of corrective justice as following from a more general theory of distributive justice, nor have I argued for it in some contractarian manner, by trying (futilely no doubt) to establish that my conception would be chosen by rational agents under certain specified conditions, and so on.

Perhaps I am mistaken in taking the meta-ethical approach to corrective justice (and to other moral concepts as well) that I have taken. But I am wrong only if some other meta-ethical view about moral predicates is correct. So someone objecting to my approach, and not merely to my execution of it, has to defend or, at least, must have in mind a different kind of meta-ethics. Perhaps a subjectivist or non-cognitivist can fault me for looking to our practices for the content of corrective justice. In the mind of either the, problem might be that corrective justice has no content (non-cognitivism), or that its content is subjective and fixed by how particular persons regard it (that my mistake is in looking to communal practices). Or a realist might fault me for looking to practices at all, for, in his view, the content of corrective justice is fixed by some set of natural facts, not by the behavior of individuals. I am unmoved, however, by the objection to middle level theory—to extracting the content of our norms and principles from the practices in which they figure—when it is advanced by those who are unprepared to defend some other meta-ethics. Many who advance this objection are apparently committed to the fashionable view that one can engage in substantive normative ethics while remaining agnostic on meta-ethical issues. This view of the relationship between meta- and normative ethics strikes me as mistaken.

I have looked to see how the concept of corrective justice figures in various practices, including tort law, as a way of getting a handle on its content. Because I am an anti-realist about moral predicates, I am committed to the view that the core of corrective justice is drawn from the practices in which it figures. And that is part of the meaning of the phrase I have employed in speaking of corrective justice as a practice—'the practice of corrective justice'—a phrase that George Fletcher claims to find wholly mysterious.[8]

There are, of course, legitimate, general concerns one might have about my kind of approach to fleshing out the content of corrective justice. Consider two: first, by focusing on the practices in which the concept figures as the source of its content, am I not just committing myself to a kind of conventionalism in which all we can say, for example, about corrective justice is that the community regards it in a certain way? Corrective justice is fixed by our practices, and, if that is the case, how can corrective justice serve as a criterion or standard for assessing our practices?

Secondly, if I focus on practices as the source of the content of corrective justice, then I will treat tort law as one such practice. If tort law helps to give content to the concept of corrective justice, in what sense can corrective justice serve as a criterion for assessing existing tort practice? In what sense can we even ask whether and to what extent existing tort practice implements the principle of corrective justice? Must not there be some distance between corrective justice and tort law in order for us to be able to answer either of these questions?

Let us consider the first question, the second being largely an extension of the general worry it raises. Unfortunately, I cannot answer this serious and legitimate concern in any detail in this brief essay. I hope the

---

[8] For a review of RISKS AND WRONGS written by someone who appears not to have read it, see George P. Fletcher, *Corrective Justice for Moderns*, 106 HARV. L. REV. 1658 (1993) (book review).

following remarks are not so cryptic as to be unhelpful. Generally, my view is that our practices contain adequate resources for critically assessing what those practices at any given time happen to be. That is, certain practices (I believe law is one of these) are conventional—that is, their content depends on what people do—but their content is not fixed by what people at a particular time happen to be doing. I like to think that in such practices 'truth outruns the practice'.

How can a practice be conventional and have resources sufficient for self assessment? Let me try to illustrate what I have in mind by exploring the well-known positivist view that law is a matter of convention or social fact. With respect to law, Hart famously held that law consists in social rules and that the *content* of social rules is fixed by convergent practice.[9] Dworkin takes this to be a statement of conventionalism, attributes it to all positivists, and powerfully exploits its shortcomings.[10] The problem is that such an account does not provide a plausible understanding of key features of legal practice, including the nature of theoretical disagreement, the existence of right answers in hard cases, and the possibility of large scale, pervasive mistake. In the Hartian view of social rules, law runs out—and discretion begins—when behavior no longer converges. Yet, is not law possible even in the face of disagreement about its content or requirements? Dworkin thinks the answer to this question is in the affirmative. If law extends beyond convergent behavior, and if the content and requirements of social rules is fixed by convergent practice, law cannot consist in social rules. Roughly, law cannot be a matter of sociology or social fact as the positivists contend; instead, it must be a matter of substantive moral argument, as Dworkin contends.

The problem, however, is not with the view that law is a matter of social fact or convention; the problem is with the Hartian conception of what a social rule or convention is, and what its requirements are. For Hart, the *content* of a social or conventional rule is fixed by the scope of convergent behavior. What a rule requires is restricted to the scope of that convergent behavior. Where convergence ends, so, too, do the duties to which the rule gives rise. This is not the way I think about social or conventional rules. In my view, conventional or social rules require both convergent behavior *and* shared understanding. There must be sufficient convergent behavior to establish the existence and core of a social rule. The shared understanding (which is typically reflected in behavior) determines the kind of practice or rule the behavior instantiates. For some practices, the understanding may be that the full content of the rules and the duties to which they give rise is fixed by the scope of convergent behavior. Participants in such practices

---

[9] H. L. A. Hart, The Concept of Law (1961).

[10] Ronald Dworkin, Law's Empire (1986); Ronald Dworkin, Taking Rights Seriously (1977).

understand that they have no duties under the rules beyond the range of convergent behavior. Let us imagine that stopping at red lights is such a practice. If most people stop at red lights, then (provided other conditions are satisfied) individuals would have a duty to stop at red lights under normal circumstances. But now suppose that many people do not stop at red lights after midnight (in the absence of other traffic), while others continue to stop even when there is no danger in merely slowing down and then moving on. Were stopping at red lights the sort of practice in which the duties imposed were fixed by the scope of convergent behavior, then individuals would have no duty to stop at red lights after midnight. Or if they had such a duty it would not be imposed by the social practice of stopping at red lights. On the other hand, if the shared understanding were that the scope of the duties imposed by the rule extended beyond convergent practice, then whether or not individuals generally stop at red lights after midnight will not settle whether they have a duty under the rule to do so. The behavior that reflects this understanding consists in the offering of arguments among participants regarding how the rule is to be understood and thereby extended. Such rules are social or conventional in spite of disagreements about their content precisely because their existence and character depends on substantial convergent behavior and a shared understanding of its character.

If I am right, then, the content of moral predicates derives from the ways they figure in various practices. That may make these concepts conventional in a familiar sense of that term. But their conventionality does not mean that the content of the predicate or rule is *fixed* by the scope of convergent behavior. Even conventional rules can have content that extends beyond the scope of convergent practice. Whether they do depends on the kind of practice involved. And that depends on the nature of the shared understanding about the kind of practice in which the participants are engaged. If the understanding is that the scope of the practice extends beyond convergent behavior—an understanding that is itself expressed in the behavior of participants offering arguments for extending the practice one way rather than another—then the practice may be one that has internal resources sufficient for self-assessment.

If this is right about certain concepts and practices, I have the beginnings of an answer to the second worry someone might have about my approach to corrective justice. Recall, that worry is that if tort law is among the practices to which we appeal in fixing the content of corrective justice, how can corrective justice be a criterion for assessing existing tort law? If the content of corrective justice depends on but is not fully fixed by existing practices, then the concept of corrective justice may yet provide a criterion for critically assessing even those practices whose existence is essential to the concept's existence. Were tort law the only practice in which claims to repair for harms suffered at the hands of others were made, then much of the content of corrective justice would be fixed by tort practice. But claims to repair are part of our ordinary moral practices as well, and substantially so. For that reason (among others) we can assess tort law in the light of corrective justice even if we recognize that the content of corrective justice is itself partially fixed by tort practice.

III. The Core of Corrective Justice

With this excursion into meta-ethics (and into the meta-ethics of corrective justice) complete, I return the focus to the concept of corrective justice. My thought is that, while there is substantial disagreement about the particulars of corrective justice, the scope of the disagreement can be easily overstated. I want to suggest that the concept has a coherent core drawn from the practices in which it figures. All viable accounts of corrective justice, whatever their substantive disagreements, are committed to the centrality of *human agency, rectification, and correlativity*. That is, first, the claims of corrective justice arise only with respect to losses occasioned by human agency. Other forms of misfortune do not fall within its domain. Different conceptions of corrective justice might differ with respect to the bounds and conditions of human agency, and why agency matters, but all share the view that only losses resulting from human agency can give rise to claims in corrective justice.

Secondly, claims in corrective justice are claims to repair or rectification. Again, different accounts are likely to pick out different objects of rectification. One way in which Ernest Weinrib's theory[11] and mine differ is that in his account the object of rectification is the 'wrong', whereas in my account it is the 'wrongful loss'. The difference between us reflects differences in our overall political and metaphysical commitments. For me, corrective justice is to be understood as a practice within a liberal political morality that emphasizes autonomy and well-being: thus, the emphasis on loss, which I think of in terms of diminished welfare. For Weinrib, the Hegelian, the important normative objects are abstract and only indirectly connected to human welfare or interests: thus, the emphasis on wrongs— understood as strongly objective metaphysical objects. Whatever our differences, both of us are committed to the importance of rectification as an element of corrective justice.

Finally, corrective justice involves correlativity of some sort. 'Correlativity' may be an unhappy phrase, but perhaps I can clarify it. The claims of corrective justice are limited or restricted to parties who bear

---

[11] *See, e.g.*, Ernest J. Weinrib, *Corrective Justice*, 77 Iowa L. Rev. 403 (1992).

some normatively important relationship to one another. A person does not, contrary to the view I once defended, have a claim in corrective justice to repair *in the air*, against no one in particular.[12] It is a claim against someone in particular. Different conceptions of corrective justice might flesh out the conditions under which individuals could come to stand to one another in the appropriate way, but all are committed to providing an account of those conditions as a way of explaining in part what corrective justice is. Some might emphasize causation: the fact that I caused your wrongful loss is enough for us to stand in a relationship such that if you have a claim in corrective justice it is against me, and if I have a duty of repair, it is to you. Some might argue that responsibility is the key concept: responsibility is connected to causation, of course, but not coextensive or cointensional with it. Someone can be responsible for the acts of others (acts and consequences he did not cause), and someone may perform acts that have untoward consequences for which he is not responsible (acts and consequences he caused, but for which he is not responsible). Some might emphasize being in the position of having been able to prevent the accident at the lowest cost (the cheapest cost-avoider). If I could have prevented your injury at a cost lower than anyone else (and I do not and you are injured), then I stand in the appropriate relationship to you that gives me a reason to repair your loss.[13] Whatever view one has about this matter, the important point is that, in every account of corrective justice, there is presumed to be a relationship between the parties that makes the claims of corrective justice appropriate to them—and not to others.[14]

IV. What Corrective Justice Is *Not*

Any account of the content of corrective justice will be both controversial and prescriptive. But we should not over-emphasize the differences at the

[12] *Cf.* Jules L. Coleman, *Tort Law and the Demands of Corrective Justice*, 67 IND. L.J. 349 (1992).

[13] For a discussion of the way in which the concept of the cheapest cost-avoider can figure in an account of corrective justice, *see infra*, text in section V, preceding note 19.

[14] I want to be perfectly honest not only about what I hope to accomplish, but also about what I have accomplished —which is considerably less. I am committed to the claim that the content of corrective justice is drawn from the practices in which it figures. I have suggested that, so conceived, the principle of corrective justice is not fully fixed by the convergent behavior of the population at any given time. Such a view allows me to treat the concept of corrective justice as both anti-realist, objective, and, therefore, critically useful. I have not fully developed the argument that practices can be conventional in the way I suppose they can be, nor have I demonstrated conclusively that the practice of corrective justice is of this sort. The plausibility of my overall argument depends ultimately on my providing those arguments in full.

Next, I claim that if we focus on the practices in which it figures, we will note three core elements: agency, rectification, and correlativity. In fact, I have not shown that these are features of our practices. That, too, remains to be done, but not here.

expense of the coherence of the core of the concept. If I am right in claiming that corrective justice requires agency, rectification, and correlativity, a variety of theories of tort law, whatever their substantive merits may be, do not involve corrective justice. Let me mention three.

First, there is my former account of corrective justice, which I called 'the annulment thesis'.[15] According to the annulment thesis, corrective justice requires annulling wrongful gains and losses. Understood in this way, the annulment thesis lacks the dimension of correlativity that I now believe to be part of the core of corrective justice.

A second account of tort law that has only recently begun to receive the attention it deserves is Stephen Perry's. In Perry's account, there is a two-step analysis.[16] First, we have to identify the class of individuals who are candidates for having the loss imposed on them. Here he relies on the important notion of 'outcome-responsibility' originally developed by Tony Honoré.[17] In Perry's view, in the typical tort both the victim and the injurer are outcome-responsible for the harm: typically, moreover, no one else is. Then the question becomes, how should the loss be allocated between these two parties? In Perry's account, only losses resulting from human agency fall within its ambit: that is entailed by the principle of outcome-responsibility. Moreover, his analysis relies on some notion of correlativity since the victim and injurer are presumed to be connected to one another through the important relationship of outcome responsibility. But his is not an account of corrective justice because it does not invoke the concept of rectification or repair. Rather, his is best seen as an approach to tort law that emphasizes a concept of 'local distributive justice', in which the principle of outcome-responsibility fixes the range within which the allocation or distribution question is raised and answered. His is an account of the distribution of loss, not the rectification of loss.

Finally, as an alternative to my conception of corrective justice, Ronald Dworkin has suggested another two-step analysis.[18] First, distinguish losses that result from human agency from other sources of misfortune or loss. Then ask the following question: What does fairness require with respect to the allocation of losses resulting from human agency? The principles for

---

[15] *E.g.*, COLEMAN, *supra*, note 12.

[16] Stephen R. Perry, *The Moral Foundations of Tort Law*, 77 IOWA L. REV. 449 (1992).

[17] Tony Honoré, *Responsibility and Luck*, 104 L.Q.R. 530 (1988).

[18] This account was suggested to me by Ronald Dworkin at a seminar at NYU Law School in the fall of 1993 as an alternative to the account I developed in RISKS AND WRONGS which was the topic of discussion in the seminar. I do not mean to attribute the view to him as his ultimate position. I bring it up, not to criticize Dworkin, but to elucidate my own views by contrasting them with several plausible alternatives. Indeed, this chapter developed primarily as a result of the discussion during that seminar, and, in particular, in response to a question of Thomas Nagel's about whether the duties of corrective justice are *natural* and, if they are, whether legal or other institutions could cancel them.

allocating loss that are required by fairness within that domain constitute the principles of corrective justice.

Whatever else can be said either in favor of or against this account, it is not an account of corrective justice. Whereas it emphasizes human agency, it ignores both correlativity and rectification. Instead of asking whether a victim has a right to recover against a particular person who stands in a certain kind of relationship to her (a relationship that makes that question meaningful and appropriate), it asks how shall a loss be allocated. In short, my previous theory of corrective justice lacks the correlativity dimension; Perry's lacks the rectification element; and Dworkin's suggestion lacks both. This does not mean that none of these 'moral ideals' is attractive or the best interpretation of important aspects of our legal practices. It means only that they are not genuine accounts of corrective justice.

V. THE PRACTICE OF CORRECTIVE JUSTICE

If I am right, any plausible account of corrective justice will emphasize agency, correlativity, and rectification. In this section, I want to fill out my own conception of corrective justice by exploring other features of the duty to repair the wrongful losses for which one is responsible. These are not features that have been emphasized by other writers, and at least some of them are likely to be quite controversial.

The duty to repair in corrective justice is pre-political and non-instrumental. As I have said on several occasions now, the content of corrective justice is neither epistemically, constitutively, nor logically independent of the moral, legal, and political practices in which it figures. Even more interestingly, whether or not the principle of corrective justice gives rise to a duty of repair in a particular community is conditional on the practices, legal and otherwise, that already exist within the community. Let me briefly explain each of these characteristics of corrective justice.

To say that corrective justice is pre-political is to say that there may be duties of corrective justice even in the absence of political institutions designed to enforce or implement them. Corrective justice cannot exist independently of all practices whatsoever, but it does not require political or legal institutions to enforce the duties to which it gives rise. So, in the absence of a state, there may be a duty of corrective justice: that is, a responsibility in morality to repair the wrongful losses for which one is responsible.

This is not to say, however, that the duty in corrective justice is a natural duty in the moral realist sense: that is, a duty whose existence is logically and constitutively independent of human practices and motivations. If a duty is natural then it imposes responsibilities on individuals regardless of how they regard themselves and independent of whatever practices they may have. The source of the duty is not human practice, but moral fact (or natural facts on which the moral fact is said to supervene or to be reducible to). One can accept the pre-political character of corrective justice without accepting the metaphysics of natural duties. And that is precisely the kind of approach I have in mind.

The duty of corrective justice is also 'non-instrumental' in an important sense. To see this, compare the duty one has to repair the wrongful losses for which one is responsible (under corrective justice) with the alleged duty one might have to repair all losses which one could avoid (in the future) at the lowest cost. The phrase 'one could avoid at the lowest cost' or 'cheapest cost-avoider' might be understood as a definition or an analysis of responsibility: the cheapest cost-avoider is all we mean by the responsible party. This is hardly an intuitively compelling characterization of the very complicated notion of responsibility, but if it is the right one, then there would be no difference between the economic and corrective justice principles stated above. In contrast, if the cheapest cost-avoider can sometimes be different from the responsible party, then it is hard to make sense of the claim that individuals who are the cheapest cost-avoiders have a duty to repair simply in virtue of their being the cheapest cost-avoider apart from such a duty figuring instrumentally in serving a desirable collective or social policy goal of reducing (or increasing) accident costs to a certain level. Imagine no such collective goal. Can it make sense to say that those people who are in fact the cheapest cost-avoiders have a duty to repair wrongful losses? Not really. But once we introduce the 'collective' goal of optimizing accident costs, such a duty makes perfectly good sense, but only instrumentally in the pursuit of the collective goal.

In my judgement, however, we need no notion of a joint goal or aspiration to make sense of the claim that those responsible for the misfortunes of others have a duty to repair them. It is part of our common-sense morality or moral practice that individuals have such a duty. That is what I mean by saying that the duty of corrective justice is non-instrumental. It does not mean that such a duty can serve no instrumental role, and in my book I indicate the way in which such a duty might figure in a liberal political theory more generally.[19]

Whereas corrective justice is both pre-political and non-instrumental, legal and political practices can affect the content of the duty corrective justice generates in many ways. Let me mention two. First, such practices can affect what behavior will count as satisfying or meeting the duty. Secondly, such practices may even cancel the duty altogether. To see how the former claim can be made out consider the duty to be *charitable*. Imagine that

---

[19] See especially the discussion of the relationship of corrective justice both to distributive justice and to stability in RISKS AND WRONGS.

there is a hurricane that leaves 100 people homeless. The cost of providing shelter turns out to be $300,000; imagine, moreover, that there are 1,000 people in the community who have a duty to be charitable, to come to the aid of the 100 homeless people. Suppose the local municipality puts a project in place to provide shelter that requires each member of the community to be burdened by the duty to contribute $300. Discharging the duty to be charitable can be accomplished by making a payment of $300 to the fund. Now, there may be other ways of discharging the duty to be charitable in this instance. Given the state-sanctioned project, giving one homeless person $300 would not count as discharging one's duty, even though providing the same amount to the general fund would. So the legal practice can sometimes determine whether an act constitutes discharging a duty whose existence does not depend itself on legal practices. I want to suggest, in effect, that the same is true of corrective justice.

Finally, and perhaps most controversially, whether one has a duty in corrective justice within a particular community can depend on the other practices in place for allocating losses. So, to use a familiar example, in New Zealand, where all accident costs (we may presume) are handled through the general tax coffers, whether they result from human agency or not, there is no practice of corrective justice. There are no duties in corrective justice to repair the wrongful losses for which one is responsible. This does not mean that there are no duties that fall to those responsible for harming others—duties that do not fall to others. Those responsible for loss may well have duties to make amends in other morally relevant ways: e.g. to apologize. It is just that there is no moral or legal duty of corrective justice to make repair. This suggests that the duty to repair is conditional on other practices.

Again, this does not mean that there is nothing we might be able to say regarding the morality of New Zealand's practices for allocating accident costs. We might point out that a practice of corrective justice tightens the bonds of community and of personal responsibility (if, in fact, it does), and that, to the extent that a community lacks a practice of corrective justice, it may risk eroding these bonds as well as the liberal ideal of community. What we cannot say, however, is that New Zealand has failed in some way simply by not having a practice of corrective justice. So even though the duties of corrective justice are non-instrumental, whether a community's not having a practice of corrective justice marks a moral shortcoming depends on what is lost morally, from the point of view of other principles, e.g. autonomy and responsibility, to which a practice of corrective justice contributes.

VI. SUMMARY

Let me see if I can sum up what I have tried to say about corrective justice. Corrective justice is, in my view, the principle that one has a duty to repair the wrongful losses for which one is responsible. In this way, the principle of corrective justice links agents with the misfortunes of others. The content of the principle is not independent of human practices with respect to it (as it would be for a moral realist). Yet the content of the principle is not fully fixed by those practices at any given time: what corrective justice requires is not solely determined by what people regard it as requiring at any give time.

Any particular conception of corrective justice will be a contestable interpretation drawn from practices, including legal ones, in which the concept figures. In the conception I offer, corrective justice requires agency, rectification, and correlativity (at a minimum). The practice of corrective justice is such that the duties imposed by it are pre-political—that is, they do not rely on legal or other political institutions for their implementation or enforcement; they are also non-instrumental, that is, they make sense independent of our having some set of collective goals (like cost avoidance) that they might serve; and while the duties of corrective justice do not depend on legal practices for their enforcement, legal and other practices may have an effect both on the content of the principle of corrective justice and whether such a duty exists at all in a particular community.

The Morality of Tort Law — Questions and Answers

TONY HONORÉ*

In relation to any social institution, after stating what general aim or value its maintenance fosters, we should inquire whether there are any, and if so what, principles limiting the unqualified pursuit of this aim or value.

H. L. A. HART[1]

I. THE QUESTIONS POSED

Hart was writing about punishment. In his view those who are puzzled about the justification of punishment should begin by disentangling a number of questions about the criminal process. It is a mistake to search for a single justification (deterrence or retribution) for the system as a whole. Moreover, once we see that a single aim will not justify every aspect of the system, we should not replace the single aim by a compound aim. We should not, for example, say that the justification of punishment is a mixture of deterrence, retribution, reform and denunciation. According to Hart, at least six questions about punishment need to be answered separately: (1) Why are certain kinds of conduct forbidden by law on pain of punishment? (2) What is the definition of punishment? (3) What general aims justify us in having a system of criminal law? (4) Who may properly be punished? (5) Subject to what mental and other conditions may a person be punished? and (6) How much punishment are we justified in inflicting? The answers to questions (4) to (6), which concern the 'distribution' of punishment, limit the extent to which it is proper to pursue the general aims that emerge in answer to question (3).

Hart meant his remark to apply to institutions other than criminal law, and it can certainly be applied to tort law. The theory of tort law is now

* Formerly Regius Professor of Civil Law, University of Oxford. I am grateful to Richard Wright for his comments on an earlier draft, the more so as my views on the moral structure of tort law are rather different from his.

[1] H. L. A. HART, PUNISHMENT AND RESPONSIBILITY: ESSAYS IN THE PHILOSOPHY OF LAW (1968), 10.

the subject of a sophisticated debate, especially in North America.[2] But has enough groundwork been done in distinguishing the various questions to be answered? This essay tries to unravel some of the questions and to suggest some answers.

Tort law and criminal law have common features. Each aims to eliminate or reduce undesirable behavior, each provides for sanctions to be imposed on those whose conduct is undesirable, and each poses difficult questions about the conditions for imposing sanctions and the extent of liability of wrongdoers. On the other hand the aims of the tort system are in some ways wider than those of the criminal justice system; and, correspondingly, the definition of tort liability differs from that of punishment.

Here are some questions about tort law corresponding to those put by Hart about criminal law. We may ask (1) Why are certain types of conduct made tortious? (2) What is the definition of tort liability? (3) What general aims justify the state in maintaining a system of tort law? (4) What justifies the person whose rights have been infringed in claiming compensation from the wrongdoer? (5) Subject to what conditions may one who by his conduct has infringed the rights of another be required to pay compensation? and (6) What limits should be placed on the extent of the duty to compensate?

Only the moral aspects of these questions will be examined. Efficiency, and its elaboration by Richard Posner,[3] are left on one side, as are problems of proof. Tort law, like the rest of law, must satisfy several values, of which efficiency in pursuing worthwhile objectives is only one.[4] Efficiency must be pursued within a morally defensible framework[5]; so we must ask, and ask first, what aims it is morally desirable and defensible to pursue by imposing tort liability.

---

[2] *See* Richard W. Wright, *Substantive Corrective Justice*, 77 Iowa L. Rev. 625 (1992) (discussing especially the work of Jules L. Coleman and Ernest J. Weinrib). *See generally* Symposium, *Corrective Justice and Formalism—The Care One Owes One's Neighbors*, 77 Iowa L. Rev. 403 (1992).

[3] *See, e.g.*, Richard A. Posner, *What Has Pragmatism to Offer Law*, 63 S. Cal. L. Rev. 1653, 1657, 1662–3 (1990).

[4] 'Tort law implements a variety of different principles and policies': Jules L. Coleman, *The Mixed Conception of Corrective Justice*, 77 Iowa L. Rev. 427 (1992) [hereinafter *Mixed Conception*]; *cf.* Jules L. Coleman, *Tort Law and the Demands of Corrective Justice*, 67 Ind. L.J. 349, 357 (1992) [hereinafter *Tort Law and Demands*].

[5] Ernest J. Weinrib, *The Case for a Duty to Rescue*, 90 Yale L.J. 247, 263 (1980); Guido Calabresi, The Costs of Accidents: A Legal and Economic Analysis (1970), 24–6, 291–308. For a view that this leaves minimal room for the pursuit of efficiency, see Richard W. Wright, *The Efficiency Theory of Causation and Responsibility: Unscientific Formalism and False Semantics*, 63 Chi.-Kent L. Rev. 553, 562–7 (1987).

II. THE QUESTIONS ANSWERED

A. The Descriptive Framework of Tort Law

The first two questions listed, though concerned with norms, call for descriptive, not normative answers.

(1) Why are certain types of conduct made tortious?

The first question Hart asked in his analysis of criminal law was why certain kinds of conduct are forbidden by law and so made crimes or offences. He gave the answer '[t]o announce to society that these actions are not to be done and to secure that fewer of them are done.'[6] Much the same may be said of conduct that by common law or statute is made a tort. When the legislature or courts make conduct a tort they mean, by stamping it as wrongful, to forbid or discourage it or, at a minimum, to warn those who indulge in it of the liability they may incur. It is true that the terms used to describe it, 'tortious' or 'wrongful', are not as strong as the term 'offence' in criminal law, and they do not carry the same stigma. But that is a matter of degree. In tort law not only actions but omissions are at times treated as wrongful; that is also the case in criminal law, for example in the law of homicide. Again, tort law sometimes treats as wrongful not an action or omission as such but the causing of harm by conduct of a potentially dangerous sort, for example selling a defective product or setting off explosives. In such cases the harm-causing action itself need not be wrongful, though it is done at the agent's risk. Criminal law also uses this technique, but mostly with the implication that the conduct is wrongful even apart from its consequences. Think of the crime (in the U.K.) of causing death by dangerous driving, dangerous driving being itself an offence, though a less serious one. The word that best covers all these cases (actions, omissions, causing untoward consequences) is 'conduct'. If conduct is understood to include them all, we can say that tort law, like criminal law, announces that certain conduct is forbidden and tries to secure that less of it takes place. Tortious conduct is generally wrongful in itself, though if no harm results no liability may be incurred. When strict liability is imposed, the conduct is generally not wrongful in itself but the wrong consists in causing harm by engaging in certain types of risky activities.

But that is not the only reason why the state and its courts make conduct tortious. One point of creating a tort, as opposed to a crime, is to define and give content to people's rights by providing them with a mechanism for protecting them and securing compensation if their rights are infringed.

---

[6] HART, *supra*, note 1, at 6.

(2) What is the definition of tort liability?

The second question follows naturally from the first. It concerns the definition of tort liability. Liability in tort (a) is imposed, if the dispute cannot be resolved without litigation, by the courts of the legal system having jurisdiction (b) at the instance of an individual whose right has been infringed (c) on a person who has committed a civil wrong (tort) against that person, and (d) normally imposes on one who has committed the wrong an obligation to pay money by way of compensation to the person whose right has been infringed.[7] One may treat as subsidiary, though theoretically important, other remedies in tort law such as mandatory orders or injunctions and, outside tort law, administrative measures which may prohibit or regulate harmful conduct and may impose pecuniary penalties for such conduct.

B. The Justifying Aims of Tort Law

The first two questions called for a description of how the system of tort law operates. The answers do not justify the existence of tort law, still less any particular part of it. The third question concerns the justification of tort law:

(3) What general aims justify the state in maintaining a system of tort law?

Two different aspects of this question need to be dealt with here: (a) is the state entitled to take steps to discourage undesirable behavior? and (b) if so, may it do so by treating certain interests of individuals as rights and giving them the legal power to protect those rights and obtain compensation if they are violated?

The tort system is one means by which the state, on behalf of the community, seeks to reduce conduct that it sees as undesirable. Others include the criminal law, education, administrative means such as licensing and inspection, differential taxes, and many more. The state not only may but must, if a society is to be viable, try to minimize at least some types of disruptive conduct. Is tort law, like criminal law, a suitable means to this end? What tort and criminal law have in common, and what distinguishes them from some other means of social control, is that they work by marking out conduct, or the failure to attain a required standard of conduct, as wrongful. On the other hand licensing, inspection, differential taxation, and rationing discourage behavior not by marking it as wrongful but by limiting opportunities to indulge in it, for example by refusing licenses for sex shops, or by denying benefits to those who do indulge in it, for example by

---

[7] *See* Wright, *supra*, note 2, at 634, n. 38.

charging more for leaded petrol. Other branches of the law of civil responsibility, such as the law of contracts or restitution, though they provide remedies for what are seen as wrongs, act primarily not by treating conduct as wrongful but in other ways. Thus, contract law mainly marks out the conditions in which agreements will be enforceable, and the law of restitution mainly specifies what is to count as an unjust benefit.

The technique of tort law therefore is to label certain things as not to be done or omitted or brought about, though in a less stigmatic way than criminal law. If the state is justified in making conduct criminal and attaching to it penalties that may include prison, it must also be justified in marking conduct as tortious and attaching to it the lesser sanction of compensation. In all societies some people behave disruptively or, without meaning to be disruptive, expose others to undue risks of injury. The state must have the right and duty to minimize the risks and remedy the disruption.

But it does not follow that the legislature or courts are right to make any particular sort of conduct tortious. That must depend on factors like those familiar in the debate about criminal law. Is the state justified in rendering tortious (or criminal) only conduct that threatens harm to others? If so, must the harm be physical/economic or should inroads on personal, emotional, and other intangible interests count as harm? This is not the place to pursue this important debate.

Assuming that the state can rightly make conduct tortious, is it entitled to do so by treating individual interests as rights and threatening economic sanctions against those who infringe the rights? Can the state properly use its resources, prestige, and power for this purpose? The question goes deep into political theory. A supporter of the rule of law, and hence of the *Rechstaat* idea,[8] is driven to a positive answer. The rule of law depends, among other factors, on a framework of individual rights that must be respected by others and by the state itself. This gives people a degree of independence from one another and from the power of government. One who accepts this ideal will think the state justified in trying to minimize undesirable behavior by a technique that treats some interests as rights and gives those who have the rights the power to avert or redress the unwanted conduct.

Assuming that this is a proper role for the state, it may also be justified, within limits, in subsidizing right-holders by setting up and paying for a framework of civil courts for the enforcement of tort claims. But even a critic who is not opposed to the rule of law can argue that to subsidize private rights in this way is not a proper use of the state's resources. While, so far as I know, there is no state in which this view has so far been taken,

[8] The idea that the state has a duty to set out and enforce certain rights of the citizen, even against itself.

it may be rash in an age of privatization to assume that no state in the future will ever refuse to subsidize the use of its courts to give effect to the tort system. In such a state, those who pursue tort claims in the courts would have to pay the cost of judicial enforcement. It would be morally and politically objectionable for a state to go even further and refuse access to its courts altogether to those wishing to bring claims in tort. Closing the courts to tort claims would be to give up an important technique for lessening undesirable conduct and would jettison a central element in the structure of rights that underlies the rule of law. Of course in some societies (past and present), more emphasis is placed on reducing bad conduct by social pressures and administrative means than on enforcing individual rights. But these societies tend to be less committed to the rule of law.

Assuming that the arguments in favor of the rule of law are persuasive, the state is justified in maintaining a system of tort law that seeks to reduce the incidence of undesirable conduct by treating certain interests of individuals as rights and providing those who have them with the legal power to avert inroads on those rights and, if they are infringed, to obtain compensation for their violation.

C. The Distribution of Tort Liability

(4) What justifies the person whose rights have been infringed in claiming compensation from the wrongdoer?

What was said in answer to question (3) is incomplete. To justify the tort system, it is not enough to show that the state is entitled to take steps to minimize undesirable behavior and to give individuals the power to protect their rights and obtain compensation if they are violated. It must also be shown that some principle or principles of justice entitle the right-holders (tort-plaintiffs) to sue the wrongdoers (tort-defendants) for compensation. For though the state may be entitled to designate certain interests as rights and certain sorts of conduct as wrongs, it cannot thereby make it *just* for the right-holders to sue the wrongdoers for compensation. It cannot by fiat create a principle of justice linking the two. The issue here then is whether there are one or more independent principles that justify tort claims against tort-defendants.

a. Corrective Justice

The principle most often cited for such an approach is that of corrective justice.[9] This can be put in various ways. On a wide view it requires those who have without justification harmed others by their conduct to put the

---

[9] Wright, *supra*, note 2, at 627–1.

matter right.[10] This they must do on the basis that harm-doer and harm-sufferer are to be treated as equals, neither more deserving than the other. The one is therefore not entitled to become relatively better off by harming the other. The balance must be restored.

I have said 'without justification' rather than 'wrongfully', not because the latter is incorrect, but to put aside the question whether to harm someone without justification is a wrong in itself[11] or whether it is a wrong only if the person doing the harm was at fault. 'Putting the matter right' (reparation[12]) is a concept that may (according to the circumstances) require the harm-doer to restore something to the person harmed, or to repair a damaged object, or (when the unharmed position cannot be restored, as it usually cannot) to compensate the harm-sufferer. Compensating in turn means doing something conventionally regarded as restoring the harm-sufferer to his unharmed position. 'Compensate' is used to cover whatever may be done to make good the loss when reparation is not literally possible; what counts as compensation is largely a matter of convention. Nothing in the idea of corrective justice requires the compensation to be in money. Though in tort law it nearly always takes that form, outside of tort law various forms of substitute provisions in kind or services are treated as proper ways of making good the harm to the sufferer.[13]

The claim to put things right lies against the harm-doer, and sometimes only the harm-doer can satisfy it, for example when it includes an apology. But in other cases, for instance when the claim is purely for money, the harm-doer can arrange for someone else to pay, perhaps through third-party insurance or the generosity of a friend. If the matter is put right in that way, the harm-doer satisfies the demands of corrective justice.[14] Moreover the loss may be covered by the harm-sufferer's own insurance, or through a state scheme, in which case the harm-doer may to that extent be freed from the need to compensate the harm-sufferer. The harm-doer

[10] The application of corrective justice to unjust gains is not dealt with here, though a similar analysis would be possible.

[11] On this wrong-in-itself view, which I prefer, the defendant's conduct may not be *wrongful* in itself, but causing harm without justification is nevertheless a *wrong* that grounds a claim for compensation. Jules Coleman expresses it differently: '[T]he duty to repair . . . wrongful losses is grounded not in the fact that they are the result of wrongdoing, but in the fact that the losses are the injurer's responsibility, the result of the injurer's agency': Coleman, *Mixed Conception, supra* note 4, at 443. Unlike Coleman, I regard the two as correlative: the losses are wrongful if and only if caused by the agent without justification.

[12] NEIL MACCORMICK, LEGAL RIGHT AND SOCIAL DEMOCRACY (1982) 212 .

[13] Contrary to Coleman, *Tort Law and Demands, supra,* note 4, at 366, Wright argues that in cases where corrective justice requires the rightful position to be restored, the mode of rectification is implicit in the grounds of recovery and liability: *see* Wright, *supra,* note 2, at 683. But, unless settled by a particular legal system, the precise content of the victim's right and the appropriate mode of giving effect to it against the harm-doer seems an open question, though the rectification must be adequate in context.

[14] Wright, *supra,* note 2, at 703.

has wrongfully caused the physical harm but, ultimately, not an economic loss. But then the harm-doer, not having satisfied the liability personally, may not unjustly be required to compensate the insurer or the state instead of compensating the harm-suffer. In law this takes the form of subrogation.

From what has been said it will be clear that in my view corrective justice is a relational principle. It can exist only when the harm-doer's wrong violates the harm-sufferer's right; the two cannot be dissociated. On this point I agree with Ernest Weinrib and disagree with the view formerly embraced by Jules Coleman. For Coleman at one time thought that there could be wrongful losses, calling for redress, in the abstract, even though one could not point to any particular wrongdoer as the person who ought to put them right.[15]

Corrective justice presupposes that the defendant has caused harm to the plaintiff. It is this doing of harm that needs to be corrected. So there must be a causal link between the defendant's conduct and the plaintiff's loss. The conduct need not be *the* cause of the harm.[16] It is enough that it is *a* cause, and there can be more than one human cause of the harm in question, in which case both (or all) harm-doers can be responsible.[17] The existence of the causal link is a *necessary* condition of corrective justice and of the duty to compensate in a tort action. It is not a *sufficient* condition, however, for two reasons. First, for compensation to be rightly claimed, there must have been no justification for inflicting the harm. If there was a justification, the person harmed cannot on the same facts be justified in claiming compensation. Secondly, though someone who harms another without justification must in principle make the harm good as a matter of corrective justice, what form his responsibility should take, whether legal or extra-legal, and subject to what further conditions,[18] remains an open question.

Since a causal link is necessary to both corrective justice and tort liability, much turns on the view we take of the responsibility of one who causes another harm. A widespread view is that a person who harms another is responsible for the harm only when he is at fault.[19] If this view is accepted, corrective justice has to be defined more narrowly than in my earlier formulation. It will require reparation or compensation only if the person causing the harm was at fault in doing so. This view would set a narrower limit to corrective justice and, in particular, would exclude strict liability in

---

[15] Not entirely abandoned in his *Mixed Conception* article, *supra*, note 4.

[16] *See, e.g.*, Stephen R. Perry, *The Moral Foundations of Tort Law*, 77 Iowa L. Rev. 449, 464, n.58 (1992).

[17] See *infra*, question (6).   [18] See *infra* question (6).

[19] *See, e.g.*, Coleman, *Mixed Conception*, *supra*, note 4, at 442–3; Perry, *supra*, note 16, at 497.

tort law.[20] On the wider view, which I favor, the importance of fault is not denied, but the fault requirement operates, so far as it does, as an independent limit to the pursuit of corrective justice rather than as an element in it. If so, it falls to be discussed under the next question (5), which concerns the conditions for imposing tort liability.

b. Outcome Responsibility

The view that those who cause harm are responsible for it even in the absence of fault fits what I have elsewhere termed outcome-responsibility.[21] On this view we are, if of full capacity and hence in a position to control our behavior, responsible for the outcomes of our conduct, whether act or omission.[22] This responsibility is an essential constituent of our character and identity, without which we would lack both achievements and failures. Lacking a positive history of what we have done and its outcome, we should at most be half-persons.[23] Outcome-responsibility figures prominently in our sense of our own agency and is important for both the theory of agency and moral theory.[24] This is not to say that we are responsible for everything that would not have happened had we not acted, or refrained from acting, as we did.[25] That would be a misconception. The conduct that grounds outcome-responsibility includes what we do but does not include our not doing all that we do not do. Under non-doing it comprises only omissions which are violations of a norm.[26]

There is nothing mysterious about this limitation of our responsibility to actions and those omissions that violate norms. When we act, we launch ourselves upon the world and implicitly choose to be responsible for what we do, including its outcome. When we do *not* act, we are responsible only so far as responsibility is thrust upon us, because society requires of us certain actions that we omit to do. Moreover, the outcomes to which outcome-responsibility applies do not consist of everything that would not have happened but for the conduct in question, but are limited to consequences

---

[20] I take strict liability to be liability without fault, whether or not the defendant was engaged in a dangerous activity. To engage in a dangerous activity gives the law a reason to impose strict liability on the person engaging in it, but it does not form part of the definition of strict liability. Wright, interpreting Aristotle, takes a different view, distinguishing between strict liability for risk and absolute liability: Wright, *supra*, note 2, at 697, n. 335. But are Aristotle's 'unjust losses' not simply those caused by another without justification, for example by accident, even if the conduct did not apparently carry with it any special risk?

[21] Tony Honoré, *Responsibility and Luck*, 104 L.Q.R. 530, 541, 545–6 (1988).

[22] *Cf.* Perry, *supra*, note 16, at 488–9. My thesis can stand on its own feet. But it is arguable that Aristotle took a similar view, viz., that wrongful, mistaken, and accidental conduct (covering both fault and strict liability) causing harm to others obliges the harm-doer to repair the harm as a matter of corrective justice. Wright, *supra*, note 2, at 697–8.

[23] The other 'negative' half of our history concerns what has happened *to* us.

[24] Perry, *supra*, note 16, at 490.   [25] As argued by Wright, *supra*, note 2, at 682.

[26] Tony Honoré, *Are Omissions Less Culpable?*, in Essays for Patrick Atiyah (Peter Cane & Jane Stapleton (eds.), 1991), 31, 36–42.

properly attributable to the conduct rather than to later voluntary or abnormal interventions by other people and events.

Outcome-responsibility serves to foster a sense of identity because it does not stretch indefinitely into the future but enables each of us to claim for ourselves, or to share with a few others, outcomes of limited extent, whether successes or failures.[27] Yet outcome-responsibility for harm to another does not by itself create a duty to *compensate*. The *form* that our responsibility for an outcome should take remains an open question. An apology or telephone call will often be enough. But outcome-responsibility is a basis on which the law can erect a duty to compensate if there is reason to do so. There will be *some* reason to do so if the conduct in question is socially undesirable and if there is also reason to treat the harm suffered as the infringement of a right.

If the outcome of conduct is harmful to another the next question is whether in the context there was a *justification* for inflicting the harm. We are sometimes justified in injuring others, for example in self-defence. When we compete we are justified in inflicting losses or setbacks on our rivals. Whether those injuries, losses, or setbacks count as 'harm' depends on whether that protean word is thought to carry with it the implication that the injury or loss has not been *justifiably* inflicted.[28] I win the 100 meters and you lose. Outcome-responsibility makes me responsible for your defeat as well as for my victory. But the nature of the race justifies me in inflicting that setback on you. The same is true of other forms of competition, for example in trade, business, politics, literature, and love. If some succeed, others fail. When, however, there is no justification for inflicting a loss on another, outcome-responsibility supports the claims of corrective justice. Since I am responsible for a loss inflicted on you without justification, I have a duty to *answer* for what I have done, and to make whatever amends are appropriate to the situation. It will then be in order for the state to

---

[27] The discussion of outcome-responsibility here fits an analysis of causal concepts by Hart and myself that need not be repeated in this essay: *see generally* H. L. A. HART & TONY HONORÉ, CAUSATION IN THE LAW (2d ed. 1985), 68–83 *passim* [hereinafter HART & HONORÉ]. Stephen Perry treats this as an analysis of responsibility rather than causation: *see* Perry, *supra*, note 16, at 503. But since our approach is regularly criticized for containing normative elements that are foreign to causatio, *see, e.g., id.*, it is worth stressing that the analysis of causal concepts that we put forward, though not normative, is functional. These causal concepts take the shape they do because they are tailored (of course not consciously) to fit certain purposes, especially explanation and the attribution of responsibility. Those purposes require them to incorporate cut-off points. Without cut-off points, both backward and forward, causal concepts would not play the prominent role they do in everyday life, because they would not serve any worthwhile purpose. But these concepts are not normative: they are neutral between different ways of behaving and different assessments of conduct. Thus, the responsibility that they serve to identify is as much responsibility for good conduct and good outcomes as for bad conduct and bad outcomes.

[28] According to Jules Coleman, the implication of 'harm' is that a legitimate interest of the plaintiff has suffered: *see* Coleman, *Tort Law and Demands, supra,* note 4, at 350.

impose tort liability to compel me to make good your loss, if my conduct was undesirable and your loss an infringement of your rights, provided that to do so is not inconsistent with other values important to maintain.[29]

c. Distributive Justice

But if outcome-responsibility supports the wider view of corrective justice,[30] we must note that the justification for imposing outcome-responsibility on those who cause harm to others rests not on corrective but on distributive justice. Perry rightly points to the distinction between outcome-responsibility from the agent's point of view—something that helps the agent foster a sense of his personal identity, character and history—and outcome-responsibility as a justification for holding people liable to others for the harmful outcome of their conduct.[31] But I do not agree with him that these two aspects of outcome-responsibility are inconsistent. The argument for holding people responsible to others for harmful outcomes is that it is fair to make the person to whom the advantages will flow from an uncertain situation over which he has some control (or which he has chosen to enter into) bear the losses that may likewise flow from that situation. It is fair to treat the agent as if he had made a bet on the outcome of his action. This argument, somewhat loosely expressed, tries to spell out what justice requires in situations of uncertainty. It is a familiar notion in legal and extra-legal contexts. For example the person to whom the income of property or a business will accrue if it does well has normally also to bear the risk of loss if it does badly. In the law of sales, when the right to income or fruits passes to the buyer, the risk of deterioration or destruction normally passes to him as well.

Aristotle and subsequent philosophers who have developed the theory of distributive justice do not expressly mention this principle of risk, no doubt because it has arisen mainly in legal contexts. But, despite appearances, the risk principle rests on a form of distributive justice.[32] Though this form of justice is generally concerned with the distribution of goods, it also covers the distribution of losses and burdens. For example, it applies to the incidence of taxation. The just distribution of burdens and losses among the members of a society requires that a criterion be found (say benefit or capacity) according to which they may fairly be allocated. There is no rea-

---

[29] See *infra*, question (5).

[30] Wider in the sense that reasons other than fault may support a duty to compensate.

[31] Perry, *supra*, note 16, at 490–1.

[32] This is not to accept Nickel's argument that corrective justice applies only to the impairment of distributively just holdings of goods: *see* James W. Nickel, *Justice in Compensation*, 18 Wm. & Mary L. Rev. 379, 381–3, 385–8 (1976); *cf.* Jules L. Coleman, *Justice and the Argument for No-Fault*, 3 Social Theory & Practice 161, 174, 180, n. 19 (1975) [hereinafter *Argument for No-Fault*]. Corrective justice applies to actual holdings, whether or not those actual holdings in justice ought to be redistributed in whole or part to other members of the community.

son why the distribution of the *risk* of gains or losses in a situation of uncertainty should not equally be part of distributive justice. To be specific, we can speak of the just distribution of risks as risk-distributive justice. It might seem at first sight that this sort of justice is not distributive, because the benefit of success and the risk of failure fall on the same person, whereas distributive justice is concerned with the allocation of assets and burdens among all or many of the members of a community. But the risk principle is entirely general. It places on *every* member of the community the burden of bearing the risk that his conduct may turn out to be harmful to others in return for the benefit to himself that will accrue should his conduct turn out as he plans. It distributes throughout society the risks of harm attributable to human conduct.

d. The Blend of Corrective and (Risk-)Distributive Justice

I therefore take corrective justice to be in one way distinct from distributive justice and in another dependent on it. It is distinct in the sense that the interests (holdings) that corrective justice protects need not be just from a distributive point of view. The filthy rich can appeal to corrective justice if their holdings are filched by the grinding poor. But to justify corrective justice involves appealing at a certain stage to the just distribution of *risk* in a society. In that respect corrective justice depends on distributive justice. Corrective justice is a genuine form of justice only because the just distribution of risks requires people to bear the risk of harming others by their conduct even when they are not at fault in doing so.[33] For this reason, corrective justice is a substantive, not a merely formal, principle. It needs, and can be given, a moral basis.

This principle of risk distribution has an intuitive appeal. It may rest on the sort of moral intuition that one cannot go behind; or it may be that deeper analysis will show that it turns on something more fundamental. At any rate, risk distribution serves to justify outcome-responsibility, and outcome-responsibility opens the door to imposing a duty of reparation in suitable cases, and so to corrective justice. This conclusion is welcome, since it puts some parts of tort liability on a morally sound basis. But it does so only when the defendant has personally infringed the plaintiff's rights. For it is only when this is the case and the harm-sufferer sues the person who is outcome-responsible for the harm that corrective justice by itself justifies the claim.

In criminal law the offender is nearly always held responsible for what he has done personally. Vicarious liability or, what comes to the same thing, the liability of corporations and other bodies for the conduct of their members, is exceptional. Tort liability is different. Many tort actions give

---

[33] How far this responsibility should be translated into strict legal liability depends on the answers to questions (5) and (6) *infra*.

effect to personal responsibility. But others follow a different pattern. They are brought, for example, against an employer for the act of an employee who, in working for him, has harmed the plaintiff. In that case outcome-responsibility and corrective justice do not serve to justify an action against the employer,[34] though they may justify one against the employee. Is some other justification available? The conventional reasons given for holding that the employer ought to bear the risk of loss within certain limits for the employee's harmful conduct in the course of his work are that the employer (i) has control over the business, including the work of employees, and (ii) stands to profit from the employee's services. A combination of these reasons, it is generally thought, justifies us in imposing vicarious responsibility on the employer. As in outcome-responsibility, the person who, in a situation of uncertainty, has a degree of control over how it will turn out, and who stands to gain if it goes in his favor, must bear the risk that it will turn out to harm another. This reasoning appeals once more to a principle of justice based on risk distribution. The justification of tort liability is, as before, a combination of corrective and distributive justice. But distributive justice now appears at two points rather than one. It does so, first, to support the outcome-responsibility of the employee and, secondly, to support the action against the employer, who has not personally harmed the plaintiff.

In the end, the justification of tort liability both against the harm-doer personally and against secondary defendants, such as employers held to be vicariously liable, rests on both corrective and (risk-)distributive justice.

(5) Subject to what conditions may one who by his conduct has infringed the rights of another be required to pay compensation?

The main questions are whether fault is, morally speaking, a necessary condition of tort liability, and whether modern conditions justify using loss spreading to support liability that may be out of proportion to the blameworthiness of a defendant's conduct. The second question is not strictly about the legal conditions of tort liability in individual cases but about a background state of affairs that may be necessary if the pursuit of corrective justice by tort law is to be morally defensible. Both questions raise the issue of how far, if at all, corrective justice should be tempered by considerations of retributive justice.

---

[34] Richard Wright argues that corrective justice requires the employer to compensate the victim 'for injuries that are tortiously inflicted in pursuance of the employer's objectives': Wright, *supra,* note 2, at 674, n. 219. But, as he himself recognizes, *id.* at 674, it is unjust to compel someone to be an insurer for the fault of another, unless he has undertaken to do so (or, I would add, the just distribution of risks requires him to do so). It seems a mere fiction to argue that the employee's act is really the employer's, or must be treated as such.

a. Retributive Justice and Fault in Criminal Law

To begin with fault, there is no doubt that, however this complex notion is interpreted, it is in general a necessary condition of conviction for a criminal offence, at any rate for a serious offence for which imprisonment is possible. One reason is that the law's prohibitions are meant to guide the potential offender's choices. Their aim is to influence conduct and their sanctions are directed at those who choose to do what the law forbids, not those who do the forbidden action without choosing to do it. If, therefore, the defendant had no choice, but was compelled to act as he did, for example if he was forced to steal against his will, it cannot be said that he *disregarded* the prohibition. He contravened it but, since he did not disregard or defy it, he should not be subject to punishment.

But the focus on choice does not stop there. If, though not compelled, the offender did not intend to do the wrong that the law forbids, he again cannot be said to have defied the prohibition. For example, if he did not mean the victim he assaulted to die, or if, oddly, he did not realize that the woman with whom he was having intercourse did not consent to it, he cannot be said to have flouted the prohibition of murder or rape, though he may have defied some lesser prohibition, say of assault or sexual harassment.

This condition of punishment, that the offender should have flouted the law, by intentionally doing what it forbids, is well settled for serious criminal cases that carry heavy penalties. This remains true though the offender, given the difficulties of proof and the desire not to reward ignorance of the law, need not have known the exact terms in which the prohibition is couched. When the wrongdoer's fault is less serious, say recklessness or negligence,[35] most legal systems will still permit lesser degrees of punishment. In these latter types of cases, the offender need not have deliberately flouted the prohibition. It is sufficient that he behaved in a way that displayed too much self-regard and too little concern for the interest of others. Indifference or unconcern, falling short of defiance, is enough. Moreover, when the penalty is only a modest fine, fault even in the sense of indifference or unconcern may be dispensed with altogether and strict liability imposed. Yet even in the case of strict liability, the defendant must have chosen to act as he did. Compulsion will exclude punishment. But given the element of choice, the case for punishment here depends on the just distribution of risks. The criminal law may properly be used to ensure that those who, acting in their own interest, create a risk to others should suffer a modest penalty for the harm that their activity brings about. For

---

[35] Offences of negligence such as negligent wounding and killing are of course commoner in civil law than common law systems, but they are by no means absent from the common law.

example the seller of milk which, unknown to him, is adulterated may properly be fined in a modest sum for selling adulterated milk. There is therefore in practice a rough correlation between the type of fault or conduct and the weight of the punishment imposed. For the most serious penalties the offender must have chosen to defy the law, for the somewhat less serious he must have chosen to act with indifference to the interests of others, and for the relatively minor he must at least have chosen to do something that is potentially harmful to others.

What has been said describes in outline the correlation between fault/conduct and penalty in most systems of criminal justice. Can this rough correlation be morally justified? It has a certain intuitive appeal. The principle on which it seems to rest is retributive. The retributive principle has, however, two aspects, both grounded in the principle of proportionality. One *requires* that a sanction be imposed that is roughly *proportionate* to the moral gravity of the conduct. The other *forbids* that a sanction be imposed that is *out of* proportion to the gravity of the conduct. It is this second, *limiting*, aspect of the retributive principle that is in play here. The limiting principle requires the sanction to be no greater than is justified by the gravity of the conduct, of which the degree of the wrongdoer's fault is perhaps the most important ingredient. Of course, the correlation is extremely rough.

It may be objected that talk of retributive principles is out of place. According to some versions of retributive justice, there can be no punishment in the absence of fault, since conduct that is free from fault does not possess even a minor degree of moral gravity. Hence, there should be no strict liability in criminal law. But a person who freely does something chooses to intervene in the world and, while what he does may display neither defiance of nor indifference to the interests of others, it may, in pursuit of his own interests, put others at risk. It seems reasonable to put conduct that exposes others to a risk that materializes—for example, selling milk that may possibly be and is in fact adulterated—at a fairly low point on the scale of misconduct on which conduct showing indifference to and defiance of the interests of others occupy the higher reaches. The behavior located low on the scale is not morally bad, and does not amount to fault, but neither is it morally indifferent; conduct that may affect others cannot be that. It is taking a chance of harming others.[36] Suitably extended, therefore, the retributive principle can surely treat as just, and not merely expedient, the imposition of minor sanctions for risk-creating conduct that goes wrong. The retributive principle, thus modified, would still

---

[36] Stephen Perry says it is based on something resembling fault: *see* Perry, *supra*, note 16, at 504. The difference is between what one should not in any case do and what one may do provided it does not turn out to be harmful to others.

require the gravity of the conduct to be roughly proportionate to the sanction.

Of course, even without this suggested extension, retribution as a theory intended to justify the criminal process has been fiercely attacked. But it has its defenders so far as sentencing is concerned, and every system of criminal justice, so far as I know, pays some attention to it at least in that context. This is not the place for a detailed discussion of the case for it; I merely assume that, in its limiting form, it has some merit. And *if* it is right to require the conduct to be of sufficient moral gravity to correspond roughly to the severity of the penalty imposed in criminal law, something similar should in principle be true in tort law as well.

b. Retributive Justice and Fault in Tort Law

How should the retributive principle apply in tort law? First, the tortfeasor, like the criminal offender, presumably ought not to be made to pay unless he has chosen to do what the law forbids. There should be no tort liability for an act done under compulsion. So much seems to be required by the fact that tort law, like criminal law, is meant to influence conduct by inducing people to abstain from undesirable behavior. But, as tort law does not impose imprisonment, there is on the retributive principle no strong case for requiring that a tortfeasor had intended to defy the law, though, if he did, the case for a sanction is strengthened.[37] Provided the behavior was selfish or inconsiderate, which negligent conduct often is, he may properly be made liable in tort. But the burdens of tort liability, though less grave than losing one's physical freedom, can be very serious, especially if the defendant is not insured.[38] In such cases, the retributive principle will not merely justify but will require fault as a condition of tort liability.

In other cases, however, fault will not be necessary. A tort defendant is often insured and in some of the commonest types of tort liability, such as motoring accidents, insurance is compulsory. Hence the defendant does not have to pay the damages personally, except to the extent that he pays them indirectly through his insurance premium. Provided that the insurance premium is modest, therefore, there seems no moral reason to require fault as a condition of liability in these cases.[39] In practice many countries, such as

---

[37] *See generally* David G. Owen, *The Moral Foundations of Punitive Damages*, 40 ALA. L. REV. 705 (1989).

[38] Or if his employer is vicariously liable for his conduct but exercises rights of subrogation against him—in practice a rare event.

[39] *See generally Argument for No-Fault, supra,* note 32, at 173–4; Jules L. Coleman, *Mental Abnormality, Personal Responsibility and Tort Liability, in* MENTAL ILLNESS: LAW AND PUBLIC POLICY (Baruch A. Brody & H. Tristram Engelhardt, Jr. (eds.), 1980), 107, 118–21, 123–4. *Cf.* Jules L. Coleman, *The Morality of Strict Tort Liability*, 18 WM. & MARY L. REV. 259, 283–4 (1976).

France and Germany, impose strict liability for transport accidents, relying on liability insurance to minimize the burden on individual defendants. Again, when the defendant is vicariously liable for the conduct of an employee,[40] the retributive principle may not require that his liability be confined to cases where the employee is at fault. Since the profit that falls to the employer is not always merely the amount that he deserves to make, but may include windfalls, an employer's vicarious liability need not be confined to accidents caused by fault on the part of the employee but may sometimes extend to harm that is purely accidental.[41]

Often, therefore, there should be in principle no moral objection to strict liability in tort law,[42] provided that it does not impose an undue burden on the defendant personally. Hence it is not surprising that the degree of care and skill required in tort law is a stringent one. The standard of negligence is nearly always objective. The defendant may therefore be held liable for faults that a reasonable person would not have committed but that he could not help because he was too rash, clumsy, or stupid.[43] Though nominally the liability is for fault, the defendant is in effect subject to strict liability. Of course, often fault is actually present, but the faults in question may be rather minor ones of inattention and slowness to react.

What has been said so far shows that corrective justice as tempered by the retributive principle supports some strict liability, but not universal strict liability. But it also shows that the line between fault and strict liability is often blurred. And even when fault is genuinely a condition of tort liability, and still more when liability is objective or strict, the compensation payable may be disproportionate to what is often a minor fault. To avoid this disproportion, the retributive principle seems to require that defendants should not be exposed to disproportionately heavy losses. If the claims of corrective justice are to be morally viable, ways must therefore be found of spreading such losses.

Insurance is a common mechanism for spreading losses, and helps at the same time to protect the plaintiff's claim to compensation. Loss spreading is indeed often achieved by a form of distributive justice that allocates burdens roughly in proportion to benefits. Those who benefit from some activity, say motoring, are made to bear a proportionate share of the losses that the activity causes, for example through compulsory third-party insurance. This is certainly not an infallible instrument of justice, since insurance

---

[40] For whose conduct the employer properly bears the risk according to principles of distributive justice.

[41] It is true that in practice legal systems tend to confine vicarious liability of employers to accidents attributable to employee fault.

[42] As Coleman has pointed out, the retributive arguments in favor of fault liability in tort law as it operates in practice are rather weak: *Argument for No-Fault, supra*, note 32, at 162–72. *But see* David G. Owen, *The Fault Pit*, 26 GA. L. REV. 703 (1992).

[43] Honoré, *supra*, note 21, at 536.

premiums may be exorbitant. Nevertheless, it helps to ensure that tort damages are in most cases not grossly disproportionate to the fault of the defendant who has caused the harm. Hence, though loss spreading (through third-party insurance) is distributive, the reason why it is needed as an adjunct to the tort system is, in part at least, to satisfy the demands of retributive justice. It serves to cushion losses which, whether defendants are at fault or not, are out of scale with the gravity of their conduct. This does not entail that loss spreading is an aim of the tort system as such, merely that some form of insurance is essential if a system of corrective justice is to operate fairly in modern conditions. Corrective justice can operate as a morally defensible system only in harness with retributive justice. This in turn may require recourse to a form of justice that distributes burdens equitably.

So, while corrective justice in isolation warrants holding people strictly liable to make good the loss to those whom they harm without justification, the tort system is not bound to translate this into a legal liability to compensate when to do so would be unduly burdensome to the defendant. On the contrary, the retributive principle requires that the burden be made roughly proportionate to the gravity of the conduct. In many instances this can to some extent be achieved by making fault a condition of liability. In others, the personal burden on the defendant must be reduced, whether he is at fault or not, by a system that redistributes losses among those who benefit from the activities that cause them. In that way full compensation for the plaintiff can be achieved, as corrective justice demands, while the personal liability of the defendant is tempered by loss distribution.

(6)   What limits should be placed on the extent of the duty to compensate?

Retributive and distributive justice are not the only moral considerations that may limit the untrammelled pursuit of corrective justice. Three other reasons are commonly given for restricting the compensation payable in tort actions: the scope of the rule violated, the foreseeability of the harm for which compensation is sought, and the conduct of the plaintiff. A fourth is more radical. It is sometimes said that tort liability should be replaced, entirely or above a certain amount, by a state compensation scheme, at least in certain areas of life.[44] What is the moral status of these arguments?

a. The Scope of the Rule Violated

A rule making conduct tortious, for example requiring dangerous machinery to be fenced, may have a limited scope. It may be that, properly inter-

---

[44] As in New Zealand, with respect to accidents.

preted, the aim of the rule is to prevent parts of the employee's body or clothes catching in the machinery rather than to prevent parts of the machinery flying out and injuring someone. There is nothing special to tort law about this need for interpretation. Every rule that makes conduct wrongful, whether in criminal law, tort law, the law of contract, trust law, or whatever, requires interpretation and the interpretation will set limits to the scope of the rule in question. When the interpretation excludes certain types of harm, the pursuit of corrective justice by the use of state judicial machinery is to that extent ruled out. But is it just to exclude, for example, certain of the plaintiff's economic, psychological, or emotional interests from the scope of a tort law rule or from tort law as a whole?

It seems that the state must be justified in imposing some limits on the type of harm for which compensation may be claimed. To require compensation for every type of harm in the context of every rule of tort law would to be impose a burdensome liability on defendants. It would be inefficient when, especially with some types of harm difficult to ascertain, the cost of imposing tort liability would much exceed the likely benefit. The legislature and courts must be entitled to take the view that some interests—say, wrongfully inflicted but trivial psychological harm—do not deserve the status of a right. Of course, the state may make mistakes in these matters, but it must surely be justified, indeed bound, to mark out such limits on liability. If the state is bound to decide what conduct should be made criminal or tortious, fallible as its judgment may be, it must also be bound to fix the limits of responsibility for various types of harm.

b. The Foreseeability of the Harm

The unforeseeability of the harm for which compensation is claimed is often put forward, particularly in tort claims based on negligence, as an independent ground for limiting the extent of the defendant's liability. The ground for this limitation is sometimes said to be that, when the liability is based on negligently failing to foresee and takes steps to avoid harm, the resulting liability should logically be restricted to the harm, or type of harm, that should have been foreseen. Thus, if the defendant should have foreseen harm by impact alone he should not be liable for the harm by fire or explosion that unexpectedly results. This argument assumes that there is never a case for placing the risk of an unexpected outcome on the person at fault in creating the risk.[45] The argument is no more convincing than the view that where it is a condition of liability that the defendant intended harm, the harm for which he is liable should be confined to what he intended. The conditions of liability (question (5) above) and the extent of liability (this question (6)) present somewhat different moral and policy

---

[45] Hart & Honoré, *supra,* note 27, at 259–5.

issues. But the retributive principle does require a rough proportion to be preserved between the degree of fault and the burden of the sanction. To rule out recovery for unforeseeable harm, or harm of an unforeseeable type, enables courts to limit the extent of the burden, though in a somewhat arbitrary way given the fluidity of the criteria used to identify unforeseeable harm after the event. But it must be stressed that the argument for proportionality weakens when the defendant does not pay the compensation personally, as in cases of insured, vicarious, and organizational liability, which bulk large in tort liability for negligence.

c. Conduct and Fault of the Plaintiff

Corrective justice suggests that the defendant's duty to compensate the plaintiff should be limited when the plaintiff's conduct, along with that of the defendant, is a cause of the harm. In that case the plaintiff as well as the defendant is responsible for the outcome. If they are both responsible, the plaintiff should bear part of the loss himself. How great that part should be will depend on whether causal contribution can be quantified. The question is controversial, though in my view the notion of causal contribution is a coherent one.[46] If causal contribution can be assessed, the plaintiff's claim, from the viewpoint of corrective justice, should be reduced proportionately to that contribution. If not, retributive principles must be taken into account.

Suppose that the plaintiff's conduct has not merely been a cause of the harm along with the conduct of the defendant, but that the plaintiff has been at fault in behaving as he did, or has acted with deliberation. Should the plaintiff's fault or deliberation bar or reduce his compensation? The plaintiff may be morally disentitled to sue, for instance because he consented to the defendant's conduct or intentionally provoked it. More difficult is the question how far his recovery should be affected by the fact that, short of intentional provocation, his fault contributed to the harm done. Does the existence of contributory fault modify the claim to compensation on the basis of corrective justice? To reduce the plaintiff's claim from what corrective justice on its own would warrant is to impose a loss on him. The retributive principle requires the loss to be not disproportionate to his fault. This sets a limit to the possible extent of the reduction, but does not settle the question whether a reduction proportionate to fault is morally required. If both plaintiff and defendant were at fault in causing the harm, the straightforward retributive principle would make both plaintiff and defendant responsible to an extent roughly proportionate to the gravity of their respective faults. Putting these considerations together, the plaintiff's claim, when both he and defendant are at fault, should be

[46] HART & HONORÉ, *supra*, note 27, at 225–35.

reduced by an amount that results in plaintiff and defendant bearing a share of the loss roughly proportionate to their respective faults, but not so as to impose on the plaintiff a loss disproportionate to his fault considered in isolation. In practice, those legal systems that apportion damages for contributory negligence adopt these criteria, or something rather like them.

d. The Replacement of Tort Liability by a State Scheme of Compensation

According to Richard Wright, the replacement of tort liability by a compulsory no-fault state compensation scheme would be inconsistent with corrective justice.[47] It would fail to impose the duty to compensate on the party who ought to bear it and would impose it on persons who, from the point of view of corrective justice at least, have no duty to bear it. The effect of such a scheme is to transfer the whole or part of the duty to compensate from the harm-doer to the taxpayer or the contributors to an insurance fund.

There is, however, an argument for doing precisely this, based on the just distribution of risks. If it is fair for everyone to have to contribute through taxes to the defense of the country, since everyone in the country benefits from its being defended, so it is fair for everyone who owns or drives a vehicle, or who benefits from the existence of a transport system, to contribute to the accident costs that such a system carries with it. To argue in this way is simply to extend to a wider group the sort of argument that leads to an employer being held liable for the harm done by his employee when engaged in working for him. Of course there is a technical difference in that, under the imagined state scheme, the harm-doer would not be liable in tort, while in the law of vicarious liability as it stands in most countries the employee remains liable even when his employer is vicariously liable. But in practice the employee is not sued, because he will usually not be able to pay the damages, or not so easily as the employer, and usually he does not even pay the insurance premium that covers the employer's potential liability for his harmful conduct. It would hardly be an injustice to take from the harm-sufferer (who is entitled to compensation from another source) a merely technical right to sue the harm-doer.

That is not to say that there is a morally compelling case for replacing tort liability by a state compensation scheme. To do so would tend to undermine the sense of personal responsibility of some potential harm-doers, just as vicarious liability tends to undermine the sense of personal responsibility of some employees. But to introduce a state compensation scheme would not in my view violate corrective justice. The propriety of corrective justice depends, I have argued, on our taking a certain view about the just distribution of risks in a society, a view for which individual

---

[47] Wright, *supra*, note 2, at 704.

outcome-responsibility provides a basis. But it is possible to take a wider view about how risks should be distributed, at least in certain areas of life. One can argue that the distribution of risks, from motoring for example, should take place at the level not of the individual but of the vehicle-owning population or the whole community. The level at which risks should be distributed in a particular area of community life seems pre-eminently a matter of political judgement.

III. THE ANSWERS SUMMARIZED

A brief summary of the suggested answers to the six questions discussed may be helpful:

(1) and (2) By the tort system the state aims to reduce the incidence of undesirable conduct by treating certain individual interests as rights and giving the right-holder the power to protect his rights and obtain compensation if they are infringed by undesirable conduct marked as a civil wrong.

(3) The state is justified in maintaining, and probably in subsidizing, a tort system and an institutional framework, including courts, to give effect to it.

(4) Subject to (5) and (6) below, tort-plaintiffs in principle are morally entitled, on the basis of corrective justice, to recover damages from tort-defendants who have without justification personally caused them harm. On a wide view, corrective justice requires those who have without justification harmed others by their conduct to put the matter right, even if they were not at fault. The reason is that we are responsible for the outcome of our conduct (outcome-responsibility) and that a just distribution of risks requires us to make good the harm our conduct causes to others in return for the benefit and credit that accrues to us when our plans come off. The case for imposing vicarious liability in tort on employers and organizations who have not personally caused the harm also rests on the just distribution of risks.

(5) But the pursuit of corrective justice must be tempered by the need to keep a proportion between the burden of compensation that falls on a defendant personally and the gravity of his conduct. There are cases in which it is unjust to hold the defendant liable in the absence of fault and in which, even if he is at fault, the extent of his personal liability should be limited by loss spreading. The moral basis for proportionality is the retributive principle, which requires that the sanction should not be disproportionate to the gravity of the conduct for which it is imposed. The argument for proportionality does not apply, or applies more weakly, when the liability is vicarious rather than personal.

(6) The pursuit of corrective justice is also tempered by the duty and power of the state to decide which harms are to count as infringing legal rights. The state is justified in reducing or refusing compensation when the harm lies outside the scope of the rule of law on which the plaintiff relies or was of an unforeseeable type the risk of which should not be imposed on the defendant. When the plaintiff's conduct contributes to the harm he suffers, the extent to which his claim should be reduced, if any, should be settled according to the principles of corrective justice and the retributive principle. Lastly, it would not be unjust, though it might be unwise, for the state to replace tort liability in certain areas by a scheme of no-fault insurance based on the just distribution of losses. The principle of corrective justice that justifies the straightforward cases of tort liability, in which the defendant has personally done the harm, has therefore to be tempered by considerations of distributive and retributive justice that limit the extent to which it can properly be applied.

PART II

PRINCIPLES AND VALUES UNDERLYING TORT LAW

Wealth Maximization and Tort Law: A Philosophical Inquiry

RICHARD A. POSNER[*]

For more than two decades I have been arguing that what I call 'wealth maximization' is the best positive and normative guide to the law of torts.[1] My purpose in this essay is to restate, refine, and amplify the philosophical version of this argument.

I. Introduction

By 'wealth maximization' I mean the policy of trying to maximize the aggregate value of all goods and services, whether they are traded in formal markets (the usual 'economic' goods and services) or (in the case of 'non-economic' goods or services, such as life, leisure, family, and freedom from pain and suffering) not traded in such markets. 'Value' is determined by what the owner of the good or service would demand to part with it or what a non-owner would be willing to pay to obtain it—whichever is greater.[2] 'Wealth' is the total value of all 'economic' and 'non-economic' goods and services and is maximized when all goods and services are, so far as is feasible, allocated to their most valuable uses.

The non-pecuniary dimension of wealth is important to emphasize, especially to noneconomists, who are prone to assume that economists care only about goods and services that are priced in the market. Yet I concede the incompleteness of 'wealth', even when so broadly defined, as a measure of social welfare. The reason is that the concept of wealth is dependent on the assignment of property rights and—what is closely related, because property rights are a source of wealth—on the distribution of wealth across persons. To illustrate from tort law, the demand for clean air and water, and hence the contours of nuisance doctrine, may vary depending on

[*] Chief Judge, U.S. Court of Appeals for the Seventh Circuit, and Senior Lecturer, University of Chicago Law School. I thank William Landes and David Owen for their helpful comments on an earlier draft.

[1] For the fullest statement of my position, see WILLIAM M. LANDES & RICHARD A. POSNER, THE ECONOMIC STRUCTURE OF TORT LAW (1987); for the most philosophical statement, see RICHARD A. POSNER, THE PROBLEMS OF JURISPRUDENCE (1990), chs. 12–13 *passim*.

[2] POSNER, *supra*, note 1, at 356–7.

whether the question is posed as whether the victim of pollution would be willing to 'sell' his 'right' to be free from pollution for a price that the polluter would be willing to pay or as whether the victim would offer to 'buy' the right to clean air or water from the polluter at a price the latter would be willing to accept. Demand is a function of income and wealth as well as of price. An indigent may not be able to pay anything for freedom from pollution, while a wealthy person may demand an astronomical price to surrender his right (if it is his right) to clean air and water.

I want to prescind from these 'baseline' problems and examine wealth maximization in the more common tort situations in which such problems are not acute. A small (or for that matter a large) change in tort doctrine is unlikely to so alter the wealth distribution that (as in my pollution example) the efficiency of the two states of doctrine cannot be compared. It is not confining, therefore, to limit consideration to cases in which a 'Hand formula' approach—an injurer in an accident situation should be liable to his victim if, but only if, the expected cost of the accident (that is, the loss, both pecuniary and non-pecuniary, caused by the accident if it occurs, multiplied by the probability of its occurring) exceeds the cost (which again might have a non-pecuniary component, such as time) of avoiding the accident—will generate the identical result whichever party to the accident has a *prima facie* right to the legal protection of his activity.

II. The Positive Theory

The idea that value should be determined in this way and used to guide social policy toward accidents and other dangerous conduct comes naturally to most economists and economically minded lawyers. The idea that it *is* the guide that the courts have used in constructing the doctrines of tort law is much more controversial, even among economic analysts. Yet it has support not only in my work and my joint work with William Landes, but in work by Ronald Coase, Guido Calabresi, Steven Shavell, and many others,[3] though few go as far as Landes and I do in defense of the descriptive adequacy of the theory. Controversial as it is, the positive side of the wealth maximization theory of tort law does not present very interesting *philosophical* problems. No doubt a philosopher of science could be engaged to evaluate the entitlement of the positive theory to call itself 'scientific' and its claims to be better supported than rival theories. And Landes's and my efforts to elide the age-old philosophical disputes over the meaning of intention and of causation by recasting these concepts in economic terms

---

[3] And lately we have seen the conversion of Richard Epstein to this view. Richard A. Epstein, *Holdouts, Externalities, and the Single Owner: One More Salute to Ronald Coase*, 36 J.L. & Econ. 553 (1993).

that do not refer to them[4] might raise some philosophers' eyebrows.[5] But the philosophical adequacy of the positive theory is not apt to trouble many people.

It is different with the normative branch of the theory. The idea that to the extent tort law departs from the dictates of wealth maximization it ought to be changed to conform to them has drawn the ire of philosophers and philosophically minded lawyers, such as Jules Coleman, Ronald Dworkin, Anthony Kronman, and Ernest Weinrib. The issues of moral and political philosophy raised by the wealth maximization theory are the focus of this essay.

III. The Normative Theory

A. Pragmatic Normativity

I begin my discussion of the normative theory with three disclaimers. First, partly for the reason given earlier (the dependence of wealth maximization on the prior assignment of property rights and on the distribution of wealth across persons), I neither assert nor believe that the theory is adequate to resolve all issues of social policy, or even all issues of tort law. Secondly, I do not believe that it can be deduced from any overarching moral theory, such as utilitarianism. And thirdly, I do not believe that wealth in the sense in which I use it, broad as that sense is (remember that it is not a pecuniary *concept* although it uses a pecuniary *metric*), has any intrinsic, non-instrumental, plausibly 'ultimate' value, as pleasure or happiness or human flourishing or a good will is thought to have in various philosophies.

All this I concede to my critics.[6] But I no longer think that these concessions weaken my position. For I have become profoundly skeptical of efforts to construct coherent moral systems. I have come to believe that in our society moral beliefs to a great extent precede, and are largely unaffected by, the reasons that can be marshaled pro and con them. It would for example be extraordinarily odd for someone to say, 'I know and believe

---

[4] We distinguish between intentional and unintentional injuries by asking whether the cost of avoidance was positive—requiring the injurer to expend resources to *avoid* it (in which case the injury was unintentional), or negative—requiring the injurer to expend resources to *cause* it (in which case the injury was intentional): Landes & Posner, *supra,* note 1, at ch. 6. And we avoid questions of whether a defendant's act was the cause or a cause of the plaintiff's injury by asking in every case simply whether imposing liability on the defendant would increase wealth: *id.* at ch. 8.

[5] E.g., see the essays in this volume by John Finnis, *Intention in Tort Law*, and Tony Honoré, *Necessary and Sufficient Conditions in Tort Law*—Ed.

[6] Most notably Ronald M. Dworkin, whose article *Is Wealth a Value?*, 9 J. Legal Stud. 191 (1980), *reprinted in* Dworkin, A Matter of Principle, (1985) ch. 12, remains the best, as well as the best-written, criticism of wealth maximization as an ethical principle.

that torturing children is bad, but I would like to know *why* it is bad.' One might or might not be able to give him a reason; but it is quite unlikely that one could affect his belief. So when Bruce Ackerman, starting from first principles, ends up advising his readers that '[t]he rights of the talking ape are more secure than those of the human vegetable,'[7] or that a fetus has fewer rights than a dolphin,[8] or that the only reason parents should be forbidden to kill their day-old infant is that they could give the infant to someone else,[9] the proper objection is not that Ackerman is 'wrong' but that he is quixotic in supposing that *argument* can or should alter people's beliefs about such things. It is unrealistic, as Swift said, to suppose that you can argue a person out of a position that he had not been argued into; and it is weak-minded to abandon a deep-seated moral belief just because you cannot think up a good retort to a clever argument.

I do not mean that people's moral beliefs never change; certainly many of mine have. But they change because of experience rather than argument. I dare say that some professional philosophers have reasoned their way into one moral position or another (vegetarianism, for example), but I think that arriving at moral beliefs through argument is rare even among philosophers and much rarer among the rest of the population.

All systematic moral theories stub their toes on the immovability of bedrock moral beliefs by argument. The consistent utilitarian has trouble showing why it might not be a good idea occasionally to hang someone known to be innocent. A Kantian who, like Ackerman, believes that only beings endowed with 'reason' have moral rights will have trouble explaining why it is wrong to kill profoundly retarded or comatose people. The greatest natural lawyer (Aquinas) reasoned himself into such conclusions as that masturbation is a worse sin than raping one's mother and that lending money at interest is condemned by the same principle that condemns sodomy.[10] A Rawlsian has trouble explaining why our brains are not a collective good. A Nozick-style libertarian has trouble explaining why gladiatorial contests are wrong. And a wealth maximizer will encounter embarrassments very similar to those that both the utilitarian *and* the Nozickian encounter as he explores such topics as slavery, discrimination, and welfare. These topics are not likely to be directly encountered in tort law, but a philosophy that is contradicted by our deep moral intuitions in various testing cases may be thought inadequate to govern any area of moral inquiry.

---

[7] BRUCE A. ACKERMAN, SOCIAL JUSTICE IN THE LIBERAL STATE (1980) 80. See discussion in POSNER, *supra*, note 1, at 336—40.

[8] ACKERMAN, *supra*, note 7, at 127. [9] *Id.* at 129.

[10] Rape is a 'natural' use of the sexual organs, masturbation an unnatural use of them. Lending money at interest is an attempt to make a barren metal (gold) breed; sodomy is an equivalently sterile employment of the reproductive organs.

It seems unlikely that the only reason for the inadequacy of moral theories as persuaders to action in our society is that no one has appeared on the scene yet who is bright enough to think up a compelling theory. A more plausible explanation, offered by Alasdair MacIntyre,[11] is that the moral beliefs of modern Americans reflect different and to a significant degree inconsistent traditions of moral thinking: Greek (Platonic, Aristotelian, Stoic, Pyrrhonian, Epicurean), Jewish, Catholic, Protestant (including Puritan), pragmatic, liberal, utilitarian, scientific (including Darwinian), Freudian, populist, frontier-individualist, humanitarian, egalitarian. These traditions are not, of course, mixed in the same proportions in every American. So varied are the mixtures, indeed, that some Americans seem actually to inhabit different moral universes from others. Very few live entirely in one tradition, moreover, and those who live in more than one are apt to have a set of moral beliefs that is internally inconsistent—for example, for abortion, sexual freedom, euthanasia, and the protection of animal predators, but against infanticide, capital punishment, economic freedom, and humans eating meat; against abortion, but for hunting and capital punishment; for close families, yet also for easy divorce; for democracy, yet also for academic privilege. So there is inconsistency both within and across individuals, and there is nothing that moral theorizing can do about it.

If this is correct, the most constructive philosophical approach to the question whether wealth maximization should guide tort law may be, rather than considering its adequacy or pedigree as a moral theory, to *relate* it to the various moral traditions that might have or imply a position on tort liability. If, as I believe, wealth maximization resonates well with several moral theories and offends none, a tort system founded on wealth maximization may deserve to command the widespread support that it does in fact seem to command in our society.[12] To put this another way, the unreflective public opinion underlying a system of tort law that can be best understood and explained in terms of wealth maximization intersects the principal moral traditions found in our society.

B. Illustrations

Limitations of space and time compel me to confine myself to a brief explanation of the compatibility of wealth maximization with five ethical theories: (1) the Pareto principle, (2) rule utilitarianism, (3) Aristotelian corrective justice, (4) Kantian deontology, and (5) Kantian egalitarianism.

---

[11] ALASDAIR C. MACINTYRE, AFTER VIRTUE: A STUDY IN MORAL THEORY (2nd ed., 1984).

[12] This approach has some affinity to Rawls's idea of 'overlapping consensus', but there is no need to consider how close the affinity is: *see* JOHN RAWLS, POLITICAL LIBERALISM (1993) lect. 4.

1. The Pareto Principle

I begin with the Pareto principle,[13] which is that a change (including a change brought about by an accident or an intentional act) is good if it makes at least one person better off and no one worse off. This is a 'liberal' principle[14] akin to Kant's and Mill's principle that everyone is entitled to as much liberty as is consistent with the liberty of all other people. The Pareto principle protects a person from harmful activities carried on by others by insisting that all persons potentially harmed by those activities consent to the effects upon them. Persons ordinarily will consent to be harmed only if they have received some form of compensation as a result of which, on balance, they are not made worse off by the harmful activity. By requiring unanimity, the Pareto principle in its pure form avoids the objections to majoritarianism.

The Pareto principle may seem inconsistent with a system of tort law that does not require strict liability for all injuries, although it makes a good fit with the provision of damages for negligent and intentional torts. Even a comprehensive regime of strict liability would be suspect to a Paretian because in the case of serious physical injuries, including death, tort compensation is rarely full compensation. And yet a tort system dominated by the negligence principle—resigned to awarding zero recovery in many cases of accidental injury and less than full compensation even in many cases in which liability is imposed, and very costly to operate (our tort system)— may nevertheless approximate Pareto optimality.

To see this requires understanding that compensation can be *ex ante*, in the form of a cost savings, as well as *ex post*, in the form of a judgment or settlement. *Ex ante* the cost (an 'expected' cost in economic jargon) of an accident has two components: the expected cost to the potential injurer of being held liable and made to pay damages for causing an injury to someone else, and the expected cost to the potential victim of being injured in an accident. The same person can, of course, be both potential injurer and potential victim; this is common in collision cases; and let me for the sake of simplicity confine attention to this class of case. Let me also eliminate any dubieties associated with the concept of an 'expected' cost by noting that expected costs can be transformed into smaller and more certain current costs through insurance: liability insurance in the case of the expected cost of being an injurer, accident insurance in the case of the expected cost

---

[13] Often referred to as 'Pareto efficiency'. The concept of efficiency implicit in the use of the criterion of wealth maximization is what is called 'Kaldor-Hicks efficiency', or sometimes 'potential Pareto efficiency'. It differs from Pareto efficiency in not requiring that persons harmed by a change be compensated. It thus lacks the aspect of unanimity that makes Pareto efficiency so attractive an ethical principle.

[14] Though it can generate illiberal implications, as shown in Amartya Sen, *The Impossibility of a Paretian Liberal*, 78 J. POL. ECON. 152 (1970); but not in the cases I discuss.

of being a victim. No one buys unlimited insurance, so the transformation of expected into current costs is not complete. Subject to this qualification, of which more shortly, an insured will want to minimize the sum of the premiums for the two types of insurance. The balance between the two costs will differ under negligence and under strict liability. The cost of liability insurance will be lower under the former because a smaller proportion of accidents create liability under a regime of negligence than under one of strict liability. But by the same token the cost of accident insurance will be higher under the negligence regime because more accidents are left uncompensated by the tort system under that regime. If, however, the *sum* of liability and accident insurance costs is lower under the negligence regime, it may be the preferred regime. And if it is preferred by *everybody* it will be Pareto optimal even though, *ex post*, some accident victims will be worse off under the negligence regime. They will be worse off because accident insurance does not always provide full compensation, if only because an accident may so reduce the utility of money to the victim that he would not pay for the right to receive insurance proceeds in the event of such an accident.[15]

I say that negligence 'may be' rather than 'is' the preferable regime in the case I have just put precisely because there are uncompensated accident costs. Even if the insured's total cost of (both accident and liability) insurance is lower under negligence, the sum of his current and expected accident costs may be higher under a negligence regime than under strict liability—or, depending on such factors as differential incentives for safety and different costs of administration, lower.

It is unlikely in any event that *everybody* will be made better off *ex ante* by any particular choice of tort doctrines. But that is true in every situation in which the Pareto concept is invoked: all 'voluntary' transactions have some third-party effects—or, if not all *individual* voluntary transactions, all *classes* of such transactions. A series of voluntary contracts between fully informed and consenting adults may alter the prices of the goods or services involved in the contracts (or prices of inputs into those goods or services) and by doing so harm other people. Still, the Pareto concept retains at least some normative force when approximated, which it might be possible to show is the case with regard to one or more doctrinal or institutional features of (or reforms in) the tort system when evaluated by the criterion of wealth maximization. If unanimity is a morally

---

[15] The clearest such case is where the victim dies in the accident. Then accident insurance proceeds will be of value to him only in so far as he is altruistic toward his survivors. Tort damages awards (funded to a large extent by liability insurance) tend to be more generous, though in many cases—the case of death for example—they still are not fully compensatory. But that is not an important consideration in a comparison of negligence and strict liability, unless the two regimes are thought to produce a different number of accidents.

attractive criterion for social action, near unanimity should be attractive too, even if less so.

2. Rule Utilitarianism

The next moral system with which I want to compare the wealth maximization theory of tort law is utilitarianism—appropriately next, because as we progressively relax the unanimity criterion of the Pareto principle we slide closer and closer to utilitarianism. I offer wealth maximization as the rule utilitarian's rule for determining tort liability.[16] The offer will be rejected out of hand by anyone who thinks rule utilitarianism inconsistent with utilitarian premises. Not imposing tort liability on an individual or a firm that had caused no injury might be a good utility-maximizing rule, but if in a particular case total utility would be maximized by departing from it in order to enhance the deterrence of harmful acts, on what *utilitarian* basis could one refuse to do so? Utilitarians give various answers. Many are variants of the proposition that whatever hypothetical departure is thrown up by the critic of utilitarianism would not in fact be utility-maximizing in the real world—to which the critic may answer that basic moral principles must, to be such, hold in all conceivable worlds—to which the utilitarian can reply that all moral theories, even one as austere as Rawls' justice as fairness, are contingent upon certain facts about the world and human nature.[17]

I do not want to get sucked into this vortex. It is enough for my purpose that many, probably most, utilitarians believe that it is infeasible to maximize utility at retail, as it were. They believe that a utility-maximizing polity would rely heavily on rules, admitting some exceptions of course but refusing to allow a general exception that would permit any rule to be waived whenever utility would be maximized by doing so. The general exception would make most people feel insecure and therefore unhappy, and, a related point, it would be difficult to find someone or some institution that could be trusted to enforce so far-reaching a discretionary power fairly and intelligently. So the general exception would not be utility-maximizing, and this in turn implies that the hypothetical cases in which applying it would increase utility are not merely hypothetical, but illusory.[18]

---

[16] I shall not discuss here the choice between rules (such as negligence) and standards (such as strict liability) in tort law. For a discussion of that distinction, see generally Posner, *supra*, note 1, at 44–8. The rule/standard choice has formal affinities to the choice between rule and act utilitarianism—information costs, for example, are a crucial consideration in both choices—but adopting wealth maximization as the rule utilitarian's 'rule' would not dictate the purely instrumental choice between rules and standards as principles of tort law.

[17] This is the line taken in Stephen W. Ball, *Uncertainty in Moral Theory: An Epistemic Defense of Rule-Utilitarian Liberties*, 29 THEORY & DECISION 133 (1990).

[18] The version of rule utilitarianism that I am defending here is similar to what Lyons calls (without pejorative intent) 'primitive rule utilitarianism': DAVID LYONS, FORMS AND LIMITS OF UTILITARIANISM, (1965) pt. 4. It is quite compatible with act utilitarianism. *Cf.* Gerald F. Gaus, *Mill's Theory of Moral Rules*, 58 AUSTRALIAN J. PHIL. 265 (1980).

It is infeasible to make *ad hoc* judgements concerning the net contribution to aggregate utility of some particular dangerous act or practice that results in injury—to measure the unhappiness caused by the injury and the unhappiness that would have been caused by the precaution that would have averted it. If utility is to be maximized with respect to accident-causing activities, it will have to be done indirectly. To the extent that the costs of a dangerous activity can be monetized through insurance and compared with the costs of minimizing the expense of insurance through changes in liability or regulation, public policies (including liability rules) designed to minimize the sum of all these costs are more likely to be utility-maximizing than policies guided by some other norm. The uninsured costs of accidents—the costs that insurance does not cover—pose greater difficulty. Yet we observe that most people contentedly assume slight risks of serious injury in exchange for modest benefits. It is unlikely that preventing them from assuming those risks, as by fixing a speed limit of 10 m.p.h. on all roadways, would be a utility-maximizing policy. The risks can be valued, and risky behavior optimized, by the tort system as follows: estimate what a person would charge to assume the risk in question (it might be the risk of being killed by a speeding driver), divide that number by the risk, and award the quotient in damages if the risk materializes.[19] So, if a person would demand $1 to be subjected to a one in a million chance of being killed, the proper award if he were killed and the defendant found liable would be $1 million; if he would demand $25,000 for a one in a hundred risk, the proper damage award would be $2.5 million. Awards calculated in this manner should give potential defendants the 'correct' incentive to take safety precautions by confronting them with the expected costs to potential victims of precautions, while a larger award would induce an excessive investment in such precautions and a smaller award an inadequate incentive.

Such a system of tort liability could not be *proved* to maximize utility, since utility is unobservable and unmeasurable. But the common-sense rule utilitarianism that I am defending is based on the idea that it is possible to make rough but adequate guesses as to what rules are likelier than the alternatives (including *ad hoc* utility-maximizing, in lieu of any rule) to be utility-maximizing, and wealth maximization is a good candidate to be that rule, at least in the area of tort law. This should not be a surprising claim, in view of the historically close connection between the economist's idea of 'wealth' and the utilitarian philosopher's idea of 'utility'.[20] Prosperity is not

---

[19] *See* LANDES & POSNER, *supra*, note 1, at 188.

[20] Economists distinguish between 'wealth' and 'utility' along the axis of certainty. The two concepts coincide for persons who are risk neutral, but for risk preferrers and risk avoiders they diverge when a choice involves a possibility rather than a certainty of wealth. A risk-averse person, for example, will prefer (get greater utility from) a 100 per cent chance of $1 than a 10 per cent chance of $10, even though the expected wealth of the two chances is the

everything, but to most people it is a lot; and because wealth maximization is not a narrowly pecuniary concept, the wealth maximizer's notion of 'prosperity' incorporates noneconomic goods, such as safety and clean air and satisfying family relations, along with economic ones. It is possible that some change in tort law would increase total utility even though it resulted in higher insurance costs and, perhaps, no decrease in accidents. This might happen if, for example, the change resulted in a transfer of income to people who gained more utility from the increment to their income than the transferors lost. So a utilitarian who thought that poor people are more likely than rich ones to be accident victims and that they have a higher marginal utility of money might favor the abolition of the defense of contributory negligence. But as there is no way to verify such conjectures, the wealth maximization approach should appeal to the rule utilitarian as a practical solution to the problem of how *feasibly* to maximize utility.

3. Aristotelian Corrective Justice

I want to turn my attention now to the moral tradition—for my purposes adequately illustrated by aspects of the moral teachings of Aristotle and of Kant—in which preference satisfaction, either on an aggregate or an individual basis, is rejected as a basis for moral or legal duties. In Aristotle's theory of corrective justice (to which two and a half millennia of further philosophizing have added rather little),[21] the duty to rectify a wrong is simply that—a duty—rather than an instrument for the achievement of a social or even personal end, such as deterrence or happiness. Aristotle's theory is entwined with the concept of *pleonexia*, or trying to get more than one's fair share. The principles of distributive justice establish some pattern of entitlements, and if someone wrongfully disturbs that pattern, corrective justice requires that the just equilibrium be restored.

This intuitively appealing principle provides a more direct route to remedying intentional torts than the wealth maximizer's approach. But when one turns to the detailed articulation of intentional-tort doctrine, the theory of corrective justice quickly runs out of steam, whereas the economic analyst can explain the defenses to these torts and why they differ in some respects from the defenses to unintentional torts, the details of the remedies (including why they differ from the remedies for other torts), the overlap with unintentional torts (such as, frequently, defamation), the relation to crime at one end and breach of contract at the other, and in short the over-

---

same. I use 'wealth' broadly to embrace 'utility' in such examples, but avoid the latter term in a philosophical discussion in order to avoid confusion with utilitarianism. The 'utility' (in the sense used by utilitarians) to a thief of a good that he could not afford to buy has no ethical status or legitimacy in wealth maximization. It is not a demand backed by an offer price.

[21] Despite efforts to do so illustrated by Symposium, *Corrective Justice and Formalism— The Care One Owes One's Neighbors*, 77 Iowa L. Rev. 403 (1992).

all pattern of liability for these wrongs.[22] Corrective justice may be in the driver's seat, but economics is required to tell the driver when to turn, stop, accelerate, and so forth.

And with regard to unintentional torts, which is to say to liability for (most) accidents, corrective justice has no thrust at all. One can if one wants speak of the speeding driver as 'pleonexic'—as wanting more than his fair share as it were of the opportunities for self-fulfillment provided by the road—but it is difficult to see what is gained by this redescription. There are numerous objections to eliminating tort liability for this or that class of dangerous accidents, as is sometimes done, for example, in workmen's compensation laws and in no-fault automobile compensation schemes. But the loss of corrective justice is not one of the objections. The reason is that, as an aspect of the general lack of detail in the theory, it is wholly unclear what institutional arrangements are entailed by corrective justice. If, as opponents of tort liability believe, some alternative regulatory scheme would control accidents more effectively—or at least as effectively, and at lower cost (or more fairly)—than the tort system, there is no purchase in Aristotle's theory for criticism. The theory does not foreclose oblique, wholesale, or otherwise non-traditional modes of rectifying injustices. It is not even clear what basis for objection an Aristotelian would have to the substitution of criminal for tort liability as the legal regime for intentional torts, if the substitution could be persuasively defended as a fairer, more effective, and cheaper method of 'correcting' this class of injustices. Even if the victim is not compensated, provided the criminal is punished severely enough, victim and criminal are once again placed on a plane of equality (and here we can sense the connection between corrective and redistributive—'eye for an eye'—justice). So maybe even in its core application,[23] corrective justice provides only weak support for tort law. But that is not the issue. All that is most important here is the consilience between a wealth maximizer's approach to tort law and that of an Aristotelian.

4. Kantian Deontology

The most emphatic insistence that moral duties shall not be based on preferences comes from the Kantians, whose basic thesis, so far as bears on my subject, is that it is wrong for one person to use another person as a means to the first person's ends—wrong therefore to use a worker's body as an input into the manufacture of goods, or a pedestrian's body as an input into one's commuting, without their consent. (If they do consent, then they are being 'used' for their own ends as well as for those of the user.)

---

[22] *See, e.g.,* LANDES & POSNER, *supra,* note 1, at ch. 6.

[23] Aristotle appears to have been concerned with what we would call intentional torts and to have contemplated their rectification by private litigation analogous to modern tort litigation.

A Kantian, whether or not of egalitarian bent, is unlikely to be pleased with the implication of a wealth maximization theory of tort law that a person should feel free to drive faster in a poor than in a wealthy neighborhood because expected accident costs are on average lower in the former (the magnitude of the loss if an accident occurs being a function in part of the income of the victim), making the optimal expenditure of time and other resources on avoiding accidents in the poor neighborhood also lower. From a Kantian perspective, this analysis appears to treat potential accident victims merely as obstacles to the ends of potential injurers.

But would an alternative system of tort law provide a *better* fit with Kantian moral principles? The Kantian, like the utilitarian, will find it infeasible to apply his principles directly to morally questionable activities, such as fast driving in poor neighborhoods. He needs a rule too. Maybe a system of tort law oriented by the principle of wealth maximization is the best approach for the Kantian. It seeks to accommodate conflicting activi-ties in such a way that the scope for productive activity is maximized. To the extent that it succeeds in this aim, tort law enjoins upon potential injur-ers and potential victims alike (and often these are the same person) due consideration for the plans, goals, choices, etc. of the other. It requires *mutual* adjustments, and if the tort system satisfies (approximates) the Pareto condition they will be (or will approximate) the mutual adjustments desired by all. An individual who consents to a system of tort law because, although it may leave him uncompensated for some accidents, on the whole it promotes his ends better than any other system would do cannot com-plain that he is a mere means to the ends of potential injurers.

5. Kantian Egalitarianism

Some Kantians might, however, want to focus on the inegalitarian impli-cations of wealth maximization that the example of driving faster in the poor neighborhood brings to the fore. As the example shows, tort law inter-preted in terms of wealth maximization tends to ratify rather than to change the pre-existing distribution of income or wealth. The victim of the negligent driver is to be put back, so far as possible, in the same position in the income distribution that he occupied before the accident; but a corol-lary is that some potential accident victims receive less consideration than others, merely because they are poorer. But an egalitarian has standing to object to this feature of tort law only if he can show that tort law is, poten-tially at least, an efficient method of making the distribution of wealth more equal—which seems unlikely. If average rather than individual damages were awarded in tort cases, poor victims would be over-compensated and their incentives to safe conduct correspondingly reduced; this consequence aside, homogenization of damages across income classes would result in a capricious redistribution of wealth from wealthy accident victims (who would receive less compensation) to poor ones. The vast majority of poor people would be unaffected. Perhaps the tort system, while wealth maximizing, is as egalitarian as it can be.[24]

IV. CONCLUSION

I have tried to show, too briefly I fear to carry full conviction, that a system of tort law guided by the norm of wealth maximization is likely to be consistent with the most influential moral traditions in our society. That does not prove that it is the right system to have, but it ought to blunt the philosophical attacks upon it.

---

[24] In this regard, the significance of the contingent fee in bringing tort remedies within the reach of all tort victims, however lacking in current assets, should not be overlooked.

The Uneasy Place of Principle in Tort Law

GEORGE C. CHRISTIE*

Lawyers have always had the urge to find some coherent logical structure in the law. One recalls Sir Edward Coke's assertion that the common law is 'an artificial perfection of reason, gotten by long study, observation, and experience.'[1] Coke was attacked by Thomas Hobbes[2] as being a proponent of what in our time would be called 'sterile formalism'. But, whatever Coke may have been driving at, throughout history the notion that the common law represents the application of general principles in some non-formalistic sense to the decision of concrete cases has always captured the imagination of the legal profession. Of course, the intensity of the urge to find principles at the core of legal development waxes and wanes in any given area of the law at any given time and, in some areas of the law, it is greater than it is in others. It is no mere happenstance that one of the most frequently cited statements in all of legal literature is Holmes' aphorism that '[t]he life of the law has not been logic: it has been experience'.[3]

In the last thirty years, however, there has been an increased interest among scholars, judges, and practicing lawyers concerned with the law of

---

* James B. Duke Professor of Law, Duke University. I wish to thank Jane Stapleton and Martin Stone for their careful reading of a draft of this paper and for their many helpful comments.

[1] SIR EDWARD COKE, FIRST INSTITUTES § 138. A fuller quote is: 'Reason is the life of the law, nay, the common law itself is nothing else but reason; which is to be understood of an artificial perfection of reason, gotten by long study, observation, and experience, and not of every man's natural reason; . . . And therefore, if all the reason that is dispersed into so many several heads, were united into one, yet could he not make such a law as the law of England is; because by many successions of ages, it hath been fined and refined by an infinite number of grave and learned men.' The *First Institutes* were, of course, a commentary on *Littleton on Tenures*. In the 'new arrangement', by J. H. Thomas in 1818 of the *First Institutes*, the quoted material appears as the first paragraph of Volume I, Chapter I.

[2] THOMAS HOBBES, LEVIATHAN, ch. XXVI, at 147–8 (Everyman edn., 1914), where Hobbes attacks Coke's assertion in *First Institutes* § 709 that a person who flees to avoid a felony persecution, but is subsequently acquitted of the felony, must nevertheless forfeit his goods because the law does not permit him, in the forfeiture proceedings, to challenge the presumption of guilt raised by his initial flight. Hobbes makes the same criticism in his *A Dialogue Between a Philosopher and a Student of the Common Laws of England*, in 6 HOBBES ENGLISH WORKS (William Molesworth (ed.), 1840), 136–7.

[3] OLIVER WENDELL HOLMES, JR., THE COMMON LAW (1881) 1.

torts to find the principles that underlie that law. Sometimes, as with some in the law and economics school, the endeavor starts out as an attempt to discover the principles that can organize legal experience and explain the decision of actual cases even if those principles were not (even 'unconsciously') in the minds of the judiciary. An example is the claim that the law of negligence can be explained on the assumption that the law is seeking to achieve the more efficient allocation of society's resources.[4] Of course, it is only a small step from the observation that the cases can be usefully organized around such a principle to the conclusion that, if not consciously, at least 'unconsciously', judges were actually motivated by such a principle. From there it is only another small step for a proponent of economic efficiency, as the key to legal development, to put forth the normative claim that judges should be motivated by such a principle.

There are other principles, however, which start out from the beginning as being primarily normative principles, even if it is thought that they also serve an explanatory purpose. Recent experience brings to mind a number of such normative principles which have been urged upon the profession by scholars and judges. If someone were to remark that most of these instances seem to be examples of the Duke of York marching ten thousand men up a hill only to march them down again, he would not be alone.[5] To see why someone might be tempted to make this observation, it will be useful to examine some of these well-known recent attempts to subject the law of torts to the discipline of principles. This is what I propose to do after a few preliminary remarks which will clear the way for the central part of the discussion.

I. SOME PRELIMINARY OBSERVATIONS ON THE USES OF PRINCIPLE IN TORT LAW

It is of course necessary to recognize that, even if we can agree on an appropriate principle, it still remains to agree on an exact canonical formulation of that principle and another matter still to agree on how that principle should be applied to concrete fact situations. By themselves, however, these are not insurmountable objections to the appeal to principle. I advert to these possible objections to make clear from the outset that it shall be no part of my thesis to claim that they are. For example, in

---

[4] Richard A. Posner, *A Theory of Negligence*, 1 J. LEGAL STUD. 29 (1972). *See also* RICHARD A. POSNER, ECONOMIC ANALYSIS OF LAW, (2d edn. 1977) pts. 1 & 2.

[5] *See* David Howarth, *Negligence after* Murphy: *Time to Re-think*, 50 CAMBRIDGE L.J. 58, 87 (1991), (who used a shortened version of this old saw). Howarth's article is primarily concerned with the state of negligence law after recent developments, many of which I will discuss below, rather than with the normative status of principle that is the focus of this paper.

McDougald v. Garber,[6] the New York Court of Appeals enunciated the principle that, in order to recover for loss of enjoyment of life—which the court considered a subcategory of pain and suffering—the injured plaintiff must have 'cognitive awareness'. No such damages could be recovered by a comatose person. What level of cognition is necessary so that the person might be held to have 'cognitive awareness' is nevertheless obviously a difficult matter. The difficulty was highlighted in the dissent's submission that the award of substantial sums for pain and suffering to a person with very slight awareness of his predicament, which the majority recognized would be permissible, can hardly be said to give effect to the policy considerations underlying the court's decision—are these second order principles or the original principle in different guise?—that general damages in negligence cases should have some 'meaning or utility to the injured person'.[7] The majority recognized the validity of the objection but declared that considerations of efficiency of application precluded the adoption of a more fine-tuned test. Whether or not one agrees with the principles adopted by the majority, its response to the dissent's argument seems fair enough. Every general principle will confront cases in which its application may run at cross purposes with its aspirations and this feature is not by itself a conclusive reason either to abandon the principle or even necessarily to refuse to apply it in those cases. The real world is not such a neat and tidy place.

A second preliminary observation is that many of the objections to the use of particular principles in the decision of tort cases arise from oversimplified characterizations of the facts of particular cases that end up making legal disputes into verbal disputes. For example, a much more important principle of modern tort law than the one at stake in *McDougald v. Garber*, and one to which I will be devoting a great deal of attention in the succeeding portions of this essay, is the principle that both the question of fault—where that is in issue—and the question of causation in modern tort law should be governed by foreseeability. The late Dean Prosser attacked the use of the concept of foreseeability, as applied to questions of legal causation, on the ground that '[i]n one sense, almost nothing is entirely unforeseeable, since there is a very slight mathematical chance, recognizable in advance, that even the most freakish accident which is possible will occur, particularly if it has ever happened in history before.'[8] Prosser's basic objection that the foreseeability test 'lacks all clarity and precision'[9] reminds one of the similar criticisms made by Judge Friendly in 1964 in *Petition of Kinsman Transit Co.*,[10] where he commented that some

---

[6] 536 N.E.2d 372 (N.Y., 1989).　　　　　　　　　　　[7] *Id.* at 375, 378.

[8] WILLIAM L. PROSSER, LAW OF TORTS (4th ed., 1971), 267. Curiously he did not make the same complaint about the use of foreseeability in determining questions of duty and fault.

[9] *Id.*　　　　　　[10] 338 F.2d 708 (2d Cir. 1964), *cert. denied*, 380 U.S. 944 (1965).

American courts had applied the foreseeability test so as to 'extend that concept to such unforeseen lengths as to raise serious doubt whether the concept is meaningful'.[11] The case cited to support this assertion was *In re Guardian Casualty Co.*,[12] in which, to quote Judge Friendly,

[T]he majority gravely asserted that a foreseeable consequence of driving a taxicab too fast was that a collision with another car would project the cab against a building with such force as to cause a portion of the building to collapse twenty minutes later, when the cab was being removed, and injure a spectator twenty feet away. Surely this is 'straining the idea of foreseeability past the breaking point,' . . . at least if the matter be viewed as of the time of the negligent act, as the supposedly symmetrical test of The Wagon Mound demands.[13]

Judge Friendly's strictures notwithstanding, the example he gives does not support the conclusion at which he wishes to arrive. First of all, any concept will, of course, present some difficulties in application. As we have already noted, this by itself is not a sufficient reason to reject it. Furthermore, the case he mentions is not at all bizarre. Of course, if one had to foresee the exact manner in which every accident occurred or the exact person who would be injured, very few things would be antecedently 'foreseeable'. But, in the type of case that Judge Friendly posited, surely it is foreseeable that a motor vehicle that travels too rapidly in an urban setting might crash into the side of a building and it is surely foreseeable that the crash itself might dislodge some of the bricks in the building or that, in the process of extracting a vehicle that has embedded itself in a structure, some bricks might be displaced which would then fall on pedestrians. If one characterizes the situation as I have—which not only does not seem unfair but seems to conform to what common sense would suggest—the accident seems neither bizarre nor unusual and certainly not unforeseeable *ex ante*. The problems with a foreseeability test to which I shall now turn are, however, not of this order and cannot be removed by more careful statement of the factual issue before the court.

II. THE MODERN ODYSSEY OF THE FORESEEABILITY PRINCIPLE

A. British Cases on Economic Loss

Once it became generally settled in England, as in the United States, that, at least in some circumstances, recovery could be had for the economic loss suffered as a consequence of negligent misrepresentation,[14] the question

---

[11] *Id.* at 724.   [12] 2 N.Y.S.2d 232, *aff'd,* 16 N.E.2d 397 (N.Y. 1938).
[13] *Kinsman,* 338 F.2d at 724–5, n.10 (citation omitted).
[14] *See* Hedley Byrne & Co. v. Heller & Partners, Ltd. [1964] A.C. 465 ; RESTATEMENT (SECOND) OF TORTS § 552 (1976).

arose whether 'pure' economic loss might not be recoverable in other types of actions based on a negligence theory. For my purposes, the judgment of the Court of Appeal in *Spartan Steel & Alloys, Ltd. v. Martin & Co.*[15] is a convenient starting point for examining the flurry of judicial and scholarly concern with the issue of when economic loss may be recovered that is only now beginning to subside.[16] Although some of the leading cases are well-known, at least in England, it may be helpful to set out briefly the evolution of judicial thinking on the legal principles that should govern in this area.

In *Spartan Steel*, the defendants' employees severed a power cable. The plaintiffs, who were the owners of a nearby factory, incurred some physical damage when molten metal in their furnaces cooled. The defendants conceded that they were liable for this damage. The plaintiffs, however, also sought to recover the loss of the profits they would have made if they could have fabricated the metal that was spoiled and sold it as finished goods. They further sought recovery for the lost profits for metal that they would have been able to melt and fabricate during the time that their factory was inoperative owing to the negligent conduct of the defendants. The trial court allowed all these items of damages. The defendants appealed against that portion of the trial court's judgment which allowed any damages for loss of profits.

The Court of Appeal allowed the claim for loss of profits on the metal that was damaged but a majority of the court denied recovery for any other loss of profits during the period that the factory was inoperative owing to absence of electric power. Lord Denning, MR, found unhelpful analyses which would deny recovery for the loss of profits on the basis that there was either 'no duty' or that the damage was 'too remote'. He thought that such tests should be discarded and that the time had come 'to consider the particular relationship in hand, and see whether or not, as a matter of policy, economic loss should be recoverable'.[17] He thus concluded that the loss of profit on the metal that the plaintiffs would have been able to process and fabricate but for the fact that their power was cut off could not be recovered 'because that was economic loss independent of the physical damage'.[18] Edmund Davies LJ. dissented on this point. He noted that it was common ground that the lost profits on the metal that was ruined in the process of fabrication and the lost profits on the metal that the plaintiffs were unable to process and fabricate 'were equally foreseeable and

---

[15] [1973] Q.B. 27 (C.A.).

[16] The flurry is continued in this volume in an essay by Peter Benson, *The Basis for Excluding Liability for Economic Loss in Tort Law*—Ed.

[17] *Id.* at 37.

[18] *Id.* at 39. Why he was prepared to allow recovery for the loss of profits on the metal that was spoiled is an interesting question. Given recent developments, that would seem incorrect.

equally direct consequences of the defendants' admitted negligence'.[19] Admittedly, the former profit was loss as a result of physical damage done to the material in the furnace at the time when the power was cut off. 'But what', he asked, 'has that purely fortuitous fact to do with legal principle?'[20] In answer to his own question he replied: 'In my judgment, nothing'.[21]

Whatever the appeal of Lord Denning's conclusion, that whether and in what circumstances there may be recovery for economic loss ultimately depends on policy considerations, developments in the House of Lords soon raised the question whether Lord Denning's approach was in point of fact the correct one. *Anns v. Merton London Borough Council*,[22] decided in 1977, involved a group of plaintiffs who were the long-term lessees of a group of flats in a housing development that had been completed in 1962. Two of the plaintiffs were original lessees, but the others acquired their leases by subsequent assignment. The block of flats had been constructed with inadequate foundations. The basis of the claim against the Merton Borough Council was that its employees had negligently inspected and approved the foundations that had been laid by the contractor although these foundations had not conformed to the Council's building code. The House of Lords affirmed the Court of Appeal's conclusion that, on the facts presented, the plaintiffs could bring an action in negligence against the Council. Lord Wilberforce, who delivered the principal speech with which all the other law lords expressed their agreement, declared that such an action could only arise 'when the state of the building is such that there is present or imminent danger to the health or safety of persons occupying it'.[23]

What gave fuel to the controversy with which we are concerned was not so much this fairly narrow holding but Lord Wilberforce's statement, citing among other authorities Lord Reid's speech in *Home Office v. Dorset Yacht Co.*,[24] that, in English law, 'the position has now been reached that in order to establish that a duty of care arises in a particular situation, it is not necessary to bring the facts of that situation within those of previous situations in which a duty of care has been held to exist'.[25] Instead, Lord Wilberforce thought, one had to ask two questions. First, was there 'a sufficient relationship of proximity or neighbourhood' such that it was 'in the reasonable contemplation' of the defendant that carelessness on his part would be likely to cause damage to the plaintiff, 'in which case a *prima facie* duty of care arises'.[26] Secondly, if that in fact were the case, one would then have to consider 'whether there are any considerations which ought to neg-

---

[19] *The Basis for Excluding Liability for Economic Loss in Tort Law* at 41.
[20] *Id.*   [21] *Id.*   [22] [1978] A.C. 728.
[23] *Id.* at 760.   [24] [1970] A.C. 1004.   [25] *Anns*, [1978] A.C. at 751.
[26] *Id.* at 751–2.

ative, or to reduce or limit the scope of the duty or the class of person to whom it is owed or the damages to which a breach of it may give rise'.[27] Among the examples which he gave of situations where such limitations might be appropriate was that of negligent misrepresentation.[28]

Although *Anns* involved physical damage to property, Lord Wilberforce's speech obviously raised the question whether the traditional distinction between pure economic loss and other sorts of loss was about to be discarded and replaced by a 'more principled' mode of analysis. For example, in 1981, in *Lexmead (Basingstoke), Ltd. v. Lewis*,[29] Lord Diplock, who delivered the only significant speech in the House of Lords, queried whether a retailer who was obliged to indemnify his buyer for sums that the buyer had to pay to third parties injured by a negligently manufactured product might not seek to recover those damages against the manufacturer with whom the retailer was *not* in privity of contract. Lord Diplock raised this query because the Court of Appeal had declared that the principle of *Donoghue v. Stevenson*[30]—under which a party, who was not in privity of contract with the negligent manufacturer of a product, could nevertheless bring an action for damages against the manufacturer—did not extend to purely economic loss. Lord Diplock went out of his way to declare that '[w]hile in the absence of argument it could not be right to express any final view, I should not wish the dismissal of the . . . appeal to be regarded as an approval by this House of the proposition that where the economic loss suffered by a distributor . . . consists of a liability to pay damages to the ultimate consumer for physical injuries . . . such economic loss is not recoverable under the *Donoghue v. Stevenson* principle from the manufacturer.'[31]

Lexmead (Basingstoke), Ltd. v. Lewis involved a case where the damage for which indemnity was sought was largely physical injury to the person, but Lord Diplock's ruminations certainly could be taken as further evidence of the siren call of a single general principle governing liability for negligence and, in particular, of the principle that liability should be determined by 'reasonable foreseeability'. In fact, this is the position that the House of Lords seemed to be in the process of adopting the very next year, 1982, when it decided *Junior Books, Ltd. v. Veitchi Co.*[32] In that case, the defendant was a subcontractor who had installed a defective floor in a factory. The owner of the factory was permitted to bring an action sounding in negligence, not only for the cost of correcting the defect but also for the foreseeable loss of profits suffered as a result, despite the lack of privity of

[27] *Id.* at 752.
[28] The House of Lords had of course declared that an action for negligent misrepresentation might be brought, even in the absence of some 'special relaionship', Hedley Byrne & Co. v. Heller & Partners, Ltd. [1964] A.C. 465, but had not yet spelled out, and may perhaps still not have—*see infra*, note 52—the limits of that liability.
[29] [1982] A.C. 225.
[30] [1932] A.C. 562 (appeal taken from Scot.).
[31] [1982] A.C. at 278.
[32] [1983] 1 A.C. 520 (1982) (appeal taken from Scot.).

contract. There was no allegation that the defective flooring created any danger to life or limb or to any other physical property. Except for a lone dissenter, all of their lordships in *Junior Books* expressed agreement with the speech of Lord Roskill. To the argument that allowing recovery in such cases would 'open the floodgates', Lord Roskill responded that although 'policy considerations have from time to time been allowed to play their part in the tort of negligence since it first developed . . ., yet today I think its scope is best determined by considerations of principle rather than of policy'.[33] He cited, with approval, the speeches of Lord Reid in *Dorset Yacht* and of Lord Wilberforce in *Anns*. Applying the criteria laid down by Lord Wilberforce in *Anns* to the facts before him, he saw 'nothing whatsoever to restrict the duty of care arising from the proximity of which I have spoken'.[34] In dissent, Lord Brandon of Oakbrook argued that the only duty the subcontractor had to the owner of the factory was to install the flooring so as to insure that there was no danger to persons or property, excluding the property in question, i.e. the floor itself.

Lord Roskill in *Junior Books* also cited a number of Commonwealth cases of which the most well-known is *Caltex Oil (Australia) Pty. Ltd. v. The Dredge 'Willemstad'*.[35] In that case, the dredge had damaged a pipeline owned by an oil refining company. The pipeline connected the refinery on one side of a bay with an oil terminal owned by the plaintiff on the other. The plaintiff's terminal depended upon the pipeline to receive oil from the refinery. The High Court of Australia held that the plaintiff was entitled to recover the foreseeable expenses it incurred in finding alternate means of getting oil to its terminal.[36]

The apparent triumph of the principle of foreseeability in the economic loss cases had been foreshadowed a few months previously in *McLoughlin v. O'Brian*[37] in which the House of Lords allowed recovery of damages for emotional distress by a mother who had not witnessed the serious injury to her children and husband in an automobile accident, but first saw them a few hours later in a dazed and battered condition in the hospital where she was also informed that one of the children had been killed. The most interesting speeches were those of Lord Scarman and of Lord Bridge of Harwich who concluded that, with regard to the question of the limits of liability for the infliction of nervous shock, there were 'no policy considerations sufficient to justify limiting the liability of negligence tortfeasors by reference to some narrower criterion than that of reasonable foreseeability'.[38] In an ironic twist, Lord Bridge of Harwich expressed regret that Lord

---

[33] [1983] 1 A.C. 520 (1982) (appeal taken from Scot.) at 539.　　　[34] *Id.* at 546.

[35] 136 C.L.R. 529 (1976) (Austl.). This case pre-dated *Anns* but was not cited in it.

[36] The High Court tried to limit the sweep of its decision by declaring that reasonable foreseeability of economic loss was not enough. There had to be a sufficient relationship of 'proximity' between the parties. 136 C.L.R. at 574—5 (Stephen J). *Cf. id.* at 553–6 (Gibbs J).

[37] [1983] 1 A.C. 410.　　　[38] *Id.* at 443.

Edmund-Davies, as he now was, whose dissent in *Spartan Steel* was the starting point of our discussion, criticized this conclusion of his. Not only did Lord Edmund-Davies criticize Lord Bridge of Harwich's conclusion, he also rather pointedly disagreed with the conclusion of Lord Scarman, who in a brief speech expressing his agreement with Lord Bridge of Harwich asked, 'Why then should not the courts draw the line, as the Court of Appeal [which denied recovery on policy grounds] manfully tried to do in this case?'[39] To which question Lord Scarman declared '[s]imply, because the policy issue as to where to draw the line is not justiciable. The problem is one of social, economic, and financial policy. The considerations relevant to a decision are not such as to be capable of being handled within the limits of the forensic process.'[40] To which Lord Edmund-Davies replied that this proposition was 'as novel as it is startling'.[41] He found it novel because it had never been mentioned in argument and 'startling because in my respectful judgment it runs counter to well-established and wholly acceptable law'.[42]

Junior Books turned out to be the zenith of the attempt to 'rationalize' the law of tort concerning the recovery of economic damages by application of the 'reasonable foreseeability' principle. The first retreat took place in *Governors of the Peabody Donation Fund v. Sir Lindsay Parkinson & Co.*,[43] a case very similar to *Anns* but with one, as it turned out, significant difference; the plaintiff was a foundation not a group of individual homeowners. In denying recovery, *Anns* was distinguished on precisely this ground. The following year, in *Candlewood Navigation Corp. v. Mitsui O.S.K. Lines, Ltd.*,[44] a time charterer sought to recover the economic loss sustained when the ship it had chartered had to be taken out of service for repairs after a collision with defendant's negligently navigated vessel. Although the case arose in Australia, the Privy Council refused to accept the reasoning of the Australian judges in the *Caltex Oil* case. Instead, citing English precedent and Justice Holmes' opinion in the *Robins Drydock* case,[45] the Privy Council reaffirmed the traditional view that the time charterer could not recover its economic loss. The proposition that a person with no physical property that was damaged could not recover in tort for economic loss consequent to the damage of property owned by another was

---

[39] *Id.* at 431.   [40] *Id.*

[41] *Id.* at 427. Lord Edmund-Davies nevertheless supported the decision to allow recovery in the case because, on policy grounds, he reached a different conclusion than had the Court of Appeal.

[42] *Id.* In a subsequent case, their lordships were able to avoid ruling on whether the principle of foreseeability would enable someone who saw a disaster 'live' on television to recover against the culpable party by reliance on the practice of the television authorities not to show pictures of suffering by recognizable individuals: Alcock v. Chief Constable of S. Yorkshire [1992] 1 A.C. 310.

[43] [1985] A.C. 210.   [44] [1986] A.C. 1 (P.C.).

[45] Robins Dry Dock & Repair Co. v. Flint, 275 U.S. 303 (1927).

then shortly thereafter also reaffirmed by the House of Lords.[46] While these developments were taking place in Great Britain, the United States Supreme Court, in *East River Steamship Corp. v. Transamerica Delaval, Inc.*,[47] held that damages for economic loss cannot be awarded in a product liability action brought in admiralty regardless of whether the action was brought under a strict liability theory or a negligence theory. The plaintiffs in that case had entered into long-term bare-boat charters of tankers that turned out to have defective turbines. The plaintiffs were not only unable to recover their lost profits while the ships were being repaired, but also were denied recovery for the cost of repairing the defective engines. The Court was unwilling to displace the operation of warranty law in an action involving commercial parties. Relying in part on *East River*, the House of Lords in 1988 then decided *D. & F. Estates, Ltd. v. Church Commissioners for England*,[48] a case involving a block of flats in which the plaster work had been done negligently by one of the subcontractors. Their Lordships held that, in the absence of a contractual relationship between the parties, the cost of repairing a defect in physical property that was discovered before the defect had caused personal injury or physical damage to other property was not recoverable in a negligence action by a remote purchaser or lessee.

Finally, in 1990, the House of Lords was presented with *Murphy v. Brentwood District Council*,[49] a case even more similar to *Anns* because the plaintiff was an individual who sought recovery for the loss he suffered in selling his house for a lower price than he would have received had it not been defective. The trial court specifically found that, in its defective state, the house had posed an imminent danger to plaintiff during the time he occupied it. In reversing the judgment of the Court of Appeal, which had affirmed the trial court's award of damages, the House of Lords held that *Anns* had been wrongly decided and that the subsequent cases relying upon it should be overruled. Lord Keith of Kinkel, with whose speech all the other law lords expressed agreement, expressly declared that 'although the damage in *Anns* was characterised as physical damage by Lord Wilberforce, it was purely economic loss'.[50] Lord Keith of Kinkel concluded that 'it is clear that *Anns* did not proceed upon any basis of established principle, but introduced a new species of liability governed by a principle indeterminate in character but having the potentiality of covering a wide range of situations, involving chattels as well as real property, in which it had never hitherto been thought that the law of negligence had any proper place'.[51] He noted that the logical implication of what he thought was 'a somewhat superficial examination of principle' in the *Anns* case was 'collision with

---

[46] Leigh & Sillavan Ltd. v. Aliakmon Shipping Co. [1986] A.C. 785.
[47] 476 U.S. 858 (1986).   [48] [1989] A.C. 177.   [49] [1991] 1 A.C. 398.
[50] *Id.* at 466.   [51] *Id.* at 471.

long established principles regarding liability in the tort of negligence for economic loss'.[52]

With the decision of *Murphy*, the Duke of York had seemingly returned to the bottom of the hill. Given this history, it has been asserted by British scholars, with particular reference to the House of Lords' decisions in *Caparo Industries PLC v. Dickman*,[53] a negligent misrepresentation case, and *Alcock v. Chief Constable of South Yorkshire*,[54] an emotional distress case, that the only general principle recognized by the House of Lords for organizing the extent of liability in negligence cases is that of 'proximity', a concept that is lacking in substance.[55] As will be seen shortly, my objections are premised not on the fact that the alternatives to reasonable foreseeability might be even more unsatisfactory but that the attempt to establish a single general principle of liability for all negligence cases—which run the gamut from physical injury to emotional distress to various kinds of economic loss—has shown itself to be as hopeless as it is unwise.

B. American Cases on Economic Loss

The same urge to resolve the question of whether economic loss should be recoverable in a tort action by subsuming it under the broader principle of reasonable foreseeability was of course felt in the United States. A small minority of state courts did in fact hold that, in product liability actions, what might be called pure economic loss was indeed recoverable.[56]

---

[52] *Id.* The *Murphy* case was then applied in *Department of the Environment v. Thomas Bates and Son, Ltd.*, [1991] 1 A.C. 499.

[53] [1990] 2 A.C. 605. Their Lordships held that shareholders who bought additional shares of a company on the basis of a negligently prepared auditor's report could not bring an action against the auditors. For a glimpse at the uncertainties of the extent of liability for negligent misrepresentation in American law, compare the California Court of Appeal's decision in *International Mortgage Co. v. John P. Butler Accountancy Corp.*, 223 Cal. Rptr. 218 (Cal. Ct. App. 1986) with the later decision of the California Supreme Court in *Bily v. Arthur Young & Co.*, 834 P.2d 745 (Cal. 1992).

[54] [1992] 1 A.C. 310. The case is discussed *supra*, note 42.

[55] *See* Jenny Steele, *Scepticism and the Law of Negligence*, 52 CAMBRIDGE L.J. 437 (1993); *see also* Howarth, *supra*, note 5. More recently, while this essay was in the process of publication, the House of Lords held, in Spring v. Guardian Assurance PLC [1994] 3 W.L.R. 354, that a former employee could bring an action against his former employer for the negligent preparation of a letter of reference that, but for the defense of qualified privilege, could have been the basis for an action for libel. Lord Keith of Kinkel dissented on the ground that the law of defamation should not be superseded by resort to the law of negligent misrepresentation. The majority relied on a mélange of factors, such as foreseeability, proximity, public policy, conceptions of fairness, etc. Unlike perhaps the British authors, I see no reason why cases involving the types of economic loss considered in the body of this essay need necessarily be decided by the same considerations governing recovery for negligent misrepresentation, let alone by those governing recovery for the negligent infliction of emotional distress.

[56] *See, e.g.*, Santor v. A & M Karagheusian, Inc., 207 A.2d 305 (N.J. 1965); Oksenholt v. Lederle Lab., 656 P.2d 293 (Or. 1982); City of La Crosse v. Schubert, Schroeder & Assocs., Inc., 240 N.W.2d 124 (Wis. 1976). *See also* J'Aire Corp. v. Gregory, 598 P.2d 60 (Cal. 1979), a case very like *Junior Books*.

Nevertheless, over time, even these courts had difficulty with this doctrine. For example, after first holding that a retail purchaser of defective 'Grade #1' carpet could recover the cost of replacing that carpet from the manufacturer, who was several steps removed from the retail purchaser in the distribution scheme and of whose name the purchaser was unaware at the time of purchase,[57] the New Jersey Supreme Court subsequently refused to apply that doctrine in an action that involved 'commercial' parties.[58]

Problems with the foreseeability principle are more starkly revealed in the contortions of the U.S. Court of Appeals for the Second Circuit in *Petition of Kinsman Transit Co.*[59] That case involved the liability arising from the following almost comically bizarre set of facts. A Great Lakes grain ship, over four hundred feet long, was moored at a wharf for the winter in the Buffalo River which runs through Buffalo, New York, into Lake Erie. Through the combined negligence of those in charge of the wharf, who failed properly to maintain the deadman, and the ship's watchman, the ship broke her moorings and struck and dislodged another even longer ship. Both ships drifted down the river until they lodged in a drawbridge that, owing to the negligence of the bridgekeepers, was only partially raised by the time the runaway ships reached it. Since the channel was only 177 feet wide at this point, the two ships wedged into the bridge, forming a dam in the ice-choked river that flooded riparian property for three miles back up the river to the starting point of the tragi-comedy.

A majority of the Second Circuit was prepared to allow all of the riparian owners whose property had been flooded to recover. Certainly, to my mind, all these damages were foreseeable consequences of a ship of that size breaking loose from her moorings in an ice-choked river. Nevertheless, the second time the case reached the Court of Appeals,[60] it held that there was no liability for the economic loss suffered by, among others, those parties whose claim was that, with the river closed to navigation, they were unable to move grain they were contractually bound to deliver to the appropriate dock. Judge Kaufman, however, did not want to rely on the traditional distinction between economic loss and physical loss, which would have easily disposed of the case despite the fact that it would have been difficult to argue that these damages were not reasonably foreseeable consequences of the original negligence. In denying recovery, Judge Kaufman held that the connection between the defendants' negligence and the plaintiffs' damages was 'too tenuous and remote' to permit recovery.[61] 'In the final analysis', he declared, 'the circumlocution whether posed in terms of "foreseeability","duty", "proximate cause", "remoteness", etc. seems unavoidable.'[62]

---

[57] *Santor*, 207 A.2d 305.
[58] Spring Motors Distrib., Inc. v. Ford Motor Co., 489 A.2d 660 (N.J. 1985).
[59] 338 F.2d 708 (2d Cir. 1964), *cert. denied*, 380 U.S. 944 (1965).
[60] 388 F.2d 821 (2d Cir. 1968).   [61] *Id.* at 825.   [62] *Id.*

He concluded by quoting from Judge Andrews' dissenting opinion in the *Palsgraf* case that ' "[i]t is all a question of expediency . . . . of fair judgement".'[63] Whether this was a more satisfying basis for deciding the case than simply dismissing the claims because they were pure economic loss is another matter. The decision of the Supreme Court of the United States in *East River Steamship Corp.*[64] indicates that in admiralty cases, which are governed by federal law, that court is content with the traditional distinction.

C. Other American Experiments with the Foreseeability Principle

The attempt to find easily articulable clear statements of principle which supposedly provide for the 'just' resolution of cases is, of course, not confined to the maneuverings concerning the issue of recovery for economic loss. An area of tort law that, at least in the United States, is giving rise to the same sorts of intellectual fumbling is that concerning so-called derivative actions. Examination of one such instance, which was also driven at least in part by notions of reasonable foreseeability, may be helpful. In *Wycko v. Gnodtke*,[65] the Supreme Court of Michigan, in 1960, held that the loss of companionship of a minor child was a compensable item of damages for the parents under Michigan's then existing version of Lord Campbell's Act which limited recovery to 'pecuniary damages'. A few years later, however, in 1970, the Supreme Court of Michigan reconsidered the issue[66] and the law returned to its pre-*Wycko* state, in which loss of companionship was not considered 'pecuniary' damage. In 1971 the Michigan legislature responded by enacting legislation, effective March 30, 1972, specifically permitting recovery for loss of society and companionship in wrongful death actions. When confronted with the question of what happened with regard to cases that had commenced before March 30, 1972, the Michigan Supreme Court then held that its decision retreating from *Wycko* was in error.[67]

Subsequent to this minuet, the Supreme Court of Michigan in *Berger v. Weber*[68] was confronted with the issue of whether a minor child could recover for the loss of the society and companionship of its mother who

---

[63] 388 F.2d at 825 (quoting Palsgraf v. Long Island R.R., 162 N.E. 99, 104 (N.Y. 1928)). In *Union Oil Co. v. Oppen*, 501 F.2d 558 (9th Cir. 1974), an oil spill case, Judge Sneed also expressed dissatisfaction with the traditional exclusion of recovery for economic loss but then tried to limit the reach of his decision, recognizing liability, to commercial fishermen for whom there were precedents for allowing recovery on a public nuisance theory. Certainly the economic losses of resort hotels, which Judge Sneed seemed to want to exclude, are as foreseeable as those of commercial fishermen.

[64] This case is discussed at note 47, *supra*.   [65] 105 N.W.2d 118 (Mich. 1960).
[66] Breckon v. Franklin Fuel Co., 174 N.W.2d 836 (Mich. 1970).
[67] Smith v. City of Detroit, 202 N.W.2d 300 (Mich. 1972).
[68] 303 N.W.2d 424 (Mich. 1981).

had been injured but not killed in an automobile accident. The court held that it could, relying on the fact that, under the wrongful death statute, children could recover for the loss of society and companionship of a parent who had been killed in such an accident. Given the existing judicial and legislative policies of the state of Michigan, the court concluded that it should recognize a child's action for the loss of society and companionship of an injured parent. A few years later, however, the Michigan Supreme Court was confronted with the question whether a parent could bring an action for the loss of the society and companionship of a child that had been injured but not killed. Perhaps to the surprise of some, and to the delight of those who felt that the decision recognizing the child's action was unwise, the court refused to allow an action by the parents for the loss of the consortium of an injured child.[69] The court specifically held that '[f]orseeability of injury alone does not mandate recognition of a cause of action.'[70] Factors such as the explosion in liability costs and the burdens imposed on the courts from multiplying the actions that can arise from a single accident must also be considered. The two dissenters argued that there was no principled way to distinguish the parents' cause of action, which the Court refused to recognize, from the child's cause of action which had previously been upheld. At least one member of the majority agreed with this latter point and argued that the *Berger* case should be overruled. Here again, we see a court determined to see legal development firmly established on the basis of 'principle' forced to retreat and, in this instance, to leave the law in an even more chaotic state.

III. THE ROLE OF PRINCIPLE IN TORT LAW

Where does all this leave us? One could continue to maintain that tort law should be directed by clear statements of principle but that the principle of reasonable foreseeability is not the correct one. Or one could insist that the principle of reasonable foreseeability is the correct principle but that the courts have made a hash of it. I do not think that either of these alternatives will work. To my mind the principle of 'reasonable foreseeability' is a good one; it just cannot do all the work that is demanded of it. Moreover, I am extremely doubtful that any better general principle of tort liability could be formulated.

Another possible reaction to the confusing farrago is to scrap the whole exercise. After all, has not Judge Andrews told us that '[i]t is all a matter of expediency'? To which I would reply, it all depends on what you mean by 'expediency'. If by expediency one means 'politics'—in the sense of using

---

[69] Sizemore v. Smock, 422 N.W.2d 666 (Mich. 1988).

power to achieve hegemony in society for a particular ideology or economic or class structure or, more prosaically, of using power to advance partisan interests and if the only criterion for judging the worth of those efforts is how successful they are—I would answer no. Thus, I do not accept the assertion that the grading of an examination by a professor or the decision of a case by a judge is the same type of decision as the decision of a legislature, on the eve of an election, on how to allocate construction funds among competing public work projects.

I am not so naïve as to believe that factors such as sex, race, class, ideological commitment, and personal advancement never influence judicial decision-makers. No matter how hard a decision-maker may try, he can never be certain that he is not unconsciously influenced by factors such as these, but the whole point of a system of law is to force the decision-maker to *justify* his decision according to some legally relevant criteria. In a previous piece, I have argued that a system of strict liability for the miscarriage of an ultra-hazardous or abnormally dangerous activity which focuses only on the degree of danger of the activity and the commonness of the activity is different from one in which the social importance of the activity is stated to be a factor of equal value.[71] It is not that the question of the social importance of the activity will not influence a decision-maker operating under the former system but that such a decision-maker must be able to make a plausible argument that the activity is or is not highly dangerous whereas a decision-maker under the latter system is not so confined. It is this narrowing of discretion, to which I am certainly not opposed, that is the essence of the rule of law and the desire so to limit discretion is certainly one of the major attractions of the resort to principle.

There is, however, another view of expediency, one that sees the term as a reference to what, at least since Aristotle, is called φρόνησις or, in English, practical wisdom. I would like to think that this is what Oliver Wendell Holmes, Jr., had at least partially in mind when he said that '[t]he life of the law has not been logic: it has been experience.'[72] Under this view, principles are not ends in themselves; they are merely devices by which human beings seek to achieve the good life. The goals and values of life are many and diverse. They are often incompatible, as even modern natural lawyers recognize and yet do not feel that they are being unprincipled in so doing.[73] Principles are useful, even essential, in helping us to resolve legal and moral dilemmas, but they are not themselves ultimates. If this type of deliberation

---

[70] *Id.* at 671.

[71] George C. Christie, *An Essay on Discretion*, 1986 DUKE L.J. 747, 764–72.

[72] HOLMES, *supra*, note 3, at 1.

[73] *See, e.g.*, JOHN FINNIS, NATURAL LAW AND NATURAL RIGHTS (1980) 81–125. [For an argument that tort law is properly based on a diversity of values that are often incompatible, see Izhak Englard, *The Idea of Complementarity as a Philosophical Basis for Pluralism in Tort Law*, this volume.—Ed.]

is what Judge Andrews had in mind when he said that '[i]t is all a matter of expediency', then he has pointed us in the right direction.

A complex normative system like the law, that is inescapably intertwined with the sometimes contradictory morality of the society in which it operates, requires the making of choices by those who function as officials of that legal system. The choices these officials make are constrained by notions of consistency—the need to articulate convincing reasons of why two cases are dissimilar; by notions of what Aquinas and the natural lawyers call 'the common good'; by notions of efficiency of administration; and by many other considerations including the sorts of principles that tort scholars discuss. As already noted, the law, of course, strives to make certain factors (such as, normally, the parties' race or sex) inappropriate for consideration. But to try to make decisions of complex cases depend solely on the application of some single 'principle' to the exclusion of all other factors is as unwise as it is unachievable. To attempt to simplify the process by trying to reduce the choices involved in deciding a case to the application of a verbal formula, such as the principle of reasonable foreseeability, may seem comforting to some, but in the end, as we have seen, leads to inconsistent decisions which only serve to reinforce the cynicism that the appeal to principle was designed to avert. It is not that the verbal formulas thus far chosen were inadequate; it is rather that the whole enterprise was doomed from the start. Social life is too rich in complicated details to permit decisionmaking by resort to these kinds of overriding abstractions. The best common-law judges have always known this, and their decisions reflect the exercise of seasoned judgment.

If, perhaps under the influence of Ronald Dworkin,[74] one nevertheless insists that the law is driven by normative principles that determine the 'correct' decision of particular cases, then Lord Scarman's sharp distinction between principle and policy, in *McLoughlin v. O'Brian*, sounds plausible, and Lord Edmund-Davies' insistence that policy has always played a role in the development of the law appears as merely a sad and regrettable reflection of the fact that this is, after all, not the best of all possible worlds. This is unfortunate. If one abandons the illusory insistence that legal development must respond to a single or at most a limited number of principles with normative sweep, then Lord Scarman's stark distinction between principles and economic and social policy disappears. Are not the propositions that economic loss should be left to the contractual arrangements worked out by the parties in the light of commercial law, or that economic loss

---

[74] It does not strike me as mere coincidence that a collection of Dworkin's essays in which he continually espoused the primacy of principle and the difference between principle and policy—RONALD DWORKIN, TAKING RIGHTS SERIOUSLY (1977)—had achieved great notoriety by the time *Junior Books* and *McLoughlin v. O'Brian* were decided in 1982. In LAW'S EMPIRE (1986), Dworkin makes frequent reference to the *McLoughlin* case and makes clear his preference for the principled approach taken by Lord Scarman and Lord Bridge of Harwich.

should be insured against by the parties concerned, every bit as much statements of principle as the proposition that, in the law of torts, the range of interests that are eligible for compensation should be determined by the principle of reasonable foreseeability?

Indeed the insistence that the foreseeability be 'reasonable' is itself capable of bringing in these other factors. 'Reasonable' foreseeability has been held to include more than the likelihood of injury; it includes as well factors such as the burden on the defendant of changing his practices in the light of the foreseeable risk.[75] Why cannot the notion of reasonableness with regard to foreseeability include the social judgement that it is unreasonable to expect the tortfeasor to be responsible for the pure economic loss suffered by someone as a result of the physical damage the tortfeasor may have caused to third parties? To some extent, the law already does this. As far as I know, no court has held that, if X negligently injures a famous footballer, X would be liable in an action brought by the footballer's employer for the loss suffered because fewer people bought tickets to the games. Like the loss in *Anns* and its progeny, the footballer employer's loss of profits is much more foreseeable than the damage for fire loss recovered in the second *Wagon Mound* case.[76] But that does not necessarily mean that the law must allow recovery in tort for these losses.

IV. CONCLUSION

We have been discussing the role of principle in the decision of tort cases and have used as the focus of this discussion the principle of reasonable foreseeability which in recent years has been put forth as the controlling factor in deciding who can recover in tort and what types of damages can be recovered in tort. It has never been my position that there is no place for principle in tort law. My submission has been rather that the inconsistent and sometimes incoherent direction that the cases attempting to apply the principle of reasonable foreseeability have taken is an inevitable consequence of the fact that we have asked too much of principles. For the appeal to principles to be useful, we must not only have more modest expectations of their role in the decision of tort cases but also perhaps a more expansive notion of what comes within the ambit of a principle. For example, under the reading that I have suggested the term 'reasonable foreseeability' no longer refers to an overriding normative *principle* driving the

[75] This after all was what the second *Wagon Mound* case was all about. Overseas Tankship (U.K.) Ltd. v. Miller S.S. Co. Pty. (The Wagon Mound No. 2) [1967] 1 A.C. 617 (P.C.). See, in particular, *id.* at 641–4, where the Privy Council incorporated into the reasonable foreseeability test the factors highlighted by Learned Hand, J, in *United States v. Carroll Towing Co.*, 159 F.2d 169 (2d Cir. 1947).

[76] [1967] 1 A.C. 617 (1966) (P.C.).

decision of concrete cases but refers rather to a mnemonic device for insuring that, in the decision of difficult cases, the decision-maker makes an appropriately informed choice, a choice that can never be mechanical but must always be governed, as well as constrained, by considerations of consistency[77] and of fairness, and, if you will, by consideration of principle in the broader sense in which I have used that term. Whether one is prepared to accept such a broad reading of the notion of reasonable foreseeability, history amply illustrates that the attempt to confine the development of tort law to the application of one overriding normative principle, which insulates the decision-maker from the responsibility for making difficult choices, is the pursuit of a chimera.

[77] In my own work I have stressed the importance of consistency among cases and have asserted that it is easier to decide whether two or more cases are significantly different from each other than to reach agreement on the single principle or rule under which they should be subsumed: *see* George C. Christie, *Objectivity in the Law*, 78 YALE L.J. 1311 (1969). I discussed some of the broader implications of this thesis in LAW, NORMS & AUTHORITY (1982). There is a good related discussion by Raz in which he stresses that what he calls 'local coherence' is about all one can expect of a legal system. Law, he asserts, is based on authority and involves choices among incommensurable values. Like morality, it can never achieve 'global coherence': Joseph Raz, *The Relevance of Coherence*, 72 B.U. L. REV. 273 (1992). *See also* Jules L. Coleman & Brian Leiter, *Determinacy, Objectivity, and Authority*, 142 U. PA. L. REV. 549 (1993). In short, it may be that all that we can achieve is a high degree of consistency among the pure economic loss cases that have formed the principle focus of this essay. To broaden our net to capture the negligent misrepresentation and negligent infliction of emotional distress cases—let alone the negligent infliction of physical damage cases—within one conceptual framework may be beyond our ken.

Tort Law in the Aristotelian Tradition

JAMES GORDLEY*

In medieval and early modern Europe, Aristotle's brief account of corrective justice in the *Nicomachean Ethics* was the starting point for those seeking a philosophical explanation of the law of torts. In the thirteenth century, Thomas Aquinas interpreted Aristotle to accommodate ideas taken from Roman and canon law. In the sixteenth and early seventeenth centuries, his interpretation was elaborated by leaders of a Thomist revival such as Tomasso de Vio, better known as Cajetan (1468–1534), Domingo de Soto (1494–1560), Luis de Molina (1535–1600), and Leonard Lessius (1554–1623). This starting point was lost in the seventeenth and eighteenth centuries when Aristotelian philosophy was attacked and eventually discredited by the founders of modern critical philosophy. Paradoxically, during this same period, many of the legal doctrines that had been based on Aristotle's ideas were inherited and disseminated throughout Europe by the founders of the Northern Natural Law School, Hugo Grotius (1583–1645) and Samuel Pufendorf (1632–94).[1] A sharp break was not made until the nineteenth century.

Though Thomas Aquinas and his intellectual successors disagreed about matters of detail, they described corrective justice in much the same way. They believed that distributive and corrective justice serve the higher purpose of advancing human welfare and yet are distinct from each other. They used an Aristotelian principle of corrective justice—that no one should gain through another's loss—to explain liability both for taking another's property and for causing another harm. They gave a unified explanation of causation and fault: one could not say a person was the cause of another's harm unless he chose to harm him by acting intentionally or negligently. They thought that to avoid negligence, a person must weigh the costs and benefits of a course of action, but they did not think the purpose of the law of negligence was to give him the proper incentives to do so.

Thomas and his followers tried to be faithful to Aristotle and to explain the law of torts. This essay is concerned only with their success in the

* Professor of Law, University of California at Berkeley. I am grateful to Professors Peter Benson, Ken Kress, Steven Sugarman, and Augustine Thompson and to my wife Barbara for their comments on this essay.

[1] For similar developments in contract law, see JAMES GORDLEY, THE PHILOSOPHICAL ORIGINS OF MODERN CONTRACT DOCTRINE (1991), 69–133.

second of these tasks. I argue that they offered a better account of tort law than contemporary tort theorists have managed. The greatest defect of their explanation was a failure to explain strict liability. Yet, as we shall see, this failure was due less to the inherent limitations of their principles than to the rather patchy set of Roman rules they were trying to explain.

I. CORRECTIVE JUSTICE AND DISTRIBUTIVE JUSTICE

According to Aristotle, distributive justice 'is manifested in distributions of honor or money or the other things that fall to be divided among those who have a share in the constitution'.[2] It follows a 'geometric proportion': each citizen receives in proportion to merit. Political regimes differ, however, on what constitutes merit: 'democrats identify it with the status of freeman, supporters of oligarchy with wealth (or with noble birth), and supporters of aristocracy with excellence.'[3]

Corrective or commutative[4] justice 'plays a rectifying part in transactions between man and man'.[5] It follows an 'arithmetic proportion': equality is maintained so that one party does not have too much and the other too little. In voluntary transactions such as sale, loan, and lease, equality is preserved when the things exchanged are of equal value. In involuntary transactions such as theft, adultery, imprisonment, and murder, the amount necessary to restore equality must be taken from one party and given to the other.[6]

Some modern tort theorists such as Ernest Weinrib and Peter Benson believe that Aristotle's concept of corrective justice is coherent only if it is cut off from his concept of distributive justice. They fear that corrective justice will lose its separate identity if the two are supposed to work together, corrective justice preserving a fair distribution of wealth that distributive justice tries to establish.[7] Perhaps they merely mean that the injustice done

---

[2] ARISTOTLE, NICOMACHEAN ETHICS V.ii 1130ᵇ (W.D. Ross trans.), *in* THE BASIC WORKS OF ARISTOTLE 935 (Richard McKeon (ed.), 1941) [hereinafter NICOMACHEAN ETHICS].

[3] ARISTOTLE, NICOMACHEAN ETHICS, *supra*, note 2, at V.iv 1131ᵇ–32ᵇ.

[4] Medieval and early modern authors called it 'commutative justice'. Since, most modern tort theorists use the term 'corrective justice', I will do so here.

[5] ARISTOTLE, NICOMACHEAN ETHICS, *supra,* note 2, at V.ii 1130ᵇ.

[6] ARISTOTLE, NICOMACHEAN ETHICS, *supra,* note 2, at V.ii 1130ᵇ–1131ᵃ; V.i 1131ᵇ–1132ᵇ.

[7] Ernest J. Weinrib, *Corrective Justice*, 77 IOWA L. REV. 403, 420 (1992); Peter Benson, *The Basis of Corrective Justice and Its Relation to Distributive Justice*, 77 IOWA L. REV. 515, 530 (1992); Richard W. Wright, *Substantive Corrective Justice*, 77 IOWA L. REV. 625, 705–6 (1992). Others have more ambiguous views. Coleman has said that corrective justice protects a distribution of entitlements against distortion. Jules L. Coleman, *Moral Theories of Torts: Their Scope and Limits: Part II*, 2 J. LAW & PHIL. 5, 6 (1983) [hereinafter *Moral Theories II*]; JULES L. COLEMAN, MARKETS, MORALS AND THE LAW (1988) 185 [hereinafter MARKETS]; Jules L. Coleman, *Tort Law and the Demands of Corrective Justice*, 67 IND. L.J. 349, 357 (1992) [hereinafter *Tort Law*]. He has also said that if I hit your car, I must compensate you as a matter

if Ann robs Bart is not that resources have been allocated to the wrong person; it is that she has enriched herself at his expense. Aristotle would agree. They say, however, that they want to understand corrective justice in terms of its 'structure' rather than any 'independent goals' or 'function' it might have.[8] They fear that otherwise concerns about the distribution of wealth could sometimes trump claims based on corrective justice. A person who had less than his fair share could take something from someone who had more.[9] These interpretations break with the broader Aristotelian tradition. In that tradition one cannot understand the structure of a thing apart from its function, final cause, or end. Consequently, according to most writers in that tradition, a person in severe need could take another's property without acting unjustly.

Aristotle explained the parts and the activities of each thing in terms of its end. The end of a human being, an animal, or a plant is the way in which it tends to behave and which its parts work in harmony to achieve. The end of a human being, which constitutes human goodness or happiness, is a manner of life appropriate for a human being in which all of one's human potential is realized. In the *Politics*, Aristotle explained that '[t]he form of government is best in which every man, whoever he is, can act best and live happily.'[10] In the *Ethics*, he described the different human virtues, including distributive and commutative justice, as different powers that enable a person to live this distinctively human life.[11] For Aristotle, to try to analyze a virtue without considering what it might contribute to such a life would have been like analyzing an organ of the body without considering what it was supposed to do.[12]

of justice even if I am richer and you are poorer than any defensible theory of distributive justice would justify. Jules L. Coleman, Risks and Wrongs (1992), 304–5 [hereinafter Risks]; Jules L. Coleman, *The Mixed Conception of Corrective Justice*, 77 Iowa L. Rev. 427, 428 (1992) [hereinafter *Mixed Conception*]. Others have thought that corrective justice presupposes a distribution of resources that is sufficiently fair to be worth preserving. John Rawls, A Theory of Justice (1971), 10—11; Wilfred J. Waluchow, *Professor Weinrib on Corrective Justice*, in Justice, Law and Method in Plato and Aristotle (S. Panagiotov (ed.), 1987), 133,156; James W. Nickel, *Justice in Compensation*, 18 Wm. & Mary L. Rev. 379, 382 (1976).

 [8] Ernest J. Weinrib, *Understanding Tort Law*, 23 Val. U. L. Rev. 485, 488 (1989); Benson, *supra*, note 7, at 530.

 [9] Ernest J. Weinrib, *Causation and Wrongdoing*, 63 Chi.-Kent L. Rev. 407, 435 (1987); Benson, *supra*, note 7, at 530; Stephen Perry, *The Moral Foundations of Tort Law*, 77 Iowa L. Rev. 449, 451–2 (1992) (semble).

 [10] Aristotle, Politics VII.i 1324a (B. Jowett trans.), in Basic Works of Aristotle, *supra*, note 2, at 1127 [hereinafter Politics].

 [11] Aristotle, Nicomachean Ethics, *supra*, note 2, at V.vii.

 [12] Similarly, according to Thomas Aquinas, distributive justice concerned what was due to the individual as a part of the whole; corrective justice governed the relationship of one part to another. Thomas Aquinas, Summa theologiae II–II, Q. 61, a. 1 (Biblioteca de autores cristianos, 3rd edn., 1963) (Leonine text) [hereinafter Summa theologiae]. Like Aristotle, he understood the relationship of part and whole teleologically. As he explained at the beginning of his commentary of Aristotle's *Ethics*, there is a 'two-fold order in things, the order of parts to the whole and the order of means to an end'. The latter is more primary than the former,

The teleological character of Aristotle's ethical theory enabled Thomas Aquinas to combine it with the traditional Judeo-Christian concern for the poor. He concluded that sometimes, indeed, concern about the distribution of wealth does change the normal operation of corrective justice. A person in urgent need can take another's property for his own use.

The *Decretum* of Gratian, one of the chief authorities for Canon lawyers, contained a text in which Saint Ambrose admonished the rich who neglected the poor: 'Let no one call his own what is common.'[13] According to the standard commentary or *Ordinary Gloss* to this text, ascribed to the Canon lawyer Johannes Teutonicus, this maxim applied literally in a state of necessity.[14] The *Gloss* cited a Roman legal text which provided that all passengers had a right to share the provisions on a ship if food ran short during a voyage.[15]

Thomas gave an Aristotelian explanation of the Canonists' conclusion. In the *Politics*, Aristotle criticized the view of his teacher, Plato, that property should be held in common. If it were, there would be perpetual quarrels, and those who labor much and get little will complain of those who labor little and get much.[16] Similarly, Thomas explained that private property was a legitimate institution because it avoided the disadvantages Aristotle had mentioned.[17] Nevertheless, Aristotle had also said that the end of external things was to meet human needs.[18] Accordingly, Thomas concluded that a person in urgent need with no other recourse may lawfully take another's property.[19]

Soto, Molina, and Lessius followed Thomas, and natural lawyers such as Grotius and Pufendorf borrowed from them. While these authors developed these ideas in different ways, they all say that by nature, or originally, or in principle, all things belong to everyone. They all describe private ownership as instituted to overcome the disadvantages of common ownership, usually the ones mentioned by Aristotle and Thomas.[20] Therefore, they

---

because it is for the sake of the end that the parts have their order: THOMAS AQUINAS, IN DECEM LIBROS ETHICORUM ARISTOTELES EXPOSITIO lib. I, lectio i, no. 1 (Angeli Pirotta (ed.), 1934) [hereinafter IN DECEM LIBROS ETHICORUM ARISTOTELES EXPOSITIO].

[13] DECRETUM GRATIANI D. 47 c. 8., *in* 1 CORPUS IURIS CANONICI (E. Friedberg (ed.), 1876).

[14] *Glossa ordinaria* to DECRETUM GRATIANI D. 47 c. 8 to *commune* (1595). Similarly, *id.* to D. 1 c. 7, to *communis omnium*; *Glossa ordinaria* to X 5.18.3 to *poenitaet*.

[15] DIG. 14.2.2.2.

[16] ARISTOTLE, POLITICS, *supra*, note 10, at II.v.

[17] AQUINAS, SUMMA THEOLOGIAE, *supra*, note 12, at II–II, Q. 66, a. 2.

[18] ARISTOTLE, POLITICS, *supra*, note 10, at I.viii, *cited in* AQUINAS, SUMMA THEOLOGIAE, *supra*, note 12, at II–II, Q. 66, a. 1.

[19] AQUINAS, SUMMA THEOLOGIAE, *supra*, note 12, at Q. 66, a. 7.

[20] DOMENICUS DE SOTO, DE IUSTITIA ET IURE LIBRI DECEM, (1553) lib. 4, q. 3, a. 1; LODOVICUS MOLINA, DE IUSTITIA ET IURE TRACTATUS, (1614) disp. 20; LEONARDUS LESSIUS, DE IUSTITIA ET IURE, CETERISQUE VIRTUTIBUS CARDINALIS LIBRI QUATUOR, (1628) lib. 2, cap. 5, dubs. 1–2; HUGO GROTIUS, DE IURE BELLI AC PACIS LIBRI TRES (de Kanter–van Hetting Tromp ed., 1939) II.ii.2; SAMUEL PUFENDORF, DE IURE NATURAE ET GENTIUM LIBRI OCTO, (1688) II.vi.5; IV.iv.4–7.

regarded the rights of a private owner as qualified, so that a sufficiently necessitous person can use another's property.[21] Lessius and Grotius add that such a person must pay for doing so if he has the resources.[22]

This conclusion is in harmony with modern law. American law recognizes a doctrine of necessity that allows a person to tie a boat to another's pier to save it in a storm although he must pay for damage to the pier.[23] Article 904 of the German Civil Code allows use of a thing against the will of the owner when 'necessary to avoid a present danger and the damage threatened by it is unreasonably large compared to the damage arising to the owner' although 'the owner may demand compensation'. The drafters of the Code explained that otherwise, it would be 'against the law for a drowning man to pull himself onto another's boat to rescue himself' or for a person 'to tear down another's fence during a conflagration to permit the entry of fire-fighting equipment.'[24] Italian law is like the German.[25] Although the French Civil Code does not mention necessity, a leading French jurist has claimed that French courts would reach such a result in practice.[26]

If Weinrib and Benson would allow the boat owner to push the drowning man back into the water, their theories are at odds, not only with modern law, but with most people's moral intuitions. If they would not, then they must smuggle a concern with human welfare into their own accounts of corrective justice which supposedly are independent of any prior conception of human welfare or advantage.[27] By so doing, they would then be allowing concerns about the distribution of wealth to trump the normal operations of corrective justice.

Weinrib and Benson have argued that if the point of corrective justice were to preserve a *just* distribution of resources, one could no longer distinguish it from distributive justice.[28] Stephen Perry agrees, provided one

---

[21] SOTO, *supra*, note 20, lib. 5, q. 3, a. 4; MOLINA, *supra*, note 20, disp. 20; LESSIUS, *supra* note 20, lib. 2, cap. 12, dub. 12; GROTIUS, *supra*, note 20, II.ii.6–7; PUFENDORF, *supra*, note 20, II.vi.5.

[22] LESSIUS, *supra*, note 20, lib. 2, cap. 16, dub. 1, nos. 2, 16; GROTIUS, *supra*, note 20, II.ii.9.

[23] Ploof v. Putnam, 71 A. 188 (Vt. 1908); Vincent v. Lake Erie Transp. Co., 124 N.W. 221 (Minn. 1910).

[24] PROTOKOLLE DER KOMMISSION FÜR DIE ZWEITE LESUNG DES BÜRGERLICHEN GESETZBUCHS, § 419, at 214 (1899).

[25] *See* CODICE CIVILE, § 2045; Angelo Venchiarutti in 4 COMMENTARIO AL CODICE CIVILE, § 2045, no. 1 (Paolo Cendon ed., 1991).

[26] JEAN CARBONNIER, 3 DROIT CIVIL (8th edn., 1975), 166–9.

[27] Ernest J. Weinrib, *Right and Advantage in Private Law*, 10 CARDOZO L. REV. 1283, 1293 (1989). For objections, see Perry, *supra*, note 9, at 482. *See* Stephen R. Perry, *Professor Weinrib's Formalism: The Not-So-Empty Sepulchre*, 16 HARV. J.L. & PUB. POL'Y 597, 606–7 (1993); Stephen Perry, *Loss, Agency and Responsibility for Outcomes: Three Conceptions of Corrective Justice, in* TORT THEORY (Ken Cooper-Stephenson & Elaine Gibson (eds.), 1993), 24, 3–5 [hereinafter *Loss*].

[28] Weinrib, *supra*, note 7, at 420–21; Benson, *supra*, note 7, at 530. The same objection is made by Wright, *supra*, note 7, at 705–6.

holds a 'simple patterned theory' of distributive justice.[29] Lessius, however, thought one could distinguish distributive from commutative justice even in a simple case in which an academic authority must distribute fellowship money among scholars according either to their poverty or to their learning. He would violate distributive justice if he disregarded the principle of proportionality that was supposed to guide the distribution. He would violate the arithmetic equality of commutative justice if he gave a scholar less that the amount that had been determined to be due to him.[30] Lessius' example shows that while one can calculate an individual scholar's share in two different ways and arrive at the same answer, the knowledge required for each calculation is different, as is the moral principle one must respect. To do distributive justice, one must know the size of the fund, the distributive principle, and the qualifications of everyone who might be entitled to a share. One must be willing to apply the distributive principle even-handedly. To do commutative justice, one needs to know that someone should receive a certain amount, however that amount may have been determined. One has to be willing to pay whatever is owed.

In any case, the Aristotelian tradition did not have a 'simple patterned theory' in which each citizen is simply entitled to the share assigned by the prevailing principle of distributive justice. Private property was supposed to prevent quarrels and to provide incentives to work. Consequently, a citizen cannot demand more resources in a democracy simply because he has less than someone else or in an aristocracy simply because he has the same amount as someone less virtuous. To obtain the advantages of a system of private property, a society will have to tolerate some deviations from the principle of distributive justice it regards as ideal.

Weinrib and Perry also object that if the point of corrective justice is to preserve a *given* distribution of resources, one must explain why accidents or natural events are allowed to change that distribution.[31] Writers in the Aristotelian tradition say little about this problem. An answer, however, seems to be implicit in their account of private property. Private property is supposed to provide an incentive to work and to prevent quarrels. To eliminate chance gains and losses, a society would have to distinguish them from gains and losses that are the result of labor and care. It may not be possible to do so. Even if it were, the attempt might lead to so many

---

[29] Perry, *supra*, note 9, at 451.

[30] LESSIUS, *supra*, note 20, lib. 2, cap. 1, dub. 4, no. 23. Molina had made a similar argument in response to the 14th century philosopher Buridan who claimed distributive and commutative justice were the same, since if the state refused to pay what was due someone as a matter of distributive justice, the failure to pay the amount due would be a violation of commutative justice: MOLINA, *supra*, note 20, disp. 12 (citing J. BURIDAN, QUAESTIONES SUPER DECEM LIBROS ARISTOTELIS AD NICOMACHUM, (1513) V, q. 7).

[31] Perry, *supra*, note 9, at 451; Weinrib, *supra*, note 7, at 420.

charges of arbitrariness as to give rise to the quarrels that a system of private property is supposed to prevent.

Moreover, some resources are more vulnerable to chance destruction than others. Some decisions about what to produce or consume are more prone to error. If everyone were fully compensated when his property was destroyed or his decisions were thwarted by bad luck, those who had chosen to hold more vulnerable types of property, or to embark on riskier projects, would use up a greater share of resources than those who did not. A person who chose to live in a glass house, to pick an extreme example, might use up five or ten houses in the same time a person in a wood house would use up one. Thus, rather than preserving a given distribution of wealth, such a system of compensation would transfer wealth from those whose property was less vulnerable to those whose property was more vulnerable, from those whose projects were more conservative to those whose projects were more adventurous.

Writers in the Aristotelian tradition do not make these arguments expressly. They seem to assume that once one adopts a system of private property, one adopts along with it the Roman rule, *res pereat domino*, an object perishes at the owner's cost. But they may have had an understandable difficulty seeing how a system of private property was supposed to work without this rule.

II. Defendant's Gain and Plaintiff's Loss

Aristotle said that in the involuntary type of corrective justice, 'the judge tries to equalize things by means of the penalty', taking away the 'gain' of one party and restoring the 'loss' of the other.[32] Though he admitted that it seems odd to speak of a 'gain' when one person has wounded another, Aristotle maintained that 'when the suffering has been estimated, the one is called loss and the other gain'.[33]

Some modern scholars have found it difficult to see how holding the defendant liable to the plaintiff is supposed to restore equality by eliminating these gains and losses. George Fletcher has observed that the person who pays compensation for harming another will be poorer than he was initially unless he happens to have profited by an equivalent amount.[34] Jules Coleman has noted that equality will not be restored if the defendant keeps a gain that he made wrongfully but without causing any plaintiff a loss.[35]

---

[32] ARISTOTLE, NICOMACHEAN ETHICS, *supra,* note 2, at V.iv 1132ᵃ.   [33] *Id.*

[34] George P. Fletcher, *Corrective Justice for Moderns*, 106 HARV. L. REV. 1658, 1668 (1993) (reviewing JULES L. COLEMAN, RISKS AND WRONGS (1992)). *See* Perry, *supra,* note 9, at 454.

[35] Jules L. Coleman, *Property, Wrongfulness and the Duty to Compensate*, 63 CHI-KENT L. REV. 451, 461-2 (1987) [hereinafter *Property*].

In the Aristotelian tradition, a first step toward an explanation was taken by the teacher of Thomas Aquinas, Albert the Great. He said that 'the one who acts has more of what he wants, and the one who suffers has less . . . and this is appropriately designated by the name gain and loss'.[36] Thomas clarified: a 'person striking or killing has more of what is evaluated as good, insofar, that is, as he fulfills his will, and so is seen to receive a sort of gain'.[37] To gain', then, means to fulfil one's will. One who has taken or used or harmed another's resources for his own ends has 'gained', and therefore must pay compensation, whether or not his ends have been achieved, and whether or not he has made a financial gain by pursuing them.

Writers in the Aristotelian tradition used this simple principle to explain the basic legal principles underlying the law of property, unjust enrichment, and tort. If one possesses another's property, even innocently, one must give it back. If one no longer has the property but has profited from its use, even innocently, one must return the profit.[38] In these cases, one is liable, as Thomas put it, 'by reason of the thing taken'.[39] If one voluntarily harms another, one is liable 'by reason of the injurious action' or 'taking'.[40] As we will see shortly, for Thomas, to harm another voluntarily meant to cause the harm either intentionally or negligently. The point of interest now is that in all of these cases, a person owes compensation because he has 'gained' at another's expense in the sense that he has fulfilled his will with another's resources.

We can see, then, despite Fletcher's objection, why corrective justice restores a pre-existing equality even when the defendant has not profited financially from the plaintiff's loss. By voluntarily harming the plaintiff, he has chosen to use the plaintiff's resources for his own ends. The pre-existing equality that corrective justice seeks to restore is a state in which each party achieves his own goals out of his own resources.

We can also see, despite Coleman's argument, why corrective justice does not require taking away the defendant's gain if the plaintiff has not suffered a loss. In that case, the defendant has not achieved his own ends at the plaintiff's expense. As Thomas noted, when corrective justice required restitution, '[t]he chief end . . . is not that he who has more than his due may cease to have it, but that he who has less than his due may be compensated.'[41] Thomas concluded that though it might be appropriate to take

---

[36] ALBERTUS MAGNUS, ETHICORUM LIBRI DECEM lib. V, tract. ii, cap. 6, no. 25, *in* 7 OPERA OMNIA (A. Bourgnet ed., 1891).

[37] AQUINAS, IN DECEM LIBROS ETHICORUM ARISTOTELES EXPOSITIO, *supra*, note 12, at lib. V, lectio vi, no. 952.

[38] CAJETAN (TOMASSO DE VIO), COMMENTARIA TO THOMAS AQUINAS, SUMMA THEOLOGICA, (1698) post Q. 61, a. 6; MOLINA, *supra* note 20, disps. 713, 718, 719; LESSIUS, *supra*, note 20, lib. 2, cap. 7, dub. 5; cap. 14, dubs. 1–2.

[39] AQUINAS, SUMMA THEOLOGIAE, *supra*, note 12, at II–II, Q. 62, a. 6.

[40] *Id.*   [41] *Id.* at II–II, Q. 62, a. 6, ad 1.

away the defendant's gain by criminal sanctions,[42] the defendant did not have to pay if the plaintiff was not harmed: for example, if plaintiff's use of his resources was unimpaired, as when the defendant took a light from the plaintiff's candle,[43] if the plaintiff was never harmed because the defendant's plan miscarried,[44] or if the plaintiff had already been compensated by another tortfeasor.[45]

Corrective justice in the Aristotelian tradition thus links the plaintiff's right to compensation and the defendant's duty to compensate: the defendant must pay because he has used up the plaintiff's resources for his own ends. Until recently, Coleman argued that there could be no such link,[46] that the proposition 'the plaintiff has lost' is 'analytically' different from the proposition that 'the defendant should be liable'.[47] It is 'logically possible', Coleman argued, that everyone would agree in advance to distribute losses without regard to fault or to establish a fund into which individuals at fault would pay and from which those who suffered losses would be compensated.[48]

Suppose, however, that the point of corrective justice is to ensure that each citizen pursues his own ends out of his own resources. That purpose would be frustrated if plaintiffs were not compensated or were compensated out of public funds.[49] Moreover, it would be distinctly odd to say that though Alice is not liable to Bill for using up $100,000 of his resources, she must contribute that amount to a fund from which Bill may withdraw it. It would be like a restaurant owner claiming he never charges patrons for their meals but he does require them to contribute an equivalent amount to a fund from which he can withdraw it. Unless one is addressing the entirely different problem of insuring plaintiffs against the risk of defendants' insolvency, it is pointless to talk about a fund.

Coleman has wanted to develop a concept of corrective justice that will not condemn no-fault compensation plans.[50] But surely, nothing in the traditional Aristotelian theory would prevent people from establishing such a plan, for example, because they wished to avoid the costs and errors of

---

[42] *Id.* at Q. 62, a. 3.   [43] *Id.* at Q. 62, a. 3.   [44] *Id.* at Q. 62, a.7, ad 2.
[45] *Id.* at Q. 62, a.7, ad 2.

[46] Coleman, *Moral Theories II, supra,* note 7, at 72; COLEMAN, MARKETS, *supra,* note 7, at 187; Coleman, *Property, supra,* note 35, at 461; Jules L. Coleman, *The Structure of Tort Law,* 97 YALE L.J. 1233, 1233 (1988) (reviewing WILLIAM M. LANDES & RICHARD A. POSNER, THE ECONOMIC STRUCTURE OF TORT LAW (1987) & STEVEN SHAVELL, ECONOMIC ANALYSIS OF ACCIDENT LAW (1987)); Coleman, *Tort Law, supra,* note 7, at 358, 366. Recently, he has abandoned this position. COLEMAN, RISKS, *supra,* note 7, at 369–71, 481 n.5; Coleman, *Mixed Conception, supra,* note 7, at 432–3.

[47] Coleman, *Property, supra,* note 35, at 461; COLEMAN, MARKETS, *supra,* note 7, at 135.

[48] COLEMAN, MARKETS, *supra,* note 7, at 135, 199.

[49] As Posner notes, if the loss does not fall on the defendant, it must fall on someone else: Richard A. Posner, *The Concept of Corrective Justice in Recent Theories of Tort Law,* 10 J. LEGAL STUD. 187, 197 (1981).

[50] COLEMAN, RISKS, *supra,* note 7, at 401–2.

litigating questions of fault. In the Aristotelian theory, as we have seen, the defendant's gains do not have to be canceled as long as the plaintiff is compensated. The citizens are free to assume voluntarily a burden that would otherwise rest on defendants as a matter of corrective justice.

III. Causation and Choice

Some classical scholars have thought that Aristotle believed that a person owed compensation for harm caused negligently as well as intentionally. My colleague, David Daube, has shown rather clearly that Aristotle had only intentionally inflicted harm in mind.[51] Daube claimed that anyone reading the *Nicomachean Ethics* without prior indoctrination by the classicists would arrive at his conclusion. He would be gratified to know that not only Thomas Aquinas but many modern tort theorists have done so.[52]

Whatever Aristotle may have meant, however, Roman law imposed liability for harm caused negligently as well as intentionally.[53] By the time that Thomas was writing, the Canon lawyers had decided that a person who injured another through negligence or a lack of due diligence was not only morally guilty[54] but under a moral obligation to compensate the victim.[55] Consequently, though Thomas understood Aristotle in the *Ethics* to be speaking of intentionally caused harm, he tried to explain liability for negligence on Aristotelian principles.

Thomas argued that harm caused intentionally was voluntary and intended directly. Harm caused negligently was voluntary and intended accidentally 'as that which removes an obstacle is called an accidental cause'.[56] In either case, compensation must be paid because the harm was caused voluntarily.

---

[51] David Daube, Roman Law: Linguistic, Social and Philosophical Aspects (1969), 131–56.

[52] Aquinas, In decem libros Aristoteles expositio, *supra,* note 12, at lib. V, lectio xiii, no. 1043; Coleman, Markets, *supra,* note 7, at 197; Posner, *supra,* note 49, at 190; Perry, *supra,* note 9, at 453. Wright's view, which seems impossible to square with the text, is that Aristotle distinguishes intent, negligence, and strict liability as grounds for the duty to pay compensation: Wright, *supra,* note 7, at 697–8.

[53] *See generally* Reinhard Zimmermann, The Law of Obligations: Roman Foundations of the Civilian Tradition (1990), 953–1049.

[54] Decretum Gratiani, *supra,* note 13, D. 50, cc. 49–50; Decretales Gregorii IX 5.10.7–13, *in* 2 Corpus Iuris Canonici, *supra,* note 13; Bernardus Papiensis, Summa Decretalium (E. Laspeyres ed., 1956) lib. 5, tit.10, §§ 5–6; Raimondus de Pennaforte, Summa de Paenitentia (X. Ochoa & A. Diez eds., 1976) lib. 2, tit. 1, § 3. *See* Stephan Kuttner, Kanonistische Schuldlehre von Gratian bis auf die Dekretalen Gregors IX (1935), 213–27.

[55] *Glossa ordinaria* to Decretales Gregorii IX (Venice, 1595) 5.36.5 *Casus*; to *non custovit*; to *reddet*; to 5.36.6 to *voluntarie*; 5.36.9.

[56] Aquinas, Summa theologiae, *supra,* note 12, at II–I, Q. 68 a. 8.

For Thomas, this conclusion followed not only from Aristotle's theory of commutative justice but also from his theory of voluntary action. Voluntary action is performed because of an internal principle. Because a human being is a rational animal, the internal principle by which he acts, and which makes his action that of a human being, is reason and will. Through reason, he understands the courses of action available to him, and through will, he chooses among them. An action is therefore involuntary in so far as a person is in ignorance, not knowing what he does, or in so far as he cannot choose, as when his body is moved by force.[57] Aristotle concluded that he could not be praised or blamed for such actions.[58] Thomas concluded that he could not be liable for them.

The feature of this account that concerns us at present is that causation or agency is identified with choice. In the case of intentionally inflicted harm, a person chooses to act so that harm will occur. In the case of negligently inflicted harm, he chooses an action that is inappropriate because harm may occur. Thomas seems to have assumed these are the only two cases in which a person voluntarily produced the harmful result. Be that as it may, a person who did not choose in any sense for the harm to occur did not cause the harm *qua* human being.

In contrast, according to some modern tort theories, a person may be liable for harm that was not the result of any choice he should or could have made differently. Supposedly, he should be liable simply if he caused the harm. In these theories, then, causation must mean something different from choice.

Just what it could mean is hard to see. No one seems to think the defendant should be liable simply because an action he voluntarily performed happened to create a risk to the plaintiff. One cannot act without creating risks, and the plaintiff's own act created a risk to himself.[59] Nor does anyone claim that the defendant should be liable simply because his body played a causal role in the accident: for example, he landed on the plaintiff after he was thrown from an upstairs window. And certainly no one believes the defendant should be liable because, absent his action, the accident would not have occurred. An accident has an infinity of but-for causes.[60]

Instead, the builders of such theories explain causation in such a way that it looks much like fault except for the absence of personal culpability or a personal choice that the harm should occur. These theorists hold the defendant liable for performing the sort of action that people ordinarily would

---

[57] ARISTOTLE, NICOMACHEAN ETHICS, *supra,* note 2, at III.i; AQUINAS, SUMMA THEOLOGIAE, *supra,* note 12, at I–II, Q. 6, aa. 1, 5, 8.

[58] ARISTOTLE, NICOMACHEAN ETHICS, *supra,* note 2, at III.i.

[59] Perry, *supra,* note 9, at 463–5; Stephen R. Perry, *The Impossibility of General Strict Liability,* 1 CAN. J.L. & JUR. 147, 169 (1988) [hereinafter *Impossibility*].

[60] *See* Perry, *Impossibility, supra,* note 59, at 169.

be at fault for performing. Then they claim that the defendant should pay because he caused any harm that occurred even if he was not at fault. They never adequately explain why, if liability does not rest on fault, fault should matter at all. In particular, they do not explain why the question whether the defendant caused the harm should depend on whether some other person would have been at fault for acting as the defendant did.

Richard Epstein has built a theory in which fault is supposed to be irrelevant. The defendant is liable if his action falls within one of four 'causal paradigms'. The paradigms, however, describe actions that people typically do not perform unless they are at fault:[61] the defendant applied force to the plaintiff's person or thing; he frightened the plaintiff; he compelled the plaintiff to act; or he created a dangerous condition that injured the plaintiff.[62] Epstein then describes defenses by which the defendant can escape liability. They look like typical cases in which a person ordinarily would not be at fault. For example, he is not liable if the plaintiff blocked his right of way, and whether the plaintiff did so depends on applicable state traffic laws.[63]

Epstein has argued that 'the proper conception of ownership compels the adoption of a strict liability principle' because ownership is typically defined in terms of inviolability which suggests protection against all invasions.[64] But Epstein's theory does not protect the owner from all invasions. It only protects the owner against invasions that typically would be culpable if committed by someone other than the defendant. Epstein does not explain why the concept of property only requires protection against these invasions.

Other tort theorists have adopted a so-called 'objective' theory of negligence. According to Oliver Wendell Holmes, Stephen Perry, and Jules Coleman, the defendant is liable without personal fault if he deviated from the standard of conduct that a reasonable person would normally observe.

Holmes argued that if 'a man is born hasty and awkward . . . his slips are no less troublesome to his neighbors than if they sprang from guilty neglect'.[65] Sometimes, Perry argues in a similar way that negligence law is 'interest-sensitive', and 'determines liability by reference to a certain level of permissible risk'.[66] On this rationale, however, all that should matter is

[61] On the normative character of Epstein's paradigms, see Weinrib, *supra*, note 9, at 417; Perry, *supra*, note 9, at 464; Posner, *supra*, note 49, at 195–6; Gary T. Schwartz, *The Vitality of Negligence and the Ethics of Strict Liability*, 15 GA. L. REV. 963, 988–9 (1981).

[62] Richard Epstein, *A Theory of Strict Liability*, 2 J. LEGAL STUD. 151, 166–89 (1973).

[63] Richard A. Epstein, *Defenses and Subsequent Pleas in a System of Strict Liability*, 3 J. LEGAL STUD. 165, 176 (1974).

[64] Richard A. Epstein, *Causation and Corrective Justice: A Reply to Two Critics*, 8 J. LEGAL STUD. 477, 500 (1979).

[65] OLIVER WENDELL HOLMES, JR., THE COMMON LAW (1881), 108.

[66] Perry, *Loss, supra*, note 27, at 46.

whether a person has created an above average level of risk. If so, he is more troublesome to his neighbors and should be held liable independently of whether he deviated from a standard of conduct that would guide a normal person, and independently of whether he chose to create this level of risk. But then there is no place to stop. The person who infects the plaintiff with a contagious disease, crashes into the plaintiff when his brakes fail through an undetectable defect, or lands on the plaintiff after being thrown out of the window creates an above average risk at the moment before impact. His presence is no less troublesome for the fact that he could not help being there.

Perry has also defended such a theory by claiming that people may be 'outcome responsible' even when they are not at fault. A person is 'outcome responsible' for events he could not help if he has voluntarily performed an act that 'contributed causally' to an injury in a way that is 'close and normatively significant' and would typically arouse in him a feeling of 'agent regret'.[67] Why such a person should be liable is left mysterious. If the defendant was not at fault, one wonders what could make his connection to the accident 'normatively significant', and how anything so illusive could be the basis of tort law.

Jules Coleman defends an objective theory on the grounds that '[t]he central concern of the principle of corrective justice is the *consequences* of various sorts of doings, not the character or culpability of the doers.'[68] Why someone should be responsible for consequences he could not prevent is again unclear. Coleman defines the defendant's conduct as 'wrongful' or 'injurious' by reference to a 'community standard' that supposedly he was unable to meet, and then asserts that it is better a loss should fall on someone who has acted 'injuriously' than on someone who has not done so.[69]

Unlike Holmes, however, Coleman claims that the reason the defendant should be liable for deviating from that standard is not simply that his conduct is dangerous but that his actions are 'the consequences of agency: the agent's causal powers'.[70] On this rationale, however, it is again difficult to

[67] Perry, *supra*, note 9, at 498–9, 503; Perry, *Loss*, *supra*, note 27, at 40–4; Stephen Perry, *Comment on Coleman: Corrective Justice*, 67 IND. L.J. 381, 399 (1992) [hereinafter *Comment on Coleman*].

[68] Coleman, *Tort Law*, *supra*, note 7, at 370. *See* COLEMAN, RISKS, *supra*, note 7, at 333–5; COLEMAN, MARKETS, *supra*, note 7, at 174; Coleman, *Mixed Conception, supra*, note 7, at 442; Jules L. Coleman, *Mental Abnormality, Personal Responsibility and Tort Liability*, in MENTAL ILLNESS: LAW AND PUBLIC POLICY (B. Brody & H.T. Engelhardt, Jr. eds., 1980), 107 [hereinafter *Mental Abnormality*]; Jules L. Coleman, *Moral Theories of Torts: Their Scope and Limits: Part I*, 1 LAW & PHIL. 371, 376–8 (1982) [hereinafter *Moral Theories I*].

[69] COLEMAN, RISKS, *supra* note 7, at 224–5, 334.

[70] Coleman, *Mixed Conception, supra*, note 7, at 442; COLEMAN, RISKS, *supra*, note 7, at 334–5; Coleman, *Tort Law, supra*, note 7, at 371; Coleman, *Mental Abnormality, supra*, note 68, at 126–31. For a negative reaction, see Ernest J. Weinrib, *Non-Relational Relationships: A Note on Coleman's New Theory*, 77 IOWA L. REV. 445, 445 (1992); for a positive reaction, see Perry, *Comment on Coleman, supra*, note 67, at 399.

see the relevance of an *objective* standard of conduct. It is odd to think that the extent of Al's causal powers depends on what Betty (and others, whose collective conduct forms the standard) can do. Moreover, according to Coleman, 'agency requires the ability to form intentions and to act accordingly'.[71] For that reason, he would not hold liable a person with bi-polar disease or catatonic schizophrenia since, according to Coleman, the former may be unable to form intentions and the latter 'to translate intentions into actions'.[72] If the reach of one's causal powers depends on one's intentions, however, it is hard to see why anyone should be liable who intended no harm to the plaintiff and tried to take every appropriate precaution to avoid harming him.

Holmes and Coleman claim that their 'objective' theory best explains modern law.[73] Actually, it does not. In American law, as in that of other major legal systems, the defendant usually is held liable if he fails to use the care a reasonable person would use.[74] Usually, however, that is the best, and, indeed, the only evidence of the care of which he was capable or would have been capable had he spent his life overcoming whatever hasty and awkward proclivities we suppose him to have inherited. In American, German, Italian, and French law, the defendant with a physical handicap will be held only to the standard of a person with such a handicap.[75] Thus the defendant will escape liability if he can point to a physical condition for which he clearly was not responsible. That is as one would expect if, in principle, personal culpability matters.

Admittedly, mental handicaps are treated differently. In German, Italian, and French law, insane persons and children may be required to compen-

---

[71] Coleman, *Mental Abnormality, supra,* note 68, at 130.   [72] *Id.* at 30–1.

[73] HOLMES, *supra,* note 65, at 107–9; Coleman, *Moral Theories I, supra,* note 68, at 377–8; COLEMAN, RISKS, *supra,* note 7, at 218–9, 333–4; COLEMAN, MARKETS, *supra,* note 7, at 174; Coleman, *Tort Law, supra,* note 7, at 370; Coleman, *Mental Abnormality, supra,* note 68, at 111–12.

[74] *See, e.g.,* W. PAGE KEETON, DAN B. DOBBS, ROBERT E. KEETON, & DAVID G. OWEN, PROSSER AND KEETON ON THE LAW OF TORTS (5th edn. 1984), 173–5 (American law) [hereinafter PROSSER & KEETON]; Peter Hanau, *in* 2 MÜNCHENER KOMMENTAR ZUM BÜRGERLICHEN GESETZBUCH, (Kurt Rebmann & Franz-Jürgen Säcker eds., 2d edn., 1985) § 276, no. 78 (German law); Luigi Gaudino in COMMENTARIO, *supra,* note 24, at § 2043, no. 8; GABRIEL MARTY & PIERRE RAYNAUD, 1 DROIT CIVIL LES OBLIGATIONS, (2d edn., 1988) § 457, at 512–4 (French law). *See generally,* KONRAD ZWEIGERT & HEIN KÖTZ, INTRODUCTION TO COMPARATIVE LAW (Tony Weir ed., 2d edn., 1987), 635–68; FRANCESCO PARISI, LIABILITY FOR NEGLIGENCE AND JUDICIAL DISCRETION (2d edn., 1992) 341–72; MARIO BUSSANI, LA COLPA SOGGETTIVA (1991).

[75] *See* RESTATEMENT (SECOND) OF TORTS, § 283C (1963); PROSSER & KEETON, *supra,* note 74, at 175–6 (American law); Hanau, *supra,* note 74, at § 276, no. 85 (German law); BUSSANI, *supra,* note 74, at 7 (French law); 3 LINA BIGLIAZZI GERI, UMBERTO BRECCIA, FRANCESCO BUSNELLI, & UGO NATOLI, DIRITTO CIVILE (1989), 702 (Italian law).

sate those they have injured.[76] In American law, the insane are also liable,[77] though children are not if they were engaged in appropriate activities and used the care to be expected of a child of similar age.[78] Except possibly in France, however, the reason does not seem to be allegiance to an objective standard of fault. In American law, an insane plaintiff is not held to an objective standard in proving contributory or comparative negligence.[79] The German and Italian Codes provide that the insane or under-age defendant is not liable because of fault.[80] Special provisions impose a duty of compensation and allow the court to award an indemnity that is 'equitable' considering the financial resources of both parties if the plaintiff cannot recover from those in charge of caring for the insane person or the child.[81] Thus in American, German, and Italian law, while the liability of the insane and of children may be a kind of strict liability, it is not simply an application of the ordinary standard of liability for fault.

IV. NEGLIGENCE

As we have just seen, one way in which Thomas integrated the Roman and Canon law concept of negligence into Aristotelian moral philosophy was to identify negligence as a voluntary action depriving another of his due. Another way he did so was to describe negligence as a failure to exercise prudence.[82]

[76] For German and Italian law, *see infra,* note 81. In France, an insane person was not liable until a 1968 statute changed the law: Law of 3 Jan. 1968, now CODE CIVIL, § 489–2. *See* MARTY & RAYNAUD, *supra,* note 74, at §§ 460, 463; Petrelli, *La responsabilità civile dell'infermo di mente nell'ordinamento francese,* 37 RIVISTA DI DIRITTO CIVILE 77–86 (1991). Children were held to the standard of a child of their own age until the decision of May 9, 1984 by the highest French judicial authority, the *Cour de cassation* meeting in *assemblée plénière.* [1984] RECUEIL DALLOZ SIREY JUR. 525. *See* Henri Mazeaud, *La 'faute objective' et la responsabilité sans faute,* [1985] RECUEIL DALLOZ SIREY CHR. 13 at 86–95 (1991); Petrelli, *supra,* at 77–86.

[77] RESTATEMENT (SECOND) OF TORTS, § 283B (1963); PROSSER & KEETON, *supra,* note 74, at 176–78; Stephanie I. Splane, *Tort Liability of the Mentally Ill in Negligence Actions,* 93 YALE L.J. 153, 155–6 (1983).

[78] RESTATEMENT (SECOND) OF TORTS, § 283A (1963); PROSSER & KEETON, *supra,* note 74, at 179–82.

[79] PROSSER & KEETON, *supra,* note 74, at 178; Splane, *supra,* note 77, at 155–7.

[80] BÜRGERLICHES GESETZBUCH [BGB], §§ 827–8; Karl Schäfer in J. VON STAUDINGER, KOMMENTAR ZUM BÜRGERLICHEN GESETZBUCH, § 828, no. 26 (Karl Schäfer & Norbert Horn eds., 12th edn., 1986) (German law); CODICE CIVILE, § 2046; Venchiarutti, *supra,* note 25, at § 2046, no. 2.1 (Italian law).

[81] BGB, § 829; CODICE CIVILE, § 2047.

[82] More technically, negligence (*negligentia*) was a lack of solicitude (*sollicitudo*) or diligence (*diligentia*). Solicitude or diligence was the virtue that enables the alert, adroit performance of the 'chief act' of prudence, *praecipere,* which could be translated as 'to command' or 'to execute'. Prudence required three 'acts': to take counsel or to consider what should be done (*consiliari*); to judge or decide what should be done (*iudicare*); and to execute this decision (*praecipere*). *See* AQUINAS, SUMMA THEOLOGIAE, *supra,* note 12, at II–II, Q. 47, aa. 8–9; Q. 54, aa. 1–2; Q. 64, a. 8.

Prudence, for Aristotle and Thomas, was a cardinal virtue. Virtues were faculties, perfected through training, which helped a person to attain his end. Through prudence a person decides how to obtain those things that are good because they contribute to his end and to avoid those that are evil because they obstruct it.[83] He weighs the magnitude of the good result he seeks against that of the evil one he avoids. Thus 'any prudent person will accept a small evil in order not to obstruct a great good'.[84] Since prudence is concerned with the 'contingencies of action', the prudent person must also concern himself with probabilities, with 'what happens in the greater number of cases'.[85]

Cajetan gave an example of how such factors might be taken into account in his commentary on Thomas' *Summa Theologiae*. A Canon law text in Gratian's *Decretum* said that parents are negligent if they fall asleep with children in their bed, and the children die because they are suffocated or crushed.[86] According to Cajetan, whether a nurse would be liable in such a case depended on the circumstances:

[If] the bed is large and there is nothing else near it, the nurse is always accustomed to find herself in the same place and position in which she put herself to begin sleeping, and the implacability of the infant required it, she seems to be excused, because it is not rational when these things concur to fear the risk.[87]

According to Thomas and Cajetan, then, a prudent person will weigh the good and evil consequences to be expected from each course of action. The fact that the baby will not stop crying otherwise can justify letting it sleep with the nurse. Indeed, the factors Cajetan expected a prudent nurse to take into account resemble those mentioned by Judge Learned Hand in *United States v. Carroll Towing Co.*[88] Hand said that a precaution should be taken if the burden it entails (B) is less that the loss that may occur (L) multiplied by the probability the precaution will prevent the loss (P).

Ernest Weinrib argued at one point that on Aristotelian principles the defendant should not be permitted to weigh these consequences. He should be liable as long as the risk he imposed on the plaintiff *went beyond a certain level*, taking account of both the likelihood of an injury and its seriousness.[89] But if that were so, negligence would no longer approximate an

---

[83] Aquinas, Summa theologiae, *supra*, note 12, at II–II, Q. 47, a. 4, obj. 1; Q. 49, a. 8; Q. 51, a. 8, ad. 1.

[84] Thomas Aquinas, De veritate Q. 5, a. 4, ad 4, *in* 9 Opera omnia, (P. Fiaccadori ed., 1859) 5.

[85] Aquinas, Summa theologiae, *supra*, note 12, at II–II, Q. 49, a. 1; a. 8 ad 3.

[86] Decretum Gratiani, *supra*, note 13, at C. 2 q. 5 c. 2.

[87] Cajetan, *supra*, note 38, post Q. 64 a. 8.   [88] 159 F.2d 169 (2d Cir. 1947).

[89] Weinrib, *supra*, note 8, at 518–9; Ernest J. Weinrib, *Right and Advantage in Private Law*, 10 Cardozo L. Rev. 1283, 1304–5 (1989); Ernest J. Weinrib, *Liberty, Community and Corrective Justice*, 1 Can. J.L. & Jur. 3, 4 (1988); Ernest Weinrib, *The Special Morality of Tort Law*, 34 McGill L.J. 403, 410 (1989). He elsewhere seems to have been attracted by a

Aristotelian conception of imprudent action or a common sense notion of fault. We do not blame a person who fails to take every possible precaution, however costly, to prevent risk from reaching a certain level, or exonerate him if he fails to take a simple precaution when the risk falls below it. Anyone would feel justified driving faster to reach a hospital in an emergency.[90]

Nevertheless, while they thought that a prudent person would weigh factors like those of the Hand formula, Thomas and Cajetan had a different idea from modern economists of what it meant to do so. Economists explain negligence law in terms of efficiency, and identify the B and L of the formula with the magnitude of social costs. Thomas Aquinas and Cajetan were discussing virtue. For them, an outcome is good or evil, and a prudent person will seek or avoid it, to the extent it furthers or detracts from the distinctively human life that is one's ultimate end. Moreover, they did not think that a prudent person could make his decision by any sort of calculus or deductive argument. A prudent person moves from the premise 'the greater evil is to be avoided' to the conclusion 'this is the proper course of action' by means of a minor premise 'this course of action avoids the greater evil', which is not itself demonstrable but is apprehended by a type of prudence (*intellectus* for Thomas, *nous* for Aristotle) which has been translated as 'understanding' or 'intuition'.[91]

To economists, it seems unscientific to claim that decisions to risk life or property can be right or wrong according to such a higher normative standard, or that people possess a moral capacity to apply this standard. For the economists, the magnitude of a cost or benefit is determined by

test that would balance the cost of taking a precaution against the level of risk. Weinrib, *supra*, note 9, at 428. *See* Perry, *Impossibility*, *supra*, note 59, at 170 (apparently favoring a level of risk test).

[90] The common law authority usually cited for the level of risk test is Lord Reid's opinion in Bolton v. Stone [1951] A.C. 850, cited by Weinrib, *supra*, note 8, at 518–19 and Perry, *Impossibility*, *supra*, note 59, at 170. The plaintiff, while standing near her house outside the cricket grounds, was hit on the head by a cricket ball. She claimed the grounds had been negligently constructed. Lord Reid did say that a person may not 'create a risk which is substantial', and that he would take no account of 'the difficulty of remedial measures': [1951] A.C. at 867. But the reason he would not take such measures into account, he said, was: 'If cricket cannot be played on a ground without creating a substantial risk, then it should not be played there at all': *id*. Possibly, all Lord Reid meant that was since one could avoid the danger in a seemingly costless way by playing cricket somewhere else, it was irrelevant that some other remedial measure, such as building a higher fence, was too expensive. That interpretation is consistent with his statement elsewhere in the opinion: 'In my judgment the test to be applied here is whether the risk of damage to a person on the road was so small that a reasonable man in the position of the appellants . . . would have thought it right to refrain from taking steps to prevent the danger': *id*. In any case, Lord Reid's speculations on when liability might be imposed if a risk were substantial had no bearing on the outcome of the case. The defendant was held not to be liable, according to Lord Reid, because the risk was not substantial.

[91] *See* ARISTOTLE, NICOMACHEAN ETHICS, *supra*, note 2, at IV.xi; AQUINAS, SUMMA THEOLOGIAE, *supra*, note 12, at II–II, Q. 49, c. 2.

individual preferences or by individual preferences backed by cash. To the extent that the economists reach normative conclusions about what the law should be, however, it is not clear why this approach is supposed to be more scientific. Indeed, it is not clear that this approach is morally or logically defensible.

Once, economists spoke like utilitarians about individual preferences, although not always consistently.[92] Preferences were psychological experiences of satisfaction or dissatisfaction. Modern economists now regard this approach as unscientific, and, in any case, it would lead to some strange conclusions. In Dickens' *Tale of Two Cities*, a rich man races a coach through a crowded street and runs down the child of a poor family. It would be odd to think that he may not have been negligent if his satisfaction is great because he really enjoys racing coaches, or if he is sadistic and enjoys running down children, and the child's loss of satisfaction is small because he is unlikely to be happy growing up in squalor.

The contemporary approach is to deny that one can compare the strength of individual preferences and to speak only about how an individual allocates whatever resources he has in accordance with his own preferences.[93] Thus Richard Posner asks what course of action would maximize 'wealth' which 'is the value in dollars or dollar equivalents . . . of everything in society. It is measured by what people are willing to pay for something or, if they already own it, what they demand in money to give it up.'[94] According to Posner, if one person walks fast and smashes another's oranges, the court would have to make a judgment as to how much the oranges were worth to the plaintiff and how much walking fast was worth to the defendant.[95] Presumably, in the case we were just considering, the court would have to compare the value the child puts on life (or the risk of it) with the value the rich man puts on racing the coach. But what does this mean?

To begin with, we are dealing with a child. In an Aristotelian world, in which prudence is a virtue that develops with time and experience, we can say that the child is too young to place a proper value on his life. On Posner's principles, however, it is hard to see why we should not treat the child like any other individual with his own individual preferences and a rather limited income. If the child would risk his life for a gumdrop, so be it.

---

[92] *See* Robert Cooter & Peter Rappoport, *Were the Ordinalists Wrong about Welfare Economics?*, 22 J. Econ. Lit. 507 (1984).

[93] For a challenge to this approach based on Aristotelian principles, see Robert Cooter & James Gordley, *The Cultural Justification of Unearned Income: An Economic Model of Merit Goods Based on Aristotelian Ideas of Akrasia and Distributive Justice, in* Profits and Morality (Robin Cowan & Mario Rizzo (eds.), 150).

[94] Richard A. Posner, *Utilitarianism, Economics, and Legal Theory*, 8 J. Legal Stud. 103, 119 (1979).

[95] *Id.* at 120.

Next, even if we were dealing with a poor person of mature years rather than a child, we still would need to know whether his life is to be valued in cash by the amount he would accept if the rich man had to pay him for endangering it, or by the amount he would offer the rich man for not doing so. Even in the first case, the result is unappealing. Whether the rich man is liable depends on whether his victim was so desperately poor as to have accepted little, and whether he is so rich, so enamored of racing, so indifferent to human life, or so genuinely sadistic, as to have paid much. Moreover, since the rich man is not liable unless he is negligent, he owes the poor person nothing as long as he would have paid an amount acceptable to the poor person even though the poor person was never offered and will never receive such an amount. Most of us deplore the terrible risks that many industrial workers once ran in return for a slight increase of their wages because of their extreme poverty. On Posner's principles, any sufficiently poor person could be exposed to the risks created by any sufficiently rich and indifferent or sadistic person for no compensation at all.

Matters are even less appealing if the life of the poor person is supposed to be valued by the amount that he would pay the rich man for not endangering him. All his wealth might be insufficient to buy protection from a risk so great that, despite his poverty, he would not choose to run it for a huge sum.

On Posner's principles, then, we do not know if the rich man is negligent until we know whether, so to speak, we should regard the racing of horses as belonging to the rich man unless the poor person can purchase it, or the freedom from risk as belonging to the poor person unless the rich man can purchase it. Posner does have a theory of how rights should initially be allocated but not one that provides a happy solution. He says that his wealth maximization principle 'ordains the creation of a system of exclusive rights' that ideally includes 'the human body and even ideas'. If transactions costs are zero, the economist is indifferent to where these rights are vested.[96] The right to the poor man's body might equally be assigned to the poor man as to the rich man. If transaction costs are positive, however, rights should be vested initially 'in those who are likely to value them most'. This, according to Posner, is the reason for giving 'a worker the right to sell his labor and a woman the right to determine her sexual partners'. Were these rights initially given to others, those who valued them most would repurchase them, and that would be a transactions cost.[97]

Even this honest but shocking fidelity to a bizarre principle does not lead to a coherent result. Whether the poor person should have the right to bodily protection against fast coach driving depends upon who would pay

---

[96] *Id.* at 125.   [97] *Id.*

more, the poor or the rich person. But in the situation we have just described, if the right were initially allocated to the poor person, he would not sell it at a price the rich driver would be willing to pay; if it were initially allocated to the rich man, the poor person would have too little money to buy it back.

Indeed, Posner's principles not only fail to explain the law of negligence but the law of intentional torts. Imagine a world in which the rights of the vast majority to sell their labor, to determine their sexual partners, and to be free from intentionally inflicted harm to their persons, together with all property rights, have been allocated to a small minority. There would be no transaction costs, because the majority would have nothing it could offer to repurchase any of these rights. Thus, on Posner's principles, even the recognition of intentional torts is not necessary to maximize wealth. It is result of a supposedly arbitrary decision as to how rights are initially distributed.

These difficulties have been raised by putting hypothetical cases in which there is an aberrational distribution of wealth or an aberrational decision maker such a child or a sadistic or indifferent rich person. The economists' principles do not lead to such absurd results as long as one can assume that the preferences of individuals are formed with prudence and that the cash that backs them is justly distributed. But that, of course, proves just the point that an Aristotelian would want to make. Their principles reach acceptable results only in so far as a society actually practices the virtues the economists reject in theory.

There is another difference between the Aristotelian account of negligence and that of modern economists. For the economists, the point of negligence law is not to compensate a person for a wrong done him in the past, but to provide the proper incentives for people to take the efficient level of precautions in the future. Tort damages function like prices in a market.

In practice, however, negligence law does not work like a market. People often act negligently even when they know that they will have to pay fully for any harm they may cause. The explanation for an Aristotelian is that prudence is a virtue we all do not perfectly possess. For an economist, however, the efficient action is supposed to follow once the incentives are right.

Moreover, in many ways, negligence law does not look like a system for providing the right incentives. Often, the damages the defendant expects to pay do not correspond to the loss the plaintiff will suffer if an accident occurs. If the plaintiff dies, the amount his family recovers in a wrongful death action is much less than the loss the plaintiff himself suffered. If the plaintiff is disabled, disfigured, or suffers great pain, the jury will be told to award damages that will compensate him as far as money will do so, but no sum of money really can.[98] An uninsured defendant can never be made to pay an amount greater than the value of his assets. And to the extent the defendant is insured, he will not have to pay the plaintiff's damages.[99] The disadvantage he will suffer when his insurance rates rise or he cannot obtain insurance is likely to be far smaller than the amount supposedly necessary to give him the right incentives. Negligence law often does not provide the right incentives but, nearly always, it does require the defendant to compensate the plaintiff if he can.

Again, if the economists are right, negligence law is addressed to what may be a fairly small fraction of the population. It can only influence the behavior of people who are sufficiently astute to act rightly when given the proper incentives, sufficiently self-serving to need these incentives to act rightly, and not sufficiently astute and self-serving to find some dishonest means of evading liability if an accident occurs. One would like to know how many such people there are. Forty years ago, when law professors were enthusiastically supporting accident insurance and no-fault compensation proposals, it seemed utterly naïve to think such programs would increase the number of accidents. Now, an entire theory of negligence law is founded on the opposite assumption about why people take precautions. Yet no one is suggesting that we do away with the institution of insurance. The Aristotelian account, in contrast, makes no such behavioral assumptions. It merely claims that if a person acted imprudently then he should be liable for precisely that reason.

V. STRICT LIABILITY

Although the Aristotelian tradition assimilated the Roman law of negligence, it never adequately explained strict liability. As we have seen, its principles were incompatible with a theory of strict liability based on mere causation. Nevertheless, one can see hints in contemporary and in earlier literature about how an Aristotelian explanation might be developed.

One of the concerns that led Epstein to his theory of strict liability sounds remarkably Aristotelian. He argued that the defendant should not be able to justify the loss imposed on the plaintiff by gains to himself.[100] Indeed, Kathryn Heidt has noted that, logically, Aristotle's theory ought to support liability for activities like disposing of toxic waste because they

---

[98] *See* Steven D. Smith, *The Critics and the 'Crisis': A Reassessment of Current Conceptions of Tort Law*, 72 CORNELL L. REV. 765, 773 (1987) (noting that it is hard to value intangible injuries and that some claims go unlitigated).

[99] IZHAK ENGLARD, THE PHILOSOPHY OF TORT LAW (1993), 44.

[100] Richard A. Epstein, *Intentional Harms*, 4 J. LEGAL STUD. 391, 398 (1975); RICHARD A. EPSTEIN, TAKINGS: PRIVATE PROPERTY AND THE POWER OF EMINENT DOMAIN (1985), 40.

harm some people and produce a gain for others.[101] Frederick Sharp, in a student note, tried to develop a theory using Aristotle's definition of corrective justice. He seems to have rested it, in part, on notions of fault: the defendant is liable because he 'departed from the restrictive standard of conduct owing to one's neighbours' and so created a hazard 'disproportionate to the expectations of citizens'.[102] Nevertheless, on Aristotelian principles, it does seem that a person might be liable simply because he sought a gain for himself by imposing a risk of loss on another.

Occasionally, some of the early modern writers groped in this direction. One of the obstacles was the rather patchy pre-modern set of strict liability rules that they were trying to explain. The cases the Roman jurist Gaius classified as quasi-tort (*quasi delictus*) or tort without fault were for the most part of the kind American law treats with the doctrine of *res ipsa loquitur*. The defendant is likely to have been at fault though there is no direct evidence. For example, the plaintiff is struck by an object thrown from the defendant's window or hung by the defendant over the street, or he is robbed while staying in the defendant's inn.[103]

There were also cases in Roman law in which the defendant would be liable if he failed to exercise an extreme diligence that went beyond what an ordinary person would observe.[104] The defendant might also be liable without fault for damage done by his animal or through the fault of his slave, although he had the option of surrendering the animal or slave to the plaintiff rather than paying damages.[105] This was not the most promising set of rules to explain by a general theory of strict liability. But there were attempts.

In the sixteenth century, Molina struggled with the rule that sometimes one could be liable for failing to exercise the most extreme diligence. Nearly all of his contemporaries said that the rule could not be explained in principle or by natural law. Molina said that one was liable in principle if the activity was so dangerous that one should not undertake it except with the intention of paying for any harm that occurred.[106]

In the next century, Pufendorf found a reason why as a matter of natural law one might be liable for the acts of an animal: 'the owner gets the profit from his animal while [the victim] suffered loss from it.'[107] The French jurist Domat repeated this explanation, though he seemed to rest

---

[101] Kathryn R. Heidt, *Corrective Justice from Aristotle to Second Order Liability: Who Should Pay When the Culpable Cannot?*, 47 WASH. & LEE L. REV. 347, 360–3 (1990).

[102] Frederick L. Sharp, Note, *Aristotle, Justice and Enterprise Liability in the Law of Torts*, 34 U. TORONTO FAC. L. REV. 84, 90 (1976).

[103] G. INST. 4.5.

[104] The phrase *culpa levissima* in DIG. 9.2.44 was interpreted to require the extreme diligence of DIG. 13.6.18 pr. and DIG. 44.7.1.4. *See* ZIMMERMANN, *supra*, note 53, at 192–3, 1027–9.

[105] DIG. 9.1; 9.4.   [106] MOLINA, *supra*, note 20, disp. 698 no. 3.

[107] PUFENDORF, *supra*, note 20, III.i.6.

liability on fault in letting the animal escape.[108] These explanations are not well thought out, but they emphasize that the defendant creates a risk through an activity from which he profits.

I believe they point in the right direction. They point toward a theory of strict liability founded on the principle that the defendant should be liable if, in order to obtain a gain for himself, he exposed the plaintiff to an especially high risk of loss. We can see the justification for such a theory if we return to the reason given earlier why a society interested in preserving a given distribution of resources would not compensate everyone for accidental losses. If it did so, people who invested in particularly vulnerable forms of property or exposed themselves or their property to especially high risks would be using up more than their share of resources. By similar reasoning, those who profit by exposing others to especially high risks will be using up more than their own share if they are not held liable.

Thus, in a sense, Epstein was right when he objected to negligence law because the defendant should not be able to justify the loss the plaintiff suffers by the gain he himself hopes to receive. As Perry has pointed out, the difficulty with Epstein's argument is that whenever an accident occurs, both parties were pursuing an activity from which they expected to benefit, and the risk of an accident was due to both of these activities.[109] One might equally well say that the plaintiff, for his own benefit, created the risk. This difficulty vanishes, however, when the defendant exposes the plaintiff to an abnormally high risk of loss. If he can justify this extra risk by pointing to his own gain, he will have achieved this gain at the plaintiff's expense. On Aristotelian principles, he should not be allowed to do so.

The case is clearest when the defendant's activity in no way benefits the plaintiff. For example, the defendant flies a glider for fun, knowing that when the wind fails he will have to land on a farmer's field, destroying his crops. The plaintiff should recover, however, even if he benefits from the defendant's activity, provided that the expected value of the harm he suffers is not perfectly correlated with the degree to which he benefits. Suppose a train occasionally throws sparks that consume the crops of nearby farmers who all use the railroad. If the railroad does not pay, the railroad will gain and the injured farmers will lose. Even if we imagine that the railroad will pass on some of this gain to the farmers through decreased fares, the farmers who ship more crops or are less exposed to sparks will still gain at the expense of those who ship less or are more exposed. The losses due to the extra risks created by the railroad will not be born by those who benefit from its presence in proportion to their benefit but by those who happen to be in the way of the sparks.

---

[108] J. DOMAT, LES LOIX CIVILES DANS LEUR ORDRE NATUREL (1713), liv. 2, tit. 8.
[109] Perry, *supra*, note 9, at 463–5. Perry, *Impossibility*, *supra*, note 59, at 169.

The train and the sparks are often used to illustrate the thesis Ronald Coase advanced in a famous article.[110] He argued that one cannot say that the farmer's loss was caused by the presence of the train any more than the presence of the crops. He then showed that from the standpoint of efficiency, if transactions costs are zero, it does not matter whether liability is placed on the railroad or the farmers. In the former case, the railroad would be willing to take any precaution that cost less than the expected value of the harm it would prevent; and in the latter case, the farmers would be willing to pay the railroad to do so.

Scholars such as Guido Calabresi have reassured us about the implications of Coase's argument by pointing out that transactions costs usually are not zero and that the railroad may be best able to determine if a given precaution is efficient or not.[111] But most people do not feel the railroad should pay because they are worried about optimizing investments in farming and transportation. They feel that otherwise an injustice will be done to the farmer. It is hard to believe Calabresi would want the railroad to escape tort liability even if it were not the best cost avoider. The Aristotelian theory identifies a reason why it is not merely efficient but just that the railroad should pay: it gained through the farmer's loss.

A theory of strict liability based on these considerations would look much like George Fletcher's theory of liability for non-reciprocal risk. According to Fletcher, 'a victim has a right to recover for injuries caused by a risk greater in degree and different in order from those created by the victim.'[112]

Unlike Fletcher's theory, the Aristotelian account would only explain strict liability in terms of non-reciprocal risk. Fletcher tries to explain intentional and negligent torts as well. The difficulty is that the defendant is liable for acting intentionally or negligently even if the risk his act creates is not 'greater in degree' than the risk created by acts that are not actionable. The defendant is liable if he shoots intending to kill even if, as at the end of Faulkner's *Snopes Trilogy*, his weapon was so defective that there was little chance of success. He is liable for negligence if he creates even a slight risk provided that the offsetting benefit of his action is even more slight. Nor can Fletcher say these risks are of a different 'order' from non-actionable risks unless he explains what is different about them and why the difference should matter from the standpoint of his theory.

Moreover, the theoretical basis for strict liability would be more clear and more solid in an Aristotelian account. This account, like Fletcher's

[110] R.H. Coase, *The Problem of Social Cost*, 3 J.L. & Econ. 1 (1960).

[111] Guido Calabresi, The Cost of Accidents (1970), 135–403; Guido Calabresi, *Transactions Costs, Resource Allocation and Liability Rules, A Comment*, 11 J.L. & Econ. 67, 71–3 (1968).

[112] George P. Fletcher, *Fairness and Utility in Tort Theory*, 85 Harv. L. Rev. 537, 542 (1972).

theory, would hold the defendant liable if he chose to engage in an activity knowing it creates an abnormally high risk of harming the plaintiff. The Aristotelian account, however, can explain why the defendant is not liable unless he knew of the risk and chose to go ahead. As discussed earlier, on Aristotelian principles one cannot attribute an action to a person unless he acted voluntarily. Fletcher claims that in his own theory the 'Aristotelian . . . categories' of compulsion and unavoidable ignorance should count as excuses.[113] But he does not explain why.

Again, the Aristotelian account can explain why the defendant is liable when the risk is abnormally high. He has gained at the plaintiff's expense. Fletcher does not base his theory on corrective justice. He rests it on the principle that 'all individuals in society have the right to roughly the same degree of security from risk'.[114] As Coleman correctly observes, on that principle everyone should have the right to compensation if he is harmed, not simply if he is hurt by a non-reciprocal risk.[115]

Another difference concerns what is meant by a risk that is 'different in order'. In the Aristotelian account, in principle, liability should be imposed on a defendant who, in pursuit of his own ends, subjected the plaintiff to an especially high risk—in Fletcher's terminology, a risk that is 'greater in degree'. To say the risk must be 'different in order', however, is simply to identify one way that courts may apply the principle pragmatically and heuristically. Human activities are so different and the risks they create so various that there is no bright line between ordinary and extraordinary risks. The law will have to make do with rough categories that work best in the generality of cases. For example, the law can impose liability on those who engage in an activity that is both less common and more risky than other activities. Roughly speaking, that is the sort of activity that is captured by Fletcher's phrase 'different in order'. In the Aristotelian account, it represents one possible and pragmatic way to apply the principle that defendant should be liable for creating an abnormally high risk.

Despite these differences, the Aristotelian account, like Fletcher's, imposes liability for non-reciprocal risk. Therefore, like Fletcher's, it can explain why modern legal systems commonly impose liability for carrying on an activity that is less typical and more dangerous than most. American courts have imposed liability for conducting an 'abnormally dangerous activity'.[116] Examples are harm caused by blasting, storing explosives, transporting large quantities of gas, and ground damage caused by aircraft. German courts have not recognized a general principle and will hold the

---

[113] *Id.* at 552.   [114] *Id.* at 550.

[115] COLEMAN, RISKS, *supra*, note 7, at 266; Coleman, *Moral Theories I, supra*, note 68, at 389; COLEMAN, MARKETS, *supra*, note 7, at 194. *Id.* at 550.

[116] RESTATEMENT (SECOND) OF TORTS, § 519 (1976); PROSSER & KEETON, *supra*, note 74, at 545–59.

defendant strictly liable only in cases recognized by specially enacted statutes. Nevertheless, the cases in which special statutes have imposed strict liability are generally those in which activities are both less typical and more risky. Examples are the operation of railroads, cars, aircraft, and electric and gas installations.[117] In Italian law, the burden of proof of negligence is reversed when the defendant has engaged in an abnormally dangerous activity.[118] Although in theory the defendant can exonerate himself, the courts have made it so difficult to do so that in practice it amounts to a kind of strict liability.[119]

An Aristotelian account of strict liability explains not only why strict liability should be imposed when activities are less common and more dangerous, but also two exceptions recognized by American courts. First, the defendant is not liable if the plaintiff's activity is abnormally sensitive.[120] For example, a defendant was not held liable for blasting when the noise alarmed the plaintiff's mink, and the mink then killed each other.[121] From an Aristotelian perspective, this exception makes perfect sense. The damage was as much due to the plaintiff's decision to pursue an activity that was abnormally sensitive as to the defendant's to pursue one that was abnormally dangerous.

Secondly, often strict liability has not been imposed when the plaintiff himself was a participant in the activity. For example, although an airline is strictly liable for ground damage when planes crash, it is not strictly liable for damage to the passengers when they collide in the air.[122] Although the owners of wild animals are usually held strictly liable, a zoo has been held liable only on proof of negligence when a visitor was bitten by a zebra,[123] and national parks have been held not liable when visitors were attacked by bears.[124] Again, the exception makes good Aristotelian sense. In these cases one can no longer say that the defendant in order to obtain a benefit of his own has imposed a risk on the plaintiff. The plaintiff and the defendant to procure a joint benefit are engaged in the activity that creates the risk. Moreover, it is an activity from which the plaintiff benefits in rough proportion to his degree of exposure to the risk. If one person flies or

---

[117] *See* ZWEIGERT & KÖTZ, *supra,* note 74, at 693–9.   [118] CODICE CIVILE, § 2050.

[119] Patrizia Ziviz in COMMENTARIO, *supra,* note 25, at § 2050, no. 1; 3 GERI, BRECCIA, BUSNELLI & NATIOLI, *supra,* note 75, at 757–9. French law is different. The French courts have imposed strict liability under Code civil, § 1384, for harm caused by objects that one has in one's custody. They have not tried to differentiate between more dangerous activities or objects and less dangerous ones. *See* ZWEIGERT & KÖTZ, *supra,* note 74, at 701.

[120] RESTATEMENT (SECOND) OF TORTS, § 524A (1976).

[121] Madsen v. East Jordan Irrigation Co., 125 P.2d 794 (Utah 1942).

[122] RESTATEMENT (SECOND) OF TORTS, § 520A (1976).

[123] City & County of Denver v. Kennedy, 476 P.2d 762 (Colo. Ct. App. 1970) (though the court explained the result by the desirability of having zoos).

[124] Rubenstein v. United States, 338 F. Supp. 654 (N.D. Cal. 1972), *aff'd,* 488 F.2d 1071 (9th Cir. 1973) (though the court explained the result by assumption of the risk).

visits a zoo or national park five times as much as another, he is roughly five times as likely to crash, to be bitten by a zebra, or to be attacked by a bear.

I hope to show in a future article that this Aristotelian account can explain other instances of strict liability as well. Liability for abnormally dangerous activities is only one pragmatic application of the larger principle that no one should gain at another's expense. Here I merely wish to show that the failure of writers in the Aristotelian tradition to explain strict liability was not due to an inherent weakness in the tradition.

VI. CONCLUSION

The Aristotelian tradition in tort law would have been impressive had it been merely a series of insights into problems so important that they are still with us. I have tried to show, however, that the insights follow from a few principles at the core of Aristotelian ethics.

At the core was the idea that human beings have an end, a manner of life in which their human potentialities are realized. As a rational animal, a person realizes this distinctively human life by understanding what an action will contribute to it, and choosing on the basis of what he understands. As a social animal, he realizes this life in co-operation with others. The object of politics is a society in which each person 'whoever he is, can act best and live happily'.

This higher concept of human welfare explains the need for distributive and corrective justice. For each person to live as he should, society must distribute resources fairly. Having done so, it must maintain the distribution. This account of justice is functional or teleological rather than purely formal. Consequently, it can explain why, when a person is in great need, the normal rules of corrective justice do not apply, and he can justly take what he needs from another person.

Because corrective justice preserves the distribution of wealth, a person who gains at another's expense must compensate the loser. In the Aristotelian account, this principle underlies the law of property, unjust enrichment, and tort. One who has another's property must give it back. One who has profited from using another's property must return the profit. One who has voluntarily harmed another, even if he has acquired nothing, has gained in the sense that he has pursued his own objectives at another's expense. He must pay for any loss he has caused.

This account of tort law links the plaintiff's right to compensation to the defendant's duty to compensate. The defendant must pay because he chose to use up plaintiff's resources for his own ends. Without that link, it would be hard to see why tort law allows the plaintiff to recover from the defendant. There would be a victim who deserves compensation and a wrongdoer who deserves punishment but nothing to explain why one should recover his loss from the other.

This account links voluntary action to causation. Because a human being is a rational animal, he only causes those results *qua* human being that he understands and chooses. Applied to tort law, this principle avoids all the blind alleys into which one can stumble by trying to impose liability for harm caused without awareness or choice.

This account explains why one can harm another voluntarily by acting negligently as well as intentionally. Negligence is a choice to imperil others beyond the extent warranted by the value of an action. In this account, as in those of modern economists, liability is imposed on a person who does not weigh risks, gains, and losses as he should. In this account, however, gains and losses are judged by a prudent appraisal of their effect on human welfare. It avoids the nightmares that come when gains and losses are merely preferences backed by cash.

The same principles, I argued, can explain strict liability. The defendant should pay if he chooses to use up plaintiff's resources for his own ends. He chooses to do so if he subjects the plaintiff to an abnormally high risk to get some benefit for himself.

Aristotle's distinction between involuntary and voluntary commutative justice may be the lineal ancestor of our own distinction between tort and contract. Our distinction derives ultimately from Gaius.[125] He was the first Roman jurist to speak generally of contract and tort rather than of what we would call particular contracts and torts. Modern scholars believe that he was following Aristotle.[126] The distinction has enduring value. If I am right, so do the principles that inspired it.

---

[125] G. INST. 3.88.

[126] ZIMMERMANN, *supra*, note 53, at 10–11; MAX KASER, DAS RÖMISCHE PRIVATRECHT (2d edn., 1971) 522; ANTHONY HONORÉ, GAIUS 100 (1962); Helmut Coing, *Zum Einfluß der Philosophie des Aristoteles auf die Entwicklung des römischen Rechts*, 69 ZEITSCHRIFT DER SAVIGNY-STIFTUNG FÜR RECHTSGESCHICHTE, ROM. ABT. 24, 37–8 (1952).

Right, Justice and Tort Law

RICHARD W. WRIGHT*

I. Explaining and Justifying Tort Liability: Giving Compensation and Deterrence a Normative Foundation

It often is said that the goals of tort law are compensation for and deterrence of loss. Without further elaboration this statement is not only unhelpful, but also misleading and inaccurate, since compensation and deterrence of all losses is normatively insupportable, descriptively implausible, and analytically impossible. There is no plausible moral argument for requiring others to compensate every person for every loss no matter how it occurred, and neither tort law nor law in general makes any attempt to achieve such universal compensation. Indeed, universal compensation of all losses, so that no one suffers any loss, is analytically impossible, since losses (like energy-matter) do not disappear, but rather are shifted (usually in transmuted form) to others, who then themselves bear uncompensated losses. Similarly, neither tort law nor law in general does or should seek to deter or prevent every loss or all risky conduct. Prevention of all risk of loss, at least in our world, is impossible. Even if everyone were to forbear all action, there would remain the risks of loss due to such inaction—e.g., death due to starvation[1] and thirst or the non-avoidance of naturally occurring risks.

The question, then, is what types of losses should be compensated and what types of risky conduct should be deterred. To answer this question, we must know the normative ground of compensation and deterrence in tort law, which in turn requires that we know the normative ground of law in general.

Many theorists assume that no single normative ground can explain or justify tort law or law in general. They argue that, especially given the complexity of modern societies and legal regimes, a plurality of competing norms (e.g., loss spreading, efficient deterrence, retribution, corrective justice, distributive justice, autonomy, and community) must be invoked to

* Professor of Law and Norman & Edna Freehling Scholar, Chicago-Kent College of Law, Illinois Institute of Technology; Visiting Fellow, Brasenose College, University of Oxford. This essay is based in part on Richard W. Wright, *Substantive Corrective Justice*, 77 Iowa L. Rev. 625 (1992), and is itself part of a larger work in progress.

[1] 'One must drive (or walk) to the store to buy one's bread'; David G. Owen, *Philosophical Foundations of Fault in Tort Law*, this volume, at 208.

explain or justify the law in general, or any particular area of law such as tort law.[2] I agree with Ernest Weinrib that any truly pluralistic theory will fail to explain or justify law in general or particular since it will necessarily be radically incoherent and indeterminate. A pluralistic (as opposed to a nihilistic) normative theory will not be completely arbitrary or lack any normative force—indeed, it suffers from a surfeit of reasons and norms. Nevertheless, when in a particular situation two or more of the pluralistic norms conflict—which usually will be the case—the theory will be normatively, descriptively and analytically arbitrary and indeterminate in terms of specifying which competing norm(s) should predominate, unless there is some foundational norm that can resolve conflicts between the competing subnorms. Yet if such a foundational norm exists, the theory at its deepest level is monistic rather than pluralistic. This is not to say that any single norm, no matter how fundamental, can explain and justify *every* aspect of the law in general, or any particular area of law. Humans are ignorant, fallible, diverse, sometimes selfish, and otherwise not always morally motivated. But a successful normative and descriptive theory of law should at least be able coherently to explain and justify the principal features of the existing law. Only a monistic foundational theory holds out any prospect of being able to do so.

The two principal monistic theories of law are (1) utilitarian efficiency theory, based on the foundational norm of maximizing aggregate social welfare, which asserts that the purpose of tort law is and should be *efficient* compensation and deterrence, and (2) the Kantian-Aristotelian theory of Right or justice, based on the foundational norm of equal individual freedom, which asserts that the purpose of tort law is and should be *just* compensation and deterrence. I believe it is clear that the equal freedom theory, rather than the utilitarian efficiency theory, provides the foundation for morality and law in general and for tort law in particular. In this essay, I elaborate the equal freedom theory underlying the concepts of Right and justice, and I argue that this theory and its constituent concept of corrective justice undergird the general structure, content, and institutions of tort law. In a companion essay, I expand and deepen the argument by shifting from the global perspective to a detailed normative and descriptive analysis of one of the central issues in tort law: the standards of care in negligence law.[3]

---

[2] For example, see the essay by Izhak Englard, *The Idea of Complementarity as a Philosophical Basis for Pluralism in Tort Law*, this volume.—Ed.

[3] *See* Richard W. Wright, *The Standards of Care in Negligence Law*, this volume.

II. The Foundational Moral Theories: (Utilitarian) Aggregate Social Welfare Versus (Kantian) Equal Individual Freedom

There are two principal types of moral theories. The first 'corporate welfare' type identifies the good with the corporate or aggregate welfare of the community or society as a whole, while the second 'equal individual freedom' type identifies the good with the equal freedom of each individual in the community or society.

The most prominent of the modern corporate welfare theories is utilitarianism, which generally is recast in the legal literature as the Kaldor-Hicks version of economic efficiency. The utilitarian efficiency theory combines a methodological individualism with a corporate substantive definition of the good. The methodological locus of value is the individual, but the good is not defined in individual terms but rather, under the foundational principle of utility or greatest happiness, as the maximization of the aggregate sum of individual welfare for the society as a whole. Each individual counts equally methodologically only, as an equal and fungible addend in the summation of aggregate social welfare. There is no independent concern about the distribution of resources or welfare. Any individual's welfare can and should be sacrificed whenever doing so would produce a greater total sum of aggregate welfare. Each individual is morally required to treat others' interests on a par with one's own. It is not permissible to prefer one's own interests or projects, or those of one's family members or friends, over those of any other person.[4]

Utilitarianism is in direct conflict with the strong and pervasive moral sense that people have of autonomy and rights, the sense that one generally should be able to prefer the interests of oneself and one's family and friends in the use of one's own resources and should not be subjected to having one's projects, resources, and welfare sacrificed merely because doing so will produce a greater aggregate welfare for others. Utilitarians have attempted to reconcile utilitarianism with the moral sense of autonomy and rights. They invoke a rule-utilitarian argument that the net benefits of any particular intrusion on autonomy or rights considered in isolation, taking into account the welfare only of the parties directly affected, would be outweighed by the widespread social insecurity and anxiety that would result if such intrusions were generally permitted.[5] However, this argument gives the principles of autonomy and right a contingent and derivative status which fails to convey their true sense or force. Moreover, under this argument, the so-called

---

[4] *See* Jeremy Bentham, An Introduction to the Principles of Morals and Legislation (rev. edn., 1823), ch. 1, §§ 1–9, ch. 4, §§ 4–6, ch. 13, § 1; John Stuart Mill, Utilitarianism (Oskar Piest ed., 1957) (1861), ch. 2 at 22–3, ch. 5 at 76.

[5] *See* Mill, *supra,* note 4, ch. 5, at 66–7, 73–9; John Austin, The Province of Jurisprudence Determined (1832) lect. 2.

'autonomy' and 'rights' of individuals still may be sacrificed if the total benefits exceed the total disutility.[6]

Moral theories based on equal individual freedom give an absolute and primary status, rather than a contingent and derivative status, to the autonomy and rights of individuals. The best known and developed of these theories is Kant's moral philosophy. The foundation of Kant's moral philosophy is the idea of free will or freedom. The idea of freedom does not imply completely unrestricted self-determination, but rather self-legislation: self-determination in accordance with universal law. Moral behavior consists in overcoming, through subjecting the maxim of one's actions to the condition of qualifying as universal law, inclinations that are in opposition to the dictates of the moral law.[7]

Freedom, and the moral personality constituted by its possession, is an inherent, internal, defining characteristic of each rational being. The possession of free will or freedom is what gives each rational being moral worth—an absolute moral worth that is equal for all rational beings:

[M]an regarded as a *person* [rather than a mere animal], that is, as the subject of a morally practical reason, is exalted above any price; for as a person (*homo noumenon*) he is not to be valued merely as a means to the ends of others or even to his own ends, but as an end in himself, that is, he possesses a *dignity* (an absolute inner worth) by which he exacts *respect* for himself from all other rational beings in the world. He can measure himself with every other being of this kind and value himself on a footing of equality with them.[8]

The supreme principle of morality (the categorical imperative) is '[a]ct only according to that maxim by which you can at the same time will that it should become a universal law', which can be reformulated as '[a]ct so that you treat humanity, whether in your own person or in that of another, always as an end and never as a means only.'[9] The categorical imperative bears some affinity to the Golden Rule, '[d]o unto others as you would have them do unto you', which in its various forms appears as a fundamental principle in many religions and moral theories. However, as Kant noted, the categorical imperative is both broader in scope and more demanding than the Golden Rule. It is morally wrong under the categorical imperative to fail to respect the absolute moral worth of anyone, including yourself, as a self-legislating rational being, regardless of whether you would allow

---

[6] For example, if the intrusions on autonomy and rights (e.g., slavery) are limited to an easily identifiable minority (e.g., blacks), so that the majority need not worry about possibly being subjected to such treatment.

[7] *See* IMMANUEL KANT, THE METAPHYSICS OF MORALS (Mary Gregor trans., 1991) (1797) *213–14, 221–3, 225–7, 379–80 & n.*, 383, 394, 397, 405.

[8] *Id.* at *434–5; see id.* at *223, 237–8.

[9] IMMANUEL KANT, FOUNDATIONS OF THE METAPHYSICS OF MORALS (Lewis W. Beck trans., 1959) (1785), *421, 429.

others to treat you without proper respect.[10] People should be treated as ends in themselves (i.e., as free and equal persons seeking to fully realize their humanity), rather than as mere means to be used to benefit others or society as a whole (as is allowed and indeed required under the utilitarian theory).

III. From Private Morality to Public Law: Kant's Doctrine of Right

In the elaboration of his moral philosophy, Kant distinguishes between a doctrine of Right and a doctrine of virtue. The doctrine of Right focuses on the external aspect of the exercise of freedom—the constraints on action required for the practical operation of freedom in the external world. The doctrine of virtue, on the other hand, focuses on the internal aspect of the exercise of freedom—one subjecting the maxim of one's actions to the condition of qualifying as universal law. The distinction between the external and internal aspects of the exercise of freedom explains the differences between the supreme principle of Right and the supreme principle of virtue, each of which is a corollary of the categorical imperative. The supreme principle of Right is 'so act externally that the free use of your choice can coexist with the freedom of everyone in accordance with a universal law', while the supreme principle of virtue is '[a]ct in accordance with a maxim of *ends* that it can be a universal law for everyone to have'.[11]

Many tort theorists (especially but not only the utilitarians) overlook Kant's distinction between the doctrine of Right and the doctrine of virtue and consequently grossly misunderstand and misstate the implications of Kant's moral philosophy for law in general and tort law in particular. To properly grasp these implications, it is necessary clearly to understand the distinctions between these two doctrines, and especially Kant's distinction between the objective nature of Right and the subjective nature of virtue (a distinction which underlies, e.g., negligence law's distinct standards of care for defendants and plaintiffs, respectively[12]).

The doctrine of Right is that part of Kant's moral philosophy that specifies which moral obligations are also legal obligations, enforceable through external coercion by others. Right consists of the authorization to obligate another through external coercion in accordance with a universal law of freedom. The concept of Right follows, Kant notes, from the idea of freedom:

---

[10] *See id.* at *430, n.14.
[11] Kant, *supra*, note 7, at *231, 395; *see id.* at *218–20, 379–80, 395–7, 406.
[12] *See* Wright, *supra*, note 3.

[I]f a certain use of freedom is itself a hindrance to freedom in accordance with universal laws (i.e., wrong), coercion that is opposed to this (as a *hindering of a hindrance to freedom*) is consistent with freedom in accordance with universal laws, that is, it is right.[13]

Right can only affect—and hence can only apply to—the external aspect of the exercise of freedom. The internal (ethical or virtuous) aspect of the exercise of freedom—one's subjecting the maxim of one's actions to the condition of qualifying as universal law—cannot be coerced by another.[14]

In the doctrine of Right, Kant is primarily concerned with justifying the move from private Right in the (notional) state of nature, which necessarily is limited to private and hence subjective enforcement, to public (juridical) Right in the civil society, which is objectively enforced by public civil authority. Kant begins by asserting one's ethical duty to assert one's moral worth in interactions with others by, among other things, resisting non-rightful coercion by those others ('protective justice'). Viewed not only as an ethical duty but also as a right, 'protective justice' encompasses what Kant identifies as the only innate Right that belongs originally to every person by virtue of his or her humanity—'*[f]reedom* (independence from being constrained by another's choice)'. Inherent in this innate Right is the authorization to use coercion against another to resist or prevent non-rightful aggression by that other against one's person or property. Yet this right exists only if one's protective conduct is 'intrinsically *right* in terms of its form'—that is, only if one has subjectively determined that one's use of coercion conforms with the principle of Right.[15]

The right of 'protective justice' is essential to the possibility of possession of external things. Through an argument by contradiction, Kant infers as a postulate of practical reason the right to acquire external things through first possession. In the state of nature, possession of external things is practically dependent on, and its extent is determined by, the would-be possessor's ability to control them by defending them against aggression by others. Yet the rightful possession thereby acquired is provisional rather than conclusive, since no person by unilateral action can conclusively bind others. Absent the universal consent of all, which can occur only in civil society, no one has any better right than any other person to acquire any

---

[13] Kant, *supra*, note 7, at *231.

[14] Although a person may be coerced into behaving externally so as to further or hinder some end, one cannot be coerced into adopting or rejecting that end as one's own: *see id.* at *219–20, 231–2, 239, 381.

[15] *See id.* at *231, 236–8, 253, 255–7, 305–6, 312. Kantian 'protective justice', which is the *ex ante*, preventive aspect of corrective justice, supplies the moral foundation for most of the self-help defenses to intentional tort actions as well as for the general availability of injunctive relief given the appropriate conditions of Right.

external thing, and the rightful limits of acquisition cannot be conclusively established.[16]

Once possession has been established, the obligation of 'commutative [corrective] justice' comes into play.[17] If a person's actions will affect the persons or property of others, those actions must conform to those others' rights—that is, they must be consistent in their external effects with the equal absolute moral worth of those others as free rational beings. Again, in the state of nature, the determination of whether one's actions conform to the principle of Right is necessarily internal and subjective.

It is the unilateral, subjective nature of private Right in the state of nature that grounds the duty to enter into civil society, in which the authorization to use coercion against others is transferred (with a few exigent exceptions such as self-defense) from each person to public institutions (public Right or 'distributive justice').[18] No matter how much good faith (virtuous respect for Right) a person displays in the state of nature in exercising his protective justice right, he will be unilaterally imposing his will on others, who may have different subjective concepts of Right, and thus his action will not fully conform with the principle of Right. In order for his use of coercion in the state of nature to be provisionally rightful, he must not only subjectively determine that his use of coercion conforms with the concept of Right, but also be willing to enter into the civil condition, where Right is objectively enforced through public civil authority. Moreover, he has the 'protective' (corrective) justice right to compel others with whom he might come into conflict to enter into the civil condition with him, if they are not willing to enter voluntarily.[19]

In sum, under the Kantian theory of morality and law, the provision of an objective mechanism for enforcing each person's Right to equal freedom is the primary (arguably sole) reason for the existence of the state. For Kant, the purpose of law and politics is no more or less than the guaranteeing of Right or justice, through public enforcement of the objective and coercively enforceable duty to act in a way that is consistent with the equal freedom of others.

---

[16] See id. at *246–7, 250–3, 256–7, 261–9.   [17] See id. at *236, 306.

[18] See id. at *306. Kant's elaboration of the doctrine of Right, like Aristotle's *Politics*, focuses on the political resources aspect of distributive justice: the creation and distribution of public offices and power. Yet he does not, as some assume, exclude or ignore the material resources aspect. He affirms the right of the people to tax the wealthy to provide for the needy, recognizes limits on original acquisition based on each person's Right to equal freedom, and notes that the duty of beneficence (an imperfect duty of virtue) usually comes into play because of the nonrightful creation of inequalities of wealth through excessive acquisitions by individuals or unjust distributions by government: see id. at *326, 454; IMMANUEL KANT, LECTURES ON ETHICS (Louis Infeld trans., 1930) (reprint of Methuen ed. 1979), 192–5.

[19] See KANT, *supra,* note 7, at *255–7, 264, 268, 307, 312.

IV. DISTINGUISHING THE TWO TYPES OF RIGHT: DISTRIBUTIVE
JUSTICE AND CORRECTIVE JUSTICE

Kant did not specifically discuss tort law or its civil law equivalent, the law
of delict. Nevertheless, as should already be clear, his doctrine of Right has
substantial and specific implications for tort liability. To further develop
those implications, it is necessary to explore in more detail the relationship
between Kantian Right and the two divisions of substantive justice (distributive and corrective) to which reference has already been made.
Corrective justice traditionally has been viewed as the ground and point of
tort law, but we will explore distributive as well as corrective justice, since
neither type of justice can be fully understood except in conjunction and
contrast with the other.

Kant considered Right and justice to be synonymous. He generally
referred to Right. We generally refer to justice rather than Right, yet with
the understanding that justice has to do with the recognition and enforcement of rights. The classic elaboration of the concept of justice appears in
book V of Aristotle's *Nicomachean Ethics*. Although Aristotle did not have
an explicit concept of 'Right' or 'rights' in the modern sense, his conception of the fundamental ground of and relationship between morality, on
the one hand, and law or justice, on the other, parallels in many respects
Kant's subsequent treatment of these issues.

Aristotle's conception of the good, like Kant's, is non-aggregative, egalitarian, and grounded in the equal absolute moral worth of each individual
as a free rational being. Aristotle emphatically rejects conceptions of the
good that are based on wealth, pleasure, or enjoyment, which are the values that are to be maximized in utilitarian efficiency theories. Instead, he
elaborates a conception of the good that is intrinsic to each individual: full
realization of one's humanity through activity in accord with a rational
principle and in accord with complete virtue over one's life. The goal of
politics is the attainment of this common good for each and every citizen
of the state, which Aristotle describes as a community of free and equal
individuals.[20] Law is the instrument by which the state achieves this common good by enforcing the requirements of justice: '[G]overnments which
have a regard to the common interest are constituted in accordance with
strict principles of justice.'[21]

Aristotle defines justice in its 'particular' sense (as distinguished from its
broader and now archaic sense of complete virtue in all our relations with
others) as the manifestation in our relations with others of the specific

---

[20] *See* Wright, *supra*, note *, at 683–5.
[21] ARISTOTLE, POLITICS III.6, at 1279a17–21 (B. Jowett trans.), in 2 THE COMPLETE WORKS
OF ARISTOTLE (Jonathan Barnes ed., 1984).

virtue of behaving equitably with respect to claims to resources, broadly conceived. He then distinguishes two distinct types of justice—corrective justice and distributive justice—which can be differentiated from one another by their respective domains of application, resources encompassed, criteria of equality, and persons covered.[22]

A corrective justice claim is grounded in an individual interaction. It encompasses the resources possessed by the parties to the interaction. The parties to the interaction are considered to be 'arithmetically' or absolutely equal regardless of their relative standing on any comparative criterion such as wealth, merit, or need. The persons potentially covered by the corrective justice claim are limited to the parties to the interaction. If one person adversely affects (or threatens) the person or resources of a second person through an interaction that is inconsistent with the absolute equality of the parties to the interaction, the second person has a bilateral corrective justice claim against the first person for rectification (or prevention) of that adverse effect.

A distributive justice claim, on the other hand, is independent of any individual interaction. It is based solely on a person's status as a member of the political community. It encompasses all the resources that exist in the community. The criterion of equality is that these resources must be distributed among the members of the community in proportion to their relative ranking under some criterion such as merit or need. The persons potentially covered by the distributive justice claim are all the members of the community.

Since justice is concerned with the attainment of the good, and Aristotle defines the common good as each free and equal citizen's full realization of his humanity through activity in accord with a rational principle and in accord with complete virtue over his life, the absolute equality of the parties in corrective justice must be conceived as an absolute moral equality based on equal freedom which prefigures Kant's foundational assumption of the 'absolute inner worth' of each person. Similarly, Aristotle's conceptions of justice and the good, reinforced by his rejection of wealth, pleasure, and enjoyment *per se* as components of the good, not only clearly preclude utilitarian efficiency conceptions of distributive justice but also point to the equal freedom of each person as the criterion of equality for distributive justice.

Aristotle declares that the most important function of the state is the 'power of deciding what is for the public interest [distributive justice], and what is just in men's dealings with one another [corrective justice]'.[23]

---

[22] *See* ARISTOTLE, NICOMACHEAN ETHICS V.1–V.4 (W.D. Ross & J.O. Urmson trans.), in 2 THE COMPLETE WORKS OF ARISTOTLE (Jonathan Barnes ed., 1984) [hereinafter ETHICS]; Wright, *supra*, note *, at 688–702.

[23] ARISTOTLE, POLITICS, *supra*, note 21, VII.8 at 1328b13–14.

Distributive justice deals with the public or communal resource-allocation issues. Its aim is a distribution of the community's resources that implements each person's right to equal freedom by giving him an equal opportunity fully to realize his humanity as a self-legislating moral being. Corrective justice, on the other hand, deals with private interactions, and it requires that those engaged in such interactions do so in a way that is consistent with the right to equal freedom of the parties to the interaction, which is reflected in the parties' presumptive equality of entitlement to their existing stocks of resources.[24]

To put it another way, distributive justice and corrective justice encompass the two different aspects of external freedom: distributive justice defines the scope of a person's positive freedom to have access to the resources necessary to realize her humanity, and corrective justice defines the scope of a person's negative freedom not to have her person or existing stock of resources interfered with by others. Together, distributive justice and corrective justice seek to assure the attainment of the good by each person by providing her with a proportionately equal share of the needed resources (distributive justice) and by safeguarding her person and existing stock of resources from actions by others that are inconsistent with the interacting parties' absolute equality (corrective justice).

The fundamental criterion of equality for both distributive justice and corrective justice is the equal freedom of each person. Distributive justice and corrective justice are aimed at the attainment of different aspects of this equal freedom—the positive and negative aspects, respectively—and thus invoke distinct criteria of proportional and absolute equality as elaborations of the fundamental criterion. Aristotle states that alleged gains and losses or excesses and deficiencies in holdings are neither correctively nor distributively unjust, respectively, even if they are deliberately caused, unless they violate one of these two criteria.[25]

For a holding—even if deliberately caused—to be unjust as a matter of distributive justice, it must vary from the person's proportionate share under the distributive criterion of equal positive freedom. Conversely, a person who (without her consent) has less than her proportionate share of holdings or goods has a distributive justice right to that share, whether or not anyone has intentionally, mistakenly, or otherwise caused her to have

---

[24] The presumptive equality of entitlement does not assume an absolute entitlement, which would be invaded by any adverse effect. Rather, it assumes that each person has an equal right to have his existing stock of resources secured against actions by others that would be objectively inconsistent with the equal freedom of all: *see infra*, notes 25 & 30 and accompanying text.

[25] *See* ARISTOTLE, ETHICS, *supra*, note 22, V.8 at 1136a1–3 (emphasis shifted): '[I]f a man harms another by choice, he acts unjustly; and these are the acts of injustice which imply that the doer is an unjust man, *provided* that the act violates proportion or [absolute] equality.'

less than her proportionate share.[26] One thus might say that distributive justice rights and duties are subject to a regime of super-absolute liability: no particular type of conduct or activity nor even a causal connection need be established to support a valid distributive justice claim.

The appropriate liability regime for corrective justice is more complex. What sorts of interactions should be said to be inconsistent with the absolute moral worth or equal negative freedom of the interacting parties? Consonant with the consent and assumption of risk doctrines in tort law, Aristotle states that neither a gain nor a loss is unjust (inconsistent with the equal negative freedom of the parties to an interaction) if the person from whom the gain came or the person who suffered the loss, respectively, freely and voluntarily consented to such gain or loss. More particularly, corrective justice is not violated by fully voluntary exchanges or gifts.[27]

The principal examples Aristotle gives of non-contractual interactions that give rise to corrective justice duties of rectification involve the intentional infliction of unconsented to injury. Yet, contrary to what is sometimes assumed, Aristotle does not limit corrective justice duties of rectification to intentionally inflicted injuries. Such duties apply, at the least, to all 'acts of injustice'. An act is unjust if it is 'voluntary'. Voluntary acts include, but are not limited to, those which the actor knows or intends will result in a loss or gain that is inconsistent with the affected party's right of equal negative freedom. Compulsion in the sense of duress or necessity (i.e., to save life or much more valuable property) does not prevent an act from being voluntary and hence unjust with respect to the losses caused to others, but may, at least in certain situations of necessity that do not involve exposing others to a risk of serious bodily harm, prevent it from being considered morally blameworthy. Ignorance will prevent an act from being voluntary only if it is ignorance of the 'particular circumstances of the action and the objects with which it is concerned', rather than ignorance of what is right or wrong. Aristotle also treats acts as being voluntary and hence unjust, despite the actors' ignorance of the particular circumstances, if the actors are responsible for their ignorance—e.g., as a result of drunkenness, failure to know 'anything in the laws that they ought to know and that is not difficult, [or failure to know] anything else that they are thought to be ignorant of through carelessness; we assume that it is in their power not to be ignorant, since they have the power of taking care.'[28] Thus unjust action encompasses not only intentionally harmful action but also subjective negligence.

Even if a person does not *act unjustly*, due to lack of actual or imputed knowledge of the foreseeable consequences, he still through involuntary

---

[26] *See id.* V.9 at 1136b15–1137a4.
[27] *See id.* V.5 at 1132b31–1133b28, V.9 at 1136a30–b14, V.11 at 1138a9–14.
[28] *Id.* III.5 at 1113b29–1114a3; *see id.* III.1, V.2 at 1131a5–9, V.8 at 1135b6–9.

ignorance may *do what is unjust* by causing an unjust holding or injury. The person who causes such an unjust holding through involuntary ignorance is said to act unjustly 'in an incidental way' rather than a blameworthy way, yet still is subject to a corrective justice duty of rectification. Aristotle divides the injuries in interaction that result from involuntary ignorance into 'mistakes' and 'misadventures'. Mistakes are injuries that were reasonably expectable given typical knowledge, but which were not expected by the actor due to his own involuntary ignorance. Misadventures are injuries that were not reasonably expectable, not because of the actor's own involuntary ignorance, but due to a general lack of knowledge that 'lies outside' the actor.[29] Liability for mistakes seems to correspond to objective negligence, while liability for misadventures would seem to be some form of strict (not absolute) liability.[30]

Injuries due to acts of injustice, being either intentional or the result of subjective negligence, ordinarily constitute wrongdoing—i.e., are morally blameworthy—and thus if sufficiently wrongful render the injurer liable to punishment in addition to rectification of any unjust loss or gain. In certain cases of duress or necessity, such acts might not be morally blameworthy and hence not deserving of punishment. Yet they still would be acts of injustice with respect to the injury inflicted on the victim and would result in the victim's being unjustly treated unless the injury were rectified. Likewise, injuries due to mistakes and (apparently) at least some misadventures are unjust losses that the injurer must rectify. But the mistakes and misadventures, being due to involuntary ignorance rather than being done with actual or imputed knowledge of the foreseeable consequences, do not ordinarily constitute wrongdoing and thus (from a moral blame viewpoint) should be forgiven rather than punished.[31]

In sum, contrary to what is sometimes asserted, the Aristotelian concepts of corrective justice and distributive justice are not empty formalist shells, which can be filled in with practically any moral content, including even utilitarian efficiency. These concepts have a non-aggregative, egalitarian substantive ethical content, prefiguring Kant's normative premise of the

---

[29] *See id.* V.8, V.9 at 1136a23–30.

[30] Liability in tort law is strict rather than being absolute or based on negligence if (unlike absolute liability) it is required that the plaintiff's injury have been caused by some special aspect of the defendant's volitional conduct that created an objectively foreseeable risk to others, but (unlike negligence) the required special aspect is not the unreasonableness of the risk. For example, there is strict liability for damage caused by the ultra-hazardous aspect of foreseeably ultra-hazardous activities. Absolute liability is excluded from corrective justice because only *unjust* gains and losses are subject to rectification. Gains and losses are unjust only if they are inconsistent with the equal negative freedom of the parties to the interaction. *See supra,* notes 24 & 25 and accompanying text.

[31] *See* ARISTOTLE, ETHICS, *supra,* note 22, III at 1109b30–34, V.8 at 1136a5–9; ARISTOTLE, RHETORIC I.13 at 1373b27-30 & 1374b4-9, I.14 at 1374b32–34 (W. Rhys Roberts trans.), in 2 THE COMPLETE WORKS OF ARISTOTLE (Jonathan Barnes ed., 1984); *supra,* text at notes 28–30.

equal absolute moral worth of each person as a free rational being, that historically has provided and continues to provide a powerful moral foundation for law in general and tort law in particular.

V. The Independence and Compatibility of Distributive Justice and Corrective Justice

As Aristotle emphasizes, distributive justice and corrective justice are two distinct and independent types of justice. Structurally, distributive justice claims are multilateral claims that are independent of any interaction and potentially apply to all the members of the community, while corrective justice claims are bilateral claims which arise from an interaction and are limited to the parties to the interaction. Substantively, distributive justice employs a criterion of relative equality, according to which resources are distributed among the members of the community in proportion to how they measure relative to one another under the appropriate distributive criterion. Corrective justice, on the other hand, employs a criterion of absolute moral equality, according to which the parties to an interaction (and their entitlements to their existing stocks of resources) are treated as equal, regardless of how much they might vary from one another under the appropriate distributive criterion or any other comparative criterion. Thus, both the structure and substance of distributive justice claims are inapposite for achieving corrective justice, and vice versa. These distinctions have important ramifications for tort law, which, given its focus on interactional injuries, is grounded on corrective justice.

Corrective justice (and hence tort law) protects against actual or threatened interactional injuries to one's person or existing stock of resources regardless of the distributive justice or injustice of the overall division of resources among the parties to the interaction or among the members of the community as a whole. The relative wealth of the parties is irrelevant to tort liability.[32] More particularly, the law recognizes a corrective justice right to rectification (including, in the absence of strict necessity, punishment of the deliberate trespasser as well as compensation of the victim) when a needy person takes property from or tortiously injures a well-off person.[33]

It is sometimes asserted that, if corrective justice truly is distinct and independent from distributive justice (rather than merely being a corollary principle which serves the subsidiary role of rectifying deviations from the

---

[32] *See, e.g.*, Vosburg v. Putney, 47 N.W. 99, 100 (Wis. 1890).

[33] *See, e.g.*, London Borough of Southwark v. Williams [1971] 2 All E.R. 175 (Eng. C.A.); *cf.* State v. Moe, 24 P.2d 638 (Wash. 1933) (criminal liability). Moreover, even trespassers, whose possession is correctively unjust with respect to the true owner, are themselves protected against trespasses by others. *See, e.g.*, Anderson v. Gouldberg, 53 N.W. 636 (Minn. 1892); Tapscott v. Cobbs, 52 Va. (11 Gratt.) 172 (1854).

just distribution), distributive justice and corrective justice are conceptually and practically incompatible. For example, Ernest Weinrib asserts that distributive and corrective justice, being conceptually distinct forms of justice, are alternative rather than complementary justificatory structures, which cannot coherently coexist in the same body of law nor simultaneously apply in any particular situation.[34] More specifically, Larry Alexander, noting Robert Nozick's argument that voluntary gifts and exchanges will upset any end-state pattern of distribution, observes that similar disruption of the desired pattern of distribution will result from the rectification of gains and losses required by corrective justice, since losses usually are not offset by quantitatively equal gains (and vice versa).[35]

In considering whether conflicts may arise between different valid justice claims, we can begin with the clear (yet sometimes contested) truth that properly implemented corrective justice claims cannot themselves be correctively unjust. For example, a person who injures a wrongful aggressor while properly exercising her corrective justice right to defend herself does not have any corrective justice obligation to compensate the aggressor, even though she injured the aggressor deliberately and without the aggressor's consent. The proper implementation of the rectification required by corrective justice simply cannot itself be a violation of corrective justice, although it is done deliberately and without the consent of the person upon whom the duty of rectification is imposed.[36] Similarly, a person who has been forced to give up some of his existing stock of resources due to a proper distributive justice (e.g., tax) assessment against him does not have any distributive or corrective justice right to have those resources restored to him, even though the resources were taken deliberately and without his consent. In each of these situations, the unconsented to loss is not only consistent with but also required by the affected individuals' right to equal freedom.

The difficulty arises when we consider whether properly implemented corrective justice claims can be consistent with distributive justice. The issue is how best to reconcile the positive and negative aspects of equal freedom that are embodied in distributive justice and corrective justice, respectively. That issue can only be resolved by invoking the fundamental norm that underlies both types of justice: the promotion of the equal freedom of each person in the community. (Note that resort to such a fundamental norm is only possible in a monistic theory of morality and law.) A proper theory of distributive justice takes account of both aspects of the equal freedom cri-

---

[34] *See* Ernest J. Weinrib, *Legal Formalism: On the Immanent Rationality of Law*, 97 YALE L.J. 949, 973–4, 979–81 & n.69, 983–5, 987–8 (1988).

[35] *See* Larry A. Alexander, *Causation and Corrective Justice: Does Tort Law Make Sense?*, 6 LAW & PHIL. 1, 2–7 (1987).

[36] *See supra*, text accompanying notes 13 & 15.

terion: first, the effectiveness of the theory in implementing equal positive freedom and, secondly, the compatibility of the theory with the maintenance of equal negative freedom (security of entitlements to one's existing stock of resources), which also is essential to freedom or autonomy.[37]

Alexander is correct when he states that corrective justice will necessarily disrupt and thus be incompatible with any *end-state* distributive justice scheme.[38] Yet, as Ronald Dworkin notes, corrective justice need not be incompatible with *beginning-state* distributive justice schemes, which provide each person with a fair proportion or amount of resources on which to build his or her life and do not thereafter try to maintain that distribution throughout the person's life.[39] The distributive justice schemes that would seem best to satisfy both aspects of the equal freedom criterion are limited, beginning-state, moderate-needs-based schemes, which focus on providing the minimum or moderate needs in terms of food, shelter, clothing, health care, education, adjustments for disabilities, and so forth that will give each person a roughly equal opportunity to lead a reasonably free and meaningful life.[40]

Properly understood, distributive justice and corrective justice are separately necessary and jointly compatible as the positive and negative aspects, respectively, of the fundamental norm of equal freedom. Contrary to Weinrib's assertion, distributive justice and corrective justice may not only coexist in the same body of law, but also apply simultaneously in the same situation. Examples include public takings of private property under the exercise of eminent domain, or private takings of private servitudes for public benefit that are authorized under nuisance doctrine in tort law. In each of these closely analogous situations, the distributive justice claim that supports the taking of the plaintiff's property is not that he has too many resources overall or, even if he does, that he is the only person who has too many resources. These prerequisites for placing the entire burden of the

[37] Nozickian libertarians, by beginning with an assumption of absolute unqualified property rights in existing holdings (despite paying lip service to the Lockean Proviso), err in disregarding the positive aspect of equal freedom, while Marxist socialists err in disregarding the negative aspect.

[38] *See supra,* text at note 35.

[39] *See* RONALD DWORKIN, LAW'S EMPIRE (1986), 297–9. Dworkin's own scheme, which would require a quantitative equality of beginning-state resources, is deficient with respect to both aspects of the equal freedom criterion. It would not properly implement equal positive freedom because it fails to take need into account—e.g., an ascetic hermit would not need nearly as many resources as an experimental physicist to pursue his projects and plans. It would undermine the security of entitlements that is the crux of negative freedom because the mandated quantitative equality of beginning resources, given constantly occurring new births, will require constantly recurring massive redistributions.

[40] *See* Thomas C. Grey, *Property and Need: The Welfare State and Theories of Distributive Justice,* 28 STAN. L. REV. 877 (1976). The same considerations should govern selection of the method of levying the burdens of a redistribution: the method chosen (e.g., taxation, eminent domain, or conscripted labor) should be the one that has the least adverse impact on the affected persons' equal freedom.

redistribution on him, without any compensation, will rarely be met. Rather, the distributive justice claim is that his property is required to accomplish some distributive objective—either redistribution of resources to those who have too little,[41] or increasing the total amount of resources in society so that everyone's distributive share can be increased[42]—and that due to the unique suitability of the plaintiff's property for this objective, an unconsented to taking rather than a voluntary sale is required to prevent him from demanding excessive compensation for his property and thus appropriating an undue share of the public benefit from the project to himself.

Since the distributive justice claim against the plaintiff is of this special sort, and is not based on his having too much or, at least, being the only one who has too much, the taking of his property without full compensation cannot be justified as a matter of distributive justice. Rather than the distributive justice objective being implemented, as in the case of proper taxation, by proportionately assessing all those who have too much and distributing the proceeds to all those who have too little, the plaintiff would be singled out, with no distributive justification, to shoulder involuntarily the full costs of the redistribution. To implement the distributive justice goal properly, those costs must be shifted from him, by fully compensating him, to those who should properly bear the distributive justice burden. If this is not done, the taking of his property without his consent is unjustified and thus gives rise to a corrective justice right to rectification (in this context, compensation).[43]

VI. THE COMPREHENSIVENESS AND COMPLETENESS OF DISTRIBUTIVE JUSTICE AND CORRECTIVE JUSTICE (HEREIN OF PUNITIVE DAMAGES IN TORT LAW)

Being the positive and negative aspects of the Right of equal freedom, distributive justice and corrective justice exhaust the possible types of substantive justice or Right. The two types differ significantly from one another in both structure and ground, as reflected in their respective domains, persons and resources encompassed, and criteria of equality. Yet each type provides a complete normative structure and ground for resolving particular claims of justice or Right that fall within its respective domain. Thus, contrary to what is assumed by some writers, there is no need to supplement distributive justice or corrective justice by postulating

---

[41] *See, e.g.*, Hawaii Hous. Auth. v. Midkiff, 467 U.S. 229 (1984).

[42] *See, e.g.*, Boomer v. Atlantic Cement Co., 257 N.E.2d 870 (N.Y. 1970); Poletown Neighborhood Council v. City of Detroit, 304 N.W.2d 455 (Mich. 1981).

[43] *See, e.g.*, Boomer *v.* Atlantic Cement Co., 257 N.E.2d 870 (N.Y. 1970).

additional types of substantive justice or by infusing some allegedly missing normative ground or principle.

It is sometimes asserted that retributive justice is a type of justice that is distinct from both distributive justice and corrective justice. However, as Aristotle clearly assumes, retributive justice is a subset of corrective justice rather than a distinct type of justice. Aristotle describes distributive justice and corrective justice as the only two kinds of justice, which govern distributions and interactions respectively. He lists a number of intentional harmings as examples of the non-consensual interactions that constitute one of the two sub-domains of corrective justice, and he prescribes punishment as part of the appropriate rectification for such subjectively wrongful interactions.[44]

When a person in an interaction with another causes a loss to him or reaps a gain for herself that is objectively but not subjectively inconsistent with his equal negative freedom—what Aristotle describes as an 'involuntary' mistake or misadventure that results in an unjust injury rather than a 'voluntary' (intentional or subjectively negligent) unjust act—there is no basis for punishment or retribution but only for requiring her to see to it that the unjust loss or gain is rectified. However, when her conduct is morally blameworthy because it is subjectively as well as objectively inconsistent with his equal negative freedom, then in addition to any nondignitary loss he may have suffered (which itself requires rectification) he also has suffered a discrete dignitary injury, which is rectified through the imposition of private retribution in the form of punitive damages that she herself must pay.[45] If, as is often the case, her conduct also constitutes a conscious flouting or reckless disregard of the rules of public peace or order, then there is an additional non-discrete injury to the dignity and security of each and every member of the civil society (or to 'the state itself'). This non-discrete injury is rectified by imposing public retribution on her in the form of a criminal sentence, which she herself must satisfy.[46]

When the retribution is for the non-discrete wrong done to all the members of society we are in the domain of criminal law. When the retribution is for the discrete wrong done to a particular individual we are in the domain of tort law. Yet tort law, unlike criminal law, is neither primarily focused on nor limited to rectification of injuries caused by subjectively wrongful (blameworthy) behavior, which invokes the retributive aspect of corrective justice. Rather, tort law focuses on rectification of private injuries caused by behavior that was objectively inconsistent with the equal

---

[44] *See supra*, text at notes 22–5, 28, & 31.

[45] *See supra*, text at notes 28–31. *Compare* David G. Owen, *The Moral Foundations of Punitive Damages*, 40 ALA. L. REV. 705 (1989).

[46] *See* ARISTOTLE, ETHICS, *supra*, note 22, V.11 at 1138a9–14; *cf.* KANT, *supra*, note 7, at *331–3.

negative freedom of the interacting parties, whether or not such behavior was subjectively blameworthy. Such rectification is based on the non-retributive aspect of corrective justice. If the defendant's behavior was also sufficiently morally blameworthy, the retributive aspect of corrective justice kicks in to provide a basis for punitive damages in addition to any actual damages.[47]

A more widespread understanding of the distinct nature and grounds of punitive damages in tort law on the one hand and criminal liability on the other, which traditionally have been conceived as discussed above, would go a long way toward clarifying and resolving much of the current debate on the appropriateness and proper scope of punitive damages in tort law.

VII. THE CORRELATIVITY OF RIGHTS AND DUTIES AND THE UNJUSTIFIED FAILURE OF PROPOSED ALTERNATIVES TO TORT LAW TO ADHERE TO THIS CORRELATIVITY

Jules Coleman argues that there is no necessary conceptual or normative link between the 'grounds of recovery', the 'grounds of liability', and the 'mode of rectification' in any coherent theory of legal responsibility.[48] However, by asserting an analytic and normative cleavage between the grounds of recovery and the grounds of liability, Coleman has failed to take the concept of a right (or a legitimate claim) seriously. A claim, as opposed to a mere statement of need, is always directed to some person (or persons or group). A legitimate claim—a claim that should be satisfied—is a claim of entitlement or right directed to that person, which assumes a correlative duty on her part to satisfy the claim. The correlativity of the right and the duty is analytic or conceptual. While there can be purely ethical duties with no correlative rights, there cannot be rights without correlative duties.[49]

The normative ground of every right is also the normative ground for its correlative duty and for the mode of rectification triggered by the infringement of that duty. Once the foundational norm of equal freedom that underlies the concept of Right is understood, and its positive and negative aspects have been elaborated in the concepts of distributive justice and corrective justice, respectively, the structure and content of the modes of rectification for infringements of distributive and corrective justice rights will be implicit in the rights themselves. Only in theories of rights such as Coleman's, in which the foundational norm underlying the concept of

---

[47] Corrective justice encompasses all interactions. It thus provides the normative foundation not only for tort law and criminal law, but also for, e.g., contract law, the law of restitution, and the transactional aspects of property law.

[48] *See* JULES L. COLEMAN, RISKS AND WRONGS (1992), 261–5, 285–8, 317, 326–8; Wright, *supra,* note *, at 665–83.

[49] *See* KANT, *supra,* note 7, at *383; MILL, *supra,* note 4, at 61–2.

Right is not elaborated, can it seem that rights are merely abstract place-holders that have no or minimal content and thus imply no particular mode of rectification when they are infringed.

It is critically important when assessing a particular legal claim to identify it properly as either a distributive justice claim or a corrective justice claim, to make sure that the claim conforms to the distinct structure and ground of the relevant division of justice.

Distributive justice claims are multilateral. To determine the resources to which a person is entitled as a matter of distributive justice, we must know both the total amount of resources that exist in the community and the person's relative ranking according to the distributive criterion in comparison with all others in the community. All those persons who have too little under the distributive criterion have distributive justice claims against all those who have too much. Thus, proper implementation of distributive justice requires concurrent assessments against all those who have too much and disbursements to all those who have too little. Allowing a person who has too little to obtain part or all of his deficiency directly and bilaterally from another person who has too much would not be a proper implementation of distributive justice. It would result in his being improperly preferred over all others who have too little and the other person's being improperly disadvantaged compared to all others who have too much. Such unequal treatment cannot be supported as a matter of distributive justice. Indeed, his unjustified unilateral attempt to satisfy his deficiency from the other's existing stock of resources would be a violation of corrective justice.[50]

Corrective justice claims are bilateral. They are claims by one person that another person has adversely affected the claimant's person or existing stock of resources by behavior that is inconsistent with the claimant's right to equal negative freedom. The injured party has a bilateral corrective justice claim against the person who injured him (and not against anyone else) for rectification of the injury.[51] The particular species of rectification—e.g.,

---

[50] *See, e.g.*, London Borough of Southwark v. Williams [1971] 2 All E.R. 175 (Eng. C.A.); State v. Moe, 24 P.2d 638 (Wash. 1933).

[51] When there are multiple parties involved in the interaction, the injured party may have claims against more than one of the other parties, and there may be counterclaims and cross-claims, but each corrective justice claim is distinct and bilateral in that it asserts a correlative right–duty relationship between two specific parties to the interaction that is distinct from any other corrective justice claims that may have arisen from the particular interaction. If two or more parties to an interaction each have distinct but related corrective justice duties to rectify the injured party's loss (i.e., joint tortfeasors, including employers and their employees), and one of the liable parties fully rectifies the loss, thereby non-voluntarily discharging the other liable parties' duties to the injured party as a side effect of discharging her own duty, she may have a restitutionary corrective justice claim for indemnification or contribution against the other liable parties: *see* RESTATEMENT OF RESTITUTION, (1936) ch. 3, topic 3; Richard W. Wright, *The Logic and Fairness of Joint and Several Liability*, 23 MEM. ST. U. L. REV. 45, 46, 61–2, 72–3 (1992).

restoration of the appropriated or injured item itself or replacement by some item, service, or money of equal value— often (but not always) may be unimportant. Yet merely offering an apology or a peppercorn for a tortiously broken leg clearly will not suffice. The required mode of rectification is the restoration by the injurer (or someone voluntarily acting on behalf of the injurer) of the injured party's preexisting stock of resources to the extent possible.

Contrary to a common misunderstanding, there is no general requirement that a corrective justice duty be discharged personally by the party who is subject to that duty.[52] Such a requirement would seem to apply only when the appropriate mode of rectification is punishment. When the appropriate mode of rectification is compensation for the unjust loss, rather than or in addition to punishment, corrective justice merely establishes the duty of the party who caused the unjust loss to see to it that the required compensation occurs. There is nothing in corrective justice which prevents that duty from being discharged voluntarily, on behalf of the party with the duty, by someone else—e.g., that party's insurer or rich aunt. Nor is there any problem from the standpoint of corrective justice if the person who discharges the duty spreads the cost of discharging that duty to others through voluntary market processes—e.g., by raising the prices of its products.

Coleman has frequently argued that, since non-retributive corrective justice duties can voluntarily be discharged on the obligor's behalf by someone other than the obligor, they also can be discharged by compulsory, no-fault, first-party or social insurance schemes.[53] This argument ignores the fundamental difference, in terms of the impact on equal negative freedom, between someone's *voluntarily* discharging another's duty and being *compelled* to discharge the other's duty. No one can justifiably be compelled to discharge another's duty in the absence of a prior voluntary contractual agreement to do so.[54] All of the examples cited by Coleman of permissible discharges of a duty by a person other than the obligor involve that other person's voluntary discharge of the duty, or, weaker yet, merely a voluntary gift to cover the loss that was not intended to (and hence will not) discharge the obligor's duty. Coleman's examples merely support voluntary participation in social insurance or no-fault compensation plans. They do not support compulsory participation in such plans or, absent explicit vol-

---

[52] This misunderstanding is especially evident in the writings of the aggregate social welfare theorists, who rely upon it to argue that corrective justice is an archaic, misguided popular illusion given the ultimate bearing of costs under our current liability regimes.

[53] *See* COLEMAN, *supra*, note 48, at 327–8; Wright, *supra*, note *, at 671–4, 680–1.

[54] Contrary to a common assumption, this proposition does not condemn the principle of vicarious liability or *respondeat superior*. An employer or other principal's 'vicarious' liability is based on the principal's own corrective justice responsibility for injuries that are tortiously inflicted by the principal's agent in pursuance of the principal's objectives.

untary waiver, the abolition of the injurer's corrective justice duty to rectify the injury to her victim.

In his recent book, Coleman dances around this problem without really confronting it, attacking instead a variety of straw arguments: e.g., that no obligation can be imposed on a person in the absence of that person's consent or wrongdoing, that wrongdoers rather than innocent individuals should be held liable for losses that neither caused, and that corrective justice duties pre-empt all other duties.[55] Persons may and do have justifiable legal duties independent of corrective justice due to the requirements of distributive justice, but not (as Coleman supposes) for reasons such as utilitarian efficiency that are inconsistent with Right and justice. Furthermore, the existence of such independent duties in no way affects the continuing validity of any particular corrective justice duty. Just as satisfaction of a particular corrective justice duty does not discharge or displace independent distributive or unrelated corrective justice duties, satisfaction of other duties of justice does not discharge or displace an independent and unrelated corrective justice duty.[56] Each duty of Right or justice must be discharged by the person subject to the duty or (unless retribution is at issue) by someone *voluntarily* acting on behalf of the person with the duty. There is no justification in Right or justice for *coercively* imposing one person's duty on another, and hence such coercion constitutes a violation of Right and (corrective) justice.[57]

This is not to say that there is no justification for state social insurance schemes. Indeed, such schemes would seem to be mandated by distributive justice. The propriety of such schemes depends on their conformity with the structural and substantive requirements of distributive justice. Yet, even if a state social insurance scheme exists as a proper implementation of distributive justice, the distributive justice arguments underlying it would not justify relieving a tortfeasor from her distinct and independent corrective justice obligation to the victim whom she tortiously injured, absent a voluntary waiver by the victim of his corrective justice rights.[58]

[55] *See* COLEMAN, *supra*, note 48, at 389–95.

[56] *See supra*, note 51, for a discussion of related corrective justice duties.

[57] Coleman ultimately asserts that corrective justice duties are not discharged, but rather extinguished or prevented from arising, by the creation of a compulsory (private or social) no-fault insurance scheme. As explained in the text, these unsupported assertions are invalid. Coleman suggests that those who 'voluntarily' accept compensation from the no-fault scheme waive any moral corrective justice right: *see* COLEMAN, *supra*, note 48, at 402–4 & n.7. But what alternative do they have, and what of those who do not accept such compensation? Coleman himself requires that any alternative compensation scheme 'conform to the relevant demands of justice and morality': *id.* at 493 n.7.

[58] Tort law's collateral source rule affirms the irrelevance to the victim's corrective justice claim against the tortfeasor of the victim's receipt of collateral payments from private or social insurance. The victim's corrective justice right against the tortfeasor is distinct and independent from his contractual corrective justice right against his private insurer or his distributive justice right under the social insurance scheme.

Compulsory no-fault first-party insurance plans not only are inconsistent with corrective justice, but also cannot be justified on distributive justice grounds. They do not attempt to allocate the costs and benefits of the no-fault plan in accordance with the covered parties' relative ranking under the distributive criterion of equal positive freedom. Premiums are universally (and usually uniformly) imposed and losses are universally compensated regardless of the resource position or needs of the persons covered. In addition, the more limited in scope such plans are (e.g., automobile accidents only), the more they fail properly to apply the distributive criterion to *all* the members of the community. Such plans are based on utilitarian loss-spreading rather than on any concept of justice.

Similarly defective are proposals to establish at-fault risk pools, according to which those who behave tortiously would pay into a common fund in accord with some retributive measure or some calculation of *ex ante* expected damages, whether or not they cause any injury, and victims injured by someone's tortious conduct would recover from the common fund. Such schemes are inconsistent with the correlative bilateral rights and duties that are a central feature of corrective justice and ignore the logical and normative correlativity of rights and duties *per se*. Although in such schemes the victim's right to recovery is grounded on tortiously caused injury, the victim's claim is made not against the person who tortiously caused the injury and thus has the correlative duty, but rather (without any normative basis) against all who have behaved tortiously whether or not they caused any injury. Conversely, tortious conduct which has not resulted in any injury is insufficient to establish a corrective justice obligation, since there has been no interference with anyone's equal negative liberty. Nor would such tortious conduct by itself, even if it resulted in injury, establish any distributive justice obligation, since distributive justice obligations are based on entirely different considerations.[59]

VIII. The Institutions of Justice

The distinct structure and content of distributive justice claims and corrective justice claims often largely determine the appropriate institutions for implementing each type of claim. Proper formulation and implementation of distributive justice claims to material resources (other than each person's own body) ideally require knowledge of the total amount of such resources in the community as well as the relative ranking of each member of the community under the distributive criterion of equal positive freedom. Given these informational needs, as well as the *ad hoc* invocation of judi-

[59] In addition to their lack of justification, such at-fault risk pools suffer from insuperable practical problems.

cial authority by litigants and the limited number of parties subject to the jurisdiction of the court in any particular legal action, the proper administration of distributive justice claims to scarce material resources (rather than non-scarce political resources such as voting rights and other civil liberties) is obviously well beyond the capacity of the courts. Only the legislature or its administrative delegee has the institutional competence to assemble, tabulate, and (re)distribute the material resources of society in accordance with the relevant distributive criterion.

Corrective justice has a much narrower domain than distributive justice. Corrective justice is only concerned with the effects of interactions on the persons and existing stocks of resources of the parties to the interaction, and it only requires that such effects be consistent with the equal negative freedom of the parties to the interaction. For corrective justice, unlike distributive justice, no community-wide counting of resources and comparative ranking of persons is required. Hence courts as well as the legislature have the capacity to implement corrective justice. Indeed, courts ordinarily would seem to be much better suited to the task. They can more readily take into account and learn from the concrete detail and variety of actual experience. If properly instituted, they are more insulated from the ebb and flow of interest-group politics. That fact plus the *ad hoc* and limited nature of their jurisdiction should make them less likely than the legislature (or its administrative delegees) to confuse corrective justice issues with distributive justice issues, utilitarian efficiency arguments, or arguments of pure self-interest. Finally, the courts' ability, not shared by the legislature, to focus on the details of numerous particular interactions makes them—or some administrative equivalent—indispensable to the general implementation of corrective justice.[60]

IX. CONCLUSION

At the core of the Kantian-Aristotelian concept of Right or justice is the normative premise that the common good to which law and politics should be directed is not the meaningless pursuit of aggregate social welfare, as assumed by the utilitarian efficiency theory, but rather the promotion of the equal (positive and negative) freedom of each individual in the community. Embodied in this concept of the good is the idea of the absolute moral worth of each human being as a free and equal member of the community,

[60] However, when the goal is widespread *ex ante* prevention of corrective justice violations, rather than *ex post* rectification or specific *ex ante* prevention, the *ad hoc* and limited nature of the courts' jurisdiction once again makes the courts, even with respect to corrective justice, less suitable institutions than the legislature and its administrative delegees. This is especially true when the widespread regulatory effort raises important distributive as well as corrective justice issues.

with an equal entitlement to the share of social resources and the security of currently held resources needed to realize his or her humanity. These normative premises resonate in Kant's moral and legal theory, in Aristotle's theory of ethics, law, and justice, and in a wide variety of ancient and modern moral and political theories.

Most people find the 'equal individual freedom' perspective of the Kantian-Aristotelian theory to be much more attractive than the 'aggregate social welfare' perspective of the utilitarian efficiency theory, at least once they understand what each of these perspectives actually means and entails. The utilitarians, and particularly the legal economists, are thus left to argue that, although the utilitarian efficiency theory may appear to be normatively unattractive, it seems to be the moral theory that actually underlies our law and politics, since it allegedly best (or even solely) explains the content of our existing laws, particularly tort law.

In this essay, I challenged that claim primarily on the global level. I elaborated the Kantian concept of Right and its corollary Aristotelian concepts of distributive and corrective justice and explored their relationship to law in general and tort law in particular. I argued that, far from being mere abstract forms with little or no substantive content, distributive justice and corrective justice, when properly understood as the positive and negative aspects of the Right of equal freedom, are comprehensive and complete normative principles for resolving claims of justice or Right that fall within their respective domains. Tort claims, being based on interactional injuries, fall within the domain of corrective justice. The primary thrust of this essay has been to demonstrate that the concept of corrective justice, understood as the negative aspect of the Right of equal freedom, explains, justifies and illuminates the general structure, content and institutions of tort law, as well as tort law's traditional status as the preferred civil liability regime for discrete non-contractual interactional injuries.[61]

---

[61] I develop the argument further in a companion essay in this volume, in which I focus on the standards of care in negligence law—the doctrinal area that is thought (incorrectly) to provide the best evidence of the alleged success of the utilitarian efficiency theory of law: *see* Wright, *supra,* note 3.

The Idea of Complementarity as a Philosophical Basis for Pluralism in Tort Law

IZHAK ENGLARD[*]

I. The Reality of Pluralism

This essay, as reflected by its title, rests upon certain premises that are controversial: it supposes both the existence and desirability of multiple aims and functions in the framework of tort law. The idea of 'complementarity' in the specific sense formulated by its founder, the Danish physicist Niels Bohr, assumes the inherently contradictory nature of the various aims and functions of the law of torts. Thus, to the extent that the rules, principles, and aims of tort law are viewed as inconsistent or 'incoherent', the concept of complementarity provides a justificatory foundation for this normative reality.

A number of modern tort theories strongly challenge the correctness of these assumptions. The objections are voiced from two different, mutually exclusive, points of view. On the one hand, the monistic approaches deny the validity of tort law's pluralistic foundations. They strive for a unitary, overarching principle of liability, be it of an instrumentalist nature, like economic efficiency,[1] or of a non-instrumentalist, right-oriented one, like that of blameworthiness predicated on a violation of some moral norm such as equal freedom.[2] Pluralism itself is viewed differently by the various monistic theorists. Some tend to deny its very existence on the positive, descriptive level. Thus, in Richard Posner's original understanding, the principle of economic efficiency, defined as wealth maximization, constitutes the key for understanding traditional common law liability rules.[3] He argued that tort law (and common law in general) can be best explained as an effort (albeit unconscious, inarticulate, and incomplete) to promote the efficient allocation of resources. Others, such as Ernest Weinrib, admit the sporadic

---

[*] Professor of Law, Hebrew University, Jerusalem.

[1] See Richard Posner, *Wealth Maximization and Tort Law: A Philosophical Inquiry*, this volume.—Ed.

[2] See Richard Wright, *Right, Justice and Tort Law*, this volume. —Ed.

[3] Posner's positions have subsequently undergone important changes, attenuating their original theoretical rigor. *See* Izhak Englard, The Philosophy of Tort Law (1993), 72 n. 34.

appearance of pluralistic approaches in tort law, caused by the introduction of distributive justice considerations into the corrective justice pattern of tort adjudication. In Weinrib's view, however, this mixing of the forms of justice is intrinsically incoherent and thus should be totally eliminated in order to maintain law's intelligibility.[4]

On the other hand, positing the reality of tort law's pluralism and incoherence, followers of Critical Legal Studies deny both the necessity and possibility of justifying concrete legal solutions. In Jack Balkin's view, for example, 'contradiction is essential because it reflects the essence of thought, and essential because it is a necessary spur to the continuing development of our moral and legal intuitions'.[5] This process of furthering moral consciousness is never-ending, since 'the more we try to systematize the law, the more the law escapes us'.[6]

It should be noted, however, that the contradictions and incoherencies inside tort law, as revealed by Balkin, are not identical with Weinrib's concern for formal consistency. Balkin's central opposition of Individualism and Communalism does not square with Weinrib's formal dichotomy of corrective justice and distributive justice. The difference between the two outlooks is most substantial: in Balkin's view the very imposition of responsibility is a communalist decision; Weinrib, on the other hand, is concerned with the justificatory forms of justice underlying the liability decision. Weinrib's concept of coherence implies the strict separation between corrective justice and distributive justice, two notions that, respectively, correspond to private law and public law. Under Balkin's approach, there seems to be no place for differentiating between private law and public law; hence, no objection could be raised against the mixture in tort adjudication of instrumentalist and non-instrumentalist considerations.

I have elsewhere critically analyzed both the monistic theories of tort liability and the rule skepticism voiced by some adherents of Critical Legal Studies.[7] Let me shortly summarize the reasons for their rejection. The reality of tort law is pluralistic, not only in the rhetorics of the courts but, as revealed by an extensive analysis of tort practices,[8] in the very essence of a multitude of liability rules. This fact removes the foundation of any positive-descriptive theory—be it based on instrumentalist assumptions or on Kantian moral premises—that pretends to ground actual tort rules on a single, comprehensive principle.[9] Richard Posner's economic principle explain-

---

[4] Ernest J. Weinrib, *Understanding Tort Law*, 23 VAL. U. L. REV. 485, 492 (1989). *See generally* ENGLARD, *supra* note 3, at 46 n. 82.

[5] J.M. Balkin, *The Crystalline Structure of Legal Thought*, 39 RUTGERS L. REV. 1, 77 (1986).

[6] J. M. Balkin, *Taking Ideology Seriously: Ronald Dworkin and the CLS Critique*, 55 U. MO. KAN. CITY L. REV. 392, 422 (1987).

[7] ENGLARD, *supra*, note 3, at 29–83.   [8] *Id.* at 123–226.

[9] Compare the observations of David G. Owen, *The Moral Foundations of Products Liability Laws: Toward First Principles*, 68 NOTRE DAME L. REV. 427, 433–4 (1993):

ing tort liability rules as 'approximations to economic efficiency' is additionally flawed by its intrinsic vagueness that renders it virtually non-falsifiable and, therefore, suspect of being ideologically driven.[10]

Monistic normative-prescriptive theories are equally wanting. The insistence on absolute economic efficiency is impracticable, given the endemic lack of information and the frequently dubious existence of deterrence. Moreover, the use of the traditional corrective-justice pattern for the exclusive purpose of attaining an end transcending the direct personal interests of the parties is problematic and bound to produce internal tensions.[11] On the other hand, Weinrib's insistence on complete theoretical purity, on the rigorous pursuit of one single value, is equally unsatisfactory. Areas of strict liability have become deeply entrenched in tort law, and the reality of insurance cannot completely be isolated from tort adjudication. The idea of efficient loss allocation should not be totally excluded from tort law, even if it does not agree with the Kantian premises of autonomy and moral responsibility. Finally, I believe, contrary to some Critical Legal Studies ideologies, that legal solutions can rationally be derived from basic principles of liability. Hence, I assume that it is possible and useful to achieve a certain measure of coherence in tort law by the elaboration of multiple, systematic principles of liability.

There is no want of theorists who admit and favor pluralistic foundations of tort liability. Combinations of justice, rights, and efficiency, of corrective justice and distributive justice, and of private law and public law, are painstakingly described, analyzed, and suggested. Evidently, there is no consensus among the writers as to the nature and content of these various notions, each starting from her own ideological and philosophical premises. But, in one respect, they all seem in accord: they remain unimpressed by Weinrib's arguments of incoherence and lack of intelligibility. Many of the pluralist tort theorists accept the mixture of objectives without inquiry into the problem of internal inconsistency. Their apparent insensitivity to coherence—further witnessed by the universally pluralistic judicial reasoning in

---

'[m]etatheories are valuable in focusing the light through a particular window upon a single point; metatheories are pernicious in shrouding the rest of the world in darkness.'

[10] ENGLARD, *supra*, note 3, at 36–7. I have similar concerns with a more recent statement of Alan Schwartz, where, criticizing Jules Coleman's tort law theory, he asserts: '[v]ictims actually can sue everyone under the economic theory whom they could sue under corrective justice and more': Alan Schwartz, *Interpreting Torts, Explaining Contracts*, 15 HARV. J.L. & PUB. POL'Y 747, 757 (1992). The first part of the statement seems to imply that all corrective justice cases can be explained on the basis of an economic principle. Compare his unqualified reference to Posner's descriptive theory: *id.* at 760. On the other hand, his methodological objections to Coleman's theory of corrective justice are persuasive.

[11] For a more detailed criticism of the cost-benefit approach, see ENGLARD, *supra*, note 3, at 37–44. For a short survey of the current economic critique of Posnerian cost-benefit analysis, see Claus Ott & H.B. Schäfer, *Emergence and Construction of Efficient Rules in the Legal System of German Civil Law*, 13 INT'L REV. OF L. & ECON. 285 (1993).

tort adjudication—indicates the paucity of support for Weinrib's stringent formalist approach.

Nevertheless, some attempts have been undertaken to justify the pluralistic foundations of tort liability in the face of Weinrib's theoretical objections. I do not refer to those theories that deny the validity of Weinrib's philosophical premises, such as the dichotomy of corrective/distributive justice. For my part, I think that this Aristotelian distinction is sound, especially if conceived in a formal-structural way as suggested by Weinrib.[12] I assume, therefore, that liability decisions based on distributive justice considerations indeed raise a serious problem of internal coherence. As a result, I disagree with Richard Wright's thesis that corrective justice and distributive justice can coexist and apply simultaneously in the same situation.[13] Wright relies on two examples in order to establish the premise of mutual compatibility. His first example concerns the public taking of private property under the exercise of eminent domain. According to Wright, the owner's full compensation by the state is a matter of corrective justice, since the just implementation of the distributive justice claim is dependent on the enforcement of the corrective justice rights of the person whose property is being taken. In my view, this analysis is erroneous: the full compensation of the proprietor, made out of public funds, constitutes an integral part of the specific redistribution of wealth resulting from the exercise of eminent domain. The owner's property is forcibly exchanged for money. This coerced sale remains an exclusive matter of distributive justice. The whole process is based upon the overriding interest of the public to use the private property in question for the common good. The taking is *ab initio* considered legitimate; hence, the ensuing compensation of the original owner cannot be conceived as the rectification of a wrong, as a matter of corrective justice.

More to the point is Wright's second example: private takings of private servitudes for public benefit as permitted under nuisance law. A good illustration is a court's refusal to grant an injunction—in view of the major public benefit of the nuisance—thus limiting the plaintiff to a damages remedy.[14] There can be no doubt that the court's reason for the denial of an injunction against the nuisance is of the nature of a distributive justice consideration. However, contrary to Wright's understanding, the actual introduction of distributive justice considerations into corrective justice tort adjudication does not establish the intrinsic compatibility of the two forms of justice. It merely demonstrates the reality of contradictory pluralistic rationales in court decisions. The thesis of this essay is that the idea of com-

---

[12] For a more recent formulation of the distinction, see Ernest J. Weinrib, *Corrective Justice*, 77 Iowa L. Rev. 403 (1992).

[13] Richard W. Wright, *Substantive Corrective Justice*, 77 Iowa L. Rev. 625 (1992).

[14] *Id.* at 708, n. 375 (citing Boomer v. Atlantic Cement Co., 257 N.E.2d 870 (N.Y. 1970)).

plementarity at once explains and justifies the apparently incoherent method of the courts.

Yet the distinctions between corrective justice and distributive justice, and their relationships to notions of private and public law, are of only secondary importance in my specific focus upon the pluralistic foundations of tort liability. My primary argument is that positive tort law is based upon polyvalent justifications that are often mutually inconsistent. Hence, for the purpose of my endeavor, it suffices to classify the pluralistic reasonings under the two headings of instrumentalism and non-instrumentalism, without regard to how well these classifications match the abovementioned categories of justice and law. Indeed, the coherence problem would remain unresolved even if we were able to categorize the multiple contrasting foundations of liability under a single conceptual heading.[15]

II. THE IDEA OF COMPLEMENTARITY

The immediate origin of the modern idea of complementarity lies in physics. Its spiritual father is the Danish physicist and Nobel Prize winner, Niels Bohr (1885–1962), who, when confronted with the problem of wave-particle duality, invented the complementarity notion for interpreting quantum mechanics. Bohr first used the term 'complementary' in public in a lecture presented at the Volta Commemoration Conference at Como, Italy, in September 1927. Bohr, who never formally defined the meaning of complementarity, described it in the later published version of this lecture[16] in the following way: '[t]he very nature of the quantum theory thus forces us to regard the space-time co-ordination and the claim of causality, the union of which characterizes the classical theories, as complementary but exclusive features of the description, symbolyzing the idealization of observation and definition respectively.'[17]

Bohr's starting point was an epistemological problem in science relating to the description of nature. Complementarity meant to convey the idea that the full understanding of physical reality may require the use of

[15] It is for this reason that I do not venture here into the complex controversy on the meaning of corrective justice. *See generally Symposium on Risks and Wrongs*, 15 HARV. J.L. & PUB. POL'Y. 621 (1992) (examining Jules Coleman's notion of corrective justice described in JULES L. COLEMAN, RISKS AND WRONGS (1992)). While I agree with Coleman's conclusion that tort law is a mixture of markets and morals, *id.* at 928, I have misgivings about a number of the theoretical premises to his tort theory: ENGLARD, *supra*, note 3, at 20, n. 30.

[16] The lecture appeared in different versions: *see* NIELS BOHR, 6 COLLECTED WORKS, 110–12 (Jürgen Kalckar ed. 1985). The version used here is that published in 121 NATURE 580 (1928) (Supplement). *See* ABRAHAM PAIS, NIELS BOHR'S TIMES: IN PHYSICS, PHILOSOPHY, AND POLITY (1991), 311–16.

[17] NIELS BOHR, *The Quantum Postulate and the Recent Development of Atomic Theory*, 121 NATURE 580 (1928) (Supplement).

contrasting, mutually exclusive models. Two or more descriptions of a thing are complementary if each alone is incapable of providing a complete description or explanation of the thing in question and both or all together provide a complete description. In quantum mechanics the wave and particle conceptions of radiation and matter together provide a complete representation of the behavior of atomic objects: each provides a suitable physical interpretation of some experimental findings, and together they provide interpretations of all experimental findings.[18] Concepts and propositions which are complementary in Bohr's sense are mutually exclusive in that the application of one such concept to a certain thing at a certain time precludes the application of the other concept to that thing at the same time. Thus, the wave and particle concepts are mutually exclusive in a logical sense, since they are conceptually incompatible.[19]

A correct understanding of Bohr's concept of complementarity in relation to quantum physics, and as its very validity are matters of fundamental controversy.[20] Bohr has alternatively been championed and criticized as positivist, realist, (objective) anti-realist, materialist, idealist, and pragmatist.[21]

Bohr himself did not seem to have too many illusions about the acceptance of his ideas by philosophers. As he remarked during his very last interview on the day before he died, half ironically, half wistfully: '[t]here are all kinds of people but I think that it would be reasonable to say that no man who is called a philosopher really understands what is meant by the complementarity description.'[22] On the other hand, in Heisenberg's

---

[18] DUGALD MURDOCH, NIELS BOHR'S PHILOSOPHY OF PHYSICS (1987), 60.

[19] *Id.* at 61. Another kind of complementarity is that of spatio-temporal descriptions and momentum-energy descriptions. See *id.* at 58, where the author calls it the kinematic-dynamic complementarity. For an analysis of the latter species, see *id.* at 80–108.

[20] *See* MURDOCH, *supra*, note 18, *passim*; HENRY J. FOLSE, THE PHILOSOPHY OF NIELS BOHR: THE FRAMEWORK OF COMPLEMENTARITY, (1985) *passim*. The debate between Einstein and Bohr is considered one of the great intellectual disputes in the history of science. One of the prominent critics of Bohr's interpretation of quantum mechanics is Karl Popper. *See* KARL R. POPPER, QUANTUM THEORY AND THE SCHISM IN PHYSICS (1982). *See also* Murdoch, *supra*, note 18, at 107, 119–20, 160; ERNST P. FISCHER, DIE ZWEI GESICHTER DER WAHRHEIT—DIE STRUKTUR NATURWISSENSCHAFTLICHEN DENKENS (1990) 102–5.

[21] JOHN HONNER, THE DESCRIPTION OF NATURE: NIELS BOHR AND THE PHILOSOPHY OF QUANTUM PHYSICS (1987) 73–4; JAN FAYE, NIELS BOHR: HIS HERITAGE AND LEGACY: AN ANTI-REALIST VIEW OF QUANTUM PHYSICS (1991).

[22] Interview with Niels Bohr by T. S. Kuhn, A. Petersen, and E. Rüdinger, November 17, 1962. *See* PAIS, *supra*, note 16, at 421. *See also* FOLSE, *supra*, note 20, at 9. On Bohr's critical attitude towards philosophers, see PAIS, *supra*, note 16, at 419–21, recounting the anecdote of Bohr's favorite definition of a philosopher: 'What is the difference between an expert and a philosopher? An expert is someone who starts out knowing something about some things, goes on to know more and more about less and less, and ends up knowing everything about nothing. Whereas a philosopher is someone who starts out knowing something about some things, goes on to know less and less about more and more, and ends up knowing nothing about everything. *See also* HONNER, *supra*, note 21, at 72.

view, Bohr was 'primarily a philosopher, not a physicist',[23]—'a judgement', as Abraham Pais observes, 'of particular interest if one remembers how greatly Heisenberg admired Bohr's physics.'[24]

From my perspective, the major interest lies in Bohr's conviction that the lesson of complementarity should be extended to fields other than atomic physics. He believed that the idea of complementarity had general epistemological importance for empirical knowledge. Since empirical sciences share the common 'problem of observation', namely, the objective description of phenomena which are observed in human experience, the framework of complementarity is relevant to all of them.[25] Bohr made significant efforts to apply complementarity, by analogy, from atomic physics to biology and psychology. He believed that the resolution of the mechanist/vitalist controversy in biology,[26] and the free will/determinist controversy in psychology (perhaps philosophy),[27] could be furthered by a complementary conception. Structure and function are pervasive concepts, and their complementary understanding might be relevant to manifold other fields of human knowledge. Bohr suggested the application of the complementarity idea broadly to human culture, including religion, art and music.[28]

The principle of polar duality in the existence, both cosmic and terrestrial, is evidently of ancient origin, and has found expression in many

---

[23] Werner Heisenberg, *Quantum Theory and Its Interpretation, in* NIELS BOHR: HIS LIFE AND WORK AS SEEN BY HIS FRIENDS AND COLLEAGUES (S. Rozental ed., 1967) 94, 95.

[24] PAIS, *supra,* note 16, at 421. In Pais' view: 'Bohr's formulation of the complementarity concept . . . makes him one of the most important twentieth century philosophers': *id.* at 23.

[25] FOLSE, *supra,* note 20, at 170.

[26] Indeed, in his very last lecture in 1962, Bohr returned to the theme of complementarity in biology, modifying his initial position, most likely in view of the advances in molecular biology: 'In the study of regulatory biological mechanisms the situation is rather that no sharp distinction can be made between the detailed construction of these mechanisms and the functions they fulfil in upholding the life of the whole organism. Indeed, many terms used in practical physiology reflect a procedure of research in which, starting from the recognition of the functional role of the parts of the organism, one aims at a physical and chemical account of the finer structures and of processes in which they are involved. Surely, as long as for practical or epistemological reasons one speaks of life, such teleological terms will be used in complementing the terminology of molecular biology. This circumstance, however, does not imply any limitation in the application to biology of the well-established principles of atomic physics'. NIELS BOHR, *Light and Life Revisited, in* ESSAYS 1958–1962 ON ATOMIC PHYSICS AND HUMAN KNOWLEDGE 26 (1963). *See* FOLSE, *supra,* note 20, at 192–3; Henry J. Folse, *Complementarity and the Description of Nature in Biological Science,* 5 BIOLOGY & PHIL. 211–24 (1990); FAYE, *supra,* note 21, at 157–63; PAIS, *supra,* note 16, at 441–4, 447. For an extensive discussion of complementarity in biology, see FISCHER, *supra,* note 20, at 125–227.

[27] *See* FOLSE, *supra,* note 20, at 175–193. On Bohr's ideas on complementarity in psychology, see generally, PAIS, *supra,* note 16, at 439–41; FAYE, *supra,* note 21, at 146–57.

[28] *See, e.g.,* Niels Bohr, *Natural Philosophy and Human Culture,* 143 NATURE 268 (1939); NIELS BOHR, *Unity of Knowledge* (1958), *in* ATOMIC PHYSICS AND HUMAN KNOWLEDGE (1961), 67, 79–81 [hereinafter *Unity of Knowledge*]; PAIS, *supra,* note 16, at 444–5. Pais correctly notes that, unlike the situation in the quantum theory, the application of complementarity to these other fields lack the quantitative support provided there by the uncertainty relations. He, therefore, suggests to use for the notion's extended applications the term of 'complementarism:' *id.* at 439.

forms. The old Chinese *T'ai-chi T'u* symbol is illustrative of that idea. The bright *Yang*[29] and the dark *Yin*[30]—the creative symbols of male and female, the active and the passive principles—twine around each other, presenting a continuous circular movement. They are one but at the same time two distinct entities accentuating each other. The two points in the diagram symbolize the idea that one force at its height already comprises the germ of its counter-force.[31] It has been claimed that the core of the ethical and spiritual insights propounded in Eastern philosophy rests essentially on the complementarity approach to the problems of life and existence, and, moreover, that relativity and quantum mechanics embody the same line of thought as one finds in the specific dialectic of Jainism.[32] No doubt, the idea that opposing principles constitute a harmonious totality can be found as well in the mystical movements of Western Monotheistic religions. However, according to his own recollection, Bohr's philosophical education that helped to shape his idea of complementarity lay in the work of William James—in particular, 'The Principles of Psychology', which had strongly impressed him in his youth.[33]

Bohr was fully aware of the antiquity of some of the roots of the conception of complementarity, especially in Eastern philosophies. When awarded Denmark's highest distinction, the knighthood in the Order of the Elephant, Bohr chose the *Yin* and *Yang* symbol for the coat of arms which tradition required him to adopt as a recipient of the award. Above its central insignia, the emblem's legend recites: *Contraria sunt complementa.*[34]

The broad epistemological significance of complementarity, as envisaged by Bohr and his followers, was its explanation of the totality of reality. The purpose was to reach a full understanding of existence. This basically pos-

---

[29] Sometimes represented as red, sometimes azure.

[30] Variously represented as black, blue, and orange.

[31] GUTORM GJESSING, COMPLEMENTARITY, VALUE & SOCIO-CULTURAL FIELD (1968), 16. FISCHER, *supra,* note 20, at 13.

[32] D. S. Kothari, *The Complementarity Principle and Eastern Philosophy, in* NIELS BOHR: A CENTENARY VOLUME (A. P. French & P. J. Kennedy eds., 1985) 325, 326.

[33] The nature of the philosophical influences upon Bohr is a matter of controversy. *See* FOLSE, *supra,* note 20, at 43–51; MURDOCH, PHILOSOPHY OF PHYSICS, *supra,* note 18, at 225–35. The most direct influence seems to have been exercised by the Danish philosopher Harald Høffding, who transmitted ideas of William James and Kierkegaard. On the influence of Høffding, see in particular, FAYE, *supra,* note 21. But see the critical attitude of PAIS, *supra,* note 16, at 423–4, and his conclusion: '[i]n summary, there is no evidence of any kind that philosophers played a role in Bohr's discovery of complementarity.'

[34] 'Opposites are complements.' The actual coat of arms is located in the church of the Frederiksborg Castle at Hillerød. *See* GERALD HOLTON, THEMATIC ORIGINS OF SCIENTIFIC THOUGHT: KEPLER TO EINSTEIN (rev. edn., 1988) 105. On the anecdotical background of the emblem's choice, see in particular, PAIS, *supra,* note 16, at 24. Bohr's awareness of Far Eastern philosophies does not mean that Bohr was necessarily influenced by them. On the other hand, Bohr referred with great respect to Buddah and Lao Tse: *id.* at 424. *See also* Hans Bohr, *My Father, in* NIELS BOHR: HIS LIFE AND WORK AS SEEN BY HIS FRIENDS AND COLLEAGUES (S. Rozental ed., 1967) 325, 337–8.

itivist notion of complementarity is insufficient for its use in the realm of normativity. In other words, the crucial question in the present context is whether complementarity can fulfil a *prescriptive* role in human life. It is one thing to explain complex cultural phenomena (inclusively legal institutions) by means of contrasting elements or mutually exclusive models;[35] it is quite another to forge rules of conduct on the basis of conflicting values. Moreover, normative questions require a uniform answer in at least two respects. First, the question of validity must be answered by a single test, since normative existence and non-existence are a logical contradiction; their combination is devoid of sense.[36] Secondly, from a practical point of view, a command that is simultaneously positive and negative constitutes a socially unacceptable directive. The notion of pluralism must, therefore, be rejected in relation to the question of a specific norm's validity on grounds of formal logic; in relation to the normative question of a certain conduct's permissibility, a uniform answer is required by reasons of practicability. On the other hand, as explained in the following section, the idea of complementarity might be put to instrumental use in shaping the content of a (single) concrete legal or moral solution to a conflict by integrating contrasting values.

It appears that Niels Bohr himself considered the extension of complementarity to the normative level to be an integral part of the lesson taught by atomic physics. Thus, he explicitly portrayed the relationship between love and justice as being subject to the principle of complementarity. An incident in his family occasioned this reflection. One day, one of his sons had committed an unforgivable deed. Bohr pondered how he could punish his child yet continue to love him.[37] In a broadcast lecture for schoolchildren, he described the problem in the following terms:

We only have to reflect by way of complementarity, as we do in using such terms as 'thoughts' and 'sentiments', in order to describe the situation in which each human being is actually placed. These terms point towards those aspects of our inner experiences which are equally essential, but which are mutually exclusive in

---

[35] Compare GJESSING, *supra*, note 31, at 13–31.

[36] On the problem of the relationship between truth and validity, and the application of the principles of logic to norms, see HANS KELSEN, ALLGEMEINE THEORIE DER NORMEN (1979), 136. On the logical contradiction between conflicting statements on the validity of a specific norm, see *id.* at 177.

[37] HOLTON, *supra*, note 34, at 133. The author quotes a first-hand report of a conversation between Bohr and J. S. Bruner that took place in 1943 or early 1944. Bruner recounts: 'The talk turned entirely on the complementarity between affect and thought, and between perception and reflection. [Bohr] told me that he became aware of the psychological depths of the concept of complementarity when one of his children had done something inexcusable for which he found himself incapable of appropriate punishment: "You cannot know somebody at the same time in the light of love and in the light of justice!" I think that those were almost exactly the words he used. He also . . . talked about the manner in which introspection as an act dispelled the very emotion that one strove to describe': FISCHER, *supra*, note 20, at 100.

the sense that even our warmest feelings completely lose their nature when we try to express them by way of clear logical reasoning. Similar situations emerge in our living together with other human beings, where neither of the terms 'justice' and 'love' can be dispensed with. Each girl and each boy understands how much 'fair play' signifies in game and sport, and that one cannot respect oneself without striving for acting mutually in a just way. But, at the same time, we must make clear to ourselves that the use of the notion of justice, in its extreme consequence, excludes love, to which we are called upon in relation to our parents, brothers and sisters, and friends.[38]

Elsewhere Bohr succinctly summarized this thought: '[T]hough the closest possible combination of justice and love presents a common goal in all cultures, it must be recognized that in any situation which calls for the strict application of justice there is no room for display of love, and that, conversely, the ultimate exigencies of a feeling of love may conflict with all ideas of justice.'[39]

III. The Implementation of the Idea of Complementarity in Law

Bohr does not provide clear guidelines as to how to resolve the *normative* problem of integrating contrasting values. As with much of his writing, including that concerning the interpretation of quantum physics, one has to struggle with the vagueness of his formulations.[40] The articulation of the

---

[38] FISCHER, *supra*, note 20, at 100 (author's translation). Compare Bohr's similar observations in his essay *Unity of Knowledge, supra* note 28, at 81: 'With respect to the organisation of human societies, we may particularly stress that the description of the position of the individual within his community presents typically complementary aspects related to the shifting border between the appreciation of values and the background on which they are judged. Surely, every stable human society demands fair play specified in judicial rules, but at the same time, life without attachment to family and friends would obviously be deprived of some of its most precious values. Still, though the closest possible combination of justice and charity presents a common goal in all cultures, it must be recognised that any occasion which calls for the strict application of law has no room for the display of charity and that, conversely, benevolence and compassion may conflict with all ideas of justice. This point, in many religions mythically illustrated by the fight between deities personifying such ideals, is stressed in old Oriental philosophy in the admonition never to forget as we search for harmony in human life that on the scene of existence we are ourselves actors as well spectators.'

[39] Niels Bohr, *Physical Science and the Study of Religions, in* STUDIA ORIENTALIA IOANNI PEDERSEN (1953), 385, 389. The author continues: 'This situation, which in many religions is mythically illustrated by the fight between divine personifications of such concepts, is indeed one of the most striking analogies to the complementary relationship between physical phenomena described by different elementary concepts which are combined in the mechanical conception of nature, but whose strict applications in wider fields of physical experience exclude each other': *id.*

[40] Examples of critical commentary on Bohr's writings include MURDOCH, *supra*, note 18, at ix: 'Bohr's interpretation [of quantum physics] is undoubtedly of major importance, but there is no universal agreement about what that interpretation is, owing largely to the notorious obscurity of his writings.'; FOLSE, *supra*, note 20, at 259: 'Bohr's published works are

idea of complementarity is a difficult enterprise, since it runs counter to deeply entrenched classical notions of comprehensiveness, uniformity, and consistency. It is no wonder, therefore, that Bohr's endeavor to expand the idea beyond physics encountered contrasting reactions.[41]

In my understanding, complementarity conveys the important message that the ubiquity of contradictions is not a destructive element in human life, but rather, through the idea of complementarity, a vital factor both for scientific progress and the development of human culture. In the normative context, however, the essential, perplexing question is how to translate into practical terms the ideal vision of harmony between contrasting principles. Law is concerned with concrete solutions; hence the delicate problem is how to determine the resolution of actual legal conflicts in conformity with the idea of complementarity. The objective of fusing conflicting principles into harmony is an attractive goal, but it is hard to implement it in practice in view of the intrinsic logical difficulty of the enterprise.

It has been suggested that complementarity involves the finding of an optimal balance between conflicting interests.[42] The weighing of interests is a commonplace procedure in the contemporary legal process, and I do not believe that the concept of complementarity is exhausted by this basically pragmatic approach.[43] Conflicting interests, as such, are not necessarily mutually exclusive in a formal-structural sense. Thus, in the framework of corrective justice, understood in Weinrib's sense as based on Kantian premises, the conflict may relate to the respective freedom interests of the two litigating parties. The law may establish a solution which constitutes a pragmatic balance of interests between the two spheres of autonomy. This kind of private solution between the injurer and the victim should not be considered as incoherent, from the formalist Weinribean perspective, since the resolution would remain strictly inside the domain of private law. Moreover, balancing contrasting instrumentalist considerations is similarly coherent from most formalist points of view. Complementarity involves conflicting interests which are formally inconsistent, like those caught by the dichotomy between corrective justice and distributive justice (or between public and private law).

such that it is easy to make out the worst possible case for complementarity. Basically Bohr's minimal acquaintance with the vocabulary and positions of traditional philosophy led him to ill-advised expressions.' *See also* HONNER, *supra*, note 21, at 72–3.

[41] For example, Abraham Pais remarks, in relation to Bohr's idea on love and justice, that this was just one of the many examples of the complementary style of thinking which have had a lasting and liberating influence on his own life: PAIS, *supra*, note 16, at 447. By contrast, in Jeremy Bernstein's view, 'such attempts at extending the principle lead to a dead end': Jeremy Bernstein, *King of the Quantum*, THE NEW YORK REVIEW, 26 Sept. 1991, at 61, 63 (reviewing ABRAHAM PAIS, NIELS BOHR'S TIMES: IN PHYSICS, PHILOSOPHY, AND POLITY (1991)).

[42] R. V. Jones, *Complementarity as a Way of Life, in* NIELS BOHR: A CENTENARY VOLUME 320 (A. P. French & P. J. Kennedy (eds.), 1985).

[43] Bohr's approach manifests a deep striving for harmony, not expediency.

Let me illustrate the point with an example taken from criminal law. Punishment of the offender may be based on moral retribution in the Kantian/Hegelian sense, or on instrumentalist reasons, like that of deterrence, general or specific. Let us assume that we have a convicted thief who, under a theory of retribution, should be imprisoned for two years. According to a theory of deterrence, on the other hand, he should be imprisoned for ten years. A court, believing in the underlying validity of both theories, might well aspire to implement both of them—as by imposing a prison term of five years. The clash is between two mutually exclusive theories, since the instrumentalist punishment ideal plainly conflicts with the autonomy-based retributive punishment ideal. The resulting 'compromise' punishment is incoherent in the sense that it is incompatible with *both* of the underlying rationales of punishment. Nevertheless, complementarity would support such a compromise solution, in a striving for pluralism through the integration of conflicting values into a concrete resolution. Integration is not to be seen as a mere pragmatic balance determined like a vector of opposing forces, each pulling in a different direction. Rather, the pluralist solution represents an effort to create a harmonious totality, optimally achieving both values in a world where conflicting values must make room for one another.

In tort liability, the idea of complementarity signifies the interdependence of corrective justice and distributive justice, each exercising a desirable limiting effect upon the other. Strict formal coherence gives way to a different, complementary harmony. Otherwise said, notions of moral rights in the Kantian sense are combined with instrumentalist objectives, forming together a concrete legal solution. Yet, the combination and accomodation of contrasting values does not suggest their inherent relativity. Instead, and rather paradoxically, it is their absolute character and independent legitimacy which renders them interdependent in a complementary way.

Has the idea of complementarity any normative significance, or is it merely an *ex post* explanation or legitimation of incoherent rules of positive tort law? Notwithstanding the difficulty of translating the idea of complementarity into practical and concrete terms, I believe that it can be used in a normative-critical sense. The importance of the concept lies in mutually restraining influence of contrasting values. Moreover, in the specific context of tort liability, it has to be acknowledged that the often opposing factors of corrective justice and distributive justice are not of equal importance. In the light of the initial bilateral setting of tort adjudication, special weight should be given to the notion of corrective justice. As a result, a solution in tort law giving undue weight to distributive considerations would violate the idea of complementarity.

For example, in resolving the causation problem in mass tort cases, the imposition of collective liability goes too far because it eliminates the core of corrective justice based on individual responsibility.[44] A distributive justice solution in this context is too commanding, and its implementation here disrupts the essence of complementarity, which strives toward harmonious coexistence of conflicting elements. The conclusion in relation to the mass tort causation problem, therefore, must be that *private* tort law constitutes an inadequate framework for the solution of the compensatory problem of mass tort victims. Instead, it is the function of *public* law to establish collective compensation schemes on the basis of society's current notions of distributive justice.

The same is true in regard to the compensation of victims of crime. Attempts to solve the predicament of crime victims through traditional tort concepts are misguided.[45] The imposition of liability upon retailers, landlords, and other private defendants, on grounds of negligent failure to prevent the commission of crimes, in many cases also exceeds the boundaries of complementarity. Here, too, excessive weight is placed on distributive justice concerns in the inherently restrictive framework of bilateral tort adjudication.

The recent discernible change of direction of many courts toward a more liability-restrictive policy indicates a growing judicial awareness of the inherent limits of tort adjudication to achieve large-scale distributive justice objectives. An explanation for this development may well lie in the idea of complementarity that, by its permanent search for harmony, endeavors to achieve a reasonable equilibrium between the conflicting elements.

IV. Conclusion

It is suggested that the inevitable incoherencies inside tort law be justified by the idea of complementarity. Its objective is to combine mutually inconsistent but legitimate legal structures and functions into integrative substantive notions of liability. So understood, the conception of complementarity offers a philosophical framework for a deeper understanding of the working of mutually restraining principles in our striving for harmony in a world of legal pluralism. Thus, an idea (re)born in human reflection about the physical world will come to bear fruit in the world of norms.

[44] ENGLARD, *supra*, note 3, at 219–26.   [45] *Id.* at 175–98.

PART III

PHILOSOPHICAL PERSPECTIVES ON TORT LAW PROBLEMS

SECTION A

Responsibility and the Basis of Liability

Philosophical Foundations of Fault in Tort Law

DAVID G. OWEN*

Fault is the basic cement of the law of torts. Fault permeates the structure of tort law doctrine, providing both definition and justification for the great majority of rules governing private responsibility for causing harm. What fault is, therefore, and how in moral theory it may claim to dominate this area of the law, are questions of fundamental importance to an understanding of tort law. 'Fault', in common parlance, is often addressed in terms of 'blame' or 'wrong': faulty conduct is 'blameworthy' or 'wrongful' conduct; a wrongdoer is subject to 'blame' or is 'at fault'. Yet, regardless of the nomenclature, the basic issues remain the same: why and how the law of torts should determine whether a particular person's conduct (more precisely, a particular person's *harmful* conduct) was blameworthy or wrongful, whether the person was at fault.[1]

In *Brown* v. *Kendall*,[2] decided in 1850, a man accidentally struck another with a stick while trying to break up two fighting dogs. Holding that negligence was necessary to liability, Chief Judge Shaw of Massachusetts officially proclaimed the central role of fault in accident law, opening a century of largely unchallenged dominance of fault in the law of torts. Within three decades of *Brown* v. *Kendall*, Oliver Wendell Holmes was able to assert authoritatively that 'the law does, in general, determine liability by blameworthiness'.[3] And as the twentieth century opened its doors, the explicitly fault-based standard of responsibility for accidents was solidly endorsed by the legal scholars of the period. Harvard Law School dean James Barr Ames, for example, noted with approval that '[t]he ethical standard of reasonable conduct has replaced the unmoral standard of acting at one's peril'.[4]

---

* Byrnes Scholar and Professor of Tort Law, University of South Carolina. For comments on an earlier draft of this essay, rather than going next door to obtain Pat Hubbard's thoughts, I went instead to Canada and England which generated beneficial suggestions from Peter Benson, Bruce Chapman, Stephen Perry, and Bernard Williams.

[1] 'Tort', from the French word for injury or wrong, derived originally from the Latin 'tortus', meaning twisted or crooked: W. PAGE KEETON, DAN B. DOBBS, ROBERT E. KEETON & DAVID G. OWEN, PROSSER AND KEETON ON THE LAW OF TORTS (5th edn., 1984), § 1 [hereinafter PROSSER & KEETON]; Peter Birks, *The Concept of a Civil Wrong*, this volume.

[2] 60 Mass. (6 Cush.) 292 (1850).

[3] OLIVER WENDELL HOLMES, JR., THE COMMON LAW (1881), 108.

[4] James Barr Ames, *Law and Morals*, 22 HARV. L. REV. 97, 99 (1908).

After about a century of virtually unchallenged dominance,[5] a small number of commentators in the 1950s began to question the legitimacy of fault as the basis of liability in certain areas of American tort law.[6] And by the late 1960s, the dominance of fault in tort law was being challenged on a variety of fronts, as no-fault automobile insurance schemes and strict products liability rapidly gained legislative, judicial, and scholarly support. As the twentieth century draws to a close, however, fault appears to have reasserted its dominance as the guiding principle of the law of torts in the United States.[7] To understand just why the concept of fault has proved so durable, and why its converse—strict liability—has proved so frail, so incapable of making lasting inroads into the heart of tort law doctrine, one must inquire into the concept of wrongdoing that underlies the law of torts.

The inquiry here into the nature of fault in tort law involves an examination of the philosophical foundations of choice, action, and harmful conduct. First to be explored are the broad ideals that give moral character to a person's actions: freedom, equality, and community or common good. Freedom (or autonomy), equality (in a 'weak' form), and community (in the 'hard' form of utility) are seen collectively to shape significantly the moral quality of human behavior. After these fundamental values are examined generally, their relative priority is next considered, followed by a consideration of the nature and ordering of the basic interests at stake in tort law. Finally, the essay focuses briefly on the more specific questions of how the underlying values help define the wrongfulness, first, of intentionally harmful conduct, and, second, of conduct that accidentally causes harm.

I. Freedom

A. The Concept of Freedom

Freedom, one may postulate with confidence, is the most fundamental, and most important, moral and political value.[8] Among modern philosophers, the one most credited with propounding this ideal is Immanuel Kant, who considered freedom to be 'the one sole and original right that belongs to

---

[5] Apart from work-place injuries, statutorily cut out of tort law and placed in workers' compensation schemes in the first few decades of this century.

[6] *See, e.g.,* ALBERT A. EHRENZWEIG, NEGLIGENCE WITHOUT FAULT (1951), *reprinted in* 54 CAL. L. REV. 1422 (1966); Fleming James, Jr., *General Products—Should Manufacturers Be Liable Without Negligence?,* 24 TENN. L. REV. 923 (1957); Charles O. Gregory, *Trespass to Negligence to Absolute Liability,* 37 VA. L. REV. 359 (1951).

[7] *See generally* David G. Owen, *The Fault Pit,* 26 GA. L. REV. 703 (1992) [hereinafter *The Fault Pit*].

[8] Much of the following is adapted from David G. Owen, *The Moral Foundations of Products Liability Law: Toward First Principles,* 68 NOTRE DAME L. REV. 427 (1993) [hereinafter *Moral Foundations*].

every human being by virtue of his humanity'.[9] While philosophers and governments of course must concern themselves to a large extent with notions of group welfare, and while selfishness is widely regarded as a vice rather than a virtue, freedom should be viewed as the first and most essential ideal within a broad philosophy of government and justice.[10]

The freedom concept rests upon the notion of free will[11]—the capacity of persons rationally to select personal goals and plans for life, and their possession of means to achieve those ends. This concept, sometimes called autonomy,[12] thus entails at least two conditions: choice and power. The design of life plans and the selection of specific goals to achieve those plans implies a range of options and opportunities, alternatives from which to choose. As a person's choices are enhanced, so too is that person's freedom. Freedom also requires power, for one must have the ability to bring one's chosen goals to fruition in order to control one's destiny, in order to be free. To be autonomous, one therefore must possess requisite mental and physical prowess and adequate physical goods and monetary resources to achieve the objectives one selects.[13]

Freedom accords persons dignity, for it permits each human to design and then to follow his own life plan, distinct from any other. The concept also forces persons to shoulder a burden, for it places responsibility upon each person to plan and live a life that is 'good' for that individual. While philosophers and theologians may debate forever the notion of what, in the abstract, constitutes the ultimate good life and its component virtues, it is each human's moral privilege—and his or her moral responsibility—to

[9] IMMANUEL KANT, THE METAPHYSICAL ELEMENTS OF JUSTICE (*Rechtslehre*) (John Ladd trans., 1965) (1797), *237 [hereinafter ELEMENTS OF JUSTICE]. Freedom, autonomy, and morality in Kant's view are all inseparably bound together: IMMANUEL KANT, FOUNDATIONS OF THE METAPHYSICS OF MORALS (L. Beck trans., 1959) (1785) *452–53 [hereinafter METAPHYSICS OF MORALS]. 'Autonomy is thus the basis of the dignity of both human nature and every rational nature': *id.* at *436. Kant viewed autonomy, freedom of the will, as 'the supreme principle of morality': *id.* at *440.

[10] *See, e.g.*, Robert B. Thigpen & Lyle A. Downing, *Liberalism and the Communatarian Critique*, 31 AM. J. POL. SCI. 637 (1987). Equality and community ideals logically presuppose the priority of freedom. 'Liberty is crucial to political justice because a community that does not protect the liberty of its members does not—cannot—treat them with equal concern': Ronald W. Dworkin, *What is Equality? Part 3: The Place of Liberty*, 73 IOWA L. REV. 1, 53 (1987) [hereinafter *What is Equality?*] (explaining '[t]he priority of liberty, under equality of resources').

[11] 'The will is free, so that freedom is both the substance of right and its goal': GEORGE W.E. HEGEL, PHILOSOPHY OF RIGHT (T. M. Knox (trans.), 1965) (1821), 20, para 4.

[12] I use the two terms interchangeably, although for some purposes there may be value in distinguishing between them. *See* JOSEPH RAZ, THE MORALITY OF FREEDOM (1986), ch. 15.

[13] *Id.* at 371–3. Conceptions of freedom vary considerably among philosophers. Having the means to be one's own master has been characterized as 'positive' freedom, as distinguished from freedom in its 'negative' form, consisting in the absence of interference with one's activities by others. For the classical formulation of this distinction, see Isaiah Berlin, *Two Concepts of Liberty*, in FOUR ESSAYS ON LIBERTY (1969), 121, *reprinted in* LIBERTY 33 (David Miller (ed.), 1991).

choose the particular life goals that he or she deems most worthwhile,[14] and to seek to achieve them through personal choice and action.

Viewed in this way, freedom is the primary moral and political ideal. It is the first condition to protecting or advancing other values, such as equality, altruism, and communal welfare. Thus, whether the ultimate goal of law is thought to be the promotion of individual well-being or the welfare of the group, the first and most important function of the law is to protect and promote freedom or autonomy.

B. Truth

Subsumed in freedom is the ideal of truth, a concept closely related to knowledge. From the time of Plato, knowledge classically has been defined as 'justified true belief'.[15] Knowledge, justification, truth, and belief thus are all functionally related. Among these concepts, however, truth is the only one that is absolute, the only true ideal.[16] Knowledge, for example, only describes the state of possessing the ideal of truth.[17] For help in resolving moral questions arising out of harmful human interactions, truth may be viewed as the correspondence of a person's beliefs with reality.[18]

The intelligent and effective selection and pursuit of goals implies an ability to perceive and comprehend things in the world and how those things interrelate according to the principles of cause and effect. No person, of course, can absolutely know the truth, which is one important reason why no one ever can be absolutely free. Humans, hampered by both physical and cerebral imperfection, can see the world but dimly, and so their choices

---

[14] For a discussion of freedom as requiring 'good' choices, see RAZ, *supra*, note 12, at 378–85.

[15] PAUL K. MOSER & ARNOLD VANDER NAT, HUMAN KNOWLEDGE: CLASSICAL AND CONTEMPORARY APPROACHES (1987), 3.

[16] Aristotle apparently viewed truth as '*more* self-evidently and fundamentally good than life': J. M. Finnis, *Scepticism, Self-Refutation, and the Good of Truth, in* LAW, MORALITY, AND SOCIETY—ESSAYS IN HONOUR OF H. L. A. HART (P. M. S. Hacker & J. Raz (eds.), 1977), 247, 249.

[17] The notions of knowledge and truth are so closely related, however, that they may be substituted for one another in most contexts. *See, e.g.,* JOHN FINNIS, NATURAL LAW AND NATURAL RIGHTS (1980), 59 (interchanging the terms 'knowledge' and 'truth', and referring to truth as 'the basic good').

[18] 'Perhaps the most ancient and certainly in all eras the most widely accepted theory of truth is the *correspondence theory*, according to which truth is *correspondence to fact'*: NICHOLAS RESCHER, THE COHERENCE THEORY OF TRUTH (1973), 5. 'The traditional correspondence theory [of truth] holds that p is true if, and only if, it corresponds to reality': D. M. ARMSTRONG, BELIEF, TRUTH AND KNOWLEDGE (1973), 113. Because the correspondence theory of truth provides epistemologists with only partial help in resolving abstract questions of knowledge, particularly in respect to the truth of propositions, it holds little interest for many modern philosophers. *See generally* THOMAS MORAWETZ, WITTGENSTEIN & KNOWLEDGE (1978), ch.3; RESCHER, *supra*, ch. I. For help in analyzing the empirical and moral problems of harmful conduct, however, which involve 'truths of fact' rather than 'truths of reason', a nontechnical definition of truth in correspondence terms appears most useful here.

of both ends and means are always frustrated by their lack of knowledge. Autonomy therefore is facilitated by the promotion of truth—improving the correspondence between people's beliefs or expectations, on the one hand, and the true world as it exists and changes, on the other.

Intentionally inflicted harm is generally based upon a subversion of truth. A person causing such harm is therefore at fault, as a preliminary matter, *not* because he has caused harm to the victim, but because of the truth-falsification means by which he has converted the victim from an autonomous person unwittingly into an object of harm. Fraud and defamation both are widely understood to be grounded in the deliberate falsification of the world, as the actor knows it to exist, to the detriment of the victim. Yet most other intentional harms are based on truth subversion, too. Whether the actor be a poisoner of candy, a burglar who cloaks himself in the mantle of the night, or an assailant who conceals a handgun in his pocket or himself behind a tree, the success of each such intentionally harmful venture—and its (preliminary) wrongfulness—rests substantially upon the prior theft of truth from the victim, as from others who might otherwise act to lend protection to the victim.

Truth, or the absence of it, also plays a powerful role both in causing accidents and in determining blame therefor. Indeed, the very word 'accident' is defined in terms of *unexpected* harm.[19] Accidental harm, then, is harm attributable to the failure of at least one person, the actor or the victim, to expect the harm, to possess the truth concerning the things that caused the harm. As an everyday example, imagine a simple intersectional collision between two cars: *A*, driving toward an intersection, sees the traffic light change from green to yellow and mistakenly believes that he can enter and clear the intersection before the light turns red. *B*, waiting on the intersecting street, enters the intersection as soon as her light turns green, mistakenly believing that it will be clear of traffic. *A* and *B* enter the intersection simultaneously, at right angles, and their cars collide. Here, the collision is attributable to the failure of both *A* and *B* to possess the truth about the status of the intersection at the time of the collision. By convention in this situation, as reflected in pre-established rules of the road, responsibility for determining the truth—and, accordingly, fault in failing to obtain it—is allocated to the person entering the intersection as the light changes from green to yellow. Here, as in myriad other contexts involving accidental harm, both causation and fault are rooted in the failure of one or both of the parties to possess the truth.

A person's ability to control his life, to live effectively within the world, is highly dependent upon the extent to which that person's vision of the

---

[19] *See, e.g.*, WEBSTER'S NEW WORLD DICTIONARY OF THE AMERICAN LANGUAGE (1964), 9 ('a happening that is not expected'). *See generally* H. L. A. HART & TONY HONORÉ, CAUSATION IN THE LAW (2d edn., 1985), 151.

world is true. Without possessing the truth in substantial measure, persons become vulnerable to both intentionally and accidentally inflicted harm. Thus, truth is a fundamentally important component of freedom that humans need to protect themselves from harm, and fault for harm is often rooted in how and why the truth is used or abused by the actor and the victim.

II. EQUALITY

A. *The Concept of Equality*

A threshold problem the law confronts in the promotion of individual freedom is the multiplicity of separate persons whose freedoms frequently collide. In a crowded world, each person's pursuit of life goals often conflicts with other persons' pursuit of their own life goals. The law therefore must draw boundaries around individuals, defining where one person's freedoms end and where another person's freedoms begin.[20] The most elementally helpful criterion for drawing such freedom boundaries in a just and enduring society is equality.[21]

How equality helps define the scope of each person's freedoms depends upon the type and strength of one's view of equality. Assume that *A* and

---

[20] This fundamental concept is nicely captured in Nozick's 'border crossing' metaphor: ROBERT NOZICK, ANARCHY, STATE, AND UTOPIA (1974), ch. 4.

[21] The equality ideal has been a profoundly important ethic in moral and political philosophy throughout the ages. It was perhaps the central ethic in Aristotle's theory of corrective justice. "[T]he law . . . treats the parties as equal, and asks only if one is the author and the other the victim of injustice or if the one inflicted and the other has sustained an injury. Injustice then in this sense is unfair or unequal, and the endeavour of the judge is to equalize it': ARISTOTLE, THE NICOMACHEAN ETHICS (J.E.C. Welldon (trans.), 1987) (bk. 5, ch. 7), 154. Equality was central to the philosophy of Kant, who considered it to be contained within the principle of freedom. KANT, ELEMENTS OF JUSTICE, *supra*, note 9, at *237–8; *see infra*, note 33. And its elemental power remains at the heart of much contemporary jurisprudence. *See generally* GERALD DWORKIN, THE THEORY AND PRACTICE OF AUTONOMY (1988), 110 ('Every moral theory has some conception of equality among moral agents'); RONALD M. DWORKIN, LAW'S EMPIRE (1986), 295–301 [hereinafter LAW'S EMPIRE]; ERIC RAKOWSKI, EQUAL JUSTICE (1991); JOHN RAWLS, A THEORY OF JUSTICE (1971), §§ 11, 32–40, 77; PETER WESTEN, SPEAKING OF EQUALITY (1990) (examining the paradoxes, rhetorical force, and various conceptions of equality); Jeremy Waldron, *Particular Values and Critical Morality*, 77 CAL. L. REV. 561, 577 (1989) ('[O]ne cannot go anywhere in serious moral thought except on the basis of some assumption about the fundamental equality of human worth.').

The innate link between freedom and equality, defined by Kant, ELEMENTS OF JUSTICE, *supra*, note 9, at *237–8, is captured succinctly by Hart: '[I]f there are any moral rights at all, it follows that there is at least one natural right, the equal right of all men to be free': H. L. A. Hart, *Are There Any Natural Rights?*, 64 PHIL. REV. 175 (1955), *reprinted in* THEORIES OF RIGHTS (Jeremy Waldron (ed.), 1984), 77. The constitutive link between equality of resources and freedom is explained in R. Dworkin, *What is Equality?*, *supra*, note 10, at 54 (arguing that 'liberty and equality are not independent virtues but aspects of the same ideal of political association', which 'strategy uses liberty to help define equality and, at a more abstract level, equality to help define liberty'). *See also infra*, note 40.

B start off equally in all respects to pursue their respective goals, and that they interact in some manner that harms *B*. A 'strong' version of equality—one that emphasizes the security of resources—might require *A* to transfer enough of his goods to *B* to restore the state of equality between *A* and *B*, based only upon the change in their respective holdings of goods from a status of equality to one of inequality.[22] A very strong version of equality, based on equality in the holdings of goods, could require this result even if *B*, not *A*, were morally responsible for the accident. A different, weaker version of equality, based on an equal right of action, might leave the loss entirely with *B*, if neither *A* nor *B* were otherwise responsible for the loss. Thus, the version of equality selected is crucial in defining limits to individual freedom.

B. Three Principles of Choice

For assistance in determining how strong or weak a version of equality is appropriate in tort law—to help ascertain moral responsibility and fault for harmful conduct—the role of human choice may usefully be examined in the recurring contexts of harmful interactions. When two people interact, the transaction often benefits them both,[23] so that actors frequently enhance the interests of other persons. Some interactions, however, are harmful to one or both affected persons. When the interaction is a harmful one, the prior choices of both persons give moral character to their actions and omissions that combined to cause the harm. At least three separate principles of choice, each bound in separate fashion to the equality ideal, may be derived from freedom principles to help define the wrongfulness of harmful conduct.[24]

The first principle of choice, based upon the equal abstract right of every person to pursue his own interests without undue interference from others, bears most significantly on harms which are intentional. This principle holds quite simply that a person should not choose to harm others solely to advance interests of his own. For example, one should not deliver an unprovoked punch in the nose, merely to show off one's pugilistic skills, allay one's anger, or win a bet. Since one person's abstract autonomy rights are equal to every other person's similar rights, an actor should not infringe another person's autonomy merely to enhance his own. For the purpose of

[22] To restore equality between the two, *A* would have to give to *B* an amount of goods equal to half of all *B's* losses. Alternatively, the state or a private insurer might transfer from a loss-pool enough communal goods to *B* to rectify the loss.

[23] Economic theorists refer to such transactions as Pareto maximizing. *See generally* Jules L. Coleman, *Efficiency, Utility, and Wealth Maximization*, 8 HOFSTRA L. REV. 509, 512–18 (1980).

[24] Whether active or passive.

achieving one's own chosen ends, in other words, one generally may not fairly choose to frustrate the vested interests—harm the vested goods—of other persons.[25] Harmful conduct may thus be viewed as unjust or wrongful, in equality terms, if the actor chose to cause the harm, knowing it to violate the victim's equal right to freedom, for the purpose of achieving the actor's ends.[26] This basic concept, which may be called the 'choice-end principle', underlies the law of intentionally inflicted harm.

When human interactions *accidentally* result in harm, rather than when harm is purposefully caused by an actor, very different choices are involved. The second principle of choice reflects the limitations of space in a crowded society, and the inevitability of collisions between separate persons pursuing their respective ends and possessing limited power, skills, and access to the truth. Moral responsibility and blame for such accidents hinge upon the nature of the prior choices of both parties to a collision. Helping frame the moral character of such choices, the abstract notion of equality helps reveal the fallacy of a common intuition that blame for accidents generally should lie upon the actor rather than the 'passive' victim.

The world in which we live is a dynamic one, where action is necessary to achieve one's goals, both to protect and to enhance one's property and satisfaction. One must drive (or walk) to the store to buy one's bread. This interest might be designated a person's 'action interest'. Each person also has another, passive form of interest, which might be called one's 'security interest'. This latter form of interest is a person's interest in maintaining his present stock of property and satisfaction against depletion.

Abstract equality suggests that action and security interests in such a world are of equal order, that the interests of an accident victim have no inherent priority over the interests of the actor. Despite an undeniable counter-intuition, an accident victim's passive security interest in maintaining his stock of goods logically should have no higher intrinsic value than the actor's affirmative action interest in protecting (and augmenting) his stock of goods.[27] Indeed, freedom of action is especially deserving of protection in a dynamic world because persons regularly must readjust through

---

[25] This principle is framed in general terms, and limited to vested goods, to allow for fair but harmful (to the loser) competition for limited economic or social goods as yet unvested and so available for competitive acquisition.

[26] 'If a person hurts another from deliberate moral purpose, he acts unjustly': ARISTOTLE, *supra*, note 21, at 172.

[27] '[T]he public generally profits by individual activity. As action cannot be avoided, and tends to the public good, there is obviously no [sound] policy in throwing the hazard of what is at once desirable and inevitable upon the actor': HOLMES, *supra*, note 3, at 95; Ernest J. Weinrib, *Causation and Wrongdoing*, 63 CHI.-KENT L. REV. 407, 428 (1987) (a property holder may not insist that his security interests are more valuable than an actor's freedom). When an accident victim suffers personal injury or death, the one obvious difference between the values of the respective interests of the actor and the victim concerns the nature of those interests. The oft-noted preference for the interest in bodily integrity is examined in part IV B, below.

action to ever-changing conditions, even if their only goal is to protect their own security.[28]

Autonomy entails the notion that a person may—indeed, must—make choices and then act upon those choices. It is a simple truism that each such action always restricts in some measure the choices available to others. If *A* chooses to move from point *x* to point *z*, and does so, he deprives *B*, standing at point *y*, of the opportunity to move to *z*. This also is true concerning decisions not to act: If *A*, standing at point *x*, decides not to move at all, he limits the opportunity of *B*, standing at point *y*, to move to *x*. Thus, whether of action or inaction, all choices of all persons diminish in some manner the available choices (and hence the freedom) of other persons, who are 'harmed' to that extent. The choices and action inherent in the very notion of individual autonomy, therefore, imply harm to other persons. This important concept, that freedom entails harm to other persons, may be called the 'choice-harm principle'. In a society devoted to autonomy and equality, the choice-harm principle suggests that no initial preference should be given to security over action.[29] And this second principle of choice undermines substantially the notion that merely *causing* harm is wrong.

The third and final principle of choice outlined here, drawing from implications of the prior two, normatively predicates fault or blame upon whether the actor's choices respected or denied the victim's equal stature as a human. This last perspective on how choice and equality fit together may be called the 'choice-blame principle'. The dual-faceted idea here, rooted in the abstract equal worth of every person, is that actors are *at fault* for choosing *without good reason* to harm other persons, or choosing to expose them to a risk of harm. As more fully explored below, one facet of this principle, the 'bad-harm' facet, holds that choosing to harm (or risk harm to) another person's vested interests without good reason violates the other person's dignity as a free and equal human—and, hence, is wrong. This principle's 'good-harm' facet is just as important: actors regularly *must*, as a practical necessity, choose to harm (or risk harm to) others for reasons that are good, and such conduct accordingly is proper.

C. Weak Equality

Together, the three principles of choice sketched out here help frame a form of equality useful in explaining fault for causing harm. Based upon the first

---

[28] *See* G. DWORKIN, *supra*, note 21, at 112 ('In general, autonomy is linked to activity, to making rather than being, to those higher forms of consciousness that are distinctive of human potential.').

[29] The choice-harm principle, therefore, is fundamentally different from John Stuart Mill's 'harm principle', which accords a higher priority to security by providing that one person may not interfere with the freedom of another except to prevent harm to others: *see* JOHN STUART MILL, ON LIBERTY (G. Himmelfarb (ed), 1974) (1859), 68–9.

two principles, the third and normative principle of choice explicitly conditions fault upon the absence of good reason for harming (or risking harm to) other persons. Central to the choice-blame principle's good-harm facet is the powerful notion that it is sometimes *proper* for one person to harm another. This conclusion suggests the propriety of some 'weak' formulation of equality, one which allows each person the maximum amount of freedom (for both security and action) consistent with an equal right of others. This form of weak equality has been aptly termed an 'equality of concern and respect'.[30] Philosophers across the ages, from Plato[31] and Aristotle[32] to Kant,[33] to Nozick,[34] and even to Rawls and Dworkin,[35] generally have accorded some such notion of weak equality a central position among moral values.

When equality is defined weakly, in terms of equality of concern and respect, it becomes subject to the criticism that it is 'empty', devoid of analytical content[36] and, so, incapable of helping to define freedom or any other ideal.[37] Yet the concept of freedom itself can be subjected to such a charge,[38] albeit less persuasively, and the charge of emptiness misses the fundamental point of equal freedom that proclaims the intrinsic and ineffable worth of every human.[39] The value of this abstract notion of equal-

[30] Although the concept derives, through Rawls, from Kant (as well as from Aquinas, Christ, and others), its statement in this form is Dworkin's. *See, e.g.,* RONALD DWORKIN, TAKING RIGHTS SERIOUSLY (1977), 182 (noting that Rawls' 'justice as fairness rests on the assumption of a natural right of all men and women to [an] equality of concern and respect . . . [possessed] simply as human beings with the capacity to make plans and give justice').

[31] *See* PLATO, LAWS VI.757 (Taylor trans.), at 143 *quoted in* WESTEN, *supra,* note 21, at 52–3.

[32] *See* ARISTOTLE, *supra,* note 21, bk. V, especially at 150–60.

[33] 'Hence the universal law of justice is: act externally in such a way that the free use of your will is compatible with the freedom of everyone according to a universal law': KANT, ELEMENTS OF JUSTICE, *supra,* note 9, at *231.

[34] Nozick may find the least use for equality among major contemporary philosophers: *see* NOZICK, *supra,* note 20, at 222–4. He is not alone, of course, in this position. *See, e.g.,* Peter Westen, *The Empty Idea of Equality,* 95 HARV. L. REV. 537 (1982). For a valuable critique of equality from a leading English legal philosopher, *see* RAZ, *supra,* note 12, ch. 9.

[35] It may seem odd for Rawls and Dworkin to be included among proponents of 'weak' equality, for they both view equality as central to their systems. *See generally* RAWLS, *supra,* note 21, at 222–4, 453–504; Ronald Dworkin, *In Defense of Equality,* 1 SOC. PHIL. & POL'Y 24 (1983). Yet they both subscribe to the notion of equal concern and respect, *see supra,* note 23, which defines the concept weakly. Although Rawls's difference principle, as expressed in his second principle of justice, is thoroughly rooted in equality, his first and 'prior' principle of justice echoes Kant's dominant concern for freedom and autonomy: 'each person is to have an equal right to the most extensive basic liberty compatible with a similar liberty for others': RAWLS, *supra,* note 21, at 60.

[36] It is at least ambiguous: WESTEN, *supra,* note 21, at 73–4.

[37] Westen, *supra,* note 34. By 'empty', Professor Westen meant that normative equality claims are *'derivative',* not *'meaningless'*: WESTEN, *supra,* note 21, at xix–xx.

[38] R. DWORKIN, *supra,* note 30, at xiii & ch. 12.

[39] *See* Erwin Chemerinsky, *In Defense of Equality: A Reply to Professor Westen,* 81 MICH. L. REV. 575 (1983); Kent Greenawalt, *How Empty is the Idea of Equality?,* 83 COLUM. L. REV. 1167 (1983). *See generally* RAZ, *supra,* note 12, at 228.

ity lies not in its substance, for it possesses little if any substantive content, but in its structure, which provides a principled basis for interpersonal comparisons that offers a powerful, initial framework for evaluating moral questions—such as blame for harmful interactions—when freedoms clash.[40]

D. Distributive and Corrective Justice

Aristotle's conceptions of distributive and corrective justice, grounded in differing notions of equality, provide a helpful initial framework of just this type.[41] 'Distributive justice' concerns the manner by which goods are distributed among persons across society, prior to individual transactions among those persons. Rather than basing such distributions upon strict equality, Aristotle argued that distributive justice requires only proportionality—a distribution of goods proportionate to a person's desert or worth.[42] The content of desert or worth, in Aristotle's view, varies according to the particular political regime and social context. In technologically advanced societies, a person's worth is measured to a large extent by his productivity which, in turn, is conveniently (if imperfectly) measured by the market. Variations among persons in productivity, accidents, and other factors result in variations over time between persons in their stocks of wealth. Under Aristotle's proportionality conception of equality, therefore, variations in holdings of wealth are not only proper, but inevitable and even necessary.

Imbalances in the proportional holdings of persons thus develop over time from various events and transactions, both voluntary and involuntary. While the development of such imbalances is a concern of distributive

[40] Consider the breadth and power of the Kantian ideal of equal freedom as lucidly expressed by Roger Pilon: 'we proceed from a [natural law] premise of moral equality—defined by rights, not values—which means that no one has rights superior to those of anyone else. So far-reaching is that premise as to enable us to derive from it the whole of the world of rights. Call it freedom, call it "live and let live," . . . the premise contains its own warrant and its own limitations. It implies the right to pursue whatever values we wish—provided only that in doing so we respect the same right of others. And it implies that we alone are responsible for ourselves, for making as much or as little of our lives as we wish and can. What else could it mean to be free?': Roger Pilon, *Freedom, Responsibility, and the Constitution: On Recovering Our Founding Principles*, 68 NOTRE DAME L. REV. 507, 509–10 (1993) (footnotes omitted).

[41] ARISTOTLE, *supra*, note 21, at 140–49. *See generally* FINNIS, *supra*, note 17, at 161–84; W. VON LEYDEN, ARISTOTLE ON EQUALITY AND JUSTICE: HIS POLITICAL ARGUMENT (1985), 13; Peter Benson, *The Basis of Corrective Justice and Its Relation to Distributive Justice*, 77 IOWA L. REV. 515 (1992); Steven J. Heyman, *Aristotle on Political Justice*, 77 IOWA L. REV. 851 (1992); Ernest J. Weinrib, *Corrective Justice*, 77 IOWA L. REV. 403 (1992); Richard W. Wright, *Substantive Corrective Justice*, 77 IOWA L. REV. 625 (1992) [hereinafter *Substantive Corrective Justice*]; Richard W. Wright, *Right, Justice and Tort Law*, this volume.

[42] Aristotle appears to have borrowed the idea from Plato, who reasoned that 'the true and best equality', in the distribution of goods, such as honor, 'deals proportionately with either party, ever awarding a greater share to those of greater worth, and to their opposites . . . such share as is fit': PLATO, *supra*, note 31, at VI.757. *See* WESTEN, *supra*, note 21, at 52–7.

justice, the internal fairness of the individual transactions themselves, and whether the law should rectify their consequences, are matters involving the entirely separate notion of 'corrective justice'.[43] Aristotle believed that this form of justice required a different (one might say stronger), 'mathematical'—rather than proportional—form of equality.[44] Thus, a thief should be required to disgorge his booty and return the goods (or equal value) to his victim in order to restore the prior proportional equality of the parties. So, too, a person *wrongfully* causing another to suffer accidental loss should be required to rectify the loss, and so restore the prior proportional relationship between the parties. This weak form of equality, which is consistent with the dominant role of freedom, thus requires compensation for losses caused by *wrongful* action, but not for other losses necessarily caused by every action.[45]

III. COMMON GOOD

A. The Concept of Common Good

In contrast to the freedom ethic, which idealizes the interests of the individual, the ethic of the common good or community[46] idealizes the collective interests of the group.[47] Although individuals comprise society, so that the promotion of communal welfare advances the interests of (at least some of) its individual members, and vice versa,[48] the community ideal of com-

[43] John Finnis argues persuasively for replacing Aristotle's 'corrective justice' phraseology with Thomas Aquinas' 'commutative justice' term, on grounds that the latter term more comfortably embraces the variety of relevant considerations seemingly excluded by the narrower, formal conception of corrective justice described by Aristotle: FINNIS, *supra*, note 17, at 178–9. After 2500 years, however, a certain presumption of correctness might be deemed to attach to a concept's name, such that it may simply be too late, as a practical matter, to change its name.

[44] Plato referred to this form of equality as 'numerical', distinguishing it from the 'proportional' or 'geometric' kind: WESTEN, *supra*, note 21, at 52–3.

[45] Recall the choice-harm principle that every action 'harms' other persons to the extent that such persons are deprived, at least hypothetically, of opportunities displaced thereby.

[46] I use the term 'community' here in a broad sense, meaning basically the same thing as common good and society. This contrasts sharply with the meaning given to the word by most 'communitarian' theorists, who consider communities to be smaller groups whose very purpose is to 'mediate' between individuals and society.

[47] Freedom and community, or something like them, are perhaps the most fundamental—and often opposing—ideals in contemporary American jurisprudence. *See, e.g.,* RONALD DWORKIN, A MATTER OF PRINCIPLE (1985), 71; Robert A. Baruch Bush, *Between Two Worlds: The Shift From Individual to Group Responsibility in the Law of Causation of Injury*, 33 UCLA L. REV. 1473, 1519–29 (1986) (contrasting 'liberal' and 'social welfare' ideals). *But see* VALERIE KERRUISH, JURISPRUDENCE AS IDEOLOGY (1991), 19 (challenging 'the individual-society dichotomy').

[48] '[T]he common good *is* the good of individuals, living together and depending upon one another in ways that favour the well-being of each': FINNIS, *supra*, note 17, at 305. Aristotle viewed the common good as 'nothing more nor less than the good of each and every citizen':

mon good subordinates the separate welfare of members individually to the broader collective welfare of the group. Autonomy has no intrinsic value within the community ideal, but is valuable only instrumentally to advance the communal interests of society.

Although the communal ethic has been waning around the globe in recent years in certain formulations as a political and economic ideal,[49] it inevitably must remain a central value in any organized society where people live closely with their neighbors. Most persons understand that a single individual cannot be allowed to hold the entire world hostage to the satisfaction of his personal wants, that individuals often must make personal sacrifices for the greater good of others.[50] Whether one labels this ethic 'altruism',[51] 'communal welfare', or something else,[52] it has been a central moral and political value in differing societies, religions, and philosophies throughout the history of the world. The community ideal was important even to Aristotle, the father of corrective justice, and to Kant, the father of modern 'liberal' theories of philosophy based on the freedom of the individual. Aristotle considered humans to be by nature social,[53] and Kant directed individuals to harmonize their personal ends with the ends of others within the community[54]—free though persons may all be, free within community.[55]

The ideal of common good is examined here from the perspectives of utility and efficiency, the 'harder' formulations of group welfare.[56] Although classical utilitarian theory on a number of grounds is flawed, and even

---

Wright, *supra*, note 41, at 685. This is an important premise of the liberal wing of communitarian theory: *see* Bush, *supra*, note 47, at 1553 (referring to this phenomenon as '[t]he paradox of the communitarian vision').

[49] As demonstrated by the spectacular collapse of Marxism and Communism in the former Soviet block nations, and with the widespread decline of socialism around the world.

[50] *See* Cass R. Sunstein, *Interest Groups in American Public Law*, 38 STAN. L. REV. 29, 31 (1985).

[51] *See* Duncan Kennedy, *Distributive and Paternalist Motives in Contract and Tort Law, With Special Reference to Compulsory Terms and Unequal Bargaining Power*, 41 MD. L. REV. 563, 584 (1982).

[52] This ethic has been referred to as 'aggregate-social-welfare (*e.g.*, utilitarian)', as distinguished from a freedom-type ethic which is 'rights-based (*e.g.*, Kantian)': Wright, *Substantive Corrective Justice*, *supr*, note 41, at 631.

[53] *See* ARISTOTLE, POLITICS (E. Barker (trans.), 1958), 5; ARISTOTLE, *supra*, note 21, at 321 ('whatever it is that people regard as constituting existence, whatever it is that is their object in desiring life, it is in this that they wish to live with their friends').

[54] KANT, METAPHYSICS OF MORALS, *supra*, note 9, at *433, 436; *see* JOHN FINNIS, FUNDAMENTALS OF ETHICS (1983), 121 (referencing Kant's third categorical imperative).

[55] More recently, John Stuart Mill celebrated the ideals of both freedom and community. JOHN STUART MILL, UTILITARIANISM, LIBERTY, AND REPRESENTATIVE GOVERNMENT (1863).

[56] Softer variations on the community ideal, sometimes viewed by communitarians in terms of 'sharing', are of little help in fashioning a scheme of responsibility based on personal accountability and fault. For a brief discussion of the limited role of sharing concepts in accident law, see *Moral Foundations*, *supra*, note 8, at 457.

arguably irrational or incoherent as a *universal* moral theory,[57] a general
and non-rigorous notion of utility serves as a useful model for values that
seek to maximize the aggregate welfare or preferences of the group.[58] The
economic notion of efficiency, which rests to a large extent upon utility, is
considered also within this context. Although incomplete as general theories of moral responsibility, principles of utility and efficiency will be seen
to provide helpful guidance in the resolution of certain tort law problems.

B. *Utility and Efficiency*

Utilitarianism may be the most prominent theory of the common good in
the recent history of Western political philosophy.[59] Consequential in
nature, this ethic evaluates the moral quality of actions, and sometimes
rules,[60] by the extent to which they maximize the average (or aggregate)
welfare of all members of society. Since every action always produces some
measure of harm as well as good, the utilitarian goal is to produce the
greatest proportion of benefits to harms, the greatest net benefit to society.
The principle of allocative efficiency, which broadly seeks to maximize
communal wealth, is an economic variant of the utilitarian ideal,[61] with
philosophical roots in hypothetical consent.[62]

Conduct causing harm is justified, according to both these theories, if the
social harm reasonably expected to result from the conduct is exceeded by
the expected social benefit. The converse is also true: conduct is wrongful

---

[57] It is particularly flawed, as a *universal* theory, in disregarding the separateness of persons. *See, e.g.,* RAWLS, *supra*, note 21, at 29; RAZ, *supra*, note 12, ch. 11. *See generally* FINNIS,
supra, note 17, at 111–18, 176–7; J. J. C. SMART & BERNARD WILLIAMS, UTILITARIANISM: FOR
AND AGAINST (1973). On its arguable incoherence as a universal theory, see FINNIS, *supra*, note
17, at 112–15, 177.

[58] 'Over a wide range of preferences and wants, it is reasonable for an individual or society to seek to maximize the satisfaction of those preferences or wants': *id.* at 111–12.

[59] *See* Ronald M. Dworkin, *Rights as Trump, in* THEORIES OF RIGHTS (Jeremy Waldron ed.
1984), 153 (postulating that 'some form of utilitarianism' is 'the most influential background
[political] justification . . . in the Western democracies'). For classical statements of utilitarianism, see JEREMY BENTHAM, AN INTRODUCTION TO THE PRINCIPLES OF MORALS AND
LEGISLATION (1789); MILL, *supra*, note 55. For a modern examination of its strengths and
weaknesses, see SMART & WILLIAMS, *supra*, note 57. For a sensitive comparison of utilitarian
and egalitarian justifications of accident law, see R. DWORKIN, LAW'S EMPIRE, *supra*, note 21,
at 288–301 (finding the egalitarian account superior).

[60] Although the application of rules may generate disutility in particular cases, the broader
principles of 'rule utilitarianism' seek to promote the general welfare over time. *See generally*
John Rawls, *Two Concepts of Rules,* 64 PHIL. REV. 3 (1955); J. O. Urmson, *The Interpretation
of the Moral Philosophy of J.S. Mill,* 3 PHIL. Q. 33 (1953). Since rule utilitarianism has little
relevance to personal moral accountability, it is accorded only slight consideration in this
essay.

[61] Explained in R. DWORKIN, LAW'S EMPIRE, *supra*, note 21, at 288.

[62] *See generally* Richard A. Posner, *The Ethical and Political Basis of the Efficiency Norm
in Common Law Adjudication,* 8 HOFSTRA L. REV. 487 (1980); Alan Schwartz, *Proposals for
Products Liability Reform: A Theoretical Synthesis,* 97 YALE L.J. 353, 357–60 (1988).

if it reasonably may be expected to produce more harm than good. These principles work equally as well in justifying intentional as well as accidental harm, but only the purist utilitarian or economic theorist would insist upon the general and exclusive application of such principles to resolve intentional harm problems where such aggregative principles are (potentially, at least) destructive of certain vital rights. In accident law, however, utility and efficiency are widely and properly viewed as central considerations in ascertaining responsibility and assessing blame.

The most renowned formulation of the utility concept in accident law is the Learned Hand standard for determining negligence, by which an actor's failure to incur a lesser burden to prevent a greater risk of harm implies the actor's negligence.[63] The Hand standard may be viewed as defining negligence in economic terms:[64] if the costs of preventing an accident are less than the costs of permitting it, the failure to incur the prevention costs is inefficient and, hence, improper. Guido Calabresi's 'cheapest cost avoider' standard, which seeks to minimize the sum of the costs of accidents and the costs of accident prevention,[65] rests similarly upon the goal of maximizing communal wealth or, the mirror image, minimizing communal waste. By placing liability upon those persons who most efficiently can prevent accidents, the law may help achieve an efficient level of expenditures on both accidents and precautionary measures.[66] Thus, principles of both utility and efficiency seek to deter accident-producing conduct that is on balance wasteful for society. Conversely, both principles encourage accident-producing conduct that produces greater benefits than harm. Yet, the important point here is the preliminary *moral* wrongfulness of behavior that foreseeably causes more harm than good,[67] which wastes communal resources, and the preliminary *moral* propriety[68] of behavior that appears likely to generate a net increase in the total stock of goods.[69]

[63] *See* United States v. Carroll Towing Co., 159 F.2d 169, 173 (2d Cir. 1947) (L. Hand, J.) (expressing the concept algebraically as B<PL implies negligence, where B is the burden or cost of avoiding accidental loss, P is the increase in probability of loss if B is not undertaken, and L is the probable magnitude or cost of such loss).

[64] 'Hand was adumbrating, perhaps unwittingly, an economic meaning of negligence': Richard A. Posner, *A Theory of Negligence*, 1 J. LEGAL STUD. 29, 32 (1972). Note, however, that the principal relevance of the Hand standard to a moral inquiry of this type lies in its demonstration of respect for the equality of other persons and for communal interests, not for any utility or efficiency that the tort law rules as so defined may themselves produce.

[65] *See* GUIDO CALABRESI, THE COSTS OF ACCIDENTS (1970), 135; Guido Calabresi & Jon T. Hirschoff, *Toward a Test for Strict Liability in Torts*, 81 YALE L.J. 1055, 1084 (1972).

[66] *See generally* CALABRESI, *supra*, note 65; WILLIAM M. LANDES & RICHARD A. POSNER, THE ECONOMIC STRUCTURE OF TORT LAW (1987).

[67] Doing violence to principles of equality and the virtue of prudence, as discussed below. *See infra*, notes 96–100 and accompanying text.

[68] The moral propriety of such behavior is preliminary because it is subject to established rights, as discussed in part IV A, below.

[69] Recall that the relevance of these social goals is limited in the present enterprise to ascertaining moral accountability for a person's choices and reflected actions and, more specifically,

IV. Ordering Values and Interests

A. Ordering Values

Although the ideals of equal freedom and the common good ('community') are both powerful touchstones for ascertaining fault in tort law, one must sometimes choose between the two values in judging the moral quality of harmful conduct. Indeed, freedom and community may be contrasted to one another as polar opposites, as noted earlier. Whether one views their opposition as partial or complete, their application to tort law problems sometimes produces conflicts which must be resolved.

Suppose a starving beggar decides to take without permission and eat a loaf of bread lying inside the open kitchen window of a wealthy and well-fed baker's house. Because the abstract autonomy of the beggar is no greater than the autonomy of the baker who owns the bread, the beggar's choice to take ('convert') the bread would violate the baker's equal abstract right to freedom and hence be wrongful when judged according to that standard. Yet, when judged by any standard of common good or community, whether utility or some softer version, the starving beggar's much greater need would seem to justify his choice and act. Such variances in result arise because of the very different underlying moral concepts: freedom celebrates the separate value of each independent person, and depends upon a strong conception of ownership, of the exclusive right to property, whereas all notions of community, soft or strong, are based at some level on aggregating—not separating—human goods. At bottom, therefore, the values of freedom (and weak equality) are directly opposed to those of community, soft or strong.

Because such conflicts do arise, it should be helpful to have a general principle of preference between the two. At least because of the logical priority of freedom to community, mentioned earlier, but also because of the greater essential moral power of freedom (and its counterpart, weak equality), it may be postulated that freedom should take precedence to community as a general principle when the two values significantly conflict.[70]

Notwithstanding freedom's general claim to prior moral value, utility remains an essential moral value to respect. Indeed, rather than being shunted to the rear as an inferior moral principle, utility (and its economic surrogate, efficiency) should be promoted to a controlling status in many

to determining when such choices and actions harming other persons may be viewed as wrongful. The search here, therefore, is not for principles of tort law that themselves promote utility and efficiency, but for principles of tort law which reflect the moral quality of an actor's choices. Thus, the kind of utility of interest here is act, not rule, utility.

[70] *See generally* CALABRESI, *supra,* note 65, at 24–6; R. DWORKIN, *supr,a* note 30, at xi (rights as 'trumps'); KANT, ELEMENTS OF JUSTICE, *supra,* note 9, at *331; RAWLS, *supr,a* note 21, at 243–8. *But see* RAZ, *supra,* note 12.

instances—those in which the guidance it can provide is strong and that of freedom weak. The guidance provided by the freedom ideal may be weak because the values it sustains are implicated only slightly, or because this abstract value (more frequently than efficiency) simply cannot provide a principled, determinate solution to a particular problem. In cases such as these, where utility (or efficiency) by contrast is able to provide guidance that is clear and strong, freedom should give way to the community ideals. This secondary, but very important, role for utility and efficiency—in providing moral substance to tort law problems when freedom fails to provide an answer—might aptly be called a 'default' role.[71]

Conflicts between freedom and common good often turn out to be minor, or indeterminate, on both sides (and sometimes turn out upon close inspection to be mirages). When this occurs, when neither ideal is implicated significantly or coherently, the law justifiably may turn instead to practicality, which is based on both freedom and utility. When the significance of moral reasoning of any type is hard to ascertain, the law should seek two results: first, to provide persons with freedom to adjust their own affairs as they deem best, on grounds of personal interest and practicality, without fear of undue legal intervention; and, second, to devise simple rules that are easy for persons to understand and apply. Moral theorizing on tort law problems, including the ascertainment of fault for causing harm, may be ordered in this manner.

B. Ordering Interests

Whether one examines problems of fault in tort law in terms of freedom or the common good, comparisons between various goods or interests inevitably arise. Often actors (and the law, in judging the wrongfulness of an actor's conduct) will have to choose between life and property, or between a risk of injury to persons and the possibility of economic gain or maybe mere convenience. In making and judging such choices, therefore, actors (and evaluators of their conduct) frequently must compare and evaluate harms (and risks of harms) to such different forms of goods or interests. And so the law has sometimes ranked such interests.

It may be helpful, in beginning an inquiry into interest ranking, to scrutinize the common assertion that the safety interests of potential victims are inherently of a higher order than the interests of actors in 'mere' property, money, or convenience.[72] Interest ordering along these lines, whereby the

---

[71] For an analogous use of the default notion, see Martin A. Kotler, *Competing Conceptions of Autonomy: A Reappraisal of the Basis of Tort Law*, 67 Tul. L. Rev. 347 (1992).

[72] *See, e.g.*, Deryck Beyleveld & Roger Brownsword, *Impossibility, Irrationality and Strict Product Liability*, 20 Anglo-Am. L. Rev. 257 (1991) (utilizing Alan Gewirth's lexical ranking of goods into three tiers, whereby a person's physical integrity is ranked as a first-tier 'basic' good, whereas wealth and convenience would be ranked as third-tier 'additive' goods).

bodily integrity interest[73] is accorded a higher abstract value than property and economic interests, has a long and deep tradition in the law of torts.[74] This ethic is rooted generally in the context of truly intentional takings, of deliberate invasions of palpably identifiable property interests known to belong to specific persons targeted by the actor—where the certainty of harm to vested 'property rights' is clear. Within this context of intentionally inflicted harm, the lexical ordering[75] of major interest categories provides a system of useful markers that serve at once to identify, define, order, and provide a bulwark of protection for society's most fundamental vested rights. And so the law declares that one may not intentionally kill or maim a human to protect some jelly jars.[76]

In judging actions causing only accidental harm, however, lexical interest ordering fits much less comfortably, for at issue here is the moral quality of choices involving mere risks to interests, often of unknown persons, that are by nature remote, contingent, and speculative. While potential victims in such a context no doubt have autonomy interests in the security of their property and bodies, the actor has an equally significant autonomy interest in being able to move about in the world, inevitably risking harm to other persons as discussed above. A person's autonomy depends as well upon his wealth[77]—of holdings of money and other property—which generally may be acquired only by actions risking harm to others. The importance of property (wealth) to a person's sense of identity, and overall autonomy, has been emphasized by philosophers across the centuries.[78]

[73] One must cautiously bear in mind the important and often subtle distinctions between notions of a person's 'interests' in safety, bodily integrity, and security; a person's (imperfect) property rights in his body; and differing conceptions of abstract 'rights' and 'property rights' variously employed by commentators on tort law theory.

[74] *See generally* RESTATEMENT (SECOND) OF TORTS (1963), §§ 77-86; PROSSER & KEETON, *supra*, note 1, at 132 ('the law has always placed a higher value on human safety than upon mere rights in property'). This premise of tort law is widely shared by the general public. 'If asked, most people would probably say that the thing of ultimate value in the world is human life': PATRICK F. MCMANUS, HOW I GOT THIS WAY (1994), 36.

[75] "This is an order which requires us to satisfy the first principle in the ordering before we can move on to the second, the second before we consider the third, and so on': Rawls, *supra*, note 21, at 43.

[76] Katko v. Briney, 183 N.W.2d 657 (Iowa 1971) (spring shotgun in vacant house injured jelly jar thief).

[77] Together with liberty, opportunity, and self-respect, Rawls classifies wealth as a 'primary good', since it is 'necessary for the framing and the execution of a rational plan of life': RAWLS, *supra*, note 21, at 433. Viewing property as a form of wealth, philosophers from the time of Aristotle have recognized its fundamental importance to the pursuit of goals by human beings. *See infra*, note 78 and accompanying text. Some philosophers, such as Alan Gewirth and Joseph Raz, accord property and other forms of wealth a lower value. *See supra*, notes 72 and 12.

[78] 'The point of property is . . . to provide an external sphere for the operation of the free will': Ernest J. Weinrib, *Right and Advantage in Private Law*, 10 CARDOZO L. REV. 1283, 1291 (1989). 'The point, in justice, of private property is to give the owner first use and enjoyment of it and its fruits (including rents and profits), [which] enhances his reasonable autonomy and stimulates his productivity and care': FINNIS, *supra*, note 17, at 173. *See generally* ARISTOTLE,

And convenience logically may not be considered trivial, for it is by definition what facilitates the achievement of a person's chosen goals. As seen above, the choice-harm principle itself is based on the equal freedom premise that one person's interest in security from accidental harm (whether to property or bodily integrity) has no greater fundamental importance than another person's freedom of action to promote his chosen goals—goals which often depend on convenience, require the use of property, and which may be stored in monetary form. Of course this concept of equality applies only to interests in the abstract, so that a person's security interests (of any type) should be protected against the action interests of another when the action interests (in convenience or other goods) are of lesser value by some fair measure. But the converse is also true, and an accident victim has no inherent moral right to derogate the actor's greater interests of any type.

An actor, therefore, in moral theory must always accord equal ('due') respect to the rights of others. This general obligation entails, first, that actors must refrain from choosing intentionally to harm, without a superior protective right, other persons' rights that are vested in any type of good—whether human life, or property, or sometimes merely economic interests.[79] In addition to this general prohibition of intentional harms, an actor moving about in a crowded world must show equal respect for the security interests of others in remaining free from accidental harm. In this context, however, in which harms to other persons' interests are not desired but only risked incidentally and abstractly as remote contingencies, substantially dependent on events beyond the actor's control, an actor has no choice but to reduce all such interests to a common denominator and value them in a calculus that also fairly values his own interests—in money and convenience, as well as other interests—necessary to the achievement of his chosen goals.

Actors must make thousands of choices every day, in which numerous potential abstract interests of known and unknown persons too numerous to count must be identified, valued (in terms of worth and risk), and balanced against a similarly vast set of outcomes desired, expected and foreseen from a contemplated course of action. Often such risk-benefit decisions must be made instantly on the spot, without opportunity for significant reflection. There can be no safety absolutes in such a rugged, real-world context where choices must be made and acted upon rapidly, one after another, all day long. The greater good of all requires that persons be permitted to

supra, note 21 (bk. 4, chs. 1–6) at 106–19; HEGEL, *supra,* note 11, paras. 41, 44, 44A; JEREMY WALDRON, THE RIGHT TO PRIVATE PROPERTY (1988).

[79] The role of tort law in protecting economic interests is explored in, e.g., PETER CANE, TORT LAW AND ECONOMIC INTERESTS (1991), and Peter Benson, *The Basis for Excluding Liability for Economic Loss in Tort Law,* this volume.

make reasonable and good faith decisions that create mere risks of harm to others without penalty if they turn out wrong. Interest ordering, based on the absolute priority of certain interests, is out of place in such a context of rough and tumble choices in an imperfect world, where life and limb (as valuable as they surely are) simply must be tossed into the same decisional scales as 'mere' property, money, and convenience. Thus, in the case of accidental harm, the equal abstract freedom interests of every person (in both action and security) are usually best accommodated—and fault is usually best determined—by principles of utility.[80]

V. Fault and Intentionally Inflicted Harm

Supported by the ideal of equal freedom, the choice-end principle posits that an actor is preliminarily blameworthy if he chooses to harm another, as discussed above. The law of intentional torts embraces this principle in the *prima facie* case—that conduct is faulty, as a preliminary matter, if it reflects a choice to cause harm to another. The good-harm facet of the choice-blame principle of choice supports the various privileges that may defeat the prima facie case.

A. The Prima Facie Case

When an actor (for no good reason) chooses to intrude into the autonomy realms of another person, he infringes the other's rights to freedom and equality in a fundamental way.[81] If an actor takes without permission ('converts') a television belonging to another person, solely because the actor does not own but wants one, the actor is but a thief. Stealing property denies its owner the freedom to enjoy the fruits of his prior labor (or good fortune), which the owner had earlier chosen to transform from labor to monetary to tangible form in the object that was stolen. Such trespasses to the property rights of others—thefts—are paradigmatic violations of the

---

[80] Accidental harm in such a context, where the actor accorded due consideration to the security interests of potential victims, thus generally should be considered 'necessary' harm within the inherent limitations of knowledge, skill, and the social calculus: *see generally* Peter Huber, *Safety and the Second Best: The Hazards of Public Risk Management in the Courts*, 85 Colum. L. Rev. 277 (1985); Christopher H. Schroeder, *Rights Against Risks*, 86 Colum. L. Rev. 495 (1985). One must remember, however, that freedom generally has priority to utility even in the accident context when such freedom interests are vested and specific, as when deriving from a pre-existing relationship of the parties based on trust.

[81] *See* Aristotle, *supra,* note 21. 'In *intending* harm, one precisely makes [losses to other persons] one's gain . . . ; one to that extent uses them up, treats them as material, as a resource for a good that no longer includes their own': John Finnis, *Allocating Risks and Suffering: Some Hidden Traps*, 38 Clev. St. L. Rev. 193, 203 (1990). 'To choose harm is the paradigmatic wrong, the exemplary instance of denial of right': *id.* at 205. *See generally* John Finnis, *Intention in Tort Law*, this volume.

equal worth of others, the type of wrong described by Aristotle in explaining the restorative purpose of corrective justice applicable to involuntary transactions.[82]

In the stolen ('converted') television example, the owner deserves compensation from the thief ('converter') because the latter deliberately chose to 'take' and appropriate for his own use something that he knew was owned by someone else. When an actor chooses to act for the very purpose of consuming property rights in goods[83] that he knows are owned by, and hence in part define, another person, he thereby consumes and merges in part the will (and hence personhood) of the owner with his own. In this way, the actor joins together in a kind of joint venture with the victim, dragging the latter (in part) along through the universe for a time and purpose defined by the will of the actor and in violation of the victim's selfhood.

This partial merger of wills, chosen only by the actor, results in a form of communion between the actor and the victim, who are to this extent conjoined into a kind of unity or 'superperson'.[84] Inasmuch as he has chosen to make himself part of this unified superperson, the actor may be seen as having inflicted the harm unto himself. Yet the resulting superperson is an illegitimate creation, for it is born as a result of a union against the victim's will. By forcing a communal integration upon the victim without consent, the actor has violated the separate, equal, and autonomous status of the victim, and in justice must act to restore the victim's separateness, the condition which gave him dignity as a human being. To achieve the separation, to undo the illicit link between the two, corrective justice and the law of torts requires the actor to return the taken property (or its monetary equivalent) to the victim, thereby restoring the victim's taken will, and to retrieve unto himself the harm he willed upon the victim.[85]

B. Privileges

The choice-blame principle, it will be recalled, conditions the wrongfulness of choices and resulting conduct on the absence of good reasons for the

---

[82] See ARISTOTLE, *supra*, note 21, at 150. *See also supra*, note 26.

[83] 'Goods' in the general sense of interests of value.

[84] See generally Richard A. Epstein, *Causation and Corrective Justice: A Reply to Two Critics*, 8 J. LEGAL STUD. 477 (1979); Weinrib, *supra*, note 27. In contrast to classical utilitarianism's effect of conflating all persons into one, criticized by Rawls (see RAWLS, *supra*, note 21, at 27), the very purpose of the superperson concept employed here is to *protect* and *enforce* distinctions between persons.

[85] Moreover, in theft as with many other forms of intentional wrongdoing, notions of both retributive and corrective justice suggest the propriety of punitive on top of compensatory damages in order fully to correct the wrong. *See generally* Bruce Chapman & Michael Trebilcock, *Punitive Damages: Divergence in Search of a Rationale*, 40 ALA. L. REV. 741 (1989); Bailey Kuklin, *Punishment: The Civil Perspective of Punitive Damages*, 37 CLEV. ST. L. REV. 1 (1989); David G. Owen, *The Moral Foundations of Punitive Damages*, 40 ALA. L. REV. 705, 718–22 (1989).

harmful conduct. To be good, reasons for intentionally inflicting harm upon another generally must be based upon some prior *protective right*— some prior entitlement to person or property belonging to the actor or another, threatened by invasion from the aggressor whom the actor harms. By perversely choosing to threaten another's vested rights, the aggressor loses in the process whatever protective rights of *his* the actor needs to sacrifice in order to repel the threatened invasion to the actor's (or third person's) rights.[86] In a sense, the aggressor's loss of rights becomes the actor's gain, since the actor thereby acquires a privilege to harm the aggressor in the exercise of the protective privilege. Such protective rights to harm another—as in the defense of oneself, of another, or of one's property— fundamentally inhere in freedom and hence in general are morally superior to utility in case of conflict, as postulated earlier.

The privilege of necessity involves a minor deviation from the general priority of freedom to utility, but it basically supports the principle. Thus, where utility suggests the propriety of consuming the lesser goods of one's neighbor to save the greater goods of one's own, as where the starving beggar steals the baker's bread in the example discussed above, the necessity privilege initially reflects the community's interest in utility by permitting the intentional invasion (and barring the usual protective rights),[87] but only with respect to lower-order property invasions. Yet the ultimate triumph is had by freedom, for the privilege does not permit the taking of higher-order goods of life or limb, and the privilege to take even lower-order goods is at best partial and incomplete, for the taker must pay the owner for the loss.[88] And so the law of torts provides the starving beggar with an initial privilege to take the baker's bread, but it holds as well that the beggar ultimately must respect the baker's rights of ownership (notwithstanding the net utility[89] of the theft) by paying for the bread. And with respect to other privileges to harm intentionally, utility is accorded scant respect; even an unproductive beggar has the right to shoot and kill a productive baker who accosts the beggar in the street and appears to threaten him with death.

Privileges to intentional torts, therefore, in their very existence reflect the general superiority of freedom to utility when the two values come in conflict, although principles of utility may play a role in defining their

---

[86] This is the idea of 'protective justice' inherent in the Kantian notion of the right to freedom. *See* Richard W. Wright, *Right, Justice and Tort Law*, this volume, at 164.

[87] Ploof v. Putnam, 71 A. 188 (Vt. 1908) (boat owner may trespass on another's dock in case of storm; dock owner may not repel trespass by casting boat adrift in Lake Champlain's high seas); Protectus Alpha Navigation Co. v. North Pac. Grain Growers, Inc., 767 F.2d 1379 (9th Cir. 1985) (dock owner could not properly cast off burning ship, preventing firefighters' access).

[88] Vincent v. Lake Erie Transp. Co., 124 N.W. 221 (Minn. 1910). *See generally* PROSSER & KEETON, *supra*, note 1, at § 24.

[89] In terms of act utility. Rule utility might oppose the theft in order to promote the security of private property holdings.

proper scope.[90] And the basic point of privileges, of the right intentionally to harm another for good reason, remains unchallenged, whether the rationale for such right-protective harm is viewed as one of freedom or utility.

VI. FAULT AND ACCIDENTAL HARM

Why the common-law rules of responsibility for accidental harm also are so solidly set in fault is explainable in terms of freedom, equality, and utility, as reflected in the second and third principles of choice. Although freedom in the accident context retains its general priority to principles of the common good, especially when the victim and the actor are tied together before the accident in some relationship, utility often operates as the controlling principle (even if only by default), especially when the parties to the accident are strangers.

Before the theory of fault in accident law is examined further, the intuitive correctness of a liability principle holding actors responsible for causing harm only when they are at fault, even when they are artificially much more powerful than their weak and vulnerable human victims, may be demonstrated by an example. Suppose that a driver, *D*, approaches an intersection with a green light in his favor. A blind person, *B*, at the moment *D* begins to enter the intersection, steps out into the cross walk from behind an ambulance, parked at the curb beside the cross walk, that has hidden *B* from *D*'s view. *D*'s car hits and injures *B*. The ambulance was parked legally for an emergency call in a No Parking zone beside the cross walk. *D* was driving with all due care and had no reason to believe that a blind person might be in the vicinity. *B*'s decision to traverse the intersection was reasonable: *B* had a good reason to cross the road, and no one was around for *B* to ask for assistance. *B* pressed the control button on the cross walk pole to change the light to red, listened for and heard the usual electronic sounds from the control box indicating that the light was changing from green to red, and had no reason to suspect that the control mechanism could malfunction and emit changing noises without actually changing the light, which in fact it did. There was no way that the control mechanism malfunction could have been anticipated or prevented by the city, the manufacturer, or anyone else.

On facts like these, where *D* was truly acting with reasonable respect for the rights of others, an intuitive sense of justice would seem to shield *D*

---

[90] As possibly in justifying the principle that an actor may not choose to harm an interest of a higher order to protect a lower one—that one may not kill or maim a poacher to protect some jelly jars, as noted earlier. Yet this principle also may be viewed simply as one of ranking rights, and hence of freedom rather than utility.

from legal responsibility for 'causing' harm to B.[91] This is so, first, because the only risks D chose to inflict on B were reasonable and, second, because B as much as D chose to risk—and hence 'caused'—the collision. Protecting D from legal responsibility for B's harm seems fair to D, and not unfair to B, who may choose to insure against the risks of such reasonably caused accidents as he might insure against all other risks of injury not attributable to the fault of others, such as from tripping on a curb.

Moral theory as well as intuition supports the conclusion that responsibility for accidental harm generally should be based on fault. In searching for an elemental theory of accident law, one might nevertheless be inclined initially toward a rule of strict liability,[92] rather than one based on wrongfulness. Under such a rule, A generally would be liable for causing harm to B, whether intentionally or accidentally. Equality might appear to demand that A correct such harm in order to restore to B what A effectively appropriated to himself by choosing to expose B to a risk of harm.[93] Indeed, if the law had assigned a prior property right[94] to B's security from harm,[95] as in the context of intentional harms discussed above, then principles of both freedom and equality would argue for corrective justice strictly to be

[91] Legal responsibility, that is, in tort law to pay B for his resulting damages. Such responsibility in tort is a stronger and otherwise quite different obligation from the form of responsibility arising from the accident, linking the actor and the victim, that may generate other weaker rights and duties, such as the actor's duty to stop and minister to the victim's special needs for immediate aid. Variations on this latter form of 'weak' responsibility, aptly dubbed 'agent-regret' by Bernard Williams, *Moral Luck, in* MORAL LUCK (1981), 20 and 'outcome responsibility' by Tony Honoré, *Responsibility and Luck: The Moral Basis of Strict Liability,* 104 LAW Q. REV. 530 (1988), are examined by both Professor Honoré and Stephen Perry in their essays in this volume. *See also* Arthur Ripstein, *Equality, Luck, and Responsibility,* 23 PHIL. & PUB. AFF. 3 (1994).

[92] This was the approach taken by Tony Honoré, *supra,* note 88, and by Richard Epstein, subject to defensive pleas. *See* Richard A. Epstein, *A Theory of Strict Liability,* 2 J. LEGAL STUD. 151 (1973); Richard A. Epstein, *Defenses and Subsequent Pleas in a System of Strict Liability,* 3 J. LEGAL STUD. 165 (1974). Among the numerous critiques of Epstein's strict liability theory, the most philosophically illuminating is Stephen Perry's. *See* Stephen R. Perry, *The Impossibility of General Strict Liability,* 1 CAN. J.L. & JURISPRUDENCE 147 (1988).

[93] That is, the security interests of B that A chose to put at risk.

[94] Philosophical problems concerning liability for harm may ultimately reduce to a question of the allocation of 'property' rights. *See, e.g.,* RICHARD A. EPSTEIN, TAKINGS: PRIVATE PROPERTY AND THE POWER OF EMINENT DOMAIN (1985), 96–8 (arguing that property rights and tort liability rights are opposite sides of the same coin); Epstein, *supra,* note 92; Weinrib, *supra,* note 27. *See generally* Guido Calabresi & A. Douglas Melamed, *Property Rules, Liability Rules, and Inalienability: One View of the Cathedral,* 85 HARV. L. REV. 1089 (1972). In the context of intentional takings, tort liability rules and property rights may indeed be seen as opposite sides of the same coin, as in the starving beggar example discussed above. Yet the property rights notion does not appear to help explain the moral or legal quality of choices to act for purposes unrelated to a victim's property holdings that produce a risk of harm to such holdings only contingently and incidentally to the actor's chosen goals. In considering the problem of responsibility for such secondary risks of harm, therefore, property rights probably need to be regarded as a separate and prior notion to the concept of liability rights.

[95] As by positing that B, standing at point y, 'owns' y—or, more precisely, that B owns at the time an exclusive possessory right in y.

applied to such a case. Yet this type of appropriation theory is logically dependent upon such a prior assignment of a property right to *B*, the victim, and upon *A*'s choice to harm that right—which thereby injects wrongfulness (under the choice-end principle) into *A*'s 'taking'. But this begs the underlying question of whether *A* is at fault and should be liable for *accidentally* causing harm to *B*, where *B*'s interests in avoiding such harm have been assigned no prior protective right, and where *A* has not chosen to cause the harm.

In such cases involving merely accidental harm, where neither the actor nor the victim has a prior right superior to the other,[96] the equality ideal may help resolve this moral conundrum. The key to resolving the conflict lies in evaluating and comparing the apparent worth of the relevant interests—those likely to be promoted by *A*'s action and those likely to be protected by *B*'s security. If *A* should know that *B*'s security from risk is more valuable than the interests (*A*'s own and those of others) that *A*'s action likely will promote, *A*'s choice to sacrifice *B*'s greater interests denies *B*'s equal worth, and so is wrongful in moral theory.[97] If, to the contrary, *A*

---

[96] Efforts to understand the philosophical aspects of corrective justice tend to run into impenetrable bedrock located at the bottom of the inquiry, framed in terms of fairness in the initial distribution of property rights. The inquiry at this point thus transforms into much broader questions of distributive justice, involving the most fundamental issues of property and political philosophy. For an introduction to these issues, *see, e.g.*, DAVID MILLER, MARKET, STATE, AND COMMUNITY (1989), ch. 2. This may well be the point at which philosophical inquiry into principles of tort law ends, and pure ethics and political philosophy begins. 'I have reached bedrock and this is where my spade is turned': LUDWIG WITTGENSTEIN, PHILOSOPHICAL INVESTIGATIONS (1953), § 217 *quoted in* Catherine Pierce Wells, *Tort Law as Corrective Justice: A Pragmatic Justification for Jury Adjudication*, 88 MICH. L. REV. 2348, 2363 (1990).

[97] An unremitting principle requiring actors always to accord the interests of others equal concern and respect to their own may be too strong for a practical, general moral or legal theory. *See generally* R. DWORKIN, LAW'S EMPIRE, *supra*, note 21, at 291–301; FINNIS, *supra*, note 17, at 304. Yet the principle unremitted is arguably what the classic 'Golden Rule' concept contemplates in abstract terms. *See, e.g.*, KANT, METAPHYSICS OF MORALS, *supra*, note 9. Moreover, when the principle of equal respect is applied to problems of *accident* law, it may be interpreted consistently with a general proposition permitting an individual ordinarily to accord primacy to his own interests as a matter of practical convenience. *See* FINNIS, *supra*, note 17, at 177 (as a matter of 'practical reasonableness', one 'cannot reasonably give equal "weight", or equal concern, to the interests of every person anywhere whose interests he could ascertain and affect'); *see also* SAMUEL SCHEFFLER, THE REJECTION OF CONSEQUENTALISM (1982). In general, an actor may fairly be considered blameworthy for causing another's accidental harm only if the actor knew or reasonably could foresee that his conduct was likely to cause more harm than good to the interests of a foreseeable class of persons of which the victim was a member. To recover damages for accidental harm, an accident victim should be required to establish that the actor's harmful behavior was *unreasonably* selfish—that (1) the actor chose to act in a manner that he should have known would expose foreseeable persons to foreseeable risks that he should have known to be more valuable than the interests of his own (and others) that he was seeking to promote, and (2) such excessive harm in fact resulted. Thus, the notion of a violation of the equal respect principle in the accident context is limited and circumscribed by linked notions of evaluation, selfish choice, action, harm, causation, and the burden of proof in law.

reasonably believes that the interests to be promoted by his action are more valuable than the interests foreseeably risked[98] thereby, then A's choice of action is proper under principles of equality.[99] Correspondingly, B's insistence in the latter case that the law require A to compensate B for his loss, under a principle of strict liability, would be to demand that B's interests be accorded more than equal worth and, hence, would be improper. The moral foundation in equality for resting responsibility for accidents upon this type of evàluative interest comparison derives from Aristotelian principles of virtue.[100] This conception of responsibility, of course, embraces also the basic calculus of risk or Hand-formula approach to fault, rooted in utility as well as equality, that has long defined responsibility for accidental harm in the law of torts. Thus, the basic ethic revealed to lie behind responsibility for accidental harm is captured in the dual-faceted choice-blame principle, that choosing to risk harm to others without good reason is blameworthy, but that so choosing for good reason is proper.

B might argue that a strict liability rule would not prevent A from promoting the greater good but would only require A to pay for, and hence 'internalize', the (lesser) costs of promoting the greater good—just as the starving beggar must pay the owner for the stolen loaf as in the intentional harm context discussed above. But the *intentional* 'taking' situation involves very different choices by the actor with respect to very different interests of the victim whom the actor targets for particular harm. No similar forced communal nexus between the wills of actors and victims occurs in cases of mere accidents. In contrast to the situation where the actor intentionally consumes goods known to belong to someone else, a person acting for a purpose unrelated to another person is, by hypothesis, not willing a communion with that person. Instead, harm caused by *accidental* encountering with other persons is by definition *unwilled*. Creating mere risks to the interests of others is an inherent and unavoidable consequence of every action, for every action entails harm (at least contingently) to others. To the extent that risks of harm from action may be deemed a necessary part of 'proper' choices of action in an uncertain world, and hence 'reasonable' according to some fair standard, they should be viewed as 'background risks' of life

---

[98] It is important to remember that the utility calculus discussed here concerns only the law of *accidents* and, hence, only *foreseeable risks* of harm to the interests of others. At the time of action, therefore, the possibility of such harm is by hypothesis contingent—an unlikely future eventuality that probably will not occur. This fact bears materially upon the moral quality of A's decision to 'sacrifice' B's interests for his own. *See* FINNIS, *supra*, note 17, at 126–7.

[99] It is also proper under related principles of utility and efficiency. *See* R. DWORKIN, LAW'S EMPIRE, *supra*, note 21, at 282. *See generally* Schwartz, *supra*, note 62. Even if A's choice proves wrong in fact, it still would be a morally proper choice if it appeared reasonable on the facts available to A at the time A acted.

[100] In particular, the virtue of *prudence*, as explained in James Gordley, in *Tort Law in the Aristotelian Tradition*, this volume.

for victims to protect against and bear.[101] Thus, *B*'s 'taking' argument, for imposing strict responsibility on *A*, is unpersuasive in cases of accidental harm.

B's compensation claim for accidental harm reasonably caused by *A* fails finally on causation grounds. As explained by the choice-harm principle discussed above, every choice to act or refrain from acting causes 'harm', at least theoretically and potentially, to other persons who commensurately are deprived of related opportunities.[102] Thus, unless the wrongfulness issue has already been resolved by a preassignment of property rights to the victim of an accident, even a 'passive' accident victim may be considered the responsible 'cause' of the harm he suffered.[103] This is because the victim, even if completely motionless at the time of the accident, made a series of deliberative choices (and resulting actions) at some time prior to the accident that were necessary antecedents to its eventuality.[104] Nothing inherent in the victim's mere 'passivity' at the precise moment of the accident is a shield from bearing moral responsibility for the intended or foreseeable consequences of such prior choices.[105]

---

[101] Potential victims often may self-insure against such risks most efficiently: *see Moral Foundations, supra,* note 8, at 484–93. On background risks, see George P. Fletcher, *Fairness and Utility in Tort Theory,* 85 HARV. L. REV. 537, 543 (1972).

[102] If *B*, standing at point *y*, chooses to remain at *y*, he deprives *A*, standing at point *x*, of the opportunity to move to *y*, thereby 'harming' *A*. If, notwithstanding *B*'s presence at *y*, *A* decides to move to *y*, resulting in a collision that causes harm, the decision of *B* as well as that of *A* may be seen to 'cause' the harm. Assuming that *B* had no prior property interest in point *y*, and assuming further that there is no good reason to prefer security (inaction) to action, then *B*'s choice to remain at *y* is just as much a cause of the collision as *A*'s choice to move to *y. See generally* Judith Jarvis Thomson, *Causality and Rights: Some Preliminaries,* 63 CHI.-KENT L. REV. 471 (1987). One's intuitive preference for the passive security interest of *B* in this situation may reflect assumptions, often unfounded, (1) that *A* intended to harm *B*, or (2) that *B* had a prior vested right in *y*. In the accident situation, the first assumption is simply wrong. The second assumption is more problematical and may derive from some rough conception of first-in-time-first-in-right: *see* Peter Benson, *The Basis of Corrective Justice and Its Relation to Distributive Justice,* 77 IOWA L. REV. 515, 584–91 (1992). Or perhaps it reflects a confusion between one's (imperfect) property rights to one's own body and one's mere interest in remaining at a particular point in space. It may be, however, that *A* rather than *B* 'owns' *y*, in which case *B*'s poaching thereon, and his obdurate refusal to move when he sees *A* coming, is as much or more the 'cause' of the collision as is *A*'s assertion of a right to occupy his *y*.

[103] *See generally* R. H. Coase, *The Problem of Social Cost,* 3 J.L. & ECON. 1, 2, 12–13 (1960); Richard A. Posner, *Strict Liability: A Comment,* 2 J. LEGAL STUD. 205, 217–20 (1973).

[104] *See generally* Tony Honoré, *Necessary and Sufficient Conditions in Tort Law,* this volume; Richard W. Wright, *Causation in Tort Law,* 73 CAL. L. REV. 1737 (1985).

[105] 'Except in unusual circumstances it can be said of any plaintiff that he made a choice to be where he (or his property) was when the harm he suffered occurred, and, just as the defendant was pursuing his own purposes in choosing to act as he did, so in making *his* choice the plaintiff was presumably attempting to further ends of his own': Perry, *supra,* note 92, at 156. '[W]e are necessarily dealing in tort law with an intersection of *two* choices to act, not with the effects for one person of a single such choice which has been made by another': *id.* at 157.

Consequently, if the law is to treat actors and victims[106] as equals, there appears to be no moral basis—in freedom, equality, or common good—for a general rule of liability that holds actors strictly accountable for accidental harm.[107] Instead, the ideals of freedom, equality, and utility all support a scheme of responsibility for accidental harm, with only small pockets of strict liability,[108] that basically is built on fault.

VII. Conclusion

The law of torts by definition concerns the law of 'wrongs'. With few exceptions, fault defines the core and borders of responsibility throughout this entire area of the law. While harm alone in some abstract sense may be viewed as a 'wrong' to the person suffering it, in most cases an actor fairly may be held accountable for making good the harm only if he was *at fault* in causing it, only if his choices that resulted in the harm fairly may be blamed. Choosing to deny another person's equal right to freedom is the most fundamental reason for such blame. While intentional harms generally are wrongful, an actor may properly choose to harm another in the exercise of his prior protective rights. In an imperfect and dynamic world, accidental harm is inevitably entailed in human freedom, such that conduct resulting in accidental harm may be considered faulty only if it results from a choice to violate another person's vested rights or the community's interests in utility. Based on philosophical foundations of this type, the law of torts rests comfortably on elemental notions of right and wrong, on principles of fault.

[106] Who might more appropriately be referred to as 'earlier actors' when they are passive at the time of harm.

[107] *See generally* Jules L. Coleman, *The Morality of Strict Tort Liability*, 18 Wm. & Mary L. Rev. 259 (1976); *The Fault Pit, supra,* note 7; Perry, *supra,* note 92; Ernest J. Weinrib, *Toward a Moral Theory of Negligence Law,* 2 Law & Phil. 37 (1983). Thus, Ames and other early tort law scholars were right in arguing for the general superiority of a rule of fault (negligence) to the 'unmoral' rule of strict liability: *see, e.g.,* Ames, *supra,* note 4.

[108] Probably for harm from commercial misrepresentations and manufacturing defects, see *Moral Foundations, supra,* note 8, and possibly from wild animals and specially dangerous activities.

Intention in Tort Law

JOHN FINNIS*

Need liability in tort be based on anything other than negligence? Is it necessary, indeed is it right, to treat *intent to harm* as a distinct basis for liability, independent of issues about reasonable foresight and the appropriate range and standards of care? Should the early-twentieth century bifurcation of torts into the intentional and the negligent be abandoned? Questions such as these cannot sensibly be answered without a clear understanding of intention as a real element in human conduct. They are questions which this essay does not undertake to settle. Its purpose is rather to indicate how academic writings as widely different as economic analysis of law and the *Restatement (Second) of Torts* have obscured the reality of intentions, and how that reality is clarified in the judicial development of doctrines as widely different as battery and conspiracy to injure in trade and labor relations.

I. INTENTION: ENDS AND MEANS OR HOPES AND DESIRES?

Intention is a tough, sophisticated, and serviceable concept, well worthy of its central role in moral and legal assessment, because it picks out the central realities of deliberation and choice: the linking of means and ends in a plan or *proposal*-for-action *adopted* by *choice* in preference to alternative proposals (including to do nothing). What one intends is what one chooses, whether as end or as means. Included in one's intention is everything which is part of one's plan (proposal), whether as purpose or as way of effecting one's purpose(s)—everything which is part of one's reason for behaving as one does. In reading the words 'plan', 'proposal', 'deliberation', and 'choice', one should ignore all connotations of formality and 'deliberateness'; in the relevant sense there is a plan or proposal wherever there is *trying*, or doing (or refraining from doing) something *in order to* bring about something or *as a way of* accomplishing something. And there is deliberation and what I am calling adoption of a proposal by choice wherever one course of conduct is preferred to an alternative which had attraction. On

* Professor of Law and Legal Philosophy, University of Oxford, and Professor of Law, University of Notre Dame.

all these matters there is a substantial and well-grounded measure of agreement among philosophers.[1]

Accordingly, common speech has many ways of referring to intentions and the intentional. It deploys not only the cognates of 'intend', but also such phrases as 'trying to', 'with the objective of', 'in order to', 'with a view to', 'so as to', and, often enough, plain 'to', and many other terms.

Consider, for example, Holmes's phrase 'prepared an injury' in dictum in *United Zinc & Chemical Co. v. Britt*:[2] 'The liability for spring guns and mantraps arises from the fact that the defendant has not rested on [the] assumption [that trespassers would obey the law and not trespass], but on the contrary has expected the trespasser and *prepared an injury* that is no more justified than if he had held the gun and fired it'.[3] Nearly thirty years earlier, Holmes had put the same point in the language of intent: a landowner who sets man-traps 'has contemplated expressly what he would have had a right to assume would not happen [that is, the trespass], and the harm done stands just as if he had been on the spot and had done it in person. His *intent* may be said to make him the last wrong-doer.'[4]

The argument had been brilliantly spelled out in Sydney Smith's famous critiques of *Ilott v. Wilkes*, the decision of the King's Bench in 1820 that a landowner who gave notice of his spring guns and man-traps[5] was not liable to trespassers injured by them. Here is one of Smith's sallies:

I do not say that the setter of the trap or gun allures the trespasser into it; but I say that the punishment *he intends* for the man who trespasses after notice is death. He covers his spring gun with furze and heath, and gives it the most natural appearance he can; and in that gun he places the slugs by which *he means* to kill the trespasser. This killing of an unchallenged, unresisting person, I really cannot help considering to be as much murder as if the proprietor had shot the trespasser with his gun . . . . Does it [matter] whose hand or whose foot pulls the string which moves the trigger?—the real murderer is he who *prepares* the instrument of death, and

---

[1] Among recent writings, see, e.g., R.A. Duff, Intention, Agency and Criminal Liability: Philosophy of Action and the Criminal Law (1990), chs. 2 & 3; Anthony Kenny, The Metaphysics of Mind (1989); Carlos J. Moya, The Philosophy of Action (1990); Alan R. White, Grounds of Liability: An Introduction to the Philosophy of Law (1985), ch. 6; Alan R. White, Misleading Cases (1991).

[2] 258 U.S. 268 (1922).

[3] *Britt*, 258 U.S. at 275, *per* Holmes J. for the Court (emphasis added).

[4] Oliver Wendell Holmes, Jr., *Privilege, Malice, and Intent*, 8 Harv. L. Rev. 1, 11 (1894) [hereinafter *Privilege*] (emphasis added). Holmes adds (*id.* at 12) that the intent in question is 'actual intention', not the 'external standard' form of 'intent' which, in his view(*id.* at 1), the law finds where there is manifest and great probability of harm.

[5] The typical man-trap was in fact a spring gun: a heavily loaded shot-gun, its trigger attached to springs and wires arranged in hidden lines along which the blast of shot would travel when anybody tripped them. Typically, such guns were set in woods and gardens to deter, disable, and punish poachers, who under the law of the day were no more than trespassers.

places it in a position that such hand or foot may touch it, *for the purposes of destruction.*[6]

Or as Smith puts it in the first of his two *Edinburgh Review* articles: 'What is the difference between the act of firing yourself, and placing an engine which does the same thing? . . . There is the same *intention* of slaying in both cases—there is precisely the same human agency in both cases; only the steps are rather more numerous in the latter case.[7] Thus both Holmes and Smith make manifest the synonymity of 'intention' with many alternative terms and phrases. Put strictly in the language of intent, their thesis is that, just as personally shooting a trespasser engaged in no act or threat of violence is simply killing or wounding with intent to kill or wound, so too setting a spring gun involves intending (conditionally but really) to do the same 'without personally firing the shot.'[8] And what one cannot lawfully, with intent, accomplish 'directly' (in person) one cannot, with the same intent, accomplish 'indirectly' (mechanically).

Now this argument was in fact put squarely by the plaintiff's counsel in *Ilott v. Wilkes*, and unanimously rejected by four well-regarded judges of the Court of King's Bench.[9] The judges' arguments to distinguish shooting by machine from shooting in person are weak. Of greater interest is the preliminary argumentation employed in two of the four judgments, argumentation to which Justice Holmes's dictum in *Britt* is a response. Chief Justice Abbott puts it thus:

I believe that many persons who cause engines of this description to be placed on their grounds do not do so with the intention of injuring any one, but really believe that the notices they give of such engines being there, will prevent any injury from occurring, and that no person who sees the notice will be weak and foolish enough to expose himself to the perilous consequence likely to ensue from his trespass.[10]

And Bayley J like this: 'Such instruments may be undoubtedly placed without any intention of doing injury, and for the mere purpose of protecting property by means of terror; and it is extremely probable that the defendant in this case will feel as much regret as any man for the injury which

---

[6] Sydney Smith, *Man Traps and Spring Guns*, 35 EDINBURGH REV. 410 (1821), *reprinted in* SYDNEY SMITH, WORKS (1859), 340, 345 [hereinafter *Man Traps*] (Smith italicized only the words 'to kill'). The passage is put on the mouth of an imaginary fifth judge in *Ilott v. Wilkes* and hence is deliberately more ponderous than Smith's own usual style.

[7] Sydney Smith, *Spring Guns*, 35 EDINBURGH REV. 123 (1821), *reprinted in* SMITH, WORKS, *supra,* note 6, at 322, 324 (1859) [hereinafter *Spring Guns*].

[8] Robert Addie & Sons Ltd. v. Dumbreck [1929] A.C. 358, 376, *per* Lord Dunedin. On conditional intentions, see JOHN FINNIS ET AL., NUCLEAR DETERRENCE, MORALITY AND REALISM (1987), 81–6, 99–100, 111–12, 124 ; John Finnis, *On Conditional Intentions and Preparatory Intentions, in* MORAL TRUTH AND MORAL TRADITION: ESSAYS IN HONOUR OF PETER GEACH AND ELIZABETH ANSCOMBE (Luke Gormally (ed.), 1994).

[9] Ilott v. Wilkes, 3 B. & Ald. 304, 106 E.R. 674 (K.B., 1820); see the opening sentences of the argument of counsel for the plaintiff-respondent, 3 B. & Ald. at 307, 106 E.R. at 676.

[10] *Id.* at 307, 106 E.R. at 676.

the plaintiff has sustained.'[11] The fallacies about intention are in each case clear enough. Chief Justice Abbott, unless he was supposing a high degree of ignorance or self-deception about the frequent[12] 'accidents' involving spring guns, clearly confuses intending with *hoping*. Landowners of the kind he envisages may well both desire and hope that no one will trespass and thus that no one will be shot, yet they clearly do intend that those (if any) who do trespass will be shot. As Sydney Smith puts the point:

> But if this be the real belief of the engineer—if he think the mere notice will keep people away—then he must think it a mere inutility that the guns should be placed at all: if he think that many will be deterred, and a few come, then he must *mean* to shoot those few. He who believes his gun will never be called upon to do its duty, need set no gun, and trust to rumour of their being set, or being loaded, for his protectio. . . . He who sets a *loaded* gun *means* it should go off if it is touched.[13]

'Means to' is another synonym for 'intends to'.

As for Bayley J's arguments, the first fails to recall that one intends not only one's ultimate ends (say, protecting one's property) but also all the means one has chosen to further those ends (say, injuring or killing poachers as a punishment, and as a deterrent to and disablement from future poaching). One's chosen means are indeed one's *proximate ends*,[14] some more and some less proximate. ('Why are you carrying that gun and wire?' 'In order to lay a man trap.' 'Why do that?' 'In order to punish, deter and disable poachers.' 'Why do that?' 'To have game for hunting.' 'Why hunt?' 'For the opportunity to show my skill and meet my friends and associates.') And Bayley J's second argument simply confuses one's forming and having an intention with one's having emotions, such as enthusiasm or vindictiveness as opposed to *ex ante* reluctance and *ex post* regret. Many crimes (and therefore batteries and other torts) of the most deliberate intent are committed with great regret, if only because of the risk of detection.

Sydney Smith's articles orchestrated the movement for reform which culminated in an Act of 1827 outlawing in England the laying of outdoor spring guns. The last and most brutally frank of the parliamentary speeches in defense of spring guns was given by Lord Ellenborough, the rising young politician son of the late Lord Chief Justice Ellenborough. But even he felt the need to veil the proximate intention of man trappers by confusing it with their motive (further end, further intention):

---

[11] *Id.* at 307, 106 E.R. at 677.

[12] *See* Hansard, 17 PARL. DEB. (2d ser.), col. 19 (23 Mar. 1827); *see also* col. 26, where the Home Secretary, Robert Peel, speaks of the 'daily accidents and misfortunes arising from the use of [spring guns as man traps]'. In *Ilott*, the victim was gathering nuts; in Bird v. Holbrook, 4 Bing. 628, 130 E.R. 911 (C.P., 1828), he was retrieving a neighbor's wandering peahen.

[13] Smith, *Spring Guns, supra*, note 7, at 325 (Smith italicized only 'loaded').

[14] For the explanation of this important feature of intention by Aristotle (who lacked the word, but scarcely an understanding of the reality) and Aquinas, see John Finnis, *Object and Intention in Moral Judgments according to St. Thomas Aquinas*, 55 THOMIST 1 (1991).

The *object* of setting Spring-guns [is] not personal injury to any one, but to deter from the commission of theft; and that object [is] as completely obtained by hitting an innocent man as a guilty one. [T]he bill [is] contrary to that principle of the English law, which [gives] a man protection for his property, in proportion to the difficulty with which it would be protected by the ordinary means.[15]

The veil is here truly diaphanous, for the argument tacitly concedes that the deterrent 'object' (intent) will be attained only by the infliction of injury or death on at least a few trespassers, culpable or innocent; such injury or death is thus intended as a means to achieving the deterrent object. And in the fundamental structure of the common law, as of sound jurisprudence, one private person's killing or injuring another with such an intent is simply a commutative injustice, whatever the killer's further purposes, objects, motives.[16] It is the sort of conduct, the sort of transaction between persons, which cannot be justified by alleged assumption of risk or by appeal to the maxim *volenti non fit injuria*,[17] fear of future greater harm, or any considerations of distributive or allocative justice as between landowners, game consumers, and poachers, whether game-seeking or (like the unlucky Ilott) nut-gathering.

When young Lord Ellenborough frankly identified a common purpose of laying spring guns as being precisely to *do harm*, as a deterrent *means* of stopping poaching, he was not inaccurate. His point is illustrated by the facts in *Bird v. Holbrook*.[18] The defendant tulip gardener testified that his reason for not posting notices was: he wanted to catch the tulip thieves, *by injuring them*. Instead, of course, he mutilated only young Bird, who was trying, in broad daylight, to help a neighbor by recapturing a peahen which had strayed into Holbrook's booby trapped garden.

II. INTENTION MISUNDERSTOOD AND REJECTED

Richard Posner made *Bird v. Holbrook* the centerpiece of his earliest published exposition of the implications of economic analysis for the common

[15] Hansard, 17 PARL. DEB. (2d ser.), col. 296 (9 Apr. 1827) (substituting direct for indirect speech).

[16] *See infra,* text accompanying notes 65–70.

[17] The maxim was a primary ground for the judgment of Bayley and Holroyd JJ in *Ilott v. Wilkes*.

[18] 4 Bing. 628, 130 E.R. 911. The facts arose before the Act of 1827, and the case was accordingly decided on the basis of the unreformed common law, which the Court of Common Pleas, *per* Best CJ (who had been the junior justice of the King's Bench in *Ilott v. Wilkes*), determined had always been in line with the Act of 1827, so far as concerned spring guns laid *without notice*. This ruling is foreshadowed by the explanation which Best J. made from the bench on 3 June 1821, in response to the excoriating attack upon him in Sydney Smith's first article against *Ilott v. Wilkes*. See *Man Traps, supra,* note 6, at 341–2.

law.[19] Indeed, this is the one case which Posner cites in his textbook treatment of the category of intentional torts.[20] Disclaiming (at that point) any normative purpose, and offering only to 'explain' the law's 'pattern',[21] Posner says that the issue in the case 'was the proper accommodation of two legitimate activities, growing tulips and raising peacocks'.[22] Spring guns may be the most cost-effective means of protecting tulips in an era of negligible police protection; but they discourage the owners of domestic animals from pursuing them onto other people's property 'and so increase the costs (enclosure costs or straying costs) of keeping animals'.[23] The challenge for the common law judges accordingly was, in Posner's view, to design 'a rule of liability that maximized the (joint) value of both activities, net of any protective or other costs (including personal injuries)'.[24]

So with a stroke the whole question of intention to injure is swept from view; not only are the 'personal injuries' homogenized into the other costs of keeping peacocks, but the fact that *these* injuries were done by one who *intended* to injure a human being (albeit not anticipated to be a mere peacock-pursuer) is treated as wholly irrelevant. The argument which had prevailed in Parliament in 1827 and subsequently in common law courts all over the United States[25] is treated as of no consequence. And explicitly so: 'intentionality is neither here nor there', according to Posner.[26] Why not? The answer is a paradigm of the *non sequitur*:

[I]t is surely not correct to say that society never permits the sacrifice of human lives on behalf of substantial economic values. Automobile driving is an example of the many deadly activities that cannot be justified as saving more lives than they take. Nor can the motoring example be distinguished from the spring-gun case on the ground that the one who sets a spring-gun intends to kill or wound. In both cases, a risk of death is created that could be avoided by substituting other methods of achieving one's ends (walking instead of driving); in both cases the actor normally hopes the risk will not materialize.[27]

In short, intending death and carelessly risking causing death are equivalent because both involve creating the risk of death; A is equivalent to B if A includes something important about B. And there are other equivocations in the passage.

---

[19] Richard A. Posner, *Killing or Wounding to Protect a Property Interest*, 14 J.L. & ECON. 201, 209 *ff*. (1971) [hereinafter *Killing or Wounding*].

[20] RICHARD A. POSNER, ECONOMIC ANALYSIS OF LAW (4th edn., 1992), 206–11 [hereinafter ECONOMIC ANALYSIS].

[21] Posner, *Killing or Wounding, supra,* note 19, at 211.

[22] POSNER, ECONOMIC ANALYSIS, *supra,* note 20, at 207.   [23] *Id.*

[24] Posner, *Killing or Wounding, supra,* note 19, at 210.

[25] *See, e.g.*, State v. Childers, 14 N.E.2d 767, 770 (Ohio 1938): 'By the overwhelming weight of authority, a person is not justified in taking human life or inflicting bodily harm upon the person of another by means of traps . . . unless, as a matter of law, he would have been justified had he been personally present and had taken the life or inflicted the bodily harm.'

[26] Posner, *Killing or Wounding, supra,* note 19, at 206.   [27] *Id.*

First, an equivocation on 'sacrifice'. Posner's use of the phrase 'sacrifice of human lives' treats as equivalent the decision to build a skyscraper, expecting that about three construction workers will fall off and be killed, and the decision to kill three construction workers to encourage the others to meet their performance targets. Secondly, an equivocation on 'hopes'. Posner's claim that, both in carelessly and in intentionally killing, 'the actor normally hopes the risk will not materialize' merely synthesizes and repeats the confusions of Chief Justice Abbott and Bayley J in *Ilott v. Wilkes*. Careless drivers hope there will be no collision *and*, that if there is, no-one will be killed. Man-trappers hope that no-one will invade their property but that anyone who does *will* be shot. And in confusing emotion with will, Posner fails to observe the emotional reluctance with which many or even most murders are committed.

Posner's writings on intention are replete with fallacies and oversights. For example, to prove that the distinction between intentional and unintentional torts is 'confusing and unnecessary', his textbook begins:

Most accidental injuries are intentional in the sense that the injurer knew that he could have reduced the probability of the accident by taking additional precautions. The element of intention is unmistakable when the tortfeasor is an enterprise that can predict from past experience that it will inflict a certain number of accidental injuries every year.[28]

It is tempting to dwell on the corrupting potential of this conception of intention. For example, one can foresee that lecturing and writing on difficult topics, unless extended beyond one's allotted measure, is certain to confuse some of one's audience. One therefore, on Posner's account, has the intention of confusing. Well then, why not throw in a few deliberate falsehoods, with (real) intent to confuse and deceive, when convenient for attaining one's legitimate educative or persuasive goals?

But the more direct objection is that Posner's conception of intention is a fiction, a faulty understanding of human action. The central reality of action in those intentional torts which Posner mentions at the outset of his subsequent treatment of them is, as he says, that 'the defendant [was] *trying* to harm the plaintiff'.[29]

In this later treatment by Posner (with Landes), however, that glimpse of reality is soon obscured and lost to sight, as the facts about intention and action get thoroughly confused with normative considerations and conclusions. Landes and Posner's first move is the right one: a rejection (albeit tacit) of Posner's earlier claim that those who conduct an enterprise knowing that

---

[28] Posner, Economic Analysis, *supra,* note 20, at 206–7 (where the conclusion that the distinction between intentional and unintentional torts is unnecessary is no longer drawn explicitly).
[29] William M. Landes & Richard A. Posner, The Economic Structure of Tort Law (1987), 149 (referring to assault, battery, and false imprisonment).

injuries are highly probable must intend the injuries. But they make this move on the basis of an economic argument whose conclusion—that no economic purpose is served by classifying the injuries from risky enterprises as intentional—is reached only with the aid of two assumptions: (1) that the risk run by the enterprise is justifiable, and (2) that the injuries are neither desired by nor beneficial to those conducting it.[30] The economic argument is thus question-begging and redundant. And the conception of intention suggested by the second assumption is unsound.

For 'desire' is never the mark of intention (unless 'desired' is given a narrow sense precisely equivalent to 'intended'). The man-trapping landowner may strongly desire that no one will trespass and be shot, yet intend that anyone who *does* trespass *will* be shot. Conversely, side-effects (effects which one is not trying/intending to bring about) may be welcome, and in that straightforward sense desired—and yet are not intended. One may choose to join the army (as conscript or as volunteer) only because it is one's legal or patriotic duty, yet welcome and thus desire, without intending, the bonus side-effects of gaining exposure to a diversity of personalities. The commanders of a bombing force may regard civilian casualties and consequent demoralization and highway-obstructing civilian refugee columns as a welcome bonus, and yet not intend them; they select only military targets, calibrate the bombs and plan the bombing runs exclusively for the purpose of destroying those targets, and desist from bombing areas containing civilians as soon as the military targets are removed.

Having declared that the operators of a *reasonably* risky railroad do not intend the deaths which they foresee as certain to be incurred by its operations over time, Landes and Posner's next move is simply to relapse into what they call 'the probability theory of intent', oddly described as a subcategory of 'deliberately inflicting an injury whether or not the injurer believes he is acting wrongfully.'[31] 'When someone does something that is overwhelmingly likely to produce a specific result, we are properly skeptical when he denies that the result was intended.'[32] But in many cases such skepticism would be wholly misplaced. Think again of lecturers who know

---

[30] *Id.* at 150, 151. [31] *Id.* at 151.

[32] *Id.* at 153. Landes and Posner add that, to accommodate cases where a result is wanted but improbable (e.g., B's trying to destroy a speeding car by dropping a boulder from a bridge), 'intent can also be inferred from any combination of probability, severity, and cost of avoidance that shows that the injury was not merely a by-product of lawful activity. B will not be heard to deny that he wanted to damage the car; there is no other plausible interpretation of his motives. . . . The critical factor is that the costs of avoidance to the injurer are low relative to the social benefits of the activity': *id.* Here questions of overall justification have completely swamped the purported discussion of intention. A realistic interpretation of motives does not depend either on knowing the costs of 'avoiding' behavior nor on the behavior's (un)lawfulness. 'By-product', however, is a concept dependent on the distinction between intention (what is intended, because an end or means within a proposal adopted by choice) and side-effect. The confusion of normative with anthropological considerations could scarcely be more complete.

that they will leave some of their audience confused; or stutterers who know that they will annoy some of their listeners; or people who wear shoes, knowing that they will wear out, or who fly the Pacific, knowing that they will get jet lag. All these undesired effects are not merely foreseeable but certain.[33]

One should return to the thought which Landes and Posner put first, and affirmed, but then (as we have just seen) rendered nonsensical. Those who intend a result, whether for its own sake or as a means to something else, are trying (however reluctantly) to bring it about. Persons so intending a result are not trying to create a risk of a result but trying to create that result. Not content to leave things to chance (to hazard, to risk), such persons are instead intervening to achieve a result they intend. As regards that result, the risk which they are concerned about is not the risk of it happening but the risk of it *not* happening. And, since we lack the capacity of making something be the case simply by willing it, the risk that the results one intends will not happen is just an inevitable side-effect or incidental concomitant of one's intention, choice, and action.

III. INTENTION: ENDS AND MEANS OR FORESEEN CONSEQUENCES?

English law takes the position that intent to harm does not render tortious conduct which but for such intent would be lawful. But the House of Lords decisions which adopted this position—*Mayor of Bradford v. Pickles*[34] and *Allen v. Flood*[35]—were marred by confusion between physical behavior and human action, between intention and feeling, and between what is intended and what is side-effect. Their broad denial of the relevance of motive was promptly, generally, and persuasively rejected in American law. Moreover, their impact has been greatly reduced by the development of a doctrine of tortious conspiracy to harm, a development which reflects a generally sounder understanding of the real character of intentions, their role in identifying what act is being done, and their distinction from motivating feelings and from knowingly causing side-effects.

Pickles's intention, in drawing off water which would otherwise have percolated into the land of the local public water-supply company, was to force the company to buy him out. The pleader's claim[36] that this involved an intent to harm the company could well have been, and to some extent was,

---

[33] One is almost tempted to call the 'probability theory' of intention, classifying such painful side-effects as intended, a pseudo-masochistic theory of intention.

[34] [1895] A.C. 587. [35] [1898] A.C. 1.

[36] The statement of claim included an allegation paraphrased in *Pickles* [1895] A.C. at 589 thus: "[He] had not a *bona fide* intention to work his minerals, and . . . his intention was to injure the appellants and so to endeavor to induce them either to purchase his land or to give him some other compensation.'

rejected as a mere misdescription. For the proposal which Pickles adopted—the idea he had in mind—was not to cause harm to the company, whether as end or means, but make his land (and/or the flow of water from it) valuable.[37] Of course, that purpose *might* have been motivated by the further purpose of damaging the company's finances—an ulterior motive which might have been an end in itself (a case of spite) or a means to some yet more ulterior purpose. But the pleadings made no such suggestion that it was.[38] So the case might have rested there. The wide dicta[39] in the House of Lords, to the effect that acts otherwise lawful cannot be made tortious by malice or other motive or intention, were gratuitous. And the accompanying dicta appealing to a symmetry between right-making and wrong-making factors—the claim that, as good motives cannot legitimate unlawful means, so bad motives cannot delegitimate lawful means[40]—sophistically ignore one of morality's most elementary principles and moral philosophy's most strategic themes. There is no such symmetry. One's conduct will be right only if *both* one's means *and* one's end(s) are right; therefore, *one* wrong-making factor will make one's choice and action wrong, and *all* the aspects of one's act must be rightful for the act to be right. The acting person's intentions must be acceptable all the way down (or up).

In *Allen v. Flood*,[41] the defendant, an official of an ironworkers' union, was sued for threatening to call his union members out, thereby 'maliciously' inducing employers to dismiss (lawfully) the plaintiffs, members of a shipwrights' union. There was evidence that the threat was issued to punish the shipwrights for having, in the past and for other employers, done ironworkers' work. Having been directed that 'maliciously' meant 'with the intention and for the purpose of doing an injury to the plaintiffs in their business', the jury found that the defendant had maliciously induced the employers to terminate the plaintiffs' contracts. The House of Lords, by a narrow majority, overturned this verdict, and their conclusion is not incompatible with an appropriately fine-grained understanding of the defendant's intentions. But the understanding of intention actually displayed in the opinions is deeply confused. In the leading judgment, for example, Lord

---

[37] *See supra*, note 36, *infra*, note 38, and *Pickles* [1895] A.C. at 595, *per* Lord Halsbury L.C., 600, *per* Lord Macnaghten.

[38] In the secondary literature, Pickles is often said to have been motivated by spite, but the trial judge, North J, made no such finding and held that he had acted out of economic self-interest. North J's finding that Pickles was in 'bad faith' meant no more than that Pickles's claims to be digging shafts for the purpose of commercial mining were insincere. *See Corporation of Bradford v. Pickles* [1894] 3 Ch. 53, 68: 'his operations are intended for the drainage of his stone, not in order that he may be enabled to work it, but in order that the Plaintiffs may be driven to pay him not to work it.'

[39] *See Pickles*, [1895] A.C. at 594, *per* Lord Halsbury L.C., 598, *per* Lord Watson, 598, *per* Lord Ashbourne, 601, per Lord Macnaghten.

[40] *See id.* at 594, *per* Lord Halsbury L.C., 599, *per* Lord Ashbourne.

[41] [1898] A.C. 1.

Watson (author of the loosest dictum in *Mayor of Bradford v. Pickles*) openly assimilates 'motive' with 'internal feelings' as opposed to 'outward acts'.[42] This approach betrays the common unsound assumption that human acts can be identified, for purposes of moral or legal assessment, independently of the acting person's intention(s). To be sure, outward *behavior* can be so identified. But countless *acts* cannot be truly identified for what they are (*prior* to assessment as right or wrong, lawful or unlawful) unless and until the outward behavior which they involve is understood as *the carrying out of such and such an intention*. Should this pat on the back be deemed a greeting, a warning, an encouragement, a condescension, a code sign to waiting police officers, or something else?

Forming and carrying out these formative and act-defining intentions is a matter of having not 'internal feelings' but a practical idea, a plan, a proposal—however instantaneous and informal—which one adopts by choice. Such a plan includes end(s) and means, perhaps very closely related (as in giving a greeting). Carrying out any plan, engaging in any conduct, has side-effects, caused and perhaps knowingly caused and fully foreseen by the acting person, yet not intended.

Inept handling of the concept of intention (under whatever name) marks most of the judgments in *Allen v. Flood*, most notably in their failure to identify the equivocation in the conception of 'malice'[43] with which the legal sources and professional discourse then current, and the trial judge's direction to the jury, confronted them. On that conception, malice includes having a purpose to 'benefit oneself at the expense of one's neighbor'. But 'at the expense of' extends equivocally to two very different cases: (1) where loss to the neighbor is the ultimate *or intermediate* object/purpose/intent (and benefit to oneself is not more than a welcome side-effect), and (2) where benefit to self is the object (and loss to the neighbor is only a foreseen, perhaps even a welcome, side-effect).[44] To be sure, the House of Lords

---

[42] '[I]n any legal question, malice depends, not upon evil motive which influenced the mind of the actor, but upon the illegal character of the act which he contemplated and committed. . . . [W]hen the act done is, apart from the feelings which prompted it, legal, the civil law ought to take no cognizance of its motive': *Allen* [1898] A.C. 1 at 94, *per* Lord Watson. 'I am altogether unable to appreciate the loose logic which confounds internal feelings with outward acts, and treats the motive of the actor as one of the means employed by him': *id.* at 98, *per* Lord Watson.

[43] *See id.* at 118–21, *per* Lord Herschell. Note the sentiments of Holmes in his letter to Pollock of October 21, 1895 in relation to *Allen v. Flood* in the Court of Appeal: 'how little importance I attach to the discussions of the run of judges, whether English or American, on matters involving general theory—beyond the *fact* that in a given jurisdiction they do so and so'; and of Pollock in his letter to Holmes of March 30, 1898 in relation to the same case in the House of Lords: 'that decision I think is the only safe one for a world of people who mostly get muddled over subtle distinctions and think them unjust whenever they can't understand': HOLMES-POLLOCK LETTERS (Mark DeWolfe Howe (ed.), 1941), I, 65, 84–5.

[44] I do not assume that wherever loss or harm to the neighbor is intended there is or should be liability. J. B. Ames, *How Far an Act May be a Tort Because of the Wrongful Motive of the*

rejected the conception of malice which involves this confusion; the judges discerned its incompatibility with the lawfulness of any winner-takes-all commercial competition.[45] Yet they did not identify the confusion's source: failure to distinguish the intention to secure all the available trade (and in this sense 'win') from the certain side-effect of such trading success—causing loss to the loser.[46]

That distinction, implicit in the competition cases from *Mogul Steamship Co. v. McGregor, Gow & Co.*[47] onwards, finally becomes an explicit and central theme when Viscount Simon L.C.'s leading judgment in *Crofter Hand Woven Harris Tweed Co. v. Veitch*[48] identifies the true question at issue:

The question to be answered . . . is not 'did the combiners appreciate, or should they be taken as appreciating, that others would suffer from their action,' but . . . 'what is the real purpose of the combination?' The test is not what is the natural result to the plaintiffs of such combined action, or what is the resulting damage which the defendants realize or should realize will follow, but what is in truth the object in the minds of the combiners when they acted as they did. It is not the consequence that matters, but purpose.[49]

Lord Simon thus avoids the term 'intention', preferring the language of 'object' or 'purpose'; but later cases and discussions often adopt his analysis while speaking synonymously of intent(ion).[50]

Actor, 18 HARV. L. REV. 411 (1905) [hereinafter *Wrongful Motive*], which is still perhaps the most helpful and illuminating treatment of the issues around *Allen v. Flood*, identifies a wide group of cases in which even a defendant with the most reprehensible motives (further intentions) escapes liability because, e.g., what he was requiring the plaintiff to do or abstain from doing was already the plaintiff's legal duty to do or not do: *id.* at 412–13, or because the defendant enjoyed legal privilege: *id.* at 413–14, or because the defendant's malevolence extended only to non-feasance in a situation where he had no duty to act: *id.* at 416, note 1.

[45] *See Allen* [1898] A.C. at 164, *per* Lord Shand, 179, *per* Lord James.

[46] Indeed, Lord Herschell, in rejecting the concept of malice, stated that lawful competitive practices include cases where, 'the very object of the defendants was to induce shippers to contract with them, and not to contract with the plaintiffs, and thus to benefit themselves at the expense of the plaintiffs, and *to injure them* by preventing them from getting a share of the carrying trade. Its express object was *to molest and interfere* with the plaintiffs in the exercise of their trade': *id.* at 140 (emphasis added). Intention and side-effect are here completely confused with each other.

[47] [1892] A.C. 25. The uncertainty with which the Lords handle intention and side-effect in this case can be exemplified by one quotation: 'there is nothing indicating an intention to injure the plaintiffs, except in so far as such injury would be the result of the defendants obtaining for themselves the benefits of the carrying trade, by giving better terms to customers than their rivals, the plaintiffs, were willing to offer': *id.* at 60, *per* Lord Hannen. Similarly, see *id.* at 36, *per* Lord Halsbury L.C.

[48] [1942] A.C. 435.   [49] *Id.* at 444–5.

[50] *See, e.g.*, Lonrho Plc. v. Fayed [1992] 1 A.C. 448, 463–8. In Lonrho Ltd. v. Shell Petroleum Co. [1982] A.C. 173, 189, Lord Diplock treats 'intent' and 'purpose' as synonymous in this context, passing in silence over his own view that in law, or at least in criminal law, foreseen results are intended (*see, e.g.*, Hyam v. Director of Public Prosecutions [1975] A.C. 55, 86). J. F. CLERK & W. H. B. LINDSELL, TORTS (R. W. M. Dias *et al.* (eds.), 16th edn., 1989), 886, n. 13, 888, n. 34, having commended the word 'object', moves easily into speaking of paramount *intention* and predominant *intent* to injure.

For English and Scottish law, the *Allen v. Flood* rule that motive or intention is irrelevant is definitively confined by *Crofter Harris Tweed* to situations where there is no combination (conspiracy).[51] Wherever there is combination, intention to harm is of decisive significance, albeit in somewhat various ways depending on whether the means employed to effect the combiners' purpose are themselves actionable or not.[52] For, even when the conspirators' chosen means are *per se* actionable without proof of intent to harm, the presence of such intent establishes that the conduct of the conspirators will not be capable of justification.[53] And where intent to harm is a prerequisite for establishing liability (because the means are not otherwise actionable), such intent is also *sufficient* to establish liability, except where that intent is merely a secondary accompaniment[54] to another predominant and legitimate purpose and is not accompanied by any unlawful act.

American tort law in this area has developed along different lines. On the one hand, the doctrine that motive cannot render tortious a lawful act has met general disfavor.[55] Even Holmes rejected it, distinguishing the relevance of motive in this context from his strong support for the 'external standard' in general negligence law.[56] And Ames's nuanced yet powerful attack upon the irrelevance-of-motive doctrine was adopted almost verbatim in what became the leading case, *Tuttle v. Buck*.[57] The opinion in *Tuttle*

[51] This tort of conspiracy to injure has recently been much described as 'anomalous' (*see, e.g., Lonrho Plc.* [1992] 1 A.C. at 463, 467), but on a larger view it is the wide doctrine of the irrelevance of intention (motive), i.e. of *Bradford Corporation v. Pickles* and *Allen v. Flood*, which is anomalous in the face not only of American and civil law but even of aspects of English common law including not only the tort of conspiracy to injure but also malicious prosecution and the type of nuisance instantiated in Christie v. Davey, [1893] 1 Ch. 316 (1892) and Hollywood Silver Fox Farm Ltd. v. Emmett [1936] 2 K.B. 468.

[52] If the means are unlawful, any intent to harm the plaintiff will suffice; if they are in themselves lawful, the intent to harm must be the combiners' predominant purpose: *Lonrho Plc.* [1992] 1 A.C. at 463, 468.

[53] 'In so far as the cases talk of a need for "just excuse" or "justification" those words seem to be no more than a description of the need for evidence (as to his trade or other legitimate interests) which a defendant can put in to meet the plaintiff's case when the latter has adduced evidence of *apparent intention* to injure on the defendant's part': CLERK & LINDSELL, *supra*, note 50, at 890–1 (citations omitted) (emphasis added).

[54] JOHN G. FLEMING, THE LAW OF TORTS (7th edn., 1987), 669–70 states that the combiners may lawfully intend harm as a means to advancing a purpose which is really or predominantly constructive. But his authority is a dissenting judgment at first instance on a motion to strike out in a 1900 case.

[55] This falls short of full-blooded repudiation. *See, e.g.,* RESTATEMENT (SECOND) OF TORTS (1977), § 870 cmt. i.

[56] 'It has been considered that, *prima facie*, the intentional infliction of temporal damage is a cause of action, which . . . requires a justification if the defendant is to escape. . . . It is no sufficient answer to this line of thought that motives are not actionable and that the standards of the law are external. That is true in determining what a man is bound to foresee, but not necessarily in determining the extent to which he can justify harm which he has foreseen': Aikens v. Wisconsin, 195 U.S. 194, 204 (1904) (citations omitted), *per* Justice Holmes for the Court. This is foreshadowed in Holmes, *Privilege*, *supra*, note 4, at 2–3.

[57] 119 N.W. 946 (Minn. 1909).

v. Buck sets out one of Lord Watson's wide dicta in *Allen v. Flood*, goes on to demonstrate its overbreadth and implausibility, and concludes with an unacknowledged transcription of Ames's clinching scenario:

> To divert to one's self the customers of a business rival by the offer of goods at lower prices is in general a legitimate mode of serving one's own interest, and justifiable as fair competition. But when a man starts an opposition place of business, not for the sake of profit to himself, but regardless of loss to himself, and for the sole purpose of driving his competitor out of business, and with the intention of himself retiring upon the accomplishment of his malevolent purpose, he is guilty of a wanton wrong and an actionable tort.[58]

On the other hand, Holmes, Ames, and the American courts failed to adopt the English position that intent to harm negatives justifiability. Instead, the relevant American tort doctrine (as Holmes desired)[59] generally embraced a position which at least in its formulation is congenial to utilitarian moral thought and far less congenial to traditional common morality: the intentional infliction of harm is actionable, whether or not there is conspiracy, if and *only if* imposing liability would be in line with the 'balance' of the conflicting interests of the litigants with the social and economic interests of society in general.[60]

IV. Constructive Intention, Real Intention, and Justice to Persons

The common law of torts and crimes has for at least two centuries been working itself free from the artificialities of objective form which were exemplified by such doctrines as felony-murder and trespassory liability for all direct injury. The process of introducing the morally relevant 'subjective' distinctions into legal doctrine has been complicated by utilitarianism. Utilitarianism had no patience with the old fictions, but it also had an agenda of its own, in which—since only 'outcomes' matter—the distinction between intention and foresight or even foreseeability has no fundamental or generally important role. So the reshaping of legal doctrine has been

---

[58] 119 N.W. 946 (Minn. 1909) at 948. *Compare* Ames, *Wrongful Motive, supra,* note 44, at 420: 'If, however, a man should start an opposition shop, not for the sake of profit for himself, but, regardless of loss to himself, for the sole purpose of driving the plaintiff out of business and with the intention of retiring himself immediately upon the accomplishment of his malevolent purpose, would not this wanton causing of damage be altogether indefensible and a tort?'

[59] *See, e.g.,* Holmes, *Privilege, supra,* note 4, at 3 (emphasis added), 'the intentional infliction of temporal damage . . . is actionable *if done without just cause'. See generally* Patrick J. Kelley, *A Critical Analysis of Holmes's Theory of Torts,* 61 Wash. U. L.Q. 681, 705–7 (1983).

[60] *See* Restatement (Second) of Torts (1977), § 870 cmts. c, e.

conducted under the shadow of the thought which Henry Sidgwick, master of the late nineteenth century's mature utilitarianism, expressed with characteristic directness: 'For purposes of exact moral or juristic discussion, it is best to include under the term "intention" all the consequences of an act that are foreseen as certain or probable.'[61]

This assimilation of what even Holmes called 'actual intention' with a merely deemed, fictitious intention has been repudiated with increasing force and clarity in English,[62] if not in American[63] criminal law. But it is installed (not without some significant modification) at the heart of American tort doctrine by the *Restatement (Second) of Torts'* definition of intent: 'The word "intent" is used throughout the Restatement of this Subject to denote that the actor desires to cause consequences of his act, or that he believes that the consequences are substantially certain to result from it.'[64] Thus the golfer whose only hope of winning at the last hole is to take a very long drive across water 'intends'—according to the *Restatement*—to miss the green and lose the ball in the pond.

The case for imposing this fiction upon the law is that outcomes do indeed matter, and people have moral responsibilities in respect of outcomes which they foresee (as highly probable) and can avoid. The case against the fiction is partly that it is indeed fiction, and partly that in common morality, as opposed to utilitarianism, those moral responsibilities are assessed by standards which—for reasons sketched in the remainder of this section—are distinct from the standards governing what one intends. The basic distinction between murder and manslaughter, as understood in modern criminal law, is only the most obvious monument to this broad distinction between types of standard.[65]

In drawing this distinction, common morality is not indifferent to outcomes. But it includes among the significant outcomes the impact of choosing and intending upon the character of the chooser. It attends to the fact that *choices last*. The proposal which one adopts by choice in forming an

---

[61] HENRY SIDGWICK, THE METHOD OF ETHICS (1874, 7th edn., 1907) (1874) 202.

[62] *See* Lord Goff of Chieveley, *The Mental Element in the Crime of Murder*, 104 L.Q.R. 30, 42–3 (1988); John Finnis, *Intention and side-effects, in* LIABILITY AND RESPONSIBILITY, (R.G. Frey & Christopher Morris (eds.), 1991), 32, 33–5, 45–6.

[63] *See, e.g.,* United States v. United States Gypsum Co., 438 U.S. 422, 445 (1978); Sandstrom v. Montana, 442 U.S. 510, 525–6 (1979): 'The element of intent in the criminal law has traditionally been viewed as a bifurcated concept embracing either the specific requirement of purpose or the more general one of knowledge or awareness.' This is the position increasingly repudiated in England.

[64] RESTATEMENT (SECOND) OF TORTS (1963) § 8A. Comment b adds: 'As the probability that the consequences will follow decreases, and becomes less than substantial certainty, the actor's conduct loses the character of intent.' This notion of *degrees of intent* dramatizes the difference between the American Law Institute's conception of 'intent' and intention as understood in common sense and philosophy.

[65] Not every detail of the definition of murder is, or perhaps need be, derived from intent to kill or cause grievous bodily harm: *see* Finnis, *supra,* note 62, at 49.

intention, together with the reasoning which in one's deliberation made that proposal intelligently attractive, *remains*, persists, in one's will, one's disposition to act. The proposal (and thus the intention) is, so to speak, synthesized into one's will, one's practical orientation and stance in the world. And this is a real, empirical (though spiritual), and inbuilt effect of one's adopting a proposal. Whatever consequences lie *outside* one's proposal, because neither wanted for their own sake nor needed as a means, are *not* synthesized into one's will. Though one may foresee these results, and may accept that one will be causing them, or the risk of them, one is not adopting them. They are side-effects, incidental risks. One may well be culpable in accepting them. But the ground of culpability will not be that one intended them, but that one wrongly, e.g. unfairly, accepted them as incidents of what one did intend.

When one intends some harm to (an)other human person or persons—when one's proposal includes, however reluctantly, some damage to (for example) their bodily integrity, or to their participation in knowledge of reality, or to their means of sustenance[66]—one is shaping oneself as one who, in the most straightforward way, exploits others. And this is so, whether one intends that harm for its own sake, as in revenge or spite, or as a means, as in killing or maiming *pour encourager les autres*, or deception for the sake of fraud, or perjury for the sake of justice, or the engineering of financial ruin for political purposes. In each case, the reality and the fulfillment of those other persons is radically subjected to one's own reality and fulfillment, or to the reality and fulfillment of some other group of persons. In *intending* harm, one precisely makes their loss one's gain, or the gain of some others; one to that extent uses them up, treats them as material, as a resource for a good that no longer includes their own.

Common, non-utilitarian morality's principle that one must never choose (intend) harm to the person of any human individual both expresses and preserves the understanding that each human individual is more than just a locus of utility or wealth (to be measured at some arbitrarily chosen future moment), or a channel or conduit for maximizing that wealth or utility (again, a maximum as measured at some *chosen* future moment). It expresses and preserves each individual person's *density*, so to speak, or *dignity*, if you will, as an equal of *everyone* else in basic rights. To choose harm to the person is the paradigmatic wrong, the exemplary instance of denial of right.

---

[66] The moral significance of intent to damage property or to harm persons in their wealth can be different from the moral significance of intent to harm persons as such, inasmuch as property and wealth are instrumental rather than basic goods intrinsic to the person, and inasmuch as in time of necessity the subpersonal resources of the world, including items of property, become common to the extent necessary to meet the emergency. *Compare* Vincent v. Lake Erie Transp. Co., 124 N.W. 221 (Minn. 1910). The obligation to pay compensation (not damages) seems to have been founded not on intent to harm but on an intentional act directly causing harm, i.e. on some sort of tacit analogy with intentional trespass to land or chattels.

A primordial and always primary (though not the only primary) function of government and law is to rectify this denial of right, this commutative injustice, by ensuring that the injurer does the injured the commutative justice of reparation.[67] No doubt there is a distributive, allocative aspect to this activity of government and the legal system. From a common stock of possible activities to be undertaken, costs incurred, and individual responsibilities to be drawn upon and distributed, the law assigns some part to this task of underwriting and guaranteeing commutative justice. Doing so is an act of distributive justice, but is ancillary to the prior, identifiable relationship of commutative injustice and potential commutative, reparative justice between the individuals. In this way, again, the dignity of the individuals, each ends in themselves (and in each basic aspect of their reality and potentiality as persons), is again expressed and preserved. So, for judges to try to decide a case like *Bird v. Holbrook* by the method commended by Posner—comparing costs (and benefits) of tulip growing with costs (and benefits) of peacock rearing—would be a denial of right.

In acts of reparative justice, government and law can be seen to have a role quite distinct from achieving any future 'end-state' state of affairs. The political community, unlike a one-project firm which must account to its shareholders at the end of the project, has no *goal*. Its success in fulfilling its responsibilities cannot be measured by any technique comparable to accounting. Success and failure are measured by quite other norms, among which the rule proscribing and rectifying intentional harm to the person is fundamental.

Moral responsibility and consequent legal liability for intentional infliction of harm are paradigmatic, exemplary. Avoiding such wrongs is only a necessary, not a sufficient, condition of acting justly. But the same respect for each individual whom one might have harmed as a means to an end carries over into, and informs, the quite different principle of fairness. Here one encounters the quite different principles of commutative injustice involved in imposing harmful foreseen side-effects on actors who fail to comply with rational principles such as the Golden Rule, in contravention of truths such as that no-one has an *a priori* superior claim on the earth's resources and no-one, therefore, has unqualified dominion over any part of them. The Golden Rule in its application involves, first, a discernment of one's feelings and then, secondly, a dispassionate rational adherence to the standard of care established by one's feelings.[68]

---

[67] Thomas Aquinas' term 'commutative justice' better embraces the variety of relevant considerations than does Aristotle's not dissimilar notion of 'corrective justice'. *See generally* JOHN FINNIS, NATURAL LAW AND NATURAL RIGHTS (1980), 178–9.

[68] *See* John Finnis, *Natural Law and Legal Reasoning, in* NATURAL LAW THEORY (Robert P. George ed., 1992), 134, 149.

Without confusing the norms of fairness with the norms outlawing certain intentions, legal thought can and does reasonably find criteria of fairness and unfairness in *analogies to the intentional.* So the wrongfulness of laying spring guns with intent to wound affords an analogue, a paradigm, for identifying as unjust the omissions of those who inherit already-laid spring guns and retain them without such intent to wound; or who allow similarly lethal and concealed conditions to persist on their land when they know that what disguises the lethality also exercises a fatal attraction or allurement to innocent strangers, including trespassers. But the range of the analogy must be controlled not by verbal or 'conceptual' considerations—word plays on 'trap', 'entrapment', etc.—but by considerations of fairness: how one wishes others to behave to oneself and one's friends; how one would behave, and would want others to behave, when one's friends or children strayed from the straight and narrow.

This conception of the fairness which is a shaping principle of commutative justice recognizes the proper role of sentiments in giving content and application to a moral principle which itself is simply rational. The normal form in which these sentiments make their presence felt in jurisprudence and legal reasoning is in the form of conventions and customs and in the far from bloodless life of the 'reasonable person' in our community here and now.[69]

And reasonable people never act (or refrain from acting) with intent to harm their neighbors. To the extent that the law continues on its centuries-long trajectory of convergence with morality, and is not deflected into the broad and easy utilitarian way (which offers to commensurate incommensurables and so can never succeed in doing more than provide rationalizations for what powerful people want),[70] judges and jurists will become less and less content with the easy-going assumption that harm done to a person by a forcible act of justified self-defense (including a private person's defense of others) is *intended.* Instead, they will become more and more interested in, and attracted to, the analysis of private defense of self or others proposed by the philosophical thinker who gave common morality and the reality of intention alike their perhaps most profound and influential discussion.[71] When defending oneself, it may of course be the case that one is intending to harm one's assailant as an end (satisfying one's hatred, spite, resentment, desire to get back one's own) or as a means (of deterring the assailant or potential assailants, or of disablement from some future revenge attack). But if one has none of those intentions, then one's *intent*

[69] *See generally* Patrick J. Kelley, *Who Decides? Community Safety Conventions at the Heart of Tort Liability*, 38 CLEV. ST. L. REV. 315 (1990).

[70] *See* John Finnis, *Commensuration and Law, in* INCOMMENSURABILITY (Ruth Chang (ed.), forthcoming).

[71] AQUINAS, SUMMA THEOLOGIAE II-II, Q. 64, a. 7.

can and should be simply to *stop this attack* by whatever means of stopping it are at hand. All the harm to the assailant, including the harm one foresees as certain, can be a side-effect, unintended. And therefore, out of respect for persons, such a side-effect should be unintended—and so, too, should be no tort, provided one acts fairly by choosing the least harmful of the efficacious means one knew or ought to have known were safely and readily available.[72]

V. Conclusion

My discussion has hinted at answers to the questions with which this essay began, questions about the very foundations and structure of tortious liability. But the argument of the essay has focussed on three preliminary issues: what intention is, independently of artificial conceptual extensions; why intention, so understood, is morally significant; and how an intent to harm is a *per se* wrong-making factor in any conduct, independently of other wrong-making factors such as negligence. The key to all these preliminary issues is the set of related distinctions between intention and desire, between behavior and action, and between intended upshot and foreseen (and even welcome) side-effect. These distinctions become clear when the forming of an intention is understood for what it is: the adopting of a proposal which, however rapidly and unselfconsciously, one has shaped in deliberation and preferred to any alternative option available for one's choice.

---

[72] *See* Finnis, *supra*, note 62, at 53–4.

The Standards of Care in Negligence Law

RICHARD W. WRIGHT*

I. MORAL FOUNDATIONS

In a prior essay in this collection, I argued that the Kantian–Aristotelian theory of legal responsibility, based on the foundational norm of equal individual freedom, is normatively much more attractive than its main competitor, the utilitarian efficiency theory. According to the equal freedom theory, each human being has an absolute moral worth as a free and equal member of the community. Thus, the common good to which law and politics should be directed is not the meaningless maximization of the aggregate utility or welfare of the society as a whole, as assumed by the utilitarian efficiency theory, but rather the creation of conditions that allow each person to realize his or her humanity as a self-legislating free rational being.[1]

The legal economists generally do not contest the relative normative unattractiveness of the utilitarian efficiency theory. They usually acknowledge that utilitarian efficiency can be at best a secondary goal that is constrained by distinct morally justifiable goals—more particularly, the pursuit of justice. However, they explicitly or implicitly assume that this constraint is minimal.[2] They also argue that, although the utilitarian efficiency theory may appear to be normatively unattractive, it seems to be the moral theory that actually underlies our law and politics, since it allegedly best (or even solely) explains the content of our existing laws, particularly tort law.[3]

---

* Professor of Law and Norman & Edna Freehling Scholar, Chicago-Kent College of Law, Illinois Institute of Technology; Visiting Fellow, Brasenose College, University of Oxford. This essay is part of a larger work in progress. I am grateful for the helpful comments of John Davies, John Finnis, and David Owen.

[1] See Richard W. Wright, Right, Justice and Tort Law, this volume.

[2] See, e.g., GUIDO CALABRESI, THE COSTS OF ACCIDENTS: A LEGAL AND ECONOMIC ANALYSIS (1970), 24–33, 291–308; WILLIAM M. LANDES & RICHARD A. POSNER, THE ECONOMIC STRUCTURE OF TORT LAW (1987), 1, 8–9, 14, 18–23, 312–13; RICHARD A. POSNER, ECONOMIC ANALYSIS OF LAW (3d edn., 1986), 11–13, 21–6.

[3] See, e.g., LANDES & POSNER, supra, note 2; A. MITCHELL POLINSKY, AN INTRODUCTION TO LAW AND ECONOMICS (1983); STEVEN SHAVELL, ECONOMIC ANALYSIS OF ACCIDENT LAW (1987); Guido Calabresi, Concerning Cause and the Law of Torts: An Essay for Harry Kalven, Jr., 43 U. CHI. L. REV. 69 (1975); Ronald H. Coase, The Problem of Social Cost, 3 J.L. & ECON. 1 (1960). But see CALABRESI, supra, note 2, at 239–87 (criticizing tort law as inefficient).

In my prior essay, I challenged the utilitarians' descriptive claim primarily on the global level. I elaborated the Kantian concept of Right and its corollary Aristotelian concepts of distributive and corrective justice and argued that these concepts explain, justify, and illuminate the general structure of tort law and its traditional status as the preferred liability regime for interpersonal injury. In this essay, I challenge the utilitarians' claim with respect to the standards of care in negligence law. Negligence liability is the most common type of tort liability and is thought to be the most obvious example of tort law's utilitarian foundation. If the utilitarian efficiency theory cannot explain negligence liability—its prime doctrinal example in its favorite field of common-law liability—it is in very serious trouble. Conversely, if the equal freedom theory can explain and justify negligence liability, it will have cleared what many see as the biggest hurdle for a nonutilitarian theory of tort liability.

II. The Unworkability of the Utilitarian 'Hand Formula'

Negligence is generally described as behavior that creates unreasonable foreseeable risks of injury. Almost all jury instructions, the vast majority of judicial opinions, and many secondary sources do not provide any test or definition of what constitutes unreasonably risky behavior, other than an often circular reference to the 'ordinary care' that would be exercised by the reasonable or prudent person in the same or similar circumstances.[4]

Legal scholars are less reticent. There is an almost universal assumption among legal scholars that a person's conduct is deemed unreasonable, and hence negligent, if and only if the foreseeable risks created by such conduct exceed its expected social utility.[5] This aggregate risk-utility test of reasonableness was most explicitly articulated in Judge Learned Hand's famous formula in *United States v. Carroll Towing Co.*: a person's conduct X is unreasonable only if P times L is greater than B, where P is the probability of an injury occurring, L is the magnitude of the injury, and B is the expected benefit of engaging in conduct X or, conversely, the expected burden or cost that would have to be borne to avoid engaging in conduct X.[6]

The assumed prevalence of Hand's risk-utility formula as the operative test of reasonableness in negligence is deemed to be the strongest evidence

---

[4] The major exception is the consumer-oriented risk-utility test for defective product designs. *See infra,* text at note 51.

[5] *See* Restatement (Second) of Torts (1963), §§ 291–3 (*but see infra,* note 43); John G. Fleming, The Law of Torts (7th edn., 1987), 102–8 (*but see infra,* text at note 33); 3 Fowler V. Harper, Fleming James, Jr. & Oscar S. Gray, The Law of Torts (2d edn., 1986), 467–82; W. Page Keeton, Dan B. Dobbs, Robert E. Keeton & David G. Owen, Prosser and Keeton on the Law of Torts (5th edn., 1984), 171–3 [hereinafter Prosser & Keeton].

[6] 159 F.2d 169, 173 (2d Cir. 1947).

of the utilitarian efficiency foundation of tort law. Under the utilitarian efficiency theory, conduct is efficient (hence reasonable and not negligent) if it maximizes the total sum of expected benefits minus costs; it does not matter who bears the costs and who gains the benefits. The Hand formula seems perfectly to reflect this view. However, there are insurmountable problems with the Hand formula even under the utilitarian efficiency theory.

The problems are both descriptive and analytic. In order to identify the efficient levels of precaution, one must focus on marginal increments in costs and benefits attributable to marginal increments in precaution, rather than the total costs and benefits of some particular suggested precaution.[7] Yet it is highly doubtful that courts engage in, or are even capable of engaging in, such marginal analysis.[8]

More significantly, even proper marginal analysis will not identify the efficient levels of precaution when the Hand formula is applied separately (as it must be) to the conduct of the defendant and the plaintiff. For example, assume that a $100 loss to the plaintiff could have been avoided by (1) a unilateral $40 precaution by the defendant, (2) a unilateral $60 precaution by the plaintiff, or (3) a bilateral $15 precaution by the defendant and $15 precaution by the plaintiff. As is almost always the case in practice, the most efficient (least total cost) option is the third, which requires bilateral precaution by both parties rather than unilateral precaution by one or the other. Yet, applying the Hand formula separately to each party's conduct, the defendant would be deemed negligent if she did not adopt option (1), since her $40 precaution would have avoided a $100 loss, and the plaintiff would be deemed negligent if he did not adopt option (2), since his $60 precaution would have avoided a $100 loss. Under the traditional negligence liability rule, according to which the plaintiff cannot recover if he is contributorily negligent, the defendant will not take any precaution, since she knows the plaintiff either will adopt option (2), in which case there will be no loss and hence no liability, or will not adopt option (2) and be barred from recovering any damages due to his contributory negligence. The plaintiff, knowing that the defendant has no (economic) reason to take any precaution, will adopt option (2)—i.e., spend $60 to avoid the $100 loss. Using the Hand formula to determine the negligence of the parties' respective conduct thus leads to the least efficient option being chosen, rather than the most efficient option.

The Hand formula will identify the efficient precaution level for one of the parties only if it is applied using the risks, burdens, and benefits that

[7] *See* John Prather Brown, *Toward An Economic Theory of Liability*, 2 J. LEGAL STUD. 323, 332–4 (1973).
[8] *See* Mark F. Grady, *A New Positive Economic Theory of Negligence*, 92 YALE L.J. 799, 806–9, 821–9 (1983).

would be expected if the other party were exercising his or her efficient level of precaution—a solution blithely assumed by the legal economists.[9] However, this solution is hopelessly circular: identifying the first party's efficient precaution level requires first knowing the second party's efficient precaution level, but the second party's efficient precaution level can be identified only if the first party's efficient precaution level is known, and so on around the circle.

Thus, from the standpoint of utilitarian efficiency, the Hand formula must be abandoned. Negligence must be defined not as a failure to satisfy the Hand formula, but rather as a failure to adopt the efficient level of precaution. As in the above example, this efficient level can only be identified by considering all the expected costs and benefits to the defendant and the plaintiff (and others) of all the possible combinations of precaution by the defendant and the plaintiff (and others) and then choosing the least cost option. Yet, as Hand himself noted, in practice it will be impossible to take into account more than a few options and their expected costs and benefits, and even for these options the expected costs and benefits generally cannot be estimated.[10] Attempting to calculate and enforce efficient precaution levels based on such highly imperfect information may very well lead to greater inefficiency rather than greater efficiency, even assuming (contrary to the usual situation) that some determinate answer is suggested by the available (imperfect) information.[11]

III. Nonutilitarian Attempts to Justify the Hand Formula

Although the legal economists' aggregate risk-utility interpretation of negligence, especially as embodied in the Hand formula, is undermined by major theoretical and practical problems, almost all legal scholars, including those critical of the utilitarian efficiency theory, assume it is descriptively correct. Critics of utilitarian efficiency generally have attempted to construct non-utilitarian arguments to explain and justify the supposed use of the aggregate risk-utility formula in negligence and other tort cases. They rely explicitly or implicitly on the fundamental Kantian moral duty to respect the equal absolute moral worth of yourself and others as rational (human) beings. This duty is assumed to require that in all your actions you must weigh the interests of others equally with your own, which leads immediately and inevitably to the aggregate risk-utility conception of reasonableness and negligence.

---

[9] *See* Landes & Posner, *supra,* note 2, at 87–91.

[10] *See* Moisan v. Loftus, 178 F.2d 148, 149 (2d Cir. 1949); *infra,* text at note 32.

[11] *See* Landes & Posner, *supra,* note 2, at 20–1, 24; Brown, *supra,* note 7, at 333–4, 340–1, 343–4.

For example, Ronald Dworkin, while not explicitly invoking Kant's (or any other) moral theory, attempts to explain the assumed use of the aggregate risk-utility formula in negligence and private nuisance cases by arguing that in such cases there are competing claims of 'abstract right' (also more accurately described as mere 'interests') which must be resolved by using the basic principle of 'equal concern and respect' to 'compromise' the competing claims so as to maximize the 'collective utility' of the parties.[12] Similarly, Ernest Weinrib, explicitly relying on Kantian moral theory, assumes that the categorical imperative, which requires one to act in accord with a maxim that one would adopt as an equal member of the 'kingdom of ends', forbids any self-preference in conception or action. He argued, until recently, that this alleged requirement of complete impartiality of interest mandates an objective 'comparison of interests' conception of reasonableness for both defendants and plaintiffs.[13] Charles Fried also purports to find in Kantian morality a requirement of complete impartiality, which he at one time used not only to justify the aggregate risk-utility conception of negligence but also to construct a social risk pool from which persons supposedly can draw, within certain unclear limits, to expose others to minor or major risk.[14]

These arguments, although meant to be non-utilitarian, are based directly on the utilitarian conception of equality, according to which treating people as equals simply means counting each person's interests equally while maximizing the total satisfaction of interests. This conception of equality is directly opposed to the Kantian conception of equal individual freedom, according to which each individual must always be treated as an end in himself rather than solely as a means to the satisfaction of the interests of others. Kant's doctrine of Right mandates proper respect for the equal absolute moral worth of others by requiring—as legal as well as ethical duties—that resources be distributed to promote each person's equal

---

[12] *See* RONALD DWORKIN, TAKING RIGHTS SERIOUSLY (rev. edn., 1978), 93–4, 98–100, 306–8. Dworkin now notes that a duty always to weigh others' interests equally with your own would completely undermine personal autonomy and is not an accepted part of ordinary morality. Yet he continues to assert that such a duty exists in negligence and nuisance cases, which allegedly involve conflicts in individuals' 'abstract legal rights' that must be resolved by applying the preferred conception of equality of concern to define individuals' 'concrete rights' in particular interactions: *see* RONALD DWORKIN, LAW'S EMPIRE (1986), 291–312.

[13] *See* Ernest J. Weinrib, *Toward A Moral Theory of Negligence Law*, 2 LAW & PHIL. 37, 40, 49–55 & note 27 (1983). Weinrib recently has been persuaded that English and Commonwealth courts usually ignore the utility side of the risk-utility formula and focus on the creation of significant foreseeable unaccepted risks to others: *see* Ernest J. Weinrib, *Understanding Tort Law*, 23 VAL. U. L. REV. 485, 518–19 & note 61 (1989), citing Stephen R. Perry, *The Impossibility of General Strict Liability*, 1 CAN. J.L. & JUR. 147, 169–70 (1988); *see also* Richard W. Wright, *Allocating Liability Among Multiple Responsible Causes*, 21 U.C. DAVIS L. REV. 1141, 1179–81 (1988).

[14] *See* CHARLES FRIED, AN ANATOMY OF VALUES: PROBLEMS OF PERSONAL AND SOCIAL CHOICE (1970), 41–4, 183–91, 196–200.

positive freedom (distributive justice) and that conduct which might affect another person's existing stock of resources be consistent with that other's equal negative freedom (corrective justice). Kant's doctrine of virtue requires—as a solely ethical duty—proper concern for the equal absolute moral worth of others as well as yourself by making their happiness one of your own ends. It does not, however, require that you weigh others' interests equally with your own in everything you do. Such a requirement would completely undermine individual autonomy and freedom.[15]

Although he is a non-utilitarian moral theorist, George Fletcher usually equates 'reasonableness' in tort law with utilitarian efficiency. In an early article, he argued that negligence and tortious conduct in general should be understood in terms of a non-utilitarian paradigm of non-reciprocal risk-creation and lack of excuse, as an alleged implementation of the right to 'equal security' that is embodied in corrective justice, rather than in terms of the utilitarian efficiency paradigm of reasonableness.[16] Now, however, Fletcher accepts the utilitarian efficiency interpretation of negligence. He claims that a 'collaborative principle' underlies the law of negligence: 'By entering into certain spheres of risk-taking, plaintiff and defendant both come under duties to act with a view to the [aggregate] costs and benefits of their actions. They become a unit, acting under an implicit obligation to optimize the [aggregate] consequences of their actions' and have 'a shared duty to find the optimal level of harmful activities'.[17]

'Ethic of care' feminists such as Leslie Bender travel the same path as Dworkin, Weinrib, Fried, and Fletcher, although they seem unaware of the destination toward which they are traveling and might be shocked to learn of their traveling companions. Bender equates the reasonableness standard in negligence and, more generally, the liberal concepts of reason, autonomy, rights, equality, fairness, and justice with a 'masculine' ethic of anti-social, self-interested, wealth-based, dehumanizing utilitarian calculation. She seeks to replace the reasonableness standard and its 'masculine' ethic with a 'feminine' ethic of care and concern for the needs and welfare of others, according to which a person in cases of both misfeasance (putting others at risk) and nonfeasance (failure to protect others from risks you did not create) should be held to a legal standard of 'conscious care and concern of a responsible neighbor or social acquaintance for another under the same or similar circumstances'.[18]

---

[15] *See* Wright, *supra*, note 1; *infra*, note 72 and accompanying text.

[16] *See* George P. Fletcher, *Fairness and Utility in Tort Theory*, 85 HARV. L. REV. 537, 537–43, 550, 556–7, 560, 569–71 (1972).

[17] *See* George P. Fletcher, *Corrective Justice for Moderns*, 106 HARV. L. REV. 1658, 1677, 1678 (1993).

[18] Leslie Bender, *A Lawyer's Primer on Feminist Theory and Tort*, 38 J. LEGAL EDUC. 3, 31 (1988); *see id.* at 25, 28, 30–36 & n. 113.

Bender's 'feminine' ethic of care might well be *less* caring than the complete impartiality requirement espoused by Dworkin, Weinrib, Fried, Fletcher, and the (mostly male) utilitarian efficiency theorists, according to which others' interests and welfare must always be treated as being equally as important as your own. Recognizing that 'we all care differently for family and friends than we do for strangers' and that 'we could not possibly have the energy to care about every person as we do our children or lovers', Bender prescribes varying levels of required care depending on the closeness of the relationship.[19] Yet, given her rejection of the 'masculine' notions of autonomy and self-interest and her emphasis on the 'feminine' ethic of care and concern for the needs and welfare of all others, it is not at all clear how she could justify such preferred treatment for one's family or friends (or oneself). Conversely, assuming a variable standard based on closeness of relationship, she seems unable to justify her proposed requirement that the concern appropriate for neighbors and acquaintances must also be afforded to strangers.

The proposed displacement of the 'masculine' ethic of reason, autonomy, rights, equality, fairness, and justice by a 'feminine' ethic of care and concern for others would seem to be, as feminists such as Catharine MacKinnon and Margaret Radin have argued, a trap for women—especially since, being a 'feminine' rather than a 'masculine' ethic, it apparently would only apply to women.[20] In a recent article, Bender seems to acknowledge this problem. She now states that 'reason has its place in tort law, but that reason is a richer and deeper concept than tort law has historically acknowledged', and she urges the usefulness of 'the reason/care paradigm' in suggesting 'reconceptualizations that make law more reflective of human experience and more responsive to concerns of justice'.[21]

IV. THE EQUAL FREEDOM STANDARDS OF CARE

If Bender were further to investigate Kantian–Aristotelian moral and legal theory, she would find a powerful elaboration of the moral and legal obligations to respect and care for the humanity in others as well as oneself that she hopes to capture in her 'reason/care paradigm'. These obligations include (although they are often overlooked) the legally enforceable duties of distributive justice and the purely ethical duties of beneficence as well as the legally enforceable duties of corrective justice.

---

[19] *See id.* at 32.

[20] *See Feminist Discourse, Moral Values and the Law—A Conversation*, 34 BUFF. L. REV. 11, 20–8, 73–4 (1985) (remarks of Catharine MacKinnon); Margaret J. Radin, *The Pragmatist and the Feminist*, 63 S. CAL. L. REV. 1699, 1699–701, 1712–19 (1990).

[21] *See* Leslie Bender, *An Overview of Feminist Torts Scholarship*, 78 CORNELL L. REV. 575, 580 (1993).

Tort law falls within the domain of corrective justice, although distributive justice considerations are interwoven in certain tort doctrines. Corrective justice aims at securing each person's existing stock of resources against conduct by others that would be inconsistent with the equal negative freedom of all. One's negative freedom—the freedom from unjustified interference with one's use of one's existing resources to pursue one's projects or life plan—will be completely undermined if one must always weigh the interests of all others equally with one's own when deciding how to deploy one's existing resources, as required by the utilitarian efficiency theory, the principle of 'equal concern and respect' as interpreted by Dworkin and others, and Bender's feminist 'ethic of care'. Under these theories, no one is treated as a distinct person with one's own life to lead. Rather each 'person' is merely a fungible addend in the calculation of some mystical aggregate social welfare. For any particular activity, it does not matter whom is being put at risk, by who, or for whose benefit; all that matters is the maximization of aggregate social welfare. This is the morally unattractive message and effect of the utilitarians' conception of reasonableness.

Under the Kantian–Aristotelian theory, which is based on the foundational norm of equal individual freedom rather than the maximization of aggregate social welfare, the respective weights to be given to an actor's interests and the interests of others who might be affected by that action will vary considerably depending on (among other factors) who is being put at risk, by whom, and for whose benefit. For example, given the Kantian requirement of treating others as ends rather than merely as means, it is impermissible to use someone as a mere means to your ends by exposing him (or his resources) to significant foreseeable unaccepted risks, regardless of how greatly the benefit to you might outweigh the risk to him. Conversely, sacrificing your interests for the benefit of someone else is regarded as morally meritorious, although not legally required, even if the risk to you greatly outweighs the expected benefit to the other person, as long as your exposing yourself to the risk does not constitute a failure to properly respect your own humanity.

It is the equal freedom conception of reasonableness, rather than the utilitarian efficiency conception, that is reflected in actual tort-law doctrines and decisions. Under the utilitarian-efficiency theory, it is as inefficient to be above the optimal level of care as to be below it: either form of divergence therefore should be considered negligent. However, consistent with the equal freedom theory, defendants and plaintiffs are only deemed negligent for being below the required level of care, not for being above it. Only when one is below the required level of care is there an impermissible interference with the rights of others (defendant's primary negligence) or a failure properly to respect one's own humanity (plaintiff's contributory negligence).

Moreover, although the utilitarian efficiency theory would apply the same aggregate risk-utility standard of care to plaintiffs and defendants in all situations, taking into account all risks and benefits to everyone, actual tort law—consistent with the equal freedom theory—applies quite different standards of care in different situations. This is evident for all three aspects of the standards of care: the risks taken into account, the perspectives applied, and the substantive criteria of reasonableness.

A. Risks Taken into Account

Different risks are taken into account in analyzing the alleged negligence of defendants and plaintiffs. The analysis of a defendant's alleged negligence focuses on the foreseeable risks *to others* created by the defendant's conduct, rather than the risks to everyone including herself, while the analysis of a plaintiff's alleged negligence focuses on the foreseeable risks *to the plaintiff himself* created by his conduct, rather than the risks to others as well as himself.[22] This differential treatment is inexplicable under the utilitarian efficiency theory, which views defendants and plaintiffs as morally and economically indistinguishable causes of the effects of their interacting activities and seeks to construct liability rules that will maximize the aggregate net benefits of such interactions, taking into account all expected costs and benefits to everyone.[23] In contrast, the equal freedom theory easily explains and justifies the different risks taken into account. As a matter of Right or justice, the defendant is liable for an interactional injury if and only if her conduct foreseeably affected the person or property of another in a manner that was inconsistent with his Right to equal negative freedom, thus generating a corrective justice obligation of rectification.[24] In the analysis of the plaintiff's contributory negligence, a quite different issue arises: whether the defendant's *prima facie* corrective justice obligation to the plaintiff should be barred or reduced because, in the light of the foreseeable risks to himself, the plaintiff failed to act with proper respect for his own humanity and thus also bears moral responsibility for his injury.[25]

B. Perspective Applied (Objective or Subjective)

Similarly, different perspectives are applied in analyzing the alleged negligence of defendants and plaintiffs. When assessing a defendant's alleged negligence, an objective perspective generally is applied: the defendant is required to take at least as much care as would be taken by the (ideal)

---

[22] *See* RESTATEMENT (SECOND) OF TORTS (1963), § 283 cmt. f, § 463 & cmt. b, § 464 cmt. f; FLEMING, *supra,* note 5, at 96, 242.

[23] *See* Coase, *supra,* note 3.   [24] *See* Wright, *supra,* note 1.

[25] *See infra,* text at notes 28–9.

prudent person with ordinary physical and mental abilities. The standard is not lowered to conform with the defendant's particular physical and mental (dis)abilities. Although a defendant with an obvious physical incapacity is not required to do what she is incapable of doing, she is required to take whatever additional precautions are necessary to reduce the foreseeable risks to others to the objectively specified acceptable level. On the other hand, although it often is not explicitly mentioned by the courts, it is generally recognized by courts and commentators that a more subjective perspective is applied when assessing a plaintiff's alleged contributory negligence.[26]

Under the utilitarian efficiency theory, a subjective perspective ideally should be applied to both defendants and plaintiffs. It would be inefficient to require all defendants or plaintiffs to attain the same level of risk reduction despite widely varying physical, mental, technical, and economic capacities to achieve such risk reduction. Instead, each defendant or plaintiff should be required to invest in care only to the point where the marginal cost of such care does not exceed the marginal benefits in reduced risk. Due to differing capacities and thus costs of care, this point will vary for each individual. It is only the very high administrative costs of attempting to apply the subjective perspective that require adoption in most instances of the objective perspective, which is assumed (but not shown) to be a second-best efficient solution for both defendants and plaintiffs. Thus, when personal (in)capacities are easily ascertainable, they should be taken into account for both defendants and plaintiffs.[27]

Under Kant's moral theory, a subjective perspective would be required if the question were the moral *blameworthiness or merit* of the defendant's or plaintiff's conduct. But, when evaluating the defendant's conduct in a tort (rather than a criminal) action, that is not the relevant question (unless punitive damages are at issue). Instead, the relevant question is the defendant's moral *responsibility* for having adversely affected someone else's person or property. As such, the question is one of objective Right rather than subjective virtue. The external exercise of freedom depends on sufficient security against interferences by others with one person and property. Regardless of measurement problems, using a subjective perspective to determine the negligence of defendants would make such security impossible, since the risks to which one could permissibly be exposed by others

---

[26] *See, e.g.,* Snider v. Callahan, 250 F. Supp. 1022, 1023 (W.D. Mo. 1966); GUIDO CALABRESI, IDEALS, BELIEFS, ATTITUDES, AND THE LAW (1985), 24–7, 32–3, 46–54, 147 note 131; FLEMING, *supra*, note 5, at 102–4, 258–60; 3 HARPER, JAMES & GRAY, *supra*, note 5, at 387–93, 421–66; 4 *id.* at 334–42; Gary T. Schwartz, *Tort Law and the Economy in Nineteenth-Century America: A Reinterpretation,* 90 YALE L.J. 1717, 1743–7, 1750–2, 1761–3 & note 333 (1981). A more subjective perspective is applied to defendants in situations in which the defendant's own rights are directly at issue. *See infra,* text at notes 46–9 and following note 70.

[27] *See* LANDES & POSNER, *supra,* note 2, at 123–6.

would depend on the subjective capacities of the particular others with whom one happens (often unpredictably) to interact. To have sufficiently secure expectations, one's rights in one's person and property must be defined by an objective level of permissible risk exposure by others which, under the moral categorical imperative and its corollary (the supreme principle of Right), must be equally applicable to all and objectively enforced. Thus, an objective standard of 'legal fault' (moral *responsibility*), rather than a subjective standard of moral *fault* (blame), is required when considering legal responsibility for the adverse effects of a defendant's conduct on the person or property of others.[28]

When the contributory negligence of a plaintiff is at issue, the question is whether the plaintiff's recovery from a defendant who infringed his rights by negligently injuring him should be barred or reduced because of the plaintiff's contribution to his own injury. Since we are concerned with an injury to the plaintiff himself, rather than an injury to the person or property of others, no issue of Right immediately arises. Instead the issue is whether the plaintiff, by exposing himself to the particular risk, failed to properly respect his own humanity and thus shares with the defendant moral responsibility for his injury. When assessing the plaintiff's moral responsibility for his own injury, the reason just given for departing from the subjective perspective of moral fault or virtue and instead applying the objective perspective of 'legal fault' or Right to the defendant's conduct does not directly apply to the plaintiff's conduct. Rather, the issue of Right arises indirectly and applies in a much more limited manner. Proper regard for the equal freedom of the defendant suggests that the plaintiff's conduct be deemed negligent and affect his right of recovery, even if it was subjectively reasonable in the light of his physical and mental capacities and beliefs, if it was unforeseeably idiosyncratic—i.e., if it fell outside the (broad) range of foreseeable behavior for the great mass of persons in similar situations. Thus, the plaintiff's conduct should be judged by a limited semi-subjective perspective rather than a fully subjective perspective.[29]

[28] Kant's doctrine of virtue, while specifying objective moral duties based on the categorical imperative, assesses the moral *blame* or *merit* of conduct in terms of one's subjective capacity and effort in attempting to ascertain and satisfy those duties. Kant's doctrine of Right, on the other hand, directly applies the objective requirements of the categorical imperative in determining one's moral and legal *responsibility* for the adverse effects that one causes to the person or property of others. Thus, as Kant repeatedly emphasizes, an action's *legality* is judged by its external conformity with the objective requirements of Right, while its *morality* is judged by one's internal subjective capacity and efforts to conform one's conduct to the objective requirements of the categorical imperative, which grounds all duties of Right and virtue: *see* IMMANUEL KANT, THE METAPHYSICS OF MORALS (Mary Gregor trans., 1991) (1797); *214, 218–32, 312, 382 n.*, 379–80, 381–3 & n.*, 389–94, 401, 404–5, 446–7, 463; Wright, *supra*, note 1.

[29] Yet the range of behavior deemed reasonable under the more subjective perspective applied to plaintiffs is sometimes very broad, especially in cases involving religious belief: *see* CALABRESI, *supra*, note 26, at 46–54.

C. The Substantive Criteria of Reasonableness

Finally, different criteria of reasonableness are used in evaluating the alleged negligence of defendants and plaintiffs in different contexts. Contrary to what is commonly assumed, the courts rarely use the aggregate risk-utility formula or any other uniform definition of reasonableness. Rather, different factors are taken into account and different weights are given to those factors depending on a number of considerations that are highly relevant under the equal-freedom theory but irrelevant under the utilitarian efficiency theory.

In an article published in 1915 that is often cited as presaging Judge Hand's formula, Henry Terry noted five factors that may be relevant, including [1] the probability and [2] the magnitude of any injury that might result from the conduct at issue and, '*in some cases, at least*', [3] the probability and [4] the magnitude of the benefit expected to be attained by such conduct discounted by [5] the probability that the benefit would be attained in the absence of such conduct.[30] In 1927, Warren Seavey warned against 'assum[ing] that we can rely upon any formula in regard to "balancing interests" to solve negligence cases', and he stated that the utility of the defendant's conduct usually is not considered or is weighted very low when the defendant for her own benefit puts another's property or especially person at risk, or intentionally interferes with the person or property of another.[31] Judge Learned Hand himself, the author of the risk-utility formula, noted that the formula's factors

> are practically not susceptible of any quantitative estimate, and the second two [L and B] are generally not so, even theoretically. For this reason a solution always involves some preference, or choice between incommensurables, and it is consigned to a jury because their decision is thought most likely to accord with commonly accepted standards, real or fancied.[32]

Similarly, after elaborating the usual academic aggregate risk-utility interpretation of reasonableness, John Fleming warns:

> But negligence cannot be reduced to a purely economic equation. . . . [I]n general, judicial opinions do not make much of the cost factor [of eliminating the risk], and for good reasons. For one thing, our legal tradition in torts has strong roots in an individualistic morality with its focus primarily on interpersonal equity rather than broader social policy. . . . [T]he calculus of negligence includes some important non-economic values, like health and life, freedom and privacy, which defy comparison

[30] *See* Henry T. Terry, *Negligence*, 29 HARV. L. REV. 40, 42–4 (1915) (emphasis added).
[31] *See* Warren A. Seavey, *Negligence—Subjective or Objective?*, 41 HARV. L. REV. 1, 8 note 7 (1927).
[32] Conway v. O'Brien, 111 F.2d 611, 612 (2d Cir. 1940), *rev'd on other grounds*, 312 U.S. 492 (1941).

with competing economic values. Negligence is not just a matter of calculating the point at which the cost of injury to victims (that is the damages payable) exceeds that of providing safety precautions. The reasonable man is by no means a caricature cold blooded, calculating Economic Man.[33]

Very little scholarly attention has been paid to the criteria of reasonableness that are actually applied in different situations. In the remainder of this essay, I attempt to begin to fill this gap. The different situations will be distinguished primarily by who put whom at risk for whose benefit and by whether the person put at risk consented to such risk exposure. More specifically, I examine the standards of care in the following (non-exhaustive) contexts: (1) defendants' treating others as means, (2) defendants engaged in socially essential activities, (3) defendant occupiers' on-premises risks, (4) defendants' activities involving participatory plaintiffs, (5) paternalistic defendants, (6) plaintiffs' self-interested conduct, (7) plaintiffs' self-sacrificing conduct, and (8) defendants' failure to aid or rescue.

1. Defendants' Treating Others as Means

The first category, the 'involuntary DPD' category, encompasses situations in which the defendant (D) put the plaintiff (P) at risk to benefit the defendant (D) or some third party, and the plaintiff did not seek to benefit directly from the defendant's risk-creating activity. Recently, a few scholars have noted that the actual test of negligence in such cases is not the utilitarians' aggregate risk-utility test but rather (consistent with the equal freedom theory) the defendant's creation of a significant, foreseeable, and unaccepted risk to the person or property of others.[34] A risk is significant, and hence unreasonable unless accepted by the plaintiff, if it is a level of risk to which an ordinary person would be unwilling to be exposed without his consent.

The best known case of this type is the British House of Lords' decision in *Bolton v. Stone*, in which the plaintiff, while standing in the road in front of her house, was seriously injured when she was struck by a ball that had been propelled by an 'exceptional' hit out of the nearby cricket grounds over an intervening house and into the street.[35] Each of the Law Lords assumed that the defendant cricket club would be liable in negligence if the risk were foreseeable and of a sufficiently high level, regardless of the utility of the defendant's conduct or the burden of avoiding creating the risk. Each lord concluded that the risk, although foreseeable, was not of a sufficiently high level to be deemed unreasonable as a matter of law, given the very low probabilities of a ball's being hit into the road and also

---

[33] FLEMING, *supra*, note 5, at 108–9 (citations omitted).
[34] *See supra*, note 13.   [35] [1951] A.C. 850, 851–2.

hitting someone on the little-used residential side street. Lord Reid was the most explicit. He stated that in order to be negligent, a risk must not only be foreseeable but also be one that a reasonable person, 'considering the matter from the point of view of safety', would consider 'material' or 'substantial':

> In considering that matter I think that it would be right to take into account not only how remote is the chance that a person might be struck but also how serious the consequences are likely to be if a person is struck; but I do not think that it would be right to take into account the difficulty of remedial measures. If cricket cannot be played on a ground without creating a substantial risk, then it should not be played there at all. . . . I do not think that a reasonable man considering the matter from the point of view of safety would or should disregard any risk unless it is extremely small.[36]

In a subsequent case, the Law Lords sitting as the Privy Council in a Commonwealth case on appeal from Australia, *The Wagon Mound (No. 2)*, held that, even when the foreseeable risk is insubstantial (small), the defendant will still be held negligent if, but only if, the risk was 'real' rather than 'far-fetched' or 'fantastic' and the defendant had no valid reason for failing to take steps to eliminate it. A valid reason could be 'that it would involve considerable expense to eliminate the risk. [The defendant] would weigh the risk against the difficulty of eliminating it.' *Bolton v. Stone*, the court said, had involved such a real but insubstantial risk. But, the court reiterated, if the risk were real and substantial, it would be unreasonable not to take steps to eliminate it, regardless of the utility of the risk or the burden of eliminating it.[37]

The Wagon Mound (No. 2) is sometimes misread as abandoning *Bolton v. Stone*'s substantial risk criterion and replacing it with the risk-utility formula. But the Privy Council clearly states that the risk-utility formula, rather than being the universal test of defendants' negligence, is applicable only in those situations in which the risk ordinarily would be considered insubstantial. If the risk is substantial, the utility of the defendant's conduct is irrelevant. The risk-utility formula is used to *expand* the defendant's liability, to encompass situations in which the risk ordinarily would be deemed insubstantial but is nevertheless deemed unacceptable because it is real, rather than fantastic, and the cost of eliminating it would be similarly

---

[36] *Id.* at 864, 867–8; *see id.* at 858–9 (Lord Porter), 861–3 (Lord Normand), 863 (Lord Oaksey), 868 (Lord Radcliffe).

[37] Overseas Tankship (U.K.) Ltd. v. The Miller S.S. Co. ('Wagon Mound (No.2)'), [1967] 1 A.C. 617, 633, 641–4 (P.C.), *per* Lord Reid. Landes and Posner ignore these statements in *Bolton* and *The Wagon Mound (No. 2)*. *See* LANDES & POSNER, *supra*, note 2, at 99. All the 'DPD' cases they discuss as alleged illustrations of the Hand formula actually turn on the significance of the foreseeable risk: *see id.* at 96–100.

small (no precise quantitative balancing of risk and utility seems to be feasible, implied or justified even in these situations).[38]

Although not usually employing language as explicit as Lord Reid's in *Bolton*, and despite sometimes employing balancing language, courts in the United States and elsewhere generally also find a defendant negligent if she created a foreseeable significant unaccepted risk of injury to the person or property of others.[39] As we previously noted, jury instructions on a defendant's negligence rarely, if ever, refer to the aggregate risk-utility formula, focusing instead on the care expected of the reasonable ordinary or prudent person who acts with proper concern for the effects of her activity on the persons and property of others. Courts have upheld jury findings of negligence even though the jury has specifically found that the benefits 'as a whole' of the defendant's conduct outweighed the risks.[40] In a careful, documented study of all nineteenth century California and New Hampshire appellate court decisions on tort liability, Gary Schwartz reports:

> The factor of private profit was seen as a reason for being skeptical, rather than appreciative, of the propriety of risky activity engaged in by enterprise. In general, the New Hampshire and California Courts were reluctant to find that economic factors justified a defendant's risktaking. Neither Court even once held mere monetary costs rendered nonnegligent a defendant's failure to adopt a particular safety precaution.[41]

Defense lawyers carefully avoid making arguments to judges or jurors that seek to justify risks imposed on the plaintiff by allegedly offsetting enhancements of the defendant's utility. Defendants that are thought to have deliberately made such risk-utility decisions are often deemed by juries and judges not only to have been negligent, but also to have behaved so egregiously as to justify a hefty award of punitive damages, as occurred in the Ford Pinto and asbestos cases.[42]

---

[38] *Cf.* Lucy Webb Hayes Nat'l Training School for Deaconesses and Missionaries v. Perotti, 419 F.2d 704, 711 (D.C. Cir. 1969) (although risk of mental patient's jumping through window in unsecured area of hospital may have been very small, it remained unreasonable and a proximate cause of patient's death if there was no good reason for allowing him to be there).

[39] *See, e.g.,* Brown v. Kendall, 60 Mass. (6 Cush.) 292, 296 (1850): '[o]rdinary care . . . means that kind and degree of care, which prudent and cautious men would use, such as is required by the exigency of the case, and such as is necessary to guard against probable danger. . . . To make an . . . inevitable accident, it must be such an accident as the defendant could not have avoided by the use of the kind and degree of care necessary to the exigency.' *See also* Depue v. Flateau, 111 N.W. 1, 2 (Minn. 1907) (stating a similar 'comprehensive principle'); *infra,* text at note 52.

[40] *See, e.g.,* Curtis v. State *ex rel.* Dep't of Transp., 180 Cal. Rptr. 843, 853–6 (Cal. Ct. App. 1982).

[41] Schwartz, *supra,* note 26, at 1757 (footnotes omitted); *see also* Gary T. Schwartz, *The Character of Early American Tort Law*, 36 UCLA L. Rev. 641, 641–3 & note 8 (1989). Schwartz's studies demolish Posner's efficiency interpretation of nineteenth century tort law.

[42] *See* Grimshaw v. Ford Motor Co., 174 Cal. Rptr. 348 (1981); Jackson v. Johns-Mansville Sales Corp., 781 F.2d 394, 399–409 & n. 12 (5th Cir. 1986); Gary T. Schwartz, *The Myth of the Ford Pinto Case*, 43 RUTGERS L. REV. 1013, 1035–8 (1991).

2. Defendants Engaged in Socially Essential Activities

While the purely private utility to the defendant of his conduct is rarely taken into account, the social utility of the defendant's conduct is taken into account in some situations, although not through a utilitarian balancing. A couple of these situations are the subject of the Wisconsin Supreme Court's illustrations of appropriate 'balancing of the social interests' in negligence cases under an 'ordinary care' jury instruction:

One driving a car in a thickly populated district, on a rainy day, slowly and in the most careful manner, may do injury to the person of another by throwing muddy or infected water upon that person. Society does not hold the actor responsible because the benefit of allowing people to travel under such circumstances so far outweighs the probable injury to bystanders that such conduct is not disapproved. Circumstances may require the driver of a fire truck to take his truck through a thickly populated district at a high rate of speed, but if he exercises that degree of care which such drivers ordinarily exercise under the same or similar circumstances, society weighing the benefits against the probabilities of damage, in spite of the fact that as a reasonably prudent and intelligent man he should foresee that harm may result, justifies the risk and holds him not liable.[43]

The court's first illustration reflects the fact that in any society certain risks—such as those posed by properly constructed, maintained, and operated electrical generation and transmission facilities, dams, trains, automobiles, and planes—will be unavoidable aspects of activities essential or important to all persons in the society. Under the supreme principle of Right (universalizable equal freedom), all members of society will be deemed to have accepted such activities and their unavoidable risks as being reasonable (but not necessarily as being immune from strict liability for damages caused to those not seeking to directly benefit from a particular risky activity). Yet, as the Wisconsin court notes, the socially important activity must be operated in 'the most careful manner' to minimize the risks to others, and the activity will be deemed reasonable only if the risks to others are not too serious (in the illustration they are de minimis) and are greatly (not merely marginally) outweighed by the activity's social utility.

The Wisconsin court's second illustration involves the operation of public emergency vehicles by defendants seeking to alleviate serious threats to people's lives or property. In such emergency situations, the defendant is

---

[43] Osborne v. Montgomery, 234 N.W. 372, 376 (Wis. 1931). *See also* RESTATEMENT (SECOND) OF TORTS (1963), § 291, which interprets reasonableness in terms of a risk-utility balance, but emphasizes in comment *d* that the legal rather than the popular evaluation of the social value of the competing interests governs and in comment *e* that '[t]he law attaches utility to general types or classes of acts as appropriate to the advancement of certain [public] interests rather than to the [private] purpose for which a particular act is done, except in the case in which the purpose is of itself of such public utility as to justify an otherwise impermissible risk.'

held to be justified in engaging in practices (e.g., driving at high speeds, on the wrong side of the road, and through traffic signals) that ordinarily would be deemed negligent, but only if she undertakes additional precautions or warnings (such as slowing down at intersections, sounding sirens, and flashing lights) so that those thereby put at risk can, without significant interference with their legitimate activities, avoid being exposed to a substantial or significant risk.[44] Defendants in emergency situations are thus treated similarly to defendants with physical incapacities, who as we have noted are not required to do what they are incapable of doing but are required to take other steps to avoid exceeding the objectively acceptable level of risk.[45]

3. Defendant Occupiers' On-Premises Risks

In a few situations, where the defendant's own rights are directly implicated, the defendant's private utility is taken into account and a semi-subjective perspective is sometimes applied. One of these situations involves risks, to persons who come on the defendant's property, that result from activities or conditions on the property. Whether formulated as distinct duties or as a single all-encompassing duty of reasonable care, the standard of care varies according to whether the plaintiff was a business invitee, a social guest, a licensee, a child trespasser, or an adult trespasser.[46] The highest, objective standard of care is required for business invitees, while the lowest, semi-subjective standard of care is required for adult trespassers. Of the various categories of on-premises plaintiffs, only business invitees are afforded approximately the same protection as off-premises plaintiffs.[47]

These distinctions are fairly easily explained and justified under the equal freedom theory, which would not require the defendant to significantly sacrifice her own interests to protect from on-premises risks those (especially adults) who have wrongfully trespassed on her property, or to go beyond providing warnings and moderate safeguards to make the premises safer for licensees or social guests than she is willing and able to make it for herself. This equal-freedom reasoning appears often in the cases. For

---

[44] In many jurisdictions, even operators of emergency vehicles are not allowed to depart from the ordinary rules of the road in the absence of explicit statutory authorization, and they must strictly comply with the additional precautions specified in the statute as a minimum requirement for avoiding being held negligent: *see* J. H. Cooper, Annotations, 82 A.L.R.2d 312 (1962) (fire department vehicles), 83 A.L.R.2d 383 (1962) (police vehicles), 84 A.L.R.2d 121 (1962) (ambulances).

[45] *See supra*, text at note 26.

[46] As more than one court has noted, the varying standards of reasonable care with respect to on-premises risks do not, as is sometimes assumed, constitute departures from or limitations on the general duty of reasonable care, but rather are elaborations of this general duty in the context of the different types of situations that may arise: *see, e.g.*, Dillon v. Twin State Gas & Elec. Co., 163 A. 111, 113 (N.H. 1932).

[47] *See* FLEMING, *supra*, note 5, at 417–53; PROSSER & KEETON, *supra*, note 5, at 386–434.

example, in the House of Lords' decision in *British Railways Board v. Herrington*, Lord Reid stated:

Normally the common law applies an objective test [to defendants]. If a person chooses to assume a relationship with members of the public, say by setting out to drive a car or to erect a building fronting a highway, the law requires him to conduct himself as a reasonable man with adequate skill, knowledge and resources would do. He will not be heard to say that in fact he could not attain that standard. If he cannot attain that standard he ought not to assume the responsibility which that relationship involves. But an occupier does not voluntarily assume a relationship with trespassers. By trespassing they force a 'neighbour' relationship on him. When they do so he must act in a humane manner—that is not asking too much of him—but I do not see why he should be required to do more.

So it appears to me that an occupier's duty to trespassers must vary according to his knowledge, ability, and resources. It has often been said that trespassers must take the land as they find it. I would rather say that they must take the occupier as they find him.

. . . [The occupier] might often reasonably think, weighing the seriousness of the danger and the degree of likelihood of trespassers coming against the burden he would have to incur in preventing their entry or making his premises safe, or curtailing his own activities on his land, that he could not fairly be expected to do anything. But if he could at small trouble and expense take some effective action, . . . I think most people would think it inhumane and culpable not to do that. . . .

It would follow that an impecunious occupier with little assistance at hand would often be excused from doing something which a large organisation with ample staff would be expected to do.[48]

More succinctly, Lord Pearson stated: 'There is also a moral aspect. . . . [T]respassing is a form of misbehaviour, showing lack of consideration for the rights of others. It would be unfair if trespassers could by their misbehaviour impose onerous obligations on others.'[49]

Under the utilitarian efficiency theory, it would seem that (contrary to the cases) defendant landowners should be at least as concerned about on-premises risks as off-premises risks, regardless of the status of the plaintiff, and indeed arguably should be subject to greater (strict or absolute) liability for on-premises risks as the usual cheapest cost avoider. The legal economists' attempts to explain the defendant landowner's greatly relaxed duty of care to trespassers as plaintiffs and, conversely, the related strict (sometimes punitive) liability of trespassers as defendants, rely on a convoluted and *ad hoc* 'encouraging market transactions' rationale that is riddled with exceptions for alleged infeasible bargaining situations.[50]

---

[48] [1972] A.C. 877, 898–9; *see id.* at 936–7 (Lord Diplock).

[49] *Id.* at 925; *see id.* at 909–10 (Lord Morris), 916 & 919–21 (Lord Wilberforce), 924–7 (Lord Pearson), 936–7 & 941–3 (Lord Diplock). *See also* Schwartz, *supra*, note 26, at 1766–7 & nn. 366 & 367 (noting the American courts' attention to such equal freedom concerns in nineteenth- and twentieth-century on-premises injury cases).

[50] *See, e.g.*, POSNER, *supra*, note 2, at 46–7, 158–9, 170–1; *cf. infra*, text at note 59.

4. Defendants' Activities Involving Participatory Plaintiffs

Another major category of negligence cases, the 'voluntary DPP' category, encompasses situations in which the defendant (D) put the plaintiff (P) at risk at least partially to benefit the plaintiff (P), and the plaintiff sought to benefit directly from the defendant's risky activity. This category includes situations in which the plaintiffs were customers of, participants in, or willing spectators of the defendant's risky activity. In these situations, the risk will be deemed reasonable even if it was substantial if it was one that the plaintiff implicitly accepted as being worthwhile given the benefits he expected to obtain from the risky activity (including the benefit of not having to pay any increased precaution costs that would likely be passed on to him). Hence, in this context a type of risk-utility test is proper under the equal-freedom theory. But the benefits taken into account are limited to those expected by the typical plaintiff, rather than also including (as the utilitarian efficiency theory would mandate) any independent utility to the defendant or aggregate social utility. Moreover, the comparison of risk and utility is not a simple quantitative comparison of non-weighted factors, as is assumed by the utilitarian efficiency theory. Depending on the values involved, the comparison may be qualitative rather than quantitative, or may involve weighted or lexically ordered factors, or both. For example, rarely, if ever, would serious risks to life or health be deemed outweighed by mere economic benefits.

There are many examples of cases in this category. Among the most common nowadays are suits by a product purchaser or user alleging defective design by the product's manufacturer. A common (but not exclusive) test of defect or reasonableness in such cases is an explicit risk-utility test, which in all but a handful of cases focuses solely on the risks and benefits to the typical consumer, rather than on any independent utility to the defendant or aggregate social utility.[51] In a typical non-product liability case, the plaintiff, a passenger on the defendant's train, apparently fainted in a washroom and received severe burns on her face when it came into contact with an exposed heating pipe under a water cooler, which pipe could only be reached by persons kneeling or lying down on the floor. Assuming that failing to guard against such an occurrence would be unreasonable if it were 'reasonably foreseeable', the court held that it was not.[52] The risk concededly was foreseeable and perhaps could have been deemed significant ('*reasonably* foreseeable'). Yet, given the very small risk, it is unlikely that the

---

[51] *See* RESTATEMENT (THIRD) OF TORTS: PRODUCTS LIABILITY (Tentative Draft No. 2, 1995), § 2 cmt. e at 24 (listing a number of consumer-related risks and benefits as relevant factors, and stating 'it is not a factor . . . that the imposition of liability would have a negative effect on corporate earnings, or would reduce employment in a given industry'); *id.* at 27.

[52] Hauser v. Chicago, R.I. & P. Ry., 219 N.W. 60, 62 (Iowa 1928).

typical passenger would have been willing to pay, through increased ticket prices, the distributed costs of eliminating the risk by shielding the pipes in every washroom on every train.

5. Paternalistic Defendants

A distinct and infrequently encountered category, the 'involuntary DPP' category, encompasses situations in which the defendant (D) put the plaintiff (P) at risk for what the defendant considered to be the plaintiff's (P's) best interest, but the plaintiff did not consent to or seek to benefit from the creation of the risk. Consistent with the equal-freedom theory but contrary to the utilitarian-efficiency theory, defendants generally are not allowed to do this without the plaintiff's consent, even if the expected benefits allegedly greatly outweigh the risks, unless the plaintiff is incapable of giving consent and there is authorized substituted consent.

The most common cases involve medical treatment. Although some jurisdictions leave to the medical profession the judgement of what risks should be disclosed to the patient, many United States jurisdictions today follow the patient-centered standard, according to which the physician has the duty to disclose risks that would be deemed material by the typical patient, or which the physician otherwise knows or has reason to know are material to the particular patient.[53] The patient-centered standard has also been approved by the High Court of Australia and the Supreme Court of Canada,[54] and was favored by Lords Scarman and Templeman in the British House of Lords' decision in *Sidaway v. Bethlem Royal Hospital.*[55]

However, a bare majority of the Law Lords in *Sidaway* affirmed the Court of Appeal's adoption of the physician-centered medical-practice standard, based on England's more paternalistic approach to doctor–patient relations and a concern that the 'transatlantic approach' was both impractical and 'would do nothing for patients or medicine, although it might do a great deal for lawyers and litigation'.[56] Nevertheless, the majority in the House of Lords agreed with the minority that the doctor's judgement on proper risk disclosure would have to give way when

[53] *See, e.g.*, Canterbury v. Spence, 464 F.2d 772 (D.C. Cir. 1972); Cobbs v. Grant, 502 P.2d 1 (Cal. 1972); *cf.* Mohr v. Williams, 104 N.W. 12 (Minn. 1905) (battery). If there was no consent at all to the medical treatment or if the consent was invalid, a battery action is appropriate. However, if the plaintiff was aware of the nature of the treatment and freely assented to it, but was not informed of attendant material risks, a negligence action is appropriate: *see, e.g.*, Sidaway v. Board of Gov'rs of Bethlem Royal Hosp. & Maudsley Hosp. [1985] A.C. 871, 883, 885, 892, 894; Reibl v. Hughes (1980) 114 D.L.R.3d 1, 10—11 (Can.); Mink v. University of Chicago, 460 F. Supp. 713 (N.D. Ill. 1978).

[54] *See* Rogers v. Whitaker, 109 A.L.R. 625 (Austl. 1992); Reibl v. Hughes (1980) 114 D.L.R.3d 1, 12–13 (Can.).

[55] [1985] A.C. 871, 882, 885–90, 903–5.

[56] Sidaway v. Bethlem Royal Hosp. Gov'rs, [1984] 1 All E.R. 1018, 1027 (C.A.) (Donaldson M.R.); *see id.* at 1030–1 (Dunn L.J.); *aff'd.* [1985] 1 A.C. at 890–5 (Lord Diplock), 895–901 (Lords Bridge and Keith).

necessary to respond fully to a patient's query about the risks involved.[57] Moreover, Lord Bridge, joined by Lord Keith, stated that, while the issue of proper risk disclosure is 'to be decided primarily on the basis of expert medical evidence', exceptional cases might arise:

[T]he judge might in certain circumstances come to the conclusion that disclosure of a particular risk was so obviously necessary to an informed choice on the part of the patient that no reasonably prudent medical man would fail to make it. . . . The kind of case I have in mind would be an operation involving a substantial risk of grave adverse consequences. In such a case, in the absence of some cogent clinical reason why the patient should not be informed, a doctor, recognising and respecting his patient's right of decision, could hardly fail to appreciate the necessity for an appropriate warning.[58]

Despite the disagreements on the doctor-centered versus patient-centered standard for determining which risks are material to the patient, it is universally recognized that the patient has the right, regardless of the doctor's opinion, to decide whether or not to undergo some medical treatment and that the doctor has a correlative duty to disclose material risks to the patient. This right and duty seem obvious under the equal freedom theory, but they are difficult to explain under the utilitarian efficiency theory.

The legal economist might argue that the medical treatment cases are low transaction-cost situations in which the doctor should be precluded from bypassing (fully informed) market bargaining by failing to disclose risk information that is knowably or foreseeably material to the patient.[59] But a patient's refusal to undergo some treatment—e.g., a refusal to accept blood transfusions because of religious beliefs or other reasons—may greatly endanger his health and life, thereby creating substantial expected disutility not only to himself but also to others economically or emotionally dependent on him. The transaction costs of negotiating with such affected third parties will generally be very high, yet the competent patient's right to refuse treatment remains clear, even though under the utilitarians' impartial calculus the aggregate benefits to the patient and others of going ahead with the treatment might be thought to greatly outweigh the psychic and/or religious costs to the patient.

6. Plaintiffs' Self-Interested Conduct

We turn now to the plaintiff's contributory negligence. The principal category, the 'PPP' category, encompasses situations such as *Carroll Towing* in which the plaintiff (P) put himself (P) at risk for his own (P's) benefit.[60] Since we are only concerned with the risk the plaintiff imposed on himself,

---

[57] *See* [1985] 1 A.C. at 895 (Lord Diplock), 898–9 (Lords Bridge and Keith).

[58] *Id.* at 900; *accord*, Bly v. Rhoads, 222 S.E.2d 783, 787 (Va. 1976).

[59] *Cf. supra*, text at note 50.

[60] In *Carroll Towing*, the plaintiff's employee, as a result of his absence for some unknown purpose, put the plaintiff's barge at risk of being damaged or sunk through negligent

no issue of Right is directly involved, but rather only whether the plaintiff failed properly to respect his own humanity and thus also is morally responsible for his injury. When engaged in such purely self-interested behavior, it would be irrational for a person to expose himself to risks which subjectively exceed the expected benefits.

As in the 'voluntary DPP' defendant category, this risk-utility test reflects the equal-freedom approach rather than the utilitarian efficiency approach. Only risks and benefits to the plaintiff are taken into account, rather than (as required by the utilitarian efficiency theory) all risks and benefits to anyone who might be affected by the plaintiff's conduct. The risks and benefits are evaluated from the subjective perspective of the plaintiff (as long as that perspective is not too idiosyncratic), rather than the objective perspective of the ideal prudent person. And the comparison of risks and benefits is not a quantitative measurement and balancing of marginal risks and expected utilities, but rather a common-sense assessment of the relevant risks and utilities, which may be and often are assessed qualitatively or lexically rather than quantitatively.[61]

7. Plaintiffs' Self-Sacrificing Conduct

This penultimate category, the 'PPX' category, encompasses situations in which the plaintiff (P) put himself (P) at risk for some third party's (X's) benefit. Under the utilitarian-efficiency theory, the plaintiff should be deemed contributorily negligent if the risks to the plaintiff (and others), objectively considered, outweigh the expected benefit to the third party (and others). Under the equal freedom theory, however, the plaintiff's willingness to sacrifice his own interests to benefit someone else is considered not only reasonable, but also morally praiseworthy, even if (under the utilitarian calculus) the risks to the plaintiff seem much greater than the expected benefit to the third party, as long as the plaintiff's conduct does not constitute lack of respect for his own humanity.

The equal-freedom theory is consistent with the cases, while the utilitarian-efficiency theory is not. Probably the most common situation is when the plaintiff puts himself at risk to rescue some helpless person who has been put in serious danger by the defendant's negligence. In these rescue situations, courts hold that, no matter how much the risk to the plaintiff may seem to exceed the expected benefit to the potential rescuee, the plaintiff's conduct is morally meritorious rather than morally blameworthy or unreasonable unless it was 'foolhardy', 'wanton', 'rash', or 'reckless'.[62]

mishandling by others: *see* United States v. Carroll Towing Co., 159 F.2d 169, 173–4 (2d Cir., 1947).

[61] *See supra,* text at notes 22–9, 32, 51–2.

[62] *See, e.g.,* Baker v. T. E. Hopkins & Son, Ltd. [1959] 3 All E.R. 225 (C.A.) ('wanton' or 'foolhardy'); FLEMING, *supra,* note 5, at 155–7 ('utterly foolhardy').

When the life of the potential rescuee is at issue, the risk to the plaintiff is considered 'foolhardy' or 'rash' only if there was no real chance of saving the potential rescuee.

One of the best known cases is *Eckert v. Long Island Railroad*,[63] which was (mis)used by Terry to illustrate the utilitarian balancing of the five factors that he identified as being relevant to a determination of a defendant's or plaintiff's negligence.[64] The rescuer in *Eckert* jumped in front of the defendant's negligently driven train to save a child on the tracks, pushing the child off the tracks just barely in time but being hit and killed himself. If we plausibly assume that the lives (L) of the rescuer and the child were equally valuable (although economists might consider the remaining life of the presumably productive adult to be more valuable than that of the as yet unproductive child), the probability of the rescuer's being killed was at least 75 per cent, the probability of the rescuer's rescuing the child was at best 25 per cent, and the probability of the child remaining on the tracks without any rescue attempt was around 90 per cent, then the risk to the rescuer ($0.750\ L$) greatly exceeded the expected benefit to the child ($0.25 \times 0.9\ L = 0.225\ L$). The court nevertheless held that the rescuer's conduct, rather than being contributorily negligent, was morally meritorious, and that it would be contributorily negligent only if it was 'rash or reckless'.[65] The utilitarian efficiency theorists ignore the *Eckert* court's 'rash or reckless' language and implausibly assume that the risk to the rescuer was less than the expected benefit to the rescuee.[66]

8. Defendants' Failure to Aid or Rescue

The last category, the 'nonfeasance DPD' category, is the reverse of the 'PPX' category that we have just discussed. It encompasses situations in which the defendant failed to aid a person who needed her help, but the defendant's failure to aid was 'nonfeasance' rather than 'misfeasance' since the defendant did not create or worsen the plaintiff's needy condition. The defendant (D) did not *put* the plaintiff at risk for the defendant's benefit, but rather let the plaintiff (P) remain at risk in order to avoid a burden to or loss of benefit by the defendant (D). In such situations, the general common law rule is that the defendant has no legal duty to aid the plaintiff. In civil-law jurisdictions and a few common-law jurisdictions, there is a limited legal (criminal law and sometimes also tort law) duty of 'easy rescue'— i.e., a duty to render aid in emergency situations to a person whose life or health is seriously threatened, if the rescuer can do so without exposing herself to significant risks or burdens. The general no-duty rule in common law jurisdictions is riddled by an expanding list of categories of persons held

---

[63] 43 N.Y. 502 (1871).   [64] *See* Terry, *supra*, note 30, at 42–4; *supra*, text at note 30.
[65] 43 N.Y. at 505–6.
[66] *See* LANDES & POSNER, *supra*, note 2, at 100–1; Terry, *supra*, note 30, at 43–4.

subject to a duty of easy rescue, usually but not always based on some 'special relationship' with the plaintiff or the plaintiff's assailant.[67]

Although it might seem efficient to impose a duty to aid whenever the expected benefits to the plaintiff outweigh the risk or burden to the defendant, if applied generally this duty could promote inefficient general laziness (the economists' 'moral hazard' problem). Thus, utilitarian efficiency theory probably would reject a general moral or legal obligation of beneficence or charity, and limit the defendant's duty to emergency situations involving significant risks to the plaintiff's life or health. It has been suggested that utilitarians might also exclude as practically unenforceable (and hence economically wasteful) any requirement that the defendant impose on herself a significant risk to her own life or health.[68] However, this exclusion would concede the lack of acceptance of the utilitarian moral theory, since under that theory a defendant should willingly incur such a risk if it were outweighed by the expected benefit to the plaintiff. In any event, utilitarian efficiency theory would require a defendant to impose significant non-health threatening burdens on herself in emergency situations involving significant risks to the plaintiff's life or health if the expected benefits to the plaintiff exceeded the burdens on her.[69] Yet no jurisdiction imposes such a duty of non-easy rescue.

Landes and Posner put forth various efficiency arguments to try to explain the lack of a general duty to attempt rescue. One argument is that a 'causation' (misfeasance) requirement, although usually irrelevant to efficiency determinations, is needed (for unexplained reasons) in this one context to avoid excessive administrative costs in identifying who would have been efficient or cheapest-cost rescuers. Another implausible argument is that a duty to rescue would inefficiently reduce the number of potential rescuers because people would avoid activities which might give rise to a duty to rescue. Yet *any* activity might give rise to a duty to rescue; to completely avoid such a duty one would have to cease to exist. Conversely, given the rare occurrence of emergency-rescue situations, even a duty of non-easy rescue should have little impact on people's choice of activities. A third implausible argument is that a duty to rescue would create a 'moral hazard' problem: that, relying on the duty to rescue, people would take insufficient precautions for their own safety or even place themselves in exigent circumstances in order to be able to sue for non-rescue.[70]

The lack of a legal duty of non-easy rescue is easily explained and justified under Kantian moral theory. No person can be used solely as a means for the benefit of others, which means that no one can be legally

[67] *See* Prosser & Keeton, *supra*, note 5, at 373–7 & nn. 21 & 31.

[68] *See* Ernest J. Weinrib, *The Case for a Duty to Rescue*, 90 Yale L.J. 247, 280–6 (1980).

[69] *See* Posner, *supra*, note 2, at 174.

[70] *See id.*; Landes & Posner, *supra*, note 2, at 143–6.

required to go beyond the requirements of Right (corrective justice and distributive justice) if such an obligation would require a significant sacrifice of one's autonomy or freedom for the alleged greater good of others. Corrective justice defines the scope of one's equal negative freedom not to have one's person or existing stock of resources adversely affected by others. It is thus limited to situations involving misfeasance, in which the defendant's conduct has put the person or property of the plaintiff in a worse position than if the defendant had not been present. Although distributive justice obligates persons with more than their just share of society's resources to redistribute that excess to those who have less than their just share, these distributive justice duties generally are multilateral rather than bilateral and thus are necessarily or best implemented through legislative and administrative (re)distribution schemes.[71] In addition to these requirements of Right, Kant specifies a duty of beneficence as one of the principal duties of virtue, but he insists that this is solely an ethical duty because it is only specifiable as an indeterminate 'broad' duty, which varies depending on each would-be benefactor's own resources and needs, rather than as a determinate (and hence legally enforceable) 'strict' duty.[72]

Thus Kantian moral philosophy, while recognizing a legal duty of distributive justice and a purely ethical duty of beneficence, rejects a general legal duty of non-easy rescue or beneficence. It is often thought to go further and to support the no-duty rule, rejecting even a duty of easy rescue.[73] Yet this is far from clear. Kant himself never addressed the issue of a limited legal duty of easy rescue. Although Kant sometimes said that the issue of need is irrelevant to Right (legal obligation), he said this in the context of distinguishing the solely ethical duty of beneficence.[74] Given Kant's fundamental focus on equal individual freedom, both negative and positive, it would seem that Kant's moral philosophy would support (indeed require) a legal duty of easy rescue, which by definition would not entail any significant burden on the defendant's substantive freedom and yet would be essential to the plaintiff's continued freedom, if such a duty could be determinately specified and practicably enforced. This legal duty could be based, given the exigent circumstances, either on distributive justice's securing of

---

[71] *See* Wright, *supra,* note 1.

[72] 'How far [the duty] should extend depends, in large part, on what each person's true needs are in view of his sensibilities, and it must be left to each to decide this for himself. For a maxim of promoting others' happiness at the sacrifice of one's own happiness, one's true needs, would conflict with itself if it were made a universal law. Hence this duty is only a *wide* one; the duty has in it a latitude for doing more or less, and no specific limits can be assigned to what should be done. The law holds only for maxims, not for specific actions.' KANT, *supra,* note 28, at *393; *see id.* at *390, 452–4.

[73] *See* Ernest J. Weinrib, *Law as a Kantian Idea of Reason,* 87 COLUM. L. REV. 472, 488–9 (1987).

[74] *See, e.g.,* KANT, *supra,* note 28, at *230.

equal positive freedom or directly on the underlying foundational norm of equal individual freedom.

The primary objection to a duty of easy rescue, even by ardent libertarians such as Richard Epstein, has been the supposed indeterminateness and impracticality of implementing such a duty. Epstein suggests the intractable difficulty of deciding who should be held liable when many people were present who easily could have aided the plaintiff.[75] Yet doctrines such as joint and several liability can be used here as in other multiple defendant situations. Epstein also suggests that it is difficult if not impossible to distinguish easy-rescue situations from non-easy-rescue situations. For example, he argues that a duty of easy rescue would require most persons to respond affirmatively to a charitable appeal for $10 'to save the life of some starving child in a country ravaged by war'.[76] But this is not true: if one had such a duty, one would be forced to respond to repeated indistinguishable claims that would quickly add up to a significant burden. The feasibility of implementing a legal duty of easy rescue seems to be demonstrated by its actual implementation in civil-law jurisdictions.

Nevertheless, there is a legitimate concern that no legal duty to rescue should be imposed in nonfeasance situations that would significantly interfere with the defendant's Right of equal freedom. I believe this concern justifies applying a subjective perspective and raising the burden of proof from 'a preponderance of the evidence' to 'clear and convincing' evidence when determining whether the rescue attempt actually would have been easy (i.e., would not have been a significant intrusion on the defendant's autonomy). In addition, I acknowledge some doubts about the justice of imposing extensive tort damages which might bankrupt the defendant when the defendant is being charged merely with nonfeasance (failure to benefit someone else) rather than misfeasance (affirmatively putting someone else at risk). Such doubts might suggest that only minor criminal penalties or significantly restricted tort damages be made available for breach of the duty of easy rescue.

V. Conclusion

The Kantian–Aristotelian theory of legal responsibility, which is based on the normatively attractive premise of equal individual freedom, explains, justifies, and illuminates the various aspects of the multiple standards of care in negligence law. On the other hand, the utilitarian-efficiency theory, which treats plaintiffs and defendants as indistinguishable and fungible

---

[75] *See* Richard A. Epstein, *Causation and Corrective Justice: A Reply to Two Critics*, 8 J. Legal Stud. 477, 491 (1979).

[76] *See* Richard A. Epstein, *A Theory of Strict Liability*, 2 J. Legal. Stud. 151, 198–9 (1973).

addends in the maximization of aggregate social welfare, is a complete failure. It not only is normatively unattractive, as sometimes is conceded, but also, contrary to what is generally assumed, fails to explain or justify any of the various aspects of the standards of care in negligence law. This failure is a critical one for the utilitarian-efficiency theory of law, which generally has offered tort law, and more particularly negligence law, as the prime illustration of the theory's own utility.

The Seriousness of Harm Thesis for Abnormally Dangerous Activities

KEN KRESS*

Risk[1] figures prominently in most recent legal analyses of potentially harmful activity.[2] Economic theorists, defining expected value as the probability (risk) of injury times the anticipated magnitude of the loss if it occurs, recommend legal rules which minimize risk (and risk-avoidance costs) as a means to the minimization of accident and accident-avoidance costs. Following Lord Reid,[3] some moral theorists define negligence as the creation of a substantial risk of harm—a level- or threshold-of-risk theory of negligence.

This essay concerns the reasons given for finding activities abnormally dangerous and therefore subject to strict liability. Once again, risk predominates. As Justice Linde states: 'Whether the danger is so great as to give rise to strict liability depends both on the probability and on the magnitude of the threatened harm.'[4] According to the received view, either small probabilities of large harms or large probabilities of small harms suffice for strict liability.[5] On this common view, whether an activity is subject to abnormally dangerous strict liability depends upon the magnitude of the expected disvalue—a function of both the probability of harm and the magnitude of the harm—that it imposes. This essay rejects the conventional risk analysis and expected-utility analysis for abnormally dangerous activities, and by implication it

* Professor of Law and University Faculty Scholar, College of Law, University of Iowa. A large number of friends and colleagues commented helpfully on this essay. I am especially indebted to Charles Fisher, James Gordley, David Jung, David Owen, Stephen Perry, Stephen Sugarman, Jeremy Waldron, Richard Wright, and participants at presentations at the University of California, Hastings, and at the Center for the Study of Law and Society, University of California, Berkeley.

[1] The term 'risk' is used inconsistently in the economic, philosophical, legal, social psychology, and risk assessment literatures. Sometimes risk means the probability that harm will occur. Other times it means expected value (or disvalue), that is, the probability that harm will occur times the expected magnitude of the loss. Sometimes it means expected benefits less expected disvalue. On occasion, it refers to the magnitude of the expected loss alone. Although the meaning of risk will vary as this essay follows the usages of alternative theories, context should make the intended meaning clear.

[2] *See, e.g.*, Stephen Perry, *Risk, Harm and Responsibility*, this volume.—Ed.

[3] In Bolton v. Stone [1951] A.C. 850.

[4] Koos v. Roth, 652 P.2d 1255, 1260 (Or. 1982).

[5] *Id.* at 1260–61; W. PAGE KEETON, DAN B. DOBBS, ROBERT E. KEETON, & DAVID G. OWEN, PROSSER AND KEETON ON THE LAW OF TORTS (5th edn., 1984), 556; RESTATEMENT (SECOND) OF TORTS, § 520(a) & (b) (1976).

raises questions about the appropriateness of its employment in other areas of tort law. Rather, this essay argues that the *magnitude of the loss* is the major factor determining which activities are abnormally dangerous.

Part I sets forth and explores an alternative to risk and expected-utility analysis for determining responsibility for abnormally dangerous activities. According to this alternative analysis, abnormally dangerous activities are defined primarily by the magnitude of the harm, and secondarily by the conditional probability that harm will occur if control of the dangerous instrumentality is lost. The *chance* that control will be lost (that the dam will break, the wild animal will escape, or the like) is, according to this alternative, of little or no significance. This is the 'seriousness of harm thesis' advocated in this essay. Part I argues that this thesis accurately explains our considered judgments about abnormally dangerous activities.

Part II considers the normative significance of the analysis presented in Part I. It explores arguments maintaining that the seriousness of harm defines whether an activity is abnormally dangerous. More precisely, this part examines arguments for employing a maximin decision rule to determine abnormal dangerousness, rather than classical expected-utility decision theory.[6] This part argues that neither expected-utility decision theory nor maximin reasoning adequately grounds abnormally dangerous strict liability. Instead, Part II claims that if the defendant imposes a particular type of risk—that if an instrumentality escapes the defendant's control then there is a moderate to high probability that a serious harm will occur—and if a harm within the scope of that particular type of risk does result, then the defendant is legally responsible for that harm. Finding certain obvious candidates for normative justification wanting, Part II leaves a full normative justification of the principle open for future inquiry.

The following methodological principles are employed in examining the abnormally dangerous activity cases. More recent decisions count for more. They are more important to explain and justify than older cases. The main types of cases to be considered are vicious animal, blasting, reservoir, rocket testing, ammunition storage, escape of gas, crop dusting, nuclear power plants, nuclear weapons and industries, oil-well drilling, pile driving, and the early English fire cases. Following the *Restatement*, the trespassing-animal cases are distinguished from the abnormally dangerous activity cases. It is unlikely that any analysis could explain all of the abnormally dangerous activity cases. Moreover, it would be surprising if an adequate justification fit *all* of the decisions, given that their authors were advocates of widely varying moral, political, and jurisprudential views and ideologies. But we need not conclude, as some critical legal scholars have, that law is

---

[6] The maximin decision rule is described *infra*, at note 45 and accompanying text.

hopelessly indeterminate, contradictory, and incoherent.[7] An explanation and justification of actual and hypothetical case outcomes, which on reflection satisfies our considered judgements, is our goal.[8]

Some cases may be discounted as mistaken. Thus, the best analysis, other things being equal, is the one which most successfully captures more of our considered judgements, weighted for importance and significance. The analysis is ultimately normative, not descriptive. This does not mean that the cases are irrelevant, for they present a subject matter for justification and possible revision. Still, as Dworkin urges, if this is to be an analysis and interpretation and not a change in subject matter, there is a limit to the number of cases which may be adjudged mistaken. Additionally, a uniform analysis is preferable to a pluralistic approach that deploys different factors in varying settings, unless a convincing explanation of the necessity and desirability of doing so is provided. Finally, a simple explanation is preferable to a complex one, particularly if the complexity appears *ad hoc*. The seriousness of harm thesis is superior to conventional analyses on each of these methodological grounds. The gains in simplicity and uniformity are particularly striking.

I. The Seriousness of Harm Thesis

A. Rejecting Uncommonness and Size of Risk as Determinants of Abnormally Dangerous Activity

Traditional analyses of abnormally dangerous activities tend to focus on one or both of two factors. First, they look to whether the activity is of a kind not ordinarily engaged in by members of the relevant community, thereby imposing risks of a kind not normally created (or encountered) by most members of the community—that is, whether the activity is uncommon and therefore non-reciprocal. Second, they look to whether the risk imposed is large.

Relying on each of these factors is a mistake. First, in many settings, such as some trespassing-cattle,[9] pile-driving,[10] and the early English fire cases,[11]

---

[7] For discussion, see Ken Kress, *Legal Indeterminacy*, 77 CAL. L. REV. 283 (1989); Ken Kress, *A Preface to Epistemological Indeterminacy*, 85 NW. U. L. REV. 134 (1990).

[8] John Rawls, *Outline of a Decision Procedure for Ethics*, 60 PHIL. REV. 177 (1951); JOHN RAWLS, A THEORY OF JUSTICE (1971), 14–21, 43–53, 578–82 [hereinafter THEORY OF JUSTICE]; Ken Kress, *Coherence and Formalism*, 16 HARV. J.L. & PUB. POL'Y 639, 651–2 (1993). *See also id.* at 648–66.

[9] Gary T. Schwartz, *The Vitality of Negligence and the Ethics of Strict Liability*, 15 GA. L. REV. 963, 985 (1981). However, as noted above, trespassing livestock are not paradigm examples of abnormally dangerous activities.

[10] Sachs v. Chiat, 162 N.W.2d 243, 245 (Minn. 1968) (plaintiff had used similar pile-driver construction technique to build damaged house; because of special soil conditions other methods of construction apparently were unavailable in this area).

[11] Turberville v. Stampe, 91 E.R. 1072 (K.B. 1697) (judgment for plaintiff for allowing fire

many or most members of the community create substantially similar, reciprocal risks, yet the courts impose strict liability. Indeed, at least one court explicitly rejected uncommonness of defendant's usage as a prerequisite to abnormally dangerous strict liability.[12] These types of cases partly undermine the descriptive power of the uncommonness prerequisite.

The normative underpinnings of reciprocity and commonness are in much worse shape than their explanatory power. George Fletcher claims that reciprocal, 'background' risks 'must be borne as part of group living,'[13] arguing that a rule of strict liability for reciprocal risks merely substitutes 'the risk of liability for the risk of personal loss.'[14] He maintains that only if some might suffer more than others in the short run and, if, moreover, those losses *should* be shifted to others, would strict liability for reciprocal, common risks make sense.[15]

Contrary to Fletcher's implication, both of these conditions are met for injury from common, abnormally dangerous activities. Not only do some suffer more than others in the short run from these activities,[16] but many (including those who die, most who have their livelihoods or homes destroyed, as well as some others with modest injuries) suffer more than others in the long run. Moreover, as this essay urges, the loss from an abnormally dangerous activity *should* be shifted to the injurer because the injurer in these cases imposes a risk of *a harm of great seriousness* which eventuates in a *loss* within the scope of that risk. Legal responsibility is predicated upon proximately causing such a harm. (A second predicate is discussed in Part I B.) Fletcher, like the instrumentalists he opposes, confuses the significance of *risk* with the significance of loss or *harm*. Lack of reciprocity and uncommonness are underinclusive prerequisites for abnormally dangerous strict liability.

Even more dominant than the uncommonness of the activity requirement

in stubble field to spread to plaintiff's close; court employs the term 'negligence' but means something closer to 'strict liability'); Musgrove v. Pandelis [1919] 2 K.B. 43, 46 ('A man was liable at common law for damage done by fire originating on his own property (1.) for the mere escape of the fire . . . (3.) upon the principle of *Rylands v. Fletcher* [although the] principle was not then known by that name, because *Rylands v. Fletcher* was not then decided') (citation omitted); *see* Garnier v. Porter, 27 P. 55, 55 (Cal. 1891) (finding no liability but noting that fires are common agricultural practice); Schwartz, *supra*, note 9, at 985.

[12] *See, e.g.*, Loe v. Lenhardt, 362 P.2d 312, 316–17 (Or. 1961) ('Such activities as crop dusting, the use of explosives in highway construction, or the use of impounded water for irrigation, are all accepted practices at appropriate times and places. We believe it is not a question where mere frequency of usage . . . should determine whether or not the activity should pay its way.'); *but see* Koos v. Roth, 652 P.2d 1255, 1263, 1265 (Or. 1982) (accepting uncommonness as a prerequisite).

[13] George P. Fletcher, *Fairness and Utility in Tort Theory*, 85 HARV. L. REV. 537, 543 (1972).

[14] *Id.* at 547.   [15] *Id.*

[16] 'If the accidentally impoverished neighbor is told that in the long run the losses will balance out, he may answer, like one economist, that in the long run we are all dead': *Koos*, 652 P.2d at 1262.

is the nearly universal requirement that an activity must create a large risk to be abnormally dangerous. In this context, 'risk' means 'expected disvalue', i.e., the probability of injury, P, multiplied by the expected loss, L. (Some courts and scholars may mean P alone.) But it bears emphasis that abnormally dangerous activity, *qua* activity, *need not be and usually is not negligent*. The *Restatement (Second) of Torts* § 519(1) provides for liability even if the actor 'has exercised the utmost care to prevent . . . harm'.[17] Indeed, where an activity is conducted negligently, we do not require either the abnormally dangerous strict liability rule or rationale to impose liability (except as a response to difficulties of proof). Negligence principles require those engaging in abnormally dangerous activity to take all reasonable safety precautions.

Under an economic interpretation of negligence, all cost-justified safety precautions must be taken. Sometimes no reasonably-priced safety precaution is available. Frequently, however, one is, and negligence rules will require its employment. Once taken, at some point the cost of the next marginal precaution, B, will exceed the marginal harm, $P \times L$, it would avoid. It therefore appears possible that actors sometimes engage in abnormally dangerous activities taking sufficient (non-negligent) precaution that the probability of injury is so small that the expected disvalue (the probability of injury, P, multiplied by the loss, L, if it occurs) is also relatively small (less than B), even where L is large.

Not only is this possible, it frequently happens and may even be the norm. For example, an actor may transport high-level nuclear wastes in several layers of the most durable protective casks, conveying them by specially designed crash-resistant vehicles, over a relatively unpopulated route. Or an actor may safely build a dam, using the latest and best technology, so that the probability that it will break is minuscule. In these situations, the probability of harm is so small that the expected disvalue ($P \times L$) imposed on the community is not greater in degree than expected disvalues which members of the community impose on the actor. Thus, the magnitude of the expected disvalue, $P \times L$, cannot explain why these activities are abnormally dangerous and subject to strict liability. *A fortiori*, since it is so small, the magnitude of P alone cannot explain abnormally dangerous strict liability in these cases.

---

[17] RESTATEMENT (SECOND) OF TORTS (1976), § 519 entitled General Principles, provides:
'(1) One who carries on an abnormally dangerous activity is subject to liability for harm to the person, land or chattels of another resulting from the activity, although he has exercised the utmost care to prevent the harm.
(2) This strict liability is limited to the kind of harm, the possibility of which makes the activity abnormally dangerous.'

B. The Seriousness of Harm Thesis Developed

What does explain liability in these cases, where a very small probability of loss and a small or modest expected disvalue regrettably eventuates in harm? The germ of the solution is contained in Blackburn J's statement in *Fletcher v. Rylands* that the water which the defendant stored in his reservoir is 'likely to do *mischief* if it escapes'.[18] Directing attention first to Blackburn J's notion of 'mischief', the seriousness of the loss, *L*, if it occurs, is the most significant factor in determining whether the activity is abnormally dangerous. The larger, more catastrophic the loss, the more likely it is to lead to fatalities or multiple injuries or massive property damage if something goes awry, the more likely it is to be an abnormally dangerous activity. *What makes an activity abnormally dangerous is the magnitude of the loss when harm does occur, not the risk (P) or the expected disvalue (P × L) imposed.* The original *Restatement of Torts* supports the significance of the magnitude of loss, defining an ultrahazardous activity in part as one that 'necessarily involves a risk of serious harm'.[19] How precisely to define the requisite loss, *L*, is a difficult question. The two most prominent candidates for such a definition are, first, the worst-case scenario—that is, the largest possible *L*—and, second, an *average* of the various possible harms—the sum of each foreseeable harm's magnitude times the chance of its occurrence, divided by the total probability that some foreseeable harm will occur.[20]

The analysis should be refined slightly to take account of the other aspect of Blackburn J's statement, that the water is '*likely* to do mischief *if it escapes*'.[21] Let P_1 be the probability that the defendant loses control of the destructive instrumentality: that 'it escapes'. Thus, P_1 is the chance that, for example, the dam will break, the rocket will veer from its course, control of the fire will be lost, or the wild animal will escape. Call P_2 the conditional probability that mischief (*L*) will occur if P_1 occurs. P_2 is the *conditional likelihood* that harm will occur *if* the instrumentality escapes—the (conditional) probability that harm will occur if the dam does break, the rocket does veer off course, or the wild animal does escape. Thus, $P_1 \times P_2 = P$. The seriousness of harm thesis maintains that the most important factor in determining whether an activity is abnormally dangerous is the magnitude of *L*.

---

[18] Fletcher v. Rylands [1866] L.R. 1 Ex. 265, 279 (emphasis added).

[19] RESTATEMENT OF TORTS (1938), § 520 (also describing uncommonness as a requirement of ultrahazardous activity).

[20] Formally, $\sum_{i=1}^{N} \dfrac{L_i P_{L_i}}{P_T}$, where L_i is the magnitude of the i-th foreseeable loss, P_{L_i} is the probability that a loss of size L_i will occur, and P_T is the (total) probability that any foreseeable harm will occur. A second (absolute) version of this second (relative) definition would omit the division by P_T, i.e., $\sum_{i=1}^{N}(L_i P_{L_i})$.

[21] *Fletcher* [1866] L.R. 1 Ex. at 279 (emphasis added).

Secondarily, the magnitude of P_2 is also a relevant consideration. If P_1 equals zero, the activity is not abnormally dangerous; it is not dangerous at all. If P_1 is not zero, only rarely (as a tie-breaker?) would P_1 be a consideration.[22] One reason is that the magnitude of L (and that of P_2) is the dominant factor in the cases where $P_1 \times P_2$ (that is, P) is minuscule. As argued above, when P is very small, neither P nor $P \times L$ is large enough to explain why an activity is abnormally dangerous. For uniformity of analysis, therefore, the magnitude of L must be the major factor even when P_1 or P is significant. Otherwise, there would be different analyses for different abnormally dangerous activities and even for the same activity engaged in at varying levels of probability of injury, P. The analysis would be *ad hoc*.

Note that L is typically large in vicious animal, blasting, reservoir, rocket testing, ammunition storage, nuclear power plant, nuclear weapons and industries, oil-well drilling, pile-driving and fire cases. L is ordinarily not so large in trespassing-animal cases, unless an entire herd trespasses and destroys the whole crop. But as the *Restatement* suggests, the trespassing-animal cases are properly distinguished from abnormally dangerous activities, and are best explained and justified on other grounds.

The conditional probability that harm will occur if control of the instrumentality is lost, P_2, is also high in these cases. One expects trouble from dam failures, nuclear accidents, escaped wild animals, oil-well fires, and the like. Harm is less probable if the activity is carried on in a remote area, but then the activity is correspondingly less likely to be abnormally dangerous.[23]

More problematic is the analysis of pile driving. It is not clear what P_1 and P_2 mean respecting pile driving. The concussion and vibration which causes damage is a known, if not intended, consequence of laying a building foundation by pile driving. It seems odd to say that one has lost control of an act of pile-driving construction because an expected concussion causes damage. Because P_1's meaning is elusive respecting pile driving, so is P_2's, since P_2 is defined in terms of P_1, as the conditional probability that harm will occur if P_1 occurs. One might argue that control is lost precisely when the concussion is great enough to cause serious damage, rather than to be merely irritating, but this contention is *ad hoc*. The least unsatisfactory resolution bites the bullet, accepts the oddity, and maintains that control is lost whenever concussion (off the actor's premises) occurs. There is

---

[22] I am indebted to Richard Wright for enlightening discussions of abnormally dangerous activities over the past several years. The usual cautions apply; the reader should not attribute my views to Wright. In particular, Wright believes that L and P_2 are of equal significance in defining abnormally dangerous activity.

[23] RESTATEMENT (SECOND) OF TORTS (1976), § 520 cmt. j; Jon G. Anderson, *The* Rylands v. Fletcher *Doctrine in America: Abnormally Dangerous, Ultrahazardous, or Absolute Nuisance?*, 1978 ARIZ. ST. L.J. 99, 126. Since P_2 and L are both smaller in remote areas, the seriousness of harm thesis explains this result.

no reason to assume that P_1 is always small. Here it is known with near certainty that concussion will occur. A similar difficulty, and perhaps equivalent analysis, would apply to concussion damage from blasting and rocket testing.

At first glance, escape-of-gas (including fumigating) and crop-dusting cases appear to be counter-examples to the seriousness of harm thesis. The gas, dust, or spray may be only mildly obnoxious or harmful. *L* is small. Nevertheless, it may be urged, the difficulty of containing the fumes or controlling drift raises the probability of harm to a level where strict liability applies.[24] *P* is large. In fact, escape-of-gas and crop-dusting cases are the exceptions that prove the rule. Rather than undermining the seriousness of harm thesis, they provide it with crucial support. Unless the gas is lethal, escape-of-gas cases are almost universally decided under *negligence* rules.[25] Similarly, nearly all jurisdictions adjudicate crop-dusting injuries under a *negligence* regime—unless the anticipated harm is especially large, as where the duster risks destroying an adjacent organic crop.[26] Rather than undercutting the seriousness of harm thesis, then, these types of cases demonstrate the thesis, and powerfully so.

Some might argue that the seriousness of harm thesis is over-inclusive on the grounds that igniting residential fires, transmitting high-voltage electrical power, and similar activities would be abnormally dangerous under its terms, since L and P_2 both are high. The argument might add that this is problematic, since the common law rejects strict liability for these activities.[27] But an over-inclusiveness argument of this sort would not in fact be problematic for the seriousness of harm thesis which would welcome abnormally dangerous strict-liability status for these activities. Notwithstanding

[24] *See, e.g., Koos*, 652 P.2d at 1261 (discussing crop dusting cases).

[25] William K. Jones, *Strict Liability for Hazardous Enterprise*, 92 COLUM. L. REV. 1705, 1737–8 & cases cited in notes. 159–67 (1992) ('With few exceptions, the courts have rejected efforts to impose strict liability for harmful emissions'); Annotation, 29 A.L.R.4th 987 (1984) (exterminator's liability); *see* Annotation, 54 A.L.R.2d 764, 768 (1957) (landowner's liability for gases or fumes); Luthringer v. Moore, 190 P.2d 1, 4 (Cal. 1948) (strict liability for escape of lethal gas).

[26] The overwhelming majority of American jurisdictions apply a negligence standard to ordinary crop-dusting cases (Louisiana, Oklahoma, and Oregon are exceptions). A handful or so hold farmers vicariously liable for the negligence of independent contractor crop-dusters. Annotation, 37 A.L.R.3rd 833, 840–9 (1971) (crop dusting liability); Anderson, *supra*, note 23, at 116; Loe v. Lenhardt, 362 P.2d 312, 315 (Or. 1961) (finding defendants strictly liable for crop dusting under an ultrahazardous/trespass theory, but noting that, 'with one exception, each of the cases we have examined found sufficient evidence of negligence on the part of the person applying the chemicals to support a verdict based upon negligence'); *but see* 3 FOWLER V. HARPER, FLEMING JAMES, JR., & OSCAR S. GRAY, THE LAW OF TORTS (2d edn., 1986) § 14.16, at 335 n. 5, 338 (suggesting that the law remains uncertain). The rationale for applying a negligence rule to these cases, according to the seriousness of harm thesis, is the comparatively modest harm resulting from a mishap. Where the damage from a mishap is expected to be serious, as where a neighboring organic farmer's crop might be completely ruined, liability is strict. Langan v. Valicopters, Inc., 567 P. 2d 218 (Wash. 1977).

[27] Jones, *supra*, note 25, at 1727, 1745–7.

their normality, the common law errs in failing to place them in the 'abnormally dangerous' strict liability classification, since there is no *morally* relevant distinction between fire and high voltage electricity and activities deemed abnormally dangerous for strict liability purposes. The seriousness of harm thesis thus reveals its normative foundation in diverging from case law in this respect.

The seriousness of harm thesis is the very model of simplicity. Two factors determine which activities are abnormally dangerous, and one—the magnitude of the loss—does the bulk of the work. By comparison, the *Restatement (Second) of Torts,* § 520, lists *six* relevant factors and provides limited guidance respecting their relative significance.[28]

The seriousness of harm thesis does *not* assert that courts do explicitly employ the magnitude of L and P_2 to *define* abnormally dangerous activities. The claim instead is perhaps more modest: that the magnitude of L and P_2 better *explain* the *outcomes* of the cases—or, to be exact, our considered judgements about the cases—than alternative justifications and explanations by courts and legal scholars. In short, the thesis explains the outcomes but not the rationales of the cases.

II. THE JUSTIFICATION OF THE SERIOUSNESS OF HARM THESIS

A. Difficulties with Bayesian Expected-Utility Decision-making and Efficiency Analysis

The size of the loss if it occurs (and only secondarily the conditional probability that loss will occur if the instrumentality escapes) successfully explains our considered judgements of the outcomes of the cases. But does this factor, the seriousness of harm, constitute a satisfactory moral justification of those considered judgements? This inquiry raises two

---

[28] RESTATEMENT (SECOND) OF TORTS (1976), § 520 entitled Abnormally Dangerous Activities, provides:
'In determining whether an activity is abnormally dangerous, the following factors are to be considered:
(a) existence of a high degree of risk of some harm to the person, land or chattels of others;
(b) likelihood that the harm that results from it will be great;
(c) inability to eliminate the risk by the exercise of reasonable care;
(d) extent to which the activity is not a matter of common usage;
(e) inappropriateness of the activity to the place where it is carried on; and
(f) extent to which its value to the community is outweighed by its dangerous attributes.'
The commentary provides that the court should weigh and balance (a)–(f), giving each factor 'the weight . . . that it merits upon the facts in evidence': RESTATEMENT (SECOND) OF TORTS (1976), § 520 cmt. *l*. One scholar has claimed 'that this is no weighting method at all. . . . [T]he commentary seems to suggest that each case is *sui generis* and . . . [no] individual decision [could affect] an entire industry': George C. Christie, *An Essay on Discretion,* 1986 DUKE L.J. 747, 768.

interdependent questions. First, how should the class of abnormally dangerous activities be defined? Second, what liability rule should apply to abnormally dangerous activities? The questions are interdependent, since the justifiable class of abnormally dangerous activities may vary with the liability rule: absolute liability, strict liability, or negligence, with or without hindsight. Conversely, the appropriate liability rule depends upon which activities are abnormally dangerous. These two questions lead naturally to a third: what justifies the answer given to the first two?

Conventional scientific thought, Bayesian probability theory, classical utilitarianism, and the law and economics movement all would recommend a cost-benefit analysis—weighing the anticipated harm ($P \times L$) against the anticipated benefits—in decision-making about abnormally dangerous (as well as other) activity. Under these approaches, liability rules should be formulated to maximize anticipated social benefits less harms, thereby encouraging efficient behavior.

Several objections to cost-benefit analysis will now be briefly stated, and then examined in detail in the rest of this part. First, the utilitarian theory underlying cost-benefit analysis presupposes that individual losses and gains are balanced off against one another in the *long run*. It presupposes a sufficient number of outcomes for the benefits of desirable activities to outweigh the costs. Yet some losses, such as death, are so large—or final—that they cannot be balanced off against later gains. Additionally, it is unclear what it means to apply *small probabilities to individual* (and not multiple) *decisions*. Bayesian decision-making[29] is on comparatively solid ground when probabilities and losses are known. Its application is problematic when these numbers are uncertain. Additionally, Bayesian theory, like classical utilitarianism, is indifferent to distributional issues—who gains and who loses. *It fails to take seriously the distinction among individuals.* Yet abnormally dangerous activity, on balance, comparatively benefits the privileged and burdens the disadvantaged. Moreover, when (1) the probabilities of various alternatives occurring are uncertain, (2) the worst-case scenario is unacceptable, and (3) improvements above a baseline are not highly valued, then decision-making which maximizes the minimum prospect[30] is preferable to expected-utility maximization. Possibly, these conditions hold respecting abnormally dangerous activities.[31] Finally, Bayesian decision-making is acceptable when the risks involved are *consented to*, but it appears problematic when the risks are *involuntarily imposed*.

---

[29] Following modern usage in political and economic theory, in this essay the term 'Bayesian decision-making' refers to expected-utility maximization, not merely to the theory of the conditionalization of subjective degrees of belief upon presentation of new evidence: *see, e.g.*, John C. Harsanyi, *Can the Maximin Principle Serve as a Basis for Morality? A Critique of John Rawls's Theory*, 69 AM. POL. SCI. REV. 594, 594 (1975).

[30] This concept is explained in Part II B, below.   [31] See Part II C, below.

These objections to cost-benefit, Bayesian methodology derive from Rawls' important critique of classical utilitarianism and defense of the maximin principle,[32] and a recent application and development of Rawls' ideas to environmental harms by Kristin Shrader-Frechette.[33] This part will first develop these and other criticisms of classical expected-utility analysis and examine whether the maximin decision rule and related arguments support the seriousness of harm thesis in social decision-making. This part concludes that classical expected-utility analysis is seriously flawed, but that the maximin decision rule is unable to justify the seriousness of harm thesis for abnormally dangerous activities. Finally, a justification for liability for abnormally dangerous activities is briefly sketched, leaving full development of a justification for future research.

Many scientists, risk analysts, and policy-makers condemn public criticism of technological risks, such as nuclear reactors, pesticides, and food additives, as hysterical and irrational since leisure-time sunburns, automobiles, skiing, and fires impose significantly greater risks. They argue that the public must misperceive the probability of harm, since any rational, informed individual would act on the basis of expected utilities.[34] To the contrary, Shrader-Frechette argues that Bayesians do not have the market cornered on rational responses to risk. Some people respond mostly to the magnitude of the worst-case scenario. Others count n lives lost in one accident as n^2. Some assess involuntarily imposed risks greater than voluntary risks of the same Bayesian magnitude. Yet others adjudge unfamiliar risks greater than familiar risks of equal Bayesian magnitude. Although conventional science would criticize these responses as irrational, Shrader-Frechette claims that these attitudes are widespread and argues that they are more philosophically justified than the views of the experts who scoff at them.[35]

Some risk assessors propose that one thousand lives lost in one accident exceed the sum of one thousand deaths one at a time. They propose that n lives lost in a catastrophic accident should be valued at n^2. Shrader-Frechette would justify this evaluation based on the social disruption and trauma involved in the catastrophe.[36] This argument suggests that fewer high-consequence risks should be tolerated, but does not impugn Bayesian statistics. It merely draws attention to controversy respecting the correct

[32] RAWLS, THEORY OF JUSTICE, *supra*, note 8, at 22–3, 152–7, 161–92, *passim*. The maximin principle is described *infra*, notes 45-46 and accompanying text.
[33] KRISTIN S. SHRADER-FRECHETTE, RISK AND RATIONALITY: PHILOSOPHICAL FOUNDATIONS FOR POPULIST REFORMS (1991). Shrader-Frechette's analysis is critiqued and refined in Jeremy Waldron, *K.S. Shrader-Frechette, Risk and Rationality: Philosophical Foundations for Populist Reforms*, 20 ECOLOGY L.Q. 347 (1993) (book review).
[34] SHRADER-FRECHETTE, *supra*, note 33, at 17, 89, 90.
[35] Waldron, *supra*, note 33, at 347–8.
[36] SHRADER-FRECHETTE, *supra*, note 33, at 90, 94.

measure of the magnitude of certain losses. If valid, it still only shows that a higher value should be placed on catastrophic consequences.

Other risk assessors note that risks that are distributed unfairly are perceived as larger than those fairly shared.[37] Moreover, an 'outrage factor' may result in imposed risks being perceived as more hazardous than voluntarily assumed risks with the same expected disutility.[38] Shrader-Frechette concedes that an individual may make decisions about his or her own life based upon expected utility. But she rejects expected utility for social decision-making regarding others because it may violate rights, or may fail to satisfy democratic principles and process concerns. She believes that a maximin decision rule is more acceptable as a social decision-maker.[39]

Consider the scientific community's ridicule of public concern about technological risks.[40] Shrader-Frechette marshals empirical evidence in support of the rationality of public perceptions of risk, arguing that the public does not misperceive the probabilities. Rather, respecting low probability, high-consequence risks, such as nuclear meltdowns, the public correctly perceives the low probability of accident. Nevertheless, the magnitude of the possible harm is nearly completely determinative of the risk perceived by the public.[41] Even if sound, however, such studies would not by themselves justify strict liability for high magnitude losses:[42] one cannot derive an ought from an is. They merely explain how and why the public views these risks as unacceptable, as Shrader-Frechette recognizes. Nevertheless, such studies do explain public support for the seriousness of harm thesis, suggesting that conventional morality supports the thesis. Since judges are members of the public whose beliefs constitute conventional morality, it is not surprising that the outcomes of their decisions are consistent with the seriousness of harm thesis, although their rationales may not explicitly mention the thesis. These studies also put us on notice and Bayesian theory on the defensive. If Bayesian theory implies that public perceptions are irrational, yet public perceptions appear rational, then perhaps Bayesian theory is incorrect. This suggests that approaches other than Bayesian social decision-making should be explored.

---

[37] Daniel Goleman, *What Should You Worry About? Probably Not What You Think*, INT'L HERALD TRIB., Feb. 3, 1994, at 8.

[38] *Id.*

[39] SHRADER-FRECHETTE, *supra*, note 33, at 105–6. The maximin decision rule is explained in Part II B, below.

[40] *See supra*, note 34.

[41] SCHRADER-FRECHETTE, *supra*, note 33, at 93–4 (citing P. Slovic *et al.*, *Facts and Fears: Understanding Perceived Risks* , in SOCIETAL RISK ASSESSMENT (Richard C. Schwing & Walter A. Albers, Jr. eds., 1980), 181, 207–8, 211 and B. Fischoff *et al.*, *How Safe is Safe Enough? A Psychometric Study of Attitudes Towards Technological Risks*, 9 POL'Y SCI. 127, 147, 149–50 (1978)).

[42] Unless, of course, legal doctrine or adjudication depends upon conventional beliefs or conventional morality.

A final example further supports the proposition that Bayesian expected-utility decision-making is not universally applicable. Consider a rational refusal of an invitation to play Russian Roulette with a five-chamber revolver. Even if the offer included a great reward if one were to win, it may still be rational to refuse to play. Now a further offer is made to play with a six-chamber revolver. The damage resulting from a self-inflicted gunshot wound to the head is so severe that the significant improvement in safety in moving from a five- to a six-chamber revolver is irrelevant to the decision whether to play.[43] The harm, not the probability of injury, is the crucial factor: 'if this is reasonable for Russian Roulette, it is hard to say that imperviousness to probabilities must be dismissed out of hand as irrational hysteria in [other] cases.'[44]

B. Comparing the Maximin Strategy to Bayesian Decision-making

These considerations parallel—but are not quite—the reasons why Rawls prefers the maximin strategy over Bayesian decision-making and classical utilitarianism. As its name implies, the 'maximin' decision rule opts to maximize the minimum possible circumstance. When choosing among alternatives each of which has multiple outcomes with differing values, the maximin decision rule recommends picking the alternative with the highest minimum-valued outcome.[45] The maximin strategy is risk averse, not expected-utility maximizing.[46] Yet the point is not that humans are inherently risk averse; not all are. Rather, the point is that maximin decision-making is rationally preferable to expected-utility maximizing under certain circumstances.[47]

[43] SHRADER-FRECHETTE, *supra,* note 33, at 95; Waldron, *supra,* note 33, at 359.

[44] Waldron, *supra,* note 33, at 359.

[45] 'The term "maximin" means the *maximum minimorum*; and the rule directs our attention to the worst that can happen under any proposed course of action, and to decide in light of that': RAWLS, THEORY OF JUSTICE, *supra,* note 8, at 154. Consider the following 'gain-and-loss' table taken from Rawls. The actor may choose any of three alternatives. Any one of three circumstances may obtain under each alternative. The (objective) value of each alternative under each circumstance is as follows:

	Circumstances		
Alternatives	c_1	c_2	c_3
a_1	−7	8	12
a_2	−8	7	14
a_3	5	6	8

Under this scenario, the maximin rule requires the actor to choose alternative a_3 because its minimum value, 5, is higher than the minimum value of the other alternatives: *id.* at 153–4.

[46] For discussion of maximin decision-making, see WILLIAM J. BAUMOL, ECONOMIC THEORY AND OPERATIONS ANALYSIS (2d edn., 1965) 531–2, 552–3; RAWLS, THEORY OF JUSTICE, *supra,* note 8, at 152–5.

[47] These circumstances are elaborated in Part II C, below. Three possible justifications and interpretations of maximin reasoning are described in Part II C, below.

Returning to Russian Roulette, if you lose in the first or second round, you will not be able to recoup your losses—death or serious brain damage—with winnings from later rounds, as you might after losing the first hand in poker. Given the size and nature of the loss in Russian Roulette, a long-run Bayesian strategy in this context clearly is inferior to a maximin decision rule. The larger the potential loss, the better the maximin strategy looks and the worse Bayesian decision-making appears. Under this circumstance, involving a very large L, non-Bayesian alternatives are attractive.

Another challenge to Bayesian statistics questions the meaning of the application of small probabilities to single, or a few, decisions. This motif along with the related one of maximin decision-making behind the veil of ignorance—the connection will be drawn out shortly—runs throughout this part. If there is a .0012 chance that a reservoir of a certain construction will give way, then an individual (or nation) with 10,000 reservoirs can expect roughly 12 floods. But what does the probability mean to an individual who constructs only one reservoir?[48] The puzzling nature of the application of small probabilities to single and small numbers of outcomes has been urged as an explanation for why heavy smokers are willing to risk a 3 percent lifetime chance of lung cancer,[49] and why educated women are willing to risk pregnancy from unprotected intercourse.[50] These considerations suggest the propriety of focusing on L, at least where P is small. In many cases, we are unable to understand the meaningfulness of the application of a small P to one or a few events, and we are therefore forced to decide on the basis of L. Once we accept the need to focus on L in these settings, then reasons of simplicity and uniformity recommend maintaining attention on L in all cases.

A Bayesian might attempt to undermine this argument. First, a heavy smoker will smoke tens or hundreds of thousands of cigarettes in his lifetime, and the woman who engages in unprotected intercourse may do so repeatedly. The above challenge to Bayesian decision-making in this context thus overlooks the possibility of combining risks. People sometimes engage in various low-probability risk-taking activities—scuba-diving, taking the Concorde, rappelling off mountains, or vacationing in New York City. These risks can be combined into medium- or long-run frequencies. Moreover, risks in these activities can be combined with those in more frequent activities—choosing ordinary or organic foods, driving fast or slowly, taking the exciting or safe roller-coaster, jogging or walking, and the like—to yield multiple activity equivalents of long-run frequencies for single activities. Additionally, whether an abnormally dangerous activity is

[48] Waldron, *supra*, note 33, at 356–7.   [49] *Id.* at 357.
[50] *Id.* (citing Kristin Luker, Taking Chances: Abortion and the Decision Not To Contracept (1975), 78–111 .

engaged in on a one-time basis or not depends upon how it and its risks are characterized: running a nuclear power plant for one year, or for each of 365 days; a .000365 risk per year, or a .000001 risk per day. The hazard of smoking may be characterized cigarette by cigarette (or even puff by puff), or in terms of a lifetime of heavy smoking. The characterization of risk frequency also depends upon whose perspective is involved—the defendant's perspective in creating the risk, or the perspective of the individual plaintiff upon whom the risk is imposed.

Yet efforts along these lines to defend Bayesian thinking from attack misconceive the phenomenology of decision-making. The woman who engages in unprotected intercourse repeatedly decides to do so separately on each occasion; she does not make a blanket decision for all or multiple future sexual activities.[51] Similarly, decisions to build a dam, scuba-dive, or rappel off mountains generally are not part of a package, but are made independently. Thus, this attempt to salvage Bayesian reasoning in low probability contexts fails.

A more powerful response on behalf of Bayesian decision-making notes that P is frequently small in cases decided under conventional *negligence* rules. Yet we do not appear to have difficulty understanding the meaningfulness of a small P in negligence cases.[52] There is no reason to think that we ignore P in those cases and decide liability only on the basis of the burden of precaution, B, the magnitude of the loss, L, and other non-P factors. Hence, the objection to the application of small probabilities to single events is not fully successful—by itself—in undermining Bayesian decision-making. But it weakens the edifice for subsequent objections. Moreover, because the difficulty in applying small probabilities to single (or a few) events is a theme running through other criticisms examined below, this objection to Bayesian theory presages these other criticisms. In particular, this objection points the way to a related, but more powerful, critique of Bayesian decision-making.

John Rawls' argument against classical utilitarianism in *A Theory of Justice* depends crucially on his rejection of Bayesian decision theory as a basis for the '*single* decision faced by persons in the "Original Position" that he uses to model the choice of principles of justice.'[53] Maximizing utility makes sense for a repeat player who expects better and worse outcomes to average out in the long run; but it is a risky bet for someone deciding on the principle that will determine with finality his life prospects: '[w]e must not be enticed by mathematically attractive assumptions into

---

[51] There may of course be some women who are exceptions, and a general decision not to protect may be engaged with respect to a particular partner. Analysis of the decision-making of smokers is complicated by its addictive qualities.

[52] Recall, however, Lord Reid's view, that P must exceed a threshold, thereby creating a substantial risk, for negligence to be present. See *supra*, note 3 and accompanying text.

[53] Waldron, *supra*, note 33, at 357.

pretending that the contingencies of men's social positions and the asymmetries of their situations somehow even out in the end.'[54]

As Rawls points out, classical utilitarianism and Bayesian theory employed as a social decision-maker assume that individual preferences can be combined for decision-making purposes into a kind of Societal Superhuman who experiences all individual, mere mortal preferences. What matters is to maximize total societal satisfactions in this Superhuman. Yet one person's gain is often at another person's expense. It may turn out that maximizing total societal satisfactions requires satisfying most of *A*'s preferences and none of *B*'s. As methods of social decision-making, classical utilitarianism and Bayesian theory fail to take seriously the distinction between persons.[55]

C. The Maximin Principle and Abnormally Dangerous Activities

Rawls recognizes that *the argument for preferring maximin to expected utility does not apply universally, but only within a limited range.*[56] First, notice that maximin gives insufficient weight to the prospect of high expected values. We would not want to maximize our minimum possible alternative outcome by one unit at a cost of ten thousand expected units. Maximin is preferable to Bayesian decision-making to the extent that the following three conditions hold: (1) there is significant uncertainty about the probabilities of the alternative possible circumstances being actualized; (2) the worst-case scenarios under alternatives other than the maximin are unacceptable; and (3) improvements above the minimum guaranteed by the maximin rule are not highly valued.[57]

Do these three conditions hold with respect to abnormally dangerous activities, justifying maximin rather than Bayesian decision-making? *Prima facie,* there is an analogy between the seriousness of harm's focus on the magnitude of the loss and the maximin rule's attention to worst-case scenarios. It might be urged that abnormally dangerous activities do frequently satisfy the three conditions to a moderately high degree. First, due to variations in material properties and modes of failure, human error, short-cuts in construction, improper procedures, or unexpected environmental conditions, it is often difficult to determine in advance the chance that the defendant will lose control of an abnormally dangerous activity.[58] The difficulty in predicting P_1 leads to a difficulty in predicting P (that is, $P_1 \times P_2$), the probability that the activity will cause harm. Even when the probability of harm is known to fall within definite parameters, the proba-

---

[54] RAWLS, THEORY OF JUSTICE, *supra*, note 8, at 171, *cited in* Waldron, *supra*, note 33, at 357.
[55] RAWLS, THEORY OF JUSTICE, *supra*, note 8, at 26–7.   [56] *Id.* at 153.
[57] *Id.* at 154–5. *See also* WILLIAM FELLNER, PROBABILITY AND PROFIT (1965), 140–2.
[58] SHRADER-FRECHETTE, *supra*, note 33, at 97; Waldron, *supra*, note 33, at 360.

bilities of the various possible magnitudes of the loss, L, may be unknown. Second, it is the very nature of abnormally dangerous activities that L can be large, or even enormous, leading to an unacceptable worst-case scenario: a nuclear meltdown might kill 150,000 people.[59] The applicability of the third condition, concerning the value of improvements over the maximin minimum, is a more difficult question. The value of such improvements would vary among abnormally dangerous activities, partly depending upon the value of the activity in comparison to any less-dangerous alternatives and upon the general extent of and distribution of social resources. The value of improvements over the maximin minimum will diminish as societal wealth and the maximin minimum grow, in consequence of the theory of the diminishing marginal utility of material goods. On balance, this argument concludes, the maximin strategy is preferable to expected-utility maximizing respecting abnormally dangerous activities. Before evaluating this argument, it will prove helpful to look more closely at the maximin decision rule.

The maximin decision rule can be interpreted in at least three different ways—a Rawlsian contractarian interpretation, and two readings of the rule as principles of rational choice. A contractarian interpretation of the maximin decision rule creates uncertainty about the alternative possible outcomes by placing the parties in the original position behind a veil of ignorance about their talents, place in society, and even the generation in which they live. These uncertainties are therefore artificially generated by contractarian methodology, by contrast to the context of abnormally dangerous activities where the uncertainty is a measure of our lack of knowledge about the activities themselves.

Rawls claims that original position methodology applies only to the basic structure of society, that is, to its constitutional and basic economic arrangements.[60] To apply contractarian methodology at the micro level to legislative and judicial rule-making would risk contradicting the directives on how to make legal rules given at the macro contractarian level. While there is no *a priori* reason why macro contractarian methods would not permit, or require, micro contractarian methods, there is also no *a priori* reason why they would not require, or permit, legal rules to be determined by non-contractarian methods like voting or adjudication. In the absence of a solid justification for micro contractarian reasoning, it is preferable to employ an alternative interpretation of the maximin decision rule in the context of abnormally dangerous activities. The artificiality of the uncertainty about the probabilities of various circumstances obtaining arising from the veil of ignorance in the contractarian setting, in contrast to the uncertainty deriving from our lack of knowledge in the context of

---

[59] Shrader-Frechette, *supra*, note 33, at 127 n. 151.
[60] Rawls, Theory of Justice, *supra*, note 8, at 7–11.

abnormally dangerous activities, further supports the decision to seek an alternative reading of the maximin rule.

A second reading of the maximin decision rule is as a principle of individual rational choice. Under the three conditions described above, it is rationally preferable to follow a maximin strategy rather than an expected-utility maximizing strategy. Legal rule-making, however, is not a matter of individual rational choice. Legal rule-making is a social enterprise which engages moral and political principles, not simply principles of individual rational conduct. For example, negligent behavior is prohibited not because it unreasonably risks injury to *oneself*, but because it unreasonably risks injury to *others*.

The best interpretation of the maximin principle in the context of legal decision-making about abnormally dangerous activities is therefore as a principle of social—not individual—rationality. The confidence we have in estimates of probabilities of alternative circumstances obtaining, the unacceptability of losses, and the evaluation of improvements over the maximin minimum, should therefore be made from a social—not individual—perspective.

Armed with this interpretation of the maximin decision rule, it appears that its application to abnormally dangerous activities is ultimately unpersuasive. Consider the first condition, that there must be good reason to discount estimates of the probabilities of various circumstances obtaining. In the Rawlsian original position, the parties have only 'the vaguest knowledge of likelihoods' since they 'have no basis for determining the probable nature of their society, or their place in it.'[61] In fact, in the original position, the parties know almost nothing about what the possible circumstances are.[62] By contrast, we have a reasonable grasp of the possible circumstances respecting abnormally dangerous activities, including, prominently, their potential social benefits, the harms they may cause and, to a lesser degree, the probability that they will cause those harms.

Moving to the second condition, the worst-case scenarios in nuclear-power-plant, ammunition-storage, and like cases appear clearly unacceptable. It is less clear that the worst-case scenario is unacceptable in wild animal and pile-driving cases. The worst-case scenario of pile driving or keeping wild animals will appear unacceptable to an *individual* subjected to the risk of death or destruction of that person's home or place of business. But this appears to result from improperly interpreting the maximin decision rule as a principle of individual rational choice, rather than rational social choice. Conceived as a *social* principle, the maximin decision rule cannot hold that any risk of death, serious injury, or substantial property damage is unacceptable. If it did, it would prohibit too much. Only losses

---

[61] Rawls, THEORY OF JUSTICE, *supra*, note 8, at 155.

[62] *Id.* For this reason, Rawls argues only that the two principles of justice are analogous to the maximin decision rule: *id.* at 152, 156.

that exceed some significant threshold are unacceptable. Thus, a significant number of those less dangerous activities conventionally considered abnormally dangerous will not meet the social maximin decision rule's criterion of unacceptability.

The third condition, whether improvements over the maximin minimum are highly valued is difficult to evaluate until a criterion for evaluating particular circumstances is selected. It seems likely that, other things being equal, improvements in efficiency are desirable. Much would need to be said about whether and why distributive considerations supplement, weigh off against, or constrain efficiency in the race for higher evaluations. This much is clear: many would be unwilling to give up the benefits of nuclear power plants, blasting, and pile driving in order to avoid their worst-case scenarios.

This brings us to the final and most telling objection to the maximin principle as a social decision-maker in the context of abnormally dangerous activities. This objection applies whichever of the three interpretations of the maximin rule is given. The maximin rule *does not recommend strict liability* for abnormally dangerous activities, it *recommends their prohibition* as a means of avoiding their worst-case scenarios.

Undaunted, the supporter of the maximin decision rule may attempt a compromise solution. While the maximin rule has force, and by itself argues for prohibition, it is not the only relevant consideration. The liberty interests of those wishing to engage in the activity and the social value of the activity must also be considered. Prohibiting activity is a rare occurrence in tort law. Unless behavior threatens an injury that would be a tort, and no remedy exists at law, injunctive relief may be unavailable.[63] For example, to enjoin a nuisance, the offense must be continuous and, moreover, unreasonable.[64] Since most abnormally dangerous activities do not meet these conditions, prohibitions generally cannot be obtained within traditional tort parameters. As a default position, as a second-best approach, or perhaps merely as a compromise of the interests of actors and victims, this argument suggests that abnormally dangerous activity should be subject to strict liability, not negligence or outright prohibition.

This second-best argument for a rule of strict liability instead of outright prohibition is a compromise view that has the virtue of explaining the positive law. It parallels the argument that the objective standard in negligence is a compromise of the plaintiff's preferred strict liability view and the defendant's preferred subjective fault (or no liability) position.[65] But both

---

[63] DAVID SCHOENBROD, *ET AL.*, REMEDIES: PUBLIC AND PRIVATE (1990), 54.

[64] Boomer v. Atlantic Cement Co., 257 N.E.2d 870 (N.Y. 1970); Jones, *supra*, note 25, at 1708.

[65] Ernest J. Weinrib, *Liberty, Community and Corrective Justice*, 1 CAN. J.L. & JURIS. 3, 11–16 (1988); Ernest J. Weinrib, *Causation Wrongdoing*, 63 CHI.-KENT L. REV. 407, 427–9 (1987); Ernest J. Weinrib, *Understanding Tort Law*, 23 VAL. U. L. REV. 485, 518–20 (1989).

these compromises have their drawbacks. Both appear to pick an arbitrary position between the plaintiff's and defendant's perspectives. Why strict liability? Why not strict liability with a contributory or comparative negligence defense? Why not a hindsight test? The compromise does not seem the resultant, sum, or outcome of the relevant arguments, but only a rough and ready compromise (point) between them. It therefore appears unprincipled, justifiable only on the coarsest administrability or salience grounds. Such a compromise approach to the seriousness of harm thesis would be contrived and *ad hoc*, and would unacceptably compromise its antiutilitarian spirit. Moreover, the compromise builds upon a weak foundation.

Although the maximin decision rule cannot ultimately justify the seriousness of harm thesis, this does not undercut the grave criticisms of Bayesian decision-making developed in Part II. Both criticisms, those that employ the maximin rule and those that do not, retain vitality.

III. CONCLUSION

The seriousness of harm thesis is in need of a normative foundation.[66] Here, only a hint of a justification can be supplied. Although this essay has followed custom in calling abnormally dangerous liability *strict*, the seriousness of harm thesis does not maintain that causation alone suffices for legal responsibility. Liability here is not the strict liability involved in what Stephen Perry has called general strict liability.[67] Instead, (1) the defendant must have created a non-zero risk that some instrumentality will escape his or her control (P_1), (2) the conditional probability that harm will ensue if control is lost (P_2) must be moderate to high, and (3) the magnitude of the loss (L) must be large. In short, the defendant must have created a non-zero probability of grave harm. It matters little whether one calls liability predicated upon this basis strict or fault-based, so long as the grounds for liability are clear. The ground is *not*, as in Bayesian theory and some case law, the size of the expected disvalue—it *is* the separate magnitudes of P_2 and L.[68] Because the seriousness of harm thesis predicates legal responsibility on the creation of a risk of great harm as well as causation, it is consistent with principles of corrective justice. It matters less whether one claims that creation of a risk of great harm is a moral fault, an objective fault, a wrongful act, or merely the predicate for legal responsibility,

---

[66] I attempt to provide this in a work currently in progress.

[67] Stephen R. Perry, *The Impossibility of General Strict Liability*, 1 CAN. J.L. & JURIS. 147 (1988).

[68] *Loe*, 362 P.2d at 317 ('The element of fault, if it can be called that, lies in the deliberate choice by the defendant to inflict a high degree of risk upon his neighbor, even though utmost care is observed in so doing').

than that one differentiates this predicate for liability from the Bayesian criterion of responsibility based upon social efficiency.

As a novel theory, the seriousness of harm thesis requires additional development and refinement.[69] What precisely are the relative roles of P_2 and L in defining abnormally dangerous activities?[70] What is the normative justification for assigning such significance to L and to P_2? While these—and other—questions await resolution, it can already be seen that 'the questions promise more than' the traditional theories provide.[71]

At the deepest level, traditional theories of abnormally dangerous activities view them as imposing a Super-risk, and being a kind of Super-negligence, no matter how much they struggle to resist these characterizations. This is most clearly revealed in the conventional focus on risk, expected disvalue, and on uncommonness as a partial proxy for unreasonable, negligent behavior. In consequence of this deep theoretical commitment, traditional views reflect a concern for consequentialist, utilitarian, and efficiency justifications which fall leaden at our feet. The seriousness of harm thesis' focus on the magnitude of the loss, L, is far more satisfying as a description and foundation for analysis of abnormally dangerous activity. Focussing on the magnitude of loss also opens the door to more fascinating normative inquiries than the tired old refrains the traditional theories provide. The conventional theories for abnormally dangerous activities should be discarded, and the seriousness of harm thesis should be substituted in their place.

[69] I attempt some of this in a more extended version of this essay currently in progress.
[70] *See supra*, note 22.
[71] To pilfer a phrase from RONALD DWORKIN, TAKING RIGHTS SERIOUSLY (1977), 44.

Aggregate Autonomy, the Difference Principle, and the Calabresian Approach to Products Liability

JOHN B. ATTANASIO*

Social and economic inequalities are to be arranged so that they are . . . to the greatest benefit of the least advantaged.[1]

[A]ct to protect the individual from severe constrictions of life plans whenever such protection requires de minimis wealth-related interference with one's own life plans.[2]

I. INTRODUCTION

Several years ago, I proposed an autonomy defense of the Calabresian approach to products liability.[3] At that time, the standard thinking was that Calabresian theory served utilitarian concerns.[4] The approach is closely identified with the Law and Economics Movement. Indeed, Guido Calabresi co-founded that movement[5] with Ronald Coase.[6] The efficiency outcomes that drive the law and economics approach are frequently con-

* Dean and Professor of Law, Saint Louis University School of Law; LL.M., Yale Law School; Dipl. in Law, University of Oxford; J.D., New York University School of Law; B.A., University of Virginia. I would like to thank John Griesbach, Cathleen Mogan, Kathleen Spartana, and Douglas Williams for their helpful comments and ideas. I would also like to thank the Saint Louis University Law Library and Joy Chatman for their wonderful research support. Finally, I would like to thank Julie Hake and Mary Ann Jauer for their diligence in typing the manuscript.

[1] This is John Rawls's famous difference principle: see JOHN RAWLS, A THEORY OF JUSTICE (1971), 302 [hereinafter RAWLS, THEORY OF JUSTICE].

[2] This is the weak principle of aggregate autonomy: see John B. Attanasio, *The Principle of Aggregate Autonomy and the Calabresian Approach to Products Liability*, 74 VA. L. REV. 677, 723 (1988).

[3] Attanasio, *supra*, note 2.

[4] *See, e.g.*, Izhak Englard, *The System Builders: A Critical Appraisal of Modern American Tort Theory*, 9 J. LEGAL STUD. 27, 34 (1980); George P. Fletcher, *Fairness and Utility in Tort Theory*, 85 HARV. L. REV. 537, 560 (1972); William H. Rodgers, Jr., *Negligence Reconsidered: The Role of Rationality in Tort Theory*, 54 S. CAL. L. REV. 1, 6 (1980). *See also* RONALD DWORKIN, A MATTER OF PRINCIPLE (1985), 267–73 (describing Calabresi as a utilitarian with distributive concerns).

[5] Guido Calabresi, *Some Thoughts On Risk Distribution and the Law of Torts*, 70 YALE L.J. 499 (1961).

[6] R. H. Coase, *The Problem of Social Cost*, 3 J.L. & ECON. 1 (1960).

nected to utilitarian concerns.[7] Some have suggested that utilitarian concerns drive not only products liability, but all of tort law.[8]

I have argued that autonomy concerns have shaped tort law more powerfully than utilitarian ones.[9] I do not reject all utilitarian influences on tort law but suggest that autonomy interests predominate.[10] With the important exception of the category refinement,[11] I maintain that the Calabresian approach strongly advances those autonomy concerns that it was commonly assumed to denigrate.

The philosophical paradigm that Calabresi serves, and really helps to illuminate, may be called the weak principle of aggregate autonomy. One formulation of the principle is: act to protect the individual against severe constrictions of life plans whenever such protection may be accomplished through de minimis wealth-related interference with the life plans of some other members of society. Put in more individualistic terms, the principle demands: act to protect the individual against severe constrictions of life plans whenever such protection requires *de minimis* wealth-related interference with one's own life plans.[12] The principle offers a broad-based justification for exacting a small amount of wealth from the producers or consumers of a product to redress the severe autonomy infringements that product accidents cause.[13]

Some more traditional autonomy theorists might call the notion of aggregate autonomy heretical. Some might charge that the aggregating move renders the principle utilitarian.[14] In my view, the aggregate autonomy principle services autonomy but with certain egalitarian constraints. The principle is concerned with the *distribution* of autonomy.

Aggregate autonomy is a step in a struggle attempting to reconcile the demands of libertarian and egalitarian theory.[15] My approach to that struggle has been deeply influenced by two highly respected scholars, Guido Calabresi and John Rawls. As noted above, the Calabresian approach to products liability supplied the window through which I glimpsed the principle of aggregate autonomy.

---

[7] In striving to maximize the resources available to society, efficiency often connects with the Benthamite form of hedonistic acts of utilitarianism. The assumption is that maximizing resources maximizes happiness.

[8] *See, e.g.*, WILLIAM M. LANDES & RICHARD A. POSNER, THE ECONOMIC STRUCTURE OF TORT LAW (1987), 15–19.

[9] Attanasio, *supra*, note 2.   [10] *Id.* at 687–93 & nn. 53–4, 707–15.

[11] By the category refinement, I mean Calabresi's proposal to predicate liability on statistical determinations of which category or party can more effectively avoid a particular type of accident: *see id.* at 715–19.

[12] *Id.* at 723.   [13] *Id.* at 727–9.

[14] For differences between the principle of aggregate autonomy and utilitarianism, see *id.* at 723–4.

[15] *See* John B. Attanasio, *The Constitutionality of Regulating Human Genetic Engineering: Where Procreative Liberty and Equal Opportunity Collide*, 53 U. CHI. L. REV. 1274 (1986).

John Rawls's magisterial work, *A Theory of Justice*, also has powerfully influenced my own struggle with libertarian and egalitarian theory. As will become apparent as the analysis unfolds, I interpret Rawls as basically an egalitarian who makes several critical moves to cabin the authoritarian aspects of strong egalitarian theories. One of his most important such moves is his design of a lexical system with liberty—albeit equal liberty—in the top sphere.

Perhaps the most renowned of Rawls' principles is his third-order difference principle. Designed to help the least advantaged members of society, it distinctly projects egalitarian concerns.[16] The difference principle inspired the principle of aggregate autonomy, which is also a lower-order[17] principle with overt egalitarian concerns. However, unlike the difference principle, the principle of aggregate autonomy incorporates autonomy concerns that are at least as important as egalitarian ones. A libertarian might react to the difference principle by saying that it exalts equality over liberty which is an impermissible move. At bottom, the debate is reduced to which value one finds more attractive in such areas as the distribution of property rights. In sharp contrast, the principle of aggregate autonomy accepts the language of liberty, or at least of autonomy which I define differently than liberty. I maintain that if one takes autonomy seriously, one would adopt something like the principle of aggregate autonomy.

To illuminate and develop further the principle of aggregate autonomy, this essay compares that principle's defense of Calabresian theory with one that might be offered by Rawlsian analysis including the difference principle. First, I briefly review the salient points of the Calabresian approach to products liability. Secondly, I explore potential Rawlsian justifications for the Calabresian approach both under *A Theory of Justice* and his recent work, *Political Liberalism*. Thirdly, I describe the principle of aggregate autonomy in greater detail and review its defense of Calabresian theory. Fourthly, I compare these two defenses in order to contrast the difference principle and the principle of aggregate autonomy. Fifthly, I try to locate aggregate autonomy within the landscapes of tort law and moral philosophy. In particular, I explore the role of the virtues. In the conclusion, I briefly reflect on the advantages of theories of the good such as aggregate autonomy over theories of the right such as the difference principle.

---

[16] For further discussion of the difference principle, see *infra*, text accompanying notes 34–7, 84–90.
[17] By lower-order principle I mean one whose dictates are trumped by concerns expressed in principles prior to it.

II. The Calabresian Approach to Products Liability

As the Calabresian approach to products liability is so widely known, I will only describe it briefly here.[18] Essentially, the approach reduces to two path-breaking ideas.

One central tenet of Calabresi's approach dictates that society should impose accident losses on whichever party can best decide whether the potential product accident is more costly to avoid or to insure against, and subsequently act on that decision.[19] Calabresi proffers this rule not only as a normative ideal but as a descriptive sketch of the way in which the products liability system in some degree already operates. For Calabresi, the best decider is strictly liable irrespective of the consequences of Learned Hand balancing[20] or other fault-based standards of responsibility.[21]

The second key to the Calabresian approach is internalization: product price should reflect accident costs attributable to that product.[22] Holding the product producer strictly liable for harms actually caused by the product will advance the internalization of the product's accident costs. Producers will consider these accident costs part of the true costs of the product and will increase the price accordingly. In this way, product price will more nearly approximate the actual, total costs of the product.[23]

These two ideas are examined in greater detail in the next two sections. The first explores whether Rawlsian theory supports the Calabresian approach to products liability. The second explores whether the principle of aggregate autonomy does.

---

[18] The watershed work detailing the Calabresian approach to tort law is Guido Calabresi, The Costs of Accidents (1970). The key article applying the approach to products liability is Guido Calabresi & Jon T. Hirschoff, *Toward a Test for Strict Liability in Torts*, 81 Yale L.J. 1055 (1972).

[19] The best decider approach incorporates the tort doctrine of assumption of risk. Calabresi & Hirschoff, *supra*, note 18, at 1065–6, 1073–4. The best decider theory allocates liability to victims in so far as they are injured as a result of assumed risks. Otherwise, it would generally allocate liability to product manufacturers: *id.* at 1070–4. *Cf.* Calabresi, *supra*, note 18, at 150–2 (describing a 'best briber' rationale in efficiency terms).

[20] By Learned Hand balancing, I am simply referring to the well-known test posited in United States v. Carroll Towing Co., 159 F.2d 169 (2d Cir. 1947).

[21] *See* Calabresi & Hirschoff, *supra*, note 18.

[22] *See id.* at 1057, nn. 10–11.

[23] Economists use the term 'externality' to describe the costs of a product or an activity that are not reflected in its price. Consequently, these costs must be borne by the society at large rather than by those who enjoy the product or activity. A classic example is pollution. *see* Paul A. Samuelson & William D. Nordhaus, Economics (12th edn., 1985), 712–21.

III. A RAWLSIAN DEFENSE OF THE CALABRESIAN APPROACH TO PRODUCTS LIABILITY

In his landmark book, *A Theory of Justice*, John Rawls seeks to reconcile the tensions between libertarian and egalitarian theory. He fashions a theory of 'the right' that he calls justice as fairness. His conception combines stringent equality of opportunity, weakened equality of condition, and 'equal liberty' trumps that modulate the authoritarian dangers of egalitarian theories.

The intricate philosophical edifice that John Rawls fashions moves to counteract 'the accidents of natural endowment and the contingencies of social circumstance as counters in quest for political and economic advantage.'[24] To mitigate arbitrary inequalities, Rawls seeks to determine how the citizens of a given society would structure the commonwealth if they were placed in the 'original position', ignorant of their individual wealth, abilities, and other resources.[25] He concludes that they would follow two sets of principles:

a.   Each person has an equal right to a fully adequate scheme of equal basic liberties which is compatible with a similar scheme of liberties for all.

b.   Social and economic inequalities are to satisfy two conditions. First, they must be attached to offices and positions open to all under conditions of fair equality of opportunity; and second, they must be to the greatest benefit of the least advantaged members of society.[26]

Rawls calls his first principle the principle of 'equal liberty'.[27] It comprehends such basic freedoms as the 'right to vote and to be eligible for

[24] RAWLS, THEORY OF JUSTICE, *supra*, note 1, at 15. Rawls does not contend that the distribution of these abilities is just or unjust. Rather, he claims that this distribution is undeserved: *id.* at 103–4.

[25] *Id.* at 17–19. This is Rawls's celebrated 'veil of ignorance'. It invests his theory with a certain universality because it enables people rationally to choose the society in which they would live without reference to selfish interests dictated by their preexisting societal position. Rawls further argues that, in response to uncertainty, individuals choose according to the 'maximin rule': that is, they prefer the least bad outcome among the worst possible outcomes: *id.* at 152–3.

[26] JOHN RAWLS, POLITICAL LIBERALISM (1993), 291 [hereinafter RAWLS, POLITICAL LIBERALISM]. This iteration of his first principle of justice is somewhat different from that articulated in *A Theory of Justice*. Rawls's final formulation of his first principle in *A Theory of Justice* required that '[e]ach person is to have an equal right to the most extensive total system of equal basic liberties compatible with a similar system of liberty for all': RAWLS, THEORY OF JUSTICE, *supra*, note 1, at 302. Rawls says that this statement was not intended to convey the notion that he was maximizing first-order liberties. His reluctance to maximize such liberties stems in part from an amorphous conception of what would be maximized, the capacity for a sense of justice or the capacity for a conception of the good. The liberties are meant to guarantee both. RAWLS, POLITICAL LIBERALISM, *supra*, note 26, at 271, 332–3.

[27] RAWLS, THEORY OF JUSTICE, *supra*, note 1, at 204.

public office[;] . . . freedom of speech and assembly; liberty of conscience and freedom of thought; freedom of the person along with the right to hold (personal) property; and freedom from arbitrary arrest and seizure as defined by the concept of the rule of law.'[28] These rights of equal liberty cannot be abridged for the welfare of the rest of society.[29]

Rawls's second set of principles—subordinate to the first— concerns the distribution of resources other than personal liberty. Although these principles do not require an equal distribution of income or wealth, they do restrict inequalities of both in certain respects.[30]

The first part of the second principle ('b') is called the principle of 'fair equality of opportunity',[31] or the principle of 'fair opportunity'.[32] This principle demands that 'positions of authority and offices of command must be accessible to all'.[33] The second part of 'b' is called the 'difference principle'.[34] It requires that society advance the interests of its least advantaged members.[35]

The principles are 'lexically' ordered. Thus, the principle of equal liberty cannot be violated to advance either the principle of equal opportunity or the difference principle. Nor can the principle of equal opportunity be abridged to advance the difference principle.[36]

The Rawlsian framework is a deontological theory describing a system of the right rather than a particular conception of the good.[37] In our pluralistic society, his conception of the right leaves to each citizen the task of working out one's own conception of the good. As a starting point, Rawls's political conception of justice seeks to provide a moral justification for the basic structure of a constitutional democracy. It draws on certain ideas fundamental to a democratic polity.[38] The constitution of his polity incorporates the principle of equal liberty, some principle of equal opportunity— which at least involves free movement and free choice of occupation, and some 'social minimum providing for the basic needs of all citizens'.[39] The legislature and other governmental institutions should, following the dictates of the equal opportunity and difference principles, work out the other aspects of these two distributive principles.[40]

---

[28] *Id.* at 61.   [29] *Id.* at 28.   [30] *Id.* at 302.   [31] *Id.* at 83.

[32] RAWLS, THEORY OF JUSTICE, *supra*, note 1, at 303.

[33] *Id.* at 61.   [34] *Id.* at 78.

[35] Although the precise definition of 'the least advantaged' is not critical to the theory, Rawls suggests that this concept might include those with less than one-half of the median income or those in 'lower' occupational classes such as unskilled workers: *id.* at 98. While he says that the definition of the least advantaged is not crucial, Rawls appears to favor the income-based standard. Rawls defines income and wealth as primary goods which are to be distributed with some notion of equality in his polity: RAWLS, POLITICAL LIBERALISM, *supra*, note 26, at 308–9.

[36] *See* RAWLS, THEORY OF JUSTICE, *supra*, note 1, at 302–3.

[37] RAWLS, POLITICAL LIBERALISM, *supra*, note 26, at 30.   [38] *Id.* at 175.

[39] *Id.* at 228.

[40] *Id.* at 228–9, 232 n. 14, 337. The constitutional convention occurs after people have

In a pluralistic society, the objects of the distributional schema are primary goods. These are goods that each person rationally may desire, first, to develop his two moral powers of 'a capacity for a sense of justice and for a concepting of the good'; and secondly, to advance his own conception of the good.[41] The primary goods are as follows:

a. The basic liberties (freedom of thought and liberty of conscience, and so on): these liberties are the background institutional conditions necessary for the development and the full and informed exercise of the two moral powers . . .; these liberties are also indispensable for the protection of a wide range of determinate conceptions of the good (within the limits of justice).

b. Freedom of movement and free choice of occupation against a background of diverse opportunities: these opportunities allow the pursuit of diverse final ends and give effect to a decision to revise and change them, if we so desire.

c. Powers and prerogatives of offices and positions of responsibility: these give scope to various self-governing and social capacities of the self.

d. Income and wealth, understood broadly as all-purpose means (having an exchange value): income and wealth are needed to achieve directly or indirectly a wide range of ends, whatever they happen to be.

e. The social bases of self-respect: these bases are those aspects of basic institutions normally essential if citizens are to have a lively sense of their own worth as persons and to be able to develop and exercise their moral powers and to advance their aims and ends with self-confidence.[42]

Neither Rawls' principle of equal liberty nor the first category of goods, described as basic liberties, seem to require any tort system at all, let alone the Calabresian approach to products liability. Rawls defines liberty narrowly to focus on the essential elements of a constitutional order.[43] His constitutional guarantee of a social minimum of basic needs also would not appear to lend much support, as welfare systems could provide such needs to incapacitated accident victims. While product accidents (as all accidents) impair the primary goods of freedom of movement and occupational choice, Rawls has narrow constitutional conceptions of these values in mind. Reductions in wealth or income suffered by accident victims may argue for some compensation and health care response using the difference principle; however, such reductions would not mandate something like the tort system.

The primary good which most powerfully argues for accident deterrence and a tort system is self-respect. Rawls suggests that this may be the most

---

resolved the principles of justice behind the veil of ignorance in the original position: *id.* at 196–7.

[41] RAWLS, POLITICAL LIBERALISM, *supra*, note 26, at 19, 180.   [42] *Id.* at 308–9.

[43] Christopher Schroeder has reached the same conclusion with regard to protection against environmental risks: *see* Christopher H. Schroeder, *Rights Against Risks*, 86 COLUM. L. REV. 495, 543 (1986).

important primary good.[44] Self-respect involves thinking that one's life plan has worth and having confidence that one can carry it out.[45] Rawls connects self-respect to our sense of our own value.[46] Product accidents can devastate one's sense of one's capacities and one's life plans. These consequences argue not only for compensation, but also for deterrence of such accidents. As the best decider and internalization aspects of Calabresian theory strongly advance deterrence and compensation, the Rawlsian edifice may support Calabresian theory.

Rawls does briefly treat accidents in *Political Liberalism*. He does not appear to differentiate between accidents with purely natural—as against human—causes. Appropriately, he says that accidents should be discussed at the legislative, rather than the constitutional, stage.[47] As the various kinds of accidents are known at this stage, the costs of treating them can be balanced in the context of total government expenditures. However, by hinging compensation on what looks a bit like cost-benefit analysis, Rawls fails to address the problem that humanly caused product accidents result in deep autonomy infringements. Autonomy theory may also suffer from Rawls's approach to compensation: 'The aim is to restore people by health care so that once again they are fully cooperating members of society.'[48] He is unclear about the need for compensation for such other damages as lost wages and pain and suffering, which accurate internalization of accident costs would require. Still, Rawls does suggest that freedom from physical pain may also be a primary good.[49] This statement may provide a step toward a justification for a tort system because freedom from pain may imply not only compensation for pain but also deterrence of the accidents that cause pain.

At bottom, the Rawlsian scheme provides no more than amorphous support for the compensation and deterrence goals of the tort system in general, and the Calabresian system in particular. Rawls may consider this area too particularized for his general theory.[50] While a defense of deterrence tort theory may be too much to expect, Rawls devotes little discussion to physical inviolability at all. In sharp contrast, the principle of aggregate autonomy counts protection of physical integrity as a core concern.

---

[44] RAWLS, THEORY OF JUSTICE, *supra*, note 1, at 396.

[45] *See id.* at 440.   [46] *Id.* at 318.

[47] I assume that Rawls would not object to common-law, judicial treatment of accidents.

[48] RAWLS, POLITICAL LIBERALISM, *supra*, note 26, at 184.

[49] Relying on an article by Thomas M. Scanlon, *The Moral Basis of Interpersonal Comparisons, in* INTERPERSONAL COMPARISONS OF WELL-BEING (Jon Elster & John E. Roemer (eds.), 1991), 17, 41.

[50] Christopher Schroeder arrives at a similar conclusion with regard to whether the difference principle, primary goods, and the distributional facets of Rawlsian theory require averting environmental risks: *see* Schroeder, *supra*, note 43, at 543–8.

IV. An Aggregate Autonomy Defense of the Calabresian Approach to Products Liability

A. Aggregate Autonomy as an Egalitarian Conception of Autonomy

Any contrast of the principle of aggregate autonomy with Rawls' difference principle must begin with some idea of how I am using the complex and rich term 'autonomy'. My unusual use of this term demands early definitional clarification. This section offers some initial approximations which will be further refined as the analysis unfolds.

As a starting point for defining autonomy, I take the widely shared vision advanced by Robert Nozick in his important book *Philosophical Explanations*. Nozick connects autonomy to the notion of free will. So characterized, autonomy resonates with a broad spectrum of philosophical and religious traditions. For Nozick, a truly free act not only advances human dignity; it also allows human beings to create new value by forming new heuristic combinations that previously had not been made.[51] Such intellectual breakthroughs allow the advancement of secular knowledge and the pursuit of transcendent truth. Unlike Kant, Nozick does not require an act to conform to the moral law in order to be truly free.

Based on the value of free will eloquently articulated by Nozick, I posit an initial working definition of autonomy as that overarching free choice that enables one to select and develop one's life plan.[52] As the discussion proceeds, I make clear that my egalitarian concept of autonomy differs from Nozick's.

In *Anarchy, State, and Utopia*, Nozick posits a rigid side constraints or boundary line version of liberty. He conceptualizes persons as being protected by relatively impervious 'side constraints' that cannot be infringed by government or private actors.[53] His theory protects a considerable range of liberty with the important limitation that one individual may not infringe on the liberty of another.[54] This notion that one's liberty extends to the point of not physically harming someone else derives from the traditional Millian notion of liberty.[55]

Perhaps more than some authors,[56] I differentiate between the concepts of liberty and autonomy. I use the term 'liberty' to describe a condition in which society imposes no immediate restrictions on individuals to pursue

---

[51] Robert Nozick, Philosophical Explanations (1981), 291–3, 519–20.
[52] Attanasio, *supra*, note 2, at 679–81.
[53] Robert Nozick, Anarchy, State, and Utopia (1974), ix.
[54] Nozick, *supra*, note 51, at 501–3.
[55] *See* John Stuart Mill, On Liberty and Other Essays (John Gray (ed.), 1991), 15.
[56] My specific distinctions between liberty and autonomy are perhaps not traditional. *See generally* Isaiah Berlin, *Two Concepts of Liberty, in* Four Essays on Liberty (1969); Nozick, *supra*, note 53; Nozick, *supra*, note 51.

chosen ends. Liberty is an instrumental value that, together with order, seeks to foster autonomy. As I have already indicated, 'autonomy' signifies the intrinsically valuable human condition that involves the right to fashion one's own life plan.

The definition of liberty that I have posited differs from the traditional Millian concept that circumscribes freedom of action in so far as it harms others. My definition of liberty permits exploration of the extent to which unfettered individual choice by one person can harm others and so actually circumscribe their autonomy.[57] This unbounded concept of liberty advances autonomy in important ways, yet constricts it in others. While the extent of convergence and divergence will vary in different contexts and is difficult to elaborate precisely, the basic idea is illuminated by what I call the liberty/order tension. This tension posits that constraining liberty, or unfettered choice, with a certain amount of order actually increases autonomy. Ideally, law—in this context, tort law—imposes a certain amount of order on unfettered choice to increase autonomy.[58]

Ultimately, the principle of aggregate autonomy seeks to maximize the number of individuals in society who have at least some minimal level of autonomy. Thus, it is concerned with the distribution of some basic level of autonomy across as many individuals as possible. Traditional libertarian autonomy theory does not concern itself with the *distribution* of autonomy except in a very remote way. Implicit in libertarian autonomy theory is the working assumption that establishing relatively impervious side constraints for each individual ensures an equal and high amount of choice for all. Missing from this central assumption is any notion that one's level of resources affects one's options in choosing life plans. The egalitarian theory of aggregate autonomy rejects this working assumption as counterfactual. Rather than avoid this reality, aggregate autonomy grapples with the dilemma that inadequate resources can severely constrict one's life plans.

The weak principle of aggregate autonomy requires small wealth infringements from members of the broader community to alleviate severe constrictions of one person's life plan. As a lower-order principle, it differentiates between property-based and more personal incursions on one's liberty, permitting only the former. This distinction reflects a priority commonly made in many areas of modern jurisprudence by allowing greater incursions on property interests than more personal interests.[59] For

---

[57] John Rawls has hinted at a similar distinction between liberty and autonomy: *see* RAWLS, THEORY OF JUSTICE, *supra*, note 1, at 254.

[58] I say increase rather than maximize autonomy because maximization may imply getting the appropriate mix of liberty and order exactly right, which is virtually impossible to do.

[59] *See* John B. Attanasio, *Personal Freedoms and Economic Liberties: American Judicial Policy, in* GERMANY AND ITS BASIC LAW (Paul Kirchhof & Donald P. Kommers (eds.), 1993) 221; *see also* Attanasio, *supra*, note 2, at 724, n. 203, 729, nn. 226, 228.

example, the principle does not allow the imposition of even slight physical harm or slight infringements on free speech to protect against severe autonomy infringements.[60] It only allows *de minimis* infringements on lower order property-based interests.[61]

The criteria of severe autonomy constrictions and *de minimis* infringements on wealth further confine the scope of the principle.[62] Indeed, these two restrictions prompt me to call the proffered principle of aggregate autonomy *weak*. Relaxing them would allow stronger principles of aggregate autonomy that eventually would approach strict equality of condition.

Strict equality of condition should be scrupulously avoided for two reasons. First, a strong theory of equality is not necessary to justify Calabresian theory. Secondly, and more importantly, strong conceptions of equality of condition have stark authoritarian fall-out that deeply infringe on autonomy. People who have lived in a Communist regime will attest to this failing. In seeking to secure some floor or baseline of equality of condition for all, the principle of aggregate autonomy engages equality of opportunity at least as much as equality of condition. Some minimum equality of condition is necessary for meaningful equality of opportunity in a market-driven competition for resources.

In the tort context, the weak principle of aggregate autonomy does not guarantee a minimum amount of resources, but restoration of the victim to the *status quo ante,* irrespective of whether this involves fewer or greater resources than minimal resources. This is a victim-specific standard. This approach is true to the tort enterprise of trying to alleviate infringements on a victim's side constraints by restoring the victim, as nearly possible, to her pre-accident condition. Of course, what is meant by restoration to that condition is a matter of some discretion in a tort law damages calculus. For example, an award for pain and suffering could vary considerably with one's conception of autonomy.

I have previously suggested that the principle of aggregate autonomy could have implications over a range of policies far broader than tort law.[63] For example, the principle might justify wealth infringements to redress not only tort misfortunes over which human beings have some control, but also hardships over which humans lack control, such as natural disaster, old

---

[60] Much intentional tort theory may be justified by a first-tier autonomy value prohibiting intentional physical violation; I am only using aggregate autonomy to justify the Calabresian approach to products liability. Exploring philosophical justifications for other parts of tort theory is beyond the scope of this chapter.

[61] I do not reject theories that balance first-order rights against each other in certain ways. For example, Rawls's principle of equal liberty permits some balancing of first-order rights: *see* RAWLS, POLITICAL LIBERALISM, *supra,* note 26, at 294–9.

[62] Occasionally, judgments rendered in products liability suits are so large that they are difficult to spread. For discussion of these exceptional cases, see Attanasio, *supra,* note 2, at 735–7.

[63] *Id.* at 729–31.

age, or genetic disability.[64] It might even require government taxation of wealth to alleviate the autonomy infringement caused by severe poverty. At some level, the first iteration of the principle could be invoked to justify many of the protections afforded by the modern welfare state. The principle does demand that even the wealth-related impositions that it requires be *de minimis*. However, the wealth-based infringement need only be *de minimis* for the particular application in question—for example, for the incursions imposed by a disability law or by food stamps. Unlike the tort context, the principle might be applied in this context to guarantee some minimum amount of resources, not restoration to the *status quo ante*. The differential treatment of accident victims—as against, for example, the poor—stems from notions of causality. Causality pinpoints the human violations of the side constraints of others with which autonomy is centrally concerned.[65] In the products liability context, individuated causality is somewhat attenuated by the involvement of many persons in the manufacturing process. Still, one can say that an entity or specific group of entities caused the harm. Moving further down the continuum, one may argue that common participation in a free market results in economic losers, or poverty. In an absurdly removed sense, congregating in one place probably advances the spread of disease. The gross attenuation of human causality and the frequent lack of a meaningful *status quo ante* in non-tort contexts may justify different patterns of compensation required by aggregate autonomy.[66]

Of course, the principle need not lead us this far. To justify Calabresian theory, but not the welfare state, the principle of aggregate autonomy may be qualified as follows: act to prevent another individual from being seriously injured by a common and normally beneficial activity (like consumption of a product) whenever such prevention requires only slight wealth-related interference with one's life plan.[67]

B. Aggregate Autonomy and Calabresian Theory

The weak principle of aggregate autonomy buttresses the duty that Calabresian theory imposes to protect the victims of product accidents. As stated earlier, the principle is a particular formulation of the liberty/order tension. In Calabresi's world, the law attempts to strike a propitious balance between liberty and order to preserve autonomy for as many individ-

[64] *See generally* John B. Attanasio, *The Genetic Revolution: What Lawyers Don't Know*, 63 N.Y.U. L. REV. 662, 711 (1988).

[65] Gross negligence which does not cause harm does not attract compensation because tort law addresses only actual harm, not risk exposure: *id.* at 731.

[66] In non-torts contexts, grossly attenuated causality may also modulate the autonomy bias for individual treatment of the disadvantaged.

[67] Attanasio, *supra*, note 2, at 729–31.

uals in society as possible. Interferences with wealth are indirect, comparatively weak impositions of order. The aggregate autonomy principle justifies *de minimis* interferences with the wealth of many to protect against and compensate the severe infringements on autonomy that accidents impose on a few through physical incapacity, physical pain, lost wages, etc. The principle legitimates the incorporation of accident costs into product price effected by the Calabresian products liability scheme. Essentially, the approach slightly narrows the choices that wealth allows by forcing product consumers, or perhaps corporate shareholders, to pay a bit more.[68]

Both the best decider and internalization aspects of Calabresian theory afford primary importance to the physical integrity of the individual. Both fit the primary autonomy concern of tort law.[69]

The best decider aspect of Calabresian theory strives to minimize injuries by devolving safety decisions on whoever might best avert accidents. By placing the ultimate decision about accidents in the hands of individuals, Calabresian theory overtly appeals to autonomy. This approach does not subordinate individual free will to a decision by the state, or even by a state-impanelled jury as required by the Learned Hand test.[70] The jury simply decides which party is the best decider to perform the Learned Hand calculus. That party—rather than the jury or other government institution—makes the accident decision.[71] Devolving such predictions on the best decider by definition entrusts them to the person who can best protect that person's own autonomy against infringement, as well as the autonomy of others. Central to such protection is superior knowledge regarding how to alleviate the autonomy infringements that liability exacts: among the victim, manufacturer, retailer, etc. the best decider has superior knowledge to elect between the options of insuring and taking additional safety precautions.[72] Allocating liability to the party with superior knowledge advances autonomy in at least four ways.

First, this superior knowledge reduces the effort necessary to make the accident decision. Extra effort reduces choice by depleting time or other resources required to participate in activities other than accident avoidance. Secondly, it renders the accident decision more accurate. Those with superior knowledge who are held liable will be less likely to suffer severe constrictions on choice by under-insuring or by spending prohibitive amounts

---

[68] For example, an employer might pay its employees less; it might charge more for the product which may well reduce sales and profits; or it might simply charge the same for the product and absorb the net reduction in income. Similarly, if required safety devices increase the purchase price of an automobile, a potential purchaser's liberty will be limited: he will be compelled either to work extra hours to pay for the car or to forgo the purchase. In either case, his choices are narrowed.

[69] For discussion of how tort law generally serves autonomy goals, see Attanasio, *supra,* note 2, at 684–705.

[70] *See, e.g.,* Calabresi & Hirschoff, *supra,* note 18, at 1074.

[71] *See id.* at 1060.   [72] *See id.* at 1070, note 54.

on safety measures. Thirdly, the best-decider approach mitigates the grave autonomy infringements that the disarray from accidents can work on product consumers. The superior knowledge of the best decider will facilitate the introduction of prompt, cost-effective safety measures to reduce the severity and number of accidents. Fourthly, the best-decider approach helps victims: even when insurance is cheaper than accident avoidance, the best decider will have superior knowledge about the kinds and levels of insurance needed to redress injuries adequately.[73]

The internalization aspect of Calabresian theory also advances autonomy. Internalizing product accident costs advances aggregate autonomy in at least four ways. First, like the best-decider approach, internalization increases information.[74] With respect to product consumers, internalization allows individuals to make more informed judgements about whether to purchase a particular product. By reflecting accident costs in a product's price, internalization helps to illuminate the true cost to consumers of a particular product. Moreover, internalization gives product sellers incentives to provide additional information in the form of warnings. The combination of price and warning information helps the potential user make more informed consumption decisions.

Secondly, internalization advances autonomy by reducing the number of autonomy infringements that consumers suffer. The internalized accident costs increase the cost of a product to the producer which can often be passed on to the purchaser. Predictably, the higher price will decrease consumption of that product and therefore decrease the number of accidents caused by that product. In this way, internalization theory endeavors to satisfy the principle of aggregate autonomy: it will constrain the liberty of consumers to purchase products to the minimum extent necessary[75] to redress the massive liberty incursions caused by those products to a comparatively small number of particular consumers.

Thirdly, incorporating accident costs into product prices using internalization generates funds for accident victims. This money can be used directly to compensate accident victims, purchase accident insurance, or otherwise help to redress the autonomy infringements occasioned by accidents.

---

[73] The insurance alternative attracts a rather piercing autonomy criticism, however. Arguably, the best decider approach consciously permits accidents, thereby sacrificing the individuals who will suffer them. Still, the law does not itself create accidents. Calabresi's theory simply acknowledges an unfortunate aspect of the human condition with which tort law always has grappled, albeit less openly. Of course, central to Calabresian thought is the notion that society will endure more or fewer accidents depending on what legal system it selects: *see* CALABRESI, *supra*, note 18, at 23; *see also* GUIDO CALABRESI & PHILIP BOBBITT, TRAGIC CHOICES (1978), 17.

[74] *See generally* JAY KATZ, THE SILENT WORLD OF DOCTOR AND PATIENT (1984).

[75] The marginal increase in price attributable to accident costs will be the lesser of the amount required to render the product safe or the amount required to insure or self-insure.

Fourthly, internalization can protect the autonomy of those who must ultimately shoulder liability. When the best decider is a product manufacturer or retailer, it more easily than consumers can often disperse the effects of the autonomy infringements. By internalizing accident losses in each product, enterprises can spread small incremental wealth losses among all consumers of the product.[76] Importantly, when enterprises encounter difficulty in spreading accident losses among consumers through internalization, they may still be able to spread such losses among shareholders.[77] The ability of enterprises to disperse losses, together with their superior knowledge of techniques for avoiding and spreading losses, helps to alleviate the liberty infringements that strict liability imposes on such enterprises. Moreover, if their actuarial foreseeability is blurry, manufacturers may have incentives to over-insure and to grow biased in favor of safety or physical inviolability.[78]

Despite the strong connections to aggregate autonomy, the Calabresian approach advances this value only imperfectly. For example, with respect to internalization, firms and consumers do not always respond to higher prices and the other economic signals that the Calabresian system emits.[79] Notwithstanding some shortcomings, however, the basic claim is modest. The Calabresian approach to products liability does not always or perfectly advance aggregate autonomy, but it does advance aggregate autonomy better than a negligence system. At bottom, it allocates small spreadable accident costs to the party who can best decide how to insure or avoid the accident.

Finally, it should be noted that neither the principle of aggregate autonomy nor Calabresian theory addresses—and certainly neither condones—the adverse autonomy effects of incorrectly imposing tort liability or calculating damages. Sometimes, judges may violate a party's autonomy by dismissing or not dismissing a particular claim. Likewise, some juries or

---

[76] As Calabresi himself has noted, the elasticity of demand for a particular product as against other less accident-prone products can affect a manufacturer's ability to spread accident losses to consumers: *see* Calabresi, *supra,* note 5, at 519–27.

[77] Accident losses can be spread among the 'owners of resources used in production', including shareholders and suppliers. In this case, however, the practicability of spreading 'depends on the availability of substitute resources whose accident costs are not as high, as well as on the alternative uses available for the resources substituted or discharged': Calabresi, *supra,* note 5, at 523. Toxic substances may present peculiar impediments to spreading. *Cf.* Richard A. Epstein, *Products Liability as an Insurance Market,* 14 J. LEGAL STUD. 645, 648–50, 664–5 (1985) (noting that toxic substances involve undifferentiated risk to large populations which impairs spreading).

[78] If manufacturers under-insure, internalization may alleviate cost overruns by spreading both past and future accident losses to consumers. Market conditions might particularly impair *post hoc* internalization of accident costs for past mishaps.

[79] *See, e.g.,* Mark J. Roe, *Corporate Strategic Reaction to Mass Tort,* 72 VA. L. REV. 1 (1986); Christopher D. Stone, *The Place of Enterprise Liability in the Control of Corporate Conduct,* 90 YALE L.J. 1 (1980).

judges may violate a plaintiff's or defendant's autonomy by improperly applying liability rules such as assumption of risk or by awarding inadequate or excessive damages. The theory of aggregate autonomy does not justify such actions.[80]

V. Comparing the Rawlsian and Aggregate Autonomy Defenses

The foregoing analysis reveals the deep debt that the principle of aggregate autonomy owes to Rawlsian theory. While the Rawlsian defense of Calabresian theory outlined in this essay explored a broad range of Rawls' theories, the difference principle was central. Moreover, the principle of aggregate autonomy builds on the difference principle more than on other parts of Rawls' schema. Consequently, my comparison of the defenses of Calabresian theory focuses on the difference principle and the principle of aggregate autonomy.

Like the difference principle, aggregate autonomy is not a first order principle. It only allows interference with a person's wealth, not with higher-order rights such as free speech, the right to vote, equal opportunity, freedom from arbitrary restraint, or freedom from intentional physical impairment. These can be protected as trumps in a lexical Rawlsian fashion.[81]

Like the difference principle, the principle of aggregate autonomy is aimed at the less fortunate among us. Unlike the difference principle, it takes a teleological rather than a deontological approach. It posits autonomy as a good to be pursued. This contrast should not be exaggerated as autonomy is a kind of pluralistic good. However, it is not a totally neutral value as some have argued.[82]

Rawls points his own conception of the right toward allowing people to achieve their own conceptions of the good in a pluralistic society. Aggregate autonomy also advances one's ability to pursue one's conception of the good, with the important constraint that one must also advance the autonomy of others, rather than simply not infringe on 'the right'. I do not posit autonomy as the only good but only as a good. For example, I believe that moral philosophy has the burden of affording guidance as to what virtues should inform the exercise of autonomy.

Much more than the difference principle, the principle of aggregate autonomy strives to provide some level of basic needs for people by posit-

---

[80] For further discussion of these problems, see Donald P. Judges, *Of Rocks and Hard Places: The Value of Risk Choice*, 42 Emory L.J. 1, 56–8 (1993).

[81] *See* Attanasio, *supra*, note 2, at 728–9. I hope to continue to develop such a schema in future articles.

[82] *See* John B. Attanasio, *Everyman's Constitutional Law: A Theory of the Power of Judicial Review*, 72 Geo. L.J. 1665, 1716 (1984).

ing a moral claim on a small amount of wealth from others who are better off. The difference principle does not guarantee any floor for basic needs.[83] Rawls himself admits that it would permit a large increase in the wealth of a few if the least advantaged benefited infinitesimally. To mitigate this problem, Rawls says that the other principles of justice as fairness operating in a competitive market system will tend to mitigate any such inequalities, particularly over time.[84] Closer in point, he imposes a requirement separate from the difference principle that society meet the basic needs of all individuals.[85] Although it is amorphous, this dictum may provide more protection for the least advantaged than the weak principle of aggregate autonomy which only allows *de minimis* wealth incursions. Still, the weak principle of aggregate autonomy can be made stronger by modulating the two key variables of severe autonomy infringements and *de minimis* wealth incursions.

Both aggregate autonomy and the difference principle have distributional concerns, but aggregate autonomy comprehends more than the distribution of income. The difference principle appears to settle on this key value at the end of the day.[86] One problem with this strategy is that income is an input rather than an outcome or result.[87] The assumption is that increasing this input will beget certain results. Moreover, in his application of the difference principle, Rawls uses income as a kind of proxy for disadvantage. This assumption does not always hold true. For example, Christopher Schroeder notes that exposure to risk does not always correlate with wealth.[88]

The lack of attention of the Rawlsian schema to accidents and physical inviolability illuminates one shortcoming of using income as a proxy for disadvantage. Autonomy appears to provide a more comprehensive measurement of the potential for human flourishing. Recognizing this shortcoming, Rawls expands the list of primary goods to include such important features as freedom from pain and self-respect, the latter of which he describes as the most important primary good. Even with the addition of these other values, however, Rawls provides inadequate support to the Calabresian system or to other accident compensation or deterrence schemes. The failure to lend strong support to preventing or compensating the serious autonomy incursions caused by product accidents illustrates the deep problem with the use of income or even wealth as a proxy for well-being.

The principle of aggregate autonomy in a partial way and the entire

---

[83] Robert P. Burns, *Rawls and the Principles of Welfare Law*, 83 Nw. U. L. Rev. 184, 241–61 (1989).

[84] *See* Rawls, Theory of Justice, *supra*, note 1, at 157–8.

[85] Rawls, Political Liberalism, *supra*, note 26, at 166, 228–9; Rawls, Theory of Justice, *supra*, note 1, at 275.

[86] *See, e.g.*, Rawls, Theory of Justice, *supra*, note 1, at 78, 285–6, 304–5.

[87] Schroeder, *supra*, note 43, at 546, note 187.   [88] *Id.* at 544–5.

Rawlsian schema in a more comprehensive way both seek to reconcile the tension between two of the paramount values in twentieth-century philosophy, liberty, and equality. The key Rawlsian move in this reconciliation cordons off one sphere of equal liberty that is primarily concerned with personal freedom. A second sphere contains the egalitarian principle of equal opportunity and the difference principle.

Rawls recognizes that the resources at one's disposal influence one's ability to effect one's aims.[89] This reality also strongly influences the principle of aggregate autonomy. In a critically important distinction, Rawls differentiates between liberty and the *worth* of liberty. This may be the key distinction between the difference principle and the principle of aggregate autonomy. The device of the worth of liberty allows the separation of liberty and equality into different spheres of the same schema.[90] However, this segregation does not adequately recognize the importance of autonomy outside the sphere of political liberty—for example, in the area of product accidents. This approach also does not afford sufficient credit to the pivotal role that resources play in the exercise of meaningful autonomy. While it borrows Rawls's spherical strategy in some respects, the principle of aggregate autonomy combines libertarian and egalitarian values in the same principle.

VI. Beyond Autonomy Rationales: The Virtues as Possible Supports for Calabresian Theory

At least one criticism of my aggregate autonomy approach is that I rest all of products liability theory—perhaps all of tort theory—on autonomy grounds.[91] I make no claim for the exclusivity of the autonomy value, only for its dominance. I freely have admitted that tort law also serves utilitarian concerns.[92] It would be empirically inaccurate to ignore the strong pull that utility exerts on tort theory. In addition to utility, the rather unconventional notion of autonomy itself incorporates values other than liberty. The paradoxical concept of aggregate autonomy explicitly incorporates such other values as equality and order.[93] Nonetheless, I myself view the weak principle of aggregate autonomy as a thin theory that does not take

---

[89] Rawls, Theory of Justice, *supra,* note 1, at 30.

[90] With regard to first-order values such as freedom of speech, Rawls combines both liberty and equality into the principle of equal liberty.

[91] *See* Martin A. Kotler, *Competing Conceptions of Autonomy: A Reappraisal of the Basis of Tort Law*, 67 Tul. L. Rev. 347, 350 (1992); David G. Owen, *The Moral Foundations of Products Liability Law: Toward First Principles*, 68 Notre Dame L. Rev. 427, 433 (1993).

[92] Attanasio, *supra* note 2, at 689–93 & nn. 53–4, 707–15.

[93] *Id.* at 684, 732–4.

us very far beyond the vaunted libertarian paradigm.[94] In a recent article, David Owen contends that a multiplicity of values—such as freedom, equality, and truth—illuminate the complex texture of products liability law.[95] I maintain that one value, autonomy, is dominant here. Moreover, to some degree other values such as truth and equality can be folded into my account of aggregate autonomy.

Truth helps to determine the extent of actual choice. One would encounter grave difficulty formulating one's life plan without accurate information. With specific regard to tort theory, choosing among risks would be difficult without accurate information. Truth influences the efficacy of such global tort policies as deterrence and such important tort doctrines as assumption of the risk. For example, one cannot assume a risk that, because of inaccurate information, one does not realize exists.

This perfunctory analysis describes truth as an instrumental value in the service of autonomy. I, of course, admit that seeking and telling the truth has intrinsic value as a virtue apart from any instrumental value that it may have in the service of autonomy. Autonomy theory provides a kind of backdrop or context that makes the exercise of virtue possible. Taken as free will, autonomy may comprise a necessary condition for the exercise of virtue: a non-autonomous act cannot be an expression of the individual's virtue, but only reflects external forces dictating behavior.[96]

In his own architecture of ascending spheres, Augustine places free will below *caritas* or perfect love. Augustine believes that free will should be informed by rectitude and love.[97] Although a good bit of talk about the virtues occupies the later parts of *A Theory of Justice*, Rawls retreats from exploring a fuller account of the good in his more recent work *Political Liberalism*. In *Political Liberalism*, he largely cabins his analysis to a discussion of the right. He seeks just institutions that will permit each person to pursue his or her own concept of the good.

Judges, juries, legislators, and other lawmakers grapple with virtues like knowledge and honesty every day. The deep challenge for legal theory and moral philosophy is to formulate accounts that can at least describe what these lawmakers are doing and hopefully help to inform their judgments.[98]

I am not saying that legal theory or moral philosophy is completely separate from the everyday thinking of legal decision-makers. Legal decision-makers also live in our modern pluralistic milieu. For this reason, I believe that more pluralistic, process-oriented values like autonomy and efficiency drive them more universally than many higher order virtues such as *cari-*

---

[94] *See* John B. Attanasio, *The Impoverished States of Law and Morality*, 64 NOTRE DAME L. REV. 773, 777–8 (1989).

[95] Owen, *supra*, note 91, at 434.   [96] *See* NOZICK, *supra*, note 51, at 291–3.

[97] *See* AUGUSTINE, THE CITY OF GOD (G. Walsh *et al.* (trans.), 1958), 542.

[98] *See generally* Onora O'Neill, *Justice and the Virtues*, 34 AM. J. JURIS. 1 (1989).

tas. Protecting each individual's autonomy helps each person to pursue his or her own life plan or concept of the good within our pluralistic framework. For better or worse, autonomy does seem to be the dominant driving force behind tort law.[99]

Tort law is shaped by moral, more than efficiency, grounds. It is, however, driven by what might be called the backdrop or background value of autonomy more than any principles like *caritas* that may inform how to use this autonomy.

VII. Postscript: The Right Versus the Good

Perhaps the central point of John Rawls's *Political Liberalism* is that members of a modern, pluralistic society can reach some agreement on a conception of the right but not on a conception of the good. Indeed, Rawls provides a justification for this enthronement of the right. The problem with this conception of society is that the right begets a rights-based mindset.[100] This rights-based mindset encourages people to pursue whatever claims against one another that they may have at their disposal.

While we may be unsure what the good society is, I suggest that each individual pursuing one's claims to the legal limit surely must be what the good society is not. We do not want to live in a society in which everyone with a tort, contract, or other claim pursues it. While Rawls does not advocate such a society, emphasizing the right over the good may produce just this result. Moral theories which stop at the right or justice in its narrow sense can bias, legitimate, or even enjoin legally pursuing whatever rights one has.

Theories of the good constrain the exercise of rights. I want to live in a society where people have forbearance, pull their punches, and do not exercise all of their rights against me, just as I do not exercise all of my rights against them. I also want to live in a society in which people care for each other as human beings, irrespective of what rights they may have or lack. Particularly in a secular society, an important burden of moral philosophy must be to advance conceptions of the good. Otherwise, our vision of the good society will be reduced to a tattered fabric woven of contract and tort rights and actions.

---

[99] Commentators on my aggregate autonomy article do not dispute this proposition. *See* Judges, *supra,* note 80; Kotler, *supra,* note 91, at 350; Owen, *supra,* note 91, at 493–8; Kathryn Dix Sowle, *Toward a Synthesis of Product Liability Principles: Schwartz's Model and the Cost-Minimization Alternative,* 46 U. Miami L. Rev. 1 (1991).

[100] *See generally* John B. Attanasio, *A Duty-Oriented Procedure in a Rights-Oriented Society,* 63 Notre Dame L. Rev. 597, 597–600 (1988).

SECTION B

Connecting Agency and Harm:
Risk, Causation, and Damage

Risk, Harm, and Responsibility

STEPHEN R. PERRY*

What is risk? Does subjecting another person to risk—or reducing his or her chance of avoiding an adverse physical outcome—constitute a distinct form of harm? What is the basis of moral responsibility for physical harm that was unintentionally caused by risky conduct? Because risk is one of the central concepts in modern tort law, any theory of torts rooted in notions of interpersonal justice and individual responsibility must come to grips with the first and third of these questions. In the light of a recent academic and judicial trend to characterize risk as harm, a response to the second question should be of interest as well. In this essay, with a view to contributing to a responsibility-based theory of tort law, I advance and defend answers to all three questions.

In section I, I offer a general analysis of risk that draws on work in the philosophy of probability. I suggest that there are two main conceptions of risk, one objective in character and the other epistemic, and that both are, in different ways, plausible candidates for explaining the moral significance that we attribute to risk. In section II, I consider the thesis that subjecting another person to risk is a form of harm distinct from any physical harm the person might suffer. This thesis is most plausible if it is understood as presupposing the objective conception of risk. Even understood in that way, however, the thesis cannot be accepted; risk does not, I argue, constitute harm in itself.

In section III, I consider moral responsibility for physical damage: under what circumstances should an agent whose risky conduct caused unintentional physical harm to another person be held morally responsible for that harm? One common argument, which I call the libertarian argument, suggests that persons should be held morally responsible for the materialization of any objective risk that their conduct creates. The libertarian argument would support a standard of absolute liability in tort law, thus requiring that liability be imposed simply for causing harm. Both the argument and the standard of absolute liability must, however, be rejected. Moral responsibility for physical harm should be grounded in a notion of epistemic rather than objective risk. This understanding of responsibility, which, borrowing a term from Tony Honoré, I call outcome-responsibility,

* Faculty of Law, McGill University. Work on this chapter was supported by a research grant from the Social Sciences and Humanities Research Council of Canada.

is consistent both with the negligence standard and with risk-based standards of strict liability such as the rule for ultrahazardous activities.

I. THE NATURE OF RISK

First, what is a risk? In ordinary language conduct is typically said to be risky when it gives rise to a chance of a bad outcome of some kind. The concept thus involves two main elements: first, a notion of chance or probability, and second, a notion of harm. The pre-theoretical concept of risk presumably does not define the relationship between these two elements in a precise way, but a natural move is to stipulate that a risk is the mathematical expectation of harm, i.e., the product of the probability of occurrence of the harm and the magnitude of the harm were it to occur ($P \times H$). For present purposes the notion of harm can be treated as unproblematic.[1] Let me loosely define harm as a setback to an interest, and an interest as an aspect of personal well-being. We may assume that independent moral arguments will determine which interests are of sufficient importance to warrant protection by the law of torts; the concept of risk can then be applied to potential interferences with the interests those arguments single out. The troublesome aspect of the concept of risk, and the one that plays the more intrinsic role in shaping its meaning, is not harm but the element of probability. The idea of risk can apply to many different types of harm or bad outcome, but what we *mean* by risk is fundamentally determined by the understanding of probability we take the concept to presuppose.

Philosophers have developed several quite different theoretical accounts of probability.[2] These theories are sometimes treated as competing and mutually incompatible, but the predominant contemporary view tends to regard probability in a pluralist light. More particularly, it has become commonplace to recognize that two distinct but non-conflicting conceptions of probability must both be recognized: one is concerned with probabilities that in some way have objective existence, while the other characterizes probabilities in terms of the current state of our knowledge and beliefs.[3] I shall call these the objective and epistemic conceptions, respectively. Ian Hacking has written that the concept of probability has possessed this 'essential duality' ever since it began to emerge in its modern

---

[1] For purposes of this chapter I treat the terms 'harm', 'injury', and 'damage' as synonymous. In some contexts, however, it is appropriate to assign them distinct meanings. *See* Stephen R. Perry, *The Moral Foundations of Tort Law*, 77 Iowa L. Rev. 449, 498 (1992).

[2] For an excellent overview, see Roy Weatherford, Philosophical Foundations of Probability Theory (1982).

[3] *See, e.g.*, Rudolf Carnap, Logical Foundations of Probability (2d ed. 1962), 19–51; David Lewis, *A Subjectivist's Guide to Objective Chance, in* 2 Philosophical Papers (1986) 83.

form in the seventeenth century.[4] Both the objective and the epistemic conceptions of probability can be given a number of different interpretations. To explain what these are, and to show why particular interpretations are particularly apposite for understanding the moral significance of risk, it will be necessary to take a short detour through the byways of the philosophy of probability.

To begin with the objective conception, people who speak of probability in an objective sense usually have in mind one or the other of two ideas. The first is the understanding of probability that emerges from the so-called relative-frequency theory of probability.[5] A probability is, on this view, just the stable relative frequency that may be exhibited by the occurrences of a given attribute within a series of events or objects in the physical world, where those events or objects can in an appropriate way be characterized as similar (e.g., the relative-frequency of .5 associated with the attribute of 'coming up heads' in a series of similar events, namely, the flips of a fair coin). The formal definition of a probability is usually given as the limit of a frequency within an infinite sequence. Despite this reliance on the notion of infinity, the relative-frequency theory regards probabilities as just a certain kind of empirical fact. The second idea people tend to have in mind when they speak of objective probability is concerned with the operation of indeterministic causal processes, such as those associated with quantum mechanics. If a particular outcome, such as the final resting place of a billiard ball, is completely determined by the preceding state of the physical universe, then the relevant causal process is deterministic. If a particular outcome, say the time at which a given uranium atom decays, is not so determined, then the causal process is indeterministic. There is no further, perhaps unknown, causal mechanism that lies behind a statement of the probability of decay. On this view a probability is again a certain kind of empirical fact, but one that has to do with the nature of causal processes.

These two senses of objective probability are related. To see the connection, first recall that a probability in the relative-frequency sense is defined with respect to a certain reference class of actual or possible events. The probability that a given coin will come up heads, for example, is defined relative to the reference class of flips of that coin. The causal processes underlying the events in the reference class could, however, be either deterministic or indeterministic. Assume that the relative frequency with which a given coin comes up heads is .5. If the causal processes involved are deterministic, then it will in principle be possible to predict whether a given coin-flip will come up heads or tails, and hence to partition the reference class in advance into two sub-classes, one consisting of all head-events and the

    [4] Ian Hacking, The Emergence of Probability (1975), 122–3.
    [5] See particularly Richard Von Mises, Probability, Statistics, and Truth (1957); Hans Reichenbach, The Theory of Probability (1949).

other of all tail-events. So far as the first sub-class is concerned, the probability of the coin coming up heads is one, whereas for the second sub-class the probability is zero. If, on the other hand, the causal processes are indeterministic, then it will not be possible to partition the reference class in this way. In an important sense the probability statement expresses an ultimate fact about the universe. But whichever of these possibilities holds, we can still meaningfully speak of the relative frequency, with respect to the original reference class of all flips of the coin, of its coming up heads. Independently of whether the relevant causal processes are deterministic or indeterministic, the relative frequency of .5 with which the coin comes up heads is an objective property of the physical world. Objective probability in the indeterministic sense is thus a special case of objective probability in the relative-frequency sense.

Of course, the other side of this coin (so to speak) is the interesting observation that objective probability can exist in a deterministic universe; probability need not be viewed as merely an epistemic phenomenon that emerges only because we can never have complete knowledge of deterministic processes. Even if the preceding state of the universe determines the outcome of any given coin flip, the statement that there is a probability of .5 that the coin will come up heads expresses a fact about the physical world. As a practical matter, of course, we cannot predict whether a coin will come up heads or tails. The result of any given coin flip can thus be characterized as 'random', and this is so whether the underlying causal processes are deterministic or indeterministic. The distinction between determinism and indeterminism turns on predictability in principle, not predictability in practice. In practice, not only might we be unable to predict particular outcomes, we might not know whether it was in principle even possible to predict outcomes, i.e., we might not know whether the causal processes were or were not deterministic. And even if we knew that outcomes were predictable in principle, this would not necessarily be particularly useful or significant information. (It would not, for example, have any effect on the various purposes for which we flip coins.) Moreover the distinction between predictability in principle and unpredictability is by no means crystal clear.[6] Taken together, these points suggest that we should treat relative frequency rather than indeterminacy as the most basic understanding of objective probability. From now on I shall accordingly employ the term 'objective probability' to mean the relative-frequency conception of probability. Reference will be made to the special case of indeterminacy as and when necessary.

---

[6] *See* Joseph Ford, *How Random is a Coin Toss?*, 36 PHYSICS TODAY 40 (April 1983). Ford maintains that a coin toss is predictable in the sense that it is describable by a finite algorithm. But it is unpredictable in the sense that the description of the initial condition requires, because chaotic processes are involved, an infinite amount of information.

Epistemic probability, like objective probability, can also be given different interpretations. For purposes of this essay, however, which is primarily concerned with risk regarded as a moral phenomenon, I shall assume that epistemic probability is best understood in terms of what I shall call the reasonableness account. The reasonableness account is based on the following two assumptions: first, that objective probabilities in the relative-frequency sense exist; and secondly, that human beings possess inter-subjectively valid standards of inductive reasoning and rational belief that are at least pragmatically justified and that permit them to discover or estimate those relative frequencies. Epistemic probability involves, according to the reasonableness account, a relation between evidentiary premises, on the one hand, and a conclusion about the way the world is, on the other. The evidence will consist, often, of partial observations of relative frequency within a sequence of (possible) objects or events that cannot be observed in its entirety, but sometimes it will take a more indirect form. The conclusion will be an estimate of relative frequency within the total sequence.[7] Epistemic probability judgments are thus estimates of objective probabilities that are based on, and relative to, a given body of evidence.[8]

According to the reasonableness account, epistemic probability judgements are capable of expressing knowledge about the world, although that knowledge will often—perhaps always—be imperfect or incomplete. The standards of reasoning assumed to be appropriate for justifying these judgements are based on the modes of probabilistic and inductive reasoning, both formal and informal, that human beings actually employ. There are a number of ways in which these standards might be characterized: one might, for example, formulate precise inductive principles that operate in conjunction with formal statistical techniques and the probability calculus; or one might seek to discover an informed consensus about the probability of a given type of event; or one might look to the probability judgements of a reasonable or representative person. Different characterizations might be suited to different purposes. Thus a formal characterization, employing sophisticated statistical techniques, might be particularly appropriate for scientific inquiry, whereas an informal characterization, based on the intuitive probability judgements of a reasonable person, might be more suitable for determining moral responsibility. A characterization along the latter

---

[7] It should be noted that even those theorists who maintain that a relative-frequency theory is the only defensible account of probability must still acknowledge the distinction between an actual frequency in the physical world and our estimate or approximation of that frequency. *Cf.* WEATHERFORD, *supra*, note 2, at 131–2, 142, 177. This distinction creates sufficient logical room to permit—in fact, to require—the development of an epistemic conception of probability along the lines of the reasonableness account.

[8] Presumably one could also regard the resulting probability judgement as an expression of the degree of rational belief that is warranted in the conclusion that the property whose relative frequency is being considered will be instantiated in a given case.

lines is, not coincidentally, reminiscent of the understanding of risk to be found in tort law.

I do not attempt in this chapter to establish the truth of the two assumptions on which the reasonableness account rests—the existence of objective probabilities, and the availability of inter-subjectively valid methods for estimating them—but they must be taken to be true if a conception of risk based on epistemic probability is to have moral significance. The first assumption ensures that epistemic judgements of risk are concerned with real possibilities of harm, while the second ensures that those possibilities are capable of being estimated by modes of reasoning that both the person who creates a risk and the person who is subjected to it can accept. If the first assumption were not true we could still formulate a non-objective conception of probability, but as the discussion below of radical subjectivism illustrates, it seems unlikely that we would be left with a morally significant concept of risk. If, on the other hand, the second assumption were not true, there would be no forms of common reasoning about risk, and little or no agreement about what risks existed and how serious they were. This would make it difficult, if not impossible, to formulate common standards of conduct relating to 'risky' behavior (whatever that term might mean in such a world).

There are other possible interpretations of epistemic probability besides the reasonableness account. In the remainder of this section I would like briefly to describe the two most influential of these interpretations, and to indicate why they are not capable of explaining or illuminating the moral significance that risk holds for human beings. Readers who do not wish to explore probability theory any further may safely take a faster but less scenic route and skip to section II.

The first of the two alternative interpretations of epistemic probability is suggested by radical versions of the subjectivist (or personalist, or Bayesian) theory of probability that has its roots in the work of F. P. Ramsey.[9] On the general subjectivist view, a judgement of probability measures a particular individual's actual degree of belief or confidence in a given proposition. The measure of degree of belief is usually understood behavioristically, by reference to the odds that the individual would be willing to accept within a coherent series of bets. Coherence is understood as conformity to the standard probability calculus. Radical versions of subjectivism, which give rise to the particular interpretation of epistemic probability with which we are now concerned, hold that coherence is the *only* constraint on rational belief. Radical subjectivists maintain that we can speak meaning-

---

[9] F. P. Ramsey, *Truth and Probability, in* FOUNDATIONS: ESSAYS IN PHILOSOPHY, LOGIC, MATHEMATICS, AND ECONOMICS (D.H. Mellor (ed.), 1978), 58. For versions of radical subjectivism, see 1 BRUNO DE FINETTI, THEORY OF PROBABILITY: A CRITICAL INTRODUCTORY TREATMENT (1974); LEONARD SAVAGE, THE FOUNDATIONS OF STATISTICS (1954), 27–68.

fully only of individual assessments of probability; there is, they assert, no such thing as probability in an objective sense.[10] This view thus places very minimal restrictions on what will count as rational belief: probability judgements can permissibly vary quite widely from person to person.

The second alternative interpretation of epistemic probability, which in some respects resembles the reasonableness account, is grounded in the so-called logical-relation (or *a priori*) theory of probability.[11] The essential idea is that probability is a logical relation between a conclusion or hypothesis about the way things are, on the one hand, and premises that set out evidence relevant to that hypothesis, on the other. Probability is taken to be a measure of the degree of rational belief in (or confirmation of) the hypothesis. The relation between premises and conclusion is understood as logical rather than psychological in character, and to that extent is taken to be an objective matter.[12] At the same time, however, probability statements are always relative to given evidence only. By treating probability statements as logical truths, this view places quite stringent restrictions on what will count as rational belief.

Neither the radical subjectivist nor the logical-relation understanding of epistemic probability seems able to explain why we attribute the moral significance to risk that we do. The radical subjectivist account assumes there is no objective conception of probability that extends beyond the weak constraints of the coherence requirement. On this view there is no general inter-subjective basis for distinguishing among risks, and hence no basis for holding someone morally responsible for risk creation. If I think that you are doing something that poses a high risk of harm, whereas you think that the risk is low or non-existent, no determinative argument (apart from considerations of coherence) could be brought to bear by either of us to show that the other was wrong. Risk thus understood would lack moral significance, because it would have no systematic and agreed-upon relation to the physical world in which consequences follow from actions. Risk would be an indication of the betting odds a given person would be willing to accept in an objectively unpredictable world, and nothing more. Perhaps, on a radical subjectivist understanding of probability, an individual's assessment of the risks his or her action poses for others might be relevant

[10] De Finetti, one of the leading radical subjectivists, formulated his central thesis in upper case letters: 'PROBABILITY DOES NOT EXIST': DE FINETTI, *supra,* note 9, at x.

[11] *See* JOHN M. KEYNES, A TREATISE ON PROBABILITY (1921); CARNAP, *supra,* note 3. The three most influential general theories of probability are the relative-frequency theory, the subjectivist theory, and the logical relation theory.

[12] It should be emphasized that probability statements are not regarded as objective in the sense presupposed by a relative-frequency theory, i.e., they are not understood as expressing facts about the physical world. They are, rather, supposed to be objective in an *a priori,* non-empirical sense: for each possible set of evidentiary premises, whether true or not, and for each conclusion about the way things might be that can be formulated in the language, there is a logically correct probability judgement that in principle is specifiable *a priori.*

to an inquiry into whether he or she had a culpable state of mind. But since in a radically subjectivist world the notion of 'acting in order to bring about an effect' might well have a meaning very different from the one we now attribute to it, even this is far from clear.

Of course radical subjectivists recognize that, for various reasons, individuals' probability judgements often converge, but they regard this as a reflection of psychological rather than physical regularities.[13] A consistent and rigorously developed radical subjectivist understanding of probability would in fact seem to have no room for our ordinary concept of physical causality, since that concept presupposes regularities in the physical world. Of course nothing in this discussion of radical subjectivism establishes that among the properties of the world are objective probabilities in the relative-frequency sense. The claim is simply that unless there are such objective probabilities, and unless our epistemic conception of probability is systematically related to them, the epistemic conception will lack moral significance.[14]

Turning now to the logical-relation understanding of epistemic probability, there are at least two reasons why it is likely to prove problematic from a moral point of view. The first concerns the fact that, on this understanding, probability judgements are not empirically verifiable statements: they are regarded, rather, as expressing an *a priori*, logical relation among propositions. As in the case of the radical subjectivist account, but for different reasons, the logical-relation understanding does not regard probability judgements as attempts to estimate relative frequencies in the physical world. As before, it is difficult to attribute moral significance to an account of epistemic probability that lacks this feature; logical truth cannot, by itself, have any moral import. Various attempts have been made by logical-relation theorists to show how and why *a priori* probability judgements can tell us something about the physical world, but we need not decide here whether any of these have succeeded. For present purposes it suffices to point out that if a systematic link between *a priori* judgements and empirically verifiable relative frequencies can be established, it is that link that will matter in an account of the moral significance of risk and not the judgements' supposed logical basis. In other words it does not matter, from a moral perspective, whether the sense of epistemic probability judgements must ultimately be explained by reference to a logical relation among propositions; the reasonableness account, which resembles the logical-

---

[13] WEATHERFORD, *supra*, note 2, at 236.

[14] It bears mention that some subjectivists, while claiming that we do not necessarily have *knowledge* of objective probabilities, do nonetheless accept that there are pragmatic standards for assessing equally coherent probability judgements as better or worse. These standards 'involve a proper respect for frequencies, arising from a proper respect for induction': Simon Blackburn, *Opinions and Chances, in* PROSPECTS FOR PRAGMATISM: ESSAYS IN MEMORY OF F. P. RAMSEY (D. H. Mellor (ed.), 1980), 175, 195.

relation theory in regarding probability as involving a relation between evidentiary premises and a conclusion about the way the world is, can simply remain agnostic on this question. What ultimately matters, from a moral point of view, is whether probability judgements are generally able, under specifiable circumstances, to serve as reliable estimates of relative frequencies in the physical world.

The second reason why the logical-relation understanding of epistemic probability is unlikely to be able to account for the moral significance of risk is that the logical relations the theory posits do not seem to be readily accessible to human understanding. Carnap, for example, proposed a very complex, language-dependent scheme of inductive logic that does not seem practically applicable by ordinary human beings except to very simple (and highly simplified) problems of probability. Difficult practical and philosophical questions also arise in specifying the formal language in which the scheme of inductive logic is to be formulated. Even if we were able to assert with some confidence that there *is* some logical relation, representing a uniquely correct probability judgement, between a given body of evidence and a given conclusion about how things might be, this fact would be of little moral significance if human beings did not generally have the capacity to reason in the requisite manner.[15]

I have argued in this section that the epistemic conception of probability, understood in terms of the reasonableness account, can plausibly be regarded as one possible point of departure for explaining why we attribute moral significance to risk creation. But I have not claimed that it is the only such point of departure. Since the reasonableness account makes essential reference to the objective conception of risk, it is plausible to think that the latter is morally significant in its own right. Perhaps it is the *only* morally significant conception of risk, and lends the epistemic conception whatever plausibility it has in this regard by means of the conceptual link between them. Thus in discussing whether risk is a distinct form of harm, and in examining the basis of moral responsibility for physical harm caused by risky conduct, it is important to ensure that neither objective nor epistemic probability is overlooked. As we shall see, the thesis that risk is a distinct form of harm is best understood in terms of objective risk, whereas moral responsibility for physical harm should be understood as being based on epistemic risk.

---

[15] Keynes, the other main proponent of a logical relation understanding of probability, took a very different approach from that of Carnap: *see* Keynes, *supra,* note 11. Keynes held, perhaps under the influence of G. E. Moore, that we have the capacity *directly* to perceive or intuit probability relations. This led him to maintain, among other things, that some probabilities are non-numerical and some non-comparative. This approach obviously ties probability judgements much more closely to actual human capacities, but it does so at the cost of rendering problematic the thesis that such judgements are logical in character.

II. Is Risk a Harm in Itself?

A number of writers and judges have suggested in recent years that subjecting another person to a risk of physical harm, or, alternatively, reducing his or her chance of avoiding an adverse physical outcome, is itself a form of harm that should be compensable in tort law.[16] It will be convenient to discuss this issue with reference to a concrete set of facts. The English case of *Hotson v. East Berkshire Area Health Authority*,[17] in which a claim for lost chance was put forward, is quite suitable for this purpose.

The facts in *Hotson* were as follows. The plaintiff suffered a fracture of his left femoral epiphysis, which the defendant health authority negligently failed to diagnose. Although the injury was correctly diagnosed and treated five days later, the plaintiff eventually developed a seriously disabling condition known as avascular necrosis. The immediate cause of this condition was a reduction in the supply of blood reaching the epiphysis. This reduction could have been caused either by the rupture at the time of the fracture of a sufficiently high proportion of the blood vessels supplying the epiphysis, or by subsequent occlusion by pressure within the joint during the five-day period before proper treatment was administered. The trial judge found as a fact that at the time the plaintiff first arrived at the defendant's hospital, there was a .75 risk that the avascular necrosis could not be avoided by proper treatment.[18] He also found that by the end of the five-day delay the avascular necrosis was inevitable, i.e., the probability of its occurrence was one. On these figures it is clear that, if the standard of proof is the balance of probabilities, the defendant's negligent diagnosis should not be treated as a cause of the plaintiff's avascular necrosis. But the plaintiff argued that the defendant had caused him to lose a .25 chance of avoiding avascular necrosis, and that this lost chance should *itself* be treated as damage compensable in tort. This argument was accepted by the trial judge

---

[16] *See* Joseph H. King, Jr., *Causation, Valuation and Chance in Personal Injury Torts Involving Preexisting Conditions and Future Consequences*, 90 Yale L.J. 1353 (1981); Richard W. Wright, *Causation in Tort Law*, 73 Cal. L. Rev. 1735, 1814–16 (1985); William M. Landes and Richard A. Posner, The Economic Structure of Tort Law (1987), 263; Jane Stapleton, *The Gist of Negligence*, pt. 2, 104 L.Q.R. 389 (1988); Herskovits v. Group Health Coop. of Puget Sound, 664 P.2d 474 (Wash. 1983) (Pearson, J., concurring); DeBurkarte v. Louvar, 393 N.W.2d 131 (Iowa 1986); Hotson v. East Berkshire Area Health Authority [1987] 2 W.L.R. 287, *rev'd.* [1987] A.C. 750; Lawson v. Laferrière, R.J.Q. 27 (Quebec 1989), *rev'd,* [1991] 1 S.C.R. 541 (Can.).

[17] [1987] 2 W.L.R. 287, *rev'd.* [1987] A.C. 750. I have criticized the thesis that risk constitutes harm in itself, along lines similar to the argument presented in this section, in Stephen R. Perry, *Protected Interests and Undertakings in the Law of Negligence*, 42 U. Toronto L.J. 247, 252–62 (1992).

[18] For the sake of convenience in exposition I shall henceforth use the terms 'risk' and 'probability' more or less interchangeably. Given our earlier definition of risk as the mathematical expectation of harm ($P \times H$), this amounts to an assumption that $H = 1$.

and by the English Court of Appeal, but it was ultimately rejected by the House of Lords.

The .75 figure represents the background risk, at the time the plaintiff first arrived at the hospital, of his contracting avascular necrosis. The .25 figure represents the augmentation of the risk brought about by the defendant's negligent conduct. Although one can speak, as courts and legal commentators tend to do, of the reduced or lost chance of avoiding the adverse physical outcome, I shall instead refer to this augmented probability as the agent-imposed risk. If the adverse physical outcome materializes, it is possible to use the antecedent risk figures to compute the probability that the outcome was caused by the agent's action. In *Hotson* the figures for antecedent risk and *ex post* probability of causation coincide, since the avascular necrosis had become inevitable by the time proper treatment was finally administered. But this is a special circumstance that will not always be present.[19] Our concern here will always be with the antecedent agent-imposed risk, rather than with the *ex post* probability that the agent caused the physical outcome. While physical harm was, on the special facts of *Hotson*, inevitable, this will not always be the case. It seems clear, moreover, that the status of agent-imposed risk as harm in itself should not depend on whether the threatened physical harm has materialized (so long, at least, as the risk has not passed). On an appropriate set of facts, a *Hotson*-type claim could thus be made even in the absence of physical harm.

The plaintiff's argument in *Hotson*, then, was that the agent-imposed risk was itself damage of a kind distinct from the physical damage (in *Hotson*, the avascular necrosis). While remaining neutral for the time being on whether this argument is sound, let me refer to the novel form of harm that the plaintiff was alleged to have suffered in *Hotson* as 'risk damage'. To assess the claim that risk damage is a true form of damage, we begin by asking whether it is epistemic or objective risk that is in issue here. To this end it will be helpful to consider the characterization of the lost chance of avoiding avascular necrosis—in our terms, the agent-imposed risk—that was accepted in *Hotson* by the House of Lords:

[Counsel] who appeared for the plaintiff . . . said that in relation to the facts of this case as found by the judge what was meant by a chance was that if 100 people had suffered the same injury as the plaintiff 75 of them would have developed avascular necrosis of the whole femoral head and 25 would not. This, he said, was an asset possessed by the plaintiff when he arrived at the authority's hospital. . . . It was this

---

[19] In general, if A is the agent-imposed risk and B is the background risk, the *ex post* probability that the agent caused the outcome is $A/(A + B)$. The *ex post* probability that a factor contributing to the background risk caused the outcome is $B/(A + B)$. In *Hotson* the figures for antecedent risk coincide with those for *ex post* probability of causation because $A + B = 1$.

asset which [counsel] submits the plaintiff lost in consequence of the negligent failure of the authority to diagnose his injury properly.[20]

This characterization of agent-imposed risk is clearly reminiscent of the objective conception of probability, which is concerned with the relative frequency of an attribute within a reference class. Here the relevant attribute is the occurrence of avascular necrosis, and the reference class is the set of (possible) persons who have suffered the 'same' injury as the plaintiff. But since the risk figures are simply the trial judge's *estimate* of the true relative frequencies, they are best regarded as instances of epistemic, not objective, risk. If the estimates turned out to be accurate, epistemic and objective risk would coincide; the relative frequency of avascular necrosis in the reference class would be .25 (objective probability), and that would be a fact of which we had knowledge (epistemic probability). Of course the figure for agent-imposed risk that comes to be accepted in a case like *Hotson* might not coincide with the true relative frequency of harm. This might happen either because a mistake in inductive reasoning occurred or because there was insufficient evidence to ensure a reliable probability judgement. In the case of a mistake in inductive reasoning the accepted figure for agent-imposed risk would not, strictly speaking, be an epistemic probability, since our definition of epistemic probability assumes compliance with the modes of reasoning sanctioned by the reasonableness account. For present purposes, however, there is no need to distinguish between these two ways in which an accepted risk figure might differ from the objective risk.

The trial judge in *Hotson* concluded that, on the facts of that case, the agent-imposed risk was .25. As it happens, there is some reason to think that his estimate might have been subject to at least one of the two forms of error just discussed.[21] Suppose for a moment that the mistake was a particularly egregious one, and that a delay of five days has no significant effect on the objective frequency with which injuries of the kind suffered by the plaintiff are treatable. The objective agent-imposed risk would then be zero. If this fact subsequently came to light, the claim that the defendant had caused risk damage to the plaintiff would no longer be plausible. This strongly suggests that risk damage must be understood in terms of objective, not epistemic, risk. That is hardly a surprising conclusion, since harm involves interference with some aspect of well-being, and such interference can ordinarily be expected to have objective existence in the physical world. In this respect physical damage is a paradigm of harm. But the point that risk damage must be understood in terms of objective risk is nonetheless worth emphasizing, for the following reason. Objective risk cannot be directly observed. We must always rely on our best estimate of the objec-

---

[20] *Hotson* [1987] 1 A.C. at 783, *per* Lord Mackay.   [21] *Id.* at 785.

tive risk, using whatever evidence is to hand. We necessarily operate, in other words, with the notion of epistemic risk. While it is true that only objective risk can plausibly be thought to constitute a form of damage, the fact that we are limited to observing objective risk through the lens of epistemic risk gives rise to the ever-present danger of confusing the two.

This brings us to the central question we must answer: *is* agent-imposed risk, understood in objective and not epistemic terms, properly regarded as a form of damage in its own right? For purposes of illustration let us assume that, contrary to what in fact appears to have been the case, the trial judge's figures in *Hotson* of .75 for the background risk and .25 for the agent-imposed risk were accurate estimates of the objective risks. Can the agent-imposed risk of .25 plausibly be characterized as a distinct form of damage, distinguishable from the physical damage that ultimately occurred in the form of avascular necrosis? Given the assumption that the relevant figures represent objective and not just epistemic risks, it follows that seventy-five of 100 persons who 'had suffered the same injury as the plaintiff' (to use the language of Lord Mackay in the House of Lords) would have developed avascular necrosis even if proper treatment had been administered right away, whereas twenty-five persons would have responded to treatment. These relative frequencies must be regarded as objective facts about the physical world which would hold even if we had no knowledge of them.

Our main concern, in determining whether risk damage is a true form of damage, is with the definition of the reference class in terms of which the pertinent relative frequencies are expressed. The reference class employed in *Hotson* was a hypothetical group of 100 representative persons who were assumed to have suffered the 'same' injury as the plaintiff. This obviously cannot mean that the injuries in the sample group are to be regarded as *precisely* the same in every respect. What must be intended, rather, is that the 100 injuries all fall under some general description of physiological states that has not been spelled out in detail but that could, if necessary, be given a more explicit formulation by reference to the plaintiff's condition at the time he was injured. Since the information that could be obtained about his condition will, inevitably, be in at least some respects incomplete, this description of physiological states will necessarily cover a *range* of cases that in various respects differ from one another. For example, since it was not known in *Hotson* what proportion of the blood vessels supplying the plaintiff's epiphysis had been ruptured at the time of the original accident, the relevant physiological description will subsume a variety of cases in which the extent of damage to the blood vessels ranges from relatively minimal to relatively severe. These variations in the extent of injury sustained will be reflected in the sample of 100 representative persons assumed to have suffered the 'same' injury as the plaintiff.

Suppose now that it was possible systematically to distinguish among different degrees of blood-vessel damage in cases of injury similar to the one sustained by the plaintiff in *Hotson*. Assuming for the moment that there is some known and more or less constant threshold of degree of damage that distinguishes treatable from untreatable injuries, it would then be possible to partition the reference class of 100 persons into the twenty-five who were treatable and the seventy-five who were not. We would also know into which sub-class the plaintiff fell. If he fell into the treatable sub-class, then it would be possible to say that the defendant, in negligently misdiagnosing his injury and sending him away without proper medical care, had causally contributed to the development of avascular necrosis. If, on the other hand, the plaintiff fell into the sub-class of persons whose injury was untreatable, it would be possible to say that the defendant had *not* causally contributed to the onset of avascular necrosis. The claim that the plaintiff suffered risk damage at the hands of the defendant must, if it is to be generally defensible, be capable of surviving such a partitioning of the reference class. The partition does not, after all, call into question the original risk figures, which have been assumed to refer to objective probabilities. The only difference between the state of affairs that obtained in *Hotson* and the circumstance we are now envisaging is that we are supposing we have sufficient knowledge to distinguish the treatable from the untreatable cases. But the claim that the plaintiff suffered risk damage must surely be independent of possession of knowledge of this kind.

In fact, the claim that the plaintiff suffered risk damage begins to look quite implausible when the treatable cases can in practice be distinguished from the untreatable cases. If the plaintiff's injury was treatable, then the defendant caused him *physical* damage; there is no reason to say that it also caused him another, separate harm that takes the form of risk damage. If, on the other hand, the plaintiff's injury was not treatable, then there is no reason to say that the defendant caused him *any* damage, whether we call it physical damage or risk damage; we can no longer plausibly maintain that he lost a chance of avoiding an adverse physical outcome. As we just saw, however, nothing should turn on whether we have the knowledge to distinguish in practice between the treatable and the untreatable cases. If the causal processes involved are deterministic then a distinction can be drawn *in principle* between the two categories of case, whether we have the knowledge to do so in practice or not, and so long as such a distinction is possible in principle, it makes no sense to claim that the plaintiff suffered, at the hands of the defendant, a peculiar, non-physical injury of the kind I have labelled risk damage. The assertion that the plaintiff suffered risk damage is simply a fiction employed to get around the practical difficulties involved in distinguishing the treatable from the untreatable cases, i.e., the difficulties in establishing causation with respect to the physical harm.

I have assumed, for the purposes of this part of the discussion, that the original risk figures in *Hotson* of .75 background risk and .25 agent-imposed risk involved objective probabilities. It is important to recognize, however, that these probabilities, like all objective probabilities, are relative frequencies that have been defined with respect to a certain *class* of persons: they are properties of those classes and not of particular individuals like the plaintiff. But it is individuals who are said to suffer risk damage, not classes of persons, and therein lies the fallacy of the claim that risk damage constitutes injury in its own right. The *Hotson* plaintiff's lost chance of avoiding avascular necrosis, because it cannot be construed as an aspect of the well-being of an individual, cannot constitute an interest of the kind tort law is concerned to protect. To come at the same point from a different direction, notice that the plaintiff cannot be said to belong to a single, canonically designated reference class in terms of which the relevant risks must be defined. Even with respect to the single incident in *Hotson*, the plaintiff belongs to an indefinitely large number of reference classes. Suppose, for example, that the plaintiff's injury was untreatable. Then he belongs to the reference class of persons with untreatable injuries, and this is so whether we can identify those persons or not. The probability of developing avascular necrosis even with proper treatment is, within *this* reference class, one, a state of affairs that is quite compatible with the fact that within the original reference class, consisting of persons with injuries vaguely similar to the plaintiff's, the probability of developing avascular necrosis even if proper treatment were administered is only .75.

Other possibilities can easily be imagined. Earlier I made the simplifying assumption that there is some more or less constant threshold of degree of blood-vessel damage that distinguishes the treatable injuries from the untreatable within the general category of injuries vaguely similar to the one the plaintiff in *Hotson* originally sustained. Let me now relax this assumption and suppose instead that the threshold varies with a number of different factors, some of which are known to us and some of which are unknown. Then various combinations of these factors will define different reference classes, although of course *we* can only refer to those classes that are defined in terms of factors we happen to know about. Suppose, for example, that two of the factors known to us are body weight and bone structure. Then we could define a reference class consisting of persons who suffer an injury of the same general kind as the plaintiff and who also have a bone structure and body weight similar to his. This class, which would presumably overlap both the class of treatable injuries and the class of untreatable injuries, would have associated with it an objective probability of inevitably developing avascular necrosis (i.e., of developing the disease even if given proper treatment) that we could expect to be different from any of the other probabilities so far considered. Relaxing the assumption of a constant threshold does not, of course, affect our earlier conclusion that someone in the position of the plaintiff in *Hotson* does not suffer any harm that can plausibly be characterized as risk damage, since we are still supposing that the relevant causal processes are deterministic. So long as this supposition holds, the treatable injuries will be distinguishable in principle from the untreatable, and this is so even though the factors that determine into which category a particular injury falls have now been assumed to be relatively numerous and complex.

The conclusion thus far, then, is that if the processes that caused or might in the future cause physical harm are deterministic, then there is no basis for saying that a person who has been put at risk by another of suffering such harm has, just by reason of being put at risk, sustained damage distinct in kind from the physical harm. In other words, in cases where determinism holds, there is no such thing as risk damage. The basis for saying that a person is at risk of suffering a certain type of physical harm is that he or she belongs to a particular reference class with which is associated a known objective probability of harm of that type. But there is nothing magical about the particular reference class selected: generally it will simply be the narrowest class, given the current state of our knowledge, for which we are able to determine with some degree of accuracy the relative frequency of the type of harm in question. If we were in a position to describe the objective probabilities associated with a still narrower reference class to which we knew the person in question also belonged, presumably we would do so. Moreover we know, given the assumption of determinism, that it is in principle possible to partition any such reference class into two subclasses, one for which the probability of physical harm is one and one for which the probability is zero. Thus, there is simply no ground for the claim that the objective probability of harm, associated with the particular reference class that we are currently in a position to describe, itself constitutes a distinct form of damage.

The natural question to ask at this point is, of course, how the analysis changes if the causal processes are *not* wholly deterministic. There does not seem to me to be any simple answer to this question, and for present purposes I will limit myself to a few observations. First, if a particular objective probability of physical harm reflects an indeterministic causal process, so that the reference class with respect to which that probability is defined cannot be further partitioned, conduct that has the effect of placing someone within the reference class in question might perhaps be characterized as having caused a distinct form of damage. The question is not straightforward, but conduct that places someone's well-being at the mercy of an indeterministic roll of the dice seems distinguishable from the situations discussed above, where the assumption was, in effect, that the risk-imposer would either definitely cause physical harm or would definitely not cause physical harm, but because of imperfect knowledge we would not be in a position to say which of these two states of affairs in fact obtained. In the indeterministic case there seems to be a true detrimental shift in position that is simply not present in the deterministic case (unless, of course, true *physical* harm in fact is caused).

The second observation is that, while there may thus be a sense in which risk-imposition does constitute damage in itself, the advocates of the risk damage thesis have not distinguished between the deterministic and indeterministic cases. Moreover in many of the fact situations in which risk damage has been alleged, the causal processes at work seem more likely to have been deterministic than indeterministic in character. This is true of *Hotson*, for example, where the House of Lords made the very plausible assumption that at the time the plaintiff arrived at the hospital *either* enough blood vessels were still intact to make his injury treatable, *or* enough had been destroyed to make avascular necrosis inevitable.[22]

The third and final observation I would make on the topic of indeterminism is that just because the causal processes underlying a given type of event are, in part or at some level, indeterministic, it does not follow that any risk associated with such an event should be treated as damage in itself. It seems clear, for example, that true indeterminism exists at the level of sub-atomic particles, but there is some reason to think that random deviations in different directions compensate for one another, in effect washing indeterminism out of the system at the macroscopic level. If that were the case then interactions among what J. L. Austin called medium-sized dry goods would, for all intents and purposes, be deterministic in character.[23] There is clearly much more to be said about the relationship between causal indeterminism and the thesis that risk-imposition is damage in itself, but these observations should at least engender caution. Even given our knowledge that indeterminism exists in the world, we generally do not have reason to treat the objective probabilities we encounter on an everyday basis as anything other than incomplete descriptions of essentially deterministic events.[24]

To repeat, my main conclusion in this section is that, at least in the case of events involving deterministic causal processes, there is no such thing as risk damage.[25] It is important, however, to emphasize the relatively

[22] *Hotson* [1987] 1 A.C. at 785, *per* Lord Mackay.

[23] Hans Reichenbach, one of the main proponents of the relative frequency theory of probability, held a thesis along these lines: *see* HANS REICHENBACH, ATOM AND COSMOS: THE WORLD OF MODERN PHYSICS (1933), 278; WEATHERFORD, *supra*, note 2, at 181.

[24] It is worth remarking that the basic tests of causation in tort law, namely, the but-for test and its more sophisticated variant, the NESS test, both appear to presuppose determinism. This is implicit in the notion of necessity that each test in different ways incorporates. For discussion of the NESS test (Necessary Element of a Sufficient Set), see Wright, *supra*, note 16.

[25] Mention should be made of *Sindell v. Abbott Lab.*, 607 P.2d 924 (Cal. 1980), since there is a sense in which that case imposed liability for risk creation (as measured by market share).

modest nature of this conclusion. I have argued that risk does not generally constitute damage, but not that there is no such thing as risk: probability in both its epistemic and objective senses is a meaningful concept, and risk is straightforwardly defined in terms of probability. Nor have I argued that liability in tort should not be imposed for risk creation as such. To support *that* conclusion a further premise is required, to the effect that tort liability should only be imposed in order to compensate for damage caused (in a but-for or NESS sense). I am generally prepared to accept this claim, or something like it, but I have not argued for it here, and the question can hardly be regarded as uncontroversial. Such a premise would be rejected by many deterrence theorists, for example, including in particular many who accept an economic interpretation of tort law.[26]

Finally, I have not argued that there should not be recovery in tort even in a case like *Hotson* itself. I have simply argued that the lost chance of .25 of not developing avascular necrosis should not be regarded as damage in its own right. There could, however, be *psychological* harm that occurs when the plaintiff in a case like *Hotson* discovers that he or she has not

---

The underlying rationale in *Sindell*, however, was to ensure that each of a group of tortfeasors pays out compensatory damages equivalent to the total amount of tortious *physical harm* that that tortfeasor can be expected to have caused in a defined category of case. Since risk is not being treated as damage in its own right, but rather as an indicator of total physical harm in a *category* of cases, the rationale of the case is not called into question by my arguments here. It is worth noting that the total-physical-harm rationale for market share liability was rejected in *Hymowitz v. Eli Lilly & Co.*, 539 N.E.2d 1069 (N.Y. 1989), where a justification based on culpability was accepted instead. For that reason *Hymowitz* is a more problematic decision than *Sindell*. A variant on the total-physical-harm rationale of *Sindell* was suggested by Weinstein, C.J., in *In re "Agent Orange" Product Liability Litigation*, 597 F. Supp. 740, 833–9 (E.D.N.Y. 1984). Given the impossibility of sorting out which individuals had contracted cancer from Agent Orange and which from background risks, the proposal was, in essence, that *all* cancer victims in the relevant group might be able to recover a share of their damages proportional to the increase in total risk created by the agent-imposed risk. The amount the defendant would have to pay out should be roughly equivalent to the physical harm it had actually caused.

[26] That risk should as a matter of *corrective justice* be compensable as such, even in the absence of physical harm, is the ultimate conclusion of a debate between Christopher Schroeder and Ken Simons. *See* Christopher H. Schroeder, *Corrective Justice and Liability for Increasing Risks*, 37 UCLA L. Rev. 439 (1990); Kenneth W. Simons, *Corrective Justice and Liability for Risk-Creation: A Comment*, 38 UCLA L. Rev. 113 (1990); Christopher H. Schroeder, *Corrective Justice, Liability for Risks, and Tort Law*, 38 UCLA L. Rev. 143 (1990). Neither Schroeder nor Simons explicitly states that risk is *harm*, but without this premise the conclusion that risk is compensable on corrective justice grounds is not very plausible. Glen Robinson also holds that risk should be compensable, but his discussion is ambiguous as to whether risk is properly treated as harm in itself. Glen O. Robinson, *Probabilistic Causation and Compensation for Tortious Risk*, 14 J. Legal Stud. 779 (1985). Landes and Posner, *supra*, note 16, at 263, expressly maintain that risk can be treated as a form of harm, but on the deterrence theory they defend this premise does not appear to be required in order to argue for the compensability of risk as such. Landes and Posner's discussion of probability is confused, in my view, by a failure to distinguish objective from epistemic probability. *See* particularly *id.* at 234–9.

received proper treatment, and perhaps this should be legally compensable.[27] More importantly, there is a very plausible argument that the lost *opportunity* to receive proper medical treatment is a distinct form of harm in its own right.[28] When the plaintiff in *Hotson* left the hospital after the initial misdiagnosis, he was relying on the defendants' supposed skill and competence in diagnosing and treating leg injuries, and if he had had any reason to doubt their competence he presumably would have gone immediately to different doctors. As a result of this reliance he lost the opportunity to receive proper treatment at a time when there was, according to our best present knowledge, at least some chance, however small, that he might have materially benefited from it. The .25 lost chance of avoiding avascular necrosis might then be regarded, not as damage in itself, but as evidence bearing on the valuation of the lost opportunity.[29]

It is, in my view, no coincidence that the tort cases in which the risk damage thesis has won any degree of judicial acceptance have all been medical malpractice actions where it was plausible to think that there had been both reliance by the plaintiff and consequent lost opportunity. We must at least consider the possibility that the approving judges really had in mind the notion of lost opportunity, not lost chance or risk, or, perhaps more plausibly in the majority of cases, that they simply failed to distinguish between these two notions. So far as I am aware, there is no case in which risk has been treated as damage in itself outside the context of a pre-existing consensual relationship involving reliance. If risk creation truly is a form of damage in its own right, it should be present even in a stranger case involving, say, a risk of disease arising from exposure to a toxic element. But the claim that risk is a distinct form of damage appears not to be advanced on facts such as these.

III. Risk and Responsibility for Physical Harm

If, as was argued in the preceding section, risk cannot be regarded as harm in its own right, then it is natural to think that moral responsibility for risky behavior should take the form of responsibility for the *physical* harm, if any, that was unintentionally caused by the conduct in question (assuming, of course, that the harm falls within the risk the conduct created). We might also consider the possibility that someone should be held morally

---

[27] *See* Lawson v. Laferrière, [1991] 1 S.C.R. 541, 558 (Can.); Ayers v. Township of Jackson, 525 A.2d 287, 295 (N.J. 1987).

[28] See further, Perry, *supra*, note 17, at 308–16.

[29] It also seems reasonable to think that medical expenses incurred to avoid or minimize a known, agent-imposed risk of suffering physical harm in the future should be recoverable in tort. Liability for pure economic loss, which as a general matter gives rise to difficulties in negligence law, is not problematic in this context. *See* Perry, *supra*, note 17, at 267–9.

responsible for simply engaging in the risky behavior, quite apart from whether harm in fact ensues, but since our present concern is with tort theory rather than criminal theory I shall limit discussion to responsibility for physical harm that an agent's conduct has actually caused. Since it will not be possible in the present chapter to consider this issue at any length, I shall concentrate on clarifying the proper understanding of risk within a theory of responsibility for causing harm, drawing on the account of risk set out in section I. We must consider two possibilities: first, that responsibility for physical harm is concerned with conduct that was risky in the objective sense, and secondly, that such responsibility is concerned with conduct that was risky in the epistemic sense.

Objective probability, and hence objective risk, is defined in terms of the relative frequency of an attribute within a reference class. Risk in this sense exists whether we know about it or not. Responsibility for harm resulting from conduct that was risky in the objective sense cannot, therefore, depend on antecedent knowledge or foreseeability. Responsibility of this kind, if it exists, is equivalent to responsibility determined solely by the fact that one's conduct *caused* harm, since if a particular action causes harm it must fall within one or more reference classes for which, whether or not we are in a position to describe those classes, the relative frequency of the relevant type of harm is greater than zero. Translated into tort terms, such responsibility would amount to a form of strict—indeed, absolute—liability. Absolute liability is often described as a matter of acting at one's own peril or risk; as the preceding discussion makes clear, it is objective risk that is at issue here.

The strongest and most influential argument for absolute liability has often been put forward by libertarians, and it fits together in a natural way with libertarian political philosophy.[30] I shall accordingly call it the libertarian argument. The essential idea is that if I choose to act in the world, I am both fully entitled to whatever gains I may make and fully responsible for whatever harms I may suffer or cause. The claim about gains leads to the standard libertarian thesis that forced redistribution is in general illegitimate. The claim about harm is the basis of the libertarian defence of a standard of absolute liability in tort law. Both claims are premised on a certain understanding of the moral significance of action. I have a *choice* about

---

[30] A version of the libertarian argument was put forward by Baron Bramwell, a 19th century English judge known for his laissez-faire ideology, in Bamford v. Turnley, 122 E. R. 27, 33 (Ex. Ch., 1862). In his early work in tort theory Richard Epstein advanced an argument very similar to Bramwell's. *See* Richard A. Epstein, *A Theory of Strict Liability*, 2 J. LEGAL STUD. 151, 157–8 (1973); Richard A. Epstein, *Intentional Harms*, 4 J. LEGAL STUD. 391, 398 (1975). For discussion of Epstein's version of the argument, see Stephen R. Perry, *The Impossibility of General Strict Liability*, 1 CAN. J.L. & JURIS. 147, 148–59 (1988). The libertarian argument seems also to be implicitly presupposed by Robert Nozick, since he assumes that an obligation to compensate arises simply from causing harm. *See* ROBERT NOZICK, ANARCHY, STATE, AND UTOPIA (1974), 71.

whether to become active in the world, and if I choose action over passivity then all subsequent consequences, both good and bad, are appropriately chalked up to my moral ledger and no one else's. Thus other persons are not entitled to share in whatever gains may accrue to me as a result of my activity,[31] but by the same token I cannot force passive by-standers to absorb any loss my activities may create. In economic jargon, agents are properly compelled to internalize the losses they cause others. In distinguishing as it does between activity and passivity, the libertarian argument thus supposes that moral consequences, both good and bad, attach not just to a decision to act in this or that way, but to a decision to act *tout court*.

In *The Common Law* Holmes criticized what is recognizably a version of the libertarian argument, which he formulated in the following way:

Every man, it is said, has an absolute right to his person, and so forth, free from detriment at the hands of his neighbors. In the cases put, the plaintiff has done nothing; the defendant, on the other hand, has chosen to act. As between the two, the party whose voluntary conduct has caused the damage should suffer, rather than one who has had no share in producing it.[32]

The main elements of the libertarian argument, including in particular the distinction between activity and passivity, are clearly present here. But Holmes rejected the argument, not just on grounds of policy—policy meaning, for Holmes, utilitarian considerations—but also because it 'offend[ed] the sense of justice'.[33] The initial premise of Holmes' counter-argument is that the reason for making the performance of an act a requirement of liability in tort is to ensure that 'the defendant should have made a choice'.[34] This premise is, of course, also one of the starting-points of the libertarian argument. But then Holmes continues: 'the only possible purpose of introducing this moral element is to make the power of avoiding the evil complained of a condition of liability. There is no such power where the evil cannot be foreseen.'[35] At this point Holmes is clearly introducing a different understanding of the moral significance of action. It is not choice as such that has moral significance, but rather choice accompanied by the power to avoid the resulting consequence. The capacity to avoid the result, rather than the mere fact of having voluntarily chosen to act, is what gives rise to moral responsibility for harm.

But why should we accept Holmes' claim that it is avoidability of the consequence, rather than the choice to act as such, that gives rise to moral responsibility for physical harm? Holmes himself has little to say on this

---

[31] The status attributed by the libertarian argument to positive externalities, i.e., benefits that flow from the agent's conduct but that accrue to other persons, is not entirely clear.

[32] OLIVER WENDELL HOLMES, JR., THE COMMON LAW (1881), 84.

[33] *Id.* at 96.   [34] *Id.* at 95.   [35] *Id.*

point, but he drops a hint, almost in passing, in his subsequent discussion of the 'argument from policy': 'A man need not, it is true, do this or that act,—the term *act* implies a choice,—but he must act somehow.'[36] This suggests that Holmes rejects, at least so far as injurers are concerned, the distinction presupposed by the libertarian argument between activity and passivity. Thus we might reconstruct his counter-argument in the following way. The libertarian argument supposes that moral significance attaches to a decision to act as such, because it supposes that persons have a true choice concerning whether to be active or passive beings. But in fact there is no such choice: the human condition is such that everyone must choose to act in some way or other.[37] Given that everyone must be active, no moral consequences can attach to action *per se*. Something more is therefore required to ground responsibility for causing harm, and that further requirement is most plausibly thought to be a capacity to avoid the harm. But there can be no such capacity unless the agent is capable of foreseeing the result. As Holmes famously put it, '[a] choice which entails a concealed consequence is as to that consequence no choice.'[38]

It is possible to take this line of thought further. The libertarian argument treats injurers as active and victims as passive, in each case by choice. Holmes responds that injurers are *necessarily* active, not active by choice, because activity is inevitable. But if that is so, then victims must be characterized as active and not just injurers. This is, in essence, the point made by Coase when he wrote that '[i]f we are to discuss the problem [of harmful interactions between two persons] in terms of causation, both parties cause the damage.'[39] The libertarian argument assumes that one person is *the* cause of harm to another, where the image is of a dominant, active party acting upon a subordinate, passive party. Coase was responding to a similar image embodied in the received economic wisdom that social costs should be internalized to *the* activity that caused them. In addition to arguing that, from an economic point of view social costs are, under certain circumstances, best dealt with by private market transactions, Coase also maintained that this image of one party acting upon the other is profoundly misleading and should be rejected. Instead, he suggested, we must see the harm in question as having been caused by the interaction of two active parties—in other words, as the product of two activities, and not just one. Thus the injury that results when a motorist 'runs down' a pedestrian should not be regarded as having been caused by one person acting unilat-

---

[36] OLIVER WENDELL HOLMES, JR., THE COMMON LAW (1881), at 95.

[37] A variant of the argument, which Holmes would probably not accept, would add that even a decision to remain motionless is, precisely because it is a voluntary decision, morally equivalent to an act in the usual sense, understood as involving muscular activity. For Holmes, '[a]n act is always a voluntary muscular contraction, and nothing else': *id.* at 91.

[38] HOLMES, *supra,* note 32, at 94.

[39] R. H. Coase, *The Problem of Social Cost,* 3 J.L. & ECON. 1, 13 (1960).

erally upon another, but rather as the upshot of two decisions to act: the motorist's decision to drive when, where and how she did, and the pedestrian's decision to walk when, where and how *he* did.

The image associated with the libertarian argument of one, active party who exerts force against another, passive party is often buttressed by an analogy with property rights, and in particular rights in land.[40] Robert Nozick's metaphor of a line or boundary that 'circumscribes an area in moral space around an individual' draws attention to this analogy in a particularly vivid way.[41] A violation of individual rights is equated with a 'border-crossing', and this notion is equated in turn with, essentially, causing harm. But the analogy with a physical border must ultimately be cashed out in terms of the distinction between an active injurer and a passive victim, and both the Holmesian and Coasean arguments call this distinction into question. In addition, the Coasean argument undermines the claim that one can pick out one of the parties to a harmful interaction as *the* cause of the harm.

I have argued elsewhere for an understanding of harmful interaction and causation that is consistent with the views of both Holmes and Coase,[42] and I need not repeat that discussion here. The point I wish to emphasize for present purposes is this. The libertarian argument, if it were valid, would justify a form of moral responsibility that was triggered by the materialization of an objective risk. But in making foreseeability the touchstone of responsibility for causing harm, Holmes is implicitly invoking a notion of *epistemic* risk. Foreseeability is a function of (possibly incomplete or only partially accurate) *knowledge* of relative frequencies, not of relative frequencies *tout court*. As Holmes makes clear, the key moral concept here is avoidability: the point of making foreseeability a requirement of responsibility for physical harm is that an agent is unable to avoid harm unless he or she can foresee it. In the absence of foreseeability, the harm is simply the unfortunate upshot of an interaction between two persons. There is no reason in justice to shift the loss from where it fell, since there is no basis for morally attributing the harm to one party rather than the other.

The reasonableness account of epistemic probability maintains that such probabilities are estimations of relative frequency that have been made in accordance with accepted standards of inductive reasoning and rational belief. Epistemic probability judgements, in so far as they presuppose intersubjectively valid standards of reasoning, can be characterized as objective. But it is natural to say that avoidability, as a moral concept, must look to a subjective capacity to avoid harm, and hence to a subjective capacity to

---

[40] *Cf.* Richard A. Epstein, *Automobile No-Fault Plans: A Second Look at First Principles,* 13 CREIGHTON L. REV. 769, 775 (1980).

[41] NOZICK, *supra,* note 30, at 57.

[42] Perry, *supra,* note 30, at 154–9; Perry, *supra,* note 1, at 461–7.

foresee it. How can this point be reconciled with the objectivity of the reasonableness account, and, indeed, with the similarly objective understanding of foreseeability in negligence law (*reasonable* foreseeability, in the language of tort)? This issue cannot be examined in detail here, but the brief answer is that we are dealing with a number of different conceptions of the objective/subjective distinction.

The notion of reasonable foreseeability in tort law is objective in its *content*: the law's determination of which risks must be foreseen by an agent is based upon, among other things, an appropriate interpretation of the reasonableness account of epistemic probability (more particularly, an interpretation expressed in terms of the judgements of an ordinary or reasonable person). The standard of due care in negligence law is similarly objective in its content: the precautions the law requires in a given situation of risk are determined by what a reasonable person, rather than the individual defendant, thinks should be done. But norms are almost always objective so far as their content is concerned; it is not up to the individual agent to decide what constitutes, say, murder. The notions of reasonable foreseeability and due care are also objective in another sense, which is that neither requires *advertence*: the individual agent need not be aware, on the particular occasion, either that he is creating unreasonable risks or taking inadequate precautions. This is, of course, an important form of the objective/subjective distinction in criminal law.

But objectivity regarding content and advertence is perfectly compatible with subjectivity regarding *capacity*, at least so long as we understand capacity in a certain way. According to the view I have in mind, which I cannot defend here but only sketch in very abbreviated form, capacity to foresee and avoid harm is appropriately understood as a *general* ability that the individual who caused a given injury ordinarily succeeds in exercising in other, similar situations.[43] Whether the person was capable of foreseeing and avoiding the harm on the particular occasion may or may not be a meaningful question, but either way it is the general capacity that matters so far as moral responsibility is concerned. The necessary assumption, then, is that most people, across a wide variety of circumstances, have the general capacity to foresee and avoid harm that the law attributes to the 'ordinary' or 'reasonable' person. The result is a form of responsibility for unintentional harm that I call, borrowing a term from

---

[43] *Cf.* Tony Honoré, *Can and Can't*, 73 MIND 463 (1964); Tony Honoré, *Responsibility and Luck*, 104 L.Q.R. 530, 549–52 (1988) [hereinafter *Responsibility*]; DANIEL C. DENNETT, ELBOW ROOM: THE VARIETIES OF FREE WILL WORTH WANTING (1984), ch.6.

[44] Honoré, *Responsibility, supra*, note 43. My understanding of outcome-responsibility differs in several important respects from Honoré's. See further, Perry, *supra*, note 1, at 488–512; Stephen R. Perry, *Loss, Agency, and Responsibility for Outcomes: Three Conceptions of Corrective Justice, in* TORT THEORY (Ken Cooper-Stephenson & Elaine Gibson (eds.), 1993), 24, 38–47.

Tony Honoré, outcome-responsibility.[44] The key moral concept that underpins such responsibility is, as Holmes suggested, avoidability. It can be contrasted with the central form of responsibility in criminal law, for which the label 'culpability' is appropriate: here the key moral concept is an intention to harm, or at least a subjective awareness that harm will or might occur. Obviously these conceptions of responsibility can overlap, since there is no reason to deny that a person who is aware of the risk he or she is creating is outcome-responsible for the resulting harm if the risk materializes. But the two conceptions of responsibility are nonetheless distinct: outcome-responsibility is, among other things, generally less blameworthy than culpability.

Outcome-responsibility, like the libertarian conception of absolute liability considered earlier, focuses on responsibility for harmful outcomes rather than on responsibility for action as such. But it differs from the libertarian conception in that it does not automatically call for an agent to whom responsibility for harm is being attributed to pay compensation. Outcome-responsibility affects reasons for action in a more diffuse fashion: in a given situation it may require the agent to apologize, for example, or to obtain assistance. It also constitutes the *basis* for a moral obligation to compensate, but in order actually to establish such an obligation further argument is necessary. In general, then, outcome-responsibility can serve as the moral foundation in tort law for either a negligence standard of care, or for a danger-based standard of strict liability such as the rule in *Rylands v. Fletcher* or the American rule for ultrahazardous activities, since both kinds of liability presuppose reasonable foreseeability. But the considerations that bear on the choice between these liability rules, as well as on their more specific formulation, are matters that must be left to another occasion.

IV. CONCLUSION

Risk is a central concept in both tort law and tort theory. In this essay I have argued that it is important to distinguish between an objective and an epistemic conception of risk. The former is grounded in the standard relative-frequency account of probability, while the latter is concerned with the evidentiary basis for judgements or estimations of relative frequency. The commonly held thesis that risk is harm in itself is most plausibly explicated in terms of the objective conception of risk. But even under this favorable interpretation that thesis must, I have argued, be rejected. Moral responsibility for the consequences of risky conduct should be understood not as responsibility for creating a risk, but as responsibility for the unintentional physical harm, if any, that ensues. Such outcome-responsibility can, however, only plausibly be attributed to a person if his or her conduct was risky in the epistemic and not just in the objective sense. This suggests in turn that within a theory of tort law based on notions of interpersonal justice and individual responsibility, foreseeability of harm ought to be considered a necessary condition of liability.

Causation, Compensation and Moral Responsibility

CHRISTOPHER H. SCHROEDER*

I. IF YOU BREAK IT, MUST YOU PAY FOR IT?

Consider this vignette:

> A young boy and his father enter a china shop to look for a birthday present for the boy's aunt. While the father inspects some serving platters, the boy ambles around the shop looking at various objects. Hearing his father call him, the boy jerks carelessly around, and as he does so his jacket brushes against a vase just hard enough to cause it to fall to the floor. The vase shatters. Chagrined, the father's eyes search out those of the nearby clerk, who has seen the whole thing unfold. The clerk silently points to a sign above the entrance to the store, which reads 'If you break it, you pay for it.'

How is the fact that some actor has caused another person to suffer a loss related to a responsibility to repair the loss? Many people believe that the store sign supplies the general answer—not the universal answer, but one that does apply to a general class of losses that occur in certain ways. For one thing, the movement of the causal agent must be a volitional act. If I pushed the child so that he helplessly crashed into the vase, it is I who caused the loss, not the child. In addition, the plaintiff must be sufficiently free from responsibility to defeat possible claims of contributory or comparative negligence, and also defenses of assumption of the risk. Also, some theory of rights must delineate the kinds of volitional harm-causing actions that give rise to liability from those that do not, because we need some way to distinguish injury resulting from a carelessly driven car, for example, from injury resulting from fair competition.

Such qualifications help make sense of tort practice, and, while their precise formulations can spark debate, the need for them is widely recognized. More controversial is whether liability for harm caused depends in some way on the defendant's behavior being deficient in some sense. This is the dispute between strict liability and negligence, which this chapter sidesteps in order to concentrate on the element of causation and the justification of the role that it plays in tort law. There is near universal agreement that that role is pivotal:

---

* Professor of Law, Duke University.

however the sphere of appropriate cases is ultimately qualified and defined, it will turn out that the criterion of causation marks a sharp, dichotomous distinction. Cases otherwise indistinguishable from one another according to all of the other relevant criteria will be treated utterly differently depending upon the presence or absence of causation. If harm has been *caused by* a human agent's volitional action of the appropriate kind, the plaintiff has a cause of action for full compensatory damages and the defendant has a duty to compensate. If the causal connection is absent, the plaintiff has no recourse at all, and the defendant has no liability of any kind. This chapter examines the justification for partitioning cases on the basis of causation.

Strict liability and negligence advocates agree that the china shop story exemplifies a paradigm case of tort liability. It is marked by the features of inadvertent volitional action, deficient so as to be considered negligent, having caused a loss to an interest protected from such action by a right. It is a loss, furthermore, that is not offset somewhere else by a gain. The interaction between the actor and the injured has been a negative-sum transaction, the exact opposite of the sort of co-operative transactions among individuals that produces gains from trade and hence a social surplus. In the latter case, society worries about just methods for distributing or allocating the gains. In the former case, what concerns society are just methods for distributing or allocating the loss.

Under these circumstances, 'If you break it, you pay for it' undoubtedly constitutes a significant rule within existing tort practice, and part of the basic structure of tort law. Not only is this duty to compensate part of tort practice, but the corrective justice literature claims that the compensation requirement is just because it is grounded on moral principle.[1]

---

[1] Implicit and explicit references to the moral basis of corrective justice are common in the literature. For example: '[corrective justice] is the moral principle external to rights that gives rights a certain content': Jules L. Coleman, *A Mixed Conception of Corrective Justice*, 77 Iowa L. Rev. 427, 437 (1992); '[i]ndividual moral responsibility [is] traditionally regarded as the province of corrective justice': Stephen R. Perry, *Comment on Coleman: Corrective Justice*, 67 Ind. L.J. 381, 398 (1992); 'at the core of Aristotle's concept of [corrective] justice is the normative premise that the good to which law and politics should be directed . . . is the idea of the absolute moral worth of each human being as a free and equal member of the community': Richard W. Wright, *Substantive Corrective Justice*, 77 Iowa L. Rev. 625, 711 (1992); '[m]y aim is to present a conception of corrective justice, to account for its nature and basis from a suitably specified moral point of view': Peter Benson, *The Basis of Corrective Justice and Its Relation to Distributive Justice*, 77 Iowa L. Rev. 515, 516 (1992); '[w]ithout any causal connection to link A with B, the selection of B as the possible defendant becomes—to use the traditional expression—morally arbitrary': Richard A. Epstein, *Luck*, 6 Soc. Phil. & Pol'y 17, 30 (1989); 'understanding corrective justice means comprehending the "morality of interaction" between a "doer and [a] sufferer"': Ernest J. Weinrib, *Causation and Wrongdoing*, 63 Chi.-Kent L. Rev. 407, 448–9 (1987); '[l]ibertarians must derive rights from a morally plausible general statement about what might constitute rights-violating behavior: *prima facie*, the obvious candidate is that one ought not to *cause harm* (at least without justification)': Mark Kelman, *The Necessary Myth of Objective Causation Judgments in Liberal Political Theory*, 63 Chi.-Kent L. Rev. 579, 583 (1987).

Notwithstanding the common repetition of the claim of moral justification for the duty to compensate, articulating the moral principle that underwrites this claim has proven extraordinarily elusive. This chapter explores why finding a convincing moral rationale for the duty to compensate has eluded our grasp. The next section breaks the paradigm tort situation into three essential elements—a victim who suffers an undeserved loss, a deficient actor, and an action that causes a loss. It argues that the most readily apparent methods for moral assessment of victims, actors, or actions, whether these elements are taken singly or in several different combinations, reveal no principles that justify such duty, and several that are actually inconsistent with it. It concludes that if the structure of tort law were based on any of the examined modes of moral evaluation, tort law would not contain the duty to compensate.

The concluding section posits a root cause of the separate difficulties described in section II, arguing that *any* justificatory strategy for the compensation requirement stands in great tension with a central principle of many moral theories. This is the principle that each individual is entitled to equal dignity and respect, or to treatment as an end in himself or herself, and not merely as a means. This principle of equal dignity and respect generates certain strictures of horizontal equity in how individuals should be treated. Corrective justice theories often acknowledge this principle in their analyses of responsibilities *prior* to the act causing loss, but not in analyzing responsibilities *after* the act causing loss, including the issue of how responsibilities for remedying the loss (if any) should be allocated. Once the demands of equal treatment are applied to that issue, an inadvertent action that causes a negative sum interaction proves to contain no features sufficient to distinguish it from other actions that receive the sharply disparate treatment called for by the duty to compensate. Under that duty, both liability and recovery rest totally and completely upon causation, but causation is often fortuitous and thus morally arbitrary. To erect sharp disparities of treatment on such a foundation violates the requirement of equal treatment implied by the conception of equal dignity and respect.

II. VICTIM, TORTFEASOR, AND ACTION

The paradigm represented by the china shop story has three essential components. First, an actor through inadvertence has acted in a manner that fails to accord with a standard of care. Secondly, an individual through no fault of his or her own has suffered a loss. Thirdly, a causal chain links the actor's action to the victim's loss. The difficulties confronting the causal claim can be illuminated by taking up each of these components and exploring the standard moral terms on which they might be evaluated.

A. The Undeserving Victim

By stipulation we are examining cases in which the plaintiff is innocent of responsibility for his or her loss. With respect to those specific actions of the plaintiff that contributed to the causal interaction with the defendant, there is nothing for which we hold the plaintiff morally responsible, or in any other way deficient. With respect to any larger appraisal of the plaintiff's character, traits, or actions, there is no basis for distinguishing him or her from other individuals with similar character, traits, or actions so as to justify the loss morally. The plaintiff has suffered bad luck. It is undeserved.

The undeservedness of the plaintiff's loss might be thought to supply the beginnings of an argument as to why some principle of law should shift the loss away from the plaintiff and onto others. While this may be so, it provides no convincing argument for the very specific sort of shifting called for by the duty to compensate, which only works to compensate losses *caused by others*. Yet persons whose losses were not caused by another human agent can and do suffer equally undeserved losses. Suppose three individuals have their car tires rotated at a tire shop, and afterwards the cars crash, causing losses. In one case, the shop employee was momentarily distracted by a sudden noise just as he was tightening one of the lug nuts, resulting in his torquing the nut too far, causing a stress fracture so that the nut subsequently broke, resulting eventually in the wheel falling off the axle. In another case, the lug nut was properly tightened, but detailed analysis after the accident reveals that it contained a defect that could not have been detected prior to its failure. In a third case, lightning struck a power pole, throwing shards of wood and metal onto the ground, one of which pierced the tire. The losses are identical in all three cases, and the victims equally undeserving. Looking at these cases exclusively from the perspective of whether or not the victims deserved the losses, the presence of human agency in one of the cases but not others provides no ground for distinguishing among them. From the victim's perspective, these individuals are all equivalently innocent. If lack of desert for the loss were the moral principle animating tort law, tort doctrine should embody a requirement quite different from the duty to compensate.[2]

---

[2] The compensation requirement creates other arbitrary distinctions among innocent victims, as well. For instance, a victim injured by a judgment-proof defendant recovers nothing, while one injured by a deep-pocket defendant gains full compensation. Critics of the tort system who view victim compensation as the most significant function of tort law regularly criticize tort for making these arbitrary distinctions: *see, e.g.*, Stephen D. Sugarman, *Doing Away with Tort Law*, 73 CAL. L. REV. 555 (1985); Marc A. Franklin, *Replacing the Negligence Lottery: Compensation and Selective Reimbursement*, 53 VA. L. REV. 774 (1967).

B. The Tortfeasor

Switching to the defendant's perspective similarly fails to reveal a mode of moral evaluation that would explain the duty to compensate. When inquiring into what consequences should accrue to an actor whose actions fall short of a standard of performance, the most straightforward moral principle is the retributive ideal, which varies the sanction to fit the severity of the failure. However, it has many times been noted that retribution and the compensation requirement are utterly incompatible.[3] For one thing, the compensation requirement treats widely disparate deficiencies identically if they cause no harm. A momentary lapse of attention and a reckless disregard for the risks of severe harm receive the same treatment. Contrariwise, the fortuity of causation in one case and not the other leads to actors who engaged in equally deficient actions receiving completely different treatment. In a fourth car accident case, the repair person torqued the lug nut too far, resulting in a stress fracture that would lead to the wheel falling off; but before the lug nut failed, a power pole downed by lightning threw metal shrapnel into the tire, causing the car to crash. Under the compensation requirement, this repair person escapes liability, while the repair person in the first car accident case does not. Because any plausible theory of retribution must vary the amount of punishment to fit the blameworthiness of the defendant's conduct, no theory of retribution justifies distinctions of this kind.[4]

In sum, the most readily apparent means for moral assessment of either the deficiency in the plaintiff's conduct or the deservedness of the defendant's loss do not provide grounds for the compensation requirement at all. To the contrary, they produce two vexing questions:

---

[3] *See, e.g.,* Larry A. Alexander, *Causation and Corrective Justice: Does Tort Law Make Sense?,* 6 LAW & PHIL. 1, 4–5 (1987) and authorities cited in *id.* at 5 n. 9; David G. Owen, *Deterrence and Desert in Tort: A Comment,* 73 CAL. L. REV. 665, 668–9 (1985); Jules L. Coleman, *On the Moral Argument for the Fault System,* 71 J. PHIL. 473 (1974).

In general, the incompatibility results from the conviction that the moral quality of an actor's action must be evaluated on the basis of facts and other constituents of practical reasoning that were known or knowable to the actor at the time of the action. One implication of this *ex ante* perspective is that whenever causal outcomes are not knowable in advance, the harm-related feature of an action relevant to moral evaluation is not the harm it causes, but rather the risk it creates: *see* Christopher H. Schroeder, *Corrective Justice and Liability for Increasing Risks,* 37 UCLA L. REV. 439 (1990).

[4] More generally, an *ex ante* approach to the moral appraisal of an actor based on his or her decisions and actions requires that such evaluation not differ on the basis of information unknowable at the time of decision and action: *see supra,* note 3. The incompatibility of the compensation requirement that the *ex ante* perspective has been noted by others. *E.g.,* Weinrib, *supra,* note 1, at 414 ('the moral quality of [the wrongdoer's] act is unaffected by whether the potential for harm that it releases actually comes to pass. Accordingly, the tort requirement of causation makes no sense if we conceive of the law as passing judgment on this moral quality as such').

(1) Why should the rules enabling compensation for loss allow recovery to an individual whose undeserved loss is caused by another human agent, to the complete exclusion of other individuals who have suffered equally undeserved losses, but not at the hands of a human agent? and (2) Why should such rules extract full compensatory damages from a human agent whose deficient conduct has caused a specific harm, to the complete exoneration of other individuals who have engaged in conduct equally deficient, but which has not caused harm?

The compensation requirement commits tort law to both those results, and there may be justifications for them. However, the two most readily apparent methods for performing a moral evaluation of the parties' conduct fail to provide such justifications. To the contrary, these moral appraisals are what have generated the questions themselves. Far from finding the moral ground for the compensation requirement, the exploration so far has set that requirement at odds with such moral evaluations.

These considerations substantially increase the burden of persuasion placed on those who argue the moral underpinnings for the duty to compensate, because these contrary moral claims cannot simply be dismissed as false leads in the hunt for those moral underpinnings. Rather, they reveal moral considerations that fight against the compensation requirement and counsel for its rejection. Proposals for norms that violate these moral considerations must explain why those violations are proper in pursuit of some more weighty purpose or value. As a result, any argument in support of the causal claim must not only be plausible *prima facie* but must also convince its hearers that these countervailing considerations ought to be overruled, and the compensation requirement adopted despite moral considerations to the contrary. Although the foregoing arguments are widely recognized in the literature, the burden of persuasion consequence of them is not.[5]

We need not pause here to consider how to resolve such a possible clash of moral principles, because the discussion thus far has failed to produce even a *prima facie* moral argument for the duty to compensate. We turn next in our search to the final essential structural component of the tort paradigm we are examining, the duty to compensate itself.

C. The Causal Connection

The fact that the deficient action of the defendant has caused harm might figure into a moral explanation in one of two ways. First, it might refocus the normative inquiry from the deficiencies in the *actor* to the deficiencies in the *action* itself. In this vein, Jules Coleman argues that '[t]he concept of

---

[5] An exception is Alexander, *supra,* note 3. Professor Alexander makes a number of observations similar to ones in this essay. He frames the question as whether or not corrective justice is compatible with either retributive or distributive justice, and he concludes that it is not.

wrongdoing implicated in the principle of corrective justice is that of fault-in-the-doing, not fault-in-the-doer. Moral culpability of the agent is not a condition of the victim's claim to repair as a matter of corrective justice.'[6] Moving away from moral culpability of the actor as the principle that grounds the duty to compensate certainly looks initially promising, because evaluating the actor's culpability has led only in the direction of the retributive ideal, which is incapable of grounding that duty.[7] Yet avoiding that dead end gains us nothing unless it leads to an argument that is itself persuasive.

To see where fault-in-the-doing takes us, we need to understand what it might mean to predicate fault of an action, rather than of an actor. Actions themselves can be deemed faulty in the sense that the action failed to conform to some functional standard. We might say that the swing of a .150 hitter in baseball is faulty, or that the foul shot motion of a basketball player who makes only 25 per cent of his shots is faulty. The ascription of fault is instrumental, relative to some function or purpose of the action. It comports with a hypothetical imperative, as in, 'if you want to raise your batting average, you will have to iron out the faults in your swing'. In the tort case, fault-in-the-doing might be ascribed in reference to the function or purpose of causing no harm. Thus, the action of the boy in the china shop is faulty in the sense that, if the boy wanted to avoid breaking the vase, he should not have acted in the faulty way that he did.

The desire to avoid harm is a desire that we should have—there is moral force behind it. So fault-in-the-doing, in so far as it expresses the thought that some element of an action increased the likelihood of harm occurring, describes the action in a morally relevant way. Yet it no more succeeds in explaining the different treatment afforded to acts that cause harm, on the one hand, and otherwise identical acts that do not, on the other hand, than did the retributive principle. This is because fault-in-the-doing can itself not distinguish between such cases. A basketball player with a faulty shooting motion can still make a foul shot once in a while; indeed, the 25 per cent shooter succeeds one time in four. His technique is nevertheless faulty, and his basketball coach will endeavor to correct it. Likewise, the .150 hitter in baseball can line a double against the fence, but it is a lucky swing. His hitting instructor still thinks, rightly, that the hitter has a faulty swing. The repair person's torquing of the lug nut in the fourth story was just as faulty as the torquing in the first one, although one caused harm and the other did not. So it is generally: fault-in-the-doing identifies an aspect of actions that can be present regardless of whether harm is caused in any specific

[6] Jules L. Coleman, *Tort Law and the Demands of Corrective Justice*, 67 IND. L.J. 349, 371 (1992).
[7] *See supra,* notes 3 & 4 and accompanying text.

instance.[8] It cannot, therefore, provide a basis for distinct treatment of harm-causing faulty actions as compared to non-harm-causing ones.

D. More Complex Strategies

To this point, we have examined each of the three structural elements of a tort-like interaction—the victim who suffers undeserved loss, the deficient actor, and the deficient action. None has produced a moral grounding for the duty to compensate, and the inquiry has actually shown that that duty is in tension with certain principles of moral appraisal. Grounding the duty must require alternative strategies. One intriguing possibility rejects the dis-aggregative approach pursued thus far in this section, and insists on taking two elements of the structure in tandem. The basic approach is *comparative*: as between an innocent victim and a deficient actor, who should bear the loss? Such comparative methodology appears in any number of tort decisions.[9] It emerges almost inevitably from the basic structure of tort practice, which pits a plaintiff against a defendant, where the question of who from among these parties should bear the loss is perhaps the only relevant question. Indeed, the very notion of corrective justice is often defined in these terms. For example, Stephen Perry observes that 'it is common ground that corrective justice is centrally concerned with the payment of compensation for certain losses that one person's conduct has caused another. . . . It is of course possible that there simply is no independent principle of corrective justice, but if there is, the obligations it yields must be both limited to injurers and correlative of victims' rights.'[10]

The answer to the comparative question comes easily only by skipping

---

[8] Perhaps, however, there are those who would insist that fault-in-the-doing identifies a feature of actions that is ascribable to actions only if they actually cause harm, but not otherwise. If this were so, then there would be no fault-in-the-doing in the torquing of the lug nut in the fourth car accident case. Likewise, when a driver momentarily looks away from the road at just the instant a child darts in front of the car, but the car narrowly misses the child anyway, there is no fault-in-the-doing—but if the car hits the child, there would be. If fault-in-the doing is truly to be a concept ascribable to actions in light of their consequences, it would be entirely unlikely that this concept could justify the duty to compensate, because it seems simply to be a redescription of the fact that the action has caused harm. To say that actions that cause harm are 'faulty' in this sense does not so much provide a moral underpinning for the duty as it raises the question why this sense of fault-in-the-doing should be relevant to the question of loss allocation at all. In addition, even if we succeeded in locating a moral claim correlated to fault-in-the-doing, we would still need to explain why that (elusive) claim ought to override the countervailing considerations based on desert and retribution, both of which are in conflict with the duty to compensate.

[9] *E.g.*, Sindell v. Abbott Labs., 607 P.2d 924, 936 (Cal. 1980) ('The most persuasive reason for finding plaintiff states a cause of action is that . . . as between an innocent plaintiff and negligent defendants, the latter should bear the cost of the injury').

[10] Stephen R. Perry, *Loss, Agency, and Responsibility for Outcomes: Three Conceptions of Corrective Justice, in* TORT THEORY (Ken Cooper-Stephenson & Elaine Gibson (eds.), 1993), 24, 38 (citation omitted).

past the prior of two distinct steps. The first step *limits* consideration of loss allocation options to choices within a certain set of persons. The second step *allocates* the loss among these eligible candidates.[11]

For comparative arguments to be solidly grounded, both steps require justification, and yet the first one is often simply assumed or built into the statement of the issue,[12] such as when the ultimate function of tort law is stated to be 'select[ing] the *responsible* causes from all the other causes'.[13] Such statements assume that there is a justification for throwing a fence around people who are linked through a causal connection, to the exclusion of all others. While it is true that our practice of tort law currently has such a structure, any moral explanation for the duty to compensate must justify that practice, not simply adopt it. Why *should* the comparison take place between these two individuals alone? Why should not others who have been equally deficient in their conduct, on the one hand, and still others who have been equally undeserving of their losses, on the other hand, be brought into the question of loss allocation? Before one can grant the correctness of tort law's answers to the comparative question, the use of the causal connection between the plaintiff and defendant as a selection device isolating these two as the exclusive objects of comparison is the crucial aspect of the practice that itself must be justified.

A comparative argument, then, needs a basis for singling out the causal agent, on the one hand, and the victim of human agency, on the other hand, for comparative moral measurement. In the currently standard terminology, what is required is an agent-relative reason for isolating victim and tortfeasor.

The most promising approach begins with an account of human agency. On this account, human beings participate in shaping the world by taking actions that we expect to have effects in the world. It would contradict our conception of ourselves as agents to deny that the *consequences* of 'our' actions are also 'ours'. This, then, is the second way the fact that harm has been caused might fit into a normative explanation for holding the defendant liable for the victim's loss.[14] Unlike the idea of fault-in-the-doing, which focused on the deficiency of the action doing the harm, agency

---

[11] Even after the first step has been taken, not everyone agrees with tort law's standard answer to the second: John E. Coons, *Compromise as Precise Justice*, 68 CAL. L. REV. 250, 257–61 (1980).

[12] An exception is Perry, *supra*, note 10. Stephen Perry is quite aware that the hardest question in corrective justice is explaining why the comparative analysis can rightly be limited to just the victim and the class of individuals who have caused the harm: *see, e.g., id.* at 38 ('What we are seeking, then, is a justification for corrective justice that incorporates these constraints [of limiting a comparative inquiry to just the victim and the injurer]').

[13] Richard W. Wright, *Causation, Responsibility, Risk, Probability, Naked Statistics, and Proof: Pruning the Bramble Bush by Clarifying the Concepts*, 73 IOWA L. REV. 1001, 1004 (1988).

[14] The other way is through the idea of fault-in-the-doing. *See supra*, note 6.

highlights the doing itself in providing the moral link between victim and tortfeasor.

Indeed, the concept of agency actually may be pre-moral, in that the existence of agency is an essential precondition that makes morality possible. If we did not have an understanding of ourselves as individuals who could anticipate the consequences of our actions and adjust our actions in virtue of those anticipations—if we did not have the capacities of prediction and control—the thought of a set of (moral) norms designed to define appropriate conduct with respect to other human beings would be quite unthinkable. Once we assume agency, however, moral judgement as we understand it does become possible.

Tony Honoré has built a theory of tort liability on such an understanding of agency. Honoré's method is ultimately not comparative, but studying it elucidates an underlying connection between agency and responsibility that can be exploited by other approaches. Honoré argues that ascribing authorship of actions and outcomes to the causing agent is fundamental to our having a personal identity. Without such an identity, in turn, the entire notion of a *someone* who could possibly be held responsible for actions would disintegrate. So 'outcome-responsibility', which means 'being responsible for the good and the harm we bring about by what we do', is 'inescapable because it is the counterpart and at the same time a constituent of our personal identity and character. We could not dispense with outcome-responsibility without ceasing to be persons.'[15]

The concept of responsibility is notoriously large, so that the particular conception of responsibility necessary for this argument must be carefully elaborated.[16] As Honoré himself notes at several places in his paper, 'outcome-responsibility' is not the same thing as the responsibility or duty to compensate for losses caused.[17] Yet he ultimately concludes that that duty is required to implement and sustain the idea of agency upon which outcome-responsibility rests. In this, I think he is mistaken, because the conception of responsibility as liability for full money damages is a much more stringent conception of responsibility than is required to support the idea of human agency. A conception of responsibility as accountability or answerability suffices, and this in the loose, general sense of an obligation to account for, or explain, one's actions. The boy in the china shop bears an obligation to answer the question 'Who did it?' by saying 'I did', and perhaps by offering an explanation, an accounting, for the action. This sense of accountability or answerability seems very close to the idea of

[15] Tony Honoré, *Responsibility and Luck*, (1988) 104 L.Q.R. 530, 530–1.

[16] The *locus classicus* for the idea that 'responsibility' has many meanings is H. L. A. HART, PUNISHMENT AND RESPONSIBILITY (1968), 211 ff.

[17] 'Contrary to what Epstein and possibly Fletcher at times seem to suggest, responsibility for a harmful outcome should not automatically involve a legal duty to compensate': Honoré, *supra,* note 15, at 541 (citations omitted).

authorship, of owning some action as one's own, and quite adequate to sustain it. Authors of actions have access to privileged information with respect to those actions that others lack. They can frequently reconstruct the practical reasoning that preceded the action, almost always better than external observers can. In so far as we must acknowledge a sense of authorship in order to sustain agency, the responsibility of discharging the burden of explanation that falls uniquely within an author's competence seems to suffice. Simply answering for one's actions by 'owning up'—saying that is mine, and this is yours—permits each person to continue to construct and maintain an evolving personal history, which Honoré says is a prerequisite for personal identity and character.[18] If this is so, then outcome-responsibility as a duty to answer is too thin a concept to bridge the gap from agency to the duty to compensate.[19] Something more is required.

When bad outcomes are involved, some have argued that outcome-responsibility may lend itself to a slightly thicker conception. Both Bernard Williams and Thomas Nagel have explored the extent to which reactive attitudes of agents and observers alike turn on how things actually turn out, so that these attitudes are markedly different with regard to careless behavior that fails to cause harm versus otherwise identical behavior that does cause serious harm.[20] The car driver who strikes a child while momentarily distracted is subject to a different moral appraisal from the car driver who, identically distracted, just misses the child. Notwithstanding the element of luck involved in such evaluations, Nagel, Williams and others contend that we have a basis for feeling differently toward the agent of harm, and for holding such an agent to a different standard of responsibility.

Nagel and Williams have certainly identified a real phenomenon, and I shall not quarrel with the legitimacy of incorporating it into an analysis of moral responsibility. Even so, a sense of responsibility suitably enlarged to include appropriately differentiated reactive attitudes that are dependent on the fortuity of causation still falls short of grounding the requirement that full compensation is owed the injured as a matter of moral judgement. For all we can tell, there is nothing to be found in the claim that such a sense

---

[18] '[A]ctions and decisions,' he writes, 'are ascribed to authors, who accordingly count as persons; and it is by virtue of these ascriptions that each of [us] has a history, an identity and a character. But there is a price to be paid for being a person. As the counterpart of this status we are responsible for our actions and their consequences, and sometimes this responsibility exposes us to legal sanctions. To ascribe personhood and responsibility to people in this way is to apply normative principles. It is not merely that others attribute to us an identity and a character, but that we are entitled to claim them for ourselves and to ascribe them to others': *id.* at 543.

[19] I am borrowing the description of conceptions of responsibility as thin or thick from Gerald J. Postema, *Risks, Wrongs, and Responsibility: Coleman's Liberal Theory of Commutative Justice*, 103 YALE L.J. 861 (1993) (book review).

[20] Bernard Williams, *Moral Luck*, in MORAL LUCK (1981), 29; Thomas Nagel, *Moral Luck*, in MORTAL QUESTIONS (1979), 24.

of responsibility exists that cannot be fully met internally by feelings of deep regret and externally by apologies or efforts to make amends that still fall dramatically short of full repair. Reactive attitudes may interact with an agent's history, character, and conscience to produce a conviction within the agent that some sort of response to harm caused is appropriate, even necessary, whether or not the specific duty to compensate is imposed.[21] The precise nature of the appropriate response to such reactive attitudes seems more heavily influenced by social custom and convention than by moral imperative.[22]

So the conception of agency cannot explain or justify the duty to compensate. Furthermore, in light of the morally based objections to that duty, the selection of such an optional doctrine seems morally repugnant, not morally grounded. Honoré thus draws too strong a conclusion when at the end of his essay he claims that the duty to compensate is grounded on the idea that '[t]o bear the risk of bad luck is inseparable from being a choosing person.'[23]

Stephen Perry has further developed the argument begun by Honoré by putting the ideas of agency and outcome-responsibility to work in a comparative inquiry involving the victim and the injurer. Perry acknowledges that 'outcome-responsibility does not necessarily carry with it an obligation to compensate';[24] however, he does argue that outcome-responsibility supplies the necessary prerequisite to an adequate grounding for that duty: a 'normative link' between particular injurers and their victims.[25]

The link thus supplied cannot by itself ground the imposition of a duty to repair, because outcome-responsibility 'may, for example, simply give rise to reasons to obtain assistance, or to express one's regret to the person harmed'.[26] What it grounds, in Perry's view, is limiting our comparative inquiry in the necessary way, to just the victim and the injurer. After that:

[t]he possibility is at least raised . . . that [the injurer] should pay full compensation, which means attempting to undo the harmful outcome entirely, to the extent that this is possible to achieve. The loss represents an interference with the victim's well-being, and it is capable of being transferred, at least up to a point, by the payment of compensation. In the nature of things, the victim will have to bear the loss if no

---

[21] On this point, see Wright, *supra*, note 1, at 682. 'Inescapably, the consequences of my volitional actions are "mine" in the sense of mere physical causation. But, by itself, this empirical fact implies nothing normative. No one's continuing status, history, or character as a person is threatened in any way by the lack of absolute moral or legal responsibility for the consequences of our actions.'

[22] 'Responsibility . . . is the product of definite social arrangements': CHARLES FRANKEL, THE CASE FOR MODERN MAN (1956), 203.

[23] Honoré, *supra*, note 15, at 553.

[24] Perry, *supra*, note 10, at 42. *See also* Stephen R. Perry, *The Moral Foundations of Tort Law*, 77 IOWA L. REV. 449, 496–507 (1992) [hereinafter *Moral Foundations*].

[25] Perry, *Moral Foundations, supra*, note 24, at 514.

[26] Perry, *supra*, note 10, at 42.

one else has a reason to shoulder it. The injurer, by virtue of her outcome-responsibility, has just such a reason. This sets the stage for a comparative inquiry of the following kind: which of these two should most appropriately suffer the interference with well-being that *either* the original loss *or* the payment of compensation necessarily entails?[27]

In this paragraph, the argument moves from the 'possibility' of full compensation from the injurer to outcome-responsibility as 'a reason' for it, a reason that seems dispositive because *as between the two of them*, the loss is 'most appropriately' placed on the injurer. However, all outcome-responsibility can supply, by Perry's own admission, is a reason for a *response*, which might take many different forms, not a reason for the duty to compensate. It is only after one fixes exclusively on victim and injurer, and insists that the answer to the question of compensation come from one or the other of them, that outcome-responsibility might conceivably provide a basis for resolving the matter. Yet nothing in the argument just quoted explains how outcome-responsibility can justify that preliminary step of isolating these two individuals for the second-step comparison. How can one individual's having *a* reason for *a* response support the elimination of *all* other compensatory alternatives from consideration? Our moral landscape contains numerous grounds for moral appraisal, including but not limited to desert and fault, that may bear on the appropriateness of providing repair and compensation. Notions of authorship and outcome-responsibility fail to justify ruling out such additional grounds as bases for compensatory measures, and hence do not support the first step necessary to get to the attempted comparative justification for the duty to compensate.

In short, to say that an actor bears a special responsibility not borne by others by virtue of his or her authorship of a harm-causing action fails to explain why no one else might bear any responsibility at all. Yet other remedial possibilities are available that would appropriately recognize the outcome-responsibility of the agent of harm. For example, the loss could be spread across all deficient actors, with the injurer paying a premium, perhaps an extra-large one. As a second example, the injurer could pay an amount correlated to his deficient action, the rest of the loss could be distributed through social insurance, and the injurer could issue an apology. For a third, the injurer could give the victim some socially determined token, acknowledging his responsibility for the mistake, but not even attempting to approximate the value of the loss, with a social insurance fund repairing all or part of the loss. The possibilities are numerous. Such possibilities seem precluded only after the comparative inquiry has been narrowed to solutions involving only injurer and victim, but nothing in the

---

[27] *Id.* at 44.

idea of authorship justifies that narrowing. Just as outcome-responsibility does not entail any particular response by an injurer, it does not entail a comparative inquiry narrowed exclusively to the injurer and the victim. In sum, the argument from agency at most supplies reasons to hold that actors who cause harm have *a* special responsibility toward bad consequences, not shared by others. Standing alone, it does not supply a reason that this special responsibility must be cashed out via the quite specific duty to compensate.

III. Equal Treatment

A theory of moral responsibility takes as one of its subjects the content and extent of individual responsibilities to prevent harm to others. The analysis of this subject and others often begins with a principle of equality, namely that every human being is entitled to be treated with equal dignity and respect.[28] By and large, corrective justice theories adopt this principle as well. For example, the obligation to treat all humans and their legitimate interests with equal dignity and respect is violated when an individual acts negligently, as in the china shop situation, because the agent has failed to accord the well-being and interests of the china shop owner an equal dignity in his practical reasoning process as his own.[29] In some such instances, a loss will be caused by that failure. The question then becomes what should be done next.

The currently standard approach to this question takes it as one of what remedy should exist for the transgression represented by the initial negligent action. However, in a more general sense, the question of what is to be done next is simply another question of responsible moral action, and thus raises issues fully on a par with those raised in giving content to the obligation to prevent harm in the first place. Under the principle of equal dignity and respect, all individuals ought to be treated equally unless some morally relevant distinction can be made among them, and this is true in answering the 'what next' question as well as all other questions of human action. The series of difficulties encountered by the duty to compensate in the preceding discussion can all be traced to a single question: is it consistent with treating human beings with equal dignity and respect to draw

---

[28] '[T]he moral character of a person's choice to act in a manner causing harm to another person is dependent upon whether the actor accorded equal concern and respect to the other's interests at the time of choice and action': David G. Owen, *The Fault Pit*, 26 GA. L. REV. 703, 720–1 (1992).

[29] *See, e.g.*, Weinrib, *supra*, note 1, at 428 ("The virtue of the negligence standard is that it regulates the relationship between [persons] on the basis of equality. . . . Thus the defendant must implicitly acknowledge . . . that [the interests of others] have the same claim to consideration as his own').

such a very sharp distinction as is called for by the duty to compensate on the basis of the single fact of causation?

In the last section, we examined both victims and agents and found that in each class individuals who are in all other relevant respects indistinguishable—moral equals, if you will—are subject to being treated entirely differently on the sole basis of the fortuity of causation, if we adopt the duty to compensate. Under that duty, the fortuity of causation must support a sharp, dichotomous distinction between two individuals, one of whom has caused harm and the other one—in all other respects indistinguishable—has not. Likewise, the fortuity of causation must support an equally sharp and dichotomous distinction between otherwise indistinguishable victims, one of whom suffers loss at the hands of a human agent, the other of whom does not. Is there a moral principle of such weight as to justify thus partitioning defendants on the one hand and plaintiffs on the other hand, who are in all other morally relevant respects equals? The fact of causation seems too slender a reed, too weak a foundation, upon which to base such sharp distinctions.

IV. CONCLUSION

The preceding discussion has sought both to explain why identifying the moral underpinnings of the duty to compensate has proven so difficult and to articulate the general challenge such a task confronts. This challenge thus far has not been met. The implications of this conclusion for the structure of tort law are not entirely clear. There are many practical or pragmatic reasons for the compensation requirement, the sufficiency of which cannot be explored here. They include the need for sound incentive structures, limitations in our capacities to acquire the knowledge necessary to identify otherwise relevant distinctions, resource constraints, a continuing commitment to a traditional private-law structure, and the requirements of social order in a world where the equal-dignity principle is not universally shared or used as a basis for action. Some or all of these, as well as other possibilities, may well be grounds enough for the duty to compensate.

Many have asserted, however, that the duty to compensate requirement follows from moral first principles. It represents quite a dramatic shift to conclude, to the contrary, that the duty to compensate *violates* first principles, although it might still be justified by second order pragmatic considerations. Yet that is the conclusion to which we have been drawn.

Necessary and Sufficient Conditions in Tort Law

TONY HONORÉ*

Argument about causation inside and outside the law is often concerned with the question: must a cause be a *necessary* condition of a result, must it be a *sufficient* condition of the result, or must it be a *necessary element in a set of conditions* jointly sufficient to produce the result? This essay supports the third view, both outside the law and inside it, whenever a sequence of physical events is in issue. A different but related idea can be used to explain reasons for human action, 'causing' or inducing people to act rather than causing things to happen. There is, I contend, no special 'legal' meaning of causation and related concepts such as inducement.

On the other hand, law alone determines when causal connection must be proved and when it can be dispensed with in legal contexts. When causal connection must be proved, law also settles what must be shown to have caused what. This is specially important in tort law. Tort law generally imposes fault liability on people who by their wrongful conduct cause harm to others; but sometimes it imposes strict liability on people whose specially dangerous activities, though not wrongful, cause others harm. The causal inquiry takes a different form depending on whether fault or strict liability is in issue.

Tort lawyers have traditionally held the view that, whatever the meaning of causal connection, the way to test whether it exists in a given case is to ask whether in the circumstances the harmful result would have occurred in the absence of the wrongful act. This is the widely adopted 'but-for' test, by which causal connection is deemed to exist between condition and consequence whenever, but for the condition, the consequence would not have occurred. The but-for test is also called the test of strong necessity.[1] It often gives what is intuitively the right answer, but it sometimes fails to do so. This test is meant to exclude those factors that had no impact on a particular course of events. But sometimes it cuts out factors that did have an impact. It serves to exclude many irrelevant conditions, but it can also exclude

---

* Formerly Regius Professor of Civil Law, University of Oxford.

[1] On strong and weak necessity and sufficiency, see JOHN L. MACKIE, THE CEMENT OF THE UNIVERSE: A STUDY OF CAUSATION (1974), 39–40, 60–6, 126–7; Richard W. Wright, *Causation, Responsibility, Risk, Probability, Naked Statistics and Proof: Pruning the Bramble Bush by Clarifying the Concepts,* 73 IOWA L. REV. 1001, 1020 (1988) [hereinafter *Pruning*].

others that are relevant.[2] Thus in some cases of 'over-determination'—cases where each of two or more independent wrongful acts alone would have sufficed to bring about the harm—the but-for test leads to the dubious conclusion that neither act caused the harm. So, if the but-for test were applied to such a case, the victim could recover from neither wrongdoer. As a way around this and other difficulties, courts have developed an alternative test of causal connection, for use in tort cases when the but-for test seems to give the wrong answer. This alternative test asks whether the condition in question was a 'substantial factor' in producing the result. But this device, which allows judges and juries to follow their intuitions, is purely pragmatic[3] and leaves the theoretical problem untouched. The 'substantial factor' notion is indefinite, if not indeterminate, and it is difficult to see how it might be fitted into a coherent theory of causation.

I. THE CAUSATION STORY:
MODERN EFFORTS TO UNRAVEL ITS MYSTERIES

In 1959 Herbert Hart and I proposed a thesis that we thought would explain the basis of and justify our intuitions in certain unusual cases, such as the over-determination situation, as well as in straightforward ones.[4] We argued that, to be a cause of an event, a prior event must be shown to be a 'causally relevant condition' of that event. Whether something more is needed to turn a causally relevant condition into a cause may for the moment be left aside; for now let it be assumed (contrary to our view) that every causally relevant condition is a cause. Our theory was that an event such as a prior wrongful act is causally relevant only if it is a necessary element in a set of conditions that is together sufficient to produce the consequence. 'A condition may be necessary just in the sense that it is one of a set of conditions jointly sufficient for the production of the consequence. It is necessary because it is required to complete this set.'[5] At least that was true, we said, of physical sequences.[6] This weak sense of 'necessary' (necessary to complete that particular set of conditions) can be contrasted with the strong necessity inherent in the but-for test. On the other hand our sense of 'sufficient' is a strong one. If the set of conditions sufficient to produce the consequence occurred, the consequence occurred; and if the con-

---

[2] Wright, *Pruning, supra,* note 1, at 1022.   [3] *Id.* at 1018–19.

[4] H. L. A. HART & A. M. HONORÉ, CAUSATION IN THE LAW (1959).

[5] *Id.* at 106 (1959).

[6] A different, though related account was needed for interpersonal transactions: H. L. A. HART & TONY HONORÉ, CAUSATION IN THE LAW (2d edn., 1985), 51–61, 125. See *infra,* notes 58–61 and accompanying text.

sequence had not occurred, the set of conditions would not have occurred either.[7]

In 1965 John Mackie applied our idea to causal 'regularities'—causal generalizations as distinguished from specific events.[8] He combined with it the doctrine of the plurality of causes. This latter theory postulates that on different occasions certain types of events—say death or road accidents—can have different causes. We discover causal regularities, and ultimately scientific causal laws, by assembling sets of conditions. Ideally, these should be such that we can say of each constituent condition that it is a necessary[9] member of a set such that, when all the members of that set are present, a particular consequence invariably follows. The conditions are jointly sufficient for the result but, in view of the plurality of causes, they may not be actually necessary for it, since there may be alternative *sets* of conditions that will produce the same consequence.[10] Mackie called such a condition— a *necessary member* of a *set* jointly sufficient (but unnecessary) to produce a given type of result—an 'INUS' (Insufficient but Necessary part of an Unnecessary but Sufficient) condition.

For example, there may be one causal regularity, by which a driver's not keeping a proper lookout plus certain other conditions is sufficient to bring about a road accident, and another causal regularity, by which going too fast plus a different set of conditions is sufficient for a road accident. If so, not keeping a proper lookout and going too fast are both INUS conditions of road accidents though, belonging to different sufficient sets,[11] neither condition is necessary to produce a road accident.

It is worth noting that sets of conditions of this sort generally have as one of their members the *absence* of counteracting or frustrating conditions. A certain dose of strychnine will, given certain bodily conditions, result in death, but only (1) in the absence of an antidote, and (2) in the absence of some other cause of death intervening before the poison takes effect. The strength of the dose, the bodily conditions, the absence of an antidote, the absence of some other intervening cause of death, etc. are all INUS members of the set of conditions that is together sufficient to result in death.

---

[7] This is to apply the reverse but-for test. Wright, *Pruning, supra,* note 1, at 1021, note 108. Richard Wright termed a condition of this sort, necessary in a weak sense but sufficient in a strong sense, a 'NESS' condition. He derived from it the NESS test, which is meant to replace the but-for test: *id.* at 1019. See *infra,* notes 16 & 17 and accompanying text.

[8] MACKIE, *supra,* note 1, at 59–63 (building to some extent on Konrad Marc-Wogau, *On Historical Explanation,* 28 THEORIA 213–33 (1962)).

[9] Mackie says insufficient (on its own), which is obvious, but also non-redundant, i.e., necessary as an element in that particular jointly sufficient set of conditions: *see id.* at 62.

[10] I have modified his terminology so far as the use of 'factor' and 'condition' are concerned, but this does not change the substance.

[11] They could also, of course, belong to the same set.

With some hesitation,[12] Mackie concluded that though this analysis of causal regularities as sets of INUS conditions often applies not only to *types* of event but to *specific* events,[13] it does not always do so.[14] He thought that at least sometimes we can say of a *specific instance* of a condition, such as not keeping a proper lookout, that it caused a collision, though we are not thereby committed to any *regularity* that would make not keeping a lookout an INUS condition of road accidents. It is not just that we and scientific experts are unable to frame a satisfactory generalization combining speed, position of the victim, visibility, road condition, etc. in the right proportions. Rather, we sometimes conclude that but for the lack of a proper lookout *this* collision would not have occurred—without believing that this was an instance of a *regularity* concerning speed, position, road condition, and the other factors. 'A singular causal statement need not imply even the vaguest generalization.'[15] If in a specific case we can back our conviction up by pointing to a set of INUS conditions, so much the better; but that is not essential.

In 1985 Richard Wright in an important paper dissented from Mackie's view on this point and, propounding the 'NESS' (Necessary Element of a Sufficient Set) test, elaborated the idea that Hart and I had originally put forward.[16] His version is only marginally different from ours. According to Wright, 'a particular condition was a cause of (contributed to) a specific result if and only if it was a necessary element of a set of antecedent actual conditions that was sufficient for the occurrence of the result.'[17] This perhaps differs from our view in one respect. Wright seems to require that *all* the conditions that belong to the set be antecedent to the result, whereas it appears to me that, to be sufficient for the result, some conditions at least can be of the sort that must persist until the result occurs. An example is the icy condition of the road as a factor in a road accident.

This difference of view, if it is one, does not affect the value of the NESS test, which is widely supported by tort theorists, and not only by them.[18] Nevertheless, Mackie is not alone in defending the but-for notion as an explanation of singular causal events. In German criminal law, Friedrich Toepel has recently published a monograph on crimes of negligence, which

---

[12] MACKIE, *supra*, note 1, at 48–50 adduces powerful arguments for a cause as something necessary and sufficient in the circumstances for its effect. *Cf.* Wright, *Pruning, supra*, note 1, at 1028–9.

[13] MACKIE, *supra*, note 1, at 65–6.   [14] *Id.* at 40—58.

[15] *Id.* at 77–8, effectively criticized by Wright, *Pruning, supra*, note 1, at 1031–4.

[16] Richard Wright, *Causation in Tort Law*, 73 CAL. L. REV. 1735 (1985) (especially 1788–1813) [hereinafter *Causation*]. *See also* Wright, *Pruning, supra*, note 1, at 1018–44.

[17] Wright, *Pruning, supra*, note 1, at 1019.

[18] *See* Wright, *Pruning, supra*, n. 1, at 1019, n. 98. For a criminal law example, see Ingeborg Puppe, *Der Erfolg und seine kausale Erklärung im Strafrecht*, 92 ZStW 863, 867–8 (1980) [hereinafter *Der Erfolg*]; Ingeborg Puppe *Die Beziehung zwischen Sorgfaltswidrigkeit und Erfolg bei den Fahrlässigkeitsdelikten*, 99 ZStW 595–6 (1987).

clearly have much in common with tort actions. Toepel supports the but-for test and dissents from the dominant view among German scholars, which rejects it.[19]

The controversy is clearly not over. In sections II and III, I explore some aspects of causal connection that are common to the NESS and but-for theories and others that divide them. The analysis focuses in particular on how far causation in tort law depends on concepts that apply outside the law, and how far it reflects normative considerations, legal or moral.

II. COMMON ELEMENTS IN THE NESS AND BUT-FOR THEORIES

Some points are, or should be, common ground between the NESS and but-for theories. First, each of these two theories embraces both a search for the *meaning* of 'causally relevant condition' and a *test* by which we can tell whether a condition is causally relevant. That is, they are both at times semantic and at times heuristic. The importance of this distinction is that we may believe that a condition was a cause of a specific event because it was a member of a set of conditions jointly sufficient to bring it about and yet not be able to say exactly what those conditions were. We may therefore *mean* by cause a condition of that sort and yet *be satisfied* in a given instance that it was a cause on the basis of the rough uniformities observed in everyday life that lead us to conclude that the presence of the condition made a difference to the outcome. We may do this though we cannot specify the INUS conditions exemplified in the case at hand.[20] No one will deny that the but-for test has in many instances a heuristic value: it often provides a quick way of testing the existence of causal connection. However, it is another matter whether it is part of the *meaning* of 'causally relevant condition' or 'cause'.

Philosophers debate whether causal connection is a relation between events or between facts.[21] An event can be described in many different ways, but a fact is tied to a specific description. That Brutus stabbed Caesar and that he betrayed Caesar describe the same historical *event* but the fact that Brutus stabbed the dictator is not the same *fact* as the fact that he betrayed him. This difference has a bearing on what a plaintiff must prove in a lawsuit. In a wrongful death action by Caesar's widow, she would have to prove, first, the fact that Brutus stabbed her husband and, second, the further fact that Caesar's death was caused by the first fact of Brutus' stabbing; it would not be enough to show that Brutus betrayed Caesar, even

[19] FRIEDRICH TOEPEL, KAUSALITÄT UND PFLICHTWIDRIGKEITSZUSAMMENHANG BEIM FAHRLÄSSIGEN ERFOLGSDELIKT (1992).
[20] *But see* MACKIE, *supra,* note 1, at 54–5 (expressing the contrary view).
[21] MACKIE, *supra,* note 1, at 258–65.

though what Brutus did could be truthfully described as betrayal, because not all forms of betrayal will found tort actions.

In my view both events and facts can be causally connected; and in law, including tort law, both events and facts can be relevant. A plaintiff must (1) identify the *event* or *events* that give rise to his claim and (2) prove that the *fact* that the defendant acted in a certain way caused the harm of which he complains. He must point to the time, place, and persons involved, which can be described in a number of ways. But then he must go on to show that some specific aspect of the events he identifies (such as the fact that the defendant drove at an excessive speed) brings the defendant within the relevant legal category and supports the conclusion that his wrongful or risk-creating conduct caused the harm of which the plaintiff complains. He must show that the element that makes the conduct wrongful or creates the undue risk was relevant to the harmful outcome for which the law provides a remedy.

Thus, if the plaintiff alleges that the defendant drove at excessive speed he must show that the fact that he drove at that such-and-such a speed, *rather than at the proper speed,* was relevant to the fact that the plaintiff suffered such-and-such injuries. Though the incident in which the defendant is alleged to have driven at an excessive speed can be described in different ways—as Dan Dawes driving down Main Street, or as the engineer in the yellow Jersey hurrying to get home—these descriptions serve merely to identify the incident in issue. Again, if the plaintiff injured in an explosion relies on strict liability for the defendant's use of explosives, he must show that the fact that the defendant used explosives was relevant to the damage for which he seeks redress, though what the defendant did can be described in various other ways — quarrying for stone, or trying out a new fuse. Law is so structured that a plaintiff must prove a connection between the facts that specify those features of the events that are both causally relevant and legally relevant in other ways.

It follows that the law determines the way in which the causal inquiry is framed. Causal connection (in German terminology *Kausalzusammenhang*) cannot be separated in cases of fault liability from unlawful connection (*Rechtswidrigkeitszusammenhang*); their separation in the writings of some German theorists is in my view a source of error. The inquiry is into whether certain faulty conduct (or risk-creating conduct entailing strict liability) caused certain harm. In a country where liability for driving an automobile depends on negligence, the legal issue will be whether the fact that the defendant *drove negligently* (e.g., without keeping a proper lookout) caused the injuries. But in a jurisdiction where automobile liability is *strict*, the question will be whether the fact that the defendant *drove* caused the harm. The answer to these two questions may be different. The defendant's driving may have caused the injury, yet his negligent driving may not have done so because his negligence made no difference to the outcome; the same collision would have occurred had he driven carefully. In tort law, the issue is not the open-ended one 'What caused this harm?' but 'Did the fact that the defendant behaved in a certain *unlawful* or *undue* risk-creating way cause it?' The first question calls for an explanation of how the harm came about, the second for an assessment of the defendant's responsibility for conduct described in categories fixed by the law.

A good illustration is the case involving the navigation of a ship by an officer who was competent and experienced but who did not possess the certificate required by law.[22] The officer navigated negligently and the ship was involved in a collision. The defendants admitted that the negligent navigation caused the collision, but they denied that the lack of a certificate was causally relevant. Had it been relevant, the amount of damages would have been greater. Given that the basis of liability was fault, it was rightly held that the lack of a certificate was irrelevant, since the officer would have navigated no better had he possessed one.

The lack of a certificate, it seems to me, would have been causally relevant had it been the case that the officer was incompetent and that, in order to obtain a certificate, he would have had to acquire the necessary competence. On the other hand, had there been strict liability for navigating the ship without a certificate, so that if the ship was navigated by a pilot without a certificate the navigation was at the defendants' risk, the navigation would have been held to have caused the collision. Since strict liability is liability not for wrongful conduct, but for engaging in certain risk-creating activity, there would have been no need in this case to show that the lack of a certificate was causally relevant. In such a strict liability case, it would have been enough that, had the ship not been navigated by X (who did not in fact possess a certificate), no collision would have occurred. In the actual case, however, what explained the collision was the fact that the ship was *negligently* navigated, not that it was navigated. There is a distinction between conduct that counts as a cause in an explanatory inquiry, on the one hand, and conduct that is made by the law a basis of liability provided it is causally connected with the harm suffered, on the other.

This point is misunderstood by Wright[23] who thinks that the Hart and Honoré criteria of voluntary human action and abnormality (in the sense of actions or events that are unusual in the context), used to distinguish causes from mere causally relevant conditions, are meant to identify tortious conduct.[24] We are said to have difficulty in accommodating strict liability, where the conduct on which liability is based (e.g., using explosives)

---

[22] The Empire Jamaica [1955] P. 52. 57-8 (Probate, Divorce and Admiralty Division).
[23] *See* Wright, *Pruning, supra,* note 1, at 1014.
[24] They are, we argue, meant to identify the *limits* of responsibility in most cases: HART & HONORÉ (2d edn.), *supra,* note 6, at 68-81.

may not be either abnormal or voluntary in the sense of intended to do harm. But the role of our criteria is to mark a backward limit in explanatory causal inquiries and only a forward *limit* to whatever responsibility is appropriate under other, normative concepts of tort law. Our causal criteria are not a substitute for the other principles of tort law that define what conduct is wrongful or entails strict liability. That depends on positive law, and varies from system to system, some systems imposing strict liability or no liability in circumstances where others insist on fault (e.g., for auto accidents). It remains true, however, that often the law for good reason designates conduct as wrongful when it is intended to do harm or is a departure from a recognized norm. In this way wrongful conduct that causes harm often coincides with what would count as a causal explanation of the harm that ensues. But in cases of strict liability, where the wrongfulness of the defendant's conduct is not in issue, there is no occasion to trace a causal path from wrongfulness to the plaintiff's harm.

A third point is that, whichever theory we adopt, a hypothetical question must be put and answered. This involves a counterfactual proposition, namely that if a condition that in fact occurred had *not* occurred, the outcome would have been so-and-so.[25] On the but-for theory, we must ask whether in the circumstances the consequence would have occurred had the condition not occurred. On the NESS theory, we must ask whether in the circumstances the condition was a necessary member of a set of conditions that was together sufficient to produce the consequence, i.e., would the remaining set of conditions have produced the consequence in the absence of the condition in issue?

But to speak of the absence of a condition, or the hypothesis that it did not occur, can mislead. It suggests that the condition we are interested in can be notionally eliminated and that we can then calculate what would have happened if only the remaining circumstances had been present. Wright says that we hypothetically eliminate the condition being tested without adding or subtracting any other conditions.[26] This view of elimination also has adherents in German legal theory, partly because theorists there tend to separate causal connection from unlawful connection. If this were the right way to test a causal hypothesis, we should indeed be comparing the real world with an imaginary world. For in the real world conduct is often a choice between alternatives. If John had not done so-and-so, he would have done something else. If he had not intervened, someone else might have, perhaps in a different way. Sometimes these alternatives would have had a bearing on the course of events we are investigating. Mackie rightly says that both necessity in the strong sense and sufficiency in the strong sense (viz., both the but-for and NESS theories) 'involve assertions

---

[25] Wright, *Pruning, supra,* note 1, at 1039–42.   [26] *Id.* at 1041–2.

about how the world would have run on if something different had been done'.[27]

But this is rather loosely expressed, for it leaves open the question, 'what *is* the something different that we must suppose to have been done?'[28] In many contexts the answer is, 'whatever in the circumstances would have occurred had the condition in question not occurred'. Sometimes there is no reason to suppose that *anything* causally relevant would have occurred in that event, and then it *looks* as if the condition in issue is simply being eliminated as causally relevant. John dropped a lighted match on some brushwood. Did he cause the destruction of the forest? To test this, we ask whether, if John had *not* dropped the lighted match, the forest fire would have occurred anyway. We begin by supposing the contradictory of the condition, viz., 'John did *not* drop the lighted match'. Often it is clear that, had he not dropped the match, whatever else would have happened would not have resulted in a fire. But the position would be different if we knew that, had John not dropped a match, David would have done so anyway. In that case, though John will indeed have destroyed the forest, he destroyed a forest that was anyhow doomed, and that may affect the forest-owner's claim. However, there usually is no reason to suppose any such alternative event and therefore no need *expressly* to substitute anything for the condition eliminated.

But this notion, that we do not substitute anything for the condition whose causal relevance we are testing, is an illusion. Suppose we want to test the assertion that Churchill kept Britain in the war in 1940. Was the fact that he was Prime Minister the cause of Britain remaining in the war? Here we cannot eliminate Churchill without substituting another Prime Minister whose hypothetical conduct of affairs would have had a bearing on whether Britain remained in the war. The contradictory of 'Churchill was Prime Minister', viz., 'Churchill was *not* Prime Minister', would have implied in the world of 1940 that someone else was Prime Minister (say Halifax); and we must then ask whether that person would have wanted and been able to convince Parliament and the British people to continue the war. The causal statement about Churchill implicitly contrasts him with this hypothetical substitute. Logically, 'Churchill was not Prime Minister in 1940' is also compatible with there being no Prime Minister at all. But it is the real world, not an imaginary world or a logical calculus, that determines what is implied in the context by the contradictory of the condition in question, and what should therefore be substituted for it in testing the counterfactual proposition. In that real world, had Churchill not been Prime

---

[27] MACKIE, *supra*, note 1, at 52.

[28] For the reasons given in the text, Wright's view and that of DAVID K. LEWIS, COUNTERFACTUALS (1973), 72–7 are unsatisfactory.

Minister, someone else would have held that office. And the someone else might or might not have kept Britain in the war.

In a legal context, the same approach may be applied, except that when the inquiry concerns the causal relevance of *wrongful* conduct, as is usual in tort claims, we must substitute for the wrongful conduct of the defendant *rightful* conduct on his part.[29] That is, when liability is based on fault, the comparison is not with what would have happened had the defendant *done nothing*, but what would have happened had he *acted properly*. The reason for making this substitution is similar to that in Churchill's case. The contradictory of 'the defendant acted wrongfully' is 'the defendant did not act wrongfully', and this is logically quite unspecific; for instance, it is compatible with his doing nothing. Once more we must turn to the features of the real world—in this case, the world of positive tort law—which tells us that what is implied by his not acting wrongfully is his acting rightfully. The reason why this is the appropriate substitution is that the aim of the legal inquiry is to discover not whether the defendant's *conduct* as such made a difference to the outcome, but whether the fact that it was *wrongful* did so.

Again, tort law normally requires the plaintiff to show that the wrongful *aspect* of the defendant's conduct was causally connected with the harm.[30] To eliminate driving at an excessive speed therefore requires us to substitute for the excessive speed driving at a proper speed, and then to ask whether that conduct would have led to the injuries that in fact occurred. Moreover, the hypothesis of rightful conduct involves supposing, not merely that the defendant drove at a proper speed, but also that the likely consequences of his doing so be taken into account. For example, if the pedestrian who was run over would have seen the defendant's automobile coming in time to avoid it, had the defendant been driving at a reasonable pace, this must be taken into account. In the same way, if someone other than Churchill had been in office, his colleagues would have been less afraid of contradicting him, and this must be taken into account in answering the historical question about 1940. In most legal contexts, the hypothetical inquiry requires that all conditions be kept steady except that we substitute rightful conduct *and* its likely consequences for the wrongful conduct of which the defendant is alleged to have been guilty.

---

[29] HART & HONORÉ (2d edn.), *supra*, note 6, at lviii–lx, 411–14; TOEPEL, *supra*, note 19, at 106.

[30] This is not the case if the law provides that, if the defendant acts unlawfully, he acts at his risk. Then, as in cases of strict liability, it has only to be shown that his action was causally connected with the harm, not that the wrongful aspect of it was so connected. HART & HONORÉ (2d edn.), *supra*, note 6, at lx–lxi. And of course there are torts, such as trespass, in which harm need not be proved.

In the context of strict liability, however, the inquiry is more like that in the dropped match case.[31] Substitution of lawful conduct is not possible and is not required in cases of strict liability, since the defendant's conduct, though it creates a risk, is not unlawful unless it causes harm. In such a case, the hypothetical inquiry thus must be whether the plaintiff would have suffered injury had the defendant not engaged in the activity (e.g., using explosives) that entails strict liability. There is normally no reason to suppose that, if the defendant had not used explosives for blasting, he or someone else would then and there have injured the plaintiff by some other means.

Both inside and outside the law, therefore, the purpose of the inquiry determines how we should frame the hypothesis to be tested. Tort law lays down what counts as wrongful conduct or conduct entailing strict liability and so what the plaintiff has to prove. It aims to protect people against wrongful infringement of their rights and exposure to undue danger. So, to ascertain whether an infringement has occurred, the wrongful conduct of the defendant must normally be compared with the notional rightful conduct that the plaintiff was entitled to expect in the circumstances. The question is whether the difference between the wrongful conduct that occurred in the real world and the rightful conduct (together with its likely consequences) that we imagine as occurring would have led to a different result in the hypothetical world that resembles the real world in all other respects. In the strict liability context, where the law protects against risks created by *lawful* conduct on the part of others, the causal inquiry is adapted to that aim.

Does the fact that in tort law we normally compare wrongful with rightful conduct show that the causal question is a *normative* question in disguise? It does not, for the inquiry into what would have occurred had the defendant obeyed a legal norm is no more normative than the question what would have occurred had the Prime Minister been someone other than Churchill. The answer to these causal inquires has no normative component. It remains the same even if we suppose that it would have been better for Britain to make peace in 1940, or that it would be better, in order to combat over-population, for those who drive automobiles to drive blindfold.

There are those who think that counterfactual propositions cannot be true or false.[32] The tort process however assumes, in my view rightly, that they can be. We can often know what, on a certain hypothesis, would probably happen in the real world. We know that if we strike a match under certain conditions a flame will appear. The statement, 'if a match is struck

---

[31] The dropped match incident might crop up in the context of negligence in tort law. In that case the comparison would be between the defendant's dropping the match and his exercising due care in regard to the match, e.g. by putting it out before throwing it away.

[32] MACKIE, *supra*, note 1, at 54; TOEPEL, *supra*, note 19, at 55.

under conditions XYZ a flame will appear', can be true or false and its truth value can be tested. Why not, also, 'if a match had been struck . . . a flame would have appeared'? The only difference is that the proposition about the past can be verified only indirectly, on the assumption that in similar conditions similar results recur. This assumption cannot itself be verified, but unless it is well-founded we cannot rely on causal regularities or scientific laws. Of course we are often uncertain what would have happened on a given occasion had the defendant acted lawfully. In such a case, though the counterfactual statement 'had X not done what he did Y would not have been harmed' is in principle still true or false, we cannot tell for certain which it is. We must then have recourse to rules of law that instruct the judge or jury to go by the probabilities and, if necessary, to fall back on rules about the burden of proof.

III. NESS VERSUS BUT-FOR: DIFFERENCES IN THE THEORIES

I now turn to some of the examples that supporters of the NESS and but-for theories interpret differently. Some concern over-determination, others indeterminacy. Over-determination cases, it will be recalled, involve two or more independent acts each of which alone would have sufficed to bring about the harm. In such cases, the separate causal processes may be similar or different, and they may culminate in harm either at the same time or successively. When (1) similar causal processes culminate in harm at the same time, the NESS and but-for theories point to different causal conclusions. But when (2) the causal processes are different or (3) one culminates in harm before the other, they point to the same casual conclusion. In cases of (4) causing or inducing people to act, neither theory is adequate, but the notion of sufficiency, in a modified form, explains why these cases are thought of as causal or quasi-causal relations.

A. Over-determination: Similar Causal Processes Culminating at the Same Time

Two similar causal processes may culminate in the same harm at the same time. Two shots, negligently but independently fired by A and B when out hunting, simultaneously hit C and destroy his left eye. Each shot was sufficient to do this without the other, and the effects of the two shots cannot be distinguished. Neither shot was necessary in the strong but-for sense, but each was necessary in the weak sense that it was a necessary member of a set of conditions together sufficient to destroy the victim's eye.[33] It

---

[33] Necessity in this weak sense is described above. See *supra*, text accompanying note 4.

would be counter-intuitive to hold that *neither A nor B* is responsible for the loss of *C's* eye. But is that because legal policy, or intuitions about 'responsibility', lead us to disregard the lack of causal connection between each shot and the loss of the eye?

Mackie, supporting the but-for theory, argues that when this type of over-determination is present the cause of the harm consists in the acts of *A* and *B* taken as a *cluster*.[34] In the absence of *both* acts, *C's* eyesight would not have been lost. But it makes no sense, he thinks, to ask which was the cause. Perhaps not, but why need we ask which was *the* cause? Cannot each shot have been *a* cause of the loss of eyesight in a sense adequate both to explain what happened causally and to ascribe responsibility to *A* and *B*? It seems that, in Mackie's view, if *A* and *B* are held liable in tort or criminal law this must be based on a legal policy that overrides the lack of causal connection, or it must rest on a special *legal* concept of cause. Indeed he says, 'whatever our actual concept may be, it is obvious that we can construct causal concepts as we wish, which may be useful for particular purposes.'[35] It is worth asking, therefore, whether in such cases of simultaneous over-determination lawyers resort to a special *legal* notion of cause.

Our concepts are tools shaped by the purposes for which we use them. Causation is used mainly for three purposes: to provide recipes, to explain events, and to allot responsibility. Its roots probably lie in the first of these. Even non-human primates develop recipes for what they want. To crack a nut, you need a stone of a certain size and weight and you must bring it down on the nut with a certain force. You learn to construct what your sophisticated cousins of a later age will call a set of conditions together sufficient to produce a given result, nut-cracking. Having assembled what seems to be a set of sufficient conditions, you whittle them down by eliminating those that trial and error show to be unnecessary. It turns out to be necessary that the stone be of a certain weight, that a certain degree of force be employed, and that the nutshell be not too thick, but unnecessary that the wind lie in a northerly direction or that the agent utter a blood-curdling whoop. The recipe is general, built up over time as instances accumulate and conditions are tested.

The discovery of conditions that are necessary members of a set sufficient to produce some result can be used to *explain* events as well as to bring them about. It can extend to events over which we have no control. We seek to discover the conditions of these events, perhaps in order to control similar events in the future, or simply to understand how the universe works. The knowledge thus acquired may come in handy, but it may be pursued for its own sake. It can be used to trace the effects of natural events

---

[34] MACKIE, *supra*, note 1, at 47. *See also*, TOEPEL, *supra*, note 19, at 71–2, 84.
[35] MACKIE, *supra*, note 1, at 58.

and inanimate forces. It can also be used to *assign responsibility*—social accountability—to human beings for the outcome of their conduct.

For all these purposes—making recipes, explaining events, and attributing responsibility—we can use the concept of the necessary members of a set of conditions together sufficient to produce a result of a given type, though we may not be able to specify or quantify all the conditions. This limited ability to specify conditions does not prevent our using causal ideas to explain events backwards in terms of previous events and conditions or to allot responsibility for conduct forward in terms of outcomes. These are not normative functions. It makes no difference whether the events to be explained, or the conduct to be assessed, is judged good or bad. It is the normative aspect of tort law, not the concept of cause, that invites us to focus on the nature and legal consequence of wrongful conduct.

What bearing has this on the problem of over-determination? The lesson is surely that the NESS test is not confined to the context of responsibility in general or tort law in particular. To revert to the two independent shots by *A* and *B* that put out *C's* eye, the acts of *A* and *B* each exemplify how to put *C's* left eye out, if that was, perhaps, the objective of snipers in a military campaign. Each shot also provides an explanation of *C's* loss of his left eye. Why, then, should not each provide a basis for assigning legal and moral responsibility to *A* and *B*? No recourse to legal policy, or to normative considerations, is needed to reach the conclusion that both A and B independently caused the harm to *C*. None of the purposes for which causal concepts are used requires us to adopt the but-for theory. There can be different recipes for attaining a given type of result, more than one of which is used on a given occasion. There can be different explanations of an event of a given type in terms of prior or concurrent conditions, more than one of which is present on a given occasion. To prevent the construction of a brick wall, one recipe is to withhold bricks, another to withhold mortar. If *A* withholds bricks and *B* independently withholds mortar, and the wall is not built or not built on time, have not both *A* and *B* prevented its construction? We do not need a special 'legal' concept of cause to deal with simultaneous over-determination by similar causal processes.

Toepel in the context of criminal law denies that either *A* or *B* is responsible for putting out *C's* left eye in a case like the shooting case.[36] Apart from pointing to the presumption of innocence, he argues that it is arbitrary to disregard *B's* shot when deciding whether *A's* was a necessary member of a set of conditions sufficient to produce the harm, and vice versa. The answer to this objection is that *B's* shot can be provisionally disregarded when we are considering the set of conditions of which *A's* shot is a member because that set *may* be sufficient without *B's* shot. The proper

---

[36] TOEPEL, *supra*, note 19, at 66, 72–5.

preliminary procedure in investigating the cause of a physical sequence of events is to assemble a set of conditions apparently sufficient to produce and hence explain the result. This we do in the light of what we know to be INUS conditions of results of that type.[37] But the set we provisionally assemble may contain some conditions that turn out to have been unnecessary for the result.

For example, the provisional set of conditions might consist of *A's* shot, the distance between *A* and *C*, the strength of the wind, the color of *A's* jacket, and *B's* shot. We then reduce the set by eliminating those conditions that were not necessary to it. This disposes of the color of *A's* jacket. *B's* shot we provisionally eliminate not because it was clearly not necessary but because our knowledge of causal regularities and scientific laws leads us to think that *A's* shot *may* have been sufficient to put *C's* eye out without *B's*. Having reduced the set so far, we then test the relevance of *A's* shot (more precisely, the fact that *A* shot negligently) by hypothetically substituting, for *A's* negligent shot, his taking proper care in shooting. We ask whether in that event *C* would have lost his eye from that set of conditions. If not, *A's* negligent shooting was a cause of *C's* loss of eyesight. But suppose that careful investigation shows that *A's* shot *missed*. In that case *A's* shot was not causally relevant to the outcome and we must construct another set of conditions, including *B's* shot, and test whether *B's* shot was a necessary member of that set of conditions which together produced the loss of eyesight. Toepel objects that this procedure involves deciding that *A's* shot was causally relevant before we test it for causal relevance.[38] That is not so. All we have decided before testing *A's* shot for relevance while provisionally omitting *B's* is that, as we know some of the INUS conditions for loss of eyesight, *A's* shot *may* on this occasion have been a causally relevant condition even in the absence of *B's* shot. It is true that the testing procedure is possible only if we know some causal regularities before we start. But we need not assume from the start that the outcome of the test will be positive.

A similar causal over-determination analysis may be applied to other cases in which two or more similar processes appear responsible for an event, for example, where two fires merge and jointly culminate in harm,[39] or where the pollution created by a number of persons independently pollutes a stream or lake.[40]

B. *Over-determination: Different Causal Processes*

In other over-determination cases the two sets of conditions involve qualitatively different causal processes, such as poisoning and dehydration, the

---

[37] See *supra*, notes 8–15 and accompanying text.
[38] TOEPEL, *supra*, note 19, at 69.
[39] Wright, *Pruning, supra*, note 1, at 1018, 1022.
[40] *See generally id.* at 1035–7.

various stages of which have been studied and can be distinguished. In that case, if we know enough about the stages by which the events came about we can generally tell, even in cases of over-determination, which causal process ran its course and which was frustrated. So in the case of the desert traveller[41]—where *A* poisons *C's* water keg, *B* empties the keg before *C* drinks the poisoned water, and *C* dies of thirst—it now seems to me that *B* causes *C's* death. I regret that, despite criticism by Mackie,[42] since endorsed by Wright,[43] the second edition of Hart and Honoré resisted this conclusion.[44] My current reasoning is that *B's* conduct introduces a condition, lack of water, that in the circumstances, including the absence of an alternative water supply, is sufficient to bring about and does bring about *C's* death from dehydration.

It is also true that *B* saved *C* from dying of poison. But this is not relevant in an explanatory inquiry, since *B's* act adequately explains how *C's* death came about (through dehydration), nor should it be relevant in a wrongful death action or prosecution for homicide. If *B*, not realizing that the water keg was poisoned, emptied it intending to harm *C* or negligently failing in his duty of care to *C*, the deceased's widow ought therefore to succeed in a wrongful death action[45]—though since *C* was doomed in any event the damages will be minimal. On the other hand, if *B* realized that the water was poisoned and emptied the keg to prevent *C* drinking the poisoned water, and believing that an alterative supply could be found in time to save *C*, *B* would still unintentionally have 'caused' *C's* death; but he would not be legally responsible for doing so. There is no need to postulate any special legal concept of cause in order to understand this type of case.

In cases of over-determination, where different causal processes are associated with the two conditions that are causal candidates, there should be no need to show that one of them was a NESS condition of death *as and how the death occurred* (e.g. by dehydration on Tuesday rather than by poisoning on Monday).[46] That would be to require establishing the very point in issue, namely how the victim's death came about. What has to be shown in a tort action is that the defendant's wrongful act caused the harm, in this· case the victim's death. We know from the way in which the law structures actions for wrongful death that what is legally relevant is death, not death

---

[41] *See* James A. McLaughlin, *Proximate Cause*, 39 HARV. L. REV. 149, 155, note 25 (1925–6); HART & HONORÉ (2d edn.), *supra*, note 6, at 239–41; MACKIE, *supra*, note 1, at 44–6.

[42] MACKIE, *supra*, note 1, at 44, 46–7.

[43] Wright, *Pruning, supra*, note 1, at 1024.

[44] HART & HONORÉ, *supra*, note 4, at 219–20; HART & HONORÉ (2d edn.), *supra*, note 6, at 239–41. *See* Mackie, *supra*, note 1, at 45–6.

[45] And, if the harm was intentional, *B* will be guilty of homicide.

[46] As suggested by Mackie, *supra*, note 1, at 46; TOEPEL, *supra*, note 19, at 70, 78–9.

at this or that time or place or by this or that process.[47] However, the plaintiff (the widow) has to *identify* the death for which she claims redress. This requires that the victim, time, and place be specified. She also has to show that the defendant's wrongful act *caused* the death, which involves showing that *some* causal process initiated by the defendant brought it about. In the water keg example, that *B's* conduct (in emptying the water keg) was a condition of *C's* death by dehydration is relevant because the process of dehydration connects *B's* act by a series of stages with *C's* death. To establish that this process occurred is relevant because, given the plurality of possible causes of death, it is necessary for *C's* widow to point to a specific causal process that links the two, and dehydration is such a process.

C. Over-determination: Harm that Has Already Occurred

Although philosophers may debate the possibility of backward causation, it seems clear that it is impossible to cause an event that has already occurred. One can flog a dead horse but not kill it. On the other hand one can kill someone who has only a moment to live, as in the case where defendants were alleged to have negligently electrocuted the deceased boy as he fell to certain death.[48] The fact that our concept of cause does not allow for causing harm that has already occurred can give rise to a problem of over-determination when the harm consists of depriving someone of future opportunities.

Suppose that *A* negligently injures *C*, a wrestler, so that he is permanently disabled from wrestling. Six months later *B* independently and negligently runs *C* over so that, even had he not been injured the first time, he would not have been able to wrestle in future.[49] That *B's* act was independent implies that the first injury did not contribute to the second, for example by preventing *C* from avoiding the second accident. What is the status of *C's* claim to loss of future earnings as a wrestler? *A*, and only *A*, is clearly responsible for what *C* would have earned in the six months following the first injury. As regards *C's* lost wrestling earnings following the second injury, however, responsibility is much less clear. *B* will plead that he did not cause *C's* disability as a wrestler even in part since *C* was permanently disabled already. Yet *A* will plead that his liability is limited to the six months' earnings alone since, as it turns out, *C* would not have been able to wrestle for more than that period in any event. If both of these arguments are accepted, *C*, having been wrongfully injured on two occasions,

[47] Wright, *Causation, supra,* note 16, at 1777–8; Wright, *Pruning, supra,* note 1, at 1025–6; Puppe, *Der Erfolg, supra,* note 18, at 863, 867–8.
[48] Dillon v. Twin State Gas & Elec. Co., 163 A. 111 (N.H. 1932).
[49] The facts are suggested by Baker v. Willoughby [1970] A.C. 467; *cf.* Jobling v. Associated Dairies [1982] A.C. 794.

obtains less than had he been injured only once, which is unsatisfactory. Yet this is not like the case of simultaneous over-determination where each agent can properly be said to have caused the same injury. Someone who claims to have lost future opportunities of earning money must show that he would have been able to take advantage of those opportunities in the absence of the wrongful act of which he complains. For example, if after six months *C* had died of a heart attack, not brought on by the earlier injury inflicted by *A*, his estate could not claim loss of earnings for the period after he was dead. A dead man cannot wrestle, and there is no reason to impose on *A* the risk that *C* could die of natural causes unconnected with *A*'s wrongful act.

There are two possible ways round this difficulty, one of which is consistent with causal principles while the other rests on a basis of risk-allocation. The first solution is to hold that there is a cause of action in tort law for depriving someone by a wrongful act of a *tort remedy* that would otherwise have been available to him. In the injured wrestler case, *B* has deprived *C* of a tort remedy against *A* for his lost wrestling earnings following the second injury. This cause of action, if it existed, would be like the suggested remedy, now much discussed, against a defendant who wrongfully deprives a plaintiff of a chance.[50] The alternative way of solving the injured wrestler conundrum is to treat *A* as guaranteeing *C* that he will not be deprived of his prospective remedy for loss of earnings by a later wrongful act of someone else. To construct such a guarantee is to provide a non-causal basis of liability, an example of the familiar principle by which the risk of harm to *C* is sometimes placed on *A*. Here the risk would be imposed on *A* as a result of *A*'s wrongdoing, just as in the law of sales risk is sometimes transferred to the seller because of his failure to deliver goods on time. The justification for putting the risk on *A* would be that it is the function of the law to protect people against wrongful invasions of their rights. Rather than let a person who has suffered two wrongs go without remedy, it is better to make the first wrongdoer guarantee him against the economic consequences of a later tort by some third person. To do this would not be to introduce a special legal sense of cause. It would be to substitute, for liability based on causing harm, liability based on risk-allocation.

D. Indeterminacy

Indeterminacy presents a difficulty for the NESS theory. If the world is indeterminate, we cannot assemble a set of conditions invariably sufficient

---

[50] *See* Wright, *Pruning, supra,* note 1, at 1067–72. A 'lost chance' case may arise, for example, if a doctor negligently fails to diagnose a progressive disease such as cancer in a timely manner, and so deprives the patient of, say, a 20 per cent chance of recovery. Causes of action along these lines, whatever their intrinsic merits, do no violence to causal principles.

to produce a given outcome. The outcome may usually follow, but there will be occasions when it does not. At most there may be a certain probability that on a given occasion the outcome will follow. An indeterminate world also presents a difficulty for the but-for theory, since in an indeterminate world we cannot accurately calculate what would have happened in the absence of a particular wrongful act. But, if it is permissible with Mackie to fall back on our intuitive grasp of but-for relationships,[51] the difficulty is less serious for the but-for than for the NESS theory.

Mackie, though leaving open whether the world really is indeterminate, argues that what we would say about causation in an indeterminate world supports the but-for theory.[52] He imagines two candy machines, both 'indeterministic'.[53] One never produces candy unless the proper coin is inserted, but does not always produce candy when it is. The other always produces candy when a coin is inserted, but sometimes does so without a coin. Applying the but-for test, Mackie thinks that we would say of the first machine that it caused the candy to appear when it did appear, but deny this for the second machine.

Mackie's argument is not convincing.[54] If we thought that the candy machine world was indeterminate we would have no reason to suppose that the first machine would not in the future behave like the second machine and produce candy without a coin being inserted, and vice versa for the second machine. We would have no reason to conclude that the insertion of the coin caused the candy to appear in the one machine but not in the other. But, though their operation may be erratic, we believe that candy machines are deterministic.[55] We explain their deviant behavior on the basis that, if the machine does not produce candy when a coin is inserted or does produce it when a coin is not inserted, the mechanism is faulty. In the first case, a counteracting factor is present; something in the machine has jammed and prevents the candy from emerging. Recall that in most sets of jointly sufficient conditions one condition is the absence of counteracting conditions.[56] In the second case, given the plurality of causes, we conclude that an alternative set of INUS conditions for the production of candy is present, which might consist for example in giving the machine a hefty kick when the mechanism is jammed.

The argument from an imagined indeterminate world does not support the but-for theory. What of the argument that the world really *is* indeter-

---

[51] *See supra,* text accompanying note 15.   [52] TOEPEL, *supra,* note 19, at 61, 90–5.

[53] MACKIE, *supra,* note 1, at 40–3, 47. By 'indeterministic' Mackie appears to mean 'indeterminate'.

[54] HART & HONORÉ (2d edn.), *supra,* note 6, at 124–5, 235 n. 56; Wright, *Pruning, supra,* note 1, at 1029; Wright, *Causation, supra,* note 16, at 1777–8; *cf.* F. TOEPEL, *supra,* note 19, at 92–3.

[55] Wright, *Pruning, supra,* note 1, at 1029.

[56] *See supra,* notes 11–12 and accompanying text.

minate? The micro-level indeterminacy associated with quantum mechanics is not in point. As Wright neatly observes, indeterminacy at this micro-level might be an obstacle to actions between fundamental particles, but it does not affect the macro-phenomena which are the law's concern. More baffling is the difficulty of tracing causal connection or something like it with human actions done for reasons—when one person provides another with a reason for doing so-and-so.[57] Although we have up to now discussed physical sequences of events as if they took place untroubled by human intervention, there are in practice few situations in tort law where a physical sequence of events is not partly determined by human decisions taken in the light of a situation as it develops.

To take an example, adapted from Mackie,[58] suppose the question is whether Alec's statement caused Bill to hit Charles. If Alec said, for instance, that Charles was having an affair with Bill's girlfriend, it would be intelligible that what he said caused Bill to hit Charles. If one objects to the use of 'caused' in a context where Bill should have controlled himself, other expressions such as 'led', 'induced', and 'provoked' could replace it. This situation is of a general type that often arises in tort law, for example in connection with false statements that induce others to invest money or persuasions that lead contracting parties to break their contracts. How should sequences of this sort, which involve providing reasons on which others act, be analyzed?

It seems impossible to suppose a set of NESS conditions that would together be sufficient to produce Bill's assault on Charles. Many people believe that human conduct is not strictly determined. If so, one cannot even in principle assemble a set of conditions sufficient to induce a person to act in a particular way. Even if human action is determined, it will still not be possible to assemble a set of conditions of this sort. This is not merely because the reactions of human beings vary. A greater difficulty is that a person who has been confronted with a similar set of conditions in the past may, in the light of that experience, react differently on this occasion. It does not follow from Bill's reaction on this occasion that he would react similarly if told the same thing again. Nor does it follow that David would react in the same way if Alec told him the same thing about *his* (David's) girlfriend. Even with a great deal of information about people's characters and background, their reactions simply are not totally predictable. Moreover, any prediction, if known by the person about whom it is made, may provide a reason for reacting differently.

[57] HART & HONORÉ (2d edn.), *supra,* note 6, at 51–61. For want of space I do not deal in this chapter with the provision of opportunities which another person exploits or the furnishing of help of which another takes advantage. These are important legally and in ordinary life but are still more remote from physical sequences than is acting on a reason provided by another.

[58] MACKIE, *supra,* note 1, at 43.

Thus, determinism in regard to human conduct, even if true, cannot reliably be *tested*. Yet Bill's reaction is *explained* by what Alec said to him, and to that extent functions as a causal (or quasi-causal) explanation. What Alec said was in some sense sufficient in the circumstances to lead Bill to react as he did. Yet if we are to speak either of 'causing' people to act or, more modestly, of influencing them in their decisions, a different account of the connection is called for.

Mackie thinks that our attitude to interpersonal transactions favors the but-for theory.[59] Had Alec not said what he did, we may be sure that Bill would not have hit Charles. But how can we tell this? Presumably because we have assembled, from our experience and that of others, not sets of INUS conditions relating to human behavior, but some loose generalizations that tell us what sorts of reasons people act on. In the present case, the only reason that could explain Bill's attack was what Alec said to him. If Bill admits that this was why he struck Charles, the diagnosis is confirmed.

But this is not enough to show that the but-for theory explains the sort of connection involved in acting for a reason. For a person usually has two or more (typically many more) reasons for reaching a decision and acting on it. A potential investor may be influenced by a false statement in a prospectus and by advice from his stockbroker. Suppose that for these two reasons he makes an ill-fated investment in Eldorado Mines. Nothing turns, it seems to me, on whether each reason was necessary or sufficient to persuade him to invest, or to dissuade him from changing his mind.[60] Would we conclude that the false prospectus did not induce him to make the investment if the advice from the stockbroker was also sufficient to persuade him to do so? If the investor is prepared to say truthfully that each of the reasons influenced him, it seems immaterial whether he is also prepared to say that, but for one of them, he would not have reached the decision he did. The reasons on which he decides and acts are precisely that—the *reasons* that, either individually or jointly, appeared to him sufficient and motivated him to decide and act.

Sam is offered a post in Middletown at an increased salary. Middletown is his wife's home town so that she wishes to return there to live. Both of these factors—the increased salary and his wife's wishes—may be reasons sufficient to induce Sam to accept the offer, in which case neither is a but-for reason. Or both may be necessary elements in a set of reasons together sufficient to persuade Sam to accept the offer. In either case, Sam acts on

---

[59] *Id.* at 131–6.

[60] *See* Australian Steel & Mining Corp. Pty. v. Corben, 2 N.S.W.R. 202, 209 (1974); HART & HONORÉ (2d edn.), *supra,* note 6, at 193; compare for criminal law, judgment of Feb. 24, 1959, BGH Gr. Sen. St., 13 Entscheidungen des Bundesgerichtshofes in Strafsachen [BGHSt] 15 (F.R.G.); *contra,* TOEPEL, *supra,* note 19, at 93.

these two reasons, which are either singly or jointly sufficient to persuade him. But along with these *reasons* that induce him to go to Middletown, there will be other *conditions* such that, had they not existed, he would have refused the offer. There are good schools in Middletown for the children; Middletown has a lively choral society. Had there not been good schools and a lively choral society, Sam would have refused the offer; but they were not his *reasons* for accepting. So far as these reasons are concerned, he might just as well have stayed where he was. But-for reasons are often not reasons *for* making a decision or acting on it, but are reasons *against not* making it. They do not cause, lead, induce, or prompt Sam to move, any more than the investor's possession of investment funds, or the existence of the capitalist system, induces him to put his money in Eldorado Mines.

It seems to me that we reach our conclusions about what caused, induced, persuaded, or provoked someone to act as he did in a way somewhat like but not identical with the way in which we reach conclusions about the causes of physical events. We cannot construct INUS conditions and NESS conditions for situations in which human beings make and act on decisions. But we know enough about the sorts of reasons that motivate us to be able often to conclude that certain factors were singly or together sufficient for the decision. All that is meant by 'sufficient' in this context is that they provide an adequate explanation of the decision and that the person who makes the decision would acknowledge, if truthful, that these were his reasons. They were sufficient for this individual in this situation, though there is no implication that they would be sufficient for him or anyone else in a similar situation on another occasion. What we mean when we speak of 'inducing', 'persuading', etc. is to refer to reasons that seemed adequate to this person on this occasion and on which he therefore acted. Some or all of them may also have been 'necessary' to the decision; and it is often a good procedure heuristically to ask whether the same decision would have been reached in the absence of a given reason. But the answer to this but-for question is not decisive of the existence of a causal or quasi-causal relation between reason and action. It is no part of the meaning of 'cause', 'induce', etc. in interpersonal transactions that the person concerned would not have acted as he did apart from the conduct of the person who is said to have induced him to act. The meaning of causal or quasi-causal connection is here closer to sufficiency that to necessity, but sufficiency not in the sense in which that term is used in regard to physical sequences, but rather in the sense of what someone regards as an adequate ground on which to decide and act in the circumstances.

IV. CONCLUSION

Why is causation important in tort law? One reason is that to insist on causal connection between conduct and harm ensures that in general we impose liability only on those who, by intervening in the world, have changed the course of events for the worse. But what is it to change the course of events for the worse? Is it to do (1) something such that in the conditions prevailing harm comes about, or (2) something in the absence of which harm would not have come about? The first interpretation is that of the NESS theory (for physical sequences); and a variant of that theory can be used to explain what it is to influence human decisions and actions. The second interpretation is that of the but-for theory.

The first interpretation is to be preferred. Causing a given harmful result means, in relation to physical events, completing a set of conditions sufficient to bring it about, i.e., providing a NESS condition of that harm. In relation to influencing human action, it means providing a reason that the human agent accepts, often along with other reasons, as sufficient to induce him to decide and act as he does (to his or someone else's detriment).

On the other hand the but-for theory, though a useful heuristic device, provides the intuitively wrong answer in certain cases of over-determination and indeterminacy. The explanation for this seems to be that our concept of cause derives ultimately from our search for recipes to bring about the outcomes we want. We look for sets of conditions that are sufficient (or, in the case of human decisions, that may be regarded by the agent as sufficient) to bring about a certain outcome. Knowledge of these sets of conditions, though nearly always imperfect, has many applications. In particular, it often enables us to explain puzzling events and, in many contexts of law, including tort law, to fix the outer limits of social responsibility for conduct.

That does not make the concept of cause a normative one. The same concept of cause is used for discovering recipes, for explaining events, and for assigning responsibility for outcomes. The normative elements are supplied by substantive tort law, which defines the conduct that entails or may entail tort liability and prescribes when causal connection between conduct and harm must be proved.

Moments of Carelessness and Massive Loss

JEREMY WALDRON*

I. Fate, Fortune & Hurt

Two drivers, named Fate and Fortune, were on a city street one morning in their automobiles. Both were driving at or near the speed limit, Fortune a little ahead of Fate. As they passed through a shopping district, each took his eyes off the road, turning his head for a moment to look at the bargains advertised in a storefront window. (The last day of a sale was proclaimed, with 25 per cent off the price of a pair of men's shoes.) In Fortune's case, this momentary distraction passed without event. The road was straight, the traffic in front of him was proceeding smoothly, and after a few seconds he returned his eyes to his driving and completed his journey without incident. Fate, however, was not so fortunate. Distracted by the bargain advertised in the shoe store, he failed to notice that the traffic ahead of him had slowed down. His car ploughed into a motorcycle ridden by a Mr. Hurt. Hurt was flung from the motorcycle and gravely injured. His back was broken so badly that he would spend the rest of his life in a wheelchair. Fate stopped immediately of course to summon help, and when the police arrived he readily admitted that he had been driving carelessly.

When Hurt recovered consciousness in hospital, the first thing he did was instruct his lawyers to sue Fate for negligence. Considering the extent of his injury, the sum he sought was quite modest—$5 million dollars to cover his medical costs, to compensate him for the extreme pain in which he would live for the rest of his life, and to make up for the earnings he could have expected from the career he was pursuing at the time. But modest or not, it was sufficient to bankrupt Mr. Fate—who, after leaving the scene of the accident and giving all his details to the proper authorities, returned to the store that had distracted him in the first place so that he could save $50 off the price of a pair of Florsheim shoes. In fact, between them, Mr. Fate and Mr. Fortune (who, oblivious to the accident, had also returned to the store) bought the last two pairs of shoes that were available at the reduced price.

* Professor of Law and Philosophy, Jurisprudence & Social Policy Program, Boalt Hall, University of California, Berkeley.

II. Fairness Preliminaries

Most of us would say it is only fair that Hurt should win his lawsuit: justice demands that Fate compensate him for the injury he caused. It is difficult, however, to go beyond this intuition and explain exactly why it is fair that Fate should be expected to come up with a sum of money this large.

Consider how the parties have been left. Apart from the lawsuit, two things have happened as a result of Fate's negligent driving: Fate is $50 better off, and Hurt is $5 million worse off. As a result of the lawsuit, however, and assuming $5 million damages is assessed by the court and paid by Fate, then Hurt will be left roughly as well off as he was before the incident, and Fate will be $4,999,950 out of pocket. Fate, in short, will be ruined. It is hard to explain why this is the fair price of a moment's carelessness.

The difficulty is exacerbated when we consider the other driver, Mr. Fortune. In terms of conduct and gain, Fortune's situation is exactly similar to that of Fate. He took his eyes off the road for the same amount of time, violating the same duty of care owed to other road users, for the sake of exactly the same advantage—a $50 savings on a pair of shoes. No one would think it appropriate to require *him* to pay Hurt $5 million; yet his behavior, morally speaking, was indistinguishable from that of Fate, from whom it seems intuitively obvious that the $5 million should be exacted.

No doubt there is something wrong with Fortune's getting away scot-free. A sharp-eyed police officer, had there been one around, would have cited him (along with Fate) for careless driving; and they both would have had to pay a small fine. But it would have been nowhere in the vicinity of $5 million. It would have been calculated to offset the attraction of the kind of small $50 gains that might entice otherwise careful motorists to engage in window-shopping while driving.

One hopes, of course, that Fate carried third party insurance; in many jurisdictions he would be legally required to do so. But I want to ignore the question of insurance, for the following reason. Insurance makes Fate's predicament easier to accept; but just for that reason, it may blur our consideration of the fairness of that predicament. For when we think about the practice of third party insurance in a case like this, there are two possibilities: either insurance transforms an unacceptable system of liability into an acceptable one; or it represents a set of privately negotiated deals that enable individuals to cope better with the demands placed on them by a system of liability that, considered by itself, is fundamentally just. In this paper, I am interested in exploring the assumption underlying the second of these alternatives: namely, that the system of tort liability, whose impact on individual injurers is ameliorated by third party insurance contracts, is in itself fundamentally just. After all, if it were not fundamentally just—i.e., if it needed the practice of third party insurance to *make* it just—then we would have to consider whether there are better ways of achieving that just outcome than by combining tort liability and third party insurance in this fashion.[1]

III. Desert in Tort Law

The case we are considering raises two questions: (a) Given that Fate has gained no more than $50 from his negligence, why exactly is it fair to require him to pay Hurt *$5 million*? (b) Given that Fate's behavior has been no more culpable than that of Fortune, why exactly is it fair to require *Fate*, but not Fortune, to pay Hurt whatever Hurt is to be paid in compensation for his loss?

The questions embarrass us by posing issues about the justice of the relationship between tort liability and what individuals deserve. Question (b) raises an issue of comparative desert, as between Fate and Fortune. Since Fate and Fortune seem equally deserving (so far as their driving is concerned), surely it is unjust to treat them differently. Question (a) raises an issue about the absolute level of desert, so far as Fate's admitted wrongdoing is concerned. Though Fate acted culpably by failing to give his driving the attention it required, the scale and character of that wrongdoing—the 'moment of carelessness' mentioned in my title—seem out of all proportion to a $5 million penalty (more than most people earn in a lifetime). The question as posed measures the scale of Fate's wrongdoing by the trivial amount he has gained (and we shall return to that issue in section IV). But we could ask it as well in terms of the brevity and evanescence of his lapse. Or we could concentrate on its mundane familiarity—

---

[1] It is important to bear in mind, throughout this discussion, that there are alternatives to the familiar system of tort liability. In New Zealand, for example, individuals are compensated for injuries caused by accidents out of a publicly-administered fund into which everyone who engages in accident-prone activities pays an annual contribution. If the incident I described in this paper had taken place in New Zealand, Hurt would not have instructed his attorneys to sue Fate. Instead he would have filled out an application to the Accident Compensation Commission and they would have paid him an amount to help him adjust to the loss he had suffered. What is more, Fate's contribution to that compensation would have been the same as Fortune's: the annual payment to the Accident Compensation Fund required of all drivers. It is possible that Fate would be fined for careless driving as a result of the accident, but in principle Fortune would be liable for that penalty too. The difference in outcomes would have been sufficiently explained by the ordinary vicissitudes of traffic policing. In all other respects, Fate and Fortune would be treated the same: and Hurt would be compensated. On the face of it, this outcome looks much better than the outcome I have posited: namely, that Hurt is compensated but only by imposing a massive loss on Fate, unmatched by anything imposed on Fortune.

which is partly the issue also raised by question (b). It is not just Fate who takes his eyes off the road from time to time: everybody does it. It led to unfortunate consequences in this case. All the same, considered by itself it does not seem like such a big deal.

Some tort theorists will contest the assumption behind my questions, the assumption that tort liability ought to be related to individual moral desert. For one thing, tort liability is often strict liability, in which considerations normally associated with desert are deemed irrelevant. Even where tort liability is not strict, i.e., even where it is based on fault, the range of admissible excuses is much narrower than, say, in the criminal law, where issues of desert are of the essence.[2] Indeed some will say that the very questions I have posed reveal the inappropriateness of transferring issues of desert from the realm of retributive justice, where they belong, to the realm of corrective justice. After all, Fate's liability to Hurt in the case I have described (and Fortune's lack of liability) is not a marginal or problematic application of tort principles: it is close to a paradigm case. If tort liability does not coincide with desert in a case like this, maybe what that shows is that moral desert is an inappropriate category of assessment when evaluating tort law.[3]

There are certainly important differences between tort liability and liability in the criminal law. Apart from anything else, the aim of compensating victims is at best secondary or incidental in criminal law, whereas it is central in torts. It would be wrong, however, to infer that individual moral desert, broadly construed, has no place in our understanding or assessment of tort liability.[4] Desert, and the associated criterion of fairness, are not concepts that can be confined like that. Think of the variety of contexts in which we say intuitively that something has gone awry because there are enormous differences in people's well-being that are unrelated to any sense of their comparative desert. The idea that how things go for a person should bear some sort of relation to how well he has acted informs our assessment of the world on all sorts of fronts. We invoke standards of fairness for assessing social arrangements of all sorts. We do not even confine it to the operation of human laws and institutions, let alone to any particular legal domain: we use it to rail against God, against nature, against dis-

---

[2] For a powerful statement of this point, see JULES L. COLEMAN, RISKS AND WRONGS (1992), 220–26.

[3] Thus Coleman cites the fact that, in tort law, 'the wrong can be very slight and the damage enormous; or the wrong can be grave and the damage minuscule', as an indication that fault in tort cannot possibly be construed as a principle of retributive justice: *id.* at 235.

[4] Compare, for example, the argument of William Prosser that many courts refuse to impose liability for unforeseeable consequences of a defendant's negligence on the grounds that to do so would be to 'impose a ruinous liability which no private fortune could meet, and which is out of all proportion to the defendant's fault': WILLIAM L. PROSSER, HANDBOOK OF THE LAW OF TORTS (2d edn., 1955), 258 *cited in* JOEL FEINBERG, DOING AND DESERVING: ESSAYS IN THE THEORY OF RESPONSIBILITY (1970), 28.

ease. We commonly argue about whether students get the grades they deserve; about whether the most deserving team won the World Series; about whether entrepreneurs deserve their profits; about who among a group of associates deserves the higher salary; and so on. In none of these cases, is an appeal to personal desert the officially determinative factor; and perhaps that is the main contrast with a system of retributive justice. But in each case, systematic and sustained dissonance between outcomes and deserts would be seen as a point against the institution in question and an appropriate basis for social criticism.

To put it another way, a gaping disproportion between individual outcomes and the morality of individual characters and conduct seems to be a primary form of unfairness, and certainly the complaint 'It's unfair' cannot be confined to the criminal law. It is true that, since Aristotle, our concept of justice has been divided among various domains—distributive justice, corrective justice, retributive justice, commutative justice, and so on—and we must expect detailed conceptions of fairness and unfairness to observe these divisions. Still, we must not let our familiarity with such distinctions blind us either to the connections that exist between the different domains of justice, or to the possibility that there are over-arching principles or intuitions of fairness and desert that entitle both corrective justice and retributive justice, for example, to be regarded as forms of *justice*.

The objection that it is inappropriate to assess the institution of tort liability in terms of a desert-based criterion of fairness would be more convincing if the institution were in better shape overall, so far as other modes of justification were concerned. But in fact tort liability is under serious challenge quite apart from the questions raised by my example. It is not at all clear that, as an institution, it deals adequately with any of the dimensions of the problems it purports to address, and many jurisdictions are seriously considering replacing the system of liability altogether.[5] (Some have already done so.) Against this background of challenge, it might be worth considering whether, for all its other faults, tort liability is a basically fair system, one that does not create outcomes for individuals that are manifestly at odds with what they may plausibly be said to deserve. But the questions raised by my example suggest that there is not even that to be said for the institution. Or, at any rate, it is the aim of this essay to consider whether tort liability can be defended on grounds of fairness, even if it cannot be defended on other grounds.

---

[5] *See, e.g.*, Marc A. Franklin, *Replacing the Negligence Lottery: Compensation and Selective Reimbursement*, 53 VA. L. REV. 774 (1967); Stephen D. Sugarman, *Doing Away With Tort Law*, 73 CAL. L. REV. 555 (1985).

IV. Inadequacy of the Annulment Theory

There is one other reason for posing the hypothetical case as I have: I want to remove entirely from consideration one superficially attractive theory about the nature and point of tort liability.

It is sometimes said that the aim of tort law is to annul wrongful gains and losses by a single transfer of wealth from an injurer-defendant who has gained from the performance of some action to a plaintiff-victim who has suffered some loss as a result of that action. If what the defendant has gained is what the plaintiff has lost, then we should be able to determine payment from the defendant to the plaintiff that will at once cancel out both the wrongful gain and the wrongful loss. This view is sometimes attributed to Aristotle, though the attribution is based on a rather free and simplistic translation of a very obscure passage in his discussion of justice in the *Nicomachean Ethics*.[6]

Whatever its provenance, the annulment theory simply collapses in the light of the questions we have posed. Question (a) indicates that there is no transfer which will both annul Hurt's wrongful loss and annul Fate's wrongful gain without occasioning further (and massive) loss to Fate. The unhappy fact is that Fate's gain is in no way the measure of Hurt's loss or vice versa:[7] there simply is no neat way of annulling both to leave things exactly as they were. The Aristotelian idea seems better suited to straightforward cases of restitution than to the massive quantitative asymmetry between the respective losses and gains of plaintiff-victims and defendant-injurers in the typical torts situation.

Question (b) compounds the case against the annulment theory. Fortune has secured as much of a wrongful gain as Fate has, but the law of torts makes no effort to annul that. Perhaps it will be said that a gain only becomes wrongful (or annullable) in the relevant sense when it is secured

---

[6] *See* Aristotle, Nicomachean Ethics (W. D. Ross (trans.), 1954), bk.5, ch 4, at 114-17.

[7] George Sher has argued, in the context of a discussion of punishment, that the extent of a miscreant's wrongful gain is necessarily proportional to the moral seriousness of his offense: 'For, in fact, a person who acts wrongly does gain a significant measure of extra liberty: what he gains is freedom from the demands of the prohibition he violates. Because others take that prohibition seriously, they lack a similar liberty. And as the strength of the prohibition increases, so too does the freedom from it which its violation entails. Thus, even if the murderer and the tax evader do succumb to equally strong impulses, their gains in freedom are far from equal. Because the murderer evades a prohibition of far greater force—because he thus "gets away with more"—his net gain in freedom remains greater': George Sher, Desert (1987), 82. I find this line of reasoning quite implausible (among other things because it seems to imply that the more wicked one's action the freer one is in performing it). Those who find Sher's argument convincing, however, may deploy it in defense of the Aristotelian theory of tort liability. If the wrongness of Fate's conduct is measured by the seriousness of the loss it occasions to Hurt, then on Sher's account the seriousness of the loss to Hurt is the proper measure of the extent of Fate's wrongful gain. Presumably the Florsheim shoes are irrelevant!

through someone else's wrongful loss. But since Fate and Fortune secured their gain in exactly the same way, it should not be said that one of them but not the other secured it at Hurt's expense: the gain would have been secured whether or not Hurt was harmed. This point has been well stated by Jules Coleman:

Negligent motoring may or may not result in an accident. Whether or not it does, individuals who drive negligently often secure a wrongful gain in doing so, namely, the 'savings' from not taking adequate safety precautions. . . . This form of wrongful gain is not, *ex hypothesi*, the result of anyone else's wrongful loss. On the other hand, if a negligent motorist causes another harm, he normally secures no *additional* wrongful gain in virtue of his doing so. . . . The wrongful gain negligent motorists secure is logically distinct from any loss they may cause others, and so the occasion of another's loss cannot be the moral basis for annulling these gains as a matter of justice.[8]

Maybe the aim of tort law is simply to annul wrongfully imposed *losses*. If so, that thesis must be separated from any claim about the importance of simultaneously annulling wrongful *gains*. It must be defended in its own right by entering plausible answers to the two questions we have posed.

V. Why Shift the Loss from Hurt to Fate?

It will be recalled that the two questions are: (a) why is it fair to impose liability of $5 million on Fate when all he has gained from his negligence is a paltry $50? and (b) why is Fate, but not Fortune, singled out for liability, when their behavior was morally speaking indistinguishable? I now want to consider a number of intuitive responses.

The answer to (a) that springs immediately to mind is that the $5 million loss imposed on Fate is not some figure plucked arbitrarily out of the air. It is the exact measure of Hurt's injury. If it is not paid to him, *he* is the one who will have to bear a $5 million loss (or its equivalent)—and that without the benefit even of a discounted pair of Florsheim shoes. Nothing is clearer than the injustice of an innocent man like Hurt having to bear a loss as grave as that.

We can emphasize this point by adding a staggeringly improbable premise to an already idealized case. Suppose that on the morning of the accident, the sun was shining, the birds were singing, and the society in which Fortune, Fate, and Hurt were living was *perfectly just, from a distributive point of view*. The reader need not agree with me about distributive justice in order to entertain this assumption; let him imagine that the society was just, according to the proper criteria of distributive justice,

---

[8] Jules L. Coleman, Markets, Morals and the Law (1988), 187.

whatever they turn out to be. If justice is equality, then Fortune, Fate, and Hurt started out with equal shares. If justice is a matter of proportionality to desert, then each already had what he merited. If the requirements of justice are no more than *suum cuique tribuere'*,[9] then each was already in possession of his own.

Now, trivial changes probably do not affect the background justice of a distribution: *de minimis non curat iustitia*.[10] But it is hard to imagine a society so prosperous that a $5 million loss inflicted out of the blue on one of its members would count as trivial. It is hard to imagine that it would not upset an antecedently just distribution. Whatever justice requires, it is fair to assume that suddenly taking away $5 million or its hedonic equivalent from the victim of an accident will be sufficient to transform a situation that is just into a situation that is less than just. For this reason, it seems clear that distributive justice requires that Hurt not be required to bear such a loss.

Unfortunately, for any argument based on distributive justice, almost exactly the same reasoning seems to apply to Fate. If Hurt's lawsuit is successful, Fate will have almost $5 million less than was allocated to him in the just distribution we are imagining. It is difficult to see how *this* could be anything other than a disruption of the justice of the *status quo ante*. Previously, Fate had a certain share of social resources; now he is impoverished. The latter state of affairs can hardly be just, if the former was.

Someone may object that a plausible conception of justice will include principles governing the allocation of losses caused by individuals in cases like this. After all, any plausible theory of justice will allow departures from a morally sanctioned initial distribution through things like voluntary gift-giving, poker games, or choices of work over leisure. The point of an initial distribution is to provide a just baseline for such individuals' choices and interactions, not to freeze a given distributive pattern in place for all time.[11] Any plausible conception of distributive justice will include ancillary principles to govern these matters. And similarly, it may be said, our theory of distribution will surely contain an ancillary principle (a principle of *corrective* justice) requiring those who cause injury to bear the losses of those whom they harm. Once a principle of this kind is put into operation—the objection continues—the fact that the resulting distribution differs from the initially just distribution is no more a reason for criticism than the fact that private gift-giving disrupts an initially just distribution. That Fate rather than Hurt should be $5 million worse off than distributive jus-

---

[9] 'Render to everyone his own.' This was one of Justinian's three fundamental maxims.
[10] 'Justice does not concern itself with trifles.'
[11] *See* ROBERT NOZICK, ANARCHY, STATE, AND UTOPIA (1974), 160 ff. *See also* Ronald Dworkin, *What is Equality? Part 2: Equality of Resources*, 10 PHIL. & PUB. AFF. 283, 292 ff. (1981).

tice initially indicated may be regarded as entirely appropriate when our conception of distributive justice is fleshed out with principles of corrective justice covering the role of choice and contingency in people's lives.[12]

I am sure that something along these lines is correct. What it shows, however, is that the justificatory burden, with respect to question (a), falls entirely on the ancillary principle of corrective justice. We shall have to consider how—in light of the challenge we have posed—such an ancillary principle can be justified. It is clear, however, that an appeal only to the disruption in the prior just distribution by Fate's causing loss to Hurt cannot justify shifting that loss to Fate: the mere fact of the disruption of an established just distribution counts as much against Fate's bearing the loss as it does against Hurt's bearing the loss.

It is tempting to say that the legal system is either imposing the loss on Fate or imposing the loss on Hurt, and the only question is which. Jules Coleman succumbs to this temptation. He argues in *Risks and Wrongs* that in tort law, 'any decision is a liability decision: losses must always fall on someone . . . . Not to impose liability on the injurer is to impose it on the victim, and vice versa.'[13]

It seems odd, however, almost to the point of incoherence, to say that a refusal by the courts to make Fate compensate Hurt would amount to the imposition of *liability* on Hurt. Liability is a two-term relation: if Fate is held liable, he is held liable *to Hurt*. To whom, on Coleman's account, is Hurt held liable, if his suit against Fate fails?

Logic aside, the claim about symmetry of liability here is quite misleading. A court that refuses to hold Fate liable for Hurt's losses makes no statement whatever about the desirability or appropriateness of Hurt's bearing that loss. Coleman says that by saying that Hurt is held liable for the loss in the absence of a judgment against Fate, he means no more than that Hurt has been determined to be in the best position to shoulder the costs occasioned by the accident.[14] But even if this is true, it confuses the meaning of the normative term 'liable' with a particular (and controversial) theory about the proper criteria for its application.[15] In any case, it is wrong to assume that in every case in which a judgment is not entered against an injurer-defendant a comparative determination has been made about his capacity and the plaintiff-victim's capacity to bear the losses

---

[12] For an excellent discussion of these matters, see ERIC RAKOWSKI, EQUAL JUSTICE (1991), 227 ff.

[13] COLEMAN, *supra*, note 2, at 223–5. (Coleman develops this as a point about strict liability. There can be no doubt that if a compensated loss to an accident victim is regarded as liability, then it is strict liability. The case against strict liability for injurers is thus diminished a little when we see that, on Coleman's account, the alternative is strict liability for victims.)

[14] *Id.* at 231.

[15] For the distinction between meaning and criteria in the case of normative terms, see R.M. HARE, THE LANGUAGE OF MORALS (1952), 94–110.

occasioned by the accident. The plaintiff's case may fail for reasons which have nothing to do with that.

My inclination is to say that if Fate is not found liable (and if nothing else is done to compensate Hurt), then the loss just lies where it fell as a result of the accident. Society has simply decided to do nothing about that given state of affairs. But Coleman contests this description. He says that the fact that the loss falls initially on Hurt is a normative conclusion of law not a statement of natural fact. '[T]he loss begins', he says, 'as the victim's "legal responsibility".'[16] This turns out to mean no more than that it is up to Hurt to initiate the process of recovering damages from Fate, and that until he acts and makes out whatever case is required, Fate will not be held liable. Now that is indeed a judgment about Hurt's legal position. The proper way to describe it, however, is as follows: (i) initially, and apart from any grounds for or the commencement of any lawsuit, Hurt has what Wesley N. Hohfeld called a *'no-claim'* against Fate correlative to Fate's lack of any background duty to pay Hurt $5 million; in the circumstances, however, Hurt's no-right is coupled with (ii) a Hohfeldian power to change that state of affairs by bringing an action in tort, such power being correlative to what Hohfeld called Fate's *'liability'* to have a duty imposed on him.[17] So there certainly are legally-defined aspects to Hurt's situation immediately after the accident. However, neither (i) nor (ii) nor their combination can plausibly be described as Hurt's having an initial 'liability' (to Fate or anyone else).

VI. The Basic Injustice of the Tort System

Coleman is on much stronger ground when he reminds us simply that '[t]ort law is unjust either to victims or injurers, probably to both'.[18] As things stand, in a system of tort law, either Hurt is going to have to suffer a great loss, uncompensated by anything received from Fate, or Fate is going to have to suffer a great loss, uncompensated by anything except the $50 shoe bargain which he gained as the benefit of his inattentive driving. Both situations seem unfair. That the first is the result of an accident together with the lack of a legal judgment against Fate, whereas the second is the result of an accident together with the imposition of a legal judgment against Fate, does not alter the fact that both seem out of all proportion to anything that the parties deserve.

It may be wrong, though, to leave the matter there. It is possible to con-

---

[16] Coleman, *supra*, note 2, at 232.
[17] For this terminology, see Wesley N. Hohfeld, Fundamental Legal Conceptions (1919), 36.
[18] Coleman, *supra*, note 2, at 221.

cede that either situation (Hurt's bearing the loss or Fate's bearing the loss) would be gravely unfair, and still insist that it is marginally less unfair to allocate the loss caused by an accident to a careless defendant than to let the equivalent loss lie where it has fallen, on his innocent victim. The lawsuit singles Fate out to bear a massive loss on the basis of the fortuitous outcome of a moment's carelessness. But if it is arbitrary to single Fate out in this way, it is even more arbitrary to allow Hurt to be singled out for such a massive loss. For Hurt is *entirely* innocent in the matter; he does not even have the taint of carelessness associated with his conduct that Fate has.[19] This is a fair point—particularly in a context in which, as Coleman says, 'we frame the question of who is to bear the costs of a particular injury to exclude everyone other than the victim and the injurer.'[20]

But why should we frame the question in that way? Given that it seems arbitrary to require *either* Fate or Hurt to bear the whole loss, and given that the morally relevant difference between them seems quite slight (it amounts to Fate's moment of carelessness and his insignificant gain), why not abandon the framework that confines our attention to the two of them, and seek a way of addressing accident costs that does not involve arbitrary elements of this sort?

That, after all, as I said at the end of section II, is the point of the questions we are asking. Is the traditional nexus between plaintiff-victim and defendant-injurer, which lies at the heart of tort law, sufficiently fair, sufficiently non-arbitrary from a moral point of view, to count as a better way of addressing the problem of accident costs than, say, a New Zealand style scheme that abandons the principle of individual liability altogether? As a society, we have the choice of instituting a scheme whereby a fee is levied on all drivers (increasing on a scale according to detected instances of careless driving) sufficient to give us a fund out of which we can make good the losses of all accident victims. This scheme has what will be to many the unattractive feature that some individuals are required to contribute to compensating losses for which they bear absolutely no causal responsibility. But we must ask whether it is, in that regard, more arbitrary or less arbitrary than the scheme we have at present.[21]

---

[19] *Id.* at 224.　　　　　　　　　　　　　　　　　　　　　　　　　　　　[20] *Id.*

[21] The point about insurance may be relevant here. It may be difficult to make a convincing argument that a scheme like the one in New Zealand would be more arbitrary than a system of tort liability, given that the effect of the latter, when taken together with the practice of third party insurance, is in effect to convert the one into something very much like the other (with minor—though even more arbitrary!—differences). Since most jurisdictions that have tort liability now insist that drivers (and others who engage in potentially dangerous activities) carry third-party insurance, they can hardly say that the New Zealand scheme is more arbitrary than tort liability would be on its own, apart from the ameliorating effects of the insurance requirement.

VII. CONSIDERING CAUSATION

Enough, for the time being, of question (a), involving the problem of comparative deserts. There is also an intuitive answer to (b), concerning the issue of the defendant's absolute desert, that will spring to the reader's mind. Fortune should not be required to compensate Hurt because Fortune did not cause Hurt's injury. Fate did, and it is this distinguishing fact of causation that explains why Fate is the one who should have to pay (if anyone should).

Causation occupies a prominent role in several contemporary theories of tort liability. Ernest Weinrib regards it as one of the two basic principles (the other related principle is the binary relation between plaintiff and defendant) around which the whole structure of tort liability is intrinsically ordered. On his view, it is essential to tort law that actions be described in terms of their causal consequences:

[T]he causation that figures in an intrinsically ordered tort law is not fragmentable into two independent segments, one dealing with what the defendant did and the other with what the plaintiff suffered. Causation refers to a sequence stretching from the defendant's act to the plaintiff's injury. The defendant's act is understood from the standpoint of its potential for injuring the plaintiff, and the injury for which the plaintiff recovers is a materialization of that potential. The doing and the suffering of harm constitute a single unbroken process. . . .

. . . Doing is significant inasmuch as someone suffers thereby, and suffering is significant inasmuch as someone has inflicted it. A doing that results in no suffering and a suffering that is the consequence of no-one's doing fall beyond the concern of tort law.[22]

On this account, it is quite misleading to say that what Fate did and what Fortune did are on a par. What Fortune did is drive carelessly, something which in itself is of no interest from a torts point of view. But what Fate did is carelessly injure Hurt by his driving. That act-description, with its tight connection between Fate's driving and Hurt's loss, raises issues of tort liability that are simply absent in Fortune's case.

All this can be conceded, without resolving anything. Actions can be described in all sorts of ways, some of them morally interesting, some of them in ways that highlight what is morally irrelevant. Weinrib has drawn to our attention the sort of description that is germane to tort liability. But of course we already knew that the torts perspective characterizes Fate's action in a way that radically distinguishes it from Fortune's, and makes Fate's ruination turn on that distinction. That is exactly the problem: whether it is fair or arbitrary to describe the issue in this way, especially

---

[22] Ernest J. Weinrib, *Understanding Tort Law*, 23 VAL. U. L. REV. 485, 512 (1989).

since such high stakes are associated with the characterization selected. Although he criticizes others for raising this question,[23] Weinrib has no answer. All he is prepared to say is this:

We would not, I think, identify as tort law a system that ignored causation in compensating for disabilities. We might perhaps rejoice if eliminating the causation requirement allowed a more general treatment of injury, where compensation was triggered by the injury itself rather than its tortious infliction. Again, however, such a more general treatment would be an alternative to tort law, not a version of it.[24]

That last point is certainly not in dispute. All we are exploring at this stage is whether the rejoicing which Weinrib mentions would be appropriate on grounds of fairness.

Maybe the fact that Fate caused injury while Fortune did not is important for what it tells us about their personal responsibility.[25] Hurt's disability will always be something that Fate was *responsible for*, always something that he will have to regard as part of his history, always something marked, so to speak, on his account. Nothing like this can be said about Fortune. Unhappily for the advocates of tort liability, however, the connection between causation and responsibility fails to establish a nonarbitrary basis for differential liability as between Fate and Fortune. For we all know that 'responsible for' is a Janus-faced term. On one side, it means little more than 'caused' (the avalanche was responsible for the destruction of the village). On the other side, it connotes culpability and liability. It is not in dispute that Fate's carelessness *was* responsible (and Fortune's carelessness was *not* responsible) for Hurt's injury in the first sense. But something more is needed to establish the relevance of the second sense of responsibility in a meaningful way.

That the extra something cannot be supplied is indicated by the following example, similar to the case of Fate and Fortune except that it involves many more drivers. Suppose there are two lanes of traffic on a freeway, the fast lane and the slow lane. Illuminated signs have warned drivers of ice and freezing rain ahead. The drivers in the slow lane, all prudent souls, reduce their speed and increase their following distances. By contrast, the drivers in the fast lane close ranks and speed up, all hoping recklessly to get home before the bad weather really settles in. But the weather deteriorates quickly: visibility falls and ice forms on the road. In a particularly treacherous patch, the reckless drivers in the fast lane find their vehicles swerving to the right. Though they all swerve out of control, some of them hit the vehicles in the slow lane, and some of them do not: it is a purely

---

[23] *Id.* at 500 (criticizing JUDITH JARVIS THOMSON, *Remarks on Causation and Liability, in* RIGHTS, RESTITUTION, AND RISK: ESSAYS IN MORAL THEORY (William Parent (ed.), 1986), 192.

[24] *Id.* at 494.

[25] For a robust insistence on the connections between causation, responsibility, and liability, see Richard A. Epstein, *A Theory of Strict Liability*, 2 J. LEGAL STUD. 151 (1973).

fortuitous matter depending on whether there happens to be a vehicle to the right of a given reckless driver at the moment his car begins to the slide. The result is chaos and carnage: wrecked cars all over the place, and a large number of careful drivers killed and injured as a result of vehicles swerving into them from the fast lane. When asked at the scene to comment on the accidents, the commander of the local highway patrol shakes his head sadly and says, 'It seems that every vehicle in the left-hand lane was travelling much too fast for the conditions. They ignored clearly posted warnings. None of them paid proper attention to the dangers of ice on the roads. The result is that fifty people have died. If the drivers in fast lane had adjusted their speed to the conditions, none of this would have happened. They should all be ashamed of themselves.'

From Weinrib's point of view, this comment is unspeakably unfair, since it lumps all of the fast drivers together, ignoring crucial distinctions of causality. The fact is that some of the drivers in the fast lane caused death and injury; others did not. Those whose speeding cars swerved into other vehicles are in a different category altogether from those whose speeding cars swerved fortuitously into empty space. The former did something altogether different from the latter: for in the former case, someone's speeding and someone's being injured are tied together as part of 'a single unbroken process',[26] whereas in the latter case these things have nothing to do with one another.

Richard Epstein has argued that it is important 'to develop a normative theory of torts that takes into account common sense notions of individual responsibility'.[27] But from a common sense point of view, the distinctions stressed in the previous paragraph are ridiculous. Everyone knows that the differences in the causal consequences of the reckless drivers' speeding are purely fortuitous, purely random, like the flip of a coin. That one driver hit, whereas another missed, the car to his right is something that fails to tell us anything interesting about the drivers' conduct, character, or credit. True, some of them will go away knowing that in any strictly causal account of what has happened in the universe, no death or injury will be associated with their driving. Weinrib thinks this is something important for them (and us) to ponder; most of us would think it fatuous, if not downright disgraceful, of the lucky drivers to take pride in this fact or to regard it as marking anything other than an arbitrary distinction between them and those whose cars happened to hit other vehicles in the pile-up. The highway patrol commander is correct: *all* of the fast drivers were reckless—the result was carnage; they *all* ought to be ashamed of themselves.

I do not want to overstate the point. It is not that causality is irrelevant, or that it does not matter what happens as a result of what we do. One can-

---

[26] Weinrib, *supra*, note 22, at 512.   [27] Epstein, *supra*, note 25, at 151.

not fully understand the significance of the indictment of recklessness in the freeway pile-up I have described, or the lesser charge of carelessness against Fate and Fortune, without focusing on causality. The reason we are required to take care in our driving is that automobiles are apt to cause injury if not handled correctly, and especially apt to cause injury if not handled with great care in adverse conditions. The reason we impose a duty of care on people like Fate and Fortune is because of the very sort of incident in which Fate and Hurt became embroiled. Similarly, we impose duties of care on all freeway drivers because of the danger that, absent such care, some of them may become embroiled in the sort of causal nexus between injurer and victim that Weinrib makes so much of. All that this illustrates, however, is that it is possible to explain the importance of causation without explaining its importance as a basis of differential liability.

VIII. Liability As A Lottery

Let us return to our first example. It seems that there is something arbitrary and unfair about singling out Fate as the careless driver who must compensate Hurt. It is true that Fate is the one who happened to injure Hurt, but that does not remove the sense of arbitrariness: that is the *basis* of the seeming arbitrariness. The question is whether it is just to permit a purely fortuitous connection drive what is, on any account, a significant and far-reaching legal decision—namely, the decision to impose a huge loss on Fate as a way of compensating Hurt.

I know of only one argument or characterization that may remove this appearance of arbitrariness, and I am not sure whether it is convincing. The argument was put forward by David Lewis, in an intriguing paper dealing with the problem of criminal attempts.[28] The law characteristically punishes people more severely for successful than for unsuccessful criminal attempts (attempts to murder someone, for example): a successful murderer may be punished by death or life imprisonment, whereas the penalty for attempted murder may be ten years or even less. Yet, in terms of both their intent and their actions, the murderer and the unsuccessful attempted murderer may be morally indistinguishable. Both, for example, may have aimed and shot at their intended victim, doing their best to see that his death resulted. It may be purely happenstance that the bullet from one of their guns happened to miss its target. The affinity between this case and the case of tort liability is obvious. We are not trying to punish Fate and Fortune, but we impose differential liability on them in light of exactly the same sort of happenstance that determines whether a criminal attempt succeeds or not. An

[28] David Lewis, *The Punishment That Leaves Something to Chance*, 18 Phil. & Pub. Aff. 53 (1989).

examination of the problem of criminal attempts may therefore cast some light on the problem of tort liability.

Lewis's attempt to make sense of an apparently arbitrary distinction turns on the notion of a *'penal lottery'*. Suppose Cain, intending to kill Abel, shoots at him in a manner that has a 60 per cent chance of causing his death. It may be felt that an appropriate punishment for this offense—appropriate, for example, on *lex talionis* grounds[29]—is to impose on Cain a 60 per cent risk of death, the same risk that he imposed on Abel. On his conviction for making the attempt (whether or not it turned out to be successful), Cain is sentenced to draw a straw from a bundle containing six short straws and four long straws. If he draws a short straw, he is put to death; if he draws a long straw he goes free.[30] It is possible, of course, that a given pair of people who receive this sentence will suffer different fates as a result: one being executed and the other going free. But though the outcomes are different, the punishment is the same. They are both exposed to the identical risk.

It is a rare case in which we can quantify with confidence the exact risk to which Cain exposed his victim. But maybe we can proceed using a re-enactment of the crime as the lottery mechanism rather than a bundle of straws. As soon as he is convicted of having tried successfully or unsuccessfully to kill someone, Cain may be taken to a setting (not unlike that in which he made his attempt on Abel's life) and shot at by a gunman whose marksmanship is as similar to Cain's as we are able to judge. Unfortunately, this procedure, too, may run into difficulties. It may be impossible to determine Cain's marksmanship exactly or to duplicate it accurately in the official gunman whose firing is the basis of our penal lottery. So the following radical suggestion might be made.

Since our objective is to impose on Cain a risk for a like risk, and since it is difficult for us to reproduce anything other than a rough approximation of the risk he imposed on Abel, why not take the outcome of Cain's actual attempt—rather than any re-enactment of it—as the basis of the penal lottery? If Abel is struck by Cain's bullet and dies, then Cain will be put to death; if Abel escapes or survives the bullet, Cain will go free. Proceeding in this way will have the advantage of exposing Cain to a risk of death (i.e. probability that death will result) which is not just similar but exactly the same as the risk to which he exposed Abel. Of course everyone is presumed to understand in this situation that the actual outcome of Cain's attempt is irrelevant to the degree of his culpability—irrelevant, that is, to what he deserves. But just for that reason, it is ideal for the purposes

---

[29] *See* Jeremy Waldron, *Lex Talionis*, 34 Ariz. L. Rev. 25, 46 (1992).

[30] Or, in a less pure but more realistic case, there might be a set minimum punishment for all who attempt to kill others, with a penal lottery determining the punishment they are to endure over and above that: *see* Lewis, *supra*, note 28, at 58.

of our lottery. What he deserves is to be exposed to exactly the risk of this event's occurring, only with his life at stake rather than Abel's. So in the event (itself irrelevant to the degree of his culpability) that Abel dies, he is put to death; in the event (also irrelevant) that Abel survives the attempt, Cain goes free. The proposal does have the odd feature that the lottery to determine punishment takes place before guilt is determined. But that hardly affects its fairness. If Cain is found not guilty of making an attempt (successful or unsuccessful) on Abel's life, he will go free and what happens to Abel—what would otherwise count as the outcome of the penal lottery—will have no effect on him.

According to Lewis, a penal lottery of this sort (in which the random outcome of the crime is used as the basis for determining the outcome of the risk imposed on the convict as punishment) is the best explication of our current practice in dealing with successful and unsuccessful criminal attempts—best in the sense that it makes that practice look less arbitrary than it would otherwise be.

I will leave others to enter final judgment on Lewis's account so far as criminal law is concerned.[31] But it raises intriguing and interesting possibilities for us, inasmuch as the difference between Fate and Fortune is similar in many respects to the differences between a successful and an unsuccessful criminal attempt. We do have to be careful with the analogy. Tort law is not criminal law, and tort liability is certainly not supposed to duplicate retributive justice. Jules Coleman warns that 'the net result of applying one's understanding of the criminal law to torts is bad philosophy and total confusion'.[32] Remember, however, that our aim is not to explicate tort liability on its own terms; if it were, we would simply say (along Weinrib's lines) that Fate injured Hurt and Fortune did not and that's that. Our aim is to see whether the apparent unfairness or arbitrariness of tort liability can be rebutted. Lewis's idea suggests a promising strategy for such rebuttal.

Both Fate and Fortune drove carelessly: they wrongfully imposed a risk of great loss on those around them. The aim of a tort system is certainly not to punish them for that; it is to recompense Hurt who suffered as a result of this carelessness. Still, we may think it a condition of the fairness of such a system that it treat Fate and Fortune equivalently. One way of doing this is to expose both careless drivers to a risk of liability exactly equivalent to the risk of loss that they imposed on the drivers around them.

Let us say that a driver who studies store windows when he drives along busy city streets (as Fate and Fortune did) imposes a 30 per cent risk of harm on the person in front of him; in three out of ten cases of such

---

[31] For some serious doubts, see Sanford Kadish, *Foreword: The Criminal Law and the Luck of the Draw*, 84 J. CRIM. L. & CRIMINOLOGY 679 (1994).

[32] COLEMAN, *supra*, note 2, at 222.

inattention, he will cause that person injury. So, whether or not he actually injures the person in front of him, it will not be unfair for him to be exposed at law to a 30 per cent risk of sustaining a loss equivalent to the injury he risked imposing on another. In the real world in which he drives in this manner, a dense and chaotic network of inscrutable physical causes determines whether or not his vehicle actually strikes the person in front. This network of causes is, if you like, the mechanism of the lottery wrongfully inflicted by the driver on the person in front of him. If the legal system is going to impose a similar lottery on the driver, in connection with the compensation of those who suffer as a result of this carelessness, it will have to come up with a statistically similar mechanism. It does not particularly matter what the mechanism is, provided it generates the requisite 30 per cent probability. Why not save time and money, then, by using the very mechanism of the lottery that the defendant imposed upon his victim as the basis of determining his liability?

Applied to our tort example, the Lewis approach might produce a kind of 'liability lottery'. Thus, Fortune is driving along with someone in front of him. He takes his eyes off the road and stares at a store window, thus imposing a 30 per cent risk of harm on the other driver. In seven out of ten such cases, we would expect nothing to happen and this time nothing does. Still, what Fortune did was wrong, and we tell him that, in our efforts to secure compensation for the victims of this sort of carelessness, it would not be unfair for him to suffer the imposition of a similar risk of loss. He asks when this imposition of risk will take place, and we tell him that it has already taken place—that we have used the interaction between him and the person in front of him as the basis of his punishment. There was a 30 per cent chance of his striking the other person, and had he done so he would have been required to pay an enormous sum of money. In fact, this contingency did not eventuate, and he can now go free. His own exposure to the compensatory risk is complete.

Fate is reproached with exactly similar negligence: by taking his eyes off the road and staring at a store window, he imposed a 30 per cent risk of harm on the driver in front of him. He, too, is told that it would be fair for him to suffer the imposition of a similar risk. He asks when this will take place, and we tell him, as we told Fortune, that it has already taken place— that we have used his interaction with the person in front of him at the time of his offense as the basis of determining his liability. There was a 30 per cent chance of a certain event occurring in that interaction, and the risk to which we exposed him was that, if that event were to occur, he was to suffer a massive loss. That event was stipulated as the event of his injuring the other person. It did take place. So, as part of his being exposed to this risk, he must now pay over a massive sum equivalent to the victim's losses. Fate may be puzzled by all this, but he can hardly complain. He wrongfully imposed a 30 per cent chance of great loss on another person and, like Fortune, he has had to suffer a similar exposure to a similar loss himself. His victim might have been lucky, but he was not. And Fate might have been similarly lucky, but he was not. That is the way it goes.

Is there anything fishy about this kind of liability lottery? As a matter of fact, we rigged the lottery so that Fate would get lucky if and only if his victim got lucky. The same liability lottery determined both outcomes. But this is essentially irrelevant. What matters from a moral point of view is that the probabilities in the two cases were quantitatively the same. The fact which explains that—that they were indeed the same spin of the same wheel—is neither here nor there.[33]

IX. IN SEARCH OF COMPENSATORY JUSTICE

I believe that a Lewis-type liability lottery approach offers the best prospect of answering the imputation of unfairness implicit in question (b). But how does it leave us with regard to question (a)? We have given an explanation of the imposition of liability on Fate but not on Fortune. They both deserve to suffer the same, and they do: only, what they suffer is the imposition of a risk, and it happens to turn out badly for Fate. Does this also take care of the problem about the sheer scale of the liability that is imposed on Fate in our example?

I am left in two minds about this. On the one hand, Fate cannot deny that what he did was wrongfully to expose Hurt to a risk of loss that was great. All he did was indulge in a moment's carelessness. Yet he knew that carelessness in such a context was wrong, and he knew why it was wrong: even a moment's negligence matters, particularly when one is driving, because a moving automobile is a very dangerous object that can inflict grave injury if it comes into contact with another vehicle. All this applies to Fortune as well. It seems that neither of them can complain about being exposed to a risk of loss this large, since they imposed a risk of exactly such loss on the others around them. If they cannot complain that the risk is unfair, then they can hardly complain that materialization of one of its contingencies is unfair.

That is one side of the story. The other side is more difficult to state. The

---

[33] Lewis argues that the only drawback of this approach is confusion: 'one and the same event plays a double role: if his victim dies, that death is at once the main harm done by his crime and also the way of losing his lottery. If we are not careful, we are apt to misunderstand. We may think that the successful attempter suffers a worse fate because he is more guilty when he does a worse harm, rather than because he loses his lottery. But it is not so: his success is irrelevant to his guilt, his wickedness, his desert, and his sentence to face the lottery—exactly as the shortness of his straw would have been, had he been sentenced to the lottery by straws': Lewis, *supra,* note 28, at 67.

lingering sense of unfairness may be captured as follows: 'why are we imposing *exactly this lottery* on Fate (and Fortune)—a liability lottery that has only two outcomes, zero loss and the loss of $5 million? Why not some lottery with a more moderate range of outcomes? Or why a lottery at all?' The answer will be that this is exactly the structure of the risk that Fate and Fortune imposed upon Hurt and others—that they would either be gravely injured or not injured at all. So there is something macabrely appropriate about the imposition of exactly this risk on them.

In some contexts, macabre appropriateness may be all there is to fairness. There is a strong strand of retributivism which holds that the imposition on a miscreant of a pain, loss, or risk which exactly matches what he imposed on his victim is a good thing in itself, as some sort of 'negation of the negation', canceling or annulling the original crime. But, as Coleman reminded us, the logic of torts is not necessarily the logic of retribution. In retributive justice, paying back the criminal for his crime is the whole point of the practice; and, depending on one's exact conception of retribution, that purpose cannot be served except by requiring the criminal to suffer just what his victim suffered. In tort, there is a different main point—namely, the compensation of the victim. It is the victim's loss we are trying to cancel or annul in tort, not the defendant's wrong.

Before we reach any conclusion, then, about the fairness of a practice of imposing a risk on every negligent person corresponding exactly to the risk that his negligence imposes on the others around him, we shall have to ask whether this is the only way or the best way of serving the main goal of tort law. If it is, then tort defendants must simply grin and bear it; the practice is necessary, and its structure can be said to match what they deserve. If it is not necessary, however, if there are other and better ways of compensating accident victims, then imposing this risk on negligent persons will seem unnecessarily retributive and arbitrary, in the sense of being insufficiently motivated by any good reason.

In fact, it is clear that there *are* better ways of compensating accident victims. We could set up a 'no-fault' scheme, levying a charge on all negligent drivers—or all drivers in general, figuring realistically that everyone will have moments of carelessness sometime in their driving career, adjusted perhaps for individual risk experience over time. If a driver protested, 'this is unfair, I'm being required to pay, even though I didn't actually *cause* any injury', we would reply by pointing out the implausibility of regarding the arbitrary vicissitudes of causation as conclusive of the issue of fairness. We would, if necessary, lay out for him the example of the drivers in the fast lane (set out in section VII, above), and the argument based on that. If he persists in his complaint, pointing to the fact that traditional tort liability makes causation central to liability as a way of disputing our claim that causality is morally irrelevant, we will reply that even in the best-justified scheme of tort law (the one described in the second half of section VIII), causation determines liability only as a lottery mechanism. In such a scheme, the nexus between causation and liability is not regarded as essential: it just happens to be the method we have adopted for ensuring that those who expose others to risks are exposed to substantially the same risk themselves. We can say to him in other words that the sheer fact of causation is not a morally relevant factor, and that even the schemes of liability in which it appears to be essential, are in fact—in their best-justified form— not schemes that really make it so.

We can state the advantages of no-fault over tort liability another way. Both schemes (no-fault compensation and tort liability) treat all negligent drivers the same. The no-fault scheme subjects them all to the same levy, while the tort scheme (in our reconstruction of it) exposes them all to the same risk. (Of course, in the latter case, as result of that equal exposure, some of them are ruined and some go scot free. But that is quite consistent with their being treated equally in the sense of being exposed to the same risk.)

We may even fine-tune the scheme, to ensure not only that like cases are treated alike but that relevantly different cases are treated relevantly differently. If there are varying degrees of negligence, then a properly administered Lewis-style tort scheme will expose equally negligent drivers to the same risk. All of those whose negligence imposes a 10 per cent risk of harm will be exposed to a 10 per cent risk of liability; all of those whose negligence imposes a 30 per cent risk of harm will be exposed to a 30 per cent risk of liability; and so on. By the same token, a well-administered no-fault scheme will adjust the levy it imposes on drivers to correlate with their driving records. Those whom the state determines (e.g. through the observations of the Highway Patrol) to be imposing on average a 30 per cent risk on other drivers will pay a heavier levy than those whom it determines to be imposing a 10 per cent risk. In this (complicated) way, both schemes treat like cases alike.

Thus, both schemes treat equals equally, and in that sense both of them satisfy principles of fairness. So how are we to choose between them? The question seems to be one for the drivers, since the victims should receive exactly the same (full) compensation, provided each scheme is perfectly administered (on its own terms).[34] Which scheme would the drivers choose—particularly if they did not know in advance (how could they?) whether their negligence was actually likely to cause injury or not?

[34] Opinions differ about how victims fare in second-best versions of these schemes. It seems clear that in the real world version of the liability lottery (with the vicissitudes of under-insurance, jury trials, and contingency fees) some victims end up with no compensation at all or considerably less than they deserve, while others get much more than they deserve. In the real version of the alternative scheme that exists in New Zealand, there is a common complaint that victims of accidents get less than they deserve in the way of compensation.

The answer seems to me to be obvious: if there was ever a case for max-imin,[35] this is it. If people opt for the liability lottery, drivers face a non-trivial chance of complete ruin if they lose—all for the hope of a gain which consists simply of not losing anything if they win. The downside is worse by orders of magnitude than the levy imposed under the no-fault scheme, and the upside of the liability lottery is only slightly better. For the sake of saving at most a few hundred dollars, drivers would be exposed to a poten-tial loss of millions. The insurance behavior of thousands of individuals who are in fact exposed to the liability lottery already gives us a clear indi-cation of drivers' preferences in regard to these alternative arrays of pay-offs.

X. Conclusion

We began with some questions about the fairness of imposing tort liability on those whose momentary carelessness happened to result in massive losses for others. Though such liability appears arbitrary from a moral point of view, we managed to cobble together an account—in terms of a Lewis-style lottery—which eliminated the appearance of unfairness. That move, however, does not amount to a vindication of tort liability. At best, it simply puts it on a par—so far as fairness is concerned—with other schemes, such as no-fault New Zealand style schemes of compensation. It remains unattractive as an alternative to schemes of the latter kind.

---

[35] Maximin refers to the following strategy for choosing among risks: if you have a choice, always choose the risk whose worst outcome is the best of the worst outcomes of all the risks available in the choice-set.

Wrongdoing, Welfare, and Damages: Recovery for Non-Pecuniary Loss in Corrective Justice

BRUCE CHAPMAN[*]

I. Introduction

Perhaps the most fundamental principle governing the award of damages in the law of torts is that it is the purpose of damages to restore the plaintiff to the position he or she would have been in had the tort not occurred—*restitutio in integrum*. Of course, it often will be very difficult to determine exactly what the appropriate measure of damages is under this principle; it often will involve, for example, very complicated predictions about what the future holds, or might have held, for the plaintiff. But the principle itself seems clear enough, and would appear to have been long accepted in the law.[1]

Recently, however, the principle has attracted the criticism of theorists of tort law from both the left and the right of the political spectrum. On the left, the compensation theorist of tort law emphasizes the needs of the injured plaintiff as they now are after the accident has occurred, and argues for economic damages to be biased towards the costs of future care. The position which the plaintiff was in before the accident occurred, or where the plaintiff might have been had there been no accident at all, is not of much concern. Indeed, this sort of theorist often sees an opportunity in the awarding of damages to do a little distributive justice, for example, arguing that similarly injured plaintiffs should receive the same basic awards for lost earnings, no matter how unequal these earnings might have been before the occurrence of the accident.[2] Yet, awards for *non-pecuniary* loss should

* Associate Professor, University of Toronto, School of Law. I am very grateful to Alan Brudner, Catherine Valcke, Stephen Waddams, and Ernest Weinrib for helpful discussions.

[1] *See, e.g.*, Livingstone v. Rawyards Coal Co. [1880] 5 A.C. 25, 39, *per* Lord Blackburn: 'I do not think there is any difference of opinion as to its being a general rule that, where any injury is to be compensated by damages, in settling the sum of money to be given for reparation of damages you should as nearly as possible get at that sum of money which will put the party who has been injured, or who has suffered, in the same position as he would have been in if he had not sustained the wrong for which he is now getting his compensation.'

[2] *See, e.g.*, PETER CANE, ATIYAH'S ACCIDENTS, COMPENSATION, AND THE LAW, (4th edn., 1987), 169–75. Feminist theorists of tort law also see an opportunity in damage awards to correct for the gender gap in earnings. *See, e.g.*, Elaine Gibson, *The Gendered Wage Dilemma in*

be modest on this theorist's view, and for much the same sort of forward-looking reason. Money damages are, by definition, of little use in compensating for non-pecuniary losses; better that scarce economic resources be allocated to what money *can* buy for the injured plaintiff, namely an adequate level of future care.

The utility of money damages has also been a concern of theorists of tort law on the right hand side of the political spectrum. Adopting an *ex ante* insurance perspective (rather than the *ex post* perspective of the compensation theorist), the economic analyst of tort law has argued that persons would not rationally insure for full compensation for non-pecuniary losses since the occurrence of such losses does not change (at the margin) the demand for money in any way.[3] To provide for such losses in damage awards, therefore, is to give something to the plaintiff which he would rather not have, at least if he has to pay for it, something which might well be true if one considers the effects of damage awards on the costs of everyone's liability insurance (e.g., where plaintiffs and defendants are in the same insurance pool) or on the prices of potentially injurious products.[4] Thus, although seeing the issue from the perspective of a consumer's willingness to pay, a perspective which depends upon, rather than abstracts from, a given *ex ante* distribution of wealth, the economic theorist of tort law nevertheless agrees with the compensation theorist that the forward-looking utility of money is a relevant consideration for awarding less in monetary damages to a plaintiff suffering non-pecuniary loss than what a strict adherence to the more backward-looking principle of *restitutio in integrum* would seem to require. Where these theorists differ is in what each would award for the costs of future care and the loss of future earnings. In direct contrast to the compensation theorist, the economist as insurance theorist, one suspects, would fully compensate for lost earnings and would argue that a plaintiff's willingness to pay *ex ante*, rather then a plaintiff's needs *ex post*, provides a proper, more modest measure of what the plaintiff ought to receive for future care.[5]

Personal Injury Damages, in TORT THEORY (Ken Cooper-Stephenson & Elaine Gibson (eds.), 1993).

[3] The insurance argument seems to have first appeared in detail in Philip J. Cook & Daniel A. Graham, *The Demand for Insurance and Protection: The Case of Irreplaceable Commodities*, 91 Q.J. ECON. 143 (1977). Early applications of the argument to the issue of damages include Samuel A. Rea, Jr., *Nonpecuniary Loss and Breach of Contract*, 11 J. LEGAL STUD. 35 (1982); and David Friedman, *What is 'Fair' Compensation for Death or Injury?*, 2 INT'L REV. LAW & ECON. 81 (1982).

[4] *See* David G. Owen, *The Moral Foundations of Products Liability Law: Toward First Principles*, 68 NOTRE DAME L. REV. 427, 475–84 (1993).

[5] This summary of the economic theorist's position on damages ignores, of course, what this same theorist would want to say about deterrence. The economist has recognized from the beginning that while the insurance perspective might argue for less than full compensation for some kinds of losses, the deterrence perspective needs to worry about the efficient avoidance of these losses, losses which are no less real and socially significant for their being

The corrective justice theorist of tort law, it would seem, would not want to address these forward-looking concerns about the utility of monetary damages. What matters for the corrective justice theorist is that the defendant has wrongfully caused an injury to the plaintiff. This injury may have different dimensions, and in particular may be made up of loss of future earnings, a need for future care, and non-pecuniary losses, but all of these are simply different factual manifestations of the defendant's same past wrongdoing and are equally significant from a normative point of view. All, therefore, should be fully compensated.[6] Or so it would appear. Certainly, the forward-looking concerns of the compensation theorist for meeting the needs of the now injured plaintiff, and for bringing about more distributive justice in some overall earnings profile, cannot concern a theorist whose backward-looking focus is on the correction of wrongdoing. Nor can it matter what damages the plaintiff might have been willing to insure; this turns too much on what the plaintiff can buy for herself *ex ante*, and not enough on what the plaintiff deserves to collect from the defendant as a matter of justice *ex post*.

In this chapter, I offer a slightly different account of what corrective justice requires for the payment of monetary damages. Specifically, I argue that, while corrective justice does require full compensation for the costs of future care, at least in so far as these involve pecuniary losses, and does require full compensation for the loss of future earnings, it does *not* require full compensation for non-pecuniary loss. This is true despite the fact that such losses have been caused by the defendant's wrongdoing and lie within its ambit. The reason for this, I argue, is that corrective justice corrects for wrongdoing within the space of rights, not welfare. While welfare under the

(typically) uninsured. Thus, on the economist's *deterrence* view, full compensation for non-pecuniary loss may be required. The different and seemingly incompatible requirements of deterrence and insurance theory have provided some economic analysts of tort law with an opportunity to explain the 'insurance crisis' that occurred in the middle part of the 1980s. *See, e.g.*, Michael J. Trebilcock, *The Social Insurance—Deterrence Dilemma of Modern North American Tort Law: A Canadian Perspective on the Liability Insurance Crisis*, 24 SAN DIEGO L. REV. 929 (1987). The incompatibility of insurance and deterrence has also led to various proposals for 'decoupling' the damage award into two sub-components, differing in what the defendant must pay and what the plaintiff should receive. *See, e.g.*, JULES L. COLEMAN, RISKS AND WRONGS (1992), 424–5. Since this chapter is more concerned with what the plaintiff should receive as an award for damages than with what the defendant should pay, the economist's insurance perspective provides a more relevant analysis than the deterrence argument.

[6] COLEMAN, *supra*, note 5, at 426, 428. The contractual side of Coleman's theory does not require the payment of damages for non-pecuniary loss (because the payments there are only those to which the plaintiff would agree, and the economist's insurance argument applies). However, the corrective-justice side of his theory (where losses are wrongfully visited upon the plaintiff outside the contract) does require full compensation for non-pecuniary loss.

For an example of a corrective-justice account of tort law damages which does *not* require full compensation for non-pecuniary losses (or even, perhaps, other sorts of losses as well), see Margaret Jane Radin, *Compensation and Commensurability*, 43 DUKE L.J. 56 (1993). This chapter analyses Radin's argument in greater detail in section IV, infra.

aspect of rights is ultimately attended to by a damages award under corrective justice, the fact that monetary damages can have no utility for the correction of non-pecuniary welfare losses under this aspect is decisive against the award of such damages.

If this argument is correct, it is of both theoretical and practical interest. As a theoretical matter, it signals a degree of consensus amongst theorists of tort law which might not have been expected. Whatever differences there might be in other respects between tort theorists, at least on this they should agree: full compensation for a plaintiff's non-pecuniary loss is not required. Perhaps more important than this, however, is the practical implication. Awards for non-pecuniary losses form a significant portion of the damages now recovered in tort actions.[7] Without them, therefore, we would live in a very different world. For any kind of tort theorist, this is an important fact of life.

II. Rights, Welfare and Damages

The most prominent of the contemporary theorists of corrective justice is Ernest Weinrib, and it is his theory of tort law which provides the focus for discussion here.[8] Other significant theorists of corrective justice or, at least, those whose theories exhibit some of the same aspects of corrective justice as does Weinrib's theory, such as Jules Coleman[9] and Stephen Perry,[10] are mentioned only in so far as their criticisms of Weinrib's account bear directly on the issue of awarding damages. As will be seen, while Weinrib's theory can withstand their critique, his response to these criticisms helps to clarify why corrective justice does not require full recovery for non-pecuniary loss.

For Weinrib, a negligence action in tort law instantiates the normative demands of corrective justice by exhibiting throughout its structure the correlativity of a special kind of doing by the defendant with the suffering of

---

[7] For example, over 60 per cent of U.S. automobile liability payments relate to non-pecuniary damages: *see* Bruce Chapman & Michael J. Trebilcock, *Making Hard Social Choices: Lessons from the Auto Accident Compensation Debate*, 44 Rutgers L. Rev. 797, 815–16 (1992).

[8] *See, e.g.*, Ernest J. Weinrib, *Causation and Wrongdoing*, 63 Chi.-Kent L. Rev. 407 (1987); Ernest J. Weinrib, *Understanding Tort Law*, 23 Val. U. L. Rev. 485 (1989) [hereinafter *Understanding Tort Law*]; Ernest J. Weinrib, *Right and Advantage in Private Law*, 10 Cardozo L. Rev. 1283 (1989) [hereinafter *Right and Advantage*]; and Ernest Weinrib, *The Special Morality of Tort Law*, 34 McGill L.J. 403 (1989). Weinrib's overall account of tort law can now be found in Ernest J. Weinrib, The Idea of Private Law (1995).

[9] Jules L. Coleman, *The Mixed Conception of Corrective Justice*, 77 Iowa L. Rev. 427 (1992); Coleman, *supra*, note 5.

[10] Stephen R. Perry, *The Moral Foundations of Tort Law*, 77 Iowa L. Rev. 449 (1992) [hereinafter *Moral Foundations*]; Stephen R. Perry, *Loss, Agency, and Responsibility for Outcomes: Three Conceptions of Corrective Justice*, in Tort Theory, *supra*, note 2, at 24 [hereinafter *Loss, Agency, and Responsibility*].

a corresponding injury by the plaintiff. In other words, the significance of wrongful doing in tort law lies in the fact that the defendant's conduct runs the foreseeable and substantial risk of a certain kind of suffering for another, and the significance of the suffering by the plaintiff lies in its being exactly the kind of suffering which lies within the ambit of that wrongful doing. Weinrib explains the role which is played by all the required elements of a successful negligence action in this way:

> The sequence starts with the potential for harm inherent in the defendant's act (hence the absence of liability for nonfeasance), and concludes with the realization of that potential in the plaintiff's injury (hence the necessity for causation). The further requirements of reasonable care and remoteness link the defendant's action to the plaintiff's suffering through judgments about the substantiality of the risk and the generality of the description of its potential consequences. Each category traces an actual or potential connection between doing and suffering, and together they translate into juridical terms the movement of effects from the doer to the sufferer. The negligence concepts form an ensemble that brackets and articulates a single normative sequence.[11]

While elegantly laid out, it is, nevertheless, remarkable that this articulation of the normative sequence of negligence only describes the sequence from its beginnings in the defendant's wrongdoing through to an end in the plaintiff's correlative wrongful loss. There is no mention here that the normative sequence carries forward into an obligation by the defendant to repair the plaintiff's loss by paying compensatory damages. It is as if the theory only provides us with an understanding of what it is to *judge* (however abstractly) possible wrongdoing in tort law, but nothing in the way of practical guidelines on how to *respond* to that judgment once we have made it. However, as Jules Coleman has pointed out, there is an important difference between, on the one hand, the duty not to wrong a person at all and, on the other hand, the duty to compensate someone you have wronged with a payment of monetary damages.[12] Coleman refers to the former as a primary duty and the latter as a secondary one, and his complaint of Weinrib's account is that the normative sequence of negligence fails to link the two.

Stephen Perry has argued that Weinrib's failure to link the two duties is more than some mere oversight, easily remedied, for example, by extending the sequence further and then running it somehow 'in reverse',[13] His argument is that Weinrib's theory of the primary duty of tort law is

---

[11] Ernest J. Weinrib, *The Jurisprudence of Legal Formalism*, 16 HARV. J.L. & PUB. POL'Y 583, 593 (1993).

[12] Jules L. Coleman, *Property, Wrongfulness and the Duty to Compensate*, 63 CHI.-KENT L. REV. 451, 469–70 (1987).

[13] *Cf.* Weinrib, *Understanding Tort Law, supra,* note 8, at 524: 'The conceptual structure of negligence law enables the court to trace the progression from doing to suffering and to reverse it by making the wrongdoer compensate the victim of the wrong.'

grounded in the abstract universality of rights rather than the particularity of individual welfare or interests. But the secondary duty to pay compensation for injury must of necessity operate in this excluded space of individual welfare or interest. As Perry succinctly puts the point: 'Compensation is for loss and loss must be understood as a degradation of an interest, but interests as such are accorded no normative significance by [Weinrib's theory of] abstract right.'[14] Thus, according to Perry, there is an unbridgeable gap in Weinrib's theory between these primary and secondary duties, a gap which, far from being merely a missing detail in Weinrib's overall account of tort law, actually 'makes tort law impossible'.[15]

However, Perry is surely wrong about Weinrib's theory and the role which it describes for individual interests or welfare. Far from manifesting the sort of indifference to individual interests which makes tort law impossible, Weinrib's theory of rights is replete with interests. Indeed, the theory requires that some such attention be given to interests if the rights of individuals are to have any determinate or actual existence in the world. In theories of rights, an interest only assumes the status of a moral good if it is an interest which has been freely chosen or determined by an agent. But, equally, an agent's potential for freedom is only real, or actual, if it is exercised as the determination of some particular interest as that agent's good. A potential for freedom which is never realized in this way is no potential at all.

Thus, the abstraction from particularity which concerns Perry and which, mistakenly, he thinks renders Weinrib's theory incapable of explaining the workings of compensatory damages, is only an abstraction from interests in particular (e.g., the special needs of someone who is seriously injured, no matter how this might have occurred) and not all particular interests.[16] Weinrib's claim that interests or welfare only have significance for corrective justice under the aspect of rights is merely a way of putting the age-old point that the right is prior to (although not exclusive of) the good, and that the good has no significance independent of, or prior to, the right.[17] The importance of this point, both as a general theoretical matter and for what it tells us about the problem of non-pecuniary loss, can be better appreciated by way of an example.

[14] Perry, *Moral Foundations, supra*, note 10, at 487.

[15] *Id.* at 488.

[16] Weinrib, *Right and Advantage, supra*, note 8, at 1288: 'Abstract right features abstraction from the particularity of willing. From the standpoint of the will in abstract right, particular acts, as well as the material circumstances and the subjective aims and interests that occasion those acts, have no standing of their own. Particular acts are only the contingent manifestations of free activity: they represent what the agent happened to choose from an array of possibilities. . . . Although a free will must, to be a will, will something, and therefore must determine itself in a particular choice, there is at this stage no choice in particular that is required by its being a free will.'

[17] For more detail on this reply to Perry, see Ernest J. Weinrib, *Formalism and Its Canadian Critics, in* TORT THEORY, *supra*, note 2, at 6, 20–3.

III. An Example With Four Variations

The significance of Weinrib's approach for considerations of individual welfare or advantage within tort law can be seen immediately from how he treats the following hypothetical example. This example is a slightly altered version of one which Weinrib has used himself to explain the relationship between rights and welfare as it exists within tort law.[18] However, the alterations to Weinrib's original example will prove useful here for the further development of some close variations. These variations will eventually take us back to the issue of recovering damages for non-pecuniary loss.

Suppose that while Smith is travelling by car to catch the ferry to the mainland, her car is negligently hit and damaged by Jones driving his car. The incident prevents Smith from catching the ferry, but this turns out to a very good thing for Smith as the ferry runs aground and sinks, drowning all passengers on board. There is no doubt, let us assume, that Smith would also have been drowned had she not had the car accident with Jones. Thus, the oddity here is that Jones's tortious conduct has actually been a net benefit for Smith; without the occurrence of the accident, Smith would have caught the ferry and now be dead.

Weinrib argues that most lawyers would agree with him that Smith can still recover from Jones in tort. Although Jones has benefited Smith with his tortious conduct, he has also violated her rights. It was her intention to use her car to catch the ferry, not to have it damaged by Jones. Moreover, Weinrib argues that the quantum of damages awarded to Smith should not be reduced because of what happened to the ferry after the car accident. While the *restitutio in integrum* principle suggests that damages should be awarded so as to put the plaintiff in the position she would have been in had the tort not occurred, the reach of this principle falls short of considering what Smith's welfare position would have been had she been on time to catch the ferry.

The point about the quantum of damages is the more interesting one for the purposes of this chapter. Why are our considerations about what might have happened to Smith's welfare 'but for' the tort not permitted to include some accounting for what her welfare would have been had she caught the ferry? The answer is that the loss for which Smith can seek compensation in tort is, as suggested by Weinrib in his response to Perry's critique, only measured under the aspect of Jones's wrongdoing or, correlatively, only as a violation of Smith's rights. Now, what makes Jones's negligent driving of his car wrong is the fact that such driving foreseeably endangers the safety of other persons and their property on the road. Thus, since Smith's damaged car falls easily within the ambit of Jones's negligence described in this

[18] Weinrib, *Right and Advantage, supra,* note 8, at 1283.

way (i.e., there is no remoteness problem), there should not be any difficulty in Smith recovering damages from Jones. Of course, it is foreseeable that such an accident also would delay Smith from reaching her destination at the ferry dock. But neither that fact by itself, nor any of the implications for Smith's welfare (positive or negative) which might attach to it, are relevant to the action in negligence.[19] Again, the point is that Smith's disadvantaged welfare is only of concern under the aspect of her rights as they have been violated by Jones, and it is no part of that wrongdoing that it might cause Smith to fail to be at some place (e.g., the ferry dock) at a certain time.[20]

The result in the case should not be any different if we vary the consequences of the sinking ferry example such that all the cars are forever lost but the passengers are saved. Here it is less clear, perhaps, that Smith has actually been benefited by Jones's tortious conduct, since Smith would not otherwise have lost her life, only her car, and that car has now been badly damaged and is in need of repair because of the accident. However, the original argument still applies, namely, that the harm to Smith's car from the collision lies within the ambit of Jones's wrongdoing and she, therefore, may recover damages. Considerations of what might have happened to Smith's welfare outside the ambit of this wrongdoing, such as that she would otherwise have lost her car, are simply not relevant.

This argument will immediately strike some as incorrect. Is it not normal legal practice to discount the value of damages which the plaintiff can

---

[19] See the discussion of 'irrelevant speeding' in H. L. A. Hart & Tony Honoré, Causation in the Law (2d edn.,1985), xxxviii–xxxix, 121–2. Hart and Honoré argue that speeding, when it only has the effect of bringing the negligent motorist to the wrong place at the wrong time (i.e., where an accident results), is irrelevant to liability in negligence because such speeding is not really a 'cause' of the accident. But this seems to involve an overly restricted account of causation. The better view would appear to be that there is causation in such a case, but not 'wrongful causation', i.e., it is no part of the wrongfulness of the defendant's speeding (and, therefore, no part of the violation of the plaintiff's rights) that the defendant might end up in some particular place at the wrong time.

[20] Cf. Weinrib, *Right and Advantage, supra,* note 8, at 1283 (citing Berry v. Sugar Notch Borough, 43 A. 240 (Penn. 1899)): 'Negligence law is concerned with the materialization of unreasonable risk, not with whether the defendant has caused the plaintiff to be or not to be at a certain place at a certain time.'

This makes the point in a very specific way, but the general thrust is clear. We need to attend to what it is that makes the defendant's negligence wrong to know what sorts of welfare claims by the plaintiff can plausibly lie within its ambit and be recoverable in tort. Often, this analysis of wrongdoing will take us well beyond foreseeability of the damage as the touchstone for liability into discussions of how we should appropriately view the purpose of the defendant's activity when that activity is performed non-negligently. While it is sometimes thought, for example, in cases of economic loss, that such a purpose test involves the use of an additional device for the limitation of what would otherwise be 'indeterminate liability', the truth is that such a concern for purpose is implicit in all cases of negligence, including the most basic of personal injury cases. For further argument to this effect, see Bruce Chapman, *Limited Auditors' Liability: Economic Analysis and the Theory of Tort Law,* 20 Can. Bus. L.J. 180, 210–3 (1992); and Bruce Chapman, *The Rational and the Reasonable: Social Choice Theory and Adjudication,* 61 U. Chi. L. Rev. 41, 99–103 (1994).

recover by the probability that the plaintiff would have suffered that loss at some time in the future anyway? The answer is 'yes', but that is not what is at issue here. Here Smith is seeking to collect for the costs of repairing her car, not for the loss of the car altogether. Where the former welfare loss, which actually occurred, lies within the ambit of the defendant Jones's wrongdoing, the latter sort of welfare loss, while it *might* foreseeably have happened (i.e., the car might have been completely destroyed by the accident with Jones), is not the sort of welfare loss about which Smith can now legitimately complain to Jones given what actually happened. But if she cannot complain about that welfare loss, so too is it the case that Jones cannot point to that kind of welfare loss (which otherwise might have happened to Smith) as an offsetting benefit for Smith of his tortious conduct. Thus, this first variation on the example stands on all fours with the original.

This discussion does suggest, however, that a second variation on the original example would be treated quite differently. Suppose that the negligently caused car accident results in the complete destruction of Smith's car and, further, that had Smith caught the ferry she would almost certainly have lost her car in any case. Now Smith is complaining of a lost car in the tort action and, under that head of damages, it *is* relevant that these damages would in all probability have been suffered in any event.[21] However, none of this analysis takes us to any consideration of Smith's welfare beyond that welfare loss she claims to have experienced under the aspect of Jones's wrongdoing. But this is what allows Jones to argue, now quite legitimately, that Smith is no worse off than she would otherwise have been without the accident and, therefore, that no damages for the lost car (or, at most, only highly discounted damages) are owing to her under the principle of *restitutio in integrum*.

A third slight variation drives this point home. Suppose now that, after the car accident in which Jones's negligence completely destroys Smith's car, Smith has her wrecked car towed onto the ferry and the car is lost when the ferry sinks. In other words, what might have happened under the second variation of the original example does actually happen here in the third. However, this cannot make any real difference, except perhaps to convert what was only the highest of probabilities (that Smith would have lost her car in any case) into a certainty.[22]

---

[21] In the well known American case, Dillon v. Twin State Gas & Elec. Co., 163 A. 111 (N.H. 1932), for example, the court discounted the plaintiff's damages to reflect the almost certain fact that the harm would have been suffered in any event.

[22] This would be consistent with the approach taken to such problems in the English cases. *See, e.g.,* Jobling v. Associated Dairies Ltd. [1981] 2 All E.R. 752 (where the 'vicissitudes of life', once they have become actual before the trial, can result in discounting the plaintiff's damages to zero). The Canadian approach, by contrast, would seem to allow for full recovery in such a situation. *See* Sunrise Co. Ltd. v. The Ship 'Lake Winnipeg' [1991] 1 S.C.R. 3 (Can.).

But now consider a fourth variation which combines aspects of the first and third. Suppose that Smith's car is only partially damaged and in need of only some repair after the accident with Jones, and that Smith gets it towed onto the ferry. Again, the ferry sinks so that all the cars on board are forever lost. What now? The original example and first variation both suggest that Smith should recover in full for the costs of repairing her car. After all, the only difference between the fourth and the first variation is that a welfare loss which was irrelevant as a high probability in the first variation has been converted into a certainty in the fourth. But the change in probabilities, as we have already seen from the third variation, should make no real difference. What does matter is whether Smith should be able to recover for the loss, and that is a function of whether the loss is the sort of loss which is embraced by Jones's wrongdoing, that is, falls within its ambit as a foreseeable *ex ante* possibility and, further, has been realized *ex post* as damages actually suffered by Smith. All of this, of course, is true in this fourth variation of the original example. Thus, on the analysis so far, Smith should recover for the costs of repairing her car even though the car has now sunk to the bottom of the sea.

Yet something does seem to have gone wrong here. Under the principle of *restitutio in integrum* the point of paying damages is to return the plaintiff to the position she would have been in had the tort not occurred. As we have already seen, however, only welfare losses and gains which lie within the ambit of the defendant's wrongdoing are properly considered in this exercise. This is what takes the losses which might otherwise have occurred in the original example (loss of life) and in the first variation (loss of car) out of consideration in the determination of damages. Equally, this is what allows what otherwise might have occurred and did occur (loss of car) in the second and third variations respectively to be all important in reducing the damages in those situations. But what if, as in the fourth variation, the plaintiff is complaining about the repair cost on a car which no longer exists because of what otherwise did occur? Now it is no longer *possible* to work the principle of *restitutio in integrum* in the space of welfare as this is informed by the defendant's wrongdoing. All that one can do here is to give money to the plaintiff, knowing that this will increase her welfare *in some other respect* (after all, money is always useful for something), but also knowing that it can have no restitutionary impact on any welfare loss as this is informed by the wrongdoing which has actually occurred to her.

This last problem is decisive against Smith recovering anything but nominal damages for her loss under the fourth variation. In all the examples to this point, the binding constraint on the payment of damages for welfare losses has been that these welfare losses are only relevant if they make their appearance under the aspect of rights which have been violated by the defendant's wrongdoing. However, where the plaintiff seeks money damages for welfare losses which now *cannot* be restored, in this case because the object of repair, the car, has itself been lost, then the only possibility which remains for money damages is for them to work in a welfare space which is uninformed by any aspect of the defendant's wrongdoing. Under this fourth variation, therefore, money damages simply cannot work on welfare losses in the normatively appropriate respect. Because this has been sufficiently decisive in earlier variations to disallow the plaintiff's recovery for such welfare losses, it should also be decisive against her recovering anything but nominal damages in the fourth variation. Nominal damages are appropriate here because they serve to recognize that the defendant has wrongfully injured the plaintiff, much in the way nominal damages do now in the law of trespass.[23]

The results of this section's analysis as it concerns the original example and the four subsequent variations are presented in summary form in the following table.

TABLE OF EXAMPLES

EXAMPLE	PLAINTIFF'S WELFARE LOSS		DAMAGES PAID
	A. In Collision	*B. On Ferry*	
Original	Damaged car	Highly probable loss of life	Full damages
First Variation	Damaged car	Highly probable loss of car	Full damages
Second Variation	Loss of car	Highly probable loss of car	Highly discounted damages
Third Variation	Loss of car	Actual loss of car	Zero or nominal damages
Fourth Variation	Damaged car	Actual loss of car	Zero or nominal damages

[23] By 'nominal' I mean only something like 'non-actual' or 'non-real', not necessarily 'small' or 'trifling'. In theory at least, it is possible that nominal damages for non-pecuniary loss could be quite large. Large nominal damages appear to be what is made possible by the Canadian Supreme Court decision in Andrews v. Grand & Toy Alberta Ltd. [1978] 2 S.C.R. 229 (Can.), where a $100,000 cap (in 1978 dollars) was imposed upon recovery for non-pecuniary loss. However, the Supreme Court seems to have been moved to award such damages as a kind of 'solace', something for which the amount of damages might vary according to the individual needs of the plaintiff. It should be clear that the provision of solace is not what is contemplated here under nominal damages, since such provision would very obviously work in a welfare space which is quite uninformed by the defendant's wrongdoing. The same might be said for any attempt to use damage awards as a measure of the plaintiff's sense of 'outrage' at the defendant's conduct, unless the payment of the money can be construed as somehow rectifying the (wrongfully caused) outrage, i.e., actually calming the plaintiff down rather than compensating for its occurrence in some other welfare space. For an interesting discussion of the possibility of compensating the plaintiff so as to calm her sense of outrage, see Radin, *supra* note 6, at 73.

IV. NON-PECUNIARY LOSS AND THE UTILITY OF MONEY

We now can see how this example might be relevant to an assessment of the plaintiff's right to recover for non-pecuniary loss. By definition, non-pecuniary losses are those for which the payment of money damages does no good. Thus, what is only contingently true in the case of the negligently damaged car—which happens subsequently to be lost forever when the ferry sinks—is universally true of non-pecuniary losses however they come about. To continue our example, assume that Jones's negligent driving causes the loss of Smith's old family portrait in the back of her car. Assume further that the portrait, while it might have huge sentimental value for Smith, has no market value at all. In these circumstances, Smith's loss is non-pecuniary and not something for which there can appropriately be any recovery beyond nominal damages.

The reason for non-recovery, again, is that money cannot work to restore a welfare loss in the normatively appropriate respect; it can only work in some other welfare space. The same result also would hold for the more usual examples of non-pecuniary loss which are somewhat further from our original example, such as past pain and suffering (for which therapy, purchasable on the market, is no good), the loss of a limb (so long as the loss does not affect future earnings, and is not the loss of the *use* of a limb for which the purchase of a prosthesis with money damages might provide some reasonable substitute), or the loss of a child. It would also, of course, be true of death or loss of the expectation of life.[24]

It is worth emphasizing, perhaps, that while this argument for very limited damages in cases of non-pecuniary loss does turn on the utility (or lack thereof) of money to the plaintiff, and in particular on the utility of the money in restoring that specific welfare loss of the plaintiff which lies within the ambit the defendant's wrongdoing, it does not turn in any way on considerations of how the plaintiff might choose to use the money. There is an important difference between, on the one hand, considering the uses to which the plaintiff *might* put the money awarded in damages and, on the other, considering what uses the plaintiff *can* put the money. The former goes to money's actual and very particular use, the latter to its overall utility.

However, this distinction is not always fully appreciated. In *H. West & Son Ltd. v. Shephard*,[25] for example, the English House of Lords considered the question whether an award for damages should be affected by the

---

[24] At common law, of course, death was not a compensable injury, either to the victim herself or to the surviving members of her family, disappointed in their expectation of continued support. The argument from corrective justice would only support the former exclusion, not the latter.

[25] [1964] A.C. 326.

fact that a permanently unconscious plaintiff would not be able to make use of any money which is awarded. Both Lord Reid[26] and Lord Devlin,[27] in dissent, were of the opinion that the plaintiff's inability to use the damages award was a relevant factor in reducing it, but the majority view, expressed in different ways by Lord Morris and Lord Pearce, was that such a consideration was irrelevant. However, both of these majority opinions confuse the use and the utility of money. Lord Morris, for example, begins with the proposition that 'it can be of no concern to the court to consider any question as to the use that *will* thereafter be made of the money awarded'[28] and follows this statement with a mix of examples which include cases where money damages could be useful (e.g., providing for medical treatment, compensating for loss of future earnings) and cases where money could be of no use at all (e.g., pain already endured, lost years of life). Lord Pearce structures his argument in the same way, that is, around the same dichotomy of actual and possible uses of money. He begins by considering a general proposition that concerns the utility of money damages (viz., 'that they *cannot* be used by her to compensate or console'),[29] but ends by claiming that 'the court does not look beyond the judgment to the spending of the damages', positing that '[w]hether the sum awarded is spent or how it is spent is entirely a matter for the plaintiff'.[30] However, the latter goes only to a contingent matter of how the plaintiff chooses to use the money within a range of unexamined possibilities, and does not address the issue with which he began, namely, what might be the possible uses for, or utility of, money in the first place. But on the view, roughly, that 'ought implies can', the utility of money is normatively important in a way that the actual use of money is not; if it is not the case that the plaintiff *can* use the money to restore the welfare loss in question, a welfare loss which is pertinent for tort consideration under the aspect of the plaintiff's violated right, it is not the case that the plaintiff *ought* to be awarded that money in compensation.[31] Nominal damages are all that can, and probably should, be awarded.

---

[26] *Id.* at 340–3.   [27] *Id.* at 363.   [28] *Id.* at 349 (emphasis added).

[29] *Id.* at 364 (emphasis added).

[30] H. West & Son v. Shepard Ltd. [1964] A.C. 326, 364.

[31] Someone might object at this point that it is possible to work with money within the welfare space made salient by the defendant's wrongdoing even though the money cannot be used to rectify the loss. In particular, one should award damages up to the point where the victim is indifferent between, on the one hand, suffering that loss and receiving the damage payment, and, on the other hand, not suffering the loss at all: *see, e.g.,* Radin, *supra,* note 6, at 59. This is certainly one way of thinking about how compensation 'makes the victim whole'. However, strictly interpreted, such an approach means that different plaintiffs who place different evaluations (or who have differently sloped indifference curves in this welfare space) on, say, damage to their car should collect different damages, despite the fact that the market price for rectifying this damage is the same for all. However, in tort law, although some plaintiffs might not care much at all about a dent in their car, the damages they collect will not be reduced on this account. This is the kernel of truth which lies at the centre of the claim made by both

Just as it is important not to confuse a plaintiff's (contingent) use of money with its overall utility, so it is also important to distinguish the idea that money may lack any utility in restoring the plaintiff's loss from the notion that money may be incommensurable with that loss. Margaret Jane Radin has emphasized incommensurability as central to her account of why corrective justice may not require full compensation for non-pecuniary loss. As the following quotation from her article suggests, there may appear to be some close affinities between her argument and the one presented here:

If corrective justice requires rectification, and if injury cannot be translated into money, how can payment of money ever amount to rectification, so as to satisfy the demands of corrective justice? The problem, an important one, has been too little noticed, perhaps because the connection between compensation and commensurability has been too little noticed. In my view, the problem will have to be dissolved rather than solved. That is, I think it most likely that the problem incommensurability poses for rectification as corrective justice will only be solved by developing an understanding of corrective justice that does not require rectification.[32]

In place of corrective justice as rectification, Radin offers corrective justice as redress:

Redress . . . means showing the victim that her rights are taken seriously. It is accomplished by affirming that some action is required to symbolize public respect for the existence of certain rights and public recognition of the transgressor's fault in disrespecting those rights. In this conception of compensation, neither the harm to the victim nor the victim's right not to be harmed are commensurate with money. They are not conceptually equated with fungible commodities.[33]

In other words, Radin argues that corrective justice as redress provides a way to restore the moral balance between the parties other than by putting the parties back into the *status quo ante,* which may not be capable of such restoration, or by putting them 'into a state equivalent in value to the *status quo ante,* which may be unachievable given the fact of incommensurability'.[34] Rather, compensation as redress restores moral balance between the parties by simultaneously symbolizing in a non-commodifiable space a respect for the plaintiff's rights and a denunciation of defendant's wrongdoing.

It should be clear that the argument in this chapter shares with Radin's an emphasis on the 'irretrievable' nature of the *status quo ante.* However, as the fourth variation on the above example also should suggest, it does not place the same emphasis on incommensurability. It is quite possible

Lord Morris and Lord Pearce, *supra,* notes 28–9, that the court does not concern itself with how the plaintiff actually *chooses* to use the damages which are awarded for rectification of a wrongful loss. This choice, of course, would turn on the plaintiff's personal evaluation of the loss (or the slope of the indifference curve), and the court's indifference to the choice signals its unwillingness to concede the objection as it is presented at the beginning of this footnote.

[32] Radin, *supra,* note 6, at 68.   [33] *Id.* at 61.   [34] *Id.* at 69.

(indeed, it seems likely) that the value of a damaged car is commensurate with money, but in the fourth variation discussed above there is, nevertheless, no recovery for this damage because the subsequent loss of the car renders recovery for that welfare loss quite useless. Money is equally useless in restoring a plaintiff's non-pecuniary losses and, therefore, damages for such losses are also not recoverable for that reason.

Of course, one possible explanation for the fact that monetary damages have no utility in restoring the plaintiff's loss could be that society believes that the loss is not properly commensurate with money and, acting on that belief, has seen to it that there is no market in which one can buy rectification of that loss as a commodity. But that need not be the only explanation. It could also be, although society is perfectly open from an ethical point of view to the commodification of some loss (for example, allowing for the purchase of a replacement in the market) that, nevertheless, no such replacements are yet available for technological reasons. Presumably, the loss of one's hearing was at some earlier time a non-pecuniary loss in this sense, but, in large part, is a great deal less so now. Equally, the loss of expectation of life from a once fatal disease may have been non-pecuniary in a way that it is not when certain cures, purchasable on the market for medical services, are made generally available. The utility of money with respect to some losses, therefore, depends much more on the presence of the good upon which the money needs to be spent, or on the availability of a market through which rectification of the loss might be bought, than does the commensurability of money with that loss.

Radin might say that this distinction continues to reflect the normatively impoverished view of corrective justice as rectification rather than redress since it still depends so much on the possible commodification of certain losses in the form of a market being available for their rectification. The loss of a child (or the loss of the ability to bear a child) is non-pecuniary, she would likely say, whatever market might be made available to 'remedy' the loss. Children, or the capacity to bear children, simply are not commodities in the way that corrective justice as rectification might suggest when the relevant markets and technologies (as for adoption or fertility) become available. However, nothing in the theory of corrective justice as rectification precludes society from making just such a normative judgement. Money's lack of utility for the rectification of wrongful loss can be explained by both normative *and* technological reasons. Where Radin's account would only imply no recovery for non-pecuniary loss in the former case, the account based on the utility of money would also have a comparable implication in the latter.

Finally, it is worth noting that Radin's account of corrective justice as redress has quite far reaching implications, some of which extend well beyond what we normally think of as the special problem of non-pecuniary loss. As already suggested, compensation as redress simultaneously symbolizes public respect for the plaintiff's rights and a denunciation of the defendant's wrong. Compensation takes the form of money, not because of money's general utility, but 'because of its importance in our culture', because of the weight we attach to it.[35] Indeed, for some entities, such as a business corporation, Radin suggests that money may be the only thing that really matters and, therefore, the only thing of significance which can be given up in redress as damages.

However, this suggests that for *any* injury the compensation required of the defendant might vary more with the characteristics of the defendant than it does with the injury suffered by the plaintiff. One is reminded here of Kant's discussion of punishment where appropriate proportionality can only be preserved 'if regard is had to the special sensibilities of the higher classes'.[36] Kant suggested that for some types of injury, for example, verbal insult, a monetary sanction may not be enough since 'someone who has a good deal of money can easily afford to make insults whenever he wishes'.[37] According to Kant, therefore, this may require that the law demand the offender to make a public apology to the person offended, 'but also at the same time to kiss his hand, even though he be socially inferior'.[38] Thus, one can imagine a range of responses to the need for public recognition of wrongdoing which are quite different from the more conventional payment of monetary damages as compensation in tort law. Indeed, as Kant's analysis suggests, money, while possibly very useful to the plaintiff for rectifying the loss, might *not* have much significance for the defendant. In such circumstances, a tort regime which focused more on the defendant's characteristics than the plaintiff's loss, and in particular concerned itself with a denunciation of the wrong which was meaningful to the defendant, might not pay much in monetary damages to the plaintiff. Thus, Radin's theory of compensation, based as it is on corrective justice as redress rather than rectification, could imply for the plaintiff quite limited recoveries of monetary damages even in those cases involving *pecuniary* loss.

V. Conclusion

In some respects it is surprising to discover that a limited right of recovery for non-pecuniary loss is an implication of Weinrib's theory of corrective justice. As the beginning of this chapter suggested, the discount on recovery for non-pecuniary loss which is characteristic of so much other con-

---

[35] Radin, *supra*, note 6, at 74.
[36] Immanuel Kant, The Metaphysical Elements of Justice (John Ladd trans., 1965), 101.
[37] *Id.*   [38] *Id.*

temporary tort law scholarship is to be found there because this scholarship views tort law and the payment of tort damages as instrumental to the achievement of some good, usually individual welfare, which has a standing independent of rights. At most, rights pose as neat conclusions to analyses which are based on these more forward-looking sorts of considerations. But Weinrib's backward-looking theory of corrective justice is steeped in an analysis of rights as prior to the good and is, therefore, quite self-consciously non-instrumental in its approach to individual welfare.

Yet this chapter shows that Weinrib's theory cannot remain purely non-instrumental throughout, at least if his account of the correlative tort sequence, which begins with the defendant's wrongdoing and embraces the materialization of that wrongdoing in the plaintiff's injury, is also to provide a coherent understanding of the defendant's obligation to repair the injury with a payment of money damages. Of course, with the materialization of wrongful loss, the only way that the defendant can recognize the plaintiff's right is by paying damages. Many times this will be enough, and other responses, such as merely issuing an apology to the plaintiff, will not be sufficient. In these cases money damages can provide for the reparation of the welfare loss as it is recognized under the aspect of the plaintiff's violated right; the apology, by contrast, only recognizes the indignity of the violation and not the underlying welfare loss.[39] At other times, and specifically when the plaintiff has wrongfully suffered a non-pecuniary loss as a result of the defendant's negligence, money damages will not be sufficient to provide the means to reparation. All that money can do here is increase the plaintiff's welfare in some respect which is irrelevant to the defendant's wrongdoing. But that, according to corrective justice, is not something to which damages in tort should attend. In such cases, therefore, only nominal damages, a kind of institutionally mandated and publicly observable apology, should be made available to the plaintiff, for that is the best that can be done.

The strict application of the principles of corrective justice, therefore, at least when they are faithful to the requirement that welfare losses only have standing to be considered in a tort action under the aspect of rights, ultimately must recognize the limited utility of money damages. On this last point at least, all of the contemporary theories of tort law seem to be agreed.

---

[39] Perry suggests that Weinrib's theory of corrective justice is consistent with the possibility of the wrongdoer offering a sincere apology to the plaintiff, and nothing more: *see* Perry, *Loss, Agency and Responsibility, supra,* note 10, at 36. Again, this follows from Perry's mistaken characterization of Weinrib's theory as only committed to the protection of rights in their abstraction, not their particularity.

The Basis for Excluding Liability for Economic Loss in Tort Law

PETER BENSON*

I. Introduction

My aim in this essay is to sketch a justification for the traditional exclusion of tort liability for certain categories of negligently caused pure economic loss. I have chosen to focus on the so-called exclusionary rule because, even after extensive scholarly discussion and despite the continuing authority of the rule, there is still little agreement as to its underlying rationale. There is even less confidence that its strict application is consistent with other aspects of the law's treatment of economic loss or with fundamental principles of tort law. By way of introduction, I will first briefly identify the main situations that raise an issue of tort liability for economic loss and then give a preliminary idea of the kind of justification that I will propose, indicating how it differs in approach from most current efforts to account for this area of tort law.

A. Classifying Economic Loss Situations

This chapter examines five different situations into which economic loss cases can be divided. In the first two situations, which may be thought of as 'exclusionary', courts hold that economic loss may not be recovered. In the remaining three situations, by contrast, courts have permitted recovery. The defining features of each of the five situations should be briefly identified.

The first 'exclusionary' situation is typified by circumstances where the defendant damages something in which the plaintiff may have a contractual interest (or something else that is less than a possessory or proprietary right) and this impairs the plaintiff's interest, causing him financial loss. (I shall refer to this as 'Situation I').[1] For example, I may have a right by

Associate Professor of Law, McGill University. I am grateful to Mahmud Jamal for his research assistance and to David Cohen and David Owen for editing the text. In particular, I wish to thank Gregory Bordan for making very helpful comments on the entire draft. The presentation of the argument changed as a result of his suggestions and, on a number of important substantive points, discussion with him enabled me to clarify my views.

[1] Cases commonly treated as coming under this first category include the following types of circumstances: Cattle v. Stockton Waterworks Co. [1874–80] All E.R. 220 (Q.B.) (plaintiff

contract with a third party, or just a liberty, to use the third party's bridge for my business purposes. As a consequence of the defendant damaging the bridge, the contract may be frustrated or I may no longer be able to exercise my liberty and I must seek alternative means to accomplish my ends, resulting in economic loss. Ever since the landmark nineteenth century English case of *Cattle*, English, American, and Commonwealth courts with very few exceptions have consistently held that in such circumstances the defendant cannot be liable in negligence for the loss, whether or not it was foreseeable. The plaintiff's claim for recovery will be dismissed for failure to state a cause of action. Financial loss that arises from physical damage to something which the plaintiff neither owns nor possesses is often referred to in the decisions and in legal scholarship as 'relational' economic loss. The rule that precludes liability here has become known as the 'exclusionary rule'.

The exclusionary rule has recently been applied by a number of the highest appellate courts in a second type of situation (hereinafter 'Situation II').[2] Here the plaintiff may have acquired a chattel, for example, that is inherently defective because of the defendant manufacturer's want of due care and, on account of the defect, the product poses a danger of injury to the plaintiff's person or property (other than the chattel) if it is put to use. The plaintiff sues the defendant in negligence for the cost of putting the chattel in a condition so that he can continue to use it free from that risk. The courts characterize the claim as one for pure economic loss for which there can be no liability.

In marked contrast to these two 'exclusionary' situations, there are three situations in which courts regularly hold that there *can* be liability. The decisions that reach this conclusion stand side by side those that apply the exclusionary rule and are of equal authority.

---

contractor must incur additional expenses to complete performance of his contractual obligations on land owned by other contracting party because of damage caused to it by defendant's negligence); La Société Anonyme de Remorquage à Hélice v. Bennetts [1911] 1 K.B. 243 (plaintiff tug owner loses remuneration under towage contract when unable to complete towage of ship when latter is sunk *en route* through defendant's negligence); Byrd v. English, 43 S.E. 419 (Ga. 1903) (plaintiff sustains financial loss when unable to operate his plant as a consequence of defendant's negligent interference with supply of electricity provided by third person under contract with plaintiff); Candlewood Navigation Corp. v. Mitsui O.S.K. Lines Ltd. [1986] A.C. 1 (appeal taken from N.S.W.) (plaintiff time-charterer claims for wasted hire paid under contract to owner of vessel and for profits lost while vessel had to be docked for repairs caused by defendant's negligence); Leigh & Sillavan Ltd. v. Aliakmon Shipping Co. [1986] A.C. 785 (plaintiff buyer sustains financial loss as result of defendant damaging goods at a time when risk, but not the property in the goods, has passed to plaintiff).

[2] *See, e.g.*, Murphy v. Brentwood Dist. Council [1990] 2 All E.R. 908 (H.L.); East River S.S. Corp. v. Transamerica Delaval Inc., 476 U.S. 858 (1986); *cf.* Sutherland Shire Council v. Heyman (1985) 60 A.L.R. 1 (Austl.). The Supreme Court of Canada, however, has recently come to a contrary conclusion. *See* Winnipeg Condominium Corp. No. 36 v. Bird Constr. Co., 121 D.L.R. 4th 193 (Can. 1995)

In the first of these 'non-exclusionary' situations (hereinafter 'Situation III'),[3] the courts allow recovery for financial loss that arises in circumstances identical to those that come under the exclusionary rule, save for the fact that the loss is deemed to be 'unavoidably' incurred by the plaintiff. In this type of situation, the loss, though economic, is analogized to physical injury to the plaintiff's person or property.

By way of illustration, I will give two Situation III examples that parallel the two kinds of circumstances that come within the exclusionary rule. First, in the context of using something that is either owned or possessed by a third party, the plaintiff involves his own property or person in such a way that it can be adversely affected if the other thing (which he does not own) is damaged, with a risk of financial loss to the plaintiff as a consequence. Suppose that the defendant damages the third party's thing and, before the plaintiff can extricate his own property from the ambit of danger, it is affected by the initial damage, causing him financial loss; or, in the process of attempting to neutralize the risk to his property, the plaintiff incurs pure financial loss. At first blush, this seems to be a case of relational economic loss because the plaintiff's interest is impaired as a result of the defendant damaging something that belongs, not to the plaintiff, but to a third party. Yet the courts do not apply the exclusionary rule but instead allow recovery where the usual requirements for negligence have been met. In the second Situation III example, a plaintiff does not know that his chattel (which the defendant manufactured) is defective and that it can cause him financial loss through its impact on his *other* property; or, on discovering that this is the case and in attempting to protect this other property from the danger, the plaintiff unavoidably sustains financial loss as a result. Here, too, the plaintiff can recover.

The two other 'non-exclusionary' situations are where the plaintiff's financial loss arises through a special relationship of justified detrimental reliance by the plaintiff on the defendant (hereinafter 'Situation IV'),[4] and where it results from the defendant's intentional interference with the plaintiff's contract with a third party (hereinafter 'Situation V').[5] To explain this contrast with the exclusionary rule, it will be essential to bring out the relevant differences between these situations and those coming under the exclusionary rule. In the case of justified detrimental reliance, the loss, which

---

[3] Examples are: Newlin v. New England Tel. & Tel. Co., 54 N.E.2d 929 (Mass. 1944); Spartan Steel & Alloys Ltd. v. Martin & Co. [1972] 3 All E.R. 557 (Eng. C.A.); and Muirhead v. Indus. Tank Ltd. [1986] 1 Q.B. 507 (Eng. C.A.). I have in mind here RESTATEMENT (SECOND) OF TORTS (1977), § 766C cmt. b, illus. 5.

[4] For example, Glanzer v. Shepard, 135 N.E. 275 (N.Y. 1922); Hedley Byrne & Co. v. Heller & Partners Ltd. [1964] A.C. 465. This basis of liability is recognized regularly in decisions where the exclusionary rule is strictly applied. See for instance *Murphy* [1990] 2 All E.R. at 920, *per* Lord Keith, at 929–30, *per* Lord Bridge, and at 934, *per* Lord Oliver. I discuss justified detrimental reliance at *infra*, text accompanying notes 48–53.

[5] Ever since Lumley v. Gye, 2 E. & B. 216 (1853).

may be purely economic, can arise from damage done to something that the plaintiff neither owns nor possesses. And where the action is for intentional as opposed to negligent interference with contract, a mere contractual right qualifies as a fully protected interest—often characterized as 'quasi-property'[6]—as against the defendant who is, of course, a perfect stranger to the contract. It is worth noting here that the analysis of contractual rights as quasi-property for the purposes of intentional tort is older than the conclusion that such rights do not constitute a protected interest in an action for negligence.

B. Justificatory Approaches

The analysis of liability in the five types of situations of economic loss just discussed—two 'exclusionary' and three 'non-exclusionary'—provides us, at least provisionally, with fixed points for which a satisfactory account must be sought. I propose to do this by elucidating a justification for the exclusionary rule. The central aim of the essay is to suggest a rationale for the rule that draws on fundamental ideas and principles which underlie all five situations of economic loss, binding them together as a coherent unity.

To make clearer the sort of explanation that I will present, it may be helpful to set it against the background of current attempts, both judicial and scholarly, to justify the exclusionary rule. These may briefly be characterized as follows: with but a few notable exceptions, they share the assumption that the rationale for the rule is not to be sought in any general conception of responsibility and fairness that is widely regarded as underlying the law of negligence and of tort law as a whole. This approach should be further explained.

When courts, especially in recent times, *explicitly* suggest a basis for the rule, they commonly refer to considerations of policy which, instead of being rooted in a general conception of liability for negligence, are explicitly viewed as constraining what would otherwise be the normal operation of basic principles of tort law. More specifically, they endorse what James called the 'pragmatic objection' to liability for economic loss, which justifies the rule on the sole basis that it provides a means of avoiding indeterminate or unlimited liability.[7] Underlying this justification is a conception of

---

[6] See, for instance, discussions and cases cited in W. Page Keeton, Dan B. Dobbs, Robert E. Keeton, & David G. Owen, Prosser and Keeton on The Law of Torts (5th edn., 1984), 981. I discuss intentional interference with contract at *infra*, text accompanying notes 54–7.

[7] Fleming James, Jr., *Limitations on Liability for Economic Loss Caused by Negligence: A Pragmatic Appraisal*, 25 Vand. L. Rev. 43 (1972). Recent English and Commonwealth judicial examples of this view include: Electrochrome Ltd. v. Welsh Plastics Ltd. [1968] 2 All E.R. 205, 208 (Glamorgan Assizes) (Geoffrey Lane J); Leigh & Sillavan Ltd. v. Aliakmon Shipping Co. [1986] A.C. 785, 816–17; Candlewood Navigation Corp. v. Mitsui O.S.K. Lines Ltd. [1986] A.C. 1, 25; and Norsk Pac. S.S. Co. v. Canadian Nat'l R.R. [1992] 1 S.C.R. 1021, 1054 ff. (Can.) (La Forest J).

liability for negligence, usually associated with the now overruled case of *Anns*,[8] that defines proximity solely in terms of the creation of a risk of foreseeable loss. It is not difficult to show that this view of liability leads to a problem of indeterminacy.

Given the evident social fact of the interdependence of economic and proprietary interests in virtue of which a practically unlimited range of interests are intertwined in an almost unlimited variety of ways, it must be reasonably foreseeable that damage to any one interest may affect other interests, however removed or indirect the impact may be. No reverberation from the initial damage, so long as it arises through this interdependence of interests, can intelligibly be distinguished as extraordinary or unforeseeable. If we combine this conclusion with the conception of liability that equates proximity with foreseeability of loss, there must be at least a *prima facie* general duty to refrain from causing economic loss, whether it is direct or indirect, relational or otherwise. The exclusionary rule is introduced to contain, and indeed to cut off, this consequence. It is needed, in other words, precisely because the conception of liability itself leads to a result which is deemed to be undesirable. Far from being mutually supportive or integrated parts of a larger conception, the understanding of liability and the exclusionary rule are thus in direct tension with each other.

As for theoretical writing, the few systematic attempts to provide a rationale for the exclusionary rule draw explicitly on economic concepts.[9] The main difficulty with this approach, in all its different versions, is that it invariably neglects or rejects certain distinctions and requirements that the cases usually treat as essential in reasoning toward their conclusions;[10] or else it introduces new considerations and lays stress on factors of which there is no trace of influence in the judgements.[11] Those who adopt this

[8] Anns v. Merton London Borough Council [1977] 2 All E.R. 492 (H.L.) was overruled in Murphy v. Brentwood Dist. Council [1990] 2 All E.R. 908 (H.L.). For a different interpretation of *Anns*, see the interesting remarks of Lord Oliver in *Aliakmon* [1985] 2 All E.R. at 56–8.

[9] For an exception to these 'policy-based' approaches, see Stephen Perry, *Protected Interests and Undertakings in the Law of Negligence*, 42 U. TORONTO L.J. 247 (1992). Limits of space preclude discussion of Perry's view, which is different from the explanation proposed here, but I hope to do so in a planned expanded version of the present chapter.

[10] E.g., W. Bishop, *Economic Loss in Tort*, 2 OXFORD J. LEGAL STUD. 1 (1982). Bishop dismisses the legal requirement of a proprietary or possessory right as economically arbitrary: '[t]he fact that the plaintiff does not own property that has suffered physical damage is economically irrelevant, as is the fact that his loss arises by way of contract': *id.* at 25. *See also* P. P. Craig, *Negligent Misstatements, Negligent Acts and Economic Loss*, 92 L.Q.R. 212, 234 (1976); RICHARD A. POSNER, TORT LAW: CASES AND ECONOMIC ANALYSIS (1982), 464–6.

[11] E.g., Mario J. Rizzo, *A Theory of Economic Loss in the Law of Torts*, 11 J. LEGAL STUD. 281 (1982). Rizzo ascribes decisive economic importance to whether a 'channelling contract' existed or could have existed between the plaintiff (who suffered relational economic loss) and a third person (who suffered injury to person or property) under which the latter could have been obliged to indemnify the former for his economic loss. My difficulty with this contention is that Rizzo does not, in my view, show that any leading decision makes this, whether explicitly or by necessary implication, the reasoned basis of its conclusion. For a similar criticism,

approach do not justify their departure from judicial reasoning on the basis of any supposed incompleteness in existing legal analysis nor do they point to any lack of fit among the considerations and principles that the law invokes. They disregard or add to the reasoning found in the cases simply because this is called for by economic theory. But this approach fails to take seriously on its own terms the very object that is supposedly under investigation, namely, the law. We are entitled to expect more from a theory that purports to be a theory of law.

The approach that I take in this essay differs fundamentally from these current efforts at justification. I shall attempt to root the exclusionary rule in a rationale that rests essentially on a conception of liability, or at least on an aspect thereof, which is presupposed throughout the law of negligence. I will try to do this by using the very categories, principles, and considerations on which courts rely in reaching their conclusions about liability. Because this account draws on and articulates ideas that are already available in the public legal culture, even if only latently, it presents itself as a *public* justification of the exclusionary rule.[12] In this way, a public justification purports to be internal to the law.

For the purposes of this essay, it will suffice if I am able to uncover in the cases a definite and coherent conception of liability that explains the exclusionary rule and to show that the conception is one which fits with the analysis of liability in the five situations of economic loss outlined above as well as with fundamental principles of negligence. My goal is to identify that conception and to make clear its essential characteristics. I shall not analyze its moral basis by explicating its underlying notion of justice or by justifying it from a moral point of view.[13] Nonetheless, I believe that the following discussion sets out the first crucial step in the elaboration of a satisfactory public justification for the analysis of liability in the central cases of pure economic loss. Given present disagreement about, and even sheer failure to explain, the rationale and scope of the exclusionary rule, it hopefully addresses a need of our public legal culture. At stake is the very possibility of a coherent, acceptable, and widely shared understanding of the reasons underpinning the law of pure economic loss and, I aim to show, of a basic and permanent feature of our conception of negligence.

---

see Robert L. Rabin, *Tort Recovery for Negligently Inflicted Economic Loss: A Reassessment*, 37 STAN. L. REV. 1513, 1535 (1985).

[12] This reference to certain features of a public justification draws on the much more developed account presented by Rawls. *See* John Rawls, Justice as Fairness: A Briefer Restatement (1990) (unpublished manuscript, on file with author); JOHN RAWLS, POLITICAL LIBERALISM (1993).

[13] I address these questions in Peter Benson, *The Basis of Corrective Justice and its Relation to Distributive Justice*, 77 IOWA L. REV. 515 (1992).

II. THE REASON FOR THE EXCLUSIONARY RULE

For more than a century, virtually uninterrupted chains of authority that developed even in detail along similar lines in the British Commonwealth and in the United States have consistently applied the exclusionary rule to actions in negligence for relational economic loss. Far from abolishing or even restricting the rule, courts took it to its natural limit, generalizing its principle and filling out its scope and application. And they did this during the same period in which they were elaborating a modern law of negligence 'that pushed liability for physical injuries toward the full extent of what was foreseeable and shattered ancient barriers to recovery based on limitations associated with privity of contract and similar restrictive concepts.'[14] On what basis did the courts reach a conclusion seemingly in direct tension with the basic tendency of the law?

A point that has been made repeatedly by both courts and scholars—and so has now become familiar—is that the law did not exclude liability on the ground that such loss is either unforeseeable or financial. The cases have made clear that, on the one hand, economic loss may be perfectly foreseeable and yet non-actionable, and, on the other, that purely economic interests will receive in certain circumstances the full protection accorded by tort law to interests in person and property.

Less widely noticed, however, is the striking fact that many, if not most, of the cases that have upheld the exclusionary rule have done so without making any reference to a pragmatic concern over extensive liability. This is especially true of the English, Commonwealth, and older American authorities. In this respect, Holmes' important opinion in *Robins*,[15] in which this consideration of policy does not appear to play any role whatever, is fully representative of the majority of cases. In fact, there are a number of decisions, among them Lord Penzance's influential speech in *Simpson*[16] and the later discussion of Widgery J in *Weller*,[17] that set out with great clarity and detail the kinds of far-reaching consequences that must follow if the plaintiff's claim is valid. Yet, these judges go on expressly to say that their rejection of the claim does not, and should not, rest on this potential for extensive liability: '[t]he magnitude of these consequences must not be allowed to deprive the plaintiffs of their rights, but it emphasises the importance of the case.'[18] Explicit judicial endorsement of the pragmatic justification, especially by English courts, is with few exceptions a recent

---

[14] James, *supra*, note 7, at 47.
[15] Robins Dry Dock & Repair Co. v. Flint, 275 U.S. 303 (1927).
[16] Simpson & Co. v. Thomson [1877] 3 A.C. 279, 289–90 (appeal taken from Scot.).
[17] Weller & Co. v. Foot & Mouth Disease Research Inst. [1965] 3 All E.R. 560, 563 (Q.B.).
[18] *Id.*

phenomenon.[19] When Lord Oliver remarked that 'as I read those cases [where recovery for economic loss was denied] it was not the `economic quality' of the damage which prevented recovery but the reason why that damage had occurred',[20] he correctly and neatly stated the general view.

A. *The Common Factor in the 'Exclusionary' Situations*

In circumstances of relational economic loss (Situation I), the 'reason why the damage has occurred' is, first, that the plaintiff has a contractual interest falling short of a proprietary or a possessory right, with respect to something owned or possessed by a third party; and, secondly, the plaintiff sustains financial loss when his interest in that thing is impaired by the defendant damaging it. For example, the plaintiff may have a contractual right against a third party to use the latter's bridge for business purposes, and the plaintiff suffers financial loss when he is no longer able to use the bridge after the defendant damages it. The courts view this set of circumstances—and nothing more—as a sufficient basis for precluding liability. The reason the law reaches this conclusion would seem, then, *prima facie* to lie in these circumstances themselves, which therefore require closer analysis.

The plaintiff's claim is with respect to an interest that arises through a contract with a third party. The plaintiff may be entitled by the contract to use, say, the third party's chattel to his advantage or to benefit from it in some way; or he may be obliged by the contract to maintain the chattel in a certain condition or to shoulder various expenses if it is damaged. As a result of the defendant damaging it, the plaintiff's advantages may be rendered less beneficial or his obligations made more onerous, giving rise to financial loss. To generalize and to simplify somewhat, we may say that the plaintiff's interest in the chattel is such that a change in the chattel's condition (caused, for instance, by the defendant's failure to use due care) will affect the use to which the plaintiff is contractually entitled or obliged to

---

[19] One early American case that does so is Connecticut Mut. Life Ins. Co. v. New York & New Haven R.R., 25 Conn. 265, 275 (1856). It might be thought that the landmark case of Cattle v. Stockton Waterworks Co. [1874–80] All E.R. 220 (Q.B.), or the widely-cited decision of Cardozo CJ in Ultramares Corp. v. Touche, 174 N.E. 441 (N.Y. 1931), are further examples. This view, I believe, is mistaken. Here, a few brief remarks will have to suffice. As for *Cattle*, I refer the reader to my remarks *infra*, text accompanying and following note 33. As regards *Ultramares*, it is important to note that Cardozo does not present the concern over extensive liability as a reason of policy that negatives or limits what, given his general conception of liability for negligence, he would otherwise view as a valid claim in tort. Rather, he sees liability 'in an indeterminate amount for an indeterminate time to an indeterminate class' as indicative of a flawed conception of duty: *id.* at 444. Moreover, he only expresses a concern of this kind in cases of claimed justified detrimental reliance by plaintiffs on defendants; he does not justify the exclusionary rule on this basis. As we will see, Cardozo's difficulty with relational economic loss lies elsewhere.

[20] Leigh & Sillavan v. Aliakmon Shipping Co. [1985] 2 All E.R. 44, 59 (Eng. C.A.).

put it, thereby reducing the benefits or increasing the burdens associated with that use.

However, the plaintiff has no proprietary or possessory right in the chattel. More specifically, the plaintiff cannot show that at the moment of the defendant's wrong, and independently of it, he possesses a proprietary or a possessory right in the chattel founded on a legally recognized ground such as demise charter, bailment, or easement.

At common law, a proprietary or possessory right in something entitles a person to exclude anyone else from using it without his consent, so long as the first person has, relative to others, a better claim to it in ownership or possession.[21] If a plaintiff lacks a proprietary or possessory right in something, he has no legal standing to constrain a defendant from intentionally using it as the defendant sees fit, even if this impairs or interferes with the plaintiff's interests. In other words, the defendant cannot be liable to the plaintiff for such harmful consequences. And if this is so when the consequence is intended, the same must be true when it is brought about by the defendant's negligence.

In addition to property and possession, there is one other possible basis of exclusive right in private law, namely, contract. However, contractual rights, in contrast to proprietary or possessory rights, are personal rights that are against a definite individual or definite individuals, so that the fact that there may be a contractual right against one person does not in itself imply that there is an exclusive right against anyone else.[22] Now in circumstances of relational economic loss, the plaintiff's *sole* exclusive right to the use of the damaged chattel is, by hypothesis, a contractual right against someone other than the defendant. Therefore, as against the defendant, the plaintiff does not have any right at all to the exclusive use of the chattel. In other words, the plaintiff has no legal grounds for complaint if the defendant intentionally or negligently damages the chattel, thereby depriving the plaintiff of its use with resulting economic loss to him.

Relative to the defendant, the legal significance of the plaintiff's contractual interest comes to this: he seeks protection of an interest in the use of something from which he has no right to exclude the defendant. This tension is identified by Holmes, who makes it the ground of his decision in *Robins*: 'justice does not permit that the petitioner be charged with the full value of the loss of use unless there is some one who has a claim to it as against the petitioner.'[23] It seems, then, that the difficulty with the

---

[21] *See* FREDERICK POLLOCK, AN ESSAY ON POSSESSION IN THE COMMON LAW, (1988) pts. I & II, at 20–5; OLIVER WENDELL HOLMES, JR., THE COMMON LAW (Mark DeWolfe Howe (ed.), 1963), 169 ff. For judicial discussion, see The Winkfield [1902] P. 42, 54–61 (Probate, Divorce and Admiralty Division) (Collins MR).

[22] I discuss this point further, *infra,* text accompanying notes 54–5.

[23] Robins Dry Dock & Repair Co. v. Flint, 275 U.S. 303, 309 (1927). *Accord,* Byrd v. English, 43 S.E. 419, 420 (Ga. 1903).

plaintiff's action is not that the loss is either unforeseeable or financial or that it carries with it a threat of indeterminate liability and so must fail as a matter of policy. Rather, the plaintiff lacks a right on which to rest the interest that forms the very basis of his claim, and this is deemed to be fatal from the standpoint of justice. Since, on this view, the problematic aspect of the claim is the absence of a right or *jus*, the rationale for the exclusionary rule may be characterized as juridical.

What is more, this same analysis seems to hold for the second situation in which courts have applied the exclusionary rule. Here, the reader may recall, the plaintiff's financial loss consists in the cost of repairing something defective which he owns so that he can continue to use it without danger of injury to himself or to his other property. The defect, we suppose, has resulted from the defendant's want of due care. We further assume that there is no contract between the parties. For example, in the important recent English case, *Murphy v. Brentwood District Council*,[24] the plaintiff purchased from a construction company a newly built house whose design had been (negligently, as it turned out) approved by the defendant council. In due course, the plaintiff noticed that the house was seriously defective, both in its structure and in its foundation. These defects posed a risk of imminent danger to the health and safety of the occupants. Unable to carry out the necessary repairs, the plaintiff decided to sell the house, subject to the defects, for an amount considerably less than its market value in sound condition. The plaintiff sued for the difference.

Among the several leading decisions that have recently denied liability in these circumstances, none is so perspicuous as Lord Oliver's speech in *Murphy*. Although the plaintiff's claim in *Murphy* was for expenditures made or needed to correct a situation involving a risk of physical injury, Lord Oliver characterized the loss as purely economic and as coming under the exclusionary rule, in this regard disagreeing fundamentally with *Anns*. He viewed the loss in this way because '[t]he injury will not now ever occur unless the plaintiff causes it to do so by courting a danger of which he is aware and his expenditure is incurred not in preventing an otherwise inevitable injury but *in order to enable him to continue to use the property or the chattel*.'[25] On this view, what the plaintiff sought to protect was an interest in being able to use something in a certain (safe) condition: the claim was for the cost of putting his defective property in shape so that he could have the benefit of its use (if only its resale value) in an improved condition. But while the plaintiff may have owned the property he wished to ameliorate, what he actually owned at the moment he discovered the defect, and the danger it posed, was just defective property. The property in an *improved* condition was not his present property or possession. It sim-

---

[24] [1990] 2 All E.R. 908 (H.L.).   [25] *Id.* at 936 (emphasis added).

ply did not yet exist. And on the facts, the plaintiff did not have against the defendant a contractual or any other right to the future possession and enjoyment of the property in a non-defective condition. Here, just as in the first situation, the fundamental difficulty with the plaintiff's claim seems to be that it was premised on his having a protected interest in the use of something over which he could not establish any right as against the defendant.

On the basis of this analysis of the two 'exclusionary' situations, we are now in a position to identify in a preliminary way what courts seem to regard as the essential difficulty with the plaintiff's claim in both: the claim is with respect to an interest *in the use of something* over which the plaintiff *lacks an exclusive right as against the defendant.* In the first situation, although not in the second, the plaintiff has a *contractual* interest in the chattel damaged by the defendant. This difference, however, is immaterial. The significance of the plaintiff's contractual interest in the first situation is simply that it establishes that his claim is, with respect to benefits or burdens, associated *with the use of* the chattel.[26] But this can be shown in other ways. For instance, the plaintiff may simply rely on the possibility of using something without having a contractual right to do so, or he may have the kind of interest in use evidenced in the defective chattel cases just discussed. Similarly, the fact that in the first situation, but not the second, there is a third party who owns or possesses the property which the plaintiff wishes to use is also an inessential difference. In both situations, the plaintiff has no right as against the defendant to have the property which he wishes to use available in a condition that is suitable for his use, whether this is because the property belongs to a third party or because what belongs to the plaintiff is only the property in a defective condition.

B. Distinguishing 'Unavoidable' Economic Loss

Thus far I have suggested a basis for the exclusionary rule by specifying what is common to the two situations (I and II) of financial loss in which the rule is applied. This conclusion must now be tested by seeing whether it is consistent with the fact that courts *permit* recovery for financial loss in certain defective property cases and in certain circumstances of relational economic loss.

In the *Murphy* case discussed above, Lord Oliver distinguishes certain circumstances in which he would *not* apply the exclusionary rule: the plaintiff can recover where he sustains financial loss 'in preventing an otherwise inevitable injury'. I take Lord Oliver to be referring here to what I identified

---

[26] This analysis of the legal significance of a contractual relation between plaintiff and third person in cases of relational economic loss contrasts with the view proposed by Rizzo, *supra,* note 11.

earlier as Situation III, in which the plaintiff attempts to insulate his *other* property from the risk imposed by his defective chattel, and he unavoidably incurs financial loss in the process of doing so. As in Situation II, the plaintiff here owns something that, because of the defendant's negligence, poses a danger to the plaintiff's person or other property. The distinguishing feature of this third situation is that as a result of—or despite—the plaintiff's efforts to avoid the danger, he unavoidably suffers financial loss. Economic loss that arises in this way is analyzed as part of physical injury to person or property and is recoverable if reasonably foreseeable.

Moreover, courts also view certain cases of *relational* economic loss in this same light. A typical situation is where the plaintiff is using something that *belongs to a third party* in such a way that if it is damaged, the plaintiff's own property may be endangered.[27] The defendant damages the third party's property and the plaintiff unavoidably suffers financial loss before he can extricate his property from the danger or as a result of his attempt to do so. Although the loss is economic and relational—because it is financial loss that is consequential on damage done to something that the plaintiff neither owns nor possesses—and so seems in this respect at least to be indistinguishable from Situation I, the exclusionary rule is not applied.[28]

How do we account for the fact that the law grants recovery in these cases of 'unavoidable' financial loss? What we must determine is whether these cases share a common feature which distinguishes them intelligibly from the circumstances that fall under the exclusionary rule. In the following discussion, I begin with and focus on 'unavoidable' *relational* economic loss. I do this because relational economic loss is the oldest and best established category of loss to come under the exclusionary rule; therefore, it is especially important to explain why certain forms of relational loss are regularly exempted from its application.

Like cases of relational economic loss that come under the exclusionary rule, 'unavoidable' relational loss also occurs because, in the context of the plaintiff using something which he neither owns nor possesses, he suffers financial loss when that thing is damaged by the defendant. For example, suppose that the plaintiff, a caterer, owns and uses a number of refrigerators that are supplied with electricity by a third-party power company under contract, and that this supply is unexpectedly interrupted during the night as a result of the defendant negligently damaging the power company's electrical cable. Unless the plaintiff can take his food out of his non-functioning refrigerators, within a brief period of time, it will spoil. To do

[27] As in Newlin v. New England Tel. & Tel. Co., 54 N.E.2d 929 (Mass. 1944) (defendant telephone company's negligently maintained pole fell on third party power company's line carrying electricity to plaintiff's mushroom farm, causing temperature rise and loss of crop).

[28] Seavey, for one, drew attention to this striking divergence from the exclusionary rule. Warren A. Seavey, Candler v. Crane, Christmas & Co.—*Negligent Misrepresentation by Accountants*, 67 LAW Q. REV. 466, 472 & n. 24 (1951).

this, however, he must pay a worker an extra fee to perform this emergency night-time work. The food is successfully removed and the plaintiff seeks to recover damages from the defendant for the extra night-time labor fee paid to the worker. Now it might be thought that in making a claim for this loss the plaintiff must invoke a right to exclude the defendant from interfering with the plaintiff's use of something which he neither owns nor possesses (the supply of electricity through the cable), making this situation indistinguishable from relational loss cases that come under the exclusionary rule. This, however, would be mistaken. The loss occurs here in a qualitatively different way. This needs to be explained.

The plaintiff's claim here involves the assertion against the defendant of a right, not to have the continued or the unimpaired use of something which the plaintiff does not own or possess, but rather to be free from injury caused to his person or property. The financial loss that is suffered by the plaintiff results just from his effort to protect his property from the very risk imposed on him by the defendant, viz., that the food will spoil if left in the non-functioning refrigerators. The financial loss here occurs through the plaintiff's property (refrigerators) being so connected with the third party's property (cable) that the former can be affected, as part of a single causal sequence, by conduct that impinges on the latter. It is certainly true, in our example, that this connection exists because the plaintiff has chosen to make use of the third party's supply of electricity. However, he need not rest his claim to recover for financial loss on a purported right to prevent the defendant from making the electrical cable unfit for his use. The claim only requires that the defendant not affect the cable in such a way that the plaintiff sustains a loss before he can (or as a result of his attempting to) extricate his property from the ambit of risk. The claim need refer only to the severing and not to the maintenance of the connection between the plaintiff's property and the thing that he is using but does not own. The fact that the injury takes place in circumstances of the plaintiff using another's thing goes only to the particular manner or causal sequence through which the injury is brought about. It does not imply a right, as against the defendant, to present or future use of the thing.

The plaintiff's action for financial loss here rests on the same implicit claim of right against the defendant as would an action against the defendant for the value of the food, supposing instead that it had spoiled before the plaintiff had a reasonable opportunity to take it out. There is no doubt that, assuming that requirements of causation, foreseeability, and so forth, were met, there could be recovery for this loss even though it was consequential on the plaintiff using something (the power company's electrical cable) which he neither owned nor possessed. It would be viewed as a case of simple injury to property. The point is that in both situations—the one involving a pure financial loss, the other property damage—the plaintiff does not have to assert implicitly against the defendant a right to the continued use and benefit of the third party's cable in order to make out his claim for recovery. The plaintiff's financial loss arising from the payment of the extra fee can be analyzed in the very same terms as a case of injury to property.

To bring out the limits of this claim for financial loss, consider the following claims by way of contrast. Suppose, for instance, that because the cable cannot be repaired for several days, the plaintiff is obliged to rent other refrigerators to preserve his food, for which expense he seeks compensation. Or secondly, suppose that the plaintiff's action against the defendant is to recover that part of the fee paid to the worker which would have been charged anyway in ordinary circumstances for removal of the food. Or finally, suppose that the plaintiff claims the profit he would have earned had he been able to continue to use his own refrigerators and to dispose of the food in his usual way. In each, the plaintiff's claim is valid only if we presuppose that he has, as against the defendant, a right to continue to receive and to benefit from the third party's electricity—and therefore a right as against the defendant to the continued use of a functioning refrigerator. The losses here happen in the same way that relational economic loss occurs in those cases that come under the exclusionary rule. These losses represent but different consequences of the materialization of the same risk that the plaintiff may lose the use of the third party's cable as a result of the defendant's negligence—something quite different from the risk that the plaintiff's food will spoil if unavoidably left in the non-functioning refrigerators. The latter risk simply no longer exists; the plaintiff has had a reasonable opportunity to remove the food unspoiled. In this respect, these claims for financial loss are not different from a claim of property loss arising in circumstances where the plaintiff has deliberately courted the risk of spoilage by putting food in his refrigerators *after* he knows them to be non-functioning. In both, the plaintiff's claim would have to rest on the same implicit assertion of right: that as against the defendant, the plaintiff has a right to the continued use of the third party's electricity.

Moreover, this analysis of 'unavoidable' relational economic loss also holds for the defective product cases distinguished by Lord Oliver as not coming under the exclusionary rule. In those cases, the plaintiff sustains a financial loss because of his effort to avoid the very risk of injury to himself or to his other property posed by a defective chattel (which he owns). The financial loss that he claims is not the cost of correcting the chattel's defect so that he can continue to use it without danger to himself or to his other property, but just the expense, if any, that he unavoidably incurs in attempting to put himself or his other property outside the ambit of perceived danger. If the plaintiff can do this (as will usually be the case) by simply ceasing to use the defective chattel once he has become aware of the danger posed, there will be no recovery. The only exception would be where, in the particular circumstances, the plaintiff has to incur costs to enable him just to cease using the chattel or to undertake further measures to protect himself or others if the danger posed by the chattel continues despite his ceasing to use it. This analysis ensures that the right claimed by the plaintiff against the defendant is not a right to the use of something that is not his (viz., the chattel in a non-defective condition), but only a right to the integrity of his person or property (other than the chattel).[29] And the fact that the chattel is owned by the plaintiff and not, as in cases of relational loss, by a third person does not affect the basic nature of the plaintiff's claim here. It is no different from a claim for 'unavoidable' relational loss.

This brief discussion of the cases of 'unavoidable' financial loss makes clear that the legal analysis which treats them differently from actions barred by the exclusionary rule turns on a difference between them that is both intelligible and categorical. Without attempting to provide a deeper justification for this legal analysis, we can still say that the circumstances which the law views as different do indeed involve different types of possible legal claims. And we can state the latter in intuitively intelligible and straightforward terms. Moreover, our discussion also explains why the real difficulty with actions barred by the exclusionary rule does not lie in the fact that they are for loss that is either economic or unforeseeable. The determining factor seems to be the *kind* of claim that the plaintiff must implicitly assert to establish his loss. It should be emphasized that an action to recover for *physical* loss to property may rest on the same kind of claim that is barred by the exclusionary rule. Suppose, for example, that the safety of the plaintiff's property depends on his being able to use something which he neither owns nor possesses, and that his property is damaged when the thing is no longer available for his use because of the defendant's want of due care. Just as there is no liability for relational economic loss that rests on an interest of this kind, so too there should not be—and is not[30]—liability for physical loss involving the same sort of interest.

Considering the difference between cases that allow recovery for 'unavoidable' financial loss and those that come within the exclusionary

---

[29] Here I am disagreeing with the dissenting opinion of Laskin, CJ, in Rivtow Marine Ltd. v. Washington Iron Works [1974] S.C.R. 1189, 1217 (Can.), *disapprov'd in* Murphy v. Brentwood Dist. Council [1990] 2 All E.R. 908 (H.L.), *and approv'd in* Winnipeg Condominium Corp. No. 36 v. Bird Constr. Co., 121 D.L.R.4th 193 (Can.1995). In my view, both this dissenting opinion and the decision of the Supreme Court of Canada in *Winnipeg Condominium* are wrong because they do not preclude liability for nonfeasance.

[30] *See, e.g.*, H.R. Moch Co. v. Rensselaer Water Co., 159 N.E. 896 (N.Y. 1928) (plaintiff's property was destroyed by fire due to defendant water company's failure to supply proper pressure at the hydrant as it was required to do under contract with city).

rule, the principle barring recovery for economic loss may be stated as follows: an action for damages must fail if it is not grounded in a right which is exclusive as against the defendant. More emphatically, the plaintiff's claim must not rest, *even in part*, on an interest that is not rooted in a right of this kind. To explain, in cases of relational economic loss barred by the exclusionary rule, the plaintiff's action may be for the diminution in value of an asset *that he owns*, the loss having resulted from the defendant injuring something else that belongs to a third person. Yet, on the foregoing analysis, the plaintiff should not recover, although the defendant has affected the value of the plaintiff's own property, if the maintenance of its value depends on the plaintiff's having the continuing use of the thing owned by the third person. While the plaintiff's claim depends merely in part on his asserting a protected interest (in the use of the third party's thing) that does not rest on an exclusive right as against the defendant, this is enough to disqualify the action. For the plaintiff to have a *protected* interest *vis-à-vis* the defendant, it must be possible to analyze that interest wholly in terms of an exclusive right against him.

Another way of articulating the reason for dismissing the plaintiff's action is to say that the loss occurs because the plaintiff has freely decided to rely on the availability of something from which he cannot rightfully exclude the defendant, and this must be at his own risk. In effect, the plaintiff has chosen to make the well-being of his person or property (financial as well as physical) dependent on the existence of certain contingent circumstances (for example, the availability of something for use) which the defendant may alter at will without violating any right in the plaintiff as against him. If loss results, it will be imputed to the plaintiff's own voluntary choice to rely, not to the defendant' conduct. On this analysis, the non-recoverability of economic loss illustrates the idea that persons are not generally responsible for the consequences of others' independent decisions to rely in this way, at least where those consequences represent the materialization of risks that were entailed by such reliance. Thus, even if it is perfectly foreseeable that there has been and will be such reliance, this alone cannot make others accountable. Something more is required. What this is I will explore later, below.

In the light of this last point, however, the following objection might be raised against our previous analysis of cases of 'unavoidable' financial loss where recovery *is* granted. When a plaintiff decides to use something (owned by a third party) in such a way that damage to it can result in the plaintiff suffering unavoidable financial loss, it may be contended that the plaintiff has also acted at his own risk and that consequently there should be no liability. To refer this objection to the earlier example, one might contend that because the plaintiff freely chose to hook up his refrigerator to the third party's power supply, he cannot reasonably hold the defendant responsible for causing a loss that happened only because the plaintiff decided to make use of the third party's electricity.

The short answer to this objection is that the defendant must regulate his conduct on the basis, first, that the plaintiff will make use of things which he may not own, thereby bringing himself or his property into relation with them; and secondly, that by damaging those things, the defendant can under certain circumstances foreseeably injure the plaintiff or his property. This must be taken as given when deciding which consequences are to be imputed to the defendant's conduct. The reason for this can be explained as follows.

The fact that every individual is *some*where and is making use of *some* external objects, with the result that he or his property is put into relation with them and is subject to being affected by conduct that affects them, is an inevitable incident of being active in the world. The thought here is *not* that persons may require certain things to meet their needs or to fulfil their purposes. A requirement of this sort would make the plaintiff's claim into one for the continued use of something, which could run afoul the exclusionary rule. The idea is rather this: as beings who exist in space and time and who are *inescapably* active and purposive,[31] persons are necessarily and always connected in manifold ways with other things which they can affect and which in turn can affect them as part of a causal sequence. More specifically, as inescapably purposive beings, persons must always be subjecting external things to their purposes—in other words, they must be making use of the latter in some way. This is also an inseparable feature of their being in the world.

If, then, in deciding which consequences are to be imputed to a defendant's conduct, we take the plaintiff to be acting *at his own risk* with respect to harms that result from damage to something else with which he is connected by such inevitable use, we in effect say to the plaintiff that others cannot be held responsible for injuring him if the loss arises through a necessary and inseparable aspect of his being a purposive agent in the world. But this would be to deny the plaintiff's standing as a rights-holder with respect to the very capacity, namely, a capacity for purposive conduct, that is usually thought to mark him off as an accountable being who can have rights and obligations. Thus, in asserting a purported liberty to injure others in this way, the defendant puts forward a claim that is directly incompatible with the very basis of right. It is no less problematic than if the plaintiff were to impute to the defendant the wholly unintended and

---

[31] Any attempt on a person's part to overcome his purposive, active nature must itself involve the very thing that he is trying to annul, namely, the exercise of his purposive capacity.

unforeseeable consequences of his actions—that is, consequences which the defendant could not possibly have chosen to avoid.[32]

This analysis applies to our example. There, the reader will recall, the plaintiff sustained financial loss as a result of his effort to protect his property (his food) from the very risk of harm created by the defendant (spoilage). In claiming compensation for the extra fee charged for the removal of the food, the plaintiff, we saw, did not have to assert an interest in the continuing use of the third party's electricity. To the contrary, by removing his food, he canceled his dependency on it. Accordingly, the fact that he happened to be using the electricity at the time of the defendant's negligence represents nothing more (but also nothing less) than the use of *some*thing at a given point in time; that is, it represents an inevitable incident of purposive conduct and must be taken as something given by the defendant in deciding what precautions to adopt in order to avoid causing the plaintiff a loss. Where the circumstances are otherwise, and the plaintiff's claim involves the implicit assertion of a right to the continued use of something in the face of the defendant's risk-imposing activity, the use is no longer inevitable in the required sense and so this conclusion does not follow.

Thus, we may provisionally conclude that cases coming within the exclusionary rule, as well as those allowing recovery for 'unavoidable' financial loss, all seem to be explicable on the basis of a simple factor—namely, whether, at the time of the defendant's wrong, the plaintiff's interest is wholly grounded in an exclusive right as against the defendant. What we must now determine is whether this requirement of an exclusive right reflects a basic underlying premise of our general conception of liability for negligence and, if so, precisely what it is. For a justification that aims to be internal to the law, a definite affirmative answer to this question is essential if the proposed explanation is to get off the ground.

III. THE EXCLUSIONARY RULE AND NONFEASANCE

An account that seeks to remain internal to the law faces here a particular difficulty. As a rule, the courts have not explicitly attempted to root the reason for the non-recoverability of economic loss in an underlying conception of negligence. What we find instead are statements that such claims are not of the requisite kind, or do not state a loss which the law regards as recoverable or that there is no legal authority to support such an action

---

[32] I suppose here, without specifying further, that the analysis of liability in tort law involves some basic notion of accountability that rests on the defendant having and exercising a capacity for purposive conduct and choice. Stated in these general terms, I believe the contention is uncontroversial.

except on the part of someone with a proprietary or possessory right of the required sort.[33] Indeed, in the very first decision that announced the exclusionary rule, the case of *Cattle*, Lord Blackburn justified the conclusion of no liability on the ground that '[n]o authority in favour of the plaintiff's right to sue was cited, and as far as our knowledge goes, there was none that could have been cited'.[34] Such reliance on authority seems on its face to be problematic. I think, nevertheless, that we should resist the all too easy temptation to dismiss these formulations as no more than failed attempts to justify the exclusionary rule. There is another, more plausible, view of the matter.

It is important to recall here that such formulations are found in long and virtually uninterrupted chains of authority in both the British Commonwealth and the United States that consistently upheld the exclusionary rule throughout the period of the development of modern negligence doctrine. What obstacle prevented all these courts over a period of more than a century from limiting or even abolishing outright the exclusionary rule, instead of expanding and generalizing its application as they did? None, it is submitted, except perhaps this: courts rejected plaintiffs' claims of this type because they viewed these claims as failing to meet, and indeed as directly colliding with, a prerequisite of liability which they already regarded as basic even before the development of a general and distinct conception of negligence in this century. That courts continued to adopt formulations of this kind to justify the exclusionary rule even while they were initiating far-reaching transformations in negligence law is at least consistent with this hypothesis. The difficulty, of course, is that for the most part the courts did not identify this prerequisite nor explain its relation to the general conception of liability for negligence which they were elaborating. So the hypothesis cannot be definitively demonstrated one way or another. On the other hand, judicial recourse to authority is precisely the kind of justification that invites further explication. If we can identify a fundamental premise of liability which was, and continues to be, presupposed throughout the law of torts but which is rarely articulated in explicit and abstract terms, and if, moreover, there is a close fit between this premise and the analysis of liability in the economic loss cases, there will be strong grounds for supposing the hypothesis to be correct. By explaining judicial reliance on precedent as congruent with a widely accepted feature of our conception of liability, the analysis can remain internal to the law even while it goes beyond the law's explicit formulations in terms of authority. Given limits of space, a brief discussion will have to suffice.

[33] *See, e.g.,* Simpson & Co. v. Thomson [1877] 3 A.C. 279, 290; Elliott Steam Tug Co. v. Shipping Controller [1922] 1 K.B. 127, 139 (Eng. C.A.); and Leigh & Sillavan Ltd. v. Aliakmon Shipping Co. [1985] 2 All E.R. 44, 60–1 (Eng. C.A.).

[34] Cattle v. Stockton Waterworks Co. [1874–80] All E.R. 220, 223 (Q.B.).

It was only in this century that the common law elaborated a distinct and general conception of negligence—one that still largely prevails to this day. According to this conception, liability is to be analyzed in terms of a relation of duty and correlative right between defendant and plaintiff.[35] In cases of non-recoverable economic loss, we saw that the plaintiff's interest is not grounded in an exclusive right against the defendant. Given the idea of the correlativity of right and duty, we can reformulate the problem with these cases in the more familiar terms of duty, as follows: what feature, if any, of our general conception of negligence precludes a duty of care in these circumstances?[36]

Certainly, it is well established that in general an individual cannot be under a duty of care toward another unless his acts or omissions impose a risk of foreseeable loss on the other. But the requirement of foreseeability does not explain the non-recovery of economic loss. For while foreseeability may be necessary to the existence of a duty of care, it is clear that it is not a sufficient condition—that there is a further quite distinct requirement which, we will see, is conceptually prior to it. A particularly explicit and clear recognition of this further requirement is found in the often-cited speeches of the Law Lords in the case of *Home Office v. Dorset Yacht*.[37] Take, for instance, this statement of Lord Diplock:

The branch of English law which deals with civil wrongs abounds with instances of acts, and, more particularly, of omissions which give rise to no legal liability in the doer or omitter for loss or damage sustained by others as a consequence of the act or omission, however reasonably or probably that loss or damage might have been anticipated.... Examples could be multiplied. You may cause loss to a tradesman by withdrawing your custom though the goods which he supplies are entirely satisfactory; you may damage your neighbour's land by intercepting the flow of percolating water to it even though the interception is of no advantage to yourself; you need not warn him of a risk of physical danger to which he is about to expose himself unless there is some special relationship between the two of you such as that of

---

[35] The classic and still the most profound elucidation of this conception is Cardozo CJ's decision in Palsgraf v. Long Island R.R., 162 N.E. 99 (N.Y. 1928). For other explicit statements of this conception, see Admiralty Comm'rs v. Steamship Amerika [1917] A.C. 38, 55 (Lord Sumner) ('for in tort the wrongful act of the defendant and an invasion of the right of the plaintiff must concur'); M'Alister (or Donoghue) v. Stevenson [1932] A.C. 562, 619 (appeal taken from Scot.) (Lord Macmillan); Seale v. Perry [1982] V.R. 193, 200 (Lush J) and 210 (Murphy J); Sutherland Shire Council v. Heyman (1985) 60 A.L.R. 1, 48 (Austl.) (Brennan J).

[36] I am agreeing here with Professor J. C. Smith that economic loss barred by the exclusionary rule raises an issue of duty rather than one of remoteness: *see* J. C. Smith, *Economic Loss and the Common Law Marriage of Contracts and Torts*, 18 U.B.C. Law Rev. 95 (1984). *See also* Attorney-General for New South Wales v. Perpetual Trustee Co., 85 C.L.R. 237, 286 (1952) (Austl.).

[37] [1970] A.C. 1004, 1027, *per* Lord Reid, 1034, *per* Lord Morris, 1042, *per* Viscount Dilhorne, and 1060, *per* Lord Diplock. For two other recent cases that state this requirement in explicit terms, see Hargrave v. Goldman (1963) 110 C.L.R. 40, 64–66 (Austl.) and Sutherland Shire Council v. Heyman (1985) 60 A.L.R. 1, 41–2 (1985) (Austl.) (Brennan J).

occupier of land and visitor; you may watch your neighbour's goods being ruined by a thunderstorm though the slightest effort on your part could protect them from the rain and you may do so with impunity unless there is some special relationship between you such as that of bailor and bailee.[38]

All these examples of no liability share a common feature: the plaintiff's claim against the defendant for loss suffered as a result of the latter's act or omission depends on the plaintiff asserting an interest which is not recognized by law. More precisely, the plaintiff must claim a right to exclude the defendant from using something which the plaintiff neither owns nor possesses (viz., the examples of withdrawing one's custom and intercepting the flow of percolating water); or he must assert a right to compel the defendant to protect his person or property from risks that are wholly independent of the defendant's conduct (viz., the failure to rescue examples). It is clear that the underlying difficulty with each of these claims is that the plaintiff cannot ground them in a notion of exclusive ownership or right; that is, in a right to prohibit others from using or injuring what is one's own without one's consent. In the first set of examples, the plaintiff does not own or possess the thing from which he wishes to exclude the defendant; in the second, the plaintiff seeks, not to prevent the defendant from using or injuring the plaintiff's thing, but to enlist the defendant's efforts to preserve it against risks which have arisen independently of his conduct. By way of explaining these long-established and widely-accepted propositions of law, we reach the following conclusion: absent a special relationship between the parties, a duty of care will not be implied unless the plaintiff's claim against the defendant is rooted in a purely negative right of exclusive ownership. This conclusion represents nothing other than the classic distinction between misfeasance and nonfeasance of which Bohlen wrote that "[t]here is no distinction more deeply rooted in the common law and more fundamental'.[39]

To prevent misunderstanding, it should be emphasized that the distinction between misfeasance and nonfeasance is not, and has never generally been viewed by the courts as, a difference between acts and omissions. An omission under certain circumstances may constitute misfeasance, just as an act in another context may be mere nonfeasance. Nor does the distinction provide an intelligible basis for treating differently physical and financial loss. It goes rather to the *form* of right in which the plaintiff's claim against the defendant must be conceived to be actionable. It must be possible to root it in a claim of exclusive right, irrespective of whether the

---

[38] *Dorset Yacht* [1970] A.C. at 1060.

[39] Francis H. Bohlen, *The Moral Duty to Aid Others as a Basis of Tort Liability*, 56 U. PA. L. REV. 217, 219 (1908). For a more recent discussion of the significance of this distinction for tort doctrine, see J. C. Smith & Peter Burns, Donoghue v. Stevenson—*The Not So Golden Anniversary*, 46 M.L.R. 147, 153 ff (1993).

content of the entitlement is physical or financial in quality. The plaintiff's loss must be a subtraction from (or injury to) something in which the plaintiff has an exclusive right—something which counts as the plaintiff's 'own'—against the defendant; but, at the same time, the plaintiff must not claim more than this purely negative entitlement to exclude the defendant. Accordingly, the law sometimes formulates this distinction as a difference between causing injury (which can give rise to liability) and withholding a benefit (which cannot).

The idea of misfeasance stipulates an essential condition that must be met if the plaintiff's loss is to be actionable as a violation of a right that can be correlative to another's duty to take care. It is the first step in conceptualizing an interest that can be the object of a duty of care. And since it establishes the existence of something that can qualify as a loss for the purposes of liability, it is conceptually prior to the further question of whether there has been foreseeable loss. The law will not imply a duty of care unless both conditions are satisfied.

The distinction between misfeasance and nonfeasance, as I have just explained it, underlies the law of torts as a whole and, in particular, is presupposed in the law of nuisance,[40] negligence,[41] and intentional wrong.[42] To satisfy the principle that there is liability only for misfeasance, a plaintiff must establish that he had the required entitlement (against which his loss will be measured) at the very moment at which the defendant's duty is alleged to have arisen. For example, in a nuisance case such as *Fontainebleau*, where the plaintiff's loss stems from the defendant's interference with the free flow of light from adjoining land to the plaintiff's premises, the law will require the plaintiff to establish a proprietary or possessory right to that flow on some recognized legal basis. Failure to establish the right will result in the court's refusal to impose a duty on the defendant to refrain from unreasonably obstructing the passage of light, even though this detrimentally affects the plaintiff by diminishing the use and value of his own property. Similarly, in circumstances of relational economic loss where the loss flows from the defendant impairing the plaintiff's use of something, the plaintiff must establish on some recognized legal ground—such as easement, demise charter, bailment, and so forth—that he

---

[40] *E.g.*, Mayor of Bradford v. Pickles [1895] A.C. 587; Fontainebleau Hotel Corp. v. Forty-Five Twenty-Five, Inc., 114 So. 2d 357 (Fla. 1959).

[41] *See supra*, note 37. In addition, see the analysis of negligence by Lord Templeman in Tate & Lyle Indus. Ltd. v. Greater London Council [1983] 2 A.C. 509, 529–31, and RESTATEMENT (SECOND) OF TORTS (1963), § 314.

[42] The classic example is intentionally inflicting economic loss on business rivals by setting up a competing enterprise and drawing away their customers. In *Dorset Yacht*, both Lord Reid (at 1027) and Lord Diplock (at 1060) include this example along with other instances of no liability for nonfeasance. The early wild-animal cases, such as Pierson v. Post, 3 Cai. R. 175 (N.Y. 1805), or Young v. Hichens (1843) 6 Q.B. 606 also illustrate the principle. See Holmes' discussion in THE COMMON LAW, *supra*, note 21, at 171 ff.

had a proprietary or possessory right in that thing.[43] This is a necessary prerequisite to establishing the existence of a relationship of proximity between the parties through which a duty of care arises. The duty is not the source of the proprietary or possessory right. On the contrary, the existence of a duty presupposes the antecedent existence of this entitlement. That the plaintiff's claim in the nuisance case displays the same basic features and involves the same difficulty as do claims for economic loss that are barred by the exclusionary rule becomes clear once we view the claim in the light of the distinction between misfeasance and nonfeasance. These decisions are but different instances of the one principle that there can be no liability for nonfeasance.

By contrast, in cases of 'unavoidable' financial loss, claims do not go beyond misfeasance. The plaintiff, we saw, need only assert a right against the defendant that he not impair or injure what belongs to the plaintiff, not a right to the continued use of something that belongs to someone else. Such claims do not rest, then, even in part, on interests that are not rooted in exclusive rights.

The distinction between misfeasance and nonfeasance has long been taken by the law as a fundamental and fixed point in the understanding of liability, both well before and throughout the development of negligence doctrine in this century.[44] This, I suggest, explains how the exclusionary rule could have been formulated prior to this period and why it was maintained unchanged during it. Moreover, with very few exceptions, courts have not articulated this distinction in general and abstract terms but rather have recognized it, without naming or conceptualizing it, in the context, and through the analysis, of particular types of circumstances. Lord Diplock's discussion is a good example of this.[45] Thus, the fact that the courts have not expressly stated that a concern over nonfeasance is the basis of the exclusionary rule is quite consistent with usual practice and does not in itself count against the proposed explanation. Still, one might wonder whether there are any judicial opinions that *explicitly* justify the exclusionary rule on this ground. To my knowledge, there have been at least two—the judgment of Cardozo CJ in *H.R. Moch Co. v. Rensselaer Water Co.*[46] and, more recently, the concurring opinions

---

[43] An excellent recent illustration of this is the American case Louisville & Nashville R.R. v. Tug M/V Bayou Lacombe, 597 F.2d 469 (5th Cir. 1979).

[44] For one historical account, see Francis H. Bohlen, *The Basis of Affirmative Obligations in the Law of Tort*, 53 U. PA. L. REV. 209, 214 ff. (1905).

[45] Another example is Deyong v. Shenburn [1946] K.B. 227, 233 (du Parcq LJ), *approv'd*, Home Office v. Dorset Yacht [1970] A.C. 1004, 1043.

[46] 159 N.E. 896, 899 (N.Y. 1928). While the plaintiff's action in *Moch* was for physical damage to property, Cardozo viewed the claim as sounding in nonfeasance. In the context of a more general discussion of the distinction between misfeasance and nonfeasance, he suggested that the application of the exclusionary rule in the well-known relational economic loss

of Lush and Murphy JJ of the Supreme Court of Victoria in *Seale v. Perry.*[47]

IV. The Fit With Detrimental Reliance and With Intentional Interference With Contract

To conclude the essay, I will briefly explain how this proposed justification for the exclusionary rule fits together with the analysis of liability in cases of justified detrimental reliance and intentional interference with contract, the last of the 'non-exclusionary' situations of economic loss that remain to be discussed.

A. Justified Detrimental Reliance

It is now firmly established that where there exists a so-called special relationship between the parties, there can be recovery for negligently caused financial loss. The decisions that first upheld and articulated this basis of liability rested it on the plaintiff's justified detrimental reliance on the defendant.[48] To make a successful claim, a plaintiff must have changed his position to his detriment as a result of the express or implied inducement by the defendant. By way of illustration, consider an example of reliance in

---

cases (such as *Robins*) reflects a concern over liability for nonfeasance. The whole discussion is exceptional for its clarity and rigor.

[47] [1982] V.R. 193, 200–2 (Lush LJ): 'A duty . . . cannot exist by itself. To the duty seen as imposed on the defendant, there must be a correlative right in the plaintiff: for either to exist, both must be capable of being identified. . . . I venture to think that it is really the problem of identifying the right which the plaintiff is entitled to have protected which underlies the difficulties of allowing actions to be brought in cases where the plaintiff has suffered and suffered only economic loss. . . . I do not regard the emphasis on property damage or personal injury in decided cases . . . as either arbitrary or restrictive. I think a consideration of the right which must be correlative to any suggested duty reveals the reason for emphasis.' In the same case, Murphy J views the exclusionary rule in tort and the rejection of third party beneficiary claims in contract as resting on the same basis: the absence of an entitlement that has been injured: *id.* at 207 ff. According to him, both types of claims sound in nonfeasance.

[48] In addition to the decisions referred to *supra*, note 4, the discussion in this section draws on such cases as Imperator Realty Co. v. Tull, 127 N.E. 263 (N.Y. 1920) (Cardozo J, concurring); Emmanuel Ayodeji Ajayi v. R. T. Briscoe [1964] 3 All E.R. 556 (P.C.); Caparo Indus. Plc. v. Dickman [1990] 1 All E.R. 568, 588–9 (H.L.) (Lord Oliver); and most recently, Henderson v. Merrett Syndicates Ltd. [1994] 3 All E.R. 506, 518–21 (H.L.) (Lord Goff). The classic article by Warren A. Seavey, *Reliance upon Gratuitous Promises or Other Conduct*, 64 Harv. L. Rev. 913 (1951), especially 925–7, is still very instructive. I have benefited from the careful discussion of the requirements for inducement in Stephen R. Perry, *Protected Interests and Undertakings in the Law of Negligence*, 42 U. Toronto L.J. 247, 281–5 (1992). Certain recent decisions have held that there can be liability absent the kind of inducement traditionally required. *See, e.g.*, White v. Jones [1995] 1 All E.R. 691 (H.L.), and Biakanja v. Irving, 320 P.2d 16 (Cal. 1958). I will not discuss the cogency of these decisions here, except to say that they seem to impose liability for mere nonfeasance.

circumstances of relational economic loss. At the invitation of the defendant, the plaintiff decides to use the defendant's (or a third party's) bridge for his business purposes. In making this decision, the plaintiff foreseeably abandons or does not undertake a course of action which would not have subjected him to the economic loss that he will suffer if his use of the bridge is disrupted. Due to the defendant's want of reasonable care, the bridge is damaged, impairing the plaintiff's use of it and causing him financial loss. In principle, there can be recovery.

In what circumstances will the law deem that the plaintiff has justifiably relied on the defendant to his detriment? First, the defendant must invite the plaintiff to rely. It is only through his voluntary conduct that the defendant can bring himself into a special relationship with the plaintiff whereby he becomes responsible for the consequences of the plaintiff's decision to rely. More specifically, it must be reasonable for the plaintiff to view the defendant as having, by word or deed, invited him to rely on the defendant for the receipt of some advantage—whether a service, a thing, or a state of affairs. In response to this invitation to rely, the plaintiff, we suppose, decides to give up some prospective or present benefit by abandoning a projected course of action or by altering his circumstances in some definite way. This decision to forego the benefit may have been expressly encouraged by the defendant or it may simply have been the foreseeable consequence of the defendant's invitation to rely. By giving up the benefit, the plaintiff exposes himself to a risk of loss, but he does this because he expects to obtain the advantage held out to him by the defendant. The plaintiff's decision to rely on the defendant is thus both reasonable and rational. In these circumstances, the law will hold that there exists a special relationship between the parties and that the defendant must exercise reasonable care either in providing the advantage in keeping with the representation or at least in enabling the plaintiff to take up again his abandoned course of action or his previous state of affairs without loss. In an action for negligence, the prior situation which the plaintiff has given up will be taken as the baseline for measuring recoverable loss. (By contrast, if there is a valid contract between the parties, the advantage which the defendant has held out to induce the plaintiff's change of position can be taken as the baseline in an action for breach of contract.) Tort law treats the prior position as a protected interest, the value of which cannot be diminished through the defendant's negligence.

The question which now presents itself is as follows: does the conclusion of possible liability in circumstances of justified detrimental reliance fit with the proposed justification for the exclusionary rule? To answer it affirmatively, we must show that recovery in such cases does not represent the imposition of liability for nonfeasance.

That there may be a fit between the two is initially suggested by the following point. In cases of economic loss (relational or otherwise), the exclusionary rule is applied subject to the proviso that the loss did not result from justified detrimental reliance by the plaintiff on the defendant.[49] But the exclusionary rule, I have argued, illustrates the idea that there is no liability for nonfeasance. Hence it is noteworthy that, in the excerpt from *Dorset Yacht* cited earlier, Lord Diplock expressly conditions the conclusion of no liability in a variety of circumstances of nonfeasance on the absence of a special relationship between the parties.[50] The parallel is striking, and it seems on its face to support the proposed justification. To see whether this is indeed so, let us return to the case of reliance in circumstances of relational economic loss and identify the difference, if any, between it and those cases that come within the exclusionary rule.

To make out his claim for loss in circumstances of reliance, the plaintiff need not assert a right to the continued use of the thing (the bridge, in our example) on which he depends but which he neither owns nor possesses. Rather, the essence of his action is that the defendant caused him a financial loss before he was able to regain the position which he foreseeably and reasonably gave up at the defendant's inducement. The only right that the plaintiff is asserting is a 'right' to return to his previous position without suffering loss, given that the defendant has not acted with due care. The fact that the plaintiff depends on the use of something which he neither owns nor possesses merely establishes the circumstances in which he can be made worse off relative to his pre-reliance position. The plaintiff's complaint is not that he has lost the benefit of such use but that he has been put in a worse position in comparison to his prior situation: the plaintiff wants to be returned to his initial position, that is, to be free from the relation of dependence. Thus, in contrast to the cases of economic loss that come under the exclusionary rule, the plaintiff here does not assert, even in part, a right against the defendant to the continued use of something that belongs to another. And while the plaintiff's dependence, being the consequence of his decision to rely, cannot be viewed as an inevitable incident of purposive activity (as it is in the cases of 'unavoidable' economic loss), it should nonetheless be imputed to the defendant rather than to the plaintiff as a matter of fairness. It would be unreasonable to allow the defendant to disown consequences foreseeably flowing from his voluntary invitation to rely and from his failure to use due care.[51] This is in contrast to the

---

[49] It is worth noting here that the court in *Cattle* [1874–80] All E.R. at 223–4, distinguished the facts in the early case of Langridge v. Levy [1837] 2 M. & W. 519 from circumstances coming under the exclusionary rule. Although a case of fraudulent misrepresentation, *Langridge* enunciated a principle of liability, *id.* at 530–1, which, if generalized, is one of liability for the foreseeable consequences of induced reliance.

[50] As does Lord Reid [1970] A.C. at 1027.

[51] See Cardozo J's statement of the underlying notion of fairness in *Imperator Realty Co.*, 127 N.E. at 266.

exclusionary situations where, I argued, the plaintiff is reasonably viewed as having acted at his own risk in making his interests dependent on the availability of something else which he neither owns nor possesses. In sum, there seems to be no contradiction between the possibility of liability in circumstances of justified detrimental reliance and the exclusionary rule.[52] Unlike actions barred by the exclusionary rule, the plaintiff's claim here seems to fall squarely within the bounds of misfeasance.

Against this conclusion however, the following important objection can be raised. In all cases of actionable justified reliance, the plaintiff alters—and indeed must have altered—his position as a result of the defendant's inducement: in reliance on the defendant's representations, the plaintiff either gives up an actual present advantage or forgoes the pursuit of a possible future advantage. In either situation, then, the plaintiff does not actually have or enjoy this advantage at the moment of the defendant's negligence. It may not even be within his actual power to do so. And he certainly does not legally possess or own it. We saw that the law treats the advantage, whether given up or simply not pursued, as setting the baseline for determining the existence of recoverable loss and views it in effect as a protected interest, the value of which specifies the plaintiff's entitlement *vis-à-vis* the defendant. This seems to entail the imposition of liability for nonfeasance. Yet this is not the case.

To see why not, it is important, first, to recall the main idea that liability for misfeasance is premised on the existence of an *exclusive right in the plaintiff as against the defendant*. Property or possessory rights, being in principle exclusive rights against the world, are also rights against the defendant. By contrast, a contract right, as I shall shortly discuss, is in contemplation of law a personal right as between two parties which is created by their combined acts of offer and acceptance (assuming the other requirements for contract formation are met). The idea of an exclusive right is thus *not* exhausted by rights of property or possession. In addition, contract makes explicit that an exclusive right between two parties may be established in and through their interaction fairly interpreted. As I will now explain, this is also true of interactions involving induced detrimental reliance.

The defendant, we suppose, has invited the plaintiff to rely on him, foreseeably inducing the plaintiff to give up or to forgo pursuing an advantage for the sake of the benefit held out. The plaintiff, we also assume, is able to show that he would in fact have kept or obtained the advantage had he not relied on the defendant's representations. In contemplation of law, the advantage, though in fact given up or not pursued, is viewed as something that could and would have been the plaintiff's at the moment of the

---

[52] Here I am disagreeing with Paul Craig's view, *supra,* note 10, at 240.

defendant's wrong but for his decision to rely. Now that decision was itself just a reasonable response to the defendant's invitation to rely, with its holding out of a prospective benefit. Seeing that it was the defendant who invited the plaintiff's reliance, it would be unfair for him to impute to the plaintiff's own decision the fact that the plaintiff did not have the advantage (because given up or not pursued) at the moment of the wrong. As a *fair* implication of his *voluntary* act of inviting reliance, the defendant should therefore be estopped from denying the following two state of affairs: first, that the plaintiff had the effective present power to keep or to obtain the advantage at the moment of the defendant's wrong; and secondly, that the plaintiff refrained from exercising this power only on condition that the defendant acted with due care. These two states of affairs, through not actually existent, nevertheless count as facts as between the parties. Taken together in circumstances of the defendant's failure to use due care, they imply on the part of the defendant a voluntary and binding acknowledgement that the plaintiff had an exclusive actual power to have and to enjoy— that is, a right to—the advantage at the moment of the defendant's wrong despite the plaintiff having given it up or not pursued it. This acknowledgement of right is imputed to the defendant as fairly implied by his voluntary conduct toward the plaintiff. Hence the conclusion that the advantage should and can count as a protected interest against the defendant for the purposes of tort law.

In reaching this conclusion, it must be emphasized that we do not hold that the plaintiff has actually acquired legal ownership or possession of the advantage—and so something that can count as a right against the world. No such acquisition has occurred. Rather, given the defendant's invitation to rely, the defendant is estopped from denying that the plaintiff has an exclusive power to have and to enjoy the advantage at the moment the defendant fails to exercise due care. The determination and the justification of the plaintiff's entitlement in reliance cases are thus strictly internal to an analysis of the fair requirements governing the defendant's conduct with respect to the plaintiff. The advantage counts as a protected interest because—and only in so far as—this is a reasonable implication of the estoppel analysis. It figures as a kind of 'quasi-property' just as between these two parties, given the specific nature of their interaction.[53] In this way, the requirement for misfeasance is met.

---

[53] 'In the negligent misrepresentation cases it may perhaps be said that a right arises in the plaintiff out of the facts of reliance by the plaintiff on the misrepresentation and an acceptance of responsibility by the defendant for the advice contained in the misrepresentation, a right which arises out of a relationship of "proximity", a para-contractual right': Seale v. Perry [1982] V.R. 193, 202 (Lush J). The explanation proposed in this chapter agrees with this remarkable judicial opinion in so far as both root the determination of the plaintiff's right in the parties' interaction. In the terms of my explanation, the necessary and sufficient conditions of the existence of the plaintiff's right are an interaction between the parties consisting in the

B. Intentional Interference with Contract

The proposed justification for the exclusionary rule holds, I have said, that the plaintiff will fail unless his interest is grounded in an exclusive right as against the defendant. Absent a special relationship or a contract between the plaintiff and defendant, the law requires that the plaintiff have a proprietary or possessory right. A mere contract right against a person other than the defendant is deemed insufficient to establish liability for negligently caused economic loss. The proposed justification for the exclusionary rule will be consistent with this legal conclusion if, but only if, in contemplation of law a plaintiff's contract right against one person (a third party) does not in itself give the plaintiff an exclusive right against some other person (such as the defendant). Until now, I have simply supposed this to be the case. I must now show that this is indeed so and indicate the conception of contract that underlies this conclusion. I will also suggest why this analysis is consistent with the fact that contract rights against third persons are treated as protected interests in actions for *intentional*, as opposed to negligent, interference with contract.

The modern common law views contract as entailing, in Corbin's words, 'a special right *in personam*, a right in the promisee against the promisor, with the correlative special duty in the promisor to the promisee of rendering the performance promised'.[54] This view holds, first, that the promisee's exclusive right is to the *performance of a promise*, not to the thing itself that has been promised; and secondly, that it is only a right *as against the person(s) who have promised*, not the world at large. The only necessary and, as it were, inherent juridical effect of a binding contract is that the promisor is no longer free to deprive the promisee of the *promised performance* without his consent. Accordingly, although a contract may give me a right to the performance of your promise, say, to deliver a horse to me, it does not confer on me a right to the horse itself. I acquire that right only when I am put in physical possession of the horse through delivery. I then, and only then, acquire a property right in the horse or a

---

defendant inviting the plaintiff to rely and the plaintiff foreseeably giving up or forgoing to pursue some advantage in reliance on the defendant. Absent the defendant's invitation, the plaintiff's reliance cannot be *justified* reliance nor the advantage a *protected* interest for the purposes of an estoppel analysis. Unless and until the plaintiff does rely, there exists no *interest* with respect to which the defendant is duty-bound to exercise reasonable care. Given the requisite interaction, the defendant is under a duty to act in such a way that the plaintiff is not wrongfully made worse off than he would have been had he not abandoned or forgone the advantage. And the plaintiff's correlative right is just to this conduct on the part of the defendant.

[54] ARTHUR L. CORBIN, CORBIN ON CONTRACTS: ONE VOLUME EDITION (1952), ch. 1, § 4, at 8. *See also* Joseph H. Beale, Jr., *Gratuitous Undertakings*, 5 HARV. L. REV. 222, (1892). For a philosophical elucidation of this conception, see IMMANUEL KANT, *The Doctrine of Right* pt. I, ch. ii, sec. ii, §§ 20 & 21, *in* THE METAPHYSICS OF MORALS (Mary Gregor trans., 1991), 93–5.

right *in rem*, and thus a right to exclude the promisor and others from using the horse without my consent. In this way, a contractual right is fundamentally different from a right *in rem* created by executed transactions or by any other conveyance of property pure and simple.

In cases of negligently caused economic loss that are barred by the exclusionary rule, the defendant damages or appropriates something in which the plaintiff may have a contractual interest, thereby affecting that interest without, however, having any intention to injure the plaintiff's contractual right. Given the purely unintentional nature of the defendant's act at least with respect to the plaintiff's interest, the only fact that can be imputed to the defendant in relation to the plaintiff is his impingement on the existence, condition, or availability of the *thing itself* (including the consequences thereof) and his only responsibility is for violations of the plaintiff's rights that result from this fact. But this impingement does not infringe any of the plaintiff's rights against the defendant because the plaintiff, having by hypothesis merely a contractual right against a third person, is entitled just to the latter's performance, not to the thing itself. Accordingly, the defendant's unintentional interference with the plaintiff's contractual interest cannot constitute a wrong against him. At most, it may lead to a breach of contract by the third person or to the frustration of their contract if performance is rendered impossible. On this analysis, then, the common law view regarding the insufficiency of contractual interests (and of course of other interests that are less than contract rights, such as mere liberties) is justified. But if this is so, on what basis can the law treat such contractual rights as protected interests—which both courts and scholars often characterize as 'quasi-property'—in cases of *intentional* interference with contract?

A clue may be found in the fact that, in the context of assignment, the law views a contractual right as a quasi-property right.[55] The reason for this is clear. As the object of an assignment, the contractual right *itself*, as distinguished from the thing, is treated by a third party as something that may be acquired as a valuable asset, but only with the consent of the one in whom it is vested. Viewed in this context, a contractual right functions no differently from any property right. The sole qualification that must be made here is that in its role as a property interest, the right is exclusive as against the assignee only, not the world in general. It is proprietary as between them in virtue of the assignee's intention, as manifested in his interaction with the assignor, to treat the contract right in this way. Now, since a contract right can be deemed to be a property interest when it is the object of a voluntary transaction of assignment, it must also be the case that it can function in this way in an involuntary transaction, when a defen-

---

[55] *See, e.g.*, ALLAN E. FARNSWORTH, CONTRACTS (1982), 745 and Corbin's discussion, *supra*, note 54, at §§ 859–61.

dant (a stranger to the contract) expressly or implicitly treats the right as a valuable asset which he can use, appropriate, or injure without the right-holder's consent. Whether there has been a wrongful taking of or injury to the contract right viewed as a quasi-property interest will crucially depend on the defendant having the necessary intention. But this is what the law requires in cases of intentional interference with contract. There must be 'malice' or some fairly specific intention that is directed at the contract right itself and that implicitly regards it as a valuable asset.[56] The plaintiff's contract right against the other contracting party counts therefore as an entitlement against the defendant because this is a fair and reasonable implication of the defendant's act and of the specific kind of interaction that has taken place between the plaintiff and defendant. This, I suggested, is also true of interaction involving induced detrimental reliance. On this basis, we account, then, for the different significance of contract rights in intentional and unintentional tort. Here also the different parts of the law respecting economic loss fit together.[57]

V. CONCLUSION

My principal aim in this chapter has been to suggest a definite answer to the question of tort liability for economic loss as this arises in the main parts of the law. Through an internal analysis of the very categories and distinctions that are present in the case law, I have tried to show that the exclusionary rule rests on a simple and principled basis, namely that actions which come under this rule involve claims sounding in nonfeasance, for which, in accordance with the general conception of negligence at common law, there cannot be liability. With this answer in hand, I have argued that the different parts of the law respecting economic loss fit together. At least in the case of liability for economic loss, tort law displays a fundamental unity.

The legal principle that there is no liability for nonfeasance articulates a severely limited idea of responsibility toward others: individuals must only not injure what already belongs to others; protected interests are defined in terms of what others have ('*suum*'), not what they need or want. And since

---

[56] See generally the very instructive discussion in Francis Bowes Sayre, *Inducing Breach of Contract*, 36 HARV. L. REV. 663, 675–86 (1923). For a more recent discussion of intention in this context, see JOHN G. FLEMING, THE LAW OF TORTS (7th edn., 1987), 656–9.

[57] Here I am answering the objection, found frequently in the literature, that the exclusionary rule should be rejected because it is premised on an arbitrary or unfounded distinction between negligent and intentional interference with contractual relations. *See, e.g.*, Charles E. Carpenter, *Interference with Contract Relations*, 41 HARV. L. REV. 728, 742 (1928); Robert G. Godwin, *Negligent Interference with Economic Expectancy: The Case for Recovery*, 16 STAN. L. REV. 664 (1964); Philip S. James, *The Fallacies of* Simpson v. Thomson, 34 M.L.R. 149, 158 & n. 44 (1971).

the duties owed to others in the law of negligence must be framed in such a way that they can be brought under misfeasance, this restricted notion of responsibility seems to specify an organizing normative principle for tort law.

The analysis undertaken in this essay is, I believe, theoretically significant in two respects. First, it gives us reason to think that the law already contains within itself the ideas and the principles with which to construct a *public* justification of the basis and the limits of the exclusionary rule. We might not have expected this conclusion in advance, given serious and increasing disagreement among contemporary jurists and scholars as to the proper resolution of this question. To get beyond present disagreement about the particular question of economic loss, the first step would seem to require that we root the justification in an idea or set of ideas which is basic to the *general* conception of negligence and which we therefore take, at least provisionally, as a fixed point in our understanding of the law. This is what I have tried to do.

Secondly, if, as I have suggested, the law of economic loss presents us with a public juridical point of view that is framed in terms of the distinction between misfeasance and nonfeasance, this provides us with a suitable starting point for further theoretical reflection. All reflection must begin with an object given to it. Theoretical reflection about law presupposes an object that embodies a *legal* point of view. The first task of theory, then, is to uncover and to identify clearly such an object. A theory that fails to begin in this way condemns itself to being irrelevant as a theory of law. Whatever else its object of cognition may be, it will not be tort law. This is the basic difficulty with the prevailing economic approaches to the exclusionary rule, briefly discussed in the Introduction. Their analyses and conclusions, however fully and rigorously worked out, are not explanations of tort law, and their prescriptions cannot be ones that tort law is obliged to recognize. If present disagreement about the basis and the limits of the exclusionary rule challenges the possibility of a public basis of justification, prevailing theoretical approaches threaten to deprive legal theory of an object for cognition. The fundamental and pervasive distinction which tort law draws between misfeasance and nonfeasance supplies us with one. The further task of theory would be the critical yet immanent examination of the object's presuppositions and its entailments. But this is beyond the scope of the present essay.[58]

---

[58] For one effort to pursue this further course of reflection, see Benson, *supra,* note 13, at 550–601.

SECTION C

Victim Responsibility for Harm

Contributory Negligence: Conceptual and Normative Issues

KENNETH W. SIMONS*

Peter, a pedestrian, negligently crosses a street without carefully checking the vehicular traffic. Doris, a motorist, negligently speeds and strikes Peter, causing him injuries. In Anglo-American jurisdictions, Peter's recovery against Doris will likely be reduced, if not eliminated, under the doctrine of contributory (or comparative) negligence. And it might seem obvious that a plaintiff who is 'at fault' should not fully recover against a tortious defendant. But the grounds for that conclusion are not at all obvious, once one considers the following problems.

First, in saying that Peter is negligent, do we mean that he acted as he should not have? (That, after all, is ordinarily what we mean when we conclude that Doris is negligent.) Or do we mean only that he should incur some of the costs of his conduct? That is, even if it is not the case that he should have acted differently, perhaps he should forfeit some of the legal damages to which he would have been entitled had his conduct not contributed to his own harm. (This, I will argue, is the important but neglected concept of plaintiff 'strict liability' or strict responsibility.)

Secondly, is the *substantive* criterion of contributory fault essentially the same as the criterion of fault towards others? And, at a deeper level, are victim and injurer fault based on similar rationales? For example, fault towards others might reflect the actor's egoism and insufficient concern for the interests of others. Does self-regarding fault reflect a similar lack of concern for others? Yet here, all of the relevant interests affected are the victim's. In what sense, then, does contributory negligence reflect insufficient concern? Alternatively, consider a utilitarian criterion of fault. Does such a criterion apply similarly to other-regarding and to self-regarding harm? (I will suggest serious reasons for doubt.) More promising is a moral parity approach, holding victims to the same standard to which they hold injurers, but this approach, too, has its difficulties. In the end, should we give

* Professor of Law, Boston University School of Law. I thank Ron Cass, Jane Cohen, Mike Conrad, Betsy Foote, Clay Gillette, Wendy Gordon, Steve Marks, Chris Marx, Liam Murphy, David Owen, Mark Pettit, Gary Schwartz, David Seipp, Kate Silbaugh, and participants in the Boston University faculty workshop for helpful advice. For a fuller analysis of some of the issues discussed in this essay, and for an examination of additional issues, see Kenneth W. Simons, *The Puzzling Doctrine of Contributory Negligence*, 16 CARDOZO L. REV. 1693 (1995).

up on the effort to develop a similar standard, and frankly acknowledge that victim 'negligence' is a radically different concept from injurer negligence?

Surprisingly, the non-economic literature on contributory fault is sparse, and pays these questions little attention.[1] My analysis in this essay is exploratory. I try to clarify and differentiate some important concepts, and to identify salient normative dimensions to the problems. Because I seriously doubt that the economic interpretation is sufficient to explain, much less justify, much of existing doctrine,[2] I have chosen not to examine the economic perspective here.

My methodology is both interpretive and normative. I attempt to elucidate and analyze the concepts underlying contributory negligence doctrine in Anglo-American law, and to place those concepts within the broader conceptual, doctrinal, and normative framework of tort law. To a large extent, the analysis is idealized: I examine the extent to which the parties' moral claims ground their legal rights and remedies, without careful regard to practical and institutional constraints.[3] However, some of the analysis might suggest reasons for altering or refining current legal doctrine.

To focus the analysis, I assume the following:

1. Both the defendant's negligence and the plaintiff's negligence causally

---

[1] Recent non-economic scholarship on tort theory, especially corrective justice scholarship, has focused almost exclusively on the justification of negligence and strict liability doctrines, and has given little attention to the plaintiff's conduct, including contributory negligence and assumption of risk. For example, Richard Epstein's early strict liability theory slights the topic of contributory negligence. RICHARD EPSTEIN, A THEORY OF STRICT LIABILITY (1980), 83–131 (rejecting contributory negligence as a separate defense, but distributing many current contributory negligence cases within the categories of causal defense (e.g., based on the victim's 'compulsion'), statutory defense, assumption of risk, and victim trespass). George Fletcher, in elucidating his non-reciprocal risk argument, only briefly mentions the doctrine, concluding that a victim who imposes excessive risks on others may justifiably be barred because it is then no longer the case that the tortious injurer has imposed nonreciprocal risks on the victim. George P. Fletcher, *Fairness and Utility in Tort Theory*, 85 HARV. L. REV. 537, 549 (1972). Fletcher also nonetheless acknowledges that the reciprocity paradigm cannot explain why a victim is considered contributorily negligent when he imposes risks only on himself: *id.* at 549 n. 44. Finally, Stephen Perry's recent writings suggest that corrective justice should be understood as posing the following comparative inquiry: among those who are causally responsible for a harmful outcome, who should pay?: Stephen R. Perry, *The Moral Foundations of Tort Law,* 77 IOWA L. REV. 449, 499, 512–13 (1992). This approach might entail reduction or forfeiture of damages due to contributory fault. To date, however, Perry has not fully spelled out the rationale for the comparative judgment.

[2] Some criticisms of the economic approach include Gary T. Schwartz, *Contributory and Comparative Negligence: A Reappraisal*, 87 YALE L. J. 697, 703–21 (1978); Howard A. Latin, *Problem-Solving Behavior and Theories of Tort Liability*, 73 CAL. L. REV. 677 (1985). In any event, I am interested in pursuing a different interpretation, one that is under-developed in the existing literature.

[3] Moreover, I focus much more on what constitutes victim negligence and victim strict responsibility and on whether such conduct should affect recovery at all than on the question of how to compare the injurer's tortious conduct to the victim's negligence or strict responsibility under a comparative fault regime.

contributed to the plaintiff's harm in a legally sufficient way.[4] This includes the notion of cause-in-fact: a reasonable precaution by either party would have avoided the entire harm that actually occurred.

2. The judgment that the plaintiff is negligent is based only on the risks of harm he creates to himself, not the risks of harm he creates to others. (Later in the chapter, I relax this assumption.)

Finally, two matters of terminology. For simplicity, I use the term 'contributory negligence' as a shorthand for either traditional contributory negligence, which was a complete bar to recovery, or modern comparative negligence, where plaintiff's negligence reduces but need not bar recovery. I also use the terms 'negligence' and 'fault' interchangeably.

I. Contributory Negligence or Contributory Strict Responsibility?

Consider first the question whether contributory negligence entails that the plaintiff should have acted otherwise. As I will explain, the concept of *injurer* fault does entail that the injurer should have acted otherwise, since injurer fault means conduct that is *deficient* relative to a standard of reasonable care. We then face the following question: Does contributory negligence rely on a similar *deficiency view* of fault?

We may conceptualize an injurer's ex ante options as follows:

(1) Do not engage in the tortious activity (e.g., do not act negligently);
(2) Engage in the tortious activity (e.g., act negligently) but pay for the harm that you cause;
(3) Engage in the tortious activity (e.g., act negligently) but *do not* pay for the harm that you cause.[5]

To say that a defendant is negligent is to say, at least, that society prefers option (1) to option (2). That is, the defendant should have acted otherwise, by taking the precaution of not engaging in the tortious activity. This interpretation supposes that defendants should not treat negligence as a legitimate option, as simply a form of pricing, per option (2). To put the

---

[4] Conventionally, both the defendant's negligence and the plaintiff's negligence must be causes-in-fact and proximate causes of the harm: RESTATEMENT (SECOND) OF TORTS (1963), § 465. Thus, ordinarily, the following propositions must hold: if Doris had acted with due care, the harm to Peter would not have occurred; if Peter had acted with due care, his harm would not have occurred; and the type of harm that occurred was reasonably foreseeable (or was sufficiently direct).

[5] I proposed this tripartite manner of conceptualizing an *injurer's* liability in Kenneth W. Simons, *Jules Coleman and Corrective Justice in Tort Law: A Critique and Reformulation*, 15 HARV. J.L. & PUB. POL'Y. 849, 875–81 (1992). 'Tortious activity' encompasses activity that creates strict as well as fault liability—e.g., it includes the faultless manufacture of a defective product.

matter in remedial terms, faulty conduct (including negligence)[6] is conduct
that society would enjoin, if that were feasible. In practice, of course, a
plaintiff ordinarily obtains only the remedy of damages. Still, the point of
that remedy is to respect, in some tangible way, the victim's right not to be
negligently injured. By contrast, cases of strict liability are instances where
society does not necessarily prefer (1) to (2), or where we actually prefer
(2); thus, we would not enjoin the activity, but we do insist that the defendant pay for the harm he has caused.[7]

On this *deficiency view* of negligence, a victim has a primary right against
the injurer not to be negligently injured. The duty of the injurer to pay damages resulting from the negligent act is secondary to the injurer's primary
duty not to act negligently. This view asserts that the injurer's conduct was
deficient relative to a standard of reasonable care—specifically, the injurer
could and should have taken a specified precaution that, *ex ante,* would be
expected to avoid the injury. The deficiency view of negligence is abstract,
and is consistent with a variety of negligence criteria and a variety of normative bases for negligence. But it does rule out some views—including
both the economic test of negligence (as usually described)[8] and, perhaps,
the prevailing English view of negligence.[9]

How does the deficiency view of negligence apply to victims? When we
conclude that a victim is contributorily negligent, do we mean that he
should have acted otherwise? Or do we believe that his conduct is permissible or even justifiable?

Reconsider the preference options above. When a plaintiff is deemed
contributorily negligent, does society prefer option (1)(no contributory negligence) to option (2)(contributory negligence but the plaintiff 'pays for' or
absorbs the relevant costs)?[10] Or are we instead indifferent? Or do we even
prefer (2) to (1)? In other words, when we say that a plaintiff was contributorily negligent for not taking a specified precaution, do we believe that
the plaintiff should have acted otherwise, and that a damage reduction is
simply one way of enforcing that moral duty? (That is, in theory, it would
be best if the plaintiff were enjoined not to act as he did.) Or do we believe
that the plaintiff has a legitimate option not to take the precaution, with
the caveat that he must suffer a damage reduction as an appropriate price

---

[6] 'Fault' in this sense encompasses negligence, recklessness, and unprivileged intentional
torts. *See id.* at 868.

[7] Private necessity, abnormally dangerous activities, and strict products liability for manufacturing flaws are all instances of 'strict liability' in this sense.

[8] However, the economic view's utilitarian criterion of faulty behavior, considered alone,
is consistent with the deficiency view: *see generally* Simons, *supra,* note 5, at 876–7.

[9] *See infra,* note 21.

[10] To capture the concept of contributory fault, the preference options must be slightly
reworded; in (2) and (3), the phrase 'pay for the harm you cause' means 'forfeit some or all
of the damages to which your fault contributes'.

for exercising that option? (That is, the plaintiff's conduct is permitted—or even to be encouraged.)[11]

Applying the deficiency view to contributory negligence suggests the following preliminary analysis. A true negligence theory of contributory *fault* supposes that the plaintiff should have acted otherwise, by taking a specified precaution; and if we do not so suppose but still believe that the plaintiff should be disentitled from full recovery, then the plaintiff's disentitlement must rest on a kind of *strict* responsibility. On such a *plaintiff's strict responsibility* theory, we are indifferent between the plaintiff taking the precaution, on the one hand, and the plaintiff not taking the precaution but suffering a reduction of damages, on the other; while on a negligence theory, we prefer that the plaintiff take the precaution. I use the term 'plaintiff's strict responsibility' as a conceptual term of art, a default category for any faultless plaintiff conduct that reduces the plaintiff's recovery.[12] Precisely which, if any, types of plaintiff's faultless conduct should have such a legal effect is a separate, and difficult, question, which I explore below.[13]

Courts have not explicitly articulated a 'plaintiff strict responsibility' rationale, but I believe that it underlies many judicial findings of 'contributory negligence'. Consider the controversial seat-belt defense. Many courts have concluded that the trier of fact can view a plaintiff's non-use of an available seat belt as a form of contributory negligence or avoidable consequence that reduces the plaintiff's damages, to the extent that the non-

---

[11] Similarly, when injurers are found strictly liable, their activity is permitted, or even to be encouraged: *e.g.*, RESTATEMENT (SECOND) OF TORTS (1976), § 520 cmt. b (explaining rationale for strict liability for abnormally dangerous activities).

[12] Jules Coleman uses the phrase 'plaintiff's strict liability' in a different sense—to describe situations in which tort law leaves the loss on the plaintiff, especially the common situation in which a rule holding a defendant liable only if he is at fault permits the nonfaulty defendant to cause harm to the plaintiff without liability: JULES L. COLEMAN, RISKS AND WRONGS (1992) 226–33. In my sense, 'plaintiff's strict responsibility' refers to a legal rule, based on the plaintiff's conduct, that leaves some of the loss on the plaintiff even though the defendant has acted tortiously. *See also* Guido Calabresi & Jon T. Hirschoff, *Toward a Test for Strict Liability in Torts*, 81 YALE L.J. 1055, 1066 (1972) (identifying assumption of risk as a form of plaintiff's strict liability).

[13] One might object that the distinction between the plaintiff's contributory negligence and the plaintiff's strict responsibility is not meaningful because, in either case, the legal consequence (forfeiture of some damages) is the same. But this objection is unpersuasive. First, a plaintiff's strict responsibility rule could have a different remedial effect than a plaintiff's contributory negligence rule—for example, assumption of risk as a form of the plaintiff's strict responsibility might result in no recovery, while contributory negligence might result in comparative apportionment. And even if the remedial effect is the same, the distinction between options (1) and (2) does illuminate the substantive criterion of plaintiff's fault, by clarifying the difference between a negligence theory and a strict liability theory. The plaintiff is negligent if, but only if, he should have acted otherwise; he is strictly responsible if that is not, or need not be, the case. And a negligence theory, unlike a strict responsibility theory, requires identifying precautions that should have been taken, and identifying the substantive ideal by which we judge what the injurer 'should' have done.

use increases the severity of his injury. But a surprising number of courts
have refused to allow juries to consider non-use of a seat belt as contributory fault.[14] One reason for these courts' hesitancy might be a judgement
that non-use of seat belts is widespread, and, in part for that reason, is not
negligent behavior that we would wish to change. And it might seem
improper to reduce a plaintiff's recovery on the basis of conduct that we
cannot say should have been otherwise.

One could, however, defend reducing the damages of a plaintiff who fails
to use his seat belt without being committed to the view that such non-use
is conduct that ought to have been otherwise. An alternative, *plaintiff's
'strict liability' or strict responsibility rule* would be this: although the plaintiff has done nothing faulty in failing to wear a seat belt, he should 'pay'
for his self-directed risky behavior to the extent of suffering a reduction in
recovery against the defendant.[15] In other words, the defendant should not
be required to 'subsidize' the plaintiff's risky behavior.[16]

Courts have explicitly recognized only one category of nonfaulty victim
behavior that can preclude recovery—assumption of risk, a doctrine that
rests on consent.[17] This failure to recognize the possibility of other categories of plaintiff's strict responsibility is surprising. For it seems that other
instances of victim non-recovery or reduced recovery, instances that do not
fit within assumption of risk doctrine, are better analyzed as a form of
plaintiff's strict responsibility. Of course, we would then need to define and
justify appropriate categories of plaintiff's strict responsibility. I explore
these questions further below.

This preliminary analysis remains incomplete, however. For it overlooks
a crucial asymmetry between the negligent defendant's duty to the plaintiff
and the negligent plaintiff's 'duty' to the defendant. A plaintiff has a pri-

---

[14] *See, e.g.*, Swajian v. General Motors Corp., 559 A.2d 1041 (R.I. 1989). Some courts are
troubled by whether failure to use a seat belt should be classified as contributory fault or
avoidable consequences. In this chapter, I generally do not distinguish contributory fault that
causally contributes to the accident itself from avoidable consequences or mitigation of damages.

[15] In a literal sense, of course, it is not the case that the victim is 'strictly liable' or must
'pay' the injurer. If the victim declines to sue the injurer, the injurer has no legal claim against
the victim. Accordingly, the phrase 'victim strict responsibility' is preferable to 'victim strict
liability', the phrase more often used in the literature. See Calabresi & Hirschoff, *supra*, note
12, at 1066. Both phrases are intended to draw an important contrast with 'victim fault', i.e.,
to denote a reason other than the victim's fault for the victim's nonrecovery or reduced recovery. I thank David Owen for emphasizing the potential confusion engendered by the 'victim
strict liability' formulation.

[16] Of course, further argument is needed in order to define and defend any victim strict
responsibility criterion, such as this criterion of liability for 'risky' behavior.

[17] *See generally* Kenneth W. Simons, *Assumption of Risk and Consent in the Law of Torts:
A Theory of Full Preference*, 67 B.U. L. Rev. 213 (1987). The consensual nature of assumption of risk explains why the seat-belt defense is not best analyzed as an instance of assumption of risk. For the passenger who declines to wear a seat belt does not consent to another
motorist not using due care: *id.* at 221 n.30.

mary right that a defendant not act in a negligent manner, a right that ideally would be protected by injunction and that, as a second-best remedy, is protected by damages. But a defendant has no independent primary right of that sort against a negligent plaintiff. Rather, a defendant has only a *conditional* right—a primary right that the plaintiff not act negligently, or a secondary right that the plaintiff bear some portion of the harm that the plaintiff negligently causes, but, in either case, a right that the defendant can exercise *only if* the plaintiff is vindicating his primary or secondary rights against the defendant. If the plaintiff chooses not to seek any remedy, the defendant has no legal right against him.

But now we have a problem. The conditional nature of the defendant's right against the plaintiff seems to undermine the deficiency view of contributory negligence itself. For the defendant's rights against the plaintiff arise only if the plaintiff seeks a remedy against the defendant. That seems like a very weak sense of 'fault', a very weak sense in which the plaintiff 'should have done otherwise'. If the plaintiff had not chosen to sue, perhaps it would no longer be the case that the plaintiff 'should have done otherwise'. Indeed, limiting a plaintiff's remedy because of his 'fault' might always be an instance of plaintiff strict responsibility, not of plaintiff negligence; for it seems that we are indifferent to whether a plaintiff acts negligently except in so far as he sues, yet it is not the case that we are indifferent to whether a defendant acts negligently except in so far as the plaintiff sues.

This objection is powerful. To meet it, we need a defensible concept of fault that can explain the sense in which a victim's purely self-regarding conduct is deficient, but that does not depend on whether the victim chooses to seek a remedy against the injurer, or even on whether the victim interacts with an injurer. The basic idea is this. When we define an *injurer's* conduct as faulty, we mean that she should have acted differently; and that moral duty helps ground a legal duty of the injurer to the victim, to be liable to an injunction or for damages. When a *victim's* conduct is faulty, we mean that he should have acted differently; but now the moral duty grounds a different, more limited legal duty. Rather than justifying a direct, unconditional legal right in any other party, the moral duty of the victim justifies only a limitation upon the victim's legal rights against the injurer.[18]

On this account, we deem the victim's conduct deficient, apart from whether the victim chooses to sue the injurer. At the same time, that deficiency is only relevant in private law if the victim does bring a lawsuit, for a simple reason: the victim's moral duty does not otherwise affect any

[18] For a careful account of the relation between moral and legal rights, see J. Raz, *Legal Rights*, in 2 PHILOSOPHY OF LAW (Jules L. Coleman (ed.), 1994), 67.

other private individual's interest to a sufficient degree to warrant legal intervention.[19]

This account still leaves us with a troubling question. How often is contributory negligence really an instance of deficient conduct, i.e., conduct that we believe should have been otherwise, even if the victim had not chosen to pursue a remedy? Often, a victim is morally entitled to act as he wishes if his conduct does not affect others[20]—as, perhaps, when he chooses not to use a seat belt. In such cases, if we still believe that his imprudent conduct should limit his legal remedies, that belief must rest on what I have called a 'victim strict responsibility' rationale. Thus, in the end, victim strict responsibility rather than victim contributory negligence might be the ground for reducing a victim's legal remedies much more often than would first appear.

II. SUBSTANTIVE RATIONALES FOR LIMITING PLAINTIFF'S RECOVERY

Thus far, I have focused on some critical conceptual issues. We have seen that the deficiency view of negligence, together with the conditional nature

---

[19] If the victim's moral duty does not create a direct legal or even moral right in another party, is it really a *moral* duty? On several defensible moral views, it is. Kant recognized moral duties to oneself, and many utilitarians would insist that the duty to maximize utility applies to choices among one's own interests as well as to choices between one's interests and another's.

[20] This condition is important, however. Sometimes the victim's conduct *does* affect or harm others, in such a way that the victim is not morally entitled to act as he wishes. I am not referring to the 'harm' the victim causes the injurer simply by increasing the injurer's potential damages to the victim—'harm' for which the injurer can receive full compensation simply by paying less in damages to the victim. Rather, I refer to two special ways that the victim's imprudence can affect the injurer, two forms of harm for which the injurer cannot so easily be compensated. Specifically, the victim's negligence sometimes causes the injurer to take special precautions (e.g., an evasive driving maneuver). And the victim also harms the injurer by implicating the injurer in the accident: if a driver's vehicle collides with a negligent pedestrian, the pedestrian victim has, through his fault, caused the driver to help bring about an accident that may cause the driver to feel guilty or, at least, 'responsible' in a non-moral sense. (For further discussion, *see* Simons, *supra*, note *, at 1709–10.)

The possibility that the victim will harm the injurer in one of these two special ways has an interesting consequence: it helps explain why the seat belt defense and mitigation of damage cases are more likely candidates for a 'victim strict responsibility' analysis than are cases where the victim's negligence contributes to the accident itself. In the latter case, these two special types of harm are much more likely. Hence, it is more likely that we really do prefer that the victim not act negligently as compared to acting negligently but suffering a reduction in his legal remedy. By contrast, we are more often indifferent about whether a victim mitigates his damages as compared to not mitigating his damages but suffering a reduction in his legal remedy. For example, a pedestrian's inattention that contributes to an accident might induce a motorist to take extra precautions, or it might cause the motorist to feel implicated as an agent of the pedestrian's harm. By contrast, a passenger's failure to wear a seat belt (or to see a doctor after the accident) does not induce others to take extra precautions, nor does it implicate the negligent motorist so directly as an agent of the harm that would have been avoided by wearing the seat belt (or by seeing the doctor).

of the injurer's right against a negligent victim, help define the meaning of contributory negligence. But these concepts do not go very far towards explaining why or to what extent a contributorily negligent plaintiff's remedy against a tortious defendant should be limited. Nor do they tell us whether the formal doctrinal criteria for victim and injurer negligence should be identical, similar, or distinct.

In the first part of this section, I explore the merits of some substantive rationales for limiting a contributorily negligent plaintiff's recovery. In doing so, I also evaluate whether the rationales justify identical or distinct formal criteria for victim and injurer negligence.[21] First, I consider a skeptical argument, based on a Kantian view of why negligence is a moral wrong. If the wrongfulness of injurer negligence is premised on the injurer's unjustifiable egoism, the argument goes, then we *cannot* explain why the victim's recovery should be limited. Secondly, I consider a utilitarian account of deficient conduct, an account which initially appears to justify similar treatment of victim and injurer negligence. Both arguments, I will suggest, are problematic. Thirdly, I consider a more promising moral parity approach, under which the victim is required to hold himself to as high a standard of conduct as the standard to which he holds the injurer. Fourthly, I examine a 'forfeiture' rationale: perhaps the reason for reducing the victim's recovery is that he justifiably forfeits his rights. Under this rationale, the legally relevant moral deficiency in a victim's conduct is quite different from the moral deficiency in an injurer's conduct; consequently, the law should employ very different criteria to define victim and injurer negligence. Fifthly, I explore whether the rationale for limiting the plaintiff's recovery changes if one relaxes the simplifying assumption that the plaintiff poses risks only to himself, and one instead assumes that he also poses significant risks to others. Finally, in the second part of this section, I examine more carefully the substantive rationales for limiting a plaintiff's recovery under a *plaintiff's strict responsibility* approach.

A. The Negligence Criterion: Injurer v. Victim

Under current doctrine, the formal criteria defining plaintiff's negligence and defendant's negligence are essentially the same.[22] Although in many

---

[21] In evaluating different understandings of negligence, I mean to include only theories consistent with the deficiency view, i.e., the view that the party should have acted differently. By contrast, consider the apparent view of the English courts that negligence consists merely in creating a reasonably foreseeable risk of harm to others, perhaps without regard to the cost of precaution. *See* Stephen R. Perry, *The Impossibility of General Strict Liability*, 1 CAN. J.L. & JURIS. 147, 169–70 (1988). This view *seems* to impose liability even if it is not the case that the defendant should have acted otherwise. If my characterization is correct, then this view is, in my terminology, a strict liability approach, not a negligence approach.

[22] *See* RESTATEMENT (SECOND) OF TORTS (1963), § 464; W. PAGE KEETON, DAN B. DOBBS, ROBERT E. KEETON & DAVID G. OWEN, PROSSER AND KEETON ON THE LAW OF TORTS (5th edn.,

cases the actual legal treatment of victims is more lenient, this is often due to differences in the factual situations of victims and injurers.[23] Still, courts occasionally intimate that creating an unreasonable risk to others is more faulty than creating an unreasonable risk to oneself.[24] Is this view justifiable? And should courts even more explicitly differentiate the formal criteria of injurer negligence and contributory negligence? Note that, if the formal rules differ, then precisely the same default (e.g., the same degree of inattention) could be judged differently depending on whether it happens to result in harm to ones self or in harm to another.

1. A Kantian View: Injurer Egoism v. Victim Non-egoism?

Consider first the following Kantian view of negligence: negligent behavior is wrongful because the negligent injurer places her own interests above the interests of her potential victims.[25] This view of negligence as unjustifiable egoism does not easily carry over to a victim's negligence, as the following example suggests.

Suppose Doris is deliberately speeding in order to arrive home earlier, and Peter is similarly refusing to look to his side because he wants to hurry across the street as quickly as possible. Both Doris and Peter are aware of the unreasonable risks of their conduct, but they each prefer so acting to the alternative of complying with tort law's demand of due care. In the following sense, their situations are asymmetrical. Doris has unreasonably

1984), 453. Section 464(1) of the Restatement (Second) provides: 'Unless the actor is a child or an insane person, the standard of conduct to which he must conform for his own protection is that of a reasonable man under like circumstances.' Comment (a) then states: 'The rule stated in Subsection (1) is essentially the same as that stated in § 283 standard of conduct required of the actor for the protection of others. The standard of conduct which determines the negligence of a defendant and the contributory negligence of a plaintiff is thus the same. . . . [H]owever, the application of this standard to particular facts may lead to different conclusions as to whether the same conduct is negligence or contributory negligence.'

[23] For example, victims are more likely to face emergencies and thus to be excused for their choices. The alleged negligence of victims is more likely to involve an affirmative duty to act, since victims are more often passive in their contribution to harm; thus, judges and juries might be more sympathetic to the victim's unreasonable decision not to rescue himself (i.e., not to rescue the injurer from causing the victim harm). Also, victims might more frequently be unaware of the unreasonable risks they run, which may be viewed as a lower level of fault than consciously creating such a risk.

[24] *See, e.g.*, Rossman v. La Grega, 270 N.E.2d 313, 317 (N.Y. 1971) ('between one whose negligent act does harm to others and one whose negligent act does harm to himself . . . the same mechanistic standard ought not to be applied undifferentially as to both') (cited in Victor E. Schwartz, Comparative Negligence (2d edn., 1986), 6).

[25] In describing this view as Kantian, I follow a familiar interpretation of Kant as speaking to the moral duty of a person not to treat the interests of others only as means to his selfish ends. On a more complex reading, Kant's legal theory is independent of his moral theory, and it is the legal theory that is most relevant to the legal duties of injurers. See Ernest J. Weinrib, The Idea of Private Law (1995), 50, 84–113. Nevertheless, I believe that Kant's moral theory remains a valuable explanation of the injurer's moral duty not to act negligently. Although additional argument is then necessary to show how that moral duty grounds a legal duty, the additional argument need not derive from Kant.

placed her own interests ahead of the interests of others. Peter has unreasonably placed certain of his own interests (arriving more quickly at a destination) ahead of other of his own interests (including personal safety). From this Kantian perspective, our disapproval of Doris is easier to explain: we are protecting the interests of others, and she is selfishly elevating her own interests over theirs.[26] Our disapproval of Peter is more puzzling. Why not permit him to rank his own interests however he likes, since he will suffer the harm? After all, by definition there can be nothing unduly 'self-serving' about his ranking of some of his own interests over other of his own interests.[27]

This distinction between defendant egoism and plaintiff non-egoism, which Gary Schwartz has helpfully articulated,[28] might appear to justify a systematically different criterion of negligence for defendants and plaintiffs. On closer inspection, however, the distinction is problematic, both factually and normatively. Factually, 'egoism' describes some cases of defendant negligence, but by no means all. For suppose a defendant treats the risk of harm she imposes on others with as much (or as little) concern as she would treat a risk of harm to herself?[29] This possibility is greatest when the defendant does not advert to the risk; forgetful or inattentive persons might possess that characteristic whether they are engaging in activities risky to

---

[26] This disapproval could be based on utilitarian as well as Kantian principles. The utilitarian approach itself has a strongly egalitarian and Kantian component, in so far as an injurer must give the same weight to the interests of others as she gives to her own: *see, e.g.,* RONALD DWORKIN, LAW's EMPIRE (1986), 291–2. For further discussion of a possible utilitarian criterion, see the next section.

[27] Here, I am emphasizing that aspect of Kantian morality that prohibits treating *others* only as means. A broader Kantian perspective might explain Peter's wrong as well as Doris's, for Kantian morality recognizes duties to self as well as to others.

We might distinguish cases of inadvertent negligence. Suppose both Doris and Peter were unaware that they were acting negligently, or were unaware of the risks that they were posing (to others or to self). For example, both were inattentive. Here, their fault seems more similar. For example, each might well have acted differently if aware of the risk. Thus, a similar criterion of negligence might properly be applied to each in such a case.

We might also distinguish cases of advertent but good faith negligence. Suppose both Doris and Peter have tried, in good faith, to act with due care, but each fails—for example, Peter is clumsy, or Doris is absent-minded. Here again, their fault seems similar, and it may be sensible to apply a similar criterion of negligence. At least, the egoism/non-egoism distinction does not justify different criteria.

[28] Schwartz, *supra,* note 2, at 722–3.

[29] Compare Richard Epstein's argument for strict liability: a strict liability rule, by requiring injurers to internalize all costs of their activities, requires them to treat harms to others as they would treat harms to themselves: EPSTEIN, *supra,* note 1, at 12–14. The problems with this argument are similar to the problems with the 'egoism' argument discussed in the text. For criticisms of Epstein, see George P. Fletcher, *The Search for Synthesis in Tort Theory,* 2 LAW & PHIL. 63, 66 (1983); Ernest J. Weinrib, *Causation and Wrongdoing,* 63 CHI.-KENT L. REV. 407, 420–2 (1987); Jules L. Coleman, *Property, Wrongfulness and the Duty to Compensate,* 63 CHI.-KENT L. REV. 451, 453–60 (1987); Perry, *supra,* note 21, at 148–59. For Epstein's response, accepting some of the criticisms, see Richard Epstein, *Causation—In Context: An Afterword,* 63 CHI.-KENT L. REV. 653, 657–64 (1987).

others or risky to themselves. But even when the actor does advert to the risk, the actor often creates risks both to the actor and to others, and often treats them with similar amounts of concern. Suppose a drunk motorist, Mary, is driving very late at night on a relatively deserted road, thus creating risks mainly to herself. If she happens to strike a pedestrian, the 'egoism' explanation of her liability rings false, for she is not treating the pedestrian's safety or concerns any more lightly than she is treating her own.[30] Moreover, sometimes both the risks and the costs of the defendant's decision whether to take a precaution are largely incurred by others; in such a case, 'egoism' cannot explain liability for an unreasonable choice. (Consider a therapist's decision not to detain a patient who threatens to harm another, or a doctor's decision not to give full warnings about medical risks to a patient.)

Normatively, as well, the distinction between defendant egoism and plaintiff non-egoism is problematic. Suppose negligent defendants usually *are* 'egoistic', i.e., they would act more prudently were they to suffer any resulting harm themselves. That, of course, is not true of negligent plaintiffs, for they *do* suffer the harm themselves. But it does not follow that we have more reason to criticize or sanction the negligence of defendants than the negligence of plaintiffs. Consider two problems. First, the 'egoism' argument seems to imply the following unpalatable result. Suppose a negligent defendant would not act differently if he knew for certain that he (rather than the victim) would be *legally liable* for the harm. In this situation, just as in the situation where he would not act differently if he knew that he (rather than the victim) personally would suffer the physical harm, it seems that he is *not* acting 'egoistically', for in neither situation is he giving undue weight to his own interests at the expense of others. Indeed, if 'egoism' were a critical determinant of negligence, then an injurer who satisfied this criterion would not be negligent—a most dubious result.

Secondly, the 'egoism' perspective fails to provide normative direction on a crucial question: what constitutes insufficient concern? Is any degree of preference for one's own interests over the interests of others wrongful? This would be an extremely stringent moral constraint.[31] Moreover, the view that people should show the same degree of concern for the interests of others as for their own interests is also problematic from the other direction. For suppose a victim shows less concern for his *own* interests than for the interests of others. It hardly follows that he is contributorily negligent.

---

[30] To be sure, the drunk motorist might also obtain a selfish and non-reciprocal benefit— the convenience of being able to transport herself after drinking. If so, the egoism justification can help explain why the conduct is faulty. Conversely, in a small number of cases a plaintiff might act strategically, engaging in risky behavior only because he believes he might obtain a tort recovery. In such a case, 'egoism' underlies his *contributory* fault.

[31] A prominent modern critique of utilitarianism emphasizes the undue stringency of such a view: *see* DAVID O. BRINK, MORAL REALISM AND THE FOUNDATIONS OF ETHICS (1989), 264–68, 273–83; DWORKIN, *supra*, note 26, at 292–3.

A parent who drives more cautiously when his children are on board is not necessarily contributorily negligent for driving less cautiously when he is alone. A generally altruistic or self-denying attitude does not make one contributorily negligent. Rather, to the extent that contributory negligence consists in unreasonable weighing of interests, it involves the plaintiff making an unreasonable choice to favor certain of his own interests over other of his own interests.[32]

The basic problem that this analysis highlights is the difficulty of establishing a baseline level of due concern, a baseline for determining whether the victim's concern or the injurer's concern is insufficient. The discussion also demonstrates that the factual scenarios for both victim and injurer negligence differ so much in the potential altruistic, egoistic, or indifferent motivations that any single explanation of the difference between victim and injurer fault is bound to fail. In the end, I believe that the 'egoism' approach does not justify a more tolerant judicial attitude towards victim negligence across the board. Rather, it might justify a more precise differentiation according to the varying factors in these different scenarios. For example, courts might make some allowance for injurers or victims who act altruistically (e.g., rescuers) or who do not personally benefit from failing to take a greater precaution (e.g., professionals in some situations).

Still, the 'egoism' perspective brings to light one important distinction between victim and injurer negligence: when the victim chooses to endanger his own personal safety rather than jeopardize another of his interests, we should be cautious before concluding that his choice is negligent. That is, a victim often faces a very difficult choice: suffer a risk of harm to his own person or property, or instead sacrifice some other personal interest (such as the interest in speedily reaching a destination, or in saving the costs of paying attention). The victim has chosen to risk suffering harm, even personal injury. The fact that the victim has made that painful choice gives serious reason for caution before characterizing the choice as negligent. The motive of self-protection is strong: a victim's failure to respond to that motive sometimes evidences a powerful countervailing value. To put the matter a little differently: epistemic modesty suggests caution before characterizing as 'unreasonable' a choice between two difficult options, both of which potentially harm one's own interests. On the other hand, if a victim's negligence is premised on his obtaining socially disvalued personal benefits of the sort that would also render an *injurer* negligent, then such sympathy and leniency are less warranted. A pedestrian who seeks the thrill of dodging speeding cars deserves less sympathy than a merely inattentive

---

[32] The example of a parent might be misleading, because the parent understandably might treat his children with more than due care. But the analysis would equally apply to a driver who is less cautious when he poses no risk of injury to others (e.g., in a deserted parking lot) than when he does pose risk to others (e.g., when driving near pedestrians).

pedestrian, for such joy-seeking risking of physical harm is socially disvalued, whether it involves risks to self or to others.

2. Utilitarian Criterion

In a formal sense, a utilitarian analysis[33] can quite easily adopt a uniform standard for victim and injurer negligence. Consider the familiar Learned Hand formula, which is often interpreted as a utilitarian metric of socially reasonable and unreasonable conduct. Formally, the Learned Hand formula applies as easily to a victim as to an injurer. An injurer is negligent if the burden of taking a precaution (a cost that is typically absorbed by the injurer) is less than the expected value of the harms that the precaution would avoid (harms that are typically absorbed, initially, by others—namely, victims). A victim is negligent if the burden of taking the precaution (again, a cost typically absorbed by the relevant actor—in this case, the victim) is less than the expected value of the harms that the precaution would avoid (harms that are now absorbed by the same actor, the victim).

Once we look beneath the surface symmetry, however, a serious problem arises. The essential justification of utilitarianism as a moral doctrine is that it explains what actions or policies are good by reference to aggregating and maximizing net utility across persons. But how can the Learned Hand doctrine (understood in utilitarian terms) apply to a single person? Do we mean that the best action for him is the one that maximizes his own utility? Although that might seem to be a simple implication of utilitarianism, it is not. For, on a utilitarian view, it is one matter to determine what each person's net 'utility' or 'good' is, and quite another to aggregate and maximize utility across persons. We might let each individual define for himself what counts as 'utility', and at the same time employ a utilitarian maximizing criterion to aggregate 'utility', so defined, over persons.[34] For example, a religious person deciding which self-regarding action is in his own best interest

---

[33] By 'utilitarian analysis', I refer to one component of the economic approach to tort law—that the measure of 'good' action (e.g., of due care) requires a consequentialist analysis of the net utility of the action (e.g., an analysis of whether the costs of taking a precaution outweigh the benefits). The other important component of the economic approach is this: the main function of liability rules is to induce optimal or 'utilitarian' conduct, so understood. The two components are independent. One might, for example, endorse a utilitarian criterion of what constitutes contributory negligence but reject the second component, believing that contributory negligence rules are unlikely to affect victims' behavior. Of course, the second component is also utilitarian in a broader sense of *maximizing* the good. Still, it is worth analyzing separately the first component, a utilitarian *measure* of the good.

[34] A number of important distinctions are embedded here. One can distinguish between prudence or rational choice as decision-procedures for an individual person, on the one hand, and utilitarianism as a social choice mechanism, on the other: *see* David Lyons, *Utilitarianism, in* ENCYCLOPEDIA OF ETHICS (Lawrence C. Becker & Charlotte B. Becker (eds.), 1992), 1261–8. More finely, one can distinguish between utilitarianism as an actual personal decision-procedure and as a criterion of rightness: BRINK, *supra*, note 31, at 256–62. And one can further distinguish between subjective and objective utilitarianism: *id.* at 211–90.

might not choose between his options in the way that a Learned Hand calculation suggests. Yet utilitarianism can certainly accommodate highly varied individual judgements of the good.

The economic approach to law usually presupposes a subjective theory of value: individuals are in the best position to decide what is in their own best interest.[35] It is therefore strange that the economic approach to the Learned Hand formula, as applied to contributory negligence, seems to adopt an objective theory of value, in so far as a victim might prefer to act in a way that the formula identifies to be 'inefficient'.

One reply is that the contributory negligence defense *does* aggregate utility across persons, for the plaintiff's duty arises only in so far as he would otherwise cause harm to another (by obtaining a remedy against a defendant). So the plaintiff's utilitarian calculus is not purely internal, after all. That calculus encompasses not only the internal burden of taking a precaution, but also the cost of not taking a precaution. And, although it is the plaintiff who most immediately incurs the latter cost, in the form of an injury to self, the defendant also incurs the cost, in the form of legal liability to the plaintiff for that injury.[36]

But I remain unconvinced. On a plausible subjective version of utilitarianism, the judgement that plaintiff is contributorily negligent depends only on the plaintiff's own internal calculus. So the question remains why the plaintiff's valuation is not considered conclusive in evaluating his utility. If the plaintiff judges that the burden of taking a precaution exceeds the expected loss in terms of self-injury (and if, as is not always the case, he is aware of the relevant burden and expected loss), then he would seem by hypothesis to obtain more expected utility from not taking a precaution than from taking a precaution. To be sure, the defendant suffers disutility from being required to pay damages to the plaintiff. And, more generally, a world without a contributory negligence defense is obviously more costly to injurers than a world with such a defense. But these are secondary issues. We first must decide whether the plaintiff has, on some justifiable utilitarian criterion, acted *wrongly*. If he has not, then we need some other theory (perhaps a form of plaintiff's strict responsibility) to explain why his conduct should require some forfeiture of damages.

We might, to be sure, apply an objective form of utilitarianism to both victim and injurer negligence. But even if adequate reasons are provided for adopting this more controversial form of utilitarianism in both contexts, a gap might remain. For such an objective theory of value might disvalue a person's causing harm to others more than his causing harm to himself, for some of the reasons discussed in the 'egoism' section, above, just as it might

---

[35] *See, e.g.*, A. MITCHELL POLINKSY, AN INTRODUCTION TO LAW AND ECONOMICS (1983), 10.

[36] I thank Steve Marks for articulating this objection.

value one's personal commitments more than his more general social obligations.[37]

Thus, the case has yet to be made that the same utilitarian criterion applicable to injurer negligence should apply equally to a victim's self-regarding negligence. Moreover, even if utilitarian theory does apply to victim negligence, the theory confronts this prominent criticism—that utilitarianism demands too much of people, requiring us to weigh the interests of all other persons as highly as we weigh our own interests.[38] The demanding nature of utilitarian aggregation seems especially troubling in so far as contributory negligence apparently obliges a victim to rescue a tortious *injurer*. Of all the people in the world who could help out the injurer, why burden the *victim*? To be sure, this complaint can be exaggerated. For the victim is not really 'required' to rescue the injurer; rather, his making reasonable efforts to do so is a condition of his obtaining a full legal remedy against the injurer. Still, the obligation, even in this conditional form, is unusually severe, in the context of tort law's general aversion to imposing duties to rescue.[39]

3. Moral Parity

Another approach, which I will call *moral parity*, asserts that what victims can legitimately expect of injurers, injurers can legitimately expect of victims.[40] In so far as a victim is seeking a remedy based on the injurer's deficient behavior, the injurer has two *prima facie* arguments: first, that the victim should be held to a similar standard of behavior; and secondly, that the victim's failure to do so should limit his recovery. The first claim is a plausible argument, one grounded in fundamental equitable principles. It is most plausible when the behaviors of victim and injurer are indeed most comparable—for example, when each has failed to pay attention *and* when each has posed risks both to self and to others. (Consider, for example, a collision between two vehicles, with each driver paying insufficient attention.) Problems quickly arise, however, whenever a dissimilarity is introduced. Some degree of inattention by a victim, for example, might be a lesser moral lapse than the same degree of inattention by an injurer, if the victim's inattention is likely to produce only self-regarding harm and the injurer's is likely to produce harm to others. (Consider a collision in which the vehicle of a daydreaming driver strikes a daydreaming pedestrian.) In

---

[37] See BRINK, *supra*, note 31, at 264–8, 273–83.   [38] *See id.* at 264–8.

[39] See Simons, *supra*, note * at 1737–44, for a more extended discussion of whether contributory negligence imposes an unduly burdensome duty to rescue.

[40] Ernest Weinrib seems to endorse a similar view of contributory negligence in his new book: *see* WEINRIB, *supra*, note 25, at 169, note 53 (arguing that contributory negligence 'expresses an idea of transactional equality: the plaintiff cannot demand that the defendant should observe a greater care than the plaintiff with respect to the plaintiff's safety'). For a discussion and rejection of the 'moral parity' approach, see Schwartz, *supra*, note 2, at 722–3.

such cases, the parity argument might have little independent justificatory force.

Moreover, it is unclear how this equitable 'parity' principle applies when the injurer's tort liability is strict or is based on intentional or reckless behavior. I doubt that the principle should be taken to its logical extreme, so that, for example, the victim is strictly responsible for the harms he causes so long as the injurer's liability is strict. But why is parity an appropriate principle for negligence but not for strict liability?[41]

If the victim has not satisfied the standard of care to which he is holding the injurer, moral parity suggest that his default should limit his recovery. But how should the recovery be limited? If we pursue the argument of moral parity literally, perhaps a simple splitting of liability makes sense, with the victim recovering half of his damages. However, a pure comparative fault apportionment (according to relative fault) also has several advantages. It allows consideration of the degree to which each party actually deviated from a standard in a given case, even if the standard (for example, requiring a reasonable degree of attention) is formally the same for both victims and injurers. More significantly, it allows variation in the underlying standard itself (for example, requiring a lesser degree of attention from victims who reasonably foresee risk only to themselves than from injurers who reasonably foresee risk only to others).

4. Forfeiture of a Remedy

The question before us is why the victim's moral duty to act differently translates into the injurer's legal right to condition the victim's remedy. Perhaps the answer is that an actor who should have acted differently justifiably *forfeits* the right to obtain a full remedy. One version of the forfeiture rationale is that any plaintiff who seeks a legal remedy must have

---

[41] Perhaps strict liability principles are special: they trump the parity principle, because they are designed to provide victims broader redress than a negligence principle provides. A related argument, which Wendy Gordon has suggested to me, is this: if a victim shows very little regard for his own interests in safety, then the injurer is entitled to show a similarly slight regard for those interests, at least to the extent of entitling the injurer to provide a lesser damage remedy. This argument, while promising, may prove too much. Suppose a victim shows essentially no regard for his own interests—for example, he engages in extraordinarily reckless and dangerous acts. It does not follow that a potential injurer is entitled, in his basic actions, to create much greater risks to such a victim than to a more prudent potential victim. Perhaps the argument makes only the more limited claim that the victim's low regard for his own interests warrants at least a partial forfeiture of his tort remedy. But even this limited claim is problematic. First, the fact that the victim values his own health or safety much less than society believes he should might be a reason for the law to compensate him as fully as possible, as a way of treating his life as valuable. Secondly, when a victim chooses an activity that endangers himself, he obtains independent value from the exercise of choice. But when an injurer treats the victim with similarly low regard, the victim has made no choice and thus obtains no such value. (I thank Clay Gillette for this last point.)

clean hands; a contributorily negligent plaintiff does not.[42] If forfeiture is a persuasive rationale, then we should examine much more carefully the reasons why *any* right-holder—whether his claim is in tort or contract, or in private or constitutional law—should suffer a loss or limitation of remedy because of his own conduct.[43]

Under a forfeiture approach, we might give up any attempt to reconcile the criteria of victim and injurer negligence. At least two strong arguments support giving up this attempt. First, the victim's legal duty not to be negligent, unlike the injurer's duty, is distinctly conditional, depending entirely on the victim's decision to seek a remedy from the injurer. Secondly, the victim might pose risks of harm entirely to himself, so it is not at all obvious that formally equal criteria (e.g., 'pay a reasonable degree of attention') have equal moral significance whether applied to victims or to injurers.

If we do give up the attempt, then the criteria of victim and injurer negligence could vary quite dramatically.[44] Victims might be considered negligent only for conduct that, if engaged in by injurers, would be considered gross negligence. Indeed, the concept of victim negligence could be extremely narrow: for example, victims might be considered negligent only in so far as their conduct creates unreasonable risks to *others*.

In the end, perhaps only the convenience and familiarity of the label 'negligence' rather than an incisive analysis of underlying rationales explain why current doctrine employs similar criteria for contributory negligence and injurer negligence.

5. Pure and Impure Victim Negligence: Risks to Self and Risks to Others

To clarify the analysis, I have assumed to this point that the victim's failure to take a reasonable precaution poses risks of harm only to himself, not to others. But many actual instances of victim negligence are not so pure. In what I will call 'impure' instances of victim negligence, the victim's failure to take a reasonable precaution poses risks to others as well as to himself. Imprudent conduct by pedestrians, for example, is a relatively pure type of victim negligence (though even here, the pedestrian's lack of care can cause injuries to others, e.g. to bicyclists and motorists who swerve to avoid the pedestrian, or who strike the pedestrian and then suffer further harm themselves). Imprudent conduct by motorists who happen to suffer

---

[42] *See* PROSSER & KEETON, *supra*, note 22; 4 FOWLER V. HARPER, FLEMING JAMES, JR., & OSCAR S. GRAY, THE LAW OF TORTS (2d edn., 1986), 276–9 (criticizing this rationale).

[43] *See, e.g.*, RESTATEMENT (SECOND) OF CONTRACTS (1979), § 350 ('damages are not recoverable for loss that the injured party could have avoided without undue risk, burden or humiliation').

[44] To warrant the name 'negligence', however, I would still insist that victim negligence satisfy the deficiency criterion and constitute a failure to take a precaution that a reasonable victim would have taken.

only injury to themselves is a more impure type of victim negligence, since the motorist's lack of care typically poses significant risks to others.

When we relax the assumption that victim negligence is pure, two questions arise. First, if the very same default—such as inattentive driving—creates both risks to self and risks to others, should both types of risk be considered when determining the victim's contributory fault? Secondly, if the answer is yes, does the circumstance that the victim created risks to others as well as to self strengthen or weaken the substantive rationale for limiting the victim's recovery?

With respect to the first question, some have given a negative answer. For example, Gary Schwartz argues that courts should ignore risks to others in deciding whether a plaintiff was contributorily negligent.[45] The rationale is that such risks are already considered in any case in which they do result in harm to another, for the 'victim' then becomes an *injurer*. On this reasoning, considering risks to others when assessing plaintiff's contributory fault is an improper form of 'double-counting'.[46]

I find this argument unpersuasive. Imagine a case in which the following is true: the risks that the 'victim' poses only to himself are not quite serious enough to make his failure to take a precaution contributorily negligent; similarly, the risks that he poses to others are not quite serious enough to make his failure to take a precaution negligent; but the combined risks do suffice to make a precaution desirable.[47] All things considered, the precaution should be taken. In such a case, compartmentalizing the risks is a mistake. But this suggests that, in every case, the risk to others is at least relevant, if not dispositive, in determining the plaintiff's own negligence.

Schwartz's concern about 'double-counting' might reflect a fear that a party who is clearly negligent with respect to others but who creates only a very small risk to himself will be found contributorily negligent, a result that Schwartz might believe to be improper. But is it? Suppose that a driver of a large car swerves dangerously around an inattentive pedestrian instead of stopping for the pedestrian. Unexpectedly, the car skids and collides into a concrete abutment. The driver then sues the pedestrian, who claims that the driver was contributorily negligent. *Ex ante*, the risks of *self*-injury from the driver's risky maneuver appear extremely small; by themselves, they would not warrant contributory fault liability. But it does not

---

[45] Schwartz, *supra*, note 2, at 723–4. John Fleming appears to agree. *See* JOHN G. FLEMING, THE LAW OF TORTS (7th edn., 1987), 242, 248, n. 51 (surveying English and Commonwealth law).

[46] Schwartz, *supra*, note 2, at 724.

[47] Employing the Learned Hand formula, suppose that the marginal cost of taking a precaution is $50, the expected value of the risks to self that the precaution would avoid is $40, and the expected value of the risks to others that the precaution would avoid is $40. (I use this formula for expositional purposes only; I do not assume that the Learned Hand formula is the best elucidation of the concept of negligence, nor that, if it is the best elucidation, it must be understood to express economic efficiency.)

follow that she is not contributorily negligent. Here, where the very same precaution (using more care in maneuvering past a pedestrian, or waiting for the pedestrian to cross) would avoid risks to others *and* to self, it would seem entirely proper to consider both types of risks when assessing the plaintiff's contributory fault.[48]

Thus, I believe that all of the risks that a person creates because of his failure to take a precaution—risks to others as well as to self—should be considered in assessing his contributory negligence. Of course, in many cases, adopting my view or Schwartz's contrary view will make no difference to the result, since the magnitude of the risks that a party creates to himself alone often will be dispositive of his contributory negligence.[49]

If I am correct, then we need to consider the second question—whether the impure rather than pure quality of a victim's negligence strengthens the rationale for limiting the victim's recovery. I believe that it does strengthen that rationale. Most generally, recall that the victim's duty not to act negligently is conditional (on the victim seeking a recovery), while the injurer's duty not to act negligently is not. And, as we have seen, it is much easier to justify a remedy against a negligent injurer than to justify a limitation upon a negligent victim's remedy. In cases of impure victim negligence, however, it is often only a fortuity whether the negligence happens to result in injury to self or injury to others. Thus, it is easier to justify limiting the remedy of a negligent victim, who could just as well have been an injurer. (This is perhaps clearest in those cases where the 'victim' is in fact also an injurer, e.g. an automobile collision where the victim's inattention actually causes harm to another as well as to himself.)

Impure victim negligence also strengthens some of the particular substantive rationales for limiting a victim's remedy. Thus, with respect to the 'egoism' argument, impure victim negligence is more likely than pure victim negligence to demonstrate unjustifiable preference for one's own interests—though it is still less probative of such a preference than is pure

---

[48] Consider this analogy. In determining an *injurer's* negligence liability, most would agree that the fact finder should evaluate the risks to foreseeable plaintiffs in several distinguishable classes, such as the classes of pedestrians and of other drivers. If the negligent driver injures a pedestrian, the pedestrian may, in demonstrating the driver's negligence, point to the risks imposed on other drivers as well as the risks imposed on pedestrians. And an injured other driver may similarly point to the risks to pedestrians. Neither can validly complain of 'double-counting'.

[49] Note the converse problem: should one be liable for negligently harming *another* if the same precaution would have avoided risks to self and risks to others, but neither set of risks is independently sufficient to justify taking the precaution? The solution might be the same— that the risks should simply be aggregated, and that the decision whether a precaution is reasonable should depend on the aggregate risks, whether those risks are to self or to others. But I confess to greater unease here, where the risks necessary to create negligence liability to others are risks to oneself, than in the situation just discussed in the text, where the risks necessary to create a contributory negligence defense are risks to others. Perhaps risks to self have less moral 'weight', for reasons discussed earlier.

injurer negligence (where the injurer poses risks of harm only to others). With respect to the utilitarian argument, impure victim negligence is more clearly socially unreasonable conduct, if one shares my doubt that pure victim negligence is necessarily undesirable from a social perspective. Finally, with respect to the moral parity argument, impure victim negligence greatly strengthens the injurer's claim that the victim's negligence is on a moral par with the injurer's negligence, as I suggested above. For it is often only fortuitous whether and to what extent the victim's default injures himself or instead (or also) injures another.[50]

B. *Plaintiff's Strict Responsibility*

Earlier, I explained the conceptual distinction between plaintiff negligence (where the plaintiff should have acted otherwise and taken a precaution), and plaintiff strict responsibility[51] where the plaintiff's recovery is reduced even though his conduct might not have been deficient. But we have yet to explore the scope and limits of the victim strict responsibility approach. Once we depart from the constraints of the deficiency approach to negligence, under which we must identify a precaution that a reasonable person would have taken, what is the criterion?

As noted earlier, tort doctrine explicitly recognizes only one category of plaintiff strict responsibility—the plaintiff's voluntary and knowing assumption of a risk. Sensibly, tort law does not recognize a broad category of plaintiff strict responsibility for all harm that a plaintiff could have avoided. The more difficult question, however, is what type of limited categories of plaintiff strict responsibility should be recognized, *beyond* assumption of risk.

One potentially significant category of plaintiff's strict responsibility consists of certain penumbral 'assumption of risk' cases. Assumption of risk would, I believe, have a much more limited scope than it presently enjoys if it were confined to cases in which its consensual rationale clearly applies.[52] But many of the assumption of risk cases that the consensual rationale cannot justify are plausible instances of plaintiff strict

[50] I have here explored whether a victim's creation of risks to others should be considered in determining the victim's negligence, and I have concluded that it should. But the creation of such risks to others also helps demonstrate that the victim is negligent and not merely strictly responsible: at least if the risks to others exceed a certain threshold, their creation helps show that the victim should have acted otherwise.

[51] In their important article, Calabresi and Hirschoff point out that assumption of risk is a form of plaintiff's 'strict liability' (or what I call plaintiff's 'strict responsibility'): Calabresi & Hirschoff, *supra*, note 12, at 1066. The authors use the analogy to argue for their own distinctive strict liability principle—the party in the best position to perform the cost-benefit analysis should be 'strictly liable' for the harm 'regardless of whether the other party "ought" to have done what he did': *id.*

[52] Simons, *supra*, note 17, at 247–8. Specifically, I believe that the consensual rationale clearly applies only when the plaintiff prefers the option that the negligent defendant actually

responsibility. Consider, for example, a plaintiff who voluntarily enters into a relationship with a tortious defendant, without consenting to a specific risk.[53] Classic examples include the defendant who lends the plaintiff a car, informing him that the brakes are bad; or the plaintiff who hitches a ride with a drunk driver. Neither plaintiff has fully assumed the risk, on my model, for each plaintiff would have preferred that the defendant had not been negligent (i.e., that he had fixed his brakes, or had not become drunk). But neither plaintiff is necessarily contributorily negligent, either. (If they acted in response to an emergency, for example, their choice to accept the danger might have been reasonable.) Thus, when courts bar recovery in such cases, they are implicitly relying on independent plaintiff strict responsibility policies.

Similarly, some instances that courts denominate 'contributory fault' are better understood as plaintiff strict responsibility. For it is often difficult to say with any confidence that a victim has acted as he should not have, given that the victim himself may incur all of the most tangible costs and benefits of his conduct. This difficulty is especially pronounced when the victim consciously chooses not to take a precaution (such as the use of a seat belt), or when unusual personal values (such as religious belief) explain the victim's choice not to take a precaution. It might not be obvious that the victim should have acted otherwise; nevertheless, we might be warranted in limiting his recovery.

Mitigation of damages cases are especially likely to exhibit these characteristics.[54] The seatbelt non-use cases may here be the paradigm. In another context, a court recently held that a Jehovah's Witness could not rely on her religious objection to a blood transfusion to justify her failure to mitigate damages. The court reasoned that the decedent could not rely on her religious beliefs to justify what would otherwise be unreasonable conduct.[55]

---

offered to the option that a non-negligent defendant would have offered. A reckless pedestrian who enjoys dodging speeding cars assumes the risk; an inattentive pedestrian who would have preferred that the motorist were not speeding does not assume the risk.

[53] *See id.* at 244–6.

[54] I find it doubtful that failure to attempt to lose weight as directed by a physician is deficient conduct, but courts have held that such a default may be considered a form of contributory fault that mitigates damages: *see, e.g.,* Tanberg v. Ackerman Invest. Co., 473 N.W.2d 193 (Iowa 1991).

[55] Munn v. Algee, 924 F.2d 568 (5th Cir. 1991). The decedent, badly injured in an automobile accident caused by the defendant's negligence, refused a blood transfusion that would have saved her life. For an extensive discussion of the case, see Note, *Reason, Religion, and Avoidable Consequences: When Faith and the Duty to Mitigate Collide,* 67 N.Y.U. L. Rev. 1111 (1992). Consider also Friedman v. State, 282 N.Y.S.2d 858 (Ct.Cl. 1967), modified, 297 N.Y.S.2d 850 (A.D. 1969). An Orthodox Jewish girl jumped from a stalled chair lift at a skiing facility rather than violate her religious duty not to remain in the lift with an unmarried male. If we assume that a 'reasonable person' would not have jumped from such a height, we might conclude that she acted unreasonably. But we should certainly be hesitant before concluding that her religious beliefs are 'unreasonable'. If we conclude that her religious beliefs

This result is more plausibly defended as follows: although the decedent's decision to honor her religious beliefs is *not* unreasonable, defendant has no duty to subsidize her choice to sacrifice her life in the name of religion.

More generally, perhaps the criteria for plaintiff strict responsibility could be derived by extrapolating the rationales for *injurer* strict liability to victims. Thus, suppose (with George Fletcher) that the defendant's strict liability is based on the defendant's imposition of non-reciprocal risks, or suppose that it is based on the defendant appropriating a non-reciprocal or special personal benefit.[56] The extrapolation approach would employ parallel criteria and limit *plaintiff's* strict responsibility to instances when the plaintiff imposes non-reciprocal risks or obtains a non-reciprocal benefit. For example, perhaps the seat-belt user is obtaining a special benefit by saving the time and trouble of buckling up, even if his not buckling up is a permissible, non-negligent choice; and he must 'pay' for appropriating that benefit, by absorbing some of the costs of his behavior.[57]

However, I doubt that the extrapolation approach is sufficient. Some of the rationales for injurer strict liability do not readily apply to victims— for example, a victim's self-regarding risk is not easily viewed as non-reciprocal. Moreover, plaintiff strict responsibility can be justifiable for reasons other than consensual assumption of risk or extrapolation from injurer strict liability policies. Consider again the Jehovah's Witness blood transfusion case. The patient's choice to decline the transfusion does not, in my view, reflect a full consent to the risk, since he would have preferred not to have been placed in that predicament by the tortfeasor's negligence.[58] Still, fairness principles plausibly justify a rule entitling the patient to decline a blood transfusion but precluding some or all of his recovery.

The failure of courts and commentators to develop arguments for plaintiff strict responsibility outside the assumption of risk context might reflect a lack of imagination. However, it might also reflect a stronger commitment to negligence as the appropriate standard of care for victims than for injurers. There is indeed evidence of such a commitment even within the nominal bounds of negligence doctrine itself. The most striking example is

do not justify her imposing the costs of her behavior on the injurer, then it is more forthright to reduce her recovery on grounds of contributory strict responsibility, rather than contributory negligence.

[56] *See* Simons, *supra,* note 5, at 863 (discussing Vincent v. Lake Erie Transp. Co., 124 N.W. 221 (Minn. 1910)).

[57] Or, in the products liability context, both the manufacturer of a product with a flaw (that due care would not prevent) and the consumer of the product might be considered strictly 'liable', i.e., they might divide the cost of the resulting harm, since each profits both from the product generally and from the manufacturer's decision not to take extraordinary care to avoid all product defects.

[58] Moreover, his choice might justify a limit upon recovery even if the patient had insufficiently specific knowledge of the risks and consequences of refusing treatment to satisfy the broader traditional assumption of risk doctrine.

the courts' greater willingness to individualize the 'objective' test of negligence for victims than for injurers.[59] For example, many courts adopt a dual standard for mental capacity.[60] When a *victim's* contributory fault is at issue, some courts will examine his actual mental capacity to determine whether the particular individual lacked the capacity to take the precaution. But when an *injurer's* fault is at issue, courts are more likely to apply an objective test. Thus, courts tend to conform the contributory negligence test to the party's genuine blameworthiness, eliminating some of the strict liability that inheres in the usual objective test of negligence. Part of the explanation might be a greater reluctance to hold victims to a standard of strict responsibility.

A final strict responsibility issue deserves brief mention here. If a plaintiff *is* held strictly responsible, should 'payment' for his risky choices mean a *complete* loss of the damage remedy that he would otherwise obtain? Note that this is the effect of traditional assumption of risk doctrine: in jurisdictions where assumption of risk doctrine retains its traditional vitality, it serves as a complete bar to recovery. However, I do not believe that the concept of plaintiff strict responsibility necessarily entails this result. More particular conceptions of plaintiff strict responsibility might suggest otherwise. Thus, the view that obtaining a special benefit from not taking care warrants strict liability might only entail that the plaintiff suffer a partial reduction in damages. For example, suppose we believe that a driver failing to use a seat belt falls into this category; it does not follow that his recovery must be completely barred to the extent that the omission caused his own harm.

III. Conclusion

These ruminations about contributory fault suggest some surprisingly undeveloped and fertile issues for future inquiry. When a plaintiff has been negligent in the sense that he should have acted otherwise, should the same criterion of negligence apply that would apply if he were creating risks only to others? Indeed, are there any persuasive reasons *not* to apply a radically different criterion of negligence? Moreover, should the plaintiff's recovery be diminished, outside the category of assumption of risk, even when the plaintiff has not been negligent? What are the justifiable criteria and limits of such plaintiff strict responsibility?

We have also seen a number of reasons for caution before concluding that a victim's self-regarding conduct is negligent. For example, a victim

[59] HARPER, JAMES, & GRAY, *supra*, note 42 at § 2210.

[60] HARPER, JAMES, & GRAY, *supra*, note 42 at § 2210; VICTOR E. SCHWARTZ, COMPARATIVE NEGLIGENCE (2d edn., 1986), 6.

often deserves special sympathy in the light of his special predicament, choosing between two evils, the immediate costs of which he must personally bear. Indeed, it might appear that the law is unfair or unduly onerous when it places significant demands on a victim with respect to his own self-regarding behavior. On the other hand, we should not forget that the victim's duty to use reasonable care is merely conditional: it applies only in case the victim seeks a remedy against the tortfeasor.

Any final resolution of these difficult issues, issues about the scope and criteria of plaintiff's negligence and plaintiff's strict responsibility, will depend in part on one's substantive views about the nature and purpose of tort liability. In this chapter, I have been largely agnostic about such views. Under any view, however, the issues resist easy analysis. The reasons that justify a victim's remedy when the injurer has been negligent simply do not suffice to justify limiting the victim's remedy when the victim has been negligent.

Afterword
What Has Philosophy to Learn from Tort Law?

BERNARD WILLIAMS*

I. TESTING COMMON SENSE: THE PICTURE

One answer to my question is that philosophy might learn from tort law the difference between practical reality and philosophical frivolity. J. L. Austin was disposed to give that answer. Austin was, like Wittgenstein and Nietzsche, struck by the irresponsibility of philosophy, its light-headed willingness to suppose that large problems could be usefully addressed by some distinctions or formulations that were simply thought up 'of a Sunday afternoon'. (There was a difference between Austin and those others: unlike them, he did more or less take it for granted that there was a subject, philosophy, which might come to conduct itself more seriously and usefully in these respects, even if he was less than clear about the form that the subject might take.)

What is this contrast? What is it that supposedly provides us with distinctions more adequate than those offered by philosophy? Austin said (with some reservations) that it was common sense or, perhaps, ordinary language, and one reason he sometimes gave for this judgement was a quasi-evolutionary one, that common sense (as I shall call it)[1] had been, at least with regard to central human concerns, under heavy selective pressure for a very long time, and the distinctions that had survived and flourished in it were likely to answer fairly reliably to human needs. This was not a very good answer, for more than one reason, and it is not easy to tell how seriously Austin took it. However, it does at least provide a starting point for thinking about something less general, a contrast drawn in similar terms between philosophy and the law. Austin also appealed to the law, and the famous article *A Plea For Excuses*, in which he sets out some of his methodological

* White's Professor of Moral Philosophy, University of Oxford; Deutsch Professor of Philosophy, University of California, Berkeley.

[1] Some philosophers of Austin's tendency may have thought that 'common sense' was consistent, self-validating, and free of ideology. The present discussion makes no such assumptions.

his methodological concerns, mentions a (rather grisly) example drawn from a nineteenth century case.[2]

If the law—for instance, the law of non-intentional torts[3]—uses certain concepts or distinctions that have been variously applied, modified, and reinterpreted within a legal tradition over a period of time, does this offer any reason at all for thinking that those concepts and distinctions provide a sound and reliable way of thinking about the relevant areas of experience? More exactly, the question is whether such facts provide any independent reason, since it might be that the legal use of certain ideas did no more than witness to what was clear anyway, that those ideas seemed obvious to common sense. If the use of certain ideas in the law does more to show that those ideas have strength than is done by the mere fact that they are part of the currency of common sense, this will have to be connected with special features of the law—with the idea, most plausibly, that the legal context is one in which a lot turns on the outcome, and hence on the arguments that lead to or legitimate legal outcomes. This is itself a kind of evolutionary argument. The sense in which 'a lot turns on the outcome' is that the issue is likely to be vigorously disputed by the parties involved, that the decision may have implications for other parties who will watch the outcome with interest, and so forth, with the result that only robustly argued conclusions, which are at least consistent with public conceptions of what makes sense in such connections, are likely to survive. I shall call this quasi-evolutionary account of the strength of some legal concepts and distinctions, the Picture.

II. Two Objections

The Picture is without doubt highly idealized. It may be suggested that it is worse than idealized, and rests, rather, on some mistake of principle. There are perhaps two main directions from which this suggestion may come. One objection is that the Picture *over*estimates the effects of legal argument. The idea here is that cases are decided on the basis of external values or principles—such as wealth maximization, utility, equal freedom—and that the legal arguments and the concepts invoked in them (fault, negligence, intention, proximity of causation, or whatever) are, at the limit, merely rhetorical decorations. The other objection is that the Picture *under*estimates the autonomy and peculiarity of legal concepts: that the require-

---

[2] J. L. Austin, *A Plea for Excuses*, in Philosophical Papers (1961); Regina v. Finney, [1874] 12 Cox 625.

[3] Much of my argument will be at a general level, where distinctions between different legal areas will not be very relevant, but the law of non-intentional torts is what I shall principally have in mind, and this has some significance in relation to a contrast with the criminal law. *See infra* note 5.

ments, purposes, and traditions of the law are special enough for its distinctions and principles to stand at a distance from common sense and from what people need to say and think in extra-legal contexts.

The two lines of objection may seem to run in opposite directions, but this is not necessarily so. One can combine them, in claiming both that legal argument is highly technical and that it fails to determine the outcome. Indeed, the suggestion may be that the reason legal argument needs to be very technical is in order to conceal the fact that it fails to determine the outcome: the technicalities provide a mystification that conceals the underlying processes. Whether the objections are combined in this way or not, they do between them threaten the Picture, which was invoked to explain how processes of the law could remind philosophy of reality by showing distinctions recognizable to common sense under pressure where much turns on the outcome. Broadly speaking, the first objection is that the distinctions invoked are recognizable to common sense, but are not under pressure; the second is that the distinctions may perhaps be under pressure (if they are not simply acting as a mystification), but they and the outcomes that they are invoked to support are only remotely related to common sense. On either showing, the idea that the law can shed light on common sense, or indeed on anything outside itself, loses momentum.

Neither objection is fatal. Even if what the first objection claims is true, it is not clear that very much follows from it for the present question. Rationalizations must have some force even to serve as rationalizations, and the rationalizations which, on this account, serve as the rhetoric of the legal process through which optimal allocations of costs are made (or whatever the supposed underlying principle or value is taken to be) must have some strength in order to discharge this role. Indeed, it may be that they will turn out to have almost as much strength as the Picture requires.

The latent economic criteria, or whatever they may be, which, according to the type of theory invoked by the first objection, determine the outcomes at the fundamental level are not *manifestly* in operation. If they were, the theory would not be controversial, and it would also have nothing new to recommend normatively, if (as some such theories do) it has that aim. The arguments that do the work at the manifest level must be the familiar ones. The theory regards them as rationalizations, but they must nevertheless do some work, since some process is actually going on at the manifest level, and that process must have some of the characteristics (of claims being argued against counter-claims and so on) that were identified in the Picture.

Of course, if the theory claims that the processes at the manifest level (conventional argument about negligence, proximate cause, and such) conceal some other criteria (economic or whatever) which actually determine the outcome, it must give some account (as all such functionalist theories must) of the ways in which those other criteria can guide, be served by, and most generally relate to the manifest level of argument. This will have certain implications about the nature of the arguments at the manifest level: such conventional arguments may, for instance, have to display a certain flexibility or porosity which allows them to respond to the functional requirements of the considerations that operate at the latent level. But if the theory can give an account of this (and it will not be a credible or interesting theory unless it can), this result itself will make the operations of the law interesting and indeed instructive to philosophy. For this porosity can scarcely be a feature of the conventional criteria simply as they are used in the law. If that were so, they could not sustain a credible rationalization. The porosity will rather have to be a feature, or at least a potentiality, of such criteria as they are used even outside the law, and this is something that philosophy should understand about them. Moreover, it may be that the porosity of the everyday common sense criteria serves to some degree the same function outside the law as (according to the theory) it serves inside the law, of allowing the criteria to be manipulated in accordance with economic or other latent considerations, and if that is so, it is equally something that philosophy should understand.

The second objection was that the arguments and concepts used in the law were too specialist, too removed from extra-legal thought, to provide philosophy with any insight into the ways in which extra-legal thought works. There are, obviously, technical aspects of the law for which this is true, but so far as the most important matters here are concerned—matters such as fault, intention, carelessness, proximate cause and consequence, and so on—the claim is simply not convincing, at least when an important concession has been made. It is true that the law must often reach a conclusion about questions to which common sense would be happy to leave the answer indeterminate—to which, indeed, in many cases, it would be unhappy to do anything but leave the answer indeterminate. There are familiar examples of this in the criminal law. If the assailant pulls the trigger in one jurisdiction and the bullet hits the victim in another, common sense may well be content to say just that much, but the law needs to decide where the victim was killed. More significantly, there are questions of an agent's state of mind, and—as an interesting if marginal consequence—of who is the criminal agent in cases, for instance, of hypnotic suggestion.[4] In all these matters, the law can be seen as *forcing the issue* relative to what I am calling common sense; though I shall suggest later that in certain connections the law may merely be a more determined accomplice of common

---

[4] This is one of several dimensions (as he recognizes) in which there are limitations to Michael Moore's project of grounding the criminal law's requirements on criminal agency in a general metaphysics of action: see MICHAEL S. MOORE, ACT AND CRIME—THE PHILOSOPHY OF ACTION AND ITS IMPLICATIONS FOR CRIMINAL LAW (1993) and for discussion, the symposium, *Act and Crime*, 142 U. PA. L. REV. 1455 (1994). On the particular issue of somnambulistic and other non-standard states, see my *The Actus Reus of Dr. Caligari, supra*, at 1661.

sense in doing this, and indeed that this is one respect in which philosophy may learn from the operations of the law.

III. FORCING THE ISSUE

The law of torts in its own ways also forces the issue, notably on the extent and directness of causation, and on questions of state of mind that present themselves in relation to such matters as intent, recklessness, and, to some extent, negligence. It has to force the issue, for a reason that superficially is the same as that for which the criminal law has to do so—that it needs a result. But that phrase, though it applies to both cases, conceals some important differences between them. The criminal law needs a result in the sense that an accused person, once he or she is accused, must be found guilty or not guilty. In tort,[5] once the action is under way, either the plaintiff or the defendant must succeed, which means in turn that one or other of the parties (or in some proportion both) must bear the cost of the loss or damage. But there is the banal difference that with crime, it is, above all, clear cases that come to court, and with tort it is, above all, hard cases. With tort, it is the legal characteristic of being a hard case that helps to get it to court in the first place, but in crime it is the arrest of a supposed criminal. Someone might say that in an absolutely ideal world all and only guilty criminals would be prosecuted,[6] but there could be no world in which it was only successful plaintiffs whose cases were heard. Tort, by its nature, must be more like a system for the allocation of costs than the criminal law is, and it follows from this that there can be systems that perform that function in a different way, such as no fault insurance systems, or, presumably, the principles of wealth maximization if they were explicitly employed.[7]

It follows that the senses in which the criminal law and tort 'have to have an answer' are rather different. In both types of case, of course, there has to be an answer, granted that the system exists and the parties are in court; but the conditions of being in court are not the same, and it is also clearer with tort than with crime what a different system might be. This makes it specially important that there should be a theory of what tort law is

[5] I am primarily concerned here with non-intentional torts, *see supra,* note 1. The distinction between intentional torts and crime raises further issues.

[6] I am not clear whether anyone takes such an ideal seriously. Anyone who did do so would have to recognize that it implies constraints on what can count as a crime.

[7] Richard Posner, in the discussion of his wealth maximization conception in *Wealth Maximization and Tort Law: A Philosophical Inquiry,* this volume, draws by implication a contrast with crime, but I am not clear what it is. 'The "utility" (in the sense used by utilitarians) to a thief of a good that he could not afford to buy has no ethical status or legitimacy in wealth maximization. It is not a demand backed by an offer price': *id.* at note 20. On the face of it, this seems to replace the platitude that unjust satisfactions have no claim in justice with the falsehood that if I cannot afford to bid for an item I can have no just claim to it.

supposed to be doing, and this in turn has consequences for its relations to philosophy. If philosophy can be instructed by the law in the terms offered by the Picture—that is to say, through seeing what distinctions and considerations prove robust in circumstances in which we have to have an answer—it will need an understanding of what the forces are that operate on the law and are expressed in it, and, in particular, of what it is for the law to have to have an answer. Philosophy, then, will not only have to attend to the principles and goals of tort law; it will also have to understand at a theoretical level why it has those principles and goals.

IV. The Place of Theory

This theoretical understanding may itself be in part philosophical, and to that extent the relations between philosophy and law will be, unsurprisingly, reciprocal. But the understanding required will also be political. In this dimension, besides the special reasons for needing a theory of what tort law is up to, namely that there are alternative systems that might perform some of its functions, there is a more general reason which tort law shares with the criminal law: that both of these operations of law involve the directed exercise of state power, and it is an aspiration of a liberal society that the operations of power should be so far as possible transparent, in at least the modest sense that their supposed legitimation should not rest on systematic misunderstanding.

This modest requirement does not imply that every political practice must be legitimated in terms of some theory, still less that all of them must be legitimated in terms of the same theory. But in a state governed by law the operations of the law represent the most direct application of power to the individual, and granted further the highly contested justifications of these operations in modern liberal societies, it is *in fact* the case that in such societies the demands of transparency are unlikely to be met without the resources of a theoretical account. Some of that account, though political, will undoubtedly overlap with the philosophical contribution and constitute part of a political philosophy.

The call on theory at this point is quite different from the idea expressed by Richard Wright in his contribution to this volume,[8] that rationality requires a theory which offers a unified, monistic, basis for both everyday morality and the law. I have argued elsewhere[9] that the aim of turning everyday morality into a theory, and indeed the idea that it has or should have a monistic basis, are misguided. The situation with political philosophy is not entirely the same, and there is more place for theory in it. The

---

[8] Richard W. Wright, *The Foundations of Legal Responsibility*, this volume.
[9] Bernard Williams, Ethics and the Limits of Philosophy (1985).

reasons for this are special to political philosophy. They are grounded both in the general point that politics is immediately involved in the application of power,[10] and also in a more local point, that legitimation in the modern liberal state requires on such matters a high level of discursive explanation.

If our aim were to develop a unitary theoretical account of everyday morality and the law on a monistic basis, these considerations would seem to favor a picture (though it would not strictly imply it) in which there was a primacy of philosophy over the law. Philosophical reflection and the theory which, on this view, it generates would be thought to make the working of the law intelligible, or to prescribe how it might be improved so as to be more intelligible. On this view, it would be a matter of what philosophy could do for the law. But on the account I am suggesting, philosophy tries to learn from the operations of the law, in conjunction with a theory of what the law is up to—a theory partly provided by philosophy itself.

V. In The Microwave

What may philosophy learn from law? The original suggestion was that it might learn the robustness of some familiar distinctions, judged from the way in which they behave under pressure, when the law 'has to have an answer'. There are indeed examples that fit this model. It is important that they are not most likely to show up in connections which from the point of view of legal theory are the most controversial. Their robustness may show up, rather, in the fact that they are taken for granted in legal argument, and are not made the focus of attack by any of the parties. Consider the matter of intent in tort or criminal law. It may indeed be controversial in a particular connection whether it matters or not that the agent intended the outcome; and it may, further, be controversial what would count as showing that he did intend the outcome (or at any rate should be treated as someone who intended the outcome). But behind all this there will be a steady stream of assumptions about situations in which it is absolutely clear that he did intend the outcome, and that it is relevant that he intended the outcome.

Again, even when it is in dispute whether the agent intended this *outcome*, the dispute itself represents him as having done *some* things intentionally. It may be thought that this is simply uninteresting, since to this

[10] Under some interpretations, of a broadly Nietzschean type, morality is also deeply involved in the application of power. I have some sympathy with those interpretations, and in some connections, such as traditional sexual morality, the claim is manifestly true. Liberation, to the extent that it may be possible, requires an understanding of those truths, and hence to some extent a theory of morality itself. But it does not require turning morality into a theory, and it is likely to be obstructed by the project of doing so: that project itself typically helps to conceal those truths.

extent the law is uncontroversially using the materials of common sense—materials, for instance, that may have been offered in evidence by citizens who are merely, in these respects, using the resources of common sense. But that is the point, that a certain store of shared interpretations and concepts survive scrutiny, every day, under legal process and provide the structure of the law's operations. They are like containers that can withstand the microwave. On any given occasion it is the stuff they contain that is the center of interest, and the legal process is directed to seeing how that stuff will turn out; but it is significant, as the Picture suggested it was, that there are some familiar materials that serve to hold and present this stuff, and have a structure that enables them, day in and day out, to withstand radiation at courtroom intensity.

However, it would be very surprising if philosophy could learn only from the less controversial parts of legal argument and doctrine, and it is itself significant that some concepts constantly cause trouble in the law and provide a focus for reinterpretation and controversy—such as the robust and persistent debate over the superiority of fault (negligence) or strict liability for accidentally caused harm. As I have already suggested, this is not only, or primarily, because it provides an opportunity for philosophy to come to the law's rescue. It may, in a certain sense, give philosophy occasion to come to the *concepts'* rescue. But if so, this will only be because philosophy can learn something about the nature of the concepts from their sufferings under the conditions of the law.

VI. Responsibility and the Voluntary

This is notably so with ideas of the voluntary and with notions of responsibility that in various ways are closely related to it. There are two truths in particular that the law may help philosophy see about these ideas.[11] One, which emerges from the experience of both the criminal law and the law of torts, is that grave problems arise for the notion of the voluntary when we seek to deepen it, to move, for instance, from issues of what on a given occasion an agent sought to bring about and of what state of mind he was immediately in (and those questions can be hard enough), to questions of how far such states of mind were normal, or normal to him, and of the extent to which he is responsible for being a person who would commit the act in that state of mind. Such lines of thought, as we all know, may rapidly lead into swamps of skepticism, some of them marked by rusting signs bearing the legend 'Free Will'.

---

[11] I have discussed these matters, with some reference both to modern law and to ancient Greek law, in Bernard Williams, Shame and Necessity (1993), ch. 3.

The other truth, one that emerges unequivocally from the law of torts, is that responsibility in the sense of a duty to compensate inevitably runs beyond responsibility for the outcome in the sense of an intention or even a desire to bring it about. Disputes about fault and the absence of justification, such as are discussed in the chapters of Tony Honoré and David Owen,[12] are concerned to ask whether there must at any rate be a grain of (something like) the voluntary on which to grow the elaborate crystal of liability; but no-one, certainly, denies that the crystal may vastly outgrow its seed.

There is a temptation to think that somehow there can be defined a notion of the voluntary which is both deep and adequate; and that, even if liability in unintentional tort could, in principle, never be made simply commensurate with what the agent in that sense voluntarily did, at least the notion would provide a foundation for thinking correctly about the ways in which liability must inevitably extend beyond it. The tendency to think in these terms can figure in the theory of the law itself. One important way in which it is displayed is by *negation*, in the idea that notions of the voluntary and of responsibility closely allied to the voluntary require a deep account, and since no such account is to be had, the law had better do without such notions altogether.

The tendency to think in this way is, I think, misguided. This is a place at which, as I put it earlier in this chapter, common sense can be in conspiracy with law or at least with certain theorists of law to 'force the issue', in this case to force the psychological and metaphysical issues beyond the superficial phenomena. Both common sense and the theory of law have some reason to sustain an idea of the voluntary as a deep notion, which has, if only we could find it, a deep account. In fact, as I have suggested elsewhere,[13] the idea of the voluntary is an essentially superficial notion, which works on condition that one does not try to deepen it. This truth, it seems to me, can be recovered from studying the law in practice, as opposed to the normative account that some theorists give of it, and examining the evasions, approximations, and misadventures which the idea of the voluntary regularly encounters there. The pressures that the law applies can in this case help philosophy to see what common sense morality and philosophy's own arguments on these subjects can help it to overlook, that the concept of the voluntary adds up to not much more than we are offered by its surface criteria, by which a voluntary act is, roughly, an intentional aspect of an act done in a normal state of mind. There is a story to be told of how

[12] Tony Honoré, *Morality of Tort Law—Questions and Answers*, and David Owen, *Philosophical Foundations of Fault in Tort Law*, both in this volume.

[13] Bernard Williams, *How Free Does the Will Need to Be?*, Lindley Lecture at the University of Kansas (1985), and Bernard Williams, *Voluntary Acts and Responsible Agents*, 10 OxFORD J. LEGAL STUD. 1 (1990), both reprinted in BERNARD WILLIAMS, MAKING SENSE OF HUMANITY (1995).

such a concept, limited as it is, has valuable work to do, in particular in the criminal law. But that story does need to be told; this is one of the points at which philosophy has to learn not only from what the law does but from a theory of what the law should be trying to do, theory to which, as I have already said, philosophy (above all, political philosophy) will have already contributed.

In the matter of liability in tort, the situation is slightly different. Here, once again, the manifest practice of the law, its struggles with concepts of fault and justification, can concentrate philosophers' minds on the reality of situations in which people can (and those in which they cannot) be fairly treated as answerable for outcomes which they did not intend and could not have foreseen. These can remind us of the many ways in which we do think in terms of 'outcome responsibility', in Honoré's phrase. In this case, it might be that further political reflection could suggest that this was not the best way for the law to try to deal with the allocation of costs; it is certainly possible that the struggles of the law with outcome responsibility could encourage us to think that the law itself might do better by shifting the emphasis to other schemes. I have no idea whether, or to what extent, this might turn out to be the case (whereas the argument for the criminal law's investment in a relatively undemanding concept of the voluntary is, I think, fairly unproblematic.)

However, even if outcome responsibility were not ultimately the best conceptual instrument for the law of torts, this would not cancel the enlightenment that philosophy can gain by looking at the law's dealings with this concept. We would still have come to see, under the law's extreme conditions, how such a concept works, and what may seem reasonable or unreasonable applications of it. We shall have seen a lot to remind us that the concept is not perfectible, and that it is probably not replaceable by a concept of moral responsibility that will eliminate responsibility for everything except what is in the immediate control of the agent's will. These remain truths about responsibility, and even if the law of torts were to decide on the basis of an improved political theory that it would be to some substantial extent better out of the responsibility business, the experience of the law, and the considerations special to the law that would be mobilized by the political theory, would still give help in understanding what we can reasonably expect of an idea of responsibility in those areas of our lives where such an idea will, unremovably, continue to have authority.

VII. Conclusion

The Picture with which I started has some truth in it. Importantly, it is not just the success of our concepts under the extreme conditions of the law that has something to tell philosophy, but also their occasional failure to survive that exposure. Philosophy will be able to learn the right lessons, however, only if there is an adequate theory (in part provided by political philosophy itself) about what features of the concepts, and what special features of the law, have contributed to those successes and failures.

Index

abnormally dangerous activities
  catastrophic accidents, evaluation of lives
      lost in 287–8
  class, defining 286
  combining risks 290–1
  cost-benefit analysis 286
  crop-dusting cases 284
  escape of gas cases 284
  harm from 155–6
  liability rule applied to 286
  maximin decision
    comparison to Bayesian decision-
        making 289–92
    contractarian interpretation 293
    individual rational choice, as principle
        of 294
    interpretation of 293
    meaning 289
    principle of 292–6
    small number of outcomes, application
        to 290
    social rationality, as principle of 294
    strict liability, not recommending
        295
  mischief, escape likely to cause 282
  mistaken cases 279
  pile driving, analysis of 283
  principles in examining cases of 278
  reasons for finding activities to be 277
  responsibility, allocating 278
  risk, meaning 281
  safety precautions 281
  seriousness of harm thesis
    additional development and refinement
        of 297
    Bayesian expected-utility decision-
        making efficiency analysis, difficulties
        with 285–9
    development of 282–5
    factors in 285
    justification 285–96
    magnitude of loss, focus on 297
    maximin strategy, comparison to
        Bayesian decision-making 289–92
    normative foundation, need for 296
    over-inclusive nature of 284
    simplicity of 285
  strict liability for 277, 295
  technological risks 287–8
  traditional theories of 297
  trespassing-animal cases 283

uncommonness and size of risk, rejection
    as determinants of 279–81
unfairly distributed risks, assessment of
    288
worst-case scenarios 294–5
accidents
  cost of treating 306
  fault central to 201
  fault, theory of 223
  meaning 205
  natural causes, with 306
  truth, involvement of 205
  utility concept, formulation of 215
  victims, compensating 406
Ackerman, Bruce 102
agency
  duty to compensate, not explaining 358
  harm, connecting to 18–23
  human 355–6
  pre-moral concept of 356
anti-realists
  belief of 59
  cognitivist 60
Aquinas, Thomas 1, 131, 134, 140–1, 145–7
Aristotle 1, 131–4, 137, 140, 145–6, 166–71,
    211
Attanasio, John 17
Austin, J.L. 487
autonomy
  abstract rights 207
  aggregate
    Calabresian theory, effect on 310–14
    comparison of defenses 314–16
    concern of 308
    distributional concerns 315
    egalitarian conception of autonomy, as
        307–10
    first order principle, not 314
    heretical notion of 300
    libertarian and egalitarian theory,
        reconciliation of 300–1, 315–16
    principle of 17
    range of policies, implications as to
        309–10
    strict equality of condition, avoiding
        309
    weak principle of 300, 308–9
  choices, acting on 209
  definition 307
  intrusion into 220
  liberty differentiated 307

autonomy (*cont.*):
 meaning 203
 products liability, defense to, *see* products
  liability
 tort law, concerns shaping 300
 truth as value in 317
 utilitarianism, in conflict with 161
 wealth, depending on 218

Balkin, Jack 184
Bender, Leslie 254–6
Benson, Peter 22–3, 132, 135
Birks, Peter 7–8
blameworthiness
 liability determined by 201
 wrong, in committing 42–5
Bohr, Niels 183, 187–93

Calabresi, Guido 2, 154, 215, 299–301
carelessness
 arbitrariness, appearance of 401
 compensatory justice 405–8
 massive loss, causing 20–1
  basic injustice of system 396–7
  causation 398–401
  desert 389–91
  fairness 388
  innocent victim, to 397
  loss, shifting 393–6
  responsibility for 399
  scenario of 387
 retribution for 406
causation
 accidental harm, of 227
 backward 379
 basic principle of 398
 but-for test 363
  indeterminacy 380–4
  NESS theory, common elements in
   367–74
  NESS theory, differences in 374–84
  over-determination 37
 carelessness causing massive loss, in
  398–401
 causal connection between events or facts
  367–8
 causal inquiry, formation of 368–73
 causal regularities 365–6
 causally relevant conditions 364, 367–9
 choice, identified with 141
 connection of actor to deficiencies of
  action 352–4
 efforts to unravel 364–7
 elimination of circumstances 370–2
 fault, resembling 141–2
 foreseeability, governed by 115
 fortuity of 361

importance, reason for 385
indeterminacy 380–4
insufficient but necessary part of
 unnecessary but sufficient condition
 365–6
mass tort cases, in 194–5
necessary element of set of conditions, as
 363, 365–6
necessary element of sufficient set (NESS)
 test 20, 366
 but-for test, common elements 367–74
 but-for test, differences in 374–84
 indeterminacy 380–4
necessary or sufficient condition of result,
 as 363
over-determination
 different causal processes 377–9
 harm already having occurred 379–80
 similar causal processes culminating at
  same time 374–7
pivotal role of 347–8
theories of 19–20
volitional act, as 347
voluntary action linked to 158
wrongful conduct, relevance of 372
Chapman, Bruce 21–2
child
 loss of companionship, recovery for
  125–6
 prudence of 148
choice
 accidental harm, in 208
 actual, trust helping to determine 317
 autonomy 209
 choice-blame principle 209–10, 220
 intention, in forming 243–4
 intentional harm, in 207–8
 principles of 207–9
 risk-benefit decisions 219
Christie, George 11
civil wrongs
 blameworthiness 42–5
 breach of legal duty, as 33–4, 37–8
 civil, use of term 40
 classification
  coherence of 47–51
  common law 31
  fourfold 31–3, 46–51
  prima facie incoherence 46–7
  Roman law 31–3
 compensation for loss 34
 concept of 33
 conduct, requirement of 41–2
 distinct category of 51
 individual complaining of 40
 law's response to 47
 legal and equitable, division between 35

meaning 39–40
morality, according to 37
notion of compensation, linked to 36
obligation arising as though from 31
plaintiff, adverse effect on 41
primary and secondary obligations 38
thesis of 33–4
two-tier structural truth 37
victim, harm to 38–41
wrong, use of term 39
Coase, Ronald 2, 154, 299, 342–3
Coke, Sir Edward 113
Coleman, Jules 2–5, 8–9, 36, 137, 139,
    143–4, 176, 178–9, 352, 395, 396, 413
combination
    intention to harm in 241
common good
    communal ethic, waning of 213
    concept of 212–14
    freedom, conflicts with 216–17
    utility and efficiency, from perspectives of
      213–15
common law
    equity, division with 34–5
    general principles, application of 113
common sense
    testing 487–8
compensation
    appropriate mode of rectification, as 178
    characteristics of defendant, varying with
      424
    comparative approach to 354
    conditions for requiring payment of 85
    corrective justice 79–80
    cost saving, as 104
    crime victims, of 195
    degradation of interest, for 414
    disparate deficiencies, treatment of 351
    duty, extent of
      conduct and fault of plaintiff 92
      harm, foreseeability of 91–2
      scope of rule 90–1
    harm caused negligently, for 140
    justification of results 352
    moral duty of 352, 354
    moral justification 348–9
    net benefit, action resulting in 415–16
    normative ground of 159
    outcome-responsibility as reason for 359
    redress, as 424
    retribution, incompatibility with 351
    right to and duty of 157
    state scheme, replacement of tort liability
      with 93
    tort practice, as part of 348
complementarity
    epistemological significance of 190–1

extension of idea of 189
law, implementation in 192–5
meaning 187–8
modern idea of 187–92
normative level, extension to 191
optimal balance between conflicting
    interests, finding 193
polar duality, principle of 189–90
quantum physics, in relation to 188
tort liability, in 194
conduct
    wrong, requirement for 41–2
conspiracy
    harm, to 237
contract
    contractual obligations 50
    failure to perform 33
    intentional interference with 430, 455–7
    liability, as explanation of 50
    obligation arising as though from 31
    rights as quasi-property 456–7
    uberrimae fidei 49
contributory negligence
    asymmetry of 466–7
    cause-in-fact, notion of 463
    complete loss of remedy 484
    concepts underlying 462
    defendant, negligence of 461
    defensible concept of fault, need for 467
    deficiency view of fault 463–8
    deficient conduct of victim 467–8
    due concern, baseline of 473
    ex ante options 464
    fault, substantive criteria of 461
    limiting plaintiff's recovery, substantive
      rationales for
      conceptual issues 468–9
      extrapolation approach 483
      injurer egoism *v.* victim non-egoism
        470–4
      injurer *v.* victim, negligence criterion
        469–81
      moral parity 476–7
      plaintiff, strict responsibility of 481–4
      pure and impure victim negligence
        478–81
      remedy, forfeiture of 477–8
      utilitarian criterion 474–6
    meaning 463
    mental capacity, dual standard for 484
    moral parity 461, 476–7
    moral responsibility 259
    non-economic literature on 462
    plaintiff, strict responsibility of 481–4
    precautions, option to take 464–5, 478–80
    pure and impure victim negligence
      478–81

contributory negligence (*cont.*):
  remedy, forfeiture of 477–8
  risk, assumption of 466, 481–2
  risks to others, ignoring 479
  seat-belt defense 465–6, 482
  self-interested conduct of plaintiffs 269–70
  strict responsibility, as 463–8
  utilitarian criterion 474–6
  victim, choices of 473
convention
  content of 64
Cooper-Stephenson, Ken 5
corrective justice
  absolute moral equality, criterion of 171
  actual or threatened interactional injuries,
    protection against 171
  agent-specific reasons for acting, imposing
    56
  aims of 256
  annulment thesis 68
  Aristotelian theory 108–9, 131
  bilateral claims 171, 177
  claims in 66
    ground of 167
    institutions for implementing 180–1
  cognitive content of 59
  compensation for future care, requiring
    411
  compensation under 36, 79–80, 354
  concern for distribution of wealth, effect
    of 134
  conduct and fault of plaintiff, compensa-
    tion dependent on 92
  content of 58, 63
  core of 66–7
  correlativity, involving 66–7
  damages 21–2
  defendant's conduct and plaintiff's loss,
    link between 80, 137–40
  distribution of wealth, preserving 157
  distributive justice
    application in same situation as 173–4,
      186
    blend with 84–5
    comparison of 132–7
    incompatibility with 172–3
  duty of 69–70
    person discharging 178–9
  duty to repair in 69
  equal negative freedom, scope of 273
  equality
    criterion of 168
    differing notions of 211–12
  fairness, principle of 246
  first principles, derivation from 62
  historical discussions of 131
  human welfare

    according to 157
    concern with 135
  individual interactions, applying to 12
  involuntary 137
  just distribution of resources by 135
  legal and political practices, effect of
    70–1
  liability regime 169
  loss
    analysis of 57
    shifting 395
  meta-ethics of 56–66
  moral predicates, content of 65
  narrow domain of 181
  negative aspect of fundamental norm of
    equal freedom, as 173, 182
  no-fault compensation plans, not
    condemning 139
  non-cognitive 63
    subjectivist 63
  objective nature of 59, 62
  particular community, duty in 71
  plaintiff's right and defendant's duty,
    linking 11–12
  political morality, in relation to 53–6
  practice of 63–4, 69–71
  pre-existing equality, restoring 138
  pre-political, being 69
  principle of 53, 78–81
  private interactions, dealing with 168–9
  pursuing of ends out of own resources,
    ensuring 139
  rectification of transactions by 132
  rectification, as 422–3
  redress, as 22, 422–4
  restitution, requiring 138
  Right, principle of 165
  role of 8
  summary of 72
  supplementation 174–5
  theorists of 412
  tort law, as means of assessing 65
  unintentional torts, in context of 109
  utility of monetary damages, concerns of
    411
  wealth maximization, compatibility with
    10, 108–9
  wrongdoing, concept of 353
  wrongful act and injury, correlation of
    412–13
criminal law
  non-discrete wrong, retribution for 175
  penal lottery 401–3
  retributive justice in 86–8
  tort law, shared features with 74

damages, *see also* compensation

analysis of situations of 419
costs of future care, biased to 409
exemplary 36
later loss or damage, effect of 418
loss of enjoyment of life, for
    cognitive awareness, requirement of
        115
money, utility of 410–11, 420–4
net benefit, action resulting in 415–16
non-pecuniary loss, for 409–10, 420–4
permanently unconscious plaintiff, for
    421
probability of future loss, discounted for
    417
punitive 176
purpose of 409
restitutionary 36
rights and welfare, in relation to 412–14
role in tort law 21
Daube, David 140
deontology
    Kantian 109–10
discourse
    cognitive 58
    objectivist and subjectivist interpretations
        58–9
distributive justice
    claim
        ground of 167
        institutions for implementing 180–1
    corrective justice
        application in same situation as 173–4,
            186
        blend with 84–5
        comparison of 132–7
        incompatibility with 172–3
    equality
        criterion of 168
        differing notions of 211–12
    human welfare, according to 157
    liability decisions based on, internal
        coherence 186
    loss, shifting 394
    manifestation of 132
    multilateral claims 171, 177
    outcome-responsibility, justification for
        imposing 83
    positive aspect of fundamental norm of
        equal freedom, as 173, 182
    public or communal resource-allocation
        168
    redistribution of excess, requiring 273
    resources, determination of entitlement to
        177
    risk, principle of 83–4
    simple patterned theory of 136
    supplementation 174–5

duty
    natural 69–70
Dworkin, Ronald 68–9, 128, 173, 253

economic loss
    American cases on 123–5
    analysis of law 457–8
    British cases on 116–23
    classification of situations 427–30
    commercial parties, cases involving 124
    defective chattel, due to 428, 436–7,
        440–1
    defendant's conduct, regulation of 443
    detrimental reliance, justified 450–5
    duty of care 118
    exclusion of liability for 22–3, 427
    exclusionary rule
        cases in which not applied 437–8
        common factor 434–7
        contractual interest, significance of 437
        justification for 430–2
        nonfeasance, in case of 444–50
        precedent, reliance on 445
        reason for 433–44
        right exclusive against defendant, action
            grounded in 442, 444
        situations of 427–8
        statement of 442
        unavoidable loss, distinguishing 437–44
        upholding of 445
    foreseeability 446
    intentional interference with contract, by
        430, 455–7
    justificatory approaches to 430–2
    loss of profits, for 117, 119
    misfeasance, due to 449
    non-exclusionary situations 429–30
    own risk, plaintiff acting at 443
    physical damage to item not owned or
        possessed by plaintiff, by 428, 434–5
    physical injury, due to 429
    policy considerations 118
    protection of property, financial loss from
        439–40, 444
    public moral point of view 458
    pure, recovery of 117
    reasonably foreseeable principle 121
    relational 428, 434, 438
    responsibility for 11
    right, assertion of 439
    right exclusive against defendant, action
        grounded in 442, 444, 453
    special relationship, arising in 429,
        450–5
    ultimate consumer, payment of damages
        to 119
    unavoidable, distinguishing 437–44

egalitarianism
  Kantian 110
  libertarian theory, reconciliation with 303
  third-order difference principle 301,
    314–16
egoism
  defendant negligence, description of 471
  injurer *v.* victim non-egoism 470–4
  insufficient concern, constituting 472–3
  liability, explanation of 472
emotional distress
  damages for 120
Englard, Izhak 3, 5, 13
Epstein, Richard 2, 142, 151, 153, 274, 400
equality
  abstract 208
  choice, principles of 207–9
  concept of 206–7
  corrective justice, *see* corrective justice
  distributive justice, *see* distributive justice
  equal liberty, principle of 303
  original position, structuring common-
    wealth when placed in 303
  resources, distribution of 304
  weak 209–11
equity
  wrongs redressed in 35

fairness
  perceptions of 388
  tort liability, defense of 391
fault
  accident law, central role in 201
  accidental harm, theory in 223–8
  action, in 353
  causation, resembling 141–2
  cement of law of torts, as 201
  corrective justice, in 92
  deficiency view of 463–8
  doing, in 353, 355
  dominance in tort law, challenge to 202
  foreseeability, governed by 115
  intentionally inflicted harm
    prima facie case 220–1
    privileges 221–3
  irrelevance, theory of 142
  meanings 201
  retributive justice, in 87–90
  self-regarding 461
  utilitarian criteria of 461
Feinberg, Joel 4
feminists
  ethic of care 254–6
Finnis, John 15–16
Fleming, John 260
Fletcher, George 2–3, 137–8, 154–5, 254,
  280

foreseeability
  American courts, application by 116
  American experiments 125–6
  economic loss, of 446
    American cases on 123–5
    British cases on 116–23
  emotional distress, damages for 120
  fault and causation, governing 115
  insubstantial real risk 262
  levels of 261
  material risks 262
  proximity, principle of 123
  reasonable 121, 129–30
    notion of 344
  requirement of responsibility for physical
    harm as 343
  risks taken into account 257
  unaccepted risk of injury, creation of 263
freedom
  common good, conflicts with 216–17
  concept of 202–4
  dignity, according 203
  free will, notion of 203
  primary moral and political ideal, as 204
  scope of 206–7
Fried, Charles 2

Gaius 31–2, 152
Gibson, Elaine 5
goods
  distributional schema, objects of 305
Gordley, James 11–12
Grotius, Hugo 1

Hacking, Ian 322
Hand, Learned formula 12, 146–8, 215,
  226, 250–5, 474–5
harm
  abnormally dangerous activity, from
    155–6
  accidental
    causation 227
    choices in 208
    equality ideal, use of 225
    fault, theory of 223–8
    responsibility, basis of 224
  chance of avoiding, loss of 330–1
  conduct causing, justification of 214
  deficiency of defendant's behavior,
    depending on 347
  definition 322
  deterministic causal processes 336, 338
  foreseeability of 91–2
  increasing likelihood of 353
  independent wrongful acts bringing about
    364
  intentionally inflicted 140, 205

choice in 207–8
moral and legal liability for 245
others, exploiting 244
prima facie case 220–1
privileges 221–3
truth, involvement of 205
justification for inflicting 82
negligently, caused 140
person causing 342
physical
probability of 336
responsibility for 339–45
proper medical treatment, loss of
opportunity to receive 339
responsibility, link to 18–23
responsibility to prevent 360
risk
as form of 321, 330–9
relation to 18
tortious conspiracy to 237
victim, to 38–41
volitional act causing 347–8
Hart, H.L.A. 9, 19, 64, 73, 364
Hegel 10
Heidt, Kathryn 151
Hobbes, Thomas 113
Holmes, Oliver Wendell 1, 142, 201, 243,
341–3
Honoré, Tony 9, 19–20, 356–7, 495–6

incoherence
prima facie 46–7
injury
injustice, due to 170
preparing 230
victim, oriented to 39
insurance
costs, certainty of 104–5
fairness, blurring 388
losses, spreading 89–90
no-fault plans 180
intention
actual 243
choice in forming 243–4
common speech, in 230–1
concept of 229
concepts distinguished from 247
constructive 242–7
desire not mark of 236
element of 235
ends and means or hopes and desires, as
229–33
fairness and unfairness, criteria of 246
fictional, repudiation of 243
foreseen consequences 237–42
harm, to cause, *see* harm
human lives, sacrifice of 235

injure, to 230–4
internal feelings, identification of 239
malice, conception of 239–40
maliciousness 238
motive, relevance of 241
object or purpose, as 240
outward behavior, identification of 239
Posner's conception of 234–6
probability theory 236–7
real 242–7
ulterior motives 238
interests
ordering 217–20

judgment
primary obligations, creating 50
justice
Aristotle, definition by 166
attainment of good, concerned with 167
compensatory 405–8
concepts of 390
proportionality to desert, as 394
recognition and enforcement of rights 166

Kant, Immanuel 1, 163–6, 202, 253–4, 273,
424
knowledge
state of possessing ideal of truth, as 204
Kress, Ken 16–17

law
logical structure, urge to find 113
monistic theories of 160
normative principles, driven by 128
Law and Economics Movement
foundation of 299
legal claim
correct identification of 177
Lewis, David 401–3
liability
basis of 14–18
dangerous activities, for 16–17
intentionally inflicted harm, for 15
no-fault, advantage of 407
symmetry of 395
tortious, *see* tort liability
liberty
meaning 307–8
Rawlsian definition of 305

MacIntyre, Alasdair 103
Mackie, John 20, 365–6, 375, 381
MacKinnon, Catherine 255
malice
conception of 239–40
massive losses
carelessness, caused by, *see* carelessness

medical treatment
  negligence in 268–9
misfeasance
  economic loss, causing 449
  essential condition of 448
  liability for 448, 455
  non-feasance distinguished 447–9, 458
mistakes
  liability for 170
moral beliefs
  change in 102
  reasons pro and con 101–2
moral responsibility
  harm, for 4
moral theories
  doctrine of Right and doctrine of virtue
    163
  equal individual theories, based on 162
  types of 161
morality
  common 243
  supreme principle of 162
Morris, Robert 2

Nagel, Thomas 357
navigation
  negligence, causally relevant conditions
    369
necessity
  doctrine of 135
  privilege of 222
negligence
  avoiding 131
  contributory, *see* contributory negligence
  deficiency view of 464
  definition 145
  description of 250
  efficiency, in terms of 147–8
  efficient level of precaution, failure to
    adopt 252
  elaboration of conception of 446
  ex ante options 463
  incentives, providing 150–1
  justification of loss 153
  Kantian view of 470–4
  Kantian-Aristotelian foundation 16
  Learned Hand formulation 215, 250–2
    nonutilitarian attempts to justify 252–5
  normative sequence of 413
  objective theory of 142–4
  precaution, levels of 251–2
  proximity, principle of 123
  prudence, failure to exercise 145–7
  reasonableness
    aggregate risk-utility interpretation 260
    defendants' treating others as means,
      where 261–3

failure to aid or rescue by defendants,
    271–4
  medical treatment, in 268–9
  occupiers' on-premises risks 265–6
  participatory plaintiffs, activities
    involving 267
  paternalistic defendants 268–9
  risk-utility test of 250–1, 253
  self-interested conduct of plaintiffs
    269–70
  self-sacrificing conduct of plaintiffs
    270–1
  situations in which applied 261
  socially essential activities, defendants
    involved in 264–5
  substantive criteria of 260–74
safety precautions, requirement of 281
standard of care
  equal freedom 255–74
  moral responsibility 258
  objective nature of 344
  perspective applied 257–9
  risks taken into account 257
  utilitarian efficiency theory, under 258
strict liability, imposing 45
uncompensated costs 105
nervous shock
  liability for 120
Nietzsche 487
nonfeasance
  misfeasance distinguished 447–9, 458
  no liability for 457
Nozick, Robert 4, 307
nuisance
  injunction, refusal to grant 186

objectivity
  convergence as precondition of 61–2
  corrective justice, of 59, 62
  minimal 61
  modest 61
  notions of 60
  strong 61
occupiers
  on-premises risks 265–6
Owen, David G. 14–15, 495
ownership
  inviolability, definition in terms of 142
  private, rights of 134–5

Pareto principle
  meaning 104
  normative force 105
  wealth maximization, compatibility with
    104–6
Perry, Stephen 18, 68–9, 135–6, 142–3, 354,
    358, 413–14

philosophy
  law, lessons from 487, 493–4, 497
pluralism
  distributional schema, objects of 305
  monistic theorists, view of 183–4
  reality of 183–7
polar duality
  principle of 189–90
political morality
  corrective justice in relation to 53–6
  liberal 54
Posner, Richard 2, 10, 148–50, 183–4,
    233–7
private law
  tort law in context of 5–6
probability
  definition 323
  epistemic 325–7
  logical-relation theory 327–9
  objective conception 323–4, 340
  radical subjectivist interpretation of
    326–8
  relative-frequency theory 323–4
  theoretical accounts of 322–3
products liability
  aggregate autonomy principle 17
  autonomy, violation of 313
  Calabresian approach to
    accident costs, incorporation into
      product price 311–12
    aggregate autonomy defense of 299,
      307–14, 310–14
    internalization aspect of 312–13
    Rawlsian defense of 303–6
    safety decisions, devolving 311
    statement of 302
    virtues as support for 316–18
  comparison of defenses 314–16
  strict liability approach 17
property
  obligation to return 138
  private, system of 136–7
protective justice
  right of 164
prudence
  cardinal virtue, as 146
  child, of 148
  failure to exercise 145–7
Pufendorf, Samuel 1, 152
punishment
  appropriate mode of rectification, as 178
  bases of 194
  justifications of 73
  retributive justice 86–8

Radin, Margaret Jane 255, 422–3
Ramsey, F.P. 326

Rawls, John 4, 17, 287, 289, 291–3, 300–1,
    303–6, 314–18
realists
  belief of 59
  convergence over time, commitment to 61
  moral 60
reparative justice
  government and law, roles of 245
rescue
  easy, duty of 271–4
  failure to aid or rescue by defendants,
    271–4
  general duty to attempt, lack of 272
  reasonableness 270–1
responsibility
  agent of harm, of 357
  basis of liability 14–18
  causal 55
  communalistic decision, imposition as
    184
  concept of 356
  duty to compensate, as 495
  grounds of recovery, grounds of liability
      and mode of rectification, link
      between 176
  harm
    connecting to 18–23
    to prevent 360
  Kantian-Aristotelian theory of 249, 274
  loss, to repair 19
  mental handicaps, treatment of 144–5
  moral, theory of 360
  outcome 81–3, 143, 344–5, 356–60, 496
  reasonable care, failure to use 144
  two-faced term, as 399
  victim, of 23–4
  voluntary, ideas of 494–7
restitution
  corrective justice requiring 138
  obligation to make 48–9
  response to event, category of 37
  Restatement of 32
    compensation requirement, incompati-
      bility with 351
retributive justice
  corrective justice, as type of 175
  criminal law, in 86–8
  fault, absence of 87
  non-discrete wrong, for 175
  tort law, fault in 88–90
Right, doctrine of
  corrective justice in 165
  doctrine of virtue distinguished 163
  equal absolute moral worth, respect for
    253–4
  exercise of freedom, affecting 164
  justice, synonymous with 166

Right, doctrine of (*cont.*):
  moral and legal obligations 163
  normative grounds of rights 176
  normative premise at core of 181
  private Right, movement to public Right
    164
  tort liability, implications for 166
risk
  abnormally dangerous activities, *see*
    abnormally dangerous activities
  agent-imposed 331–3
  augmentation by negligence 330–1
  combining 290–1
  conceptions of 321
  creation, liability in tort for 338
  damage 331–4, 337
  epistemic 343, 345
  epistemic probability, based on 326
  foreseeability, *see* foreseeability
  harm
    as form of 321, 330–9
    relation to 18
  indeterministic causal processes 337
  lottery, as 401–5
  moral significance 327, 329
  nature of 322–9
  non-reciprocal, liability for 154–6
  objective 345
    estimate of 332–3
  objective probabilities, involving 335
  physical damage, responsibility for 339–45
  potentially harmful activities, analyses of
    277
  treatable and untreatable cases, distin-
    guishing 334
  unfairly distributed, assessment of 288
  victim, assumption by 466, 481–2

Schroeder, Christopher 19
Schwartz, Gary 471
Seavey, Warren 260
self-respect
  accident deterrence, argument for 305
  meaning 306
Sharp, Frederick 152
Simons, Kenneth 23–4
social rule
  content of 64
society
  good, agreement on perception of 318
state social insurance schemes
  justification of 179
strict liability
  abnormal or voluntary conduct, not
    based on 369–70
  abnormally dangerous activities, for 277,
    295

Aristotelian account, basis in 154–6
Aristotelian theory failing to explain
  151
causal inquiry in 372–3
costs of greater good, internalizing 226
desert, irrelevance of 390
exceptional excuses 42
frailty of 202
historical explanations of 151–3
plaintiff, of 461
plaintiff participating in activity, where
  156
pre-modern rules 152
principle of 153
tort law, entrenched in 185

Terry, Henry 260
Thompson, Judith Jarvis 4
tort
  breach of legal duty 8
  causative event, as category of 36
  comparative approach to 354
  definition 7
  equitable wrongs, exclusion of 34
  essential elements 19
  fault-based theories of recovery 14
  injustice of system 396–7
  intentional 154
  theory, evolution of 3
tort law
  annulment theory 392–3
  basis of liability 14–18
  criminal law, shared features with 74
  descriptive framework 75–6
  desert in 389–91
  economic theory of 57
  efficiency of 74
  foreseeability, *see* foreseeability
  goals of 159
  incidence of undesirable conduct,
    reducing 94
  issue, forcing 491–2
  judicial enforcement, cost of 78
  justification of 159–60
  justifying aims of 76–8
  Kantian moral principles, fit with 110
  legal argument, overestimation of effects
    of 488
  loss, shifting 393–6
  monistic approaches to 183
  moral grounds, shaped by 318
  multiplicity of norms 13
  normative foundation 12
  philosophical perspectives 13–24
  philosophy of
    Anglo-American scholarship 2
    discipline, as 3

disciplines, bringing together 25
evolving conception of 3–4
history of 1
interbreeding 24
nature and realm of 7–9
practical reality and philosophical
    frivolity, difference between 487
relationship of 25–6
pluralism 183–7
principle
    role in 126–9
    use of 114–16
principles and values underlying 9–13
urge to find 114
private law, in wider context of 5–6
reasonableness
    equal freedom, conception of 256
    utilitarian efficiency, equated with
        254
requirement to compensate 348
retributive justice and fault in 88–90
strength and distinctions of legal
        concepts, account of 488
    autonomy and peculiarities, underesti-
        mation of 488
    legal argument, overestimation of
        effects of 488
    objections to 488–91
    rationalizations 489
    specialist, being 490
system, purpose of 76
theory of 73–4
place of 492–3
    threshold aim 9
tortious, conduct being 75
traditional concepts, application of 488
utilitarian concerns 316
wrongful and rightful conduct, compari-
    son of 373
wrongful losses, role in rectifying 5
tort liability
    absolute 340
    agency, based on 356
    complementarity, idea of 194
    criminal liability, differences in 390
    defendant's conduct and plaintiff's loss,
        link between 80
definition 35, 76
    desert, connection with 389–91
    distribution of 78–94
    distributive justice 83–6
    economic loss, *see* economic loss
    fault, imposition of 363
    insurance of 88–9
    lottery of 401–5
    outcome-responsibility 81–3
    paradigm case of 348–9

performance of act as requirement for 341
personal responsibility 85
pluralistic foundations, theorists favoring
    185–6
reality of situation, concentration on 496
relative wealth, irrelevance of 171
state compensation scheme, replacement
    with 93
strict 89
utility, maximizing 107
tortfeasor
    isolation, agent-relative reason for 355
    special responsibility of 359
    standard of performance, falling short of
        351
    victim, moral link with 356
trespass
    onerous obligations, imposing 266
    spring guns and man-traps, notice of
        230–3
    wrong, as 39
trust
    accidents, role in 205
    extent of actual choice, determining 317
    ideal of 204–6
    subversion of 205

unjust enrichment
    restitution, obligation to make 48–9
    wrong, as 32
utilitarianism
    agenda of 242
    autonomy and rights, in conflict with 161
    classical, Rawls' argument against 291–2
    common good, theory of 214
    contributory negligence, criterion for
        474–6
    efficiency theory 161
        normative unattractiveness of 249
    equality, conception of 253
    justification of 474
    rule, comparison with wealth maximiza-
        tion 106–8

values
    ordering 216–17
vicarious liability
    justification 85
victim
    contributory negligence, *see* contributory
        negligence
    harm to 38–41
    isolation, agent-relative reason for 355
    passivity of 342–3
    responsibility of 23–4
    tortfeasor, moral link with 356
    undeserving 350

voluntary action
  causation, linked to 158
  theory of 141
  treatment of 169

Waldron, Jeremy 20–1
wealth
  autonomy depending on 218
  distribution of 134
  maximization 10
    Aristotelian corrective justice, compatibility with 108–9
    economic efficiency, principle of 183
    ethical theories, compatibility with 103
    Kantian deontology, compatibility with 109–10
    Kantian egalitarianism, compatibility with 110
    meaning 99
    moral theory
adequacy as 103
    not deduced from 101
    normative theory 101–11
    Pareto principle, relationship with 104–6
    poor persons, value of life of 149–50
    positive theory 100–1
    pragmatic normativity 101–3
    property, notion of 108
    rule utilitarianism, comparison with 106–8

social policy issues, not resolving 101
  theory of 148–50
  tort situations, in 100
non–pecuniary dimensions 99
property rights, connection with 99
social welfare, as measure of 99
value, meaning 99
Weinrib, Ernest 3–6, 12, 132, 135–6, 146, 160, 172, 183–6, 193, 398–400, 412–15, 424–5
welfare
  corporate theories 161
  damages, in relation to 412–14
  human, concept of 157
  natural disasters, in case of 54–5
  reasons for acting with effects on 54–6
  social, wealth as measure of 99
Williams, Bernard 25–7, 357
Wittgenstein 487
Wright, Richard 12, 16, 20, 186, 366, 369, 492
wrong
  blameworthiness 42–5
  civil, *see* civil wrongs
  law of 228
  thought, committed by 42
  use of term 39

Yin and Yang 190